ISLAND *of* ANGELS

ISLAND *of* ANGELS

THE GROWTH OF THE CHURCH ON KOSRAE
KAPKAPAK LUN CHURCH FIN ACN KOSRAE
1852 - 2002

BY
ELDEN M. BUCK

WATERMARK
PUBLISHING

Department of Education
Henry E. Robert, Director
Kosrae State
Federated States of Micronesia

ISBN 0-9753740-6-0

Library of Congress Cataloging-in-
Publication Data

Buck, Elden M.
    Island of angels : the growth of the
church on Kosrae : kapkapak lun
church fin acn Kosrae, 1852-2002 / by
Elden M. Buck.-- 1st ed.
        p. cm.
1. Kosrae (Micronesia)--Church history.
I. Title: Growth of the church on Kosrae.
II. Title: Kapkapak lun church fin acn
Kosrae, 1852-2002. III.
Title.
    BR1495.M625B83 2005
    279.66--dc22

2005024394

Cover design by Nancy Watanabe
Cover photo, Elden Buck
Design and production by Gonzalez Design

Watermark Publishing
1088 Bishop Street, Suite 310
Honolulu, HI 96813
Telephone: Toll-free 1-866-900-BOOK
Web site: www.bookshawaii.net
e-mail: sales@bookshawaii.net

Printed in Korea

FOR MY WIFE,
MARY ALICE HANLIN BUCK
...WHO INTRODUCED ME TO KOSRAE
AND SHARED WITH ME
HER LOVE FOR THE ISLAND
AND ITS PEOPLE

Sixteen-year-old Alice at Wot, 1949

- CONTENTS -

In Memory of

PASTOR ALIK ISAAC
...WHO AS SENIOR PASTOR
DURING MY YEARS ON THE ISLAND
EXEMPLIFIED FOR ME THE GENTLE
YET STEADFAST AND TOTAL COMMITMENT
TYPICAL OF KOSRAEAN CHRISTIANS

NIPASTU SRUE FRANK SKILLING
...WHO MIRRORED FOR ME THE DIGNITY,
BEAUTY, COMPASSION,
AND LOYAL DEVOTION EMBODIED
IN SO MANY OF
THE WOMEN OF KOSRAE

PASTOR ERAFE TOSIE
...WHO AS A YOUNG MAN
TYPIFIED FOR ME THE INDUSTRY,
GRACIOUSNESS, AND GENEROSITY-OF-SPIRIT
COMMON AMONG KOSRAEAN MEN

The island of Kosrae lies five degrees above the equator in the central Pacific, 2,476 miles southwest of Hawai'i. It is the easternmost of the Caroline Islands—its nearest neighbor, tiny Pingelap Atoll, 144 miles to the northwest. In ancient times, its 42-square miles of land area was a kingdom, with its own monarch and nobles; its own language, customs, and traditions. Now, Kosrae is one of four island states that form the Federated States of Micronesia, and home to 8,060[1] people, the large majority of whom identify themselves as Christians related to the Kosrae Congregational Church.[2]

With joyfully contagious optimism, the people of this isolated, but wonderfully active, part of God's world bask in the multiple revelations of the Divine Presence among them. Their churches are full; their children and young people participate enthusiastically; their culture is permeated with both the discipline and the freedom revealed in the life and teachings of Jesus Christ. They experience and acknowledge the reality of God's blessing.

On August 21, 2002, the Church on Kosrae celebrated its 150th anniversary. Sesquicentennial festivities included prayers of thanksgiving, jubilant singing, and the retelling of countless stories from pulpit and stage describing the people and the processes God used to mold Kosraeans into the Christian community they are today.

Kosraeans are keenly curious about the history of their Church. They listen eagerly to stories shared by elders in family groups and classrooms. They avidly read what little information they can find that sheds light on their past. Intrigued, they work at filling the blanks in the record and tracing the chronology of church-related organizations and positions of leadership.

In the months leading up to the sesquicentennial, several leaders of the Church on Kosrae approached me with the suggestion that I compile the facts of their history to mark the occasion. They anticipated a volume that would not only preserve their story, but also honor their past and acknowledge the Family of Faith they have become.

This idea excited and challenged me. I am an American clergyman, a member of the United Church of Christ/Congregational, and have enjoyed a long association with the Kosraean Church. While teaching on Kosrae during the early 1960s, I became increasingly fascinated by the unique vibrancy of their Church and did some research into the historic records. At the time the leaders made their request, I already possessed a great deal of resource material—and I had just retired from active ministry, which meant that I had time to devote to such a project. In addition, my wife, Alice, was coordinating a new translation of the Kosraean Bible and spending considerable time with the project's Editorial Committee on Kosrae. I felt the nudge of God's timing. I would write the book.

I was intrigued by a suggestion that Alice offered from her perspective as a Bible translator, that the book could be yet another postscript to the New Testament Book of Acts: accounts of dedicated men and women who carried, received, and lived out God's Good News, providing continuation of the story of how the gospel has spread to the "ends of the Earth."

Though there have been mistakes and misunderstandings, as well as periods of darkness and pain, as the century and a half of Christianity unfolded, it has not been my purpose to launch a critique or to offer an in-depth analysis. Rather, with the Christians of Kosrae, I rejoice in the way that God has used human beings in very human situations to nurture into being the Church on Kosrae. Reporting the contributions of these willing—and sometimes not so willing—vessels of God's Spirit is what I have attempted to do. I have written and assembled materials with the intention of presenting a clear and beneficial history of their Church for the people of Kosrae. Secular history—the stage upon which the story of the Church unfolds—is included as it impacts and is impacted by the Christian message.

Also, I am very eager for non-Kosraeans to have the opportunity to become acquainted with this distinctive, church-oriented community, which thrives on its own remote mountaintop of faith. So, for non-Kosraeans too, this book is written.

The story is told chronologically, with each chapter building on the era that preceded it. I have included brief, informal observations, as well as lengthier, definitive paragraphs of many different writers, both from within and without the Church. I want my readers to see what others have had to say through the years about this island and its Church.

I am immensely grateful to Kosraean friends who have shared memories, impressions, and knowledge of their heritage, and have let me peruse rare family papers. I have tried to honor Kosraean sensitivities and traditional courtesies, but I ask forbearance from Kosrae's people when I have strayed into topics or used illustrations they find embarrassing or unacceptable for public discourse. As I am an American, and the great majority of those whom I quote were and are Americans, this story is filtered through the eyes and understanding of non-Kosraeans. Some day a Kosraean will write the incredible story from the Kosraean perspective, adding insight and giving it a welcome and essential balance.

Foreign travelers are always captivated by their first glimpse of Kosrae. I have included a number of these descriptions and initial reactions, which are almost always filled with hyperbole. As people do everywhere, Kosraeans tend to take the beauty of their own homeland for granted—though they have many songs and sayings that celebrate the cool breezes, abundant water, delicious fruits, and many other aspects of their island in which they recognize God's hand. Perhaps reading the impressions of others will remind them of the value and significance of this precious resource—their island home.

A word about the format: As will become clear to the reader, Kosraeans have had an affinity for the English language from their first contact with English speakers, and most of today's Kosraeans have been educated in that language. I want Kosraean readers to experience the original impact of the observations of my sources, so the book is in English. English is used also for the benefit of those who want to know the story, but cannot read Kosraean. To acknowledge all Kosraean readers, however, and as a means of paying tribute to the soft, distinctive, and melodious language which enfolds their culture, each chapter begins with a summary of that chapter in Kosraean.

A word about the title: Over the past 150 years, a number of foreign observers have either implied or made specific references to Kosrae as appearing to be an island of angels. The British scholar F. W. Christian was one of the first to suggest this during his visit in 1896. In 1935, the American writer Willard Price made several explicit references to Kosrae as "The Isle of the Angels." He noted the absence of orphans and needy elderly, the manner in which food was regularly shared with neighbors, the custom of wearing white on Sundays, the policy of no work on that day, and the non-existence of crime. At the close of World War II, 1st Lt. George D. Olds III, of the U.S. Coast Guard, alluded to the "angel island" analogy in letters he wrote from Kosrae to his family in New Jersey.

Kosraeans may wonder, perhaps laugh, and even recognize some irony in the allusion to them as angels. It is a Western concept, but it serves my purpose of calling attention to the singular prominence of the Church on Kosrae and to the strict, yet simple, adherence of Kosrae's people to its precepts as they understand them.

This dynamic Christian Church, existing on one of the most isolated and breathtakingly beautiful islands in the world, includes 90 percent of the population and is the predominant influence in society. A vital, workable Christianity sustains not only the gentle Kosraean people, but also the government agencies that regulate community life. It is a story that I am eager to tell.

So here it is—a gift for the people of Kosrae. It is their story, and they have been intimately involved in the process of putting it together. My desire now is that they thrill at the record, receive inspiration from the saints who have gone before, and gain new insights into their amazing legacy.

Elden M. Buck
Claremont, California

---

[1] Population projection for 2002 from the 1994 census of Kosrae. An estimated 4,000 Kosraeans live in other areas of Micronesia, in Hawai'i and the mainland United States (Kosrae State Census Report, Oct. 1996, p. 131). A population of 7,686 was recorded in 2000 (2000 Federated States of Micronesia [FSM] Census of Kosrae, chapter 2, p. 13)

[2] In the 2000 census of Kosrae, which included Filipino workers and other non-Kosraean residents, 89.1 percent were listed as "Protestant/Congregational Christians." Other categories included 1.8 percent Roman Catholic, 8.9 percent other denominations/religions, and 0.2 percent no religion or refusals (2000 FSM Census of Kosrae, chapter 7, p. 46)

– ACKNOWLEDGMENTS –

As this writing project is concluded, I thank God, not only for guiding me to an endeavor that has been immensely fulfilling, but for surrounding me with an amazing array of people who have assisted, prodded, and inspired me throughout the entire process.

I am very grateful to the late Dr. Alan R. Tippett, Australian Methodist missionary to the Solomon Islands and Fiji, who guided me in my studies at the Institute of Church Growth, Northwest Christian College, sharing his insights and helping me put into perspective my pages of research gleaned from the American Board archives of the early years of the Micronesia Mission. I am also grateful for the help of the librarians at the Hawaiian Mission Children's Society Library and the Hawaiian Historical Society, Honolulu. Fr. Francis X. Hezel, S.J., and those who work with him at the Micronesian Seminar library on Pohnpei were very helpful.

I owe a debt of gratitude to Pastor Takeo Likiaksa, Chairman of the Kosrae Congregational Church Council, who was particularly supportive from the beginning to the end of this project. Many other Kosraean friends shared time and information with me, including—on numerous occasions—Pastor Siosi and Nipastu Diana Aliksa, Pastor Natchuo Andrew, Deaconess Alwina Aruo, Pastor Ben Benjamin, Pastor Kun Caleb, Deaconess Hattie Conrad, Pastor Salik and Nipastu Anako Cornelius, Deacon Singkitchy George, Yosimi Idosi, Pastor Hirosi and Nipastu Mitchigo Ismael, Pastor Nena T. Kilafwasru, Deacon Akiwo Likiaksa, Akiko Nena, Deacon Tulenna Palsis, Deacon Roger Skilling, Kemwel Tilfas, Richard Tolenoa, and Tulensru Tupak.

Theodore E. Sigrah let me peruse journals kept by his grandfather, Pastor John Paliknoa Sigrah, Kosrae's last king; and Hashime Vicente Taulung shared with me papers recently retrieved from the jungle-buried cornerstone of Wot's 1909 mission school building.

Maeva Hipps made a wealth of information available to me, generously sharing notes, articles, and journal entries penned by her grandparents, Irving and Mary Channon. Irving and Carol Selvage—she is a grand-niece of Elizabeth and Jane Baldwin—shared information concerning those missionary sisters. At Majuro, Mary Lanwi—a Marshallese student at Wot during the 1930s and, with her husband Isaac, in charge there during the Second World War—recounted her experiences for me.

Just before her sudden death from bile duct cancer in June 2004, my wife Alice drew the sketches which are used to mark the beginning of the Kosraean and English sections of each chapter. I am deeply indebted to her for these, and for the love and support she constantly extended to me. Alice also assisted with the translations of the chapter summaries, as did Pastor Walton Palik and Pastor Lyndon Abraham. I also want to thank Aren Palik at Guam, Aaron F. Sigrah at Kosrae, and Becky Dornon in California for helping me decipher the various computer problems I encountered.

My brother-in-law, Don Roberds, read an early draft and gave me valuable suggestions. My daughters—Lisa Buck Haley and Lauren Buck Medeiros—went through sections of the manuscript, sharing comments and ideas that I grate-fully received. Both daughters, who chattered Kosraean from their earliest years, overflow with the songs and demeanor of their island heritage. I draw much strength from them.

I was greatly encouraged by Grant Ismael, Director of Kosrae's Tourist Bureau, who trusted my work and directed me to George Engebretson of Watermark Publishing in Honolulu. I sincerely thank George and his talented colleagues at Watermark for their tremendous help in getting the book into print—and so attractively packaged. I extend hearty thanks to Director Henry Robert of Kosrae's Department of Education who was the primary mover in get-ting the book published. I am exceedingly grateful to Patricia Cataldo, for many years editor of the *Kwajalein Hourglass*, for her conscientious work as my copy editor. I have been fortunate, not only to benefit from her considerable exper-tise as a writer and editor, but to profit from her calm and discerning observa-tions of culture, human nature, and the quirks of history. I am endebted to Dr. Robert C. Kiste, Director Emeritus of the Center for Pacific Islands Studies at the University of Hawai'i, for reading the completed manuscript and providing the paragraph on the back cover.

Last of all, I extend my deepest appreciation to my Finpal family—Meuser and Charity Sigrah, their children and grandchildren—who not only took me into their home, but into their hearts. Most of this book was written in the room they so graciously made available to Alice and me during our lengthy stays on Kosrae.

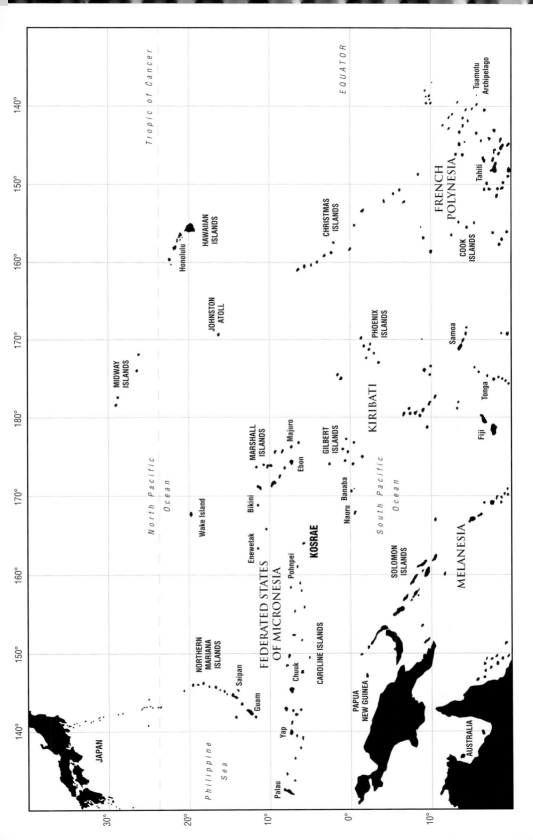

– THE SETTING –

ACN KOSRAE
MEET LIKI 1852

Kut fin lumahla tuka nukewa fin meoa se inge Pacific, Kosrae el arulana fusr—tuh finne ouinge, tausin tausin yac somla sie "volcano" tuh fokelik ac pisryak, na pa orala acn Kosrae. Fineol soko ma fulat oemeet Kosrae, Finkol, oasr fit 2,064 fin kof uh yak. Mutunte, eol soko ma fulat akluo, oasr fit 1,946 fulata. Fineol inge ac infalfal inmasrlo, sessesla ke sacn folfol finsroa. Acn Kosrae rauniyukla ke eka se ma musaiyukyak ke tausin tausin yac somla ke kain in wet srisrik pukanten se. Oasr lulu se su arulana mihs inmasrlon tuka se inge ac fin eka ah.

Ke sripen wet srisrik inge pa orala eka uh oru tia ku in moul in kofonot, acn ma infacl uh soror we orala inya sasla nu meoa. Infacl ma yohk emeet Kosrae pa Infal Innem, Infal Finkol, Infal Okat ac Infal Yela.

Tiana kalem lah pia pacl se mwet uh tuku sun acn Kosrae. Nunkeyuk mu mukul ac mutan ma sun acn Kosrae emeet elos kalkal ke oak srisrik liki mutunfacl roto me yac 2,000 somla. Elos tuh konauk lah arulana kasrup fokon acn uh, wi kof loslos ac lulu ma rauniyak tuka uh su arulana pukanten ik kac—sie acn na wowo in muta we.

Ke puseni mwet Kosrae, elos sifacna oakiya ouiya fal nu ke mutangalos fin acn selos,oayapa kas lalos ac facsin lalos ke ouiyen sou uh oakwuki fwil nu ke fwil. Elos orala calendar se lalos wi fasr lun malem, su akilenya ma sikyak ke kais sie fong ke malem se. Oasr mwet suksuk su orek pwapa ac nununku mukuikui fin acn uh, ac oasr sie tokosra su leum faclos.

Oayapa, ke yac eufoko nu ke itfoko somla, mwet meet inge tuh koanela acn tupasrpasr ke tuka Lelu in orala inkanek, ac pot ma elos etoatyak ke eot wen. Pa inge acn in muta lun tokosra ac mwet suksuk fulat. Acn se inge sie acn pwengpeng ke sramsram matu in acn Pacific.

Mwet matu Kosrae meet ah tuh alu nu sin inut mutan se pangpang Sinlaku, su elos lulalfongi mu el pa oru mos uh in kap ac in oasr kosrani. Oasr pac inut saya, na mwet tol mukul ac mutan—su pangpang Kolo Folfol—pa akkalemye ma lungse lun inut inge uh. In we sac, moul lun mwet Kosrae uh oan ye ku lun inutnut ac ma mwet tol lalos uh pangon oal. Oayapa tokosra ac mwet suksuk uh elos akkohsye mwet Kosrae ke ma sap upa lalos, wi pac ouiya puspis in sunak ma mwet uh tuh enenu in akfalye.

Ke sie tausin yac, wangin mwet saya sun acn Kosrae in aklokoalokye mwet
we. Na ke yac 1500 kutu, mwet Europe elos mutawauk in kalkal fin meoa loes
liki acn selos ke oak nes okoalos. Mwet Spain ac Portugal pa liyauk acn Kosrae
emeet. Tuka nukewa inmasrlon acn Marshall ac acn Philippine (oana Palau,
Yap, Chuuk, Pohnpei, Kosrae) elos ekin "Caroline Islands." Yac luofoko toko,
ke 1804, captain se fin oak America soko el fahkak lah el liye acn Kosrae. Ke
ma el simusla kac, el pangon acn Kosrae "Strong's Island" ke sripen el lungse
akfulatye governor lun acn Massachusetts in pacl sac, su inel pa Caleb Strong.
Ke 1824 ac 1827 acn France ac Russia tuh supwala kutu mwet "scientist" in lutlut ke ouiyen moul lun mwet in acn Pacific. "Scientist" inge simusla ma puspis
ke ouiyen moul lun mwet Kosrae, ac elos konauk lah mwet Kosrae elos mwet
misla ac arulana kulang. Elos tuh motko mu pisen mwet Kosrae in pacl sac oasr
ke mwet 6,000.

Ke yac 1830 mwet America tuh mutawauk in kalkal in acn Pacific in sukok
loat, mweyen kiris ac sri kac oasr sripa nu selos. Tukun yac singoul toko oasr
foko oak in fakfuk loat kalkal in acn Pacific. Mwet orekma fin oak inge elos
mwet na likkeke ac kupatol, ac pukanten selos lungse nimnim. Ke sripen wo
molsron lun acn Kosrae, mwet fin oak inge elos ac oai we in sukok mongo ac
kof ac etong—ac oayapa sukok mutan. Ma elos sang nu sin mwet Kosrae pa
mitmit, tuhla, ac oayapa nuknuk. Kutu selos maskin kain in mas ma tia sikyak
Kosrae meet.

Mwet fakfuk loat inge elos sripauk lokoaklok na yohk, pwanang mwet
Kosrae tia sifil kulang nu selos ku kasrelos. Pus pacl aset inge akukuin ac
anwuk nu sin mwet Kosrae—inkaiyen pacl uh ma ke sripen mukul fin oak uh
sruinkuiya mutan Kosrae. Pukanten mwet kinet ac oasr mwet misa. Oasr pacl
mwet Kosrae elos esukak oak okoan mwet fakfuk loat inge, ac uniya mwet fac
in folokin ma koluk elos oru nu selos. Pukanten mwet Kosrae misa ke sripen
anwuk inge, oayapa ke elos weak mas sasu nu selos. Ke 1840 mwet na 1,700
lula fin acn Kosrae.

Pulan pacl se inmasrlon 1830 nu ke 1852 pa sie pacl in ongoiya lulap ac fohsak nu sin mwet Kosrae ke sripen anwuk ac mas. Tusruktu oasr pac mwe kasru
nu sin mwet Kosrae in pulan pacl sac—pa ke kufwen sroasr osra ac oayapa kutu
kalmac sasu ma elos tufahna lohng. Ke sripa inge nukewa arulana ekla moul
lun mwet Kosrae, pwanang elos tia ku in folok nu ke ouiyen moul lalos meet. Na
mea elos ku in oru in karinganang facsin lalos sifacna, ke ma nukewa ma sikyak
inge oru patokyuk elos in kupasryang nu sin mwet in mutunfacl saya?

Alu matu lun mwet Kosrae, su oakwuki ke ma elos lulalfongi mu oal, tuh
munasla ke elos liye ke mwet sac uh arulana pilesru ma oalkinyuk, a wangin
ma sikyak nu selos. Pwelung ke alu lalos kunanula oetenyak.

Insien mwet Kosrae arulanu akola nu ke Pweng Wo.

MAP OF
KOSRAE
FEDERATED STATES
OF MICRONESIA

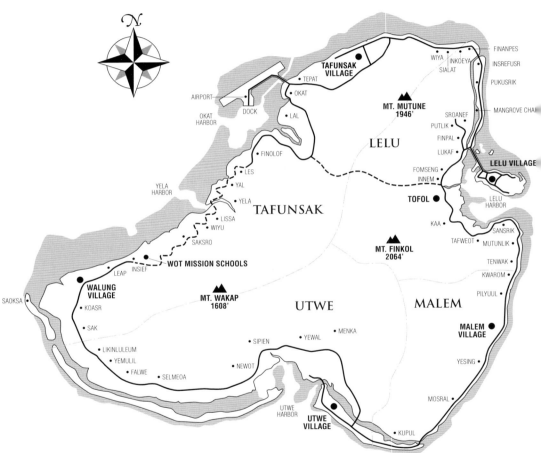

N

FINANPES
INSREFUSR
PUKUSRIK
MANGROVE CHAI

WIYA
INKOEYA
SIALAT

SROANEF
PUTLIK
FINPAL
LUKAF

LELU VILLAGE

FOMSENG
INNEM

LELU HARBOR

TAFUNSAK VILLAGE

TEPAT
OKAT

AIRPORT
DOCK

OKAT HARBOR

LAL

MT. MUTUNE 1946'

LELU

TOFOL

KAA

SANSRIK

FINOLOF

YELA HARBOR

LES
YAL
YELA

TAFUNSAK

LISSA
WIYU
SAKSRO

WOT MISSION SCHOOLS

LEAP
INSIEF

WALUNG VILLAGE

KOASR

SAK

SAOKSA

MT. WAKAP 1608'

MT. FINKOL 2064'

TAFWEOT
MUTUNLIK

TENWAK
KWAROM

PILYUUL

MALEM

MALEM VILLAGE

UTWE

MENKA
YEWAL

SIPIEN

LIKINLULEUM
YEMULIL
FALWE
SELMEOA

NEWOT

YESING

MOSRAL

UTWE HARBOR

UTWE VILLAGE

KUPUL

LEGEND:

————— Existing Road

- - - - - Proposed Road

-·-·-·- Municipal Boundary

● Village

〰〰 Coral Reef & Reef Shelf

KOSRAE
BEFORE 1852

A KOSRAEAN MYTH

And this is the way it was: In the earliest of times Kapuntolu, a great sea serpent, lived in a large cave at Kusrasrik, Okat, near Finelof. One day a lump began to grow on the massive forehead of the sea serpent. It grew and grew and grew until it burst open, and when it did, a pretty baby girl emerged.

Kapuntolu loved her little girl and took attentive care of her. The child developed into a beautiful young woman with lovely, long hair, fine features, and graceful bearing. Because of the daughter's great beauty, Kapuntolu was afraid for anyone to see her. Kapuntolu would not allow her daughter to wander far from their home at Kusrasrik.

The daughter was obedient and industrious. Kapuntolu could not easily gather food because of her enormous size, so the daughter did that chore for both of them. One day while the daughter was alone fishing, the king passed by in his canoe. The startled girl began to run away, but the king commanded his servants to capture her. Smitten by her beauty, the king insisted on taking her immediately to Lelu and making her his wife.

When evening came and the girl did not return, her mother began to worry. Slowly, she crawled down into the water, calling as she went. There was no answer. She climbed a mountain and then returned to the water. In her frantic search, she continued to go back and forth—up one mountain, back to the water, up another, down again—day after day, calling. When she tired, she curled up in the water to sleep. In each place Kapuntolu crawled up a mountain, the weight of her body formed a valley; her sleeping places became harbors; and where she dragged herself through the water a lagoon was created around the edge of the island.

Finally the sea serpent reached Lelu. That evening, her daughter left the king's compound to throw rubbish into the water of Lelu Harbor. There she saw her mother. Both of them were overjoyed. The daughter told her mother that she was now married to the king. Kapuntolu ordered her daughter to instruct the king to prepare a house for her so that she could be near by. The king commanded his men to build a four-story house for his mother-in-law. When it was completed, the sea serpent coiled herself inside where she could peer from a window at the top.

The young queen was glad to have her mother close, and everything went fine until one day the king decided to see what kind of a mother his wife had and why she needed such a large house. He poked his head into the house and heard Kapuntolu say, "Seek and find!" The king was so startled and ter-rified when he saw the huge sea serpent that he ran back to his home at Yat. He ordered the women there to take his young wife at once across the bay to Tafweyat to bathe. When the women had left with the queen, the king ordered his men to burn the house where Kapuntolu lived.

As the daughter was bathing in the river with the women, a cinder floated from the sky and dropped on her knee. Instantly she sensed that something was amiss with her mother. She rushed back to Lelu in time to see Kapuntolu's house consumed in flames. Screaming, she ran toward the blazing building, knowing that her mother was trapped inside. Those standing by realized that the young woman intended to jump into the fire. Quickly, they grabbed her by her beautiful, flowing hair, saving her from the horrible fate of her mother.[1]

Thus, according to a Kosraean legend, the valleys, harbors, and lagoon of the island came into existence.

AN ISLAND IN THE SEA

Kosrae [pronounced ko-SHRY, as in "eye"] is geologically young when com-pared with other islands in the Pacific, but the awesome volcanic explosions that gave it birth ceased millenniums ago. Forty-two square miles in area, the island is more or less triangular in shape—the mountains spiraling out in three directions from a common core. At the center is Mt. Finkol [FIN-coal], rising 2,064 feet above the level of the sea, its lofty head often hidden within a coronet of clouds. Mt. Mutunte [muh-TUHN-tay], Kosrae's second highest peak at 1,946 feet, is in the northeast corner of the triangle, separated from Mt. Finkol by the Okat-Innem isthmus.

Kosrae is encircled by a reef—a calcium wreath built by colonies of micro-scopic coral polyps which attach themselves to volcanic islands at sea level. As the island weathers and settles, these tiny animals build upon the skeletons of their ancestors in a continuous effort to remain in the sunlight at the water's surface. Thus, the gradual sinking of the high island is accompanied by contin-ued upward growth of the coral around it.

The volcanic origins of the much older Marshall Islands have completely disappeared below the surface, each leaving only a "necklace" of small coral islands dotting a reef that encloses a calm lagoon—a "lake within the ocean." Kosrae's reef girds the island at varying distances from the shore—sometimes as close as 50 feet, never further than 800 yards. A placid tideland occupies the coral shelf between the island and the outer edge of the fringing reef.

The erect, craggy interior of Kosrae is criss-crossed with valleys and ravines, each with a rushing stream at its heart. A number of these streams take on river-like proportions as they draw close to the sea. There are spectacular waterfalls and a myriad of freshwater springs, some of which bubble up through the saltwater lagoon. And everywhere there is lavishly abundant vegetation, nourished by an annual rainfall of more than 200 inches. Just five degrees above the equator, Kosrae is far enough north to receive mild trade winds, but is south and east of the major typhoon zone. The weather is humid, and extremes in temperature rare.[2]

The largest four rivers on Kosrae form deep-water harbors where they pass through the lagoon from the island to the ocean. Coral, unable to grow in fresh water, is absent where the rivers enter the sea. Thus, nature provided channels through the reef. The harbors at the mouths of the Okat [OH-cat] and Yela [YELL-lah] rivers on the northwest side of Kosrae, and the Finkol River on the south, are exposed, but provide anchorage in calm weather. The Innem [IN-nem, as in "them"] River to the east empties into Lelu Harbor, which is sheltered within a circle of mountains. The small island of Lelu provides this harbor's north shore and is the location of Kosrae's traditional administrative center.

THE FIRST KOSRAEANS

The Pacific Ocean, with thousands of islands scattered across its vastness, was the last great area of the world to be entered by humans. Indonesia and the Philippine Islands were settled as far back as 50,000 years ago, but century after century, the enchanting islands to the east and south remained the homes of only birds and insects, flowers and trees.

When it was that the first people finally penetrated Micronesia, and what manner of people they were, is not known, though it is known that there were human inhabitants on Saipan in the Mariana Islands by 1500 BCE. The western Caroline Islands were probably settled by this time as well, since they would be the logical stepping-stones to Saipan from populated areas to the south-west.[3] Recent archaeological discoveries in the Marshall Islands suggest that those islands, as well as the Gilberts (Kiribati) and islands within the eastern Carolines, were also settled by then, from the south.[4]

For more than a thousand years, the Asian continent and the Philippines to the west, the great lands of Borneo, Celebes, and New Guinea to the southwest,

and the Melanesian labyrinth to the south slowly poured their racial elements
into the melting pot of Micronesia.[5] Gradually, throughout those centuries preceding the birth of Jesus, canoe-loads of pioneering men and women migrated
eastward and northward, sometimes by circuitous routes. Pushed from the
shores of old homelands by expanding populations, wars, or famine, these
knowledgeable seafarers resolved to find new homes. Occasionally fishermen
were unwittingly swept away on strange currents and deposited on uninhab-
ited islands. Rather than by any concerted or large-scale movement, island after
island was settled by unorganized trickles of brave and determined individuals
and families. And so the first people reached the shores of Kosrae.

Shortly before the advent of Christianity, the last of the migrating groups to
enter the Pacific Islands came from the west, using the malaria-free Caroline,
Marshall, and Gilbert Islands as stepping stones to Polynesia in the east and
leaving their influence on the islands as they passed.

Following the various waves of migration that populated it, Kosrae was left
more or less alone for countless generations, though legends indicate sporadic
contacts with islands as far away as Yap, 1,515 miles to the west.

THE ISLAND BECOMES A HOME

The black-haired, brown-skinned people who came to be known as
Kosraean were shorter and more delicately built than their Polynesian cousins
and had faintly Asian facial characteristics.[6] The Kosraean men were all farmers and, in addition, specialized in one of four trades: fishing, cooking, house-
building, or canoe-making, with a son generally following the same line of work
as his father.[7]

The principal cutting tools were polished adzes made of stone and shell.
Slings and traps were used in hunting wild fowl. Their one gardening tool was
an all-purpose stick, three to five feet in length, which was used for digging,
husking coconuts, and carrying stalks of bananas, bunches of breadfruit, or
bundles of leaves. The Kosraean people were industrious, but did not need to
work hard for food and shelter, thus their technologies, in general, remained
simple.

Shellfish of all descriptions and numberless species of shallow-water fish
in a multitude of dazzling colors abounded in the streams, lagoon, and reefs of
Kosrae. Women fished together out on the tideland, using woven fiber nets hung
within large, pliable frames. As they encircled a school, the fish were snared in
the nets—removed and bitten to stun them—then placed in baskets the women
had tied to their waists and which hung behind them. Men used wooden spears,
diving for fish in the harbors or outside the reef. Fish tranquilizing—spread-

ing anesthetizing sap in the water rendering fish incapable of moving out of reach—and torch fishing at night were other popular methods used.

The ocean around Kosrae contained varieties of tuna and other fish common to the open sea, as well as sea turtles of several kinds. These were always available to the more adventurous, who were willing to take their canoes beyond the confines of the reef. This was not common, however, because the food supply inside the reef was so abundant.

LELU'S ANCIENT CITY

The flat part of Lelu [LEH-luh, as in "level" and "lull"]—the off-shore island which, with the main island, formed the Lelu Harbor basin—was constructed by inhabitants of Kosrae on the reef shelf to the west of Lelu's small mountain. This extensive fill area—built up during the 14th and 15th centuries—was threaded with a number of canals and stone-paved roadways defining the large, rectangular enclosures that comprised Lelu's lowland. Some of the walls of these enclosures were mammoth, composed of lengths of unworked columnar basalt erected in log cabin fashion, sometimes exceeding 20 feet in height. Similar walls and canals were built at Nan Madol on Pohnpei, 365 miles to the northwest. Kosraean folklore includes stories of a Kosraean army loyal to a master clan, called the Saudeleurs, who, it was said, controlled both the Lelu and Nan Madol dynasties during a bygone era.

Lelu's spectacular walls encircled or otherwise delineated the living areas of Kosrae's king and his family, and those of the highest ranking chiefs and their families. There were also two royal burial compounds and sacred courtyards which held small "spirit-houses" related to Kosrae's animistic religion. The entire area—the ruling center of Kosrae's feudal society—was under a rigid taboo that excluded most Kosraeans, except persons who were specifically required for labor or to present tribute.[8] For those who were summoned to appear in Lelu, there were myriad regulations to determine their movements, demeanor, and even vocabulary.

A LUNAR CALENDAR

Through the generations, early Kosraeans not only created the splendid walls, waterways, streets, and court yards of Lelu Island, they also devised an elaborate calendar that noted separately the nights of the lunar month. Each of the 30 nights had its own name. Memorizing these, the people knew which nights were most favorable for catching certain kinds of fish or crabs, on which nights it was best to remain close to home because of marauding spirits, and on

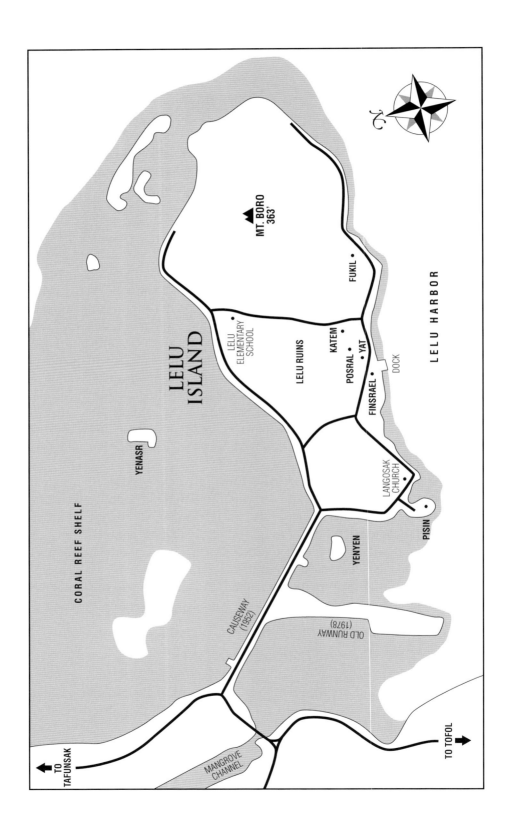

which nights love-making was most apt to produce a son.

The Kosraean names for the nights of their lunar calendar, with a much-abbreviated list of the significance of each as applied here primarily to fishing, are:

1st	Maspang	new moon
2nd	Musalum	new moon
3rd	Musaan	new moon
4th	Museit	good fishing
5th	Musaoal	poor fishing
6th	Lotloto	poor fishing
7th	Mutaoal	good for turtle catching
8th	Sriafong	phosphorescence, poor fishing
9th	Arfoko	fish gathering by species
10th	Sakanpur	good for gathering house timber
11th	Lofsan	good crab catching
12th	Olwen	good crab catching
13th	Fakfong	good fishing
14th	Mesr	planting day
15th	Eel	planting day
16th	Lulti	good fishing
17th	Kuwulah Sie	good fishing
18th	Kuwulah Luo	good fishing
19th	Sopasr	fish producing eggs
20th	Apnuk	fish in separate schools
21st	Sopasr	fish full of eggs
22nd	Osrlun	all fish now in species groups
23rd	Kusaf	fish in species groups
24th	Sunak	fish hiding
25th	Sroanpur	fish hiding beneath hanging branches
26th	Arpi	fish releasing eggs
27th	Lil	fish returning to the sea
28th	Srupup	regrouping of species
29th	Lunguni	dark of the moon
30th	Lungalan	dark of the moon[9]

FARMING AND COOKING

The number and kinds of plants cultivated by the Kosraeans for food were never large—breadfruit, coconut, wetland taro, and bananas being the four primary crops. The green, melon-sized breadfruit was gathered by men who climbed high into the trees and picked the fruit with the aid of a long, forked picking-pole. Breadfruit was usually cooked in a ground oven when almost ripe, though the ripened fruit could be kept indefinitely in fermentation pits.

Coconuts were used in many different ways. Recipes included the use of grated coconut and the "cream" squeezed from it. The juice of the green nut was a popular, refreshing drink. The young flower stalk was tapped for its sweet sap, which was drunk as it was, or condensed into a molasses-like syrup, or fermented to make sakara, "coconut toddy."[10] The coconut palm was an important source of cordage, fuel, and basketry. Several kinds of indigenous bananas, not considered especially tasty, were usually cooked green and used as auxiliary food during the breadfruit off-season. Pandanus fruit, sugarcane, tapioca or manioc, and yams were other plant foods customarily used.

Dogs and chickens were kept and used to supplement the vegetable diet. Doves, as well as a species of parakeet and other birds, were traditionally sources of protein. A small variety of rat was sometimes baked and eaten. There were strong taboos against the eating of river eel, because it was considered the sacred emblem of one of the noble clans.

The three principal ways of cooking were the ground oven, or oom, open-fire boiling, and roasting. In the ground oven, black basalt stones were placed on top of firewood and heated thoroughly. After the fuel had been consumed, the hot stones were spread out in a pit with the use of large wooden tongs. The halved breadfruit or other food was then placed on top of the stones and covered with layer after layer of banana or taro leaves. Fires were lit by the "fire plow" method—a hard stick was rubbed back and forth rapidly in a groove in a larger, softer piece of wood until friction ignited the sawdust produced.[11]

The cooked food could be eaten as it was, but breadfruit, taro, bananas, and tapioca were often pounded into a pudding, straight or mixed together, wrapped in banana leaves, and baked in the ground oven. Boiling was sometimes achieved by placing heated stones into wooden or shell containers filled with water and food. Pottery was only rudimentarily developed because a low grade of clay unsuitable for firing was all that was found on Kosrae.

Kosrae was covered with lush, virgin forest, and many kinds of trees could be used for both fire and building purposes. Mangrove was the favorite source of firewood, because it burned long with a hot flame. It was also popular for building, because the wood was hard and heavy and more resistant to rot than the common land trees. Mangrove trees grew interlaced in the brackish sea water along the shores and estuaries. Except for varieties of lizards, no reptiles infested these swamps and woodlands, so wood and food were gathered without fear.

SHELTER AND APPAREL

Four main types of buildings were erected by the Kosraean people—sleeping houses, cook houses, canoe houses, and feast or meeting houses. The style of construction was roughly the same for all of these building and involved a wooden frame lashed together with coconut-husk cord and covered with thatch. Platforms of basalt rock or coral blocks and earth were usually created as a sort of foundation for the sleeping houses, and sleeping decks inside were devised of reeds lashed tightly together. Woven pandanus mats were used as mattresses and also as covers. Walls were made of plaited coconut fronds, braided reeds, or nipa palm thatch. A type of siding made of hibiscus or mangrove poles bound together was also used.

Dugout canoes, with outriggers extended to the right on booms, were used for fishing and traveling around the island or through the mangrove swamp channels at high tide. Breadfruit was a favorite canoe-building wood, although there was some ambivalence because the healthiest fruit-bearing trees made the best canoes.

Children and young adolescents wore no clothing. Adult males wore a narrow loincloth, finely woven, often with complicated designs. The women made these on simple looms, using fibers from the inner bark of the wild hibiscus or from the trunks of certain varieties of bananas. It was a time-consuming chore. Skirts made from the fiber of unopened coconut palm fronds, as well as wraparounds of woven pandanus, were worn by both men and women. Specially woven decorative belts, called tol, were considered to be of high value, and were worn on ceremonial and other festive occasions.

THE TRADITIONAL FAMILY

Family ties were especially close. No specific terms were used for "aunt," "uncle," "niece," "nephew" or "cousin." The term "father" included uncles, "mother" included aunts, "sister" and "brother" took in cousins, and "son" and "daughter" covered nieces and nephews. A son brought his bride home to his father's house, where they remained in an extended family arrangement with their own growing children, at least until the father of the extended family died.

Pre-marital sexual activity was condoned by parents, though they frowned upon such a relationship when it did not involve a potential spouse for the child. Marriages were arranged by the families of the boy and girl, usually while they were still children—the opinions of uncles, aunts, and grandparents carrying the same weight as those of the actual parents. Elaborate food offerings and other gifts were exchanged between two families thus contracted.

Bonds between brothers and sisters, including cousins, were particularly strong. Certain taboos controlled their relationships, such as a brother kept ignorant of his sisters' romantic liaisons. Marriage between first and second cousins was prohibited, and discouraged between third, and even fourth, cousins. Extreme loyalty kept siblings close throughout their lifetime.

The bonds between siblings were often strengthened by the adoption of one another's children. Particularly if an older sibling was childless, he or she might adopt the child of a younger sibling—though brothers and sisters with children of their own might also adopt in this way. In another form of adoption, an adult would frequently give a child to his or her aging parents to assist them and provide companionship. There was no formality concerning adoption; children simply went to live with their adoptive parents, often remaining in the same extended household as their natural parents. An adopted child was usually treated as considerately as other children, but discrimination could occur in the inheritance of land. Since family ties were not usually broken by adoption, adopted children almost always knew who their natural parents were—or at least who their birth mother was. Upon reaching maturity, children sometimes returned to their birth parents, especially if those parents had ample land to pass on to them.[12]

In some ways, marrying in Kosraean society was like the marriage of families. A man had secondary sexual rights with his wife's sisters and his brothers' wives, a further manifestation of the solidarity of brothers and sisters. Still, basic monogamy was the usual pattern, with a couple remaining together through life. Polygamy was practiced, however, by the Kosraean chiefly families. For social reasons tied to land ownership and prestige, the king would often marry, in addition to his own wife, the widow of his predecessor.[13]

KOSRAEAN SOCIETY DEVELOPS

Because of the isolation of their island, Kosraeans developed a social structure and language distinct from those of other Micronesians. They had one of the best-organized political units found anywhere in the Pacific—the whole island being united under a single king. The Kosraean people were divided into four social strata: king, high titled chiefs, lower chiefs or land managers, and commoners.[14]

The king was chosen partly for hereditary rank and partly for achievement and ability. Including the king, there were some 18 high chiefs or nobles. When coming into a chieftainship, the noble gave up his own name and took instead the title of his rank. The wife of each noble had a corresponding title.

The highest nine ranks were:

I.   Tokosra [TAH-goh-shra, as in "rap"] - king
     Kasra [KAH-shrah, as in "raw"] - queen
     (Fisrak - children of the king and queen)
          The four chiefs responsible directly to the king:
          Sikein   Sinikein - his wife
          Siku   Sikupe - his wife
          Simuta   Sikatinmuta - his wife
          Sifusra   Sinifusra - his wife
II. Kanku [CON, as in "conference"-kuh] - prime minister/general
     Kasrainnap - his wife
          The three chiefs directly responsible to the kanku:
          Sipa   Sipape - his wife
          Sigrah (Sigurah) Siminlik - his wife
          Suwarku   Sinalik - his wife[15]

The king was chosen by the chiefs from among themselves. Often, when a vacancy appeared in the roster of chiefs, each one of lower rank advanced a step. All of these men were members of the highest three clans of Kosrae—Ton, Pwenma, and Lisrngi—the clan affiliation passing through the mother. These ranking officials all lived near the king, within the various enclosures designated by their titles, on the off-shore island of Lelu. They had servants to do their work, but they, themselves, were often talented fishermen, canoe builders, or wrestlers.

The king was considered to have absolute power, but in fact the chiefs could and did lead revolts, occasionally deposing a king who abused his power. After being selected, the king had the right to fill vacancies among the chieftainships from his own partisans in the various noble families, so the longer he remained in office, the more secure his position became.

The wives of these nobles lived lives of relative ease. As they seldom left their homes, their skin tone was shades lighter than that of other Kosraean women. When one of them ventured outside her husband's compound, she was carried piggy-back. A maid walked behind to hold a woven pandanus tray on which the lady's hair, which was never cut, was carefully folded to keep it from touching the ground. Others did all household chores, including the care of children, so chiefly women tended to be heavy. Their legs were often crippled from lack of activity, because they sat with their legs folded under them most of the time.

None of the common people from the large island of Kosrae were allowed to set foot on Lelu Island except by specific command, and then they could not stand upright or talk above a whisper. The Posral [po as in "pole"-SHRAL, as in "all"], Yat [yacht], and Katem [CAT-tem, as in "temper"] areas of Lelu were the private domains of the king and the kanku, and even the chiefs stooped low when on these grounds. Servants crawled on hands and knees. Every day, a different commoner was compelled to supply food for the king and his family. Others were designated to provide the daily fare for the ranking chiefs. These food-providers were under penalty of death if they failed to comply. With considerable trepidation, those bringing food would wend their way by canoe through the Lelu Island canals to specific openings or pass-throughs in the massive walls, where they would place the required offerings.

The harsh reality for Kosrae's commoners was in considerable contrast to the leisurely existence of the nobles. The work of providing for the chiefly families on Lelu Island was closely monitored, heavy, and constant. The population of Kosrae is estimated to have been close to 6,000 before 1800. The island was divided into 57 administrative districts, each with its own chief or headman, called mwet kahki. These areas and their chiefs were divided by the king among the higher ranking nobles and chiefs, who acted as the king's representatives. The king also retained two or three sections under direct personal control. The chief of a section was appointed by the high chief to whom his section was assigned, though his position was also in part hereditary.[16]

Periodically, the king would make visits, called puloa, to the villages around the large island. On these occasions, the commoners, led by their mwet kahki, would prepare a huge feast and celebration for the king. Each feast was held in a large thatched pavilion constructed especially for that purpose. Within the pavilion, platforms with floors made of reeds were built several feet above the ground—one for the king, another for the kanku, and so on down the order of rank. The food was divided into portions for each noble and a specific name, corresponding to rank, was given to each portion. In another area arranged in similar fashion, the queen and lesser ladies of nobility enjoyed their part of the feast.

The delicacy of choice was fafa: taro pounded until gummy and covered with a sugarcane-sweetened coconut sauce. Elaborate ceremonies were connected to its preparation. Guests enjoyed saka or kava, a drink made from the pounded roots of a large pepper plant containing a mild narcotic. Selections from a heritage of chants and songs were sung. These had a range of only a few notes, variation and complexity being introduced by rhythm and syncopations in the shift from one note to another.[17] Canoe races and wrestling matches often took place in connection with feast days.

If the king was pleased with the food, decorations, and entertainment provided him by those within a certain district, he would pass out gifts of mwek—shells or mother-of-pearl "money" of varying values, as well as woven mats and fiber cloth.

A unique honorific vocabulary was used by commoners when addressing a person of high rank. To address the king, everyone, including nobles, was required to speak with exaggerated slowness, using a laryngeal whisper produced as the breath was inhaled instead of exhaled. No person's head could be above the king's, nor was anyone allowed to look directly into his face. When a king died, his body was placed in one of the two ingeniously constructed stone pits, Insru and Inol, located within the Lelu complex of canals and compounds. There, an honor guard stood watch for months; when only bones remained, they were taken up and scattered on the water in the deep tidal pool next to the tiny islet, Yenasr [YEN-nahsh], not far from Lelu's north shore.

Strict courtesy rules, known as sunak [su, as in "sunny"-NAK, as in "knock"], were observed among all Kosraean families, as well. Sisters used a distinct vocabulary when addressing their brothers. Women were required to walk several paces behind their husbands and to leave the trail when a man approached to pass. A woman was also compelled to keep her head at all times on a level lower than the head of any man near her. If a man was sitting on the mat, this particular regulation required that she pull herself into his presence practically on her stomach. Any type of shouting was held to be in very poor taste.

RELIGION OF SINLAKU

The animistic religion of Kosrae centered around the worship of a breadfruit goddess, Sinlaku [sin-LACK-kuh]. Her favorite dwelling place was said to have been at the foot of the high waterfall at Yekela. There were many lesser spirits, called inut [EE-noot, as in "noon"], represented by different sites around the island, such as peculiar outcroppings of volcanic rock, cliffs, caves, strange mountain formations, or old, gnarled trees. Especially feared were the spirits of the dead. Even loved and respected members of the family, it was believed, returned after death to plague and pester. Sorcery was practiced to a considerable extent, and there was much superstition in the daily lives of the people. Death was dreaded, and the crowing of a rooster at dusk was understood to be a sure sign that the end was near for a close relative. A fish flopping into a moving canoe signaled that some feared event was taking place back home.

The religious leaders on the island were called kolo folfol—blue skins—because they were heavily tatooed and because of the color of the eels they handled during certain sacred ceremonies. These were the priests and priestesses of the goddess Sinlaku, and of a lesser god, Nusinsrat. The kolo folfol were not of the noble families, nor did they have their center of religious activities in Lelu. They gathered at Menke, in Infal Alu—the Valley of Worship—high in the mountains between the Lelu and Utwe [OOT, as in "hoot"-way] harbors. There were paths over the mountains leading to Menke from settlements around the edge of Kosrae like the spokes of a wheel.

The head of religious rites was chosen anew at periodic gatherings as participants slashed gashes on their foreheads with stones. The one who produced the greatest amount of blood was understood to be that period's high priest or priestess. Participants drank saka and sakara and, in a state of trance, would pronounce prophesies and give instructions.

The adherents of this religion were said to have been greatly helped by inut, who would perform for them great physical feats, such as moving huge stones from distant quarries to sites of worship. Along with these spirits, the priests were believed to be in league with giants, called kot, and elves, referred to as fufusr. These latter two were not the source of such extreme anxiety as were the invisible spirits, but they reappear continually in Kosraean mythology as annoying mischief-makers. The priests and priestesses were respected by the king and his chieftains, but their power was much stronger among the common people on the large island in the midst of whom they lived and worked. It was believed that they had authority over certain spirits. They were the magicians involved in most of the sorcery and the guardians of the intricate system of taboos relating to planting, fishing, and marriage.

There were those outside the circle of priests who possessed the recipes for secret remedies. These recipes included mixtures of certain herbs that often had medicinal properties. The knowledge of the correct ingredients was considered to be the private information of a given family and was guardedly passed from parent to child. The priests and priestesses, however, were the "witch doctors." They knew the formulas for potions which, when drunk, could break an evil spell. They knew, too, how to weave and construct the fetishes that Kosraeans would hang in obvious places to ward off unfriendly spirits during pregnancy or some other vulnerable time.

The people of Kosrae lived in a constant state of apprehension because of their king and his complete domination over them. They lived in terror of the multitude of spirits which they believed surrounded them, and in continuous intimidation by the blue skins who exerted such powerful influence over the details of their lives.

EUROPEANS FIND KOSRAE

During the latter part of February 1521, Fernando Magellan sailed through Micronesia on the first voyage to circumnavigate the globe, passing not far from Kosrae itself. Remarkably, Magellan traveled right through the Pacific island world, from southeast to northwest, sighting only an atoll or two, until Guam appeared on the horizon on March 6 of that year. Thus began the so-called "Era

of Discovery," with Spanish and Portuguese seamen dominating the oceans during the 16th century.

The first recorded sighting by a foreigner of the high islands in the eastern
part of the Carolines was in 1529, when Alvaro de Saavedra, a Spaniard, passed
through on his way from Mexico to the Moluccas in Indonesia. During the latter
part of that century, other Spanish adventurers visited the region but showed
little interest in the inhabitants of the islands among which they sailed. They
were concentrating, rather, on finding the quickest route between the Philippine
Islands and Peru.

One hundred years later, the 2,000-mile-long archipelago that stretched
between the Marshall Islands to the east and the Philippine Islands to the west
came to be known as the "Caroline Islands" to honor King Charles II of Spain
(1665-1700).[18] Then, as they grappled with the process of mapping the islands
and peoples of the Pacific, European explorers and anthropologists gave the
name "Micronesia" to the western part of the central Pacific that included the
Gilbert, Marshall, Caroline and Mariana islands. The name was derived from
the Greek words "micro" meaning "small" and "nesos" meaning "island."[19]

During most of the 17th and 18th centuries, the people of Kosrae, Pohnpei,
and the other islands in this part of the Pacific, continued their traditional ways,
mostly ignored by those on passing ships. Sporadic contacts did take place, but
few reports of them exist. The dawn of the 19th century, however, brought in
a new era and, with it, the guarantee of a dramatic upheaval in the traditional
island way of life. The Pacific became the whalers' bonanza.

Only a few whaling ships reached the proximity of Kosrae during the first
few years of the new century, but they did come. The initial recorded sighting
of Kosrae by Westerners was in 1804, when an American whaleship captain
aboard the *Nancy* noted it in his journal and gave it the name "Strong's Island,"
after Caleb Strong, governor of his home state of Massachusetts. This name was
used by outsiders in reference to Kosrae throughout the entire 19th century.
Kosrae's highest peak, Mt. Finkol, is still indicated on some ocean charts and
maps as "Mt. Crozier," named for the *Nancy's* captain.

VISITS OF THE *COQUILLE* AND THE *SENYAVIN*

Two much more significant events took place two decades later. On June
5, 1824, Capt. Louis Isidore Duperrey, commanding the French ship *Coquille*,
anchored in Okat Harbor. He went ashore with his men and stayed 10 days.
Though it is almost certain that others had landed previously, Capt. Duperrey
was the first to record the event. On December 7, 1827, the Russian explorer
Fyedor Lutke, captain of the ship *Senyavin*, entered Okat Harbor and spent three

weeks on Kosrae. Both Capt. Duperrey and Capt. Lutke reported the Kosraeans to be friendly. The islanders liked the Europeans, and the affection was reciprocated.[20] In spite of this, however, the Kosraeans tried to keep their women out of reach of the visiting sailors when it became obvious that the sailors were trying to approach them.

Capt. Lutke was intrigued by a young chief, Nena [NEIGH-na, as in "Nan"], and his friend, Oa, who boarded the *Senyavin*, and he noted, "Their gaiety was most attractive. Nena stood out by a certain nobility in his manners as well as by a strange impishness." On the ship, Nena refused to walk unless he was holding on to Lutke. Oa, who impressed the Russian captain as being remarkably intelligent, immediately began to act like a European—to sit on a chair and to spit in the spittoon. "They tried to discover the purpose of everything. The piano excited their curiosity, and Oa brought up a chair and began to accompany the piano player. Then he raised the top to find out how the piano was made. At the forge, he was the first to understand that one of the crew was making a knife."[21]

When Capt. Lutke went to Lelu, he used a well-traveled overland trail that crossed from Okat to Innem. Likiak, a village chief, accompanied him and was described by Lutke as "outstanding in his eagerness to help. His never failing cheerfulness made everyone love him. During the walk he was always beside me; part of the time he carried my gun, part of the time my instruments, and they could not have been in better hands."[22]

Arriving on the other side of the island, Capt. Lutke and his entourage were astonished—as were Capt. Duperrey and his men three years earlier—to find the neatly graveled roads, the canals, and the numerous high-walled compounds of Kosrae's capitol, Lelu. Lutke met the king and spent three evenings as a guest of the high chief Siba in his Lelu compound.[23] Fortuitously, among those from the *Coquille* who accompanied Capt. Duperrey were two artists whose names were Fredrick H. Von Kittlitz and Aleksandr Postel. The finely detailed sketches made by these two men captured for posterity scenes and articles of Kosraean society as it was in 1824.

A. P. Lesson, a naturalist aboard the *Coquille*, described having difficulty with the king and the higher ranking chiefs, and noted in his papers his dislike for them. Unaware of local custom, the newcomers undoubtedly slighted Kosrae's nobility and felt their disapproval. The king and chiefs in Lelu's great enclosures behaved like the aristocrats they were, and not like the Kosraean commoners who had won the esteem of the visitors by, among other things, "the attentions they lavished so eagerly on us."

Lutke noted that there was never a day that the Kosraeans did not bring breadfruit and other varieties of fruit to them in their temporary camp on the islet Mutuniel in Okat Harbor. So many Kosraeans visited the ship that there was hardly room to move around. There were a few thefts and other minor provocations. Capt. Lutke was annoyed when some Kosraeans, noting his aversion to lice, laughingly pretended to pluck some from their heads and toss them at him![24]

Those aboard the *Coquille* and the *Senyavin* introduced metal to Kosrae. Axes, cooking pots, knives—especially the machete—were quickly prized by Kosraeans. The crew of the *Coquille* left a pregnant pig on Kosrae. It was the first pig the Kosraeans had seen.[25]

"WALUNG" AND "KOSRAE"

The name Walung or Ualung [WA-lung, as in "wax" and "lung"], began appearing on charts and maps as the indigenous name for the island—the result of miscommunication. Foreign navigators, eager to know what the inhabitants called their particular place at 5.20 degrees north and 163 degrees east in the midst of the vast Pacific, stood on Lelu Island and gestured across toward the southwest side of the harbor where the large island loomed. Kosraeans standing with the newcomers responded with "Walung," a word used to designate less populated areas—the "country," as opposed to "urban." Places on the "edge of activity" or isolated from "action," were called "Walung." Any member of Lelu's chiefly community considered most parts of the large island as "Walung."

Some years later when the mistake was discovered and the actual name for the island became known, foreigners did not pronounce "Kosrae" properly and so misspelled it as "Kusaie" [koo-SIGH]—a name used by non-Kosraeans until 1977.

For countless generations "Kosrae" had been the name that included all areas within the encircling reef. The large, primary island with its spectacular mountains and winding valleys; the smaller island of Lelu with its acres of artificial canals and compounds; the historic islets of Yenyen and Yenasr on the tideland north of Lelu; the sandy islets that hug Lelu's eastern shore; Mutuniel in Okat Harbor, and Kiel at Okat's entrance; Srukames, standing alone on the western reef shelf; and the extended string of palm-covered sandbars that cover the southern reefs—all of these were and are Kosrae.

INCURSION OF THE WHALERS

Between 1830 and 1840 the whaling industry intensified. Hundreds of vessels were ploughing the Pacific from the Arctic to the Antarctic in search of the great sperm whales. Oil boiled from the fat of these huge mammals, and their bones—used, among other things, for corset stays—were valued in English and New England society. Most of the whaling ships were from Nantucket, Massachusetts, and New Bedford, Connecticut, though there were Australian and English whalers as well.[26]

Most of the time whaling fleets kept to the open seas, but when a ship did put ashore, the effect on that community was stupefying. A hundred or so lusty fellows suddenly turned loose on a quiet village after months of poor rations, hard discipline, and back-breaking work—away from the sight of women and the smell of rum—had to have been difficult, indeed, for either captain or king to control.

Few islands escaped the visits of whalers, but some of them, such as Moorea in the Society Islands, Upolu at Samoa, Hiva Oa in the Marquesas, and Kosrae in the Carolines, were especially popular because of the beauty and hospitality of their women.[27] More and more ships found their way to Kosrae as word of its concealed harbor at Lelu, its ample supply of food, water, and firewood, as well as its beautiful women, spread from ship to ship. Many reports made a special point of commenting on the docility and congeniality of the Kosraean people as compared to that of some of their Micronesian neighbors.

In the mid 1800s, Kosrae's King Lupalik I [lu, as in "lull"-PAUL-lick], referred to by the whalers as "Good King George," explained his theory of Kosrae's popularity: "Because plenty good-looking gal, schooner stop Strong's Island."[28] Kosraean women were sometimes torn from the arms of their husbands by drunken, gun-toting sailors. Just as sad were those who were "sold" for a night by fathers and husbands for a length of cloth, a shiny machete, or a bottle of liquor. These Kosraean men paid a much higher price for these items than their naivete allowed them to realize. With the debauchery came venereal disease, a curse that would continue to torment Kosrae for decades.

Other white man's illnesses also added to the destruction of this island's people. Though venereal diseases took the greatest toll, measles and pulmonary infections were also prevalent. The lack of knowledge of what is termed hygiene, coupled with the fact that Kosraeans had no natural immunity, made them extremely susceptible and the diseases all the more devastating. A few captains tried conscientiously to isolate sick passengers and sailors from the islanders, but others would deliberately abandon such people in the midst of the oblivious and vulnerable Kosraeans.

To visitors who would listen, King George (Lupalik I) lamented the loss of the days when old age was common and the laughter of children was prevalent everywhere.[29] Old people and infants alike had become scarce in all parts of Kosrae by the late 1830s.

In 1824, the French crew of the *Coquille*, and in 1827, the Russians aboard the *Senyavin*, had specifically noted the absence of weapons among the Kosraeans, whom they described as peaceful and friendly. But the era of good-will was drawing to a close. As a consequence of the reprehensible treatment the Kosraeans had too often suffered at the hands of visiting white men, the natural friendliness and generosity initially extended to visitors began to disappear. Tales of the hostility of Kosraeans began circulating among foreigners in the Pacific.

NOT ALL SHIPS WELCOMED

The history of visiting ships and crews in the 1830s illustrates the changing attitude of the Kosraeans. In January 1835, the crew of the whaler *Waverly* was killed and the ship burned in Lelu Harbor. It was said that Capt. Cathcart had forcibly carried the daughter of a chief on board and, when she resisted him, had her thrown overboard, where she drowned. Some months later, Capt. John Gordon Scott and 14 members of his crew aboard the trading vessel *Honduras* were attacked and killed. A few surviving members of that crew managed to escape on their ship to Pohnpei.[30]

Capt. C. Hingston of the London whaleship *Falcon* reported being at anchor in Lelu Harbor for 120 days in 1837 without experiencing trouble. But another London ship, the *Harriet*, commanded by Capt. Charles Bunker, was mysteriously burned in Okat Harbor and the crew massacred in 1842. The following year, five whalers stopped in the same harbor and were not bothered.[31] There were suggestions that white renegades temporarily living on Kosrae had instigated the ship attacks.[32]

WHALERS CONTINUE TO VISIT

In spite of the stories—some true, some fabricated—whalers called with ever more frequency at Kosrae. They usually stayed for a week or two, but sometimes were forced to remain for much longer periods because the channel into Lelu Harbor became dangerous for sailing vessels when the wind was blowing into the passage. Between December 1850 and October 1852, the *Emily Morgan*, commanded by Capt. Prince Ewer, visited Kosrae four times. Arriving the second time, on March 30, 1851, the crew was surprised to find the *Mary Frazier* still in port, having been "windbound" for three months. An English bark, the *Maria Laura*, was also there—and it was April 23 before the three ships could finally get out of the harbor.[33]

As the numbers of Western sailors visiting Pacific islands increased, kings and chiefs often found it profitable to keep a foreigner near to handle trade with ships and give advice on the use of foreign goods.[34] Usually these men were a stubborn, uncouth lot who used liquor excessively, paid little attention to island social organization and customs, violated taboos, and helped reduce the prestige of the very chiefs for whom they worked. Many of them set up small trading establishments and intentionally took advantage of the islanders who craved the amazing and superior products of the newcomers. The concepts of credit and debt were not understood and traders often used the innocence of the islanders to keep them in a state of servitude.[35]

A number of such men lived at various times on Kosrae. Capt. Isaac B. Hussey, a resident from 1837 to 1840, was the first. He returned in 1850 with David Kirtland, and together they set themselves up as the "official" traders of the island. In 1852, however, Capt. Hussey and his Kosraean cabin boy were murdered in a mutiny during a whaling voyage aboard the *William Penn*. This boy was among the first of many Kosraeans who left home, never to return. He was greatly mourned when word of his death finally reached his family.

Mr. Kirtland remained on Kosrae, and for a while was the only foreign resident. Then, in July 1852, two American sailors jumped ship in Lelu Harbor, swelling the white population to three.

IN NEED OF GOOD NEWS

The traumatic upheaval that occurred within the old social structure on Kosrae during the first 50 years of the 19th century induced the disintegration of the ancient religious system. The very presence of the foreigners had caused it to waver. White men demonstrated in their every action that they were not subject to the power of the customary taboos and could defy them with no fear of reprisal. The practices and materials introduced by these men had nothing to do with what had been held sacred and obligatory throughout the generations. Even Sinlaku, the breadfruit goddess, had somehow become insignificant.

A story told and retold among the Kosraeans describes a conclave which, it was said, took place among Sinlaku and her spirit-henchmen just prior to the arrival of the ship that brought the first missionaries. These inut talked of a new and mightier spirit whose imminent arrival would destroy their own power. They themselves would have to leave. ☩

Notes - The Setting:

1.   Flora Aliksa, daughter of King John Sigrah, wrote her recollection of this myth at the author's request, June 1963, translated from Kosraean
2.   Myron Kerner, U.S. Weather Bureau, Honolulu, personal correspondence, March 1963
3.   Herold J. Wiens, *Pacific Island Bastions of the United States*, 1962, pp. 8-12
4.   Harvey Gordon Segal, *Kosrae: The Sleeping Lady Awakens*, 1989, p. 4
5.   Willard Price, *Japan's Islands of Mystery*, 1944, p. 15
6.   Wiens, pp. 12-13
7.   Benjamin G. Snow, unpublished correspondence, Dec. 25, 1852
8.   Ross Cordy and Teddy John, "Interpretive Guidebook Leluh Ruins," Leluh Ruins Landowners Corporation, Kosrae Historic Preservation Office, 1984, p. 3
9.   Department of Education, "Kosrae's Lunar Calendar," Tofol, Kosrae, Jan. 2002
10. John L. Fischer, *The Eastern Carolines*, 1957, p. 84
11. Ibid, p. 93
12. James L. Lewis, "Kusaiean Acculturation 1834-1948," p. 49
13. Snow, Dec. 25, 1852
14. Cordy and John, p. 2
15. Conversation with Sikein Aliklof, June 7, 1962
16. Fischer, p. 179
17. Fischer, p. 204
18. Fairfield Osborn, editor, *The Pacific World*, "Its vast distances, its lands and the life upon them, and its peoples," W. W. Norton & Company, Inc., New York 1944, p. 156
19. Ibid, p. 24
20. Fischer, p. 22
21. Micronesian Area Research Center, "Kusaie In the Nineteenth Century," Univ. of Guam, undated, p. 3
22. Ibid, p. 3
23. Ross Cordy, "The Lelu Stone Ruins (Kosrae, Micronesia)," p. 18
24. "Kusaie In the Nineteenth Century," p. 4
25. Segal, p. 48
26. Albert W. Atwood, "Revealing Earth's Mightiest Ocean," National Geographic Society's New Map of the Pacific Ocean, 1943, p. 9
27. Douglas L. Oliver, *The Pacific Islands*, 1951, p. 77
28. Snow, unpublished correspondence, 1853
29. Ibid
30. Francis X. Hezel, S.J., *Foreign Ships in Micronesia*, Saipan, 1979, p. 90
31. "Kusaie In the Nineteenth Century," pp. 5, 6
32. Segal, p. 74
33. "Kusaie In the Nineteenth Century," p. 6
34. Oliver, p. 25
35. Wiens, p. 25

NUNAK YOHK KE CHAPTER 1
1852

Oak soko pangpang *Caroline* tuh oai Kosrae ke Sunday, August len 21, 1852. Mwet singoul tolu tuh wema oak soko ah, na oasr mwet singoul sie orekma fin oak ah. Sianyan tolu tuku America me—inelos pa Benjamin ac Lydia Snow, Luther ac Louisa Gulick, ac Albert ac Susan Sturges. Sianyen luo tuku Hawai'i me—inelos pa Daniel ac Doreka Opunui, ac Berita ac Deborah Kaaikaula. Mwet se ma kol u se inge pa Ephriam Clark, su mwet sropo se ke Kawaiaha'o Church in acn Honolulu, ac el pa sifen u se ma fosrngakin missionary inge nu Micronesia. Mwet luo saya ma wi tuku pa James Kekela, sie pac pastor Hawai'i, ac John Gulick, tamulel lal Luther Gulick.

Mukul America se tuh muta fin acn Kosrae in pacl sac, inel pa David Kirtland. El tuh som nu fin oak soko ah ke srakna oan meoa in kasrel Captain Holdsworth in utyak ke molsron Lelu.

Yac se mwet missionary tuku sun acn Hawai'i pa 1820. Mwet inge elos supweyuk sin Congregational Church in acn America. Mwet Hawai'i pukanten elos lohng kas in luti lalos ac forla mwet Christianla. Na yac tolngoul luo toko mwet Christian Hawai'i, wi mwet Christian America, tuh supama un mwet missionary fin *Caroline* inge nu Micronesia. Elos tuh lohng sramsram ke lokoalok lulap ma sikyak fin acn Kosrae ac Pohnpei ke sripen orekma koluk lun mwet fakfuk loat, na elos arulanu pakomuta. Elos pulakin lah God El kololos in som nu ke tuka luo inge in kasru mwet we, ac in fahkak Pweng Wo ke Christ nu selos. Elos oayak Honolulu ke July 15, 1852.

Ke lotutang in Monday, August len 22, missionary inge srola weacn in acn Lelu, ac Mr. Kirtland el pwanulos nu yorol Awane Lupalik I. Tokosra se inge eteyuk yurin mwet kalkal in acn Pacific ke ine se inge: "Good King George." Tokosra el arulana kulang ke el paing missionary uh. Elos lut mweyen el etu kutu kas English, oayapa yohk ma el etu ke acn sayen acn Kosrae. Ke elos sramsram yorol elos akilen lah el sie mwet lalmwetmet ac el oayapa mongfisrasr ac inse pusisel ke el kol mwet lal.

Pastu Clark el siyuk lah tokosra el ku in lela kutu selos in muta orekma fin acn Kosrae, na tokosra el topuk mu sie mukul ku in muta. Ke missionary inge elos sifil sroang nu fin *Caroline*, elos tuh sulela Pastu Snow in pa mukul sac. Lydia, mutan kial, ac oayapa mwet Hawai'i luo, Daniel ac Doreka Opunui, elos ac oelul pac muta.

Len itkosr toko, *Caroline* el oayak in som nu Pohnpei, ac missionary nukewa wi. Elos sun acn we ke September len 6. Tokosra fin acn Madolenihmw el lela Mr. Gulick, Mr. Sturges, Mr. Kaaikaula, wi mutan kialos, in mutana Pohnpei.

Benjamin ac Lydia Snow, ac Daniel ac Doreka Opunui, elos folokla nu Kosrae. Ap nukewa lalos titila liki oak ah, na oak soko ah oayak in fulokla nu Hawai'i. Tokosra el sang tuka na srisrik se pangpang Pisin nu sin missionary tuh elos in muta we. Ke pacl se aknasnasyeyuk acn Pisin ac lohm selos musaiyuk, mwet akosr inge tuh muta yurol Mr. Kirtland.

"Good King George" el tuh wulela mu el ac oanu sie papa nu selos.

– CHAPTER ONE –

THE MISSIONARIES ARRIVE
1852

THEIR DESTINATION KOSRAE

Early on the morning of August 20, 1852, five men and five women, thousands of miles from their homes, stood at the railing of the brig *Caroline*, gazing at the distant outline of the island of Kosrae. They knew it as "Strong's Island" or "Kusaie," the destination they had long hoped to reach. It appeared rugged and mysterious, a gray silhouette against the horizon. Together they bowed their heads in a prayer of thanksgiving for the safe and sure leading of God.

For hours the small group remained on watch, joined at times by the other three passengers, as well as by various members of the 11-man crew. Voices were sparked with the enthusiasm of youth. The eagerness of these young people to land, however, seemed unappreciated by the sailing vessel. With little wind, progress was exasperatingly slow.

It was mid-afternoon by the time they could see breakers foam-etched along the encircling reef. Some of the men climbed into the rigging for a better look and shouted their observations down to their companions. The sun, blazing through a cloudless sky, was reflected on the water and shimmered from the metallic-green top of the mangrove swamp which bordered the shore in a thick, luxuriant fringe.

But it was not until dawn the next day that the *Caroline* stood off the narrow channel marking a natural passage through the reef into the harbor on the east side of the island. The passengers, their weariness eclipsed by anticipation, had remained on deck most of the night, talking softly to one another or standing silently, eyes straining toward the looming shadow. Now they were rewarded as the ribbon of coral sand that traced the harbor's entrance dazzled in the rising sun. Profuse coconut palms trimming the beach, their bursts of fronds high atop stark classic trunks, bowed outward. To the sea-weary voyagers it was a gesture of welcome.

The ship had been seen, for it was only a short time before the travelers noticed a whaleboat being rowed through the swells toward them. Six men were straining at the oars, three men of the island and three unkempt white men.

Pulling alongside, these strangers labored to synchronize the wild heaving of their boat with the pitching of the ship. The oldest of the white men grabbed his chance and clambered aboard by way of the rope ladder lowered to him. He shook hands with Capt. H. J. Holdsworth, introducing himself as David Kirtland of Baltimore, Maryland. He had been on Kosrae working as a trader since deserting a whaling ship two years before. He explained that the other two white men had jumped their ships only a few weeks earlier. The three of them were the only foreign residents on the island.

For a fee of five dollars, Mr. Kirtland offered his assistance to Capt. Holdsworth in piloting the ship safely to anchorage. Tensely the passengers watched as he barked sharp, minute directions to the mate at the wheel. The ship inched its way between the great coral heads, those craggy sentinels of the reef that pinched the channel just below the surface. Everyone on board was aware that this reef—monumental and powerful but deceptive in the luminous turquoise water—had already ripped open the hulls of at least a dozen ships.

Once inside the snug, secluded harbor that had made this island famous with seamen throughout the Pacific, the passengers relaxed in wide-eyed admiration of the beauty surrounding them. Two miles long and half a mile wide, the harbor centered a new and lovely world. Mountains rose sharply on three sides. Lush tropical foliage clung to slopes, which in places were perpendicular. With the highest peaks, the forest stabbed at the sky.

People could be seen running to and fro on the beaches, some gesturing toward the ship as the *Caroline* dropped anchor a quarter of a mile from the north shore. Outrigger canoes were pushed from their sheds by some who, like the group at the rail, were anxious for a closer look.

But the day was Sunday, and the passengers were missionaries. There would be no landing that day. Word was sent with Capt. Holdsworth to Kosrae's high chief, King Lupalik I—known around the Pacific and beyond as "Good King George"—that the visitors would come ashore the next morning to greet him. The curious in the canoes, a few with shirts covering portions of their shiny brown bodies, paddled silently in the vicinity of the vessel. They gazed intently at those seated in a circle on the quarter deck, sheltered from the sun by a large awning stretched on the rigging. They watched as one of the strangers stood to read to the others from a large book. Then, with open mouths and necks stretched forward, they listened for the first time to hymns of the Christian faith.

The Rev. Ephraim W. Clark, pastor of Kawaiaha'o Church in Honolulu and the oldest man aboard the *Caroline*, led the worship service. Mr. Clark was the executive secretary of the sponsoring mission organization in Hawai'i. On this voyage he was accompanying five missionary couples to their newly assigned field of service.

Benjamin and Lydia Snow, married less than a year, were from Maine. Benjamin, 34—known as Galen to his wife and close associates—was the oldest of the five young missionary men. He had come to the islands against the wishes of his father, for whom he had been named, after graduating from Bowdoin College and Bangor Seminary. Benjamin Snow was a tall, sensitive-looking man with a short beard. His eyes were deeply set, penetrating and unswerving in their gaze, their blue magnified by the square, rimless glasses he wore.

Lydia Buck Snow was a foot shorter than her husband and three years his junior. She had already been teaching school for 15 years when she married him in September 1851. Robust and energetic, she wore her long brown hair gathered in a net at the back of her neck. Lydia had withstood well the rigors of the many weeks at sea, though at times she found herself longing for her mother, and seven brothers and sisters, in Robbinston, Maine. They had become an especially close-knit family after her father, Ebenezer Buck, had drowned when the children were young.

Another bride and groom, Luther and Louisa Gulick, sat with the Snows on the deck of the *Caroline* that Sunday in Kosrae's jade and emerald harbor. Luther, born and reared in the Hawaiian Islands by missionary parents, had been to Massachusetts to study theology and medicine. Now the 24-year-old doctor was anxious to begin putting his knowledge to work. Luther's teenage brother, John Gulick, and a recently married couple from Ohio, Albert and Susan Sturges, completed the American group on board.

Joining the Americans in worship were two dedicated Hawai'ian missionary couples, Daniel and Doreka Opunui and Berita and Deborah Kaaikaula, sent by the Church in Hawai'i to be coworkers in the Micronesia Mission. They looked handsome but uncomfortable in the tight, dark, voluminous clothing which they, like their American colleagues, wore.

WHY THEY CAME

Five weeks earlier—on July 15—this band of pioneer missionaries had sailed from Honolulu. Their departure for the part of the western Pacific known as Micronesia had been the culmination of the prayers and plans of many Christians in Hawai'i and New England.

The first Protestant missionaries had reached the Hawaiian Islands in 1820. Just 32 years later, the young Church there was reaching out toward the 2,000 tiny islands south and west along the equator. Geographically, these islands were divided into four principal groups: the Gilbert Islands (Kiribati), the Marshalls, the Carolines and the Marianas. Instinctively it was felt that outreach does not wait to develop after a church has matured, but is present from the start. When family, clan, and then populations of neighboring islands had been evangelized, these Hawaiian Christians looked still farther for people with whom to share their new faith.

By 1852, the London Missionary Society, which began its Pacific work in 1797, had missionaries firmly established in the Society Islands. Their work had spread through southern Polynesia to Samoa. The Wesleyan Missionary Society's people were at work among the Maoris of New Zealand, the Tongans, and the Samoans, and had begun to reach into Melanesia. Members of the Church Missionary Society were at work in Fiji and had made a few scattered beachheads on other Melanesian islands. Spanish Jesuit priests had been working in the southern Marianas since 1668, but the rest of Micronesia—its infinitesimal islands spread across three million square miles of ocean—was as yet without a Christian witness.

It was the American Board of Commissioners for Foreign Missions/ Congregational, headquartered in Boston, Massachusetts—the oldest Protestant mission board in the United States—that sent the first missionaries to Hawai'i. Now it joined hands with its child, the Hawaiian Evangelical Association, by appointing the Snows, the Gulicks, and the Sturgeses to take part in the Micronesia venture.

Benjamin and Lydia Snow and Luther and Louisa Gulick had sailed for Hawai'i from Boston in November 1851, aboard the *Esther May*, and two months later the Sturgeses had followed aboard the *Snow Squall*. The new missionaries suggested to the executive secretary of the American Board that they be sent via the newly opened land route across Panama to avoid the long and tedious voyage around the southern tip of South America. Permission was not granted. "Missionaries to Micronesia need the discipline of a voyage around the Horn," they were told.[1]

Fourteen Hawaiian couples had volunteered to accompany the three American couples, but only two had been selected. The newly formed Hawaiian society accepted as its representatives a school teacher, Daniel Opunui, and his wife, Doreka, and Berita Kaaikaula, a deacon in the Hawaiian Church, and his wife, Deborah.

Sea captains related spine-tingling tales of Micronesia and said they would not "give a straw" for the lives of foreign men and women who tried to live there. Earlier that same year the crew of the ship *Inga*, out of New Bedford, Connecticut, had been massacred by the natives of Nauru, an island not far south of those which the missionaries had chosen as their destination. There were reasons for these atrocities, of course. Slavers, called blackbirders, were enticing naïve islanders into the holds of their ships, closing the hatch covers, and sailing away with their cargo of slaves. With grappling hooks, other seamen from nations considered to be Christian upset native canoes as they came along side, fished out the surprised men, and carried them off to be sold at so much per head in Mexican and Peruvian guano mines. And everywhere these new-comers to Micronesia went, they left a legacy of diseases for which the island populations had no acquired immunity.

Undaunted by these stories—indeed, more determined because of them—the missionary group continued its preparations for sailing from Hawai'i. The Hawaiian Mission Children's Society pledged support of the Gulicks, because the doctor had grown up in Hawai'i. Lahainaluna Seminary promised to support their distinguished alumnus Daniel Opunui and his wife. The Second Church of Honolulu, Kaumakapili, assumed support of the Kaaikaulas. The American Board of Commissioners for Foreign Missions had already underwritten support of the Sturgeses and the Snows. In solemn ceremonies on July 6, 1852, in Kawaiaha'o Church, these 10 pioneers were consecrated to a new field of service, banded together as the Mission Church of Micronesia.

On sailing day, a multitude of friends gathered at the Honolulu dock to give the couples a warm, encouraging send off. The Hawaiian society had leased and renovated a small brig for the mission undertaking, re-christening it the *Caroline* for one of the Micronesian island groups. The Rev. Peter Gulick and his wife, Fanny, embraced their son and daughter-in-law in a proud, tearful farewell. Berita and Deborah Kaaikaula bravely bade their two young children goodbye. The youngsters were to stay in Honolulu with relatives. Climbing aboard to sail the round trip with Ephraim Clark as a fraternal delegate of the Hawaiian Churches was the admired Pastor James Kekela, who would later take the Gospel to the Marquesas Islands.

As the moorings were released and the *Caroline* slipped slowly from the dock, hundreds of voices began to sing:

> Waft, waft, ye winds, His story;
> And you, ye waters, roll
> Till like a sea of glory
> It spreads from pole to pole.[2]

Leading those voices raised in song was that of King Kamehameha III. And securely within Mr. Clark's case on board the brig was a letter written by Hawai'i's Christian king to be read to the kings of the islands of Micronesia:

Kamehameha III of the Hawaiian Islands, Hawai'i, Maui, Molokai, Lanai, Oahu, Kaua'i and Ni'ihau, King, sends greetings to all chiefs of the westward, called Caroline Islands, Kingsmill Group, etc.

> *Peace and happiness to you all, now and forever.*
> *Here is my friendly message to you all:*
> *There are about to sail for your islands some teachers of the Most High God,*

Jehovah, to make known unto you His Word for your eternal salvation. A part of them are white men from the United States of America, and a part of them belong to my islands. Their names are as follows: B. G. Snow and wife; L. H. Gulick and wife; A. A. Sturges and wife; E. W. Clark, J. T. Gulick, Opunui and wife; Kaaikaula and wife; and Kekela; H. Holdsworth is captain of the vessel.

I, therefore, take the liberty to commend these good teachers to your care and friendship, to exhort you to listen to their instructions, and seek their acquaintance. I have seen the value of such teachers. We, here on my islands, once lived in ignorance and idolatry. We were given to war, and we were very poor. Now my people are enlightened. We live in peace, and some have acquired property. Our condition is very greatly improved on what it was once, and the Word of God has been the great cause of our improvement. Many of my people regard the Word of God Jehovah, and pray to Him, and He has greatly blessed us. I advise you to throw away your idols, take the Lord Jehovah for your God, worship and love Him, and He will bless and save you. May He make these new teachers a great blessing to you and your people, and withhold from you no good thing.

Kamehameha III[3]

After a brief stop at Kaua'i, the *Caroline* sailed in a southwesterly direction, with Micronesia as its goal. Conditions on board the little ship were extremely cramped. The passengers shared the hold as a common cabin. In spite of seasickness, the group studied as they could throughout the month-long voyage and discussed at length with members of the crew and with each other their hopes and dreams, pondering all they had heard about the people to whom they journeyed.

Susan Sturges wrote of the voyage, "Our little craft was heavily laden and every inch of space was filled, so there was no room on board for exercise. Our Hawaiian cook, who was also the steward, did not understand a word of English and knew nothing of cooking. We three women made all the bread, etc., that graced our table, and as we sifted flour and baked in our 6' x 10' galley, struggling often with seasickness, we thought we were getting a little more of the 'discipline' which our dear Secretary thought we needed! However, we were young and strong and bore the hardship bravely. I look back on that voyage as one of the happiest seasons of my life."[4]

Many days passed before the *Caroline* entered Micronesia and sailed through the low coral atolls of the Marshall and Gilbert groups. They went ashore on several of these atolls, but were especially intent on reaching the high volcanic islands of the eastern Carolines: Pohnpei and Kosrae. Pohnpei was known as "Ascension Island" to Western sailors, who called Kosrae "Strong's Island" after Caleb Strong, a former governor of Massachusetts. Stories were recounted in the seaports of Hawai'i, California, New England, and Australia of these two islands and the havoc being inflicted upon them by men who, like the missionaries themselves, hailed from Boston and Honolulu. Several tales of Kosrae's high chief, Good King George, had reached their ears and it was his island that was their first destination.

MISSIONARIES MEET "GOOD KING GEORGE"

In the harbor at Kosrae, after breakfast on Monday morning, August 22, the missionary men helped their wives into the ship's boat, anxious now to make the acquaintance of Good King George and to meet the Kosraean people. Those brave and curious islanders who had ventured into the proximity of the *Caroline* seemed to the missionaries to be more lithe and gentle than the people they had seen on Butaritari in the Gilberts a week and a half before. Certainly they were not the wild-eyed, hostile savages described in stories. The newcomers could not help being encouraged by the smiles, however tentative, on the faces of the Kosraeans already glimpsed.

They were rowed to Lelu, an island within the embrace of the larger island's mountains. With its own lesser peak, Lelu formed the northern boundary of Kosrae's famed and sheltered harbor. Here the king and other chiefs resided with their families. But as the missionaries docked at the tidy rock wharf to which they had been directed, they were struck by the absence of people and activity. All was calm and still. They ceased their talking as they stood wondering which way to turn. Capt. Holdsworth and David Kirtland advised them to wait.

From an opening in a great bamboo enclosure 10 yards inland, a middle-aged man appeared, stooped low, his feet making no sound as he made his way toward them across the graveled surface of the wharf. He was dressed in a stiff brown skirt woven of pandanus fiber. Keeping his crouched position and using a slow sweeping gesture with his fingers and hand pointed downward, he motioned for the visitors to follow him. Inside the bamboo courtyard, the guide dropped to his hands and knees. No one else was seen and nothing was heard as, wide-eyed and amazed, the missionary party was led by this man who crawled forward toward the largest of the orderly thatch-roofed houses within the compound.

There was a porch across the front and along one side of this house, with flooring of bamboo poles. In the middle of the front was a door approximately five and a half feet high. A second opening, about three feet square, led in from the side of the house. On the porch, "like a Patriarch in the door of his tent," sat Good King George.[5] They judged him to be in his late 40s, though his tight muscular body and thick black hair suggested a younger man. Much to their surprise, he greeted them with a plain English "Good morning."

Dr. Gulick later described the meeting. "As we each in order shook his hand, he again wished us a good morning with a very pleasant smile, quite indicative of refinement. We stood about this door for a few minutes and then were asked to enter by another door" at the side of the house, through which the missionaries had to proceed in a low, stooped manner as the opening was only three feet high.

Inside, a square, sunken fireplace occupied the center of the room, and the king's treasure—pearl fishhooks, shell ornaments, stone adzes, guns, a ship's lantern, a dipper carved from coconut wood, and some water-color prints—were arranged neatly on shelves between the mangrove posts. Along one side of the room, foreign chests provided seating for the visitors.

MISSION EXPLAINED TO THE KING

Luther Gulick proceeds:

We then gave the presents we had brought; namely, a red blanket, two red shirts, several yards of turkey red material, and a pair of scissors for the Queen who sat on the floor beside the chest on which her husband was seated. She was fondling her infant granddaughter. With these we also gave a Hawaiian Bible and hymn book, with a copy of Cheever's Island World, *which contained a portrait of King Kamehameha III of the Hawaiian Islands and sketches of Hawaiian island localities. We thought this a very appropriate present, coming, as we did, from those islands where God's Word had been so productive of good.*

After this presentation, Mr. Clark told him our aims and wishes, that some of the party would like to stay with him for several months until their ship could go to Honolulu and return. He said they had some food on the vessel, but it was not enough for these several months ahead, and therefore they would be dependent on him for fresh provisions and for some building materials to make homes for themselves, and perhaps they would need some land for cultivation. It seemed questionable whether the King understood more than a fraction of all this, though some parts he evidently comprehended.

Mr. Kirtland, the pilot and interpreter, then explained our wishes further, which the King received in the same placid, pleasant, noncommittal but politely assenting way in which he had heard all our remarks. We could see that he was not displeased, yet we did not know more.

As Mr. Clark questioned him concerning his thoughts on missionaries, the king answered: "Bad captains tell me missionaries bad; good captains tell me missionaries good." The missionaries marveled at the unexpected insight of the king. And they were delighted when, asked if he would permit missionaries to remain on Kosrae, the king said: "Like one white man come; not many. If many come, rum come, fight come. Me all like quiet; no tap coconut tree Kusaie."[6] Later the missionaries were to discover that Good King George had indeed prohibited the drinking of intoxicating beverages on Kosrae. Both the making of kava and the production of the alcoholic toddy obtained from coconut sap had been illegal for several years.

During this audience with the king, one of his sons, a youth who wore no clothing, crept into the room on his hands and knees to take the infant from the queen. While clutching the child to his chest, he backed out of the room in the same manner in which he had entered.

Dr. Gulick's description of the meeting continued:

We now fell into a pleasant chit-chat. He ordered coconuts and water for us, and after about two hours we asked permission to look about his premises. He gave his ready consent and accompanied us. In one house he told us the body of his daughter [Srue Neporu] was kept, who died three months since. He spoke of it with a cast of sadness. He kept women in the house constantly to watch over and anoint the body. He did not ask us to enter, for the door was closed. We spent two hours in looking about, and then bade the King "good morning."

The King's whole aspect and countenance were very pleasing. There was such mildness, with evident decision and meditative intelligence, that we could not but have a feeling of respect. His only dress was a faded flannel shirt. His wife had on a short small cotton gown. Beside himself and his wife there were no islanders present. One or two came at his call, crouching on their hands and knees, and retired immediately.[7]

SELECTION OF THE SNOWS AND OPUNUIS

Returning to the *Caroline*, the 10 members of the Micronesia Mission, with pastors Clark and Kekela, sat down to discuss the king's willingness for one white man to remain on his island. After some deliberation, Benjamin and Lydia Snow accepted the assignment. It was further decided that Daniel and Doreka Opunui would remain with them. For the present both couples would stay on the ship, continuing to Pohnpei with their colleagues so that the entire group could see the situation that awaited on that island.

Benjamin and Lydia Snow were excited by the prospects of settling on Kosrae and were anxious to discuss the details with Good King George. Early Tuesday morning they returned to the king's Lelu dwelling. A piece of land would be needed on which to build a home for them and one for the Opunuis, with room to raise a garden. They were relieved and heartened when the king not only promised them land—a little island of their own, attached to the west end of Lelu by a narrow causeway—but insisted that he would build the houses for them while they were on Pohnpei.

As the king escorted them back to the wharf, the Snows noticed that the few people they saw all sat with their heads bent towards the king as he passed them. None of them spoke. Mr. Snow wrote, "I never saw such deference paid to any mere man, yet with no apparent haughtiness on his part. He is a model of quiet, unostentatious simplicity; he speaks and understands English so as to be able to converse quite well on common themes. I was surprised to discover a high moral tone, though on spiritual things he is of course a heathen."[8]

A LOOK AT KOSRAE

While the Snows were on Lelu in the royal enclosure, Luther and Louisa Gulick had taken their seats in an outrigger canoe with four paddlers assigned to them by Good King George. It was a narrow dugout, 25 feet in length, its hull stained rust-red. One of the youths directed the doctor to sit in front of the two beams which projected out to the right, holding the outrigger. Louisa sat just behind him. The guides, two in the bow and two in the stern, each held a spear-like paddle. They rowed in flawless rhythm, correcting the course of the craft by swinging the paddles over their heads to the other side without missing a beat.

The Gulicks were taken first into a twisting, shaded channel through a mangrove swamp. The foliage was thick, with giant ferns cascading from the jumble of branches to which they clung. The quiet was intense—even the paddles, masterfully handled, made no sound. The young American couple gazed about them in wide-eyed wonder.

Forty-five minutes later, Luther and Louisa were assisted from the canoe by two of their escorts, who led them through a mass of coconut palms and pandanus trees and across a stretch of sand to the crystal-clear lagoon beyond. There they were helped back into the canoe, which the other two youths had carried from the swamp and placed in the shallow waters of the rising tide.

For an hour the two visitors watched intrigued as the canoe carried them past the settlements of Kosrae's north shore. Thatch-roofed dwellings could be seen through the trees. Smoke curled above cook houses. Children grinned and waved from the sparkling beach. Then once again the newlyweds were helped from the canoe. Their smiling guides beckoned them to follow along a well-worn path that ran inland from the waterfront. After a long, brisk, and sometimes strenuous hike through lush and steamy jungle, they found themselves back at Lelu Harbor.

That night Luther Gulick wrote in his diary of the delightful day he and Louisa had spent, completely at the mercy of "four naked, friendly heathen."

Though the young men wore loin cloths and carefully observed the rules of modesty required by their culture, to these missionaries—so far from all that was familiar and considered proper—the youths were "naked."

FIRST IMPRESSIONS

Benjamin Snow later commented in his own journal: "We were told that many of the people could speak some English. We found, however, that it was a very broken English, but we were surprised that a people having so little intercourse with the Americans and British, should have learned even that much. This surprise diminished, however, when we saw more of their power of observation and wonderful inquisitiveness."[9] Albert Sturges wrote to a friend in Honolulu at how astonished he was to find "the people speaking English, and so familiar with our customs. They must have a wonderful aptness to learn."[10]

Mr. Snow's journal entry continued:

Polygamy was unknown among them, in so far as we could learn. Labor was honorable among all classes, from the King to the lowest subject. There seemed to be four trades for the men; namely, fishing, cooking, house building, and boat building. It was a rule for the son to follow the trade of his father, though there were some who became skillful in several trades. The present King was a fisherman and still pursued his old employment. So far as we could judge, the chiefs and nobility were as industrious as the common people, if not more so.

It was habitual, perhaps required, that the people approach the King on hands and knees, and when he passed they sat with their heads inclined toward him. If he spoke to them their answers were in a slow monotone, so low that he often had to ask them a second time. If they were at work they dropped all business until he had passed, and they never looked directly at him. In and about his premises everything was in order, and the people were docile and mild. The women were industrious and performed only indoor work.

The King's sympathies seemed to be quite pro-American. He appeared to have some knowledge of our cities and seaports. The harbor was large and safe. The soil was exceedingly rich and fertile. The mountains were about 2000 feet high and well wooded to the top.[11]

The missionaries aboard the *Caroline* learned that a French naval vessel, the *Bayonnaise*, had visited Kosrae two years before. Members of the French party surveyed Okat Harbor, placing some buoys and markers there. In exchange for provisions, they gave the Kosraeans potatoes, rice, and beans for planting.

But when Capt. Jurien de la Graviere requested that a few Kosraeans go back with them to France to study Catholicism and then return as missionaries, the king refused. He had heard rumors about the French that he did not like. British and American captains had told him of the French methods used in conscripting islands into their own empire, so he declined to go along with their request. The missionaries, therefore, felt that it was providential that this same king seemed so agreeable toward the establishment of their mission among his people.

However, the king did express his concern that the missionaries might interfere in matters of government and weaken his authority. Benjamin Snow assured him that this would not happen. They would be there, he told him, to teach the Bible, not to rule. When he explained to the king that the Bible commanded them to "fear God and honor the King," the king was so impressed that he went to his chest and brought out the Bible that the missionaries had given him, wanting to see the actual passage. Benjamin Snow found the place in Romans where Paul declares, "For rulers are not a terror to good conduct, but to bad," (13:3, King James Version), and showed it to the king.

"That's first rate," the king said, using an expression that the missionaries found to be very common among the Kosraeans. Mr. Snow promised to talk more about it after the mission had been established, and the king seemed pleased.

A bit later, the queen said to the Snows in her broken English, "The King speak me, he like your talk very much. He say very straight, very good!"[12]

SHIPBOARD BANQUET FOR THE KING

On one of the final afternoons that their ship was anchored in Lelu Harbor, the missionaries invited the Kosraean king to share a meal with them on board. Lydia Snow described the scene in a letter to friends in Hawai'i:

Perhaps you would like to know how we entertained our Royal Guest. The Captain ordered the Caroline's flags hoisted. Soon after the King came and had exchanged salutations with the company, we had our dinner, which consisted of boiled beef and pork, baked beans, bread and butter, potatoes and bananas cooked. For dessert we had apple pie, plum duff and cheese. But while we were seated, one of the King's men brought some native pudding prepared by the King's cooks of taro and banana with a sort of icing of pounded coconut. We ate the King's pudding and he ate our apple pie.

After sitting for some time, we repaired to the deck and listened to music from the melodian accompanied by voices, Galen's and Mrs. Gulick's. The King appeared interested in this and examined the instrument very closely to see in what way the music was made. After this our daguerreotypes were shown to him and if only you could have seen his face as he was examining them. He said they were "fuss rate!"

Just before sunset, Mr. and Mrs. Sturges, Mrs. Gulick, Mr. Snow and I, with two natives, went to the little island which is to be the Missionaries' future home.

We found that it was a beautifully fertile little island like the others, and contained probably about one and a quarter acres.[13]

MISSIONARY TEAM CONTINUES TO POHNPEI

On August 28, after a week at Kosrae, the *Caroline* set sail for Pohnpei, 365 miles to the northwest, with the entire missionary party on board. The missionaries knew the experience of the people of Pohnpei with intrusive whalers was similar to that of the Kosraeans. They did not know that there had been earlier attempts to introduce Christianity.

Members of a Protestant missionary family were aboard an English ship out of Australia—the *John Bull*, John Henry Rowe, Captain—and were lost in 1825 when the vessel was wrecked in a storm on one of Pohnpei's reefs. Some said they were on their way to Kosrae. A Catholic priest, Father Desire Maigret, was landed on Pohnpei in 1837 by the schooner *Notre Dame de Paix*, Capt. M. Grombeck out of Honolulu. He worked for seven months without success and was removed by the same ship in 1838.[14] Later generations of Pohnpeians repeated tales of his kindness.[15]

It was about noon on September 6 when, within sight of Pohnpei, the missionaries saw several canoes racing toward the *Caroline*. Given stories they had heard in Honolulu, there were some misgivings among those aboard about how they might be received. But the canoes were filled with eager would-be pilots who helped to guide them into "beautiful and wildly picturesque" Madolenihmw Harbor, where they anchored about 5 o'clock that evening.[16]

More than 30 canoes surrounded the little ship, while 12 white men, as well as the high chief of the Madolenihmw tribe, clambered aboard. Through Lewis Corgat, a white men who served as interpreter, the chief indicated that it would be good for them to stop at Pohnpei. That was good news! The missionaries were also surprised and relieved when Mr. Corgat agreed to make repairs on the *Caroline* "to the amount of more than sixty dollars, and refused pay, saying that instead of the ship being indebted to him, he was indebted to it for bringing the missionaries."[17]

Years later, Susan Sturges remembered the missionaries' arrival at the two high islands of the Eastern Carolines: "We found Kusaie and Ponape dressed in their robes of richest green, with almost endless variety of scenery, caused by mountain, valley, plateau, river and waterfall, to be indeed, 'gems of the ocean'; their skies much given to weeping, but the tears soon forgotten, because succeeded by the brightest of smiles. Darkness, however, covered the people... To a careless observer the proofs of intellect seemed very small; but close acquaintance showed many natural traits, the development of which into strength and beauty and excellence, under the direction of God's grace, it has been our privilege to watch."[18]

Though they were now in Micronesia in faith and faithfulness, such promise could not be imagined by those young adults aboard the *Caroline* in September 1852. But they sincerely believed themselves to be God's emissaries. With determination and grit, they initiated their ministries.

The Gulicks, the Sturgeses and the Kaaikaulas disembarked on Pohnpei, and—three weeks after departing Kosrae—the missionary brig returned Benjamin and Lydia Snow and Daniel and Doreka Opunui to their assigned place of service. Though Good King George expressed his pleasure at seeing the two couples again, nothing had been done toward building the promised houses. The king's time had been consumed by three whaling ships that had been in port while the *Caroline* was away at Pohnpei.

MISSIONARIES MOVE IN WITH MR. KIRTLAND

At first the missionaries were disappointed—though both of the Snows later agreed that it was for the best. With Benjamin there to supervise the construction, their house would be more to their liking. In the meantime, the king instructed the two couples to move in with David Kirtland.

Mr. Kirtland had yet to build a house for himself during his three years on Kosrae. Home for him was a large open area under a thatch roof, filled with items salvaged from wrecked ships and stolen from others. He had also erected a crude but useable bowling alley in which visiting sailors were entertained. The tousled beachcomber accepted the king's plan and told the weary missionaries that they were welcome to stay with him. But the coarse runaway sailor from Maryland and the trim young minister from Maine had little they could say to one another.

Lydia Snow watched dejectedly as sailors from the *Caroline* pushed to make room in the midst of Mr. Kirtland's collection for her boxes and trunks. These were possessions she had brought halfway around the world to help make a home for Benjamin and herself. She gasped as lizards and rats, routed from their nests and hiding places, scampered to find new quarters. Though this shed was some distance from the king's houses, it was still considered to be on royal ground. The taboo involved would at least spare them the crowds of inquisitive onlookers and perhaps thieving would not be a problem.

CAROLINE RETURNS TO HAWAI'I

Later, blinking back tears, Lydia stood on the Lelu wharf beside her husband waving her handkerchief slowly in the air. With Daniel and Doreka, the Snows watched the *Caroline* weigh anchor, slip through the channel, and pass out of sight, beginning the long return trip to Hawai'i with Ephraim Clark, James Kekela, and young John Gulick on board. Standing with the missionaries was Good King George, whose last words to Mr. Clark had been a message for King Kamehameha: "I will be all same father to missionary."[19]

Good King George kept his word. ✚

Notes - Chapter 1

1. William E. Strong, *The Story of the American Board*, Boston, 1910, p. 232
2. Reginald Heber, "From Greenland's Icy Mountains," 1819
3. E. Theodora Crosby Bliss, "Micronesia: Fifty Years in the Island World," Boston, 1906, p. 4
4. Ibid, p. 4
5. Benjamin Snow, personal correspondence to Rufus Anderson, Sept. 1, 1852
6. Bliss, p. 6
7. David & Leona Crawford, *Missionary Adventures in the South Pacific*, 1967, pp. 37-38
8. B. Snow, Sept. 1, 1852
9. Albert A. Sturges, personal correspondence to Samuel Damon, Sept. 28, 1852
10. Crawford, pp. 39-40
11. B. Snow, Sept. 1, 1852
12. Ibid
13. Lydia Vose Buck Snow, personal correspondence, in "Incidents In The Life of Mrs. Benjamin G. Snow," Mary Hitchcock Snow, ed, for the Woman's Board Jubilee, Honolulu, June 1931
14. Francis X. Hezel, S.J., *Foreign Ships in Micronesia*, Saipan, 1979, p. 42
15. John L. Fischer, *The Eastern Caroline*s, New Haven, 1957, pp. 25-26
16. Bliss, p. 6
17. Ibid
18. Susan Sturges, in "A History of Missionary Work in Micronesia 1852-1910," Mary A. Marvin, ed, Lancaster, Massachusetts, 1873-1910, Vol. I, p. 11
19. B. Snow, *The Missionary Herald*, ABCFM Boston, July 1858, p. 2

NUNAK YOHK KE CHAPTER 2
1852-1855

Benjamin Snow ac Daniel Opunui eltal tuh wi mwet orekma su Tokosra Lupalik I—su pangpang pac "Good King George"—el tuh pakiya in musai lohm seltal ac in aknasnasye acn Pisin. Eltal mole-la tuka se pangpang Yenyen ma oan apkuran nu Pisin tuh eltal in orek ima we.

Mr. Snow el mutawauk in orek alu yurin mwet Kosrae ke Sunday se emeet ma el muta Kosrae —pa October len 17, 1852. Acn se elos alu we pa nien srital "bowling" lal Mr. Kirtland, na tok kutu, elos alu ke lohm mongo sasu se lun Tokosra Lupalik. Tusruktu, Mr. Snow el tia arulana pangon mu fal in orek alu ke lohm luo inge, na pa el otela mu el ac orekmakin lohm sel sifacnu fin acn Pisin tuh in nien alu lalos.

Tokosra Lupalik ac oayapa mwet puspis sin mwet Lelu elos wi alu ke Sunday nukewa. Ke pacl in pre safla ke alu uh, Pastu Snow el siyuk mwet nukewa in tuyak. Sie ma oal oemeet me yurin mwet Kosrae pa elos in tia tuyak suwohs ye mutun tokosra. Tusruktu Tokosra Lupalik el sap mwet uh in tuyak oanu ma missionary el fahk. Oasr pac ma sap luo ma sa na oakwuki sin missionary uh. Sie pa mwet uh in tia orekma ke len Sunday. Mwet nu kemwa arulanu engan kac. Ma se akluo ah pa mukul Kosrae in tia sifilpa lela mutan uh in som nu fin kutena oak fakfuk loat ma kawuki in molsron nukewa fin acn Kosrae. Mwet uh elos insemwowo pac ke ma sap se inge.

Pastu Snow el arulana engan ke el liye lah Tokosra ac kutu mwet Lelu saya elos pwar in lohng Pweng Wo ke Christ. Ke January 1853, oasr mwet 75 nu ke 130 su wi alu ke Sunday nukewa. Oasr pacl Tokosra Lupalik ac Benjamin Snow eltal amei ke sripen facsin laltal tiana oana sie. Tusruktu, Tokosra el srakna kulang nu sin missionary uh, ac Mr. Snow el arulanu kasrel Tokosra yohk ke pacl oasr lokoalok yurin mwet fakfuk loat.

Oasr tulik mukul se natul Tokosra—inel pa Lupalikkun. El pa awowo se nutin Tokosra—el yac 10 matwa ke Tokosra el supwalla in muta yurin Mr. ac Mrs. Snow. Eltal tuh arulana lungse tulik se inge, su eltal pangon "Little George." Eltal oral oana in tulik na pwaye se natultal.

Pusiyen mwet suksuk in pacl sac elos tia insese nu ke ma Mr. Snow el oru, na elos torkaskas kacl nu sel Tokusra. Ma inge mwe asor nu sin Tokosra mweyen mwet suksuk inge elos sou fototo lal, a el oru mu Mr. Snow el kawuk se lal.

Benjamin Snow ac Daniel Opunui eltal sramteak lutlut se fin acn Pisin in luti mwet uh kas English. Tusruktu tukun malem ekasr na, mwet uh mutawauk alsrangesr kac. Na tia paht toko, tui na.

Ke sripen pus na mwet fakfuk loat fahsr na nu Kosrae, Mr. Snow el mutawauk in orek alu pac yurin mwet kalkal inge.

Doreka Opunui el oswela tulik mukul se ke July 1853—tusruktu malem se na toko, ke August len 4, Daniel Opunui, el misa. Tufahna sun yac se tukun missionary inge tuh oai fin acn Kosrae. Daniel Opunui el pukpuki fin acn Yenyen.

Ke kapin 1853, oasr lohm fahsu se musaiyuk apkuran nu ke lohm sel Tokosra ke acn se pangpang Posral, Lelu. Ke December 1853, mwet alu nukewa fin acn Lelu elos mutawauk in tukeni alu in lohm sasu sac. Pa inge lohm alu se emeet fin acn Kosrae.

Tokosra Lupalik I el misa ke September len 9, 1854. Mr. ac Mrs. Snow eltal arulana asor yohk. Mr. Snow el akilen lah Tokosra Lupalik el tuh sie mwet lulalfongi. Wen se ma matu natul Tokosra Lupalik, su Kanku in pacl sac, el solla in tokosra. Inel pa Tokosra Sru III. El tuh suli u se pangpang Kolo Folfol in oru alu in akwalyalak nu ke tokosra. Mr. Snow el arulana supwar ke ma se inge. Tusruktu mwet kol lun u sac kui in nunak lalos ke sripen Tokosra el orekmakunulos. Elos som in orek lokoalok nu sel Mr. Snow fin acn Pisin, tuh ngetnget kou lun missionary sac oru elos sangeng ac kaingla.

Benjamin Snow ac Lydia Snow eltal tuh supwarla ke yac 1854 ac 1855. Sie sripa pa eltal asorella Good King George (Lupalik I) su tuh arulanu kulang nu seltal ac kasreltal yohk. Sie pac sripe an pa puslana mwet Kosrae misa ke kain in mas sasu puspis. Apkuran in wanginla mwet wi alu. Pisen mwet Kosrae ke 1855 sun mwet na 1,106.

Tusruktu oasr sie ma missionary elos enganak kac: mwet Kosrae singoul sie elos mutawauk in tukeni fin acn Pisin yurin missionary ke wik nukewa tuh elos in pre. Mwet kol lun u se inge pa sianyan se—Kutuka ac Notwe. Yok finsrak lal Benjamin Snow mu in pal na sa mwet luo inge ac baptaisla.

CHAPTER TWO

EARLY STRUGGLES AND VICTORIES
1852-1855

For long silent minutes, Benjamin and Lydia Snow and Daniel and Doreka Opunui stood on Lelu's stone wharf, their minds leaping nostalgically ahead of the *Caroline* to its Honolulu destination. Then they fell into step single file down the trail which led to Mr. Kirtland's shed. It was October 16, 1852, and this would be their first night to sleep ashore at Kosrae.

Lydia and Doreka began preparations for supper, while their husbands gathered and chopped the firewood. It was a lonely evening for the missionaries. They had little in common with the three coarse-mouthed American men on the other side of the reed partition. They felt no hostility from the citizens of Lelu who peered at them through the darkness, but the growing awareness of their isolation from family and friends, and the dimension of the task before them, seemed overwhelming.

Yet their prayers that night were prayers of gratitude for the divine providence of God, for they were convinced that God had led them to Kosrae. They considered the conditions remarkably favorable for the introduction of the Christian Gospel. They had often said, "New Englanders damned the island. Now, with God's help, New Englanders will redeem it."

The missionaries had discovered that the Kosraeans referred to their king by the ancient title "tokosra" and that the current monarch's given name was "Lupalik." Nevertheless, they continued to refer to their new friend as "King George," as other foreigners did. During the first 30 years of the 19th century, when the whaling industry was getting started, two of the kings of England had been George III and George IV. To British and American seamen, who were not a highly educated lot, "George" seemed an appropriate name for a king. Making no effort to learn his actual name, these sailors began referring to Lupalik as "King George" soon after he was elevated as the Kosraean monarch in 1837, the year Victoria became Queen of England. Later, as accounts of his graciousness and generosity spread, "Good" was prefixed to Lupalik's title. By 1852 even some of his own people were referring to him as "Good King George."

King George arrived early the next morning to escort the missionaries to Pisin, the tiny islet 100 feet off the western tip of Lelu that he had promised them for their use before they left for Pohnpei. It was less than half an acre in size—not a bit more than one acre, as the missionaries had first estimated—and was joined to Lelu Island by a footpath that crossed a narrow stone and coral causeway. Beaming, the king explained that he was giving this land to them. From now on it would be theirs. In a letter to his superiors in Boston, Benjamin Snow commented, "It might be charming if nature did not almost run mad with luxuriance! Pisin is a singularly pleasant location, getting the breeze from both entrances of the harbor—a great blessing in a climate where the thermometer stands at 80 degrees day and night."[1]

The four newcomers were delighted with their own private island. Because the word "Pisin" [PEA-seen] sounded to American ears like "pigeon," the Snows decided to call the gift property Dove Island. They had already seen the native Kosraean dove and heard its soft call and, because the dove was a familiar metaphor for peace, the name seemed suitable for their home among the Kosraeans. Immediately they began clearing the land of its dense mantle of tropical growth. Within the miniature jungle they were pleased to discover 40 coconut palms and two large breadfruit trees.

During that first month, while Pisin was being prepared, the Snows and Opunuis continued to live at David Kirtland's. Benjamin Snow described their lodgings:

Such a mingling together of pigs, dogs, cats, rats, lizards, old barrels, old boxes, ropes, paddles, bottles, guns, rags, old bits of canvas, and mosquitoes we never before experienced. And then the felicity of being in a rainy latitude under a leaking roof, so that while eating we would be obliged to remove our table to a less drenching spot, and while sleeping (or trying to) we would change our pillows to the other end of the bed that they might be kept a little dryer, and let our feet take the shower bath.

Add to this the necessity of boxing, or tying up everything eatable in napkins to keep it from the legion of ants and other insects, to say nothing of cooking in a little Dutch oven over a fire of green wood made on the ground! Some might think it strange that in such circumstances we could find a daily cup of pleasure, and have hearts to thank God that we were brought to such a place. We do indeed think it a goodly heritage to be privileged to minister to these people.[2]

MISSIONARIES MOVE TO PISIN

The king sent carpenters, who worked alongside the missionaries in the construction and cleaning projects on Pisin. It was decided to concentrate first on a house for the Snows—in fact, a separate house for the Opunuis was not built for another six months. The workers floated timbers across the harbor and tied them in place with strips of pliable bark. Other helpers sat on the recently cleared ground and wove reed walls and sewed roofing thatch. On November

13, four weeks after the departure of the *Caroline*, the two couples left Mr. Kirtland's cluttered premises to take up residence in their own dwelling.

The missionaries moved into a house which was rectangular and large, with a small room built into each of the four corners. The design of the interior created a central space in the form of a Greek cross. Two of the little rooms were bedrooms—one used by the Snows and one by the Opunuis—Benjamin Snow used the third as his study and the fourth was a storeroom. The cross section served as parlor, sitting room, dining room, school room and church combined.

Benjamin described their new home as "a good native house 26' x 36'. The eaves are so high that I can walk in and out at the doors standing upright with my hat on. The covering of the walls is woven reed, only the sections lap a little like clapboard so that the wind has less effect upon us, and we are not so open to the gaze of outsiders. It is floored with reeds like the King's house. I have four large doors, 3' wide, in the middle of the four sides of the house, which afford good air and light."³ Later, the house was encircled with a wide veranda. The missionary women did their cooking together in an outdoor kitchen, sheltered from the sun and rain by a thatched roof.

And it did rain! American seamen sometimes referred to Kosrae as "The headquarters of squalls." A month after his arrival, Benjamin Snow quipped in a letter to a friend, "It is charmingly cool here when it rains, and that is said to be eleven months and thirty days out of a year!"⁴

Two weeks after they had moved to Pisin, Lydia Snow wrote, "We are feeling quite at home. Dove Island is indeed a beautiful place and more comfortable than any I have seen about here. We feel much happier here than we expected to be. I don't know what I should do without Doreka. She is a real treasure—so kind and cheerful. She knows how to do a great many things and manifests a desire to learn more. Opunui has more difficulty in talking with us, and we sometimes fear his silence is produced by discontent, but we hope not. We are all improving in ability to converse with each other. The King is very kind indeed to us. He sends us fish, breadfruit and coconuts in abundance, and has sent one turtle and occasionally other things."⁵

King George was particularly pleased when Mr. Snow assured him that English would be taught to commoners as well as to the chiefs, and he seems to have taken a certain pride in looking out for the welfare of the missionaries. The missionaries were pleased, too, with the mildness, docility and industriousness of the Kosraeans, and they optimistically took up "the tasks of learning Kosraean, teaching English and converting the people."⁶

THE GARDEN ON YENYEN

The missionary men were eager to plant their gardens. They obtained Yenyen, an islet not far from Pisin, for this purpose. It was rumored that the purchase price was two red shirts. Since Pisin had been a part of the area artificially filled 500 years earlier, when Lelu Island was greatly enlarged by the Kosraean ruling class, there was little soil on it. Yenyen, on the other hand, was a natural island with good soil. The missionary farmers learned that part of the island had been an ancient burial ground. It was not difficult to get things to grow, but they continually had to battle Yenyen's infestation of rats and crabs. They were relieved that there were no snakes to worry about.

Benjamin Snow and Daniel Opunui were struck by the fertility of Kosraean soil and the variety of its products. Not only coconuts and breadfruit, but pandanus, bananas in several varieties, yams, taro, sugarcane, arrowroot, sago and soursop, oranges, limes, pineapple, and guava were all there to reward even a minimum of cultivation. Some of these foods were indigenous while others had been introduced over the previous 25 years.

FIRST SUNDAY SERVICES

From his first Sunday on Kosrae—October 17, 1852, the day after the *Caroline* set sail for Honolulu—Benjamin Snow conducted Christian services for King George and his family, the chiefs and their families.

He wrote, "As King George has no chapel built yet, I incline very much to occupying Mr. Kirtland's bowling alley for a chapel, especially as he never allows any gambling in it, nor allows any rolling on the Sabbath. If swords are going to be beaten into plowshares, why not bowling alleys converted into chapels?"[7]

A printer aboard the *Emily Morgan*, which visited Kosrae on numerous occasions, mentioned the popularity of this bowling alley in his description of an 1851 stop-over at Kosrae. "The king and the chiefs spent a great part of their time there, and had become very expert players. The king might often be seen 'rolling a string' with one of the foremast hands of the different ships."[8]

But the bowling alley proved to be an unsatisfactory place of worship. Also, a large, newly erected cook house on the royal premises at Posral, which King George offered to the missionary for church purposes, did not meet Mr. Snow's criteria. Though the residents of Lelu were attending in large numbers, he felt uncomfortable conducting services in places predominantly used to entertain sailors or to prepare the king's meals. He made the decision that, until a building could be dedicated specifically as a church, he would use the house on Pisin. So, on December 12, after eight Sundays in temporary facilities, the fledgling

Lelu congregation began meeting in the large, accommodating living room of the missionaries' home.

The young American pastor was flattered by the courteous attention of the people, as they sat quietly before him in an attitude of deep concentration. Later he realized that they understood much less of his sermons—which he preached in what he referred to as "Strong's Island English"—than he thought they did. The quiet, good conduct was actually their usual behavior when they were in the presence of the king—and the king never missed a Sunday service!

At the close of one of the first services, the missionary pastor—rather absent-mindedly, he later admitted—asked everyone to stand for the benediction as was commonly done in New England churches. The king stood, but no one else moved. There was some embarrassed giggling and averting of eyes. Others pretended not to hear. The missionary described what happened in a letter to Mr. Clark: "I soon saw what a fix I was in, but as the thing was undertaken, I thought it of no small importance to get it through. I made it a strictly religious question, between doing homage to their King or homage to God. I told them to forget the King and Queen and think only of God in this act. The proposition, being very decidedly seconded by the King, finally prevailed. After much confusion they all got to their feet and stood, though some were in the windows, some nearly out of doors, and nearly all with their backs to the King and Queen, and their faces covered with their hands, as though they were perpetrating some very disgraceful business."[9]

Following the service an impatient Benjamin Snow made it plain to King George that in subsequent meetings he would expect the attitude of the people to be different. By the next Sunday the king had given his orders to his chiefs, and through them to the people of Lelu. Mr. Snow was relieved to note that when calling for them to stand for the benediction, his congregation "had quite conquered their scruples and stood as properly as any civilized audience!"[10]

There were other changes, too, which the missionary felt would be necessary. It was the king's responsibility, Mr. Snow told him, to see that these reforms were initiated. Among the new rulings was one hailed with much joy by everyone. There was to be no more work on Sunday! Benjamin Snow was elated. He felt that the order would prove to be of great physical and moral benefit. The fact that this Sabbath reform took place so soon after the arrival of the missionaries is evidence of Benjamin Snow's dominant personality, but it also speaks of the prestige and sensitivity of the king.

The tall, bearded American with his serious, steady gaze regarded himself as God's spokesman. He stood before King George and the chiefs as a prophet and patriarch. His unique dedication and his strange religion, though far from being understood, were attractive to the king. King George quickly came to the conclusion that this young man from New England was a friend and a needed ally. The missionary's strange, eccentric manner would have to be tolerated. There were advantages to having Benjamin Snow in Lelu.

INTEREST IN THE MISSIONARIES' MESSAGE INCREASES

From 75 to 130 people were attending Sunday morning worship by December 1852. The king would often punish irregular churchgoers by having them clear sizable pieces of jungle land on Monday. Delinquents could be counted on to be present the following Sunday.

At times the king would interrupt the lengthy sermons in an effort to explain to his people what the missionary was saying, or with speeches of his own unrelated to the Scripture text. Sometimes he would give a short lecture on temperance. Mr. Snow described one of these discourses as "pithy and to the point, making a clean sweep of everything, including tobacco." Another time the gist of his interruption was that "man made rum and tobacco, but God made water and coconuts!"[11]

After the service on December 19, the missionaries were mystified when the people quickly left Pisin without the usual shaking hands all around which they had learned to do with exuberance. They were soon back, however, and others were with them. They were in a cheerful mood, laughing and talking with each other. Each one carried several large woven palm-frond baskets of coconuts, baked breadfruit, and banana leaf-wrapped packages of other cooked food or fish—far more than enough to feed everyone. Puzzled by this sudden extravagant display and not knowing what else to do, the Snows helped redistribute the gifts among the donors. This seemed to satisfy everyone, wrote Mr. Snow, "as it was according to their custom. If this generous act was intended to indicate their interest in me, or my work, it was certainly very pleasing; and I don't know of any other reason. I thought this the best Sabbath we had seen."[12]

When 1853 dawned, the new residents of Kosrae were feeling hopeful and affirmed in their mission. Of Sunday, January 2, Benjamin Snow noted in his journal:

Today I spoke more of Christ and his love—the way he manifested it to his enemies. It seemed to interest them deeply; and the King came in after the others had retired to ask me more particularly about it. Each Sabbath's labor leaves its mark of advance so as to encourage and strengthen our faith.

Mr. Kirtland was present for the first time on Sabbath January 9. I took the Ten Commandments, dwelling particularly upon the Sixth, Seventh and Eighth. I did not mince matters at all with the Seventh—and have never seen a more ready and hearty response than nearly all gave to the proposition to make their women a tabooed article to sailors and others. They seem to be most truly "waiting for God's Law." The King grasped my hand, and with tears in his eyes, said "We thank you, plenty thank you, very much thank you"—to which the Queen joined, saying to Mrs. Snow, "Every woman, every gal like plenty hear Mr. Snow talk all same."[13]

Indeed, more and more women—who were customarily bare-breasted—were attending worship as they were able to find lengths of material for dresses. Very quickly the strict new teacher had made it clear that he considered it indecent for a woman to be present in a Christian meeting without some foreign clothing to cover her. So Lydia Snow helped them make dresses from long strips of calico folded over, with holes cut for the head. The sides were sewed up, leaving openings for the arms. Mr. Snow commented in his journal, "This dress, contrasted with the almost naked condition of their native wear, gives them quite an air of civilization."[14]

KING GEORGE AND BENJAMIN SNOW

As he had promised, King George accepted the role of protector for his new friends. At the same time, Benjamin Snow placed himself in the role of teacher, confidant, and critic to the king. Though the two men were drawn to one another, each was often a source of annoyance and frustration to the other.

King George was an intelligent, mild man who had been one of the lower chiefs until, in 1837, he led a successful revolt against a particularly despotic tyrant, King Sru II. King George had been a fisherman and wanted to return to that trade following the rebellion. Instead, he was elevated to the position of king—as Lupalik I—by the grateful Kosraeans. During his years as king, he found great pleasure in getting away by himself in a small outrigger to fish.

By the end of March 1853, aspects of the king's behavior began to irritate Benjamin Snow—although the king seemed happiest when doing favors for the missionaries. The missionary was particularly disgusted when the king would appear in church trying vainly to conceal a high state of intoxication.[15]

This demeanor lead to a serious conflict between the youthful missionary and Kosrae's popular king concerning the whaling ships which so frequently entered the quiet waters of Lelu Harbor. Though the king had outlawed the drinking of liquor on the island, it was apparent that he found it difficult to resist temptation himself. As they were accustomed to doing throughout the Pacific, many sea captains used liquor as a bribe to obtain women for themselves and their men. After a few drinks, the enthusiasm with which King George endorsed the Seventh Commandment would diminish.

This practice greatly angered Benjamin Snow, who conscientiously trained his spyglass on vessels anchored in the harbor. Pisin was ideally located. It commanded an excellent view of all that went on within the harbor and at the king's wharf. When the king ordered men to take their wives and daughters to the ships at night, Mr. Snow himself would often go out to denounce the captains, round up the women, and bring them home again—stopping at Posral long enough to give an intoxicated King George a sound tongue-lashing. Sternly, the missionary threatened to leave Kosrae if the king did not stop sending women to the ships, while Lydia tearfully entreated the king to give up the evil practice.

The king did not appreciate his friend meddling in his affairs, but he did not want to risk losing the missionaries. In other matters there was often much the slender white man did to champion the Kosraean cause against unscrupulous visitors. Also, both the king and David Kirtland hoped that Mr. Snow would use his influence to get a medical doctor placed on the island. So King George would make an effort to reform. For a number of years prior to the arrival of the missionaries he had been biased toward Americans and Protestantism, so he accepted the inconveniences along with what he considered to be the advantages.

But King George not only had to deal with Benjamin Snow, he also had to placate the chiefs, for Mr. Snow was also very critical of the behavior of some of them. They, in turn, would complain to the king. When he became the ruler, King George had given most of the chiefly titles to members of his family. All of his brothers and his sisters' husbands had been made chiefs. By 1853 only one of his brothers was still alive, but several of the king's older sons and nephews held positions of high rank. His oldest son had been elected to the position of kanku, second in rank only to the tokosra. Consequently, when King George opposed the chiefs it was very much a family matter.

THE CHILDREN OF KING GEORGE

Lupalik I had fathered five sons. The eldest, called Sefot, was the kanku and later, upon the death of his father, became King Sru III. The names of the next three sons were Tulensru, Aliksa, and Kilafwa.[16] All of them died as relatively young men. The youngest son, Lupalikkun, was a 10-year-old boy in 1853. Two of the king's daughters—Kenye Kitinwak and Sepe Awe—outlived their siblings. The third, Srue Neporu, had died as a young woman shortly before the arrival of the missionaries.

YOUNG LUPALIKKUN JOINS THE SNOW HOUSEHOLD

In March 1853, Mr. Snow wrote to Ephraim Clark, the mission executive who had accompanied the missionaries to Micronesia, of their life on Pisin:

I think you would hardly recognize the place, it is so changed. The bushes and vines and large stones are cleared off nicely and Opunui is building a fine wall all around the edge of Dove Island. We have three pigs—one from a sea captain, one from the Kanku, and one from the King. The King has let me have two boys to get breadfruit, wood, and water.

We have sort of adopted the King's youngest son, Lupalikkun [lu, as in "lull," -PAUL-lik, as in "lick"-kun, as in "gun"], whom we call George. He occasionally visits the King, but is evidently more attached to us. He eats with us at our table with all the propriety of a good boy at home. He is a smart, active, bright little fellow, and quite a guardian angel to us, as no natives feel at liberty to loaf about us, much less to be fingering any of our things, while he is about.[17]

Benjamin and Lydia Snow grew to love this pleasant Kosraean lad. Lydia especially valued the comradeship he provided her. He was alert and inquisitive, eager to help by running errands, bringing crabs to boil, and sweeping leaves from the yard each morning. Often Lupalikkun was visited at Pisin by another boy his age—his friend, Tulensru. The Snows were captivated by the way the two boys tried to use English with each other as they worked and played together, since English was obviously the language of Dove Island.

KOSRAE'S FIRST SCHOOL

The ability of the people of Lelu to pronounce English words with accuracy impressed Benjamin Snow. Kosraean was not spoken in any other part of Micronesia, and the number of people remaining on Kosrae was so small—approximately 1,300 at this time—that Mr. Snow concluded there was little reason to place any emphasis on the use of the Kosraean language. Rather, he would concentrate on the introduction of English. After getting settled at Pisin, the Snows, with the help of Daniel and Doreka Opunui, started a school for the purpose of teaching English to the children and young people of Lelu.

The classes proved extremely popular when they were first organized and even many of the older people came along with the eager students to observe and listen. But only a few months had passed before the onlookers were no longer around and attendance became sporadic among the 30 registered boys and girls. No inducement seemed sufficient. Finally the missionaries discontinued their school. This was particularly disappointing to Benjamin Snow, who considered it out of the question to create a system of writing the Kosraean language. He continued to hold informal English and singing classes for the few who showed interest. He also found a bit of encouragement when he discovered that some of the former students would trace the alphabet in the sand, thus teaching their letters to others who had not attended school.

CONFLICTS WITH CHIEFS AND SAILORS

During their first year at Kosrae, Mr. Snow made no effort to preach on the large island across the harbor from Lelu. He confined his work to the king, the chiefs, and members of the noble families who made their homes in the private basalt rock enclosures on the smaller island. For this reason, he had little contact with the blue skins—the priests of the goddess Sinlaku—who kept to themselves among the commoners on the large island.

However, friction continued to build up between the young missionary and some of the lower chiefs, who resented his influence over the king. Dissension increased also between Mr. Snow and foreign sailors who persisted in finding Kosrae's snug harbors. No amount of cajoling lessened the eagerness of the chiefs for the knives, cooking pots, clothing, and other articles the seamen carried with them. Relentlessly, Benjamin Snow objected to the methods of trading practiced by the chiefs and sailors, strenuously protesting the use of women for bartering purposes. He received no direct opposition from David Kirtland to his program of reformation, but neither did his fellow American give him any encouragement.

FRICTION WITH WHALERS CONTINUES

On Sunday, March 20, 1853, the whaleship *Paragon* out of Nantucket, commanded by Capt. Thomas Nelson, was wrecked at the entrance to Lelu Harbor's channel with some loss of life. For many of the Kosraeans, this tragedy confirmed the wisdom of the new no-work-on-Sunday rule. Several residents of Lelu were heard commenting, "No good sail Sunday!"[18]

Those sailors who survived the wreck set up camp on the beach at Sansrik [SAN, as in "sand"-shrook, as in "look"], located across the harbor from the royal Lelu compound. Within two months most of the stranded men had left Kosrae on other vessels, intent on moving on or convinced by the king that they were not welcome. But the *Paragon's* sullen second mate, William Covert, refused to leave. The house he built for himself became the rendezvous for the worst of visiting sailors.

The conviction was growing in Benjamin Snow's mind that he had been called to work, not only among the Kosraeans, but also among the sailors who were stopping at Kosrae in increasing numbers. When captains would permit, he held religious services aboard the vessels. He also conducted services for sailors in his Pisin home and on Sunday afternoons at William Covert's place across the harbor. Ceaselessly, the vigorous young man worked at bettering the relations of the Kosraeans with the crews of these whaling ships. He wrote reports which were published in *The Friend* in Hawai'i, naming ships and listing the captains he felt took advantage of the islanders.

Mr. Snow's superior in Hawai'i expressed his concern to his counterpart in the American Board offices in Boston. Was the zealous missionary on Kosrae going too far with his criticism? "Peculiar caution is necessary in speaking in PRINT of the white men scattered up and down in these islands. Scarcely anything too bad can be said of many of them, yet such is their connection with the commencement of missionary activity in these islands, that it is very undesirable to excite their hostility further than is absolutely necessary."[19]

Benjamin Snow refused to mince words—still, he was caught in a moral dilemma. Lack of clothing was often used as an excuse for not attending church—and it was the whalers who brought clothing to the Kosraeans.

THE SNOWS AND THEIR HAWAIIAN COLLEAGUES

It had been specifically stated in the mission agreement that the Hawaiian missionaries were to be considered as co-workers by the Americans and not as domestics. In practice this was an uneasy ideal to achieve, complicated by the fact that Daniel and Doreka Opunui had a more difficult time communicating with the Kosraeans than had been anticipated. The mission planners in Honolulu had assumed a similarity between Hawaiian and the languages of Micronesia that did not exist. As the Opunuis spoke little English, and the Snows did not speak Hawaiian, communication was awkward between them—and Benjamin and Lydia were using a pidgin English with the Lelu Kosraeans that was next to impossible for Daniel and Doreka to comprehend or use.

Often, especially in the earliest months of their relationship, it seemed that the two missionary men had only their Christian faith in common. Constantly together—isolated from family and friends, and unfamiliar with each others' customs—they found that irritations and misunderstandings were easily exaggerated. The tireless American was annoyed by what he perceived to be the easygoing work habits of his Hawaiian companion. "He quite vexes me, when I want him to hurry a little, by seeming to be knocked into such confusion that he has to stop entirely to get his reckoning and then trudges on anew."[20] At times, Benjamin Snow longed for an American colleague to help him.

Daniel Opunui found it exceedingly difficult and frustrating to work with a man as strong-willed and set in his ways as the impatient New Englander. The new life on Kosrae was frequently painful for both Daniel and Doreka. They wrote to Berita and Deborah Kaaikaula on Pohnpei that the Snows treated them like servants.

Gradually, however, Benjamin and Daniel began to appreciate each other, as did Lydia and Doreka. Benjamin Snow wrote, "I am most happy in being able to report so favorably of our Hawaiian Associates and hardly know how, in our circumstances, we could get along without them. We have great confidence in their Christian character and their exemplary lives are a constant sermon."

Doreka, Mr. Snow continued, was always cheerful and ready to learn, while Daniel was grave, thoughtful, fond of study, willing to work, slow, very exact, and plodding. "And I suspect I love him all the better for his stability. It is a treat to see him laugh, and he laughs the hardest at the soberest things."[21]

It was a great relief for both couples when, in mid-1853, Daniel and Doreka moved from their small corner room in the Snow's house and into their own home a few yards away. It was not long after that move that Doreka gave birth to a son whom she and Daniel named Galen, after Benjamin Galen Snow.

DEATH OF DANIEL OPUNUI

None of the residents of Pisin were ready for the tragedy that struck their little band on August 4, 1853—a year to the month after their arrival on Kosrae. Daniel Opunui died suddenly of "inflamation of the brain." Mr. Snow wrote, "I have lost friends at home, near and dear ones, but now my only brother is taken, and I am left alone. There is none to take his place."[22]

Daniel Opunui was buried in the mission garden on Yenyen. Doreka's feelings of loss and loneliness, so far from her Hawaiian home and family, were heavy—though her little Galen was a great source of comfort to her, and she was kept busy with his care. Both Benjamin and Lydia Snow felt that Doreka's conduct throughout the ordeal of her husband's sudden illness and death was a testimony to the Christian hope which upheld her.

RAROTONGAN CHRISTIANS VISIT

Two months later the Snows received another indication of the potential of island Christians. A company of Christian sailors, natives of the island of Rarotonga, arrived aboard the *Duke of Cornwall*, bound for Sydney. The American missionaries were much impressed to see these "civilized natives" dressed modestly in clean clothing, fruit of the mission begun in 1822 in the Cook Islands by the celebrated John Williams. Benjamin and Lydia were encouraged through the fellowship they had with the Rarotongans in prayer, and they thrilled at the way the young visitors sang.

LELU'S FIRST CHURCH BUILDING

The Christian Rarotongans made a deep impression on the people of Lelu as well. Church attendance was stimulated to the point that the king felt it necessary to provide the congregation with a larger meeting house. In December 1853 the Lelu worshipers—none of whom were as yet baptized members of the church—moved from the mission house at Pisin and began meeting for the first time in a long thatch pavilion near the king's home at Posral. It was the first building on Kosrae erected expressly as a church.

KOSRAE ESCAPES SMALLPOX,
BUT OTHER DISEASES CONTINUE UNABATED

On March 8, 1854, Benjamin Snow received word that a Capt. B. C. Elridge of New Bedford, Connecticut, had anchored his ship, the *Margarete Scott*, in Kosrae's south harbor, and that three sailors on board were suffering from smallpox. Enraged, the missionary went at once to Utwe and demanded that Elridge weigh anchor immediately. He reprimanded the captain for his negligence in permitting Kosraeans on board his vessel and allowing members of the crew on shore when such a condition existed. The *Margarete Scott* sailed the next day, destination unknown. It is tragic that from May to September of that year smallpox ravaged Pohnpei, killing a staggering two-thirds of that island's population. Miraculously, Kosrae escaped.

Other diseases, however, were taking their toll on Kosrae. Benjamin Snow wrote to his home board, "We have come too late! Death has done its heaviest work among them. A little remnant is left of this noble people to tell us of their former glory and their deeds of renown. And what we do for these must be done quickly, for they are fast dropping away."[23]

From the first, the American missionary was struck by the industry of the Kosraean people. He found them to be "close observers and wonderfully inquisitive." But of what value was their diligence in the light of the rapid decline of their race? This decline, brought on primarily by the introduction of venereal diseases and epidemics of influenza, caused the missionaries great distress.

Mr. Snow wrote to his colleagues in Hawai'i: "It is almost incredible how rapidly this people have dwindled away, nor has the tide ceased to ebb. The King knows the vessel and the very man who sowed the first seeds of the wasting disease—God only knows who and how many have been engaged in it since. Oh, deliver me from their awful doom! It is no wonder to us who are out here and know what is done, and who do it, that these Islands have been so little known to the civilized world, though they have been long known and frequently resorted to by a certain class of the seagoing world. I am glad that the night of darkness is drawing towards morning."[24]

DEATH OF GOOD KING GEORGE

On September 9, 1854, death came to King Lupalik, the missionaries' Good King George. Though he and the New England pastor had often quarreled, they had become firm friends, and Benjamin Snow felt the loss deeply. The alarmed young man had been beside the king almost continually during the final illness. He wrote:

I called again, in a drenching rain, and found him in much pain, and weak. But the interview I had with him was more satisfactory than any previous one. In my journal for that day I wrote, "The King says he feel no all same as before." He thinks he has given everything to Christ, and that Christ has accepted him. Oh, how glorious it would be to see this people turning unto the Lord, and rejoicing in the glory of God!

The following Sabbath, the King sent three men to the three most important places on the large island to see that no work was done. This looked like a hopeful beginning of a religious life, though he had done something of that sort before. When I went to hold a religious service with him, I found him in great bodily distress. I prepared some black pepper tea for him, which soon relieved him, so that he was able to sit up. He was quite unwilling to have me leave till I had prayed and talked with him. Before I left, I inquired in respect to his feelings. He replied, "This morning me feel first rate; last night all same." I thought it became me to walk softly, when the Spirit was thus teaching, lest I should quench "the smoking flax."

On the 20th of August, he told me that when he had been in very great pain, as soon as he could fix his thoughts on Christ, he was quite unconscious of his sufferings, for the joy he felt in thinking of Christ. He thought his sickness was not unto death, for he was not an old man yet, but felt himself to be in the prime of life. He seemed much interested in that idea of old Cyprian, I think it was, "Christ is a ladder to climb to God on."

On the 27th of August, I spoke to him of baptism and the Lord's Supper. He expressed a strong wish to be baptized, as soon as it should be proper; but he preferred to wait till he could do it in the church, that his people might see the act. He was also desirous to partake of the holy supper. There was no unfavorable change in his feelings, subsequently, that I am aware of. At one time he seemed delighted with the thought that, by and by, some of his people would be able to go to other islands to tell them of Christ, as we were doing among his people.

From all these things you may wonder why I should have a moment's doubt of the genuineness of the change wrought upon his heart. But from my long and very intimate acquaintance with him, I have felt obliged to look with much suspicion upon all his acts. His passion and his weakness were a desire to please everybody, especially those whom he loved. I do not know, however, that he acted this double part in any of this last month's experience. But I greatly desired to see the genuineness of his hope put to the test of a practical life. Yet my confidence was so strong in him, that if I had thought his end was so near, I should have felt it my duty and my privilege to administer baptism and the holy supper, ere he left us.

The morning we learned of his death, and for a day or two before, the moistened eyes about the missionary's house seemed as when a beloved father is leaving for a better home. He was faithful to his promise, "I will be all same father to missionary." His dying charge to his son and the other chiefs was, "Take good care of the missionary."[25]

Instead of being left exposed in one of the royal pits within the ancient Lelu enclosures in the customary way, the king was given a Christian burial. After Queen Notwe Sruh tenderly wrapped the dead monarch's head in the shawl Lydia Snow had given her the year before, the family sheathed the body in woven pandanus mats tied with coconut cord. Benjamin Snow said a graveside prayer, and the body was lowered into the grave, covered with more mats and finally with earth.

ACCESSION OF KING SRU III

With the death of King Lupalik I, church attendance fell to practically nothing. One of the chiefs, the Sesa, threatened to get rid of the missionaries now that their protector was gone. Uneasy, Benjamin Snow began to campaign to have the Kanku, the oldest of the dead king's sons, chosen to take his father's place. Word was passed among the chiefs that if the Sesa were to rule, the missionary would leave the island. After two months of indecision, the Kanku was elected by the chiefs as King Sru [shrew] III.

But a short time later Benjamin Snow was chagrined to learn that, as the new king's wife was not of royal blood, he had chosen a second wife, his aunt—Srue Nueliki—to be his official queen. Mr. Snow's protests were in vain since the old queen insisted on her son's prerogative to take another wife.

The new king further dismayed the missionary by reviving some of the practices that had been abolished by his father. How could there be a coronation ceremony without priests of the old religion presiding over it? At the command of the chiefs—some of them relieved and pleased with the king's decree—people began coming across the harbor from the large island, bringing the traditionally required baskets of food to Posral for the crowning.

On November 13, as everyone watched, two of the blue skin priests "made magic" over orange leaves and inserted them through the lobes of the new king's ears. Wreaths of flowers were placed on the heads of the king and queen while their titles were proclaimed—the new Tokosra and the new Kasra! The priests supervised as the tributes of food that had been brought by the subjects of the chiefs was distributed, on behalf of the king, back to the chiefs. A similar distribution, on behalf of the queen, was made to the wives of the chiefs and other high ranking women.[26]

While the rituals and food exchanges were taking place, Benjamin Snow stood outside the royal pavilion warning everyone within earshot of the punishment that would fall on King Sru's head. The people pretended not to hear him and a great feast that lasted several days ensued. Later, Mr. Snow was somewhat consoled to learn that the king's new marriage was one of political expedience. King Sru disliked his aunt and had no intention of living with the new queen as her husband.

CONFRONTATION WITH THE BLUE SKINS

Leaders from among the blue skin priests and priestesses on the large island, reinvigorated by the invitation to officiate at the coronation and the subsequent relaxed mood among the Lelu chiefs, decided to accost the beleaguered missionary on his home ground. They came across the harbor in a flotilla of canoes and, though they did not dare set foot on Lelu uninvited, planned to invade Pisin for whatever mischief they could inflict there.

But as they rounded the half-acre island to approach its landing, they were met by the tall, stern-faced missionary who stood on the stone steps, legs spread apart and arms folded across his powerful chest. He did not say a word, but his sharp blue eyes, magnified through the square, rimless glasses he wore, seemed to pierce their very flesh. They stopped paddling. The young priest in the bow of the lead canoe shot a pole through the shallow water to the bottom, breaking the progress of his craft. The pale foreigner's gaze did not waver nor weaken. The blue skins, their knowledge of the missionary and his powers limited to hearsay, their familiarity with varieties of demon-hexing suddenly too ample, knew they could go no further. As fast as they could turn their canoes, they were off in the direction from which they had come.

LONELINESS AND DESPAIR

Though relations with the chiefs were at an all-time low, Mr. Snow was determined that the reforms begun by Good King George be continued. The present king was often drunk, harshly beating his commoner wife and flogging his men for the smallest offenses. He avoided the missionary, who nonetheless kept busy publicly denouncing whatever sin he perceived in Lelu village. Mr. Snow was especially adamant in his condemnation of Sunday work and Sunday visiting. He learned that King George's widow, the queen mother, Notwe Sruh, was sleeping with his old enemy, the Sesa, but she remained impassive to the diatribes of the ardent young missionary.

Discouragements multiplied, and loneliness began to weigh heavily upon the Snows. Lydia went about her work at Pisin with reddened eyes. They had been on Kosrae for over two years and had yet to receive their first mail from the officers of the mission board or from loved ones in the United States. Still more disheartening was word which came piecemeal from various whaling ships out of Honolulu. The mission ship, *Caroline*, had been sold, and no plans had been announced for a replacement.

Benjamin Snow began writing letters: Why was the ship sold without consulting the ones to whom it was the only lifeline? Where were the additional personnel promised to them? "If you cannot send a doctor, send my younger sister, or Mrs. Snow's sister, or a pious farmer and his wife. We need associates! The whole Pacific is vastly more ready for Christian laborers than Christian laborers can be found to enter it."[27]

INTRODUCING KUTUKA AND NOTWE

The meager numbers attending the various worship services and classes added to the depression of those days, though there was an edge of hope. Eleven persons were gathering regularly at Pisin with the Snows and Doreka Opunui for prayer meetings. A married couple among them, Kutuka [cut-TUH-ca, as in "cat"]and Notwe [NOTE-way], gave the dejected Benjamin Snow some cause for rejoicing as he watched the development of "a Christian spirit within them."

UPS AND DOWNS

Six pleasant days in December 1854, during which Albert and Susan Sturges paid a surprise visit to Kosrae, did much to revive the lonely couple. The Sturgeses, too, enjoyed the visit. They were impressed with the Snows' cow—a gift some months earlier from a generous whaling captain, and kept "in a little yard in a stone wall"—and were amazed that Lydia Snow was able to churn milk into butter twice a week.

Dring an influenza epidemic in January 1855, Queen Srue Nueliki died. This solved, for a time at least, the appearance of polygamy which Benjamin Snow refused to condone. But the blue skins, smarting from the rebuke they had suffered on the shores of Pisin, used the epidemic against Mr. Snow. The missionary had visited the large island just prior to the outbreak of the illness, and he was loudly accused of being the cause of that disaster, which took 50 lives in the first months of the new year.

Benjamin and Lydia Snow, however—despite their loneliness and depression—enjoyed good health. His letters frequently made grateful mention of this. "Our health is almost uniformly good, though my Lydia is looking somewhat worse for wear. As for myself, I can't say. Mrs. Snow must report on me. I assure you we know not how to be sufficiently thankful for this best of our Heavenly Father's mercies. For this matter of health caused more fears and misgivings on my part, about being isolated and alone, than all others."[28]

CENSUS OF 1855

In June 1855 Benjamin Snow made a trip around Kosrae for the specific purpose of taking a census. He found a total population of 1,106, dividing it as follows:

large island men: 396	Lelu men: 103
large island women: 279	Lelu women: 89
large island boys: 109	Lelu boys: 34
large island girls: 70	Lelu girls: 26

He counted 243 houses on the large island and 89 canoes. There were 105 houses on Lelu Island, 43 canoes and 5 boats. He found 96 individuals who were ill. During the previous 12 months, 113 persons had died. He saw only one infant.[29]

This census seemed to verify the missionary's conviction that within 10 years the sod would cover the last of the Kosraean race. Mr. Snow was greatly disheartened. He commented, "They have lost all of their ancient vigor."

It was at this time that the fervent young man, pressured by what he considered a matter of time, made an important decision. "I have undertaken to preach entirely in the Kusaien language," he wrote. "Whether this has anything to do with the increase of numbers of late, I much doubt."[30] ✦

Notes - Chapter 2

1.   Benjamin Snow, unpublished correspondence, ABCFM, Boston 1852
2.   B. Snow, personal correspondence to Mrs. Ives, Honolulu, Oct 7, 1952
3.   B. Snow, personal correspondence to Ephraim Clark, Honolulu, March 7, 1853
4.   B. Snow, personal correspondence to Mrs. Ives, Oct. 7, 1852
5.   Lydia Snow, personal correspondence, to Mrs. Ives, Honolulu, Nov. 27, 1852
6.   James L. Lewis, "Kusaiean Acculturation 1824-1848," p. 28
7.   B. Snow, personal correspondence, to Samuel Damon, Honolulu, Oct 14, 1852
8.   J. D. Jones, *Life and Adventure in the South Pacific by a Roving Printer*, New York, 1861, quoted by James L. Lewis in "Kusaiean Acculturation 1824-1948," p. 27
9.   B. Snow, personal correspondence to E. Clark, Honolulu, March 7, 1853
10. B. Snow, personal journal, 1852
11. B. Snow, personal correspondence to E. Clark, March 7, 1853
12. Ibid
13. Ibid
14. B. Snow, personal journal, 1853
15. Lewis, p. 29
16. B. Snow, "Primu Kusaie–Buk in Lutlut ke Rid," 1875, p. 51
17. B. Snow, personal correspondence to E. Clark, March 7, 1853
18. David and Leona Crawford, *Missionary Adventures in the South Pacific*, 1967, p. 63
19. E. W. Clark, personal correspondence to R. Anderson, Boston, archival (Houghton Library) ABCFM, Nov. 4, 1852
20. B. Snow, personal journal, 1853
21. Albertine Loomis, *To All People*, 1970, p. 68
22. B. Snow, personal journal, 1853
23. B. Snow, unpublished correspondence, ABCFM, Boston 1853
24. B. Snow, *The Friend*, Honolulu, Sept. 17, 1853
25. B. Snow, *The Missionary Herald*, ABCFM Boston, July 1858, pp. 218-219
26. "Kusaie In The Nineteenth Century," University of Guam, undated, p.14
27. B. Snow, personal correspondence, 1854
28. B. Snow, personal correspondence to E. Clark, March 7, 1853
29. B. Snow, personal correspondence, 1855
30. Ibid

NUNAK YOHK KE CHAPTER 3
1855-1862

Ke October 1855 oak soko ma us mwe kuka tuh oai Kosrae. Inen oak soko ah pa *Belle*. Mwet missionary sasu akosr wema oak soko ah— George Pierson el taktu se, ac mutan kial pa Nancy. J. W. Kanoa el sie mwet Hawai'i ac mutan kial pa Kaholo. Mr. ac Mrs. Snow eltal arulana engan ke mwet sasu inge su tuku in welulos ke orekma lalos.

Ke April 1856, oak Marshall lulap limekosr tuh sun paka se. Elos pahtpat na meoa twe sun acn Kosrae. Mwet Marshall eungoul tolu muta fin oak ekasr inge. Ke pacl elos orekma in aksasuye acn musalla ke oak okoalos, Dr. Pierson el mutawauk in lutlut kas Marshall yorolos. Meet liki el sun acn Kosrae, Dr. Pierson el tuh srola ke kutu tuka in acn Marshall, ac el tuh pulakin lah God El pangnol elan sie missionary nu sin mwet Marshall. Ke pacl se pacna inge, Mr. Kanoa el lutlut kas Gilbert yurin mwet Gilbert luo su muta Kosrae, mweyen el ke som luti Wosasu nu sin mwet Gilbert.

Mwet fakfuk loat elos srakna orek lokoalok yurin mwet Kosrae, ac mas ma tuku sayame uniya pac mwet puspis. Mr. Snow el sang kuiyal in kasru mwet Kosrae in lain mwe ongoiya inge. Tokosra Sru III el misa in September 1856, ac Tokosra Alokoa el aolul.

In yac sac pacna, Mrs. Pierson el oswela tulik mutan se su eltal sang inel Salome, ac Mrs. Snow el oswela tulik mutan se, su eltal sang inel Caroline. Lupalikkun, wen natul "Good King George," el srakna muta Pisin yurol Mr. ac Mrs. Snow. Sie tulik mutan su matwel na Lupalikkun el muta pac yurin missionary inge in kulansupweltal. Inel pa Kat Otnaur, tuh Mr. ac Mrs. Snow eltal pangnol "Kittie." Kutuka ac Notwe eltal wi pac muta Pisin. Mr. Snow el mutawauk in supwala sianyan se inge nu Sansrik in orek alu yurin mwet we. Oasr pacl kutu sin mwet Sansrik elos aksruksrukeltal, tusruktu eltal tia fuhleak in oru orekma se itukyang kuneltal.

In July 1857, kutu mwet selu America su muta Sansrik, wi kutu mwet Rotoma su muta Tenwak, elos pwapani in sisella Tokosra Alokoa. Tokosra el lohng ke pwapa lun u se inge, na ke elos som nu Lelu in anwuk ke July len 9, Tokosra ac mwet foko lal lainulos ac folokunulos nu Sansrik. Ke malem luo mwet ma orek lokoalok inge kofla illa liki inkul selos Sansrik ke sripen mwet lun Tokosra raunela acn elos muta we. Mr. Snow ac Dr. Pierson eltal tuh kasru u luo inge kewa—eltal onoela mwet kinet, ac suk inkanek in akmisyela inmas-rlolos. *Morning Star* se emeet tuh oai Kosrae ke September 8. Captain Moore ac mwet orekma lal elos kasrel Tokosra Alokoa ac mwet lal in kutongya akukuin se ma orek. Tia paht toko, supweyukla u se ma orek lokoalok liki acn Kosrae. Mukul Rotoma luo, Tosie ac Fatiki, eltal mutana Kosrae ke sripen eltal wo ac kasru mwet Kosrae. Mwet Kosrae elos tuh pangon *Morning Star* sac "Peace Maker."

Ke November 3, 1857, Dr. Pierson ac sou lal som liki acn Kosrae nu Marshall, ac Mr. Kanoa ac sou lal som nu Gilbert. Mrs. Snow el oswela tulik mukul se ke March 9, 1858, ac eltal sang inel Fredrick Galen. Len akosr toko, Mrs. Snow el masak ac lukunna misa.

In May 2, 1858 Kutuka ac Notwe eltal baptaisla. Mwet luo inge pa mwet Christian emeet fin acn Kosrae. In September, Tokosra Alokoa el misa ac Lupalik II el aolul in tokosra. Sie tulik mukul Utwe el weang mwet ma muta Pisin yorol Mr. ac Mrs. Snow. Inen tulik se inge pa Likiaksa. Ke yac se inge, mwet na 830 lula Kosrae.

In 1859 Mr. Snow el baptaisella Lupalikkun ac mutan luo su tia kalem inel-tal. Mr. Snow el lohngak lah meet liki Kutuka el tuh baptaisla, el tuh welul Kat motul. Mutan kial Kutuka oayapa Doreka Opunui, eltal wi etu ma se inge tuh eltal okanla tia fahk. Mr. Snow ac Mrs. Snow eltal arulana supwarla sel Doreka ac Notwe. Mr. Snow el sap Kutuka ac Notwe in tuyak ye mutun mwet nukewa su wi alu Lelu in fahkak ma eltal tuh oru, ac in siyukyuk nunak munas. Ma se inge tuh arulana upa, tusruktu eltal oru oana ma Mr. Snow el sapkin. Tok, Kutuka ac Notwe sifilpa touyak nu ke mwet in church. Doreka ac tulik mukul se natul tuh folokla nu Hawai'i. Ke Lupalikkun el yac 17 el siyuk sel Mr. Snow elan fuhlella elan tila muta Pisin. Mr. Snow el sifacna nunku mu oasr tafongla lal Lupalikkun, ouinge el fuhlella elan som, ac fili el liki church. Eltal kewa arulana asor.

In 1859, Tokosra Lupalik II el sifilpa musaela lohm alu se su Tokosra Lupalik I el tuh musaela fin acn Posral ke 1853. Ke 1860 pisen mwet fasr wi alu ke Sunday pa mwet 30. Mwet ma muta Sansrik lac nu Utwe tuh engan in lohng kas in luti lun missionary liki mwet ma muta Pukusrik lac nu Okat. Pisen mwet Kosrae kiluki nu ke mwet 748. Yac se pacna inge Mr. Snow el simusla sie book srisrik in kas Kosrae pangpang Primu, in luti mwet uh in rit. El oayapa mutawauk in lungasla kutu kas in Bible: Matthew 5:3-11, Pre lun Leum, ac Psalm 23.

Mwet Christian in acn Boston su orek pwapa ke mukuikui lun mission-ary, elos sapla tuh Benjamin ac Lydia Snow in som nu Ebon in acn Marshall in orekma we. Meet liki eltal som, Mr. Snow el lungasla Gospel lal John. Inen mwet se su kasrel ke leng pa Salpasr. Puseni mwet wi alu ke church in acn Lelu, oayapa Sansrik. In pacl sac, mwet ma fasr wi alu Sansrik elos pus liki mwet ma fasr wi alu Lelu. Mwet Lelu singoul limekosr baptaisla in 1861, ac mwet eu baptaisla in 1862—oalkosr mwet Lelu, ac sie mwet Sansrik su mwet se emeet in baptaisla we.

Mr. Snow ac sou lal som liki acn Kosrae nu Marshall ke August 25, 1862— yac singoul na fal tukun elos tuh oai Kosrae. Elos usal Salpasr ac mutan kial in kasrelos fin acn Ebon. Oasr pac sie mukul fusr Lelu welultal oayak. Inel pa Paitok. Mr. Snow el liye lah wo sifal Paitok ke lutlut, na pa el lungse supwalla nu Hawai'i. Mr. Snow el sang Kutuka in liyaung alu fin acn Sansrik. Likiaksa el srisngyuki in karingin acn Pisin ac oayapa liyaung alu fin acn Lelu. Pisen mwet ma baptaisla ac oaoa mwet lun church fin acn Kosrae in pacl sac pa mwet 30. Onkosr selos pa mutan fusr onkosr inge: Srue Tafweyat, Tulpe Pisin, Sepe Nuarpat, Kat Otnaur, Wa Inkoeya, ac Notwe Kras.

CHAPTER THREE

THE FIRST KOSRAEAN CHRISTIANS
1855-1862

MISSIONARY CO-WORKERS ARRIVE

The Snows had sent letters from Kosrae with the occasional whaleship captain they felt they could trust. Those in charge of the mission in Hawai'i and the United States, however, were hesitant to send mail to the Snows aboard ships whose destinations were not specifically known or with captains of dubious reputation. So, for 37 months, mail for the missionaries accumulated in the Honolulu offices of the Hawaiian Evangelical Association.

Then the mission executives in Hawai'i were introduced to a Capt. Handy, who was sympathetic to the missionary cause. He was preparing to sail from Honolulu aboard his trading ship, the *Belle*, on a voyage through Micronesia. He agreed to sell space to the mission board, not only for missionary mail and cargo, but for two missionary couples—one American and one Hawaiian. They embarked from Honolulu in May 1855.

During June, July, August, and September, Capt. Handy went from island to island in the Gilberts and Marshalls trading goods for coconut oil and copra. It was not until October 6 that the *Belle* sailed into Lelu Harbor. In the hold were not only much-needed supplies for the Snows, but letters for them from the mission boards, their families, and friends. It was their first mail from beyond Micronesia since arriving at Kosrae. Benjamin Snow learned that his mother had been dead two years.

Also on board the *Belle* were the colleagues for whom the Snows had long been praying—Dr. George and Nancy Pierson, plus Hawaiian missionary J. W. Kanoa, his wife Kaholo, and their infant son, Seoti. Mr. Snow's heartfelt description of their arrival was published in *The Missionary Herald*:

Come with me, a few moments, and "rejoice with those that do rejoice." Last Saturday morning, October 6, report came of a "ship outside." "O dear, more trouble! When will our sorrows have an end?" Still, for some unexplainable reason, I had an unusual flow of happy feelings; so much so that I spoke of them to Mrs. Snow, and remarked that I was to have a greater trial with that ship's company than usual, or there was something very good coming of it.

The busy work of Saturday was going on till the ship made her appearance at the entrance of the harbor. My glass was in instant requisition to see what could be made of her. The survey was not continued long before I discovered a man not in a sailor's rig. And presently I saw him helping a lady up the side of the ship to look out. The distance being great, I judged from the movement, that it was Dr. Gulick and wife.

Instantly Dove Island rung with the shouts of their names. Soon there was an alternate eyeing of each other with our glasses, and answering each other's swing of the hat. But as I met my Lydia about her work I found her eyes looked red and watery, and her voice seemed failing her. In due time my boat was manned with boys, and as I got nearer the ship I found I had mistaken the man. Dr. Gulick was not Dr. Gulick, but somebody else. Yet he looked earnestly enough, to be more than ordinarily interested in me, and as soon as I struck the deck, the greeting answered to a missionary's and the name, to one we had long been looking for.

So many thousand questions crowd upon the mind, that nothing seems to be asked, nor much answered, and yet in a few minutes we know a good deal of each other. —But this won't do, we must go ashore. "Where's the mail?" The bag and little packages are soon found, and on our way ashore I learned that they had been having a blessed revival on board. The three mates had been born again, and a temperance society had been formed in the forecastle. —We are getting near the little stone wharf, and the company are reported at suitable speaking distance.

But your imagination must fill up the scene when Dove Island received "the feet of him that bringeth good tidings and publisheth peace." Let us enter the cottage—"the lone missionary's home." Those "whose hearts and hopes are one," are not very formal in their introductions, for you would think it but the meeting of old friends; yet it would seem they had been long separated, else why do the sisters hang upon each other's necks with weeping.

"Well, talk on awhile, while I look at the letter bag,"—and I fumble my pockets for a knife to cut the strings. But the "not yet" of my wife brings the prodigal to himself, and the knife is laid by, the Bible is sought—the family are all together—it looks like family worship, except that the family is suddenly enlarged and we sit less formally than usual.

The 103rd Psalm is read; I then stop to look at those whom God had sent us, remarking that I had frequently said I should want to spend the first hour in sitting and looking at them. But their faces are already familiar, so Brother Pierson reads the hymn,

> *Tis by the faith of joys to come,*
> *We walk through deserts dark as night;*
> *Till we arrive at heaven our home,*
> *Faith is our guide, and faith our light.*[1]

MISSION MEETING CANCELED

Benjamin Snow had heard rumors of the possibility of a mission-sponsored ship arriving, and he was eager to travel to Pohnpei to meet with his colleagues for a meeting of the Micronesia Mission. When he learned from those aboard the *Belle* that the board disapproved of a meeting of the mission at this time, proposing that such a meeting take place instead in 1857, Mr. Snow wrote in frustration to Ephraim Clark of the Hawaiian Evangelical Association:

"If I were not getting the reputation of being rather crusty in some of my communications, I would write as I feel and speak out as I think—though it might cost me a sharp rebuke! If Micronesian affairs are to be managed at Honolulu and not in Micronesia, let us know that. While we love you like your children, you must allow us to plan and work like men. But when you allow us no possible means for consultation or comparing of notes and experiences only once in five years—and this at the very outset of our work, it is easy to see that but little unity of action can be secured and we shall become as Dr. Pearson says, 'Micro-Missions Mission' instead of 'Micronesian Mission!'"[2]

UNEXPECTED COMPANY

Six months later an incident of far-reaching consequence took place. Five large, storm-damaged canoes appeared in April 1856, carrying 93 Marshall Islanders. Swept from a planned course between two of their atolls, the Marshallese men, women, and children had drifted at the mercy of the sea for 15 days, the last five without food or water. They were welcomed reluctantly by the Kosraeans, who feared their arrival was cover for an attack.

The young doctor, on the other hand, viewed their appearance as the divine will of God. George and Nancy Pierson had gone ashore on several of the Marshall atolls as they sailed toward Kosrae aboard the *Belle*. That they had actually met some of these marooned Marshallese on those brief visits was to them providential. The coincidence served to confirm Dr. Pierson's growing conviction that his own calling lay among the people of the Marshall Islands—the people whom he had seen at such close range during his months with Capt. Handy.

As the Marshallese slowly gained the confidence of their cautious Kosraean hosts, they began negotiating for trees to build the canoes they needed to return to their home islands. They settled temporarily near Kosrae's south harbor in areas they named for their home atolls—names which the Kosraeans kept: Ebon, Likiep and Selus [Jaluit]. The Kosraeans watched in fascination as the canoes began to take shape. Compared to their own simple, light dugouts, these deep-hulled canoes were elaborate, ingeniously crafted of hand-hewn boards laced and sealed one above another. Not blessed with a high island's expanses of fertile land, the Marshallese compensated for their sparse and sandy soil by concentrating on the sea. Raised on a lush, productive island, the Kosraeans could not match the highly developed skills of Marshallese sailors, fishermen, and canoe builders.

The Marshallese attended church services regularly while they were on Kosrae and seemed to enjoy them. "Not being able to understand the letter, they went through the form to perfection," wrote Mr. Snow. "When I put out my hands in benediction, out went their hands as gracefully as an experienced parson. We have been having full benedictions since their arrival!"[3]

Along with curious Kosraeans, George Pierson, the slender American doctor, spent every spare moment he could in the temporary Marshallese settlement. He was determined to take advantage of this unexpected happening by learning as much of the Marshallese language as he could. When the Marshall Islanders set sail in four immense canoes on August 18—carrying with them several Marshallese who had been previously stranded on Kosrae—two of their company remained behind with Dr. Pierson to help him continue his study of their language.

George Pierson's enthusiasm for his Marshallese project cost him the solidarity he had originally enjoyed with his more experienced associate. Benjamin Snow had grave misgivings about Dr. Pierson's plans. He resented the way the doctor neglected him and their joint projects among the Lelu villagers in order to cement Marshallese ties. Mr. Snow was further irritated by what he called the doctor's "bull-headedness—an inability to reason or to accept criticism." In fact, the slim but robust minister felt that the doctor was much too frail to make an effective missionary anywhere!

That the ideal missionary companion he had mentally created during the long months alone did not materialize with the arrival of George Pierson was felt keenly by Benjamin Snow, who still missed the assistance of the conscientious Opunui and the companionship he had enjoyed with Good King George.

STRANGE COINCIDENCE

While the Piersons and the Snows made a concerted effort to live in support of one another, Dr. Pierson and the Hawaiian missionary, J. W. Kanoa, were having problems reminiscent of those Benjamin Snow and Daniel Opunui had initially experienced four years earlier. Kanoa had a more forceful personality than his fellow Hawaiian, Opunui, and he had a clear sense that his was a call to work among the people of the Gilbert Islands. He had also been aboard the

Belle as it sailed through the Marshall and Gilbert groups those months before reaching Kosrae, and—as George Pierson had felt God's nudge to work among the Marshallese—J. W. Kanoa felt that nudge just as surely to work among the Gilbertese.

Then—as Dr. Pierson's feelings concerning service in the Marshall Islands had been confirmed for him by the chance arrival of those canoe-loads of Marshallese people—an uncannily similar incident did the same for Kanoa. Two Gilbert Islands men were picked up from a drifting canoe by the crew of a whaling ship and deposited at Kosrae. As George Pierson had enthusiastically begun to learn the Marshallese language from the stranded Marshallese, so J. W. Kanoa eagerly began the study of Gilbertese with Tekaoti and Marie. Ironically, just as Benjamin Snow felt abandoned in his zeal for the work on Kosrae by George Pierson, so George Pierson now felt abandoned by J. W. Kanoa.

MULLING THE WHALER DILEMMA

As his father before him, King Sru III refused to allow the making of liquor on Kosrae. But he drank heavily himself of the generous gifts lavished upon him by ingratiating ship captains who sought water, firewood, fresh produce, and shore leave for their pent-up sailors.

The whaling industry was now at its peak in the Pacific and whalers were stopping at Kosrae in ever-increasing numbers. In the spring of 1856, Mr. Snow noted that more than 75 ships had visited Kosrae since his arrival in 1852. With these ships came all of the confusion and upheaval that the wild carousing of undisciplined men could dump upon a peaceful island community.

That fall, Mr. Snow wrote of this situation in an article later published in *The Friend*:

During the second week of this month we had 20 ships in our harbor, all sperm-whalers. The first three came in on the 8th and 9th of September—the last four came in the 5th of October. Such a fleet makes our harbor look quite like a port of entry.

As I have cruised about the beach and paddled around the harbor, I have fre-quently remarked upon the well-behaved and orderly deportment of the sailors; but, by the yelling and hooting we heard some nights, when a little liquor had been obtained from ships, I was led to suspect we should see a different state of things had there been a few grogshops on the beach. But some men will run away. Our rugged mountains and deep glens look inviting to them. They say they are badly used. I have known men to run away who said they were well used. Some have been trying it from these ships.

But Kusaie is a bad place for runaways. They can't stay run! Quite a number left one ship; some got sick of it and came back; others had to be hunted up and, showing fight, one of them got badly mauled by the natives—a rib or two broken, and his life endangered. Then, what were a handful of sickly natives against such a posse of excited and revengeful white men?

...The more I see and learn of the depredations and outrages practiced upon the poor, defenseless natives, the less I wonder at their occasional cruelties to shipping and to whites. In nine cases out of ten, I venture to say it is revenge for previous wrongs done them, or it is self-defense. Any depredations may be made upon a poor Kusaien—his coconut trees robbed, his canoe stolen, his house plundered; and if he asks for redress, he gets a kick, a cuff, or a curse—not by everyone, I am most happy to say, but by many—far, far too many of those who visit them. While if one of these poor fellows is caught stealing a shirt, or a knife, or a biscuit, the whole ship is down on him, and if he gets ashore with his head on and no bones broken, he may consider himself a lucky chap. Why this inequality of justice?

But the great death-blight with us underlies all this. When the first ship of this fall fleet came into the harbor, Mrs. Snow and I were making a tour of the island. Our first news from it was at daybreak the next morning, of men passing us in post-haste, by order of a chief, to get women to go on board ship! A few Sabbath evenings after that, as some Kusaien took a sailor on board a bark, they saw four native women on board of her. I would these were all; but we have too good evidence that it is far otherwise. I am thankful that I can say it is not so with all.

Is it to be wondered at that our people are gone, and the race ruined? Rather, it is a wonder that any are left! At the rate of diminishing for the last year, in less than ten years the sod will cover the last of the Kusaien race! Who cares? Who weeps for a lost race? Surely not the destroyers, except it be that there is no longer a work of death for them!

And with such facts, what shall we hope for in our efforts to elevate and save the native race in the Pacific? It is time the difficulties were laid open to the Christian world, and the true state of things looked at, face to face. There is "darkness upon the face of the deep." We need the "Spirit of God to move upon the face of the waters." God says now, as he said at the beginning, "LET THERE BE LIGHT!"[4]

DEATH OF KING SRU III
AND ACCESSION OF KING ALOKOA

On September 30, 1856, King Sru III died in another of the influenza epidemics—though it was rumored that he had been killed by the man who succeeded him. All 14 ships in Lelu Harbor flew their flags at half-mast in his honor. The men of the Lelu clans elected a high-ranking chief, the Sesa, to take Sru's place as the next king. Benjamin Snow was appalled. There had been no mutual trust or rapport between him and Sru III, but this Sesa—who now became King Alokoa [ALL-oh-kwah]—had been one of King George's "worst foes," and Mr. Snow considered him "an unprincipled scamp!"

TWO MISSIONARY DAUGHTERS BORN ON PISIN

Benjamin Snow and George Pierson made every effort to cooperate with each other, but the difference in their personalities, styles of ministry, and interpretation of missionary work made harmonious living difficult. Moreover, there was the crowded condition of Pisin. There were now 16 residents living on the tiny islet.

Both Lydia Snow and Nancy Pierson had given birth to daughters. Salome Pierson arrived August 31, 1856, becoming the first white child—though the second missionary child—to be born on Kosrae. Four months later, on December 22, Caroline Snow was born, named for the ship that had brought her parents to Kosrae four years earlier. Mr. Snow wrote, "The love and attentions bestowed upon her are very like those other parents are wont to bestow upon their first born!"[5]

As a result of an upswing in interest following the arrival of the Piersons and Kanoas the year before, Benjamin Snow had reopened his English school at Pisin. Now he decided to discontinue his school once again—at least for the time being. It was true that he was disappointed with the truancy of his pupils and that he complained about the lack of books, but he was primarily preoccupied with his new daughter and the building of another house to help handle Pisin's growing population.[6]

In addition to the two American missionary families on Pisin, there were the Hawaiian missionaries. With Doreka and Galen in their tiny house were J. W. Kanoa, Kaholo, and their son, Seoti. Their daughter, Emma, was born at Pisin on January 8, 1857, swelling the number of infant girls on the islet to three. A Lelu boy, Palikkun, lived with the Hawaiian missionaries as their helper.

Young Lupalikkun, the youngest son of Good King George, was an integral part of the Snow family. Though he was now 14, Benjamin and Lydia continued to call him "Little George" and loved him dearly. And there was Kat, a Lelu girl who had been living with the Snows for several years and worked as their housekeeper. To their American ears, "Kat" [cat]—a common Kosraean name—seemed inappropriate for a girl, so they called her "Kittie." Kutuka and his wife, Notwe, had also become residents of Pisin. They, too, assisted the Americans as domestic helpers and were considered by their missionary pastor to be the closest of all Kosraeans to Christian baptism.

KUTUKA AND NOTWE BEGIN PREACHING

So confident was Benjamin Snow of these two determined seekers that, toward the end of 1856, he began sending Kutuka and Notwe to Sansrik, the settlement on the large island across the harbor from Lelu, to conduct Sunday services. Kutuka had little confidence in his ability to handle such an assignment, but he was surprised and pleased by the interest of the people. As many as 50 persons would turn out for these services, intent upon observing the newly acquired talents of their two fellow Kosraeans. Occasionally, Mr. Snow would accompany Kutuka and Notwe. During this period, the missionary described the Kosraeans on the large island as thoroughly superstitious but evincing some interest in Christianity.

The antagonism of the blue skin priests and priestesses of Sinlaku was soon aroused by these Sunday visits. They had not been overly concerned while Mr. Snow confined his work to Lelu, but now they took offense at his trespassing with his disciples into what they considered their own territory. People began to ridicule Kutuka and Notwe when they visited the large island, pointing at them and calling Kutuka "Peter" to tease him. They hooted at those among their acquaintances who seemed to be attracted by the new teaching. Kutuka and Notwe courageously continued their assignment, though only a few brave persons were now attending their Sansrik services.

After some time had passed, however, a man and his wife in the settlement of Pilyuul, on the southeast coast of the large island, began listening to these two determined missionaries from Lelu. The man, Pose, and his wife, Kenye, had been ardent worshipers of Sinlaku. Their growing fascination with the missionaries' message greatly encouraged Kutuka and Notwe—and also the Snows and Piersons when this interest was reported to them.

Then Pose was stabbed in the shoulder by a swordfish while trolling in the ocean. His neighbors considered this a sure sign of Sinlaku's anger and, at first, so did Pose. The blue skins immediately capitalized on the incident and demanded that Benjamin Snow and his teachers refrain from coming to the large island. Mr. Snow refused to listen to these warnings and hurried to Pilyuul, accompanied by Dr. Pierson, to treat the wounded man. The two missionaries remained vigilantly with their patient until he began to recover from his wound. Benjamin Snow and his helpers were begrudgingly allowed to continue the services on the large island of Kosrae.

MEASURING SUCCESS

As 1857 dawned, the missionaries were unsure of how to measure the success of their work. Benjamin Snow noticed and was grateful for the development of Christian commitment in the lives of Kutuka and Notwe, and he was delighted with the progress that George and Kittie were making in their studies. Both children were apt learners and impressed the Snows with their gentle, cooperative attitudes.

On March 18, Mr. Snow wrote, "I preach every Sabbath to a varied and not very numerous congregation. The attention is all the way from sleepiness to very marked and thoughtful interest. Dr. Pierson and his family are very constant and respectful hearers, probably not greatly edified with my native lingo. King Alokoa is more of a go-to-meeting hand, and more generous in his attentions to us than was King Sru III. Another chief died a few days since—he was formerly King George's Steward, Jack Sru—and I have some hope he died a believer."[7]

A PLOT AGAINST THE KING

During his four years on Kosrae, William Covert had gathered quite a colony around him at Sansrik across the harbor from Lelu. Francis C. Lawton, an African-American from New Bedford; William Johnston, an English blacksmith; and John Hathaway, a young sailor from Rhode Island, had been with Covert for several years. Covert, Lawton, and Hathaway had Kosraean women living with them, by whom they had children. Johnston's wife was Pohnpeian.

Also, 13 men from Rotuma, a lone island north of the Fiji group, were living in the Tenwak settlement not far beyond Sansrik. A number of these men had lived on Kosrae for a considerable length of time, having deserted whaling ships and taken wives from among the Kosraeans. One of them, known as "Rotuma Tom," worked as an assistant to the trader, David Kirtland, and had become competent in piloting ships in and out of Lelu Harbor. Two others, Tosie and Fatiki, were industrious, friendly, and respected by their Kosraean neighbors. The remaining 10, though diligent in their gardening and fishing, were mistrusted by the Kosraeans because they spent so much time with Covert and his gang at Sansrik.

This group of outsiders was annoyed by the prestige enjoyed by King Alokoa and the chiefs of Kosrae. William Covert was especially jealous of the king's influence and the power that went with it. Covert thought that, because he was the senior resident seaman and leader of Kosrae's foreign community, all captains of ships that entered the harbor should report to him. Instead, most of them reported to the king at Lelu.

The Rotumans and Covert were provoked as well by the various rules that King Alokoa and his predecessors had made in an effort to curtail their activities and those of other foreigners living on Kosrae. Secretly they began scheming to overthrow the Kosraean monarchy and usurp the rule of the island. Guns and ammunition, received in trade or stolen from ships, were collected at Covert's Sansrik compound. Soon quite an arsenal had been assembled.

HOSTILITIES BEGIN

During the pre-dawn hours of July 9—led by Rotuma Tom, who knew the harbor—Covert and his co-conspirators silently rowed from Sansrik to their planned point of attack on Lelu Island. To their great surprise, King Alokoa and his men were waiting for them. Four Rotumans and one Kosraean were killed before the troublemakers were driven back to the other side of the harbor. The wives of several of the Rotumans had told fathers and brothers of the conspiracy and word had reached the king. Foolishly, the Rotumans and Americans had taken for granted that their wives knew nothing of the plot since plans had been discussed only in the Rotuman and English languages.

A siege began. Covert, Johnston, and Lawton, with their families, plus the remaining Rotumans, locked themselves in William Covert's house. John Hathaway, the frail young sailor from Rhode Island, had moved to Pisin several months earlier, where Lydia Snow was trying to nurse him back to health. David Kirtland, his sailor companions having long since moved on from Kosrae, was afraid that the Kosraeans would attack him, because—like the leader of the insurrection—he was an American. He hurried to Sansrik with his Kosraean wife, Srue, urging the Snows and the Piersons to do the same.

Immediately Benjamin Snow made his own position known. He would stand with King Alokoa, while doing all within his power to convince Covert and the others of the error of their ways. Also, he would help any who were wounded, no matter from which side of the harbor they came. The foreigners in the house at Sansrik were certain that the Kosraeans would turn against the Americans at Pisin.

But the king was pleased with Mr. Snow's stand and insisted to the missionary that it was not the Americans nor the Englishman he wanted to destroy. As long as they remained in company with the Rotumans, however, they would be in danger of their lives. A cannon, which had been salvaged from a shipwreck, was mounted by the king's men on a large canoe and taken out into the harbor within range of William Covert's house. Though it was fired repeatedly, practically sinking the canoe with each blast, there was never a direct hit. No one knew how to aim it!

Benjamin Snow and George Pierson made almost daily trips from Pisin to Sansrik with their white flag flying. The blue skin priests whispered that the missionaries were providing ammunition to the renegades. What the two men were doing was tending to the wounded and trying to reason with the assaulted. But the men at Sansrik were so terrified of the several hundred angry Kosraeans—who, with their knives, clubs, and guns, surrounded the compound behind two hastily built stone walls—that they were not inclined to follow the missionaries outside.

Finally, on July 29, William Covert permitted Mr. Snow to take his little half-Kosraean daughter, Mary, back to the shelter of Pisin. Johnston's Pohnpeian wife accompanied them. On August 8, a second Kosraean was killed—shot from Covert's house as he tried to sneak up from behind one of the stone walls. On the 11th, another Kosraean was killed in the same manner. On the 22nd, Francis Lawton, wounded and seriously ill, allowed Benjamin Snow to take him to Pisin, where Dr. Pierson could better care for him. On the 31st, David Kirtland, accompanied by Srue, was persuaded that he would be safe with the missionaries.

During the siege, which continued for two months, Benjamin Snow reported church attendance in Lelu as being well above average. He used the opportunity to preach against war and about the evils of hate and killing. But he was disappointed at learning one day that King Alokoa had secretly returned to some of the traditional practices. The Tokosra did not object to the prayers of his subjects who were worshiping with Mr. Snow, but felt that the ancient incantations might help, too. Mr. Snow increased his efforts to convert the king, whom he saw daily, and he earnestly prayed for the appearance of a ship. William Covert was also hoping for a ship. Perhaps he could convince the captain of his perceived mistreatment and have help with his plan to overthrow King Alokoa and the chiefs. This might well have happened if a captain amenable to such a plan had been the first to bring his ship into Lelu Harbor. But the *Commodore Mom's*, which arrived on September 7, was commanded by Capt. Lewis H. Lawrence, a Christian gentleman from New Bedford, who had his wife and 3-year-old son on board with him. After hearing from King Alokoa, Benjamin Snow, and George Pierson, Capt. Lawrence took his stand with them.

ARRIVAL OF THE *MORNING STAR*

Before the *Commodore Mom's* captain could meet with Covert and the others who remained blockaded in the Sansrik house, September 8 dawned, and into the harbor sailed a second ship. It was the long-anticipated missionary vessel, the *Morning Star*, on its maiden voyage through Micronesia. A brig weighing 156 tons, the ship had been built in Mystic, Connecticut, at a cost of $18,351, the money raised by American Sunday School children. On board with Capt. Samuel G. Moore were Mr. and Mrs. Hiram Bingham, Jr.—son and daughter-in-law of the pioneer missionary to Hawaiʻi—and Mr. and Mrs. Edward Doane, coming to join the Micronesia Mission. Also aboard was the senior Mr. Gulick, traveling to see his son and family on Pohnpei. Hiram Bingham, Jr., wrote of that arrival:

We dropped anchor in one of the beautiful harbors of Kusaie. What a feast to our weary eyes was this gem of the Pacific—so green, so romantic, so lovely! All about us there rose abruptly hills and mountains, covered to their very summits with the densest verdure. Beneath coconut and breadfruit and banana and banyan trees nestled the picturesque dwellings of the natives. Here and there a light canoe passed rapidly along, bearing the rich, spontaneous fruits which had only to be gathered as they were needed. Snow-white birds sailed gracefully along, at a dizzy height, toward the dark mountainsides.

On a lovely islet, which the missionaries called Dove Island, stood the cottage of Mr. Snow; and not far off was the house of Dr. Pierson. Oh, how beautiful was this seclude spot! It might have been called a fairy scene. We could not help thinking of the words, "Where every prospect pleases." Too soon, however, we felt the force of those other words, "And only man is vile." A house was pointed out to us where a few white men and several natives of Rotuma had been for many days blockaded by the Kusaiens. Some of them had designed to kill the king and take the island; and the missionaries had good reason to believe that these reckless men had wished to destroy their lives.

But God had mercifully preserved His servants thus far. Before our arrival several of the insurgents had been slain; and others had taken refuge in the house to which I have referred. You will not wonder that our brethren were very glad to see the Morning Star, *for which they had been looking so earnestly! It was a great relief to them to have the little packet so near them, ready for any emergency. She brought mail, moreover, that contained the first tidings of their friends for more than a year.*

We soon assembled in Mr. Snow's house to thank our heavenly Father for all his "mercy and truth." And through His gracious influence our little vessel was soon made a peacemaker.[8]

THE PEACEMAKER

On the morning of the 10th, a meeting was held on board the *Morning Star* between King Alokoa, the chiefs, and William Covert. Looking on as witnesses were Capt. Moore, Capt. Lawrence, George Pierson, Hiram Bingham and Mr. Gulick. Benjamin Snow acted as interpreter. The king refused Covert's request to remain on the island. He, William Johnston, and all but two of the Rotumans were to leave on the first available transportation.

That same day, at the urging of Capt. Lawrence, King Alokoa signed into law the following statements:

    1) I will restore deserters to ships for a fair compensation.

    2) I will allow sick to be put ashore.

    3) All foreigners who want to stay ashore temporarily or permanently must gain my permission.

For many years after this significant event, Kosraeans continued to refer to the *Morning Star* as the "Peacemaker," even as this vessel and those that followed it continued to fly the signature white flag "having a star in the center and directly under it the word 'Morning'—and in the right hand corner a dove, all in dark blue, which stood out vividly against the white."[9]

FIRST OFFICIAL MEETING
OF THE MICRONESIA MISSION

The *Morning Star* sailed on the 15th, taking the Snows, the Piersons, Doreka Opunui, the Kanoas, and the five missionary children plus George and Kittie [Lupalikkun and Kat], to attend a meeting of the Micronesia Mission at Pohnpei. It had been five years since Benjamin and Lydia Snow began their life on Kosrae, and this was their first trip away. George and Nancy Pierson, who had been on Kosrae two years, were accompanied by their two Marshallese language teachers. The *Morning Star* carried four of the Rotumans to Pohnpei, but Capt. Moore had decided against endangering his passengers by transporting Covert and Johnston.

At Pohnpei, the first general meeting of the Micronesia Mission was held. The assembled missionaries were greatly invigorated by their shared stories, worship, and fellowship. It was decided that Edward and Sarah Doane and George and Nancy Pierson would immediately begin work in the Marshall Islands. Hiram and Minerva Bingham and J. W. Kanoa and Kaholo were assigned to the Gilbert Islands. The Snows and Doreka Opunui would return to Kosrae, and the Sturgeses and Gulicks would remain at Pohnpei.

MISSIONARIES AND OTHERS DISPERSE

Back home, the Snows were relieved to learn that William Covert and William Johnston had been taken from Kosrae several weeks earlier by Capt. Alfred M. Coffin aboard the *Roscoe* out of New Bedford. The three remaining unwanted Rotumans had been sent away with them, leaving Tosie and Fatiki on Kosrae to resettle peaceably with their wives and children at Tenwak. Francis Lawton, the African-American from among Covert's gang, died at Pisin of his war wounds on October 29 and was buried at Yenyen.

Having waited until the Pierson and Kanoa families could complete preparations for their move from Kosrae, the *Morning Star* set sail for the Gilbert and Marshall Islands on November 3. After two years, during which seven missionaries had lived together on Pisin, Doreka Opunui was once again the only colleague of Benjamin and Lydia Snow.

DEATH OF DAVID KIRTLAND

David Kirtland died in March 1858. He had lived in Lelu village for more than eight years and was appreciated for his work as Kosrae's trader and harbor pilot. After the siege at Sansrik he had tried to live a different life, telling Mr. Snow that he "desired nothing so much as to become a Christian." He had abandoned some of his habits, such as swearing and kava drinking, and had "commenced a life of prayer." In addition to the Snow family, the sickly John Hathaway of Rhode Island was now the only remaining white foreigner on Kosrae.

BIRTH OF FREDDIE SNOW

On March 9, 1858, Lydia Snow gave birth to her second child—a boy they named Fredrick Galen. The birth was normal, but on the 13th Mrs. Snow hemorrhaged severely and was desperately ill for several days, giving the missionary family at Pisin a very bad scare. To a colleague in Honolulu, Mr. Snow wrote, "There was no physician to call nor any kind mother or skillful nurse to consult. But He who careth for the sparrows thought kindly of us and spared the mother to the little ones and the wife to the husband."[10]

SNOW FAMILY AT PISIN

Caroline, or "Carrie" as the family called her, was described by her father as "a delicate child, though healthy," while Fred was "a strong, husky boy." "Carrie's eyes are blue as the bluest…while Freddie has dark hair, dark eyes and is less white than Carrie." The parents delighted in the company of their children, and their father commented, too, on how "greatly attached" his children were to each other. One visitor to Kosrae wrote of seeing a large sea turtle come out of the water at Pisin each morning and lumber up to the house for breakfast, then return carrying the two children on its back. Just before it headed for deep water, they would jump off, with much excited laughter. The entire family had good times together—and they joked that Kosrae was the only place in the tropics that had eight feet of Snow the year round!

Benjamin Snow was occasionally described by those who did not know him well as humorless and stern. But there was another, equally authentic dimension to him. He was a caring father and husband, and he and his family—including those few Hawaiians and Kosraeans who were part of the more intimate scene at Pisin—were happy together. His sometimes dictatorial or patriarchal manner fit quite easily into an existing Kosraean pattern and was one of the reasons he was accepted and admired. His soft heart was a match as well. His private letters and journals, as well as his published articles, portray a disciplined man who was also sentimental, with a self-deprecating sense of humor. His rigid exterior sheltered a sympathetic nature.

Mr. Snow criticized his missionary colleagues on Pohnpei for keeping their children away from the Pohnpeian people. His was the opposite view. He welcomed Kosraeans into his home and allowed his Freddie and Carrie to go out among them—often in the company of George and Kittie, the Kosraean young people he considered his children's brother and sister. Kat Otnaur, or "Kittie" as she was known to the family, was a big help with the children. She and Lupalikkun, or "Little George," were now 16 years old.

A third Kosraean teenager living with the Snows was Likiaksa [lick-key-AAK-saa], an adolescent boy from Utwe. Though Benjamin Snow found it necessary on one occasion to discipline Likiaksa for "playing checkers with the neighbors," both he and Lydia described the boy as an obedient, helpful, and friendly youngster. Since the missionary's efforts to evangelize had been almost exclusively with the chiefly classes on Lelu, it is noteworthy that Mr. Snow chose to include this boy from Utwe in his Pisin family.

CAUSES FOR REJOICING

May 2, 1858, was a day of profound thanksgiving for Benjamin and Lydia Snow. Kutuka and his wife, Notwe, were baptized by Pastor Snow, making them officially the first two members of the Church on Kosrae. This cause for rejoicing took place five years and nine months after the arrival of the missionaries.

Another joy reported by Mr. Snow during 1858 concerned a "missionary meeting" he had conducted describing Christian work being carried on in Sri Lanka, then known as Ceylon. The people of Lelu were so moved by Mr. Snow's report that they gave their first offering for foreign missions. It consisted of $2.20 in cash, four chickens, a duck, some eggs and some sweet potatoes. "And this from a people who six years before had not heard of Christ!"[11]

CENSUS OF 1858

Introduced illnesses were still decimating Kosrae's citizenry. The population of the island now stood at 830, 518 males and 312 females.

NEWS OF DEATHS

King Alokoa died in September 1858, the third monarch to pass from the scene since the Snows had been on the island. The Kanku was elevated by the chiefs as King Lupalik II. Lupalik II was a grandson of King Nena, the third son of the great King Sa I who had ruled at the turn of the century. To the distress of Benjamin Snow, Lupalik II retained Alokoa's queen, Kenye Inrakunut, as his second wife and adhered firmly to many of the old ways.

In late January 1859, a passing ship brought news of the death on the 14th of that month of Berita Kaaikaula of the Pohnpei mission. His widow, Deborah, later married Hawaiian missionary Hezekiah Aea and worked beside him for many years in the Marshall Islands.

MR. SNOW BEGINS BIBLE TRANSLATION

For the first time, Mr. Snow wrote to the American Board in Boston that he was beginning translation into the Kosraean language of various passages of Scripture, such as the Beatitudes, the Lord's Prayer, and the Twenty-third Psalm. Also, he requested a hand press. Once he began, he gave himself unsparingly to this task.

MEMBERS ADDED TO THE CHURCH

In February, several women were received into church membership. These included an invalid, name unknown, who was received in a "pleasant and solemn service" in her own home shortly before she died. Two more women, whose names are also unknown, were baptized by Pastor Snow in May and accepted into church membership. The missionary had planned to baptize young Lupalikkun at the same time. Earlier he had written, "Our dear George we hope has become a child of grace. We expect to receive him to Christian fellowship at our next communion."[12] However, Lupalikkun was caught taking a biscuit without asking and temporarily denied baptism. Later in the year, after expressing penitence, he was baptized and accepted into full membership of the church.

During 1859 Mr. Snow worked at preparing a primer in Kosraean to help the people recognize and read words of their own language. For several years he and Lydia had been working on an orthography, and now Mr. Snow would use it in print for the first time. As he wrote and otherwise organized the little primer, he used the names of six Kosraean women as an exercise in sight-reading and pronunciation. He made no comment on who these women were, why he chose to list them, or what they were to him or to the young Church on Kosrae. In Kosraean folklore, however, these six women are understood to be among the earliest converts to Christianity: Srue Tafweyat, Tulpe Pisin, Sepe Nuarpat, Kat Otnaur, Wa Inkoeya and Notwe Kras.[13] The names of one other woman and two men are sometimes included in this revered group: Sepe Srikin, Alik Kinsensoa, and Aliksa Lupalik, a son of Good King George.

KUTUKA RISKS HIS LIFE

On April 1, the ship *Lexington*, commanded by Capt. James Fisher out of Nantucket, was wrecked outside Lelu's harbor. Kutuka risked his life to swim with a line to the stricken ship, thus saving all on board. This act impressed the Kosraeans, who attributed Kutuka's bravery to his recent baptism. The shipwrecked sailors, who would otherwise have drowned or been killed on the jagged coral, were also impressed and grateful.

MR. SNOW REQUIRES PUBLIC CONFESSION OF SINS

Late in 1859, the Snows received what they considered to be their most severe blow yet. They discovered that Kittie had secretly entertained Kutuka on several occasions in Doreka Opunui's house right there at Pisin, with the knowledge of both Doreka and Notwe, Kutuka's wife. Kittie was immediately sent home to her family at Otnaor. The affair had taken place before Kutuka and Notwe were accepted for church membership, but Benjamin Snow felt it his "duty to require them to make public confession of their sins. It was a severe trial for them to do it, especially Notwe."

Mr. Snow wrote out Kutuka's confession, giving—as he phrased it—full particulars, and insisted that he and Notwe stand and ask forgiveness when the missionary read the statement in church. Those before whom they stood included approximately 10 baptized members of the church. Others who were gathered that day were not themselves church members, but were the interested and the curious. In Kosraean custom, requiring such a specific and public acknowledgment was almost incomprehensible. There were strict traditional formulas for admitting wrong and seeking forgiveness within prescribed family boundaries. For a woman in particular, having to describe anything of a sexual nature before a group that undoubtedly included brothers and male cousins, was beyond imagination. Reporting this incident, Mr. Snow wrote that this "was the right line to take with the Kusaiens, although it might not be in an enlightened community."[14]

Thus began the practice of requiring public confession by church members caught in the "great sin of the Pacific"—which, for Benjamin Snow, included any sexual act by any individual outside of his or her marriage. The missionary could not have been aware of what a major, lasting feature of the Church on Kosrae this practice of public confession would become.

Mr. Snow included in his report to the mission board that year: "Two of the little church had been guilty of falsehood and concealment of iniquity and were publicly disciplined. Their penitence seemed sincere and after a time they were restored to their former standing. Those cases of discipline gave the missionary an opportunity to enforce the teachings of the Bible in relation to the easily besetting sins of the natives, and to set forth, in a practical and forcible manner, the demands of Christianity upon life. The difference between Christian TRAINING of children, and the heathen NO TRAINING, was shown in a way that all could comprehend."[15]

Several months after they had been restored to church membership, Kutuka and Notwe were again suspended—this time for taking some whale oil from a wrecked ship. Mr. Snow required them to make several more public confessions before he would reinstate them.

Doreka Opunui, with her 7-year-old son, Galen, continued in her home on Pisin for more than six months, awaiting the next trip of the *Morning Star* to take her to her family in Hawai'i. The Snows were kind to her, but their relationship was strained, their trust in her having been broken. Never again would they enjoy the warm camaraderie built through years of shared trial and service. Palikkun, the boy who had served as the Opunuis' houseboy and could use the English language well, moved in with the Snow family when Doreka and Galen left Kosrae.

LUPALIKKUN LEAVES PISIN

Benjamin and Lydia Snow were heartsick when Lupalikkun, in late 1859, informed them that he no longer wished to remain at Pisin. They suspected that he, too, had fallen into the "great sin of the Pacific." Though it was normal for a Kosraean young man of his age to begin the search for a mate, Lupalikkun and Benjamin Snow were trapped by the incompatibility of their cultures. Mr. Snow proceeded to dismiss the 17-year-old youth from church membership and, sorrowfully, allowed his "Little George" to leave Pisin.

REBUILDING THE CHURCH AT POSRAL

In spite of their earlier misgivings, the missionaries found King Lupalik II to be kind, and they considered him a "friendly neighbor"—yet they thought him the least responsive to their message of any who had ruled since the beginning of the mission. He did instruct his carpenters to rebuild the church—a large, open, thatched pavilion—that King George had erected at Posral in December 1853. An average attendance of 30 in 1860 did not begin to match the numbers that Benjamin Snow had enjoyed eight years before, when the congregation sometimes soared to near 200. But when visitors from the ships were present, there were still the curious who could be expected to swell the number of those attending Sunday services.

OBSERVATIONS OF A VISITOR

During five days in June, Samuel C. Damon, editor of *The Friend*, along with several others from Honolulu, visited Kosrae aboard the *Morning Star*. Mr. Damon wrote:

The King was almost the first Kusaien to whom we were introduced, for we found him at church before the audience had assembled. Soon after we entered, an audience gathered of about one hundred. The men were seated cross-legged upon mats, in the rear. The King and three high chiefs were seated upon benches at the right. The females and children were in front of the missionary—while the missionary's family and visitors sat to the left of the desk.

A manuscript collection of hymns was handed us, and others received the same, for a Kusaien had never as yet looked upon a printed page of his language. (This gratification was later afforded him, however, as the Morning Star *brought three hundred copies of a small primer and hymn book printed in the Kusaien language.) Mr. Snow gave out the hymns and conducted the services after the usual method in our congregations, excepting that he called upon the visitors for some remarks which were interpreted. The audience was respectful and attentive. The utmost decorum prevailed during the exercises. The closing hymn was the translation of that familiar English Hymn, "The Savior Calls—Let Everyone Attend the Heavenly Sound."*

After the morning exercises were closed, the Sabbath School convened when about twenty-five remained. At the afternoon service, gathered what Mr. Snow denominates "his Christian congregation." Among them appeared Kutuka and family, who for some years has professed a strong attachment to the gospel. Several others are affording the gratifying evidence of having been born again, and stand as candidates for church membership, while others show an inquiring state of mind. Kutuka evinces a strong determination to make his light shine. He has commenced itinerating through the villages upon the island, and appears to make known among his benighted fellow islanders the truths of the gospel.

On the following Wednesday afternoon, a most interesting prayer meeting was held at the house of the missionaries, when native Christians and strangers from abroad "felt it good to be there." There was distributed for the first time, copies of PRINTED hymns in Kusaien.

In addition to Mr. Snow's labors at the station, he is accustomed to make tours—preaching from village to village. The whole south side of the large island seems much inclined to receive missionary labors, while the northern part is opposed and holds on to its former superstitions.

The Kusaiens are able to employ intelligently a great number of English words. This they had acquired from foreigners—principally with seamen. So great was their knowledge of English when the missionaries landed upon the island, that Mr. Snow endeavored for nearly four years after commencing his mission to preach in "broken" English, or Anglo-Kusaien. He endeavored to teach the English language in school, but finally abandoned the experiment, and fell back upon the language of the natives. He found it exceedingly difficult to communicate religious truths in this mixture of Kusaien, English, Spanish, Hawaiian and other languages.

We were surprised in mingling among the natives to find so many of them who were able to speak in the jargon which has been introduced. Their ability to pronounce some of the difficult sounds of the English language was very remarkable. We tested their ability by requesting a man who had never left the island to pronounce such words as "Mississippi," "Shalmanezer" and several other words in which sibilants abound. He could do it, with the utmost ease.

Mr. Snow is preparing a Grammar of the Kusaien language, which he finds to possess many peculiarities. It is a language abounding with words signifying deferential respect for those in authority, especially for chiefs. It is amusing to witness these people maintaining a species of refined intercourse, and delicate respect for one another. When they speak it is in a quiet undertone, very far removed from a rude, boisterous and hilarious turn of mind.

They are seldom, if ever, known to engage in insolent and angry discussion. When one becomes angry with another, he does not vent his anger by outrageous language and violent blows, but quietly turns away and refuses to speak with the offending party! A Kusaien can receive no greater insult than for a neighbor to refuse to speak to him. We asked Mr. Snow how a Kusaien would exhibit his anger toward a person who had offended him. He replied, "By refusing to speak to him." If with us Americans "Silence gives consent," with the Kusaiens "Silence shows contempt."

The names of individuals are not changed from the cradle to the grave, unless the person is exalted to become a chief. Then the common name is dropped and he or she goes by the official name. Every male chiefish title has a corresponding female title.

The inhabitants of Kusaie are rapidly diminishing in numbers.[16]

CENSUS OF 1860

On December 29, Benjamin Snow completed yet another census, finding a total of 748 persons—523 on the large island and 225 on Lelu.

Adult males and older boys: 411
Adult females and older girls: 258
Younger male children and infants: 37
Younger female children and infants: 42

The death rate had slowed somewhat—and there were more babies than three years before. Mr. Snow concluded his official report, "This certainly is a hopeful phase for the restoration of the race, and I desire to thank God that it is so."

Privately, Mr. Snow was dismayed by the number of disfigured women he saw as he made his tour, many formerly beautiful faces now hideously deformed and eaten away as a result of untreated venereal disease. And though he was encouraged by the increase in the number of infants—and by the fact that baby girls outnumbered baby boys—his unspoken fear was that the Kosraean race would be gone within a few years and the island inhabited instead "only by white men and low-islanders."

A consequence of Kosrae's dwindling population was the deterioration of the traditional chiefly system. Many of the lower titled positions had lapsed and, as fewer and fewer men were available to fill them, some of the higher ranks were also vanishing. The great enclosures of Lelu, defined by massive walls—and the ancient canals and roadways that linked them—were gradually abandoned. Instead of living in the flat interior of Lelu, the chiefly inhabitants began building their homes along the perimeter of the small island.

The cultural requirement that formerly brought commoners across the harbor with donations of food for designated chiefs was discontinued. There was still ample food obtainable on the lush green island and in its teeming waters, but the numbers of people had simply gotten too small to maintain the old ways of gathering, preparing, and sharing. As every family was touched by death and those who remained were often enfeebled by illness, just feeding one's own family became a burden which, historically, it had never been.

The deaths of so many people within a comparatively short time, as well as the very presence of the whalers and the missionaries, insured the end of Kosraean life as it had been lived before the upheavals of chaos and change arrived with the 19th century.

SNOWS TRANSFERRED TO THE MARSHALL ISLANDS

During this time the Micronesia Mission, with the concurrence of the American Board and the Hawaiian Evangelical Association, made the decision to relocate Benjamin and Lydia Snow to the Marshall Islands—an area considered more favorable than Kosrae to church growth. The Piersons, due to the doctor's ill health, had been forced to leave the Marshall Islands and return to the United States, and the death of Edward Doane's wife, Sarah, had left Pastor Doane at Ebon as the lone American missionary in those islands.

Benjamin Snow sent an urgent letter to the mission director in Honolulu. "What shall I say to their Macedonian cry? Ought we to leave Kusaie?" Though they understood and acquiesced to the action taken by their colleagues and superiors, both of the Snows were heavyhearted. So much remained to be done on Kosrae.

The Kosraeans, especially those in Lelu, were alarmed by news that the Snows would be departing. They began attending church services in greater numbers. Fifteen members were added to the church by baptism in 1861. Each of them, as were the other baptized members of the church, was from Lelu. But the numbers at the weekly services that Kutuka and Notwe conducted on the large island was growing, until they were having more in their services than Mr. Snow was having in Lelu.

THE WORK ESCALATES

Pastor Snow accelerated his Bible translation work, concentrating on the Gospel of John. The little primer that he had prepared and distributed among the people in 1860 had proven very popular. Many Kosraeans—particularly those in Lelu—were eagerly learning to read the words of their own language. Mr. Snow was determined to produce at least one of the four Gospels in the Kosraean language as quickly as possible. He spent hours in his Pisin study working on this project, much of the time in the company of a young man named Salpasr [SAL, as in "salad"-pasr, as in "ash"], whose comprehension and discernment were proving to be of much value in the translation process. Together, they worked through the Gospel of John.

In early 1862, nine more individuals were baptized and added to the church rolls—eight of them from Lelu, but the ninth the first convert from the large island. While these successes were gratifying to Mr. Snow, his pending move to Ebon left him feeling pressured and depressed. At one point he thought that he might be obliged to disband the young Church on Kosrae. More of its members had fallen into "sins of the flesh" and he feared that the church would be unable to continue without him. As had now become the custom, the missionary required the offenders to make public confession of their offenses in the presence of the entire congregation—a group composed of the few baptized members, plus many seekers—before their reinstatement to church membership could be considered. It was almost impossible to keep an accurate count of official church members as death was common, and the revolving door that accommodated the drop-outs, as well as those being welcomed back into the fold, continued to whirl.

DISHEARTENING NEWS

The Snows were disheartened during 1862, as were their Micronesia Mission colleagues, by rumors that the directors of the American Board were planning to abandon involvement in the Pacific. American churches were distracted by the Civil War, and funds were low. The young churches in Micronesia, the directors declared, had reached the "self-propagating stage." Then a passing vessel brought word that the *Morning Star* was to be sold. The rumors later proved to be greatly exaggerated, but at the time, the isolated, overburdened missionaries were much distressed.

As if these discouragements were not enough, the "floating scourges," as Mr. Snow called the whaling ships, seemed more numerous and destructive than ever. Simultaneously, King Lupalik II and the chiefs were resorting to various low expedients to hinder the work. Though, as the missionary prepared for his departure to Ebon, the king tried to dissuade him. "Who will make Sunday? Who will teach us and help us?"

SNOWS PREPARE TO LEAVE KOSRAE

The last few months for Benjamin and Lydia Snow on Kosrae were bittersweet. They wanted the time to sit with individual members of the church, to share warnings and words of encouragement. They longed for the opportunity to talk with those who seemed close to making their Christian commitments. But the more mundane took precedence, as Benjamin made plans with Likiaksa for the upkeep of Pisin and Yenyen, and Lydia sorted and packed with her helpers. There was a fledgling church that needed to be equipped to be on its own and a missionary household to be prepared for a major move.

Mr. Snow was particularly concerned about his Bible translation project. He was determined that this important task not come to an abrupt end because of his move. He decided that Salpasr, the young man who helped him translate the Gospel of John, would go with the family to Ebon to help the missionary refine his translation of the Gospel of Matthew. Salpasr would be accompanied by his young wife, who would assist the Snow family in their new home.

A third Kosraean was also invited to travel with them—a youth named Paitok [PIE-tok, as in "token"]. The plan was to send Paitok on to Honolulu aboard the *Morning Star*. Mr. Snow wrote to the head of the mission in Hawai'i:

Paitok is a young man of much promise in the way of learning, especially books. He reads English quite readily and has done it thus far on his own. He is quite teachable in his manners, at least he has always appeared so to us. It is our thought that if some way could be provided for him in the way of schooling he might be prepared to do great good to his people...

It is much in the light of an experiment for anyone to go from one of these islands to such a place as Honolulu, with no particular friend to care for him and look after him. Let me suggest that while he is there, if a candidate for Kusaie is waiting a chance to come down, he and Paitok be together all they can in order for the Hawaiian to be picking up the Kusaien language. I am sending herewith the Gospel of John to be printed and you may find Paitok of some service in proofreading where the letters of the words may be doubtful in my writing. If he notices errors in the spelling, such as the italic letters, so let him note them. I would not have him change the text as I have not had him with me as a translator.[17]

"We had a church meeting in Lelu that last Saturday," wrote Mr. Snow, "and examined four more for church membership. These were received and baptized, together with an infant child, the following Sabbath—a day of deep and hallowed interest, that last communion day with our dear little church on Kusaie."[18]

DAY OF DEPARTURE

On August 25, 1862—10 years almost to the day since they had sailed into Lelu Harbor aboard the *Caroline*—the Snows sailed away toward the Marshall Islands on the *Morning Star*.

It was a sad day for the Kosraean people. Some stood silently on Lelu's stone wharf watching the figures of Mr. and Mrs. Snow, Carrie, and Freddie, decrease in size as the ship slowly moved away. Others got into their canoes to follow the ship to the harbor entrance. There had been numerous upheavals and changes for the Kosraeans during those previous 10 years. Many of these changes had been brought on by the presence of the devout, single-minded missionary and the Message he had shared with them. Other changes had been easier to endure because he and his family were there.

The reflections that filled the minds of Benjamin and Lydia Snow as the *Morning Star* moved slowly toward the harbor entrance were especially poignant. They remembered Good King George and others close to them in the early years, who were no longer living. Their Pisin home—Dove Island—so full of memories, was clearly visible from where they stood on deck. And they could see Lupalikkun, their beloved Little George grown to a young man of 20 years, standing soberly at the edge of the crowd. Their hearts ached because of their estrangement from him.

The years on Kosrae had not been easy, and from their point of view, not particularly successful—but the Gospel seed had been planted. There in the center of those gathered on shore were 30 baptized believers. Benjamin and Lydia Snow thanked God for each of them—for Kutuka and Notwe, who would continue to guide the growing flock across the harbor on the large island. As she shook hands with the Snows in farewell, Notwe had simply and beautifully expressed their budding faith: "Jesus will be our missionary now!"[19]

They thanked God for dedicated, conscientious young Likiaksa, who, with the departure of Benjamin Snow, was now caretaker of Pisin.Though just barely out of his teens, Likiaksa had also been designated by Mr. Snow as leader of the Lelu disciples.

They breathed prayers of thanksgiving for Srue Tafweyat, Tulpe Pisin, Wa Inkoeya, Sepe Nuarpat, Notwe Kras, and their own Kat "Kittie" Otnaor who had been reinstated to church membership—six faithful young women who were among the very earliest to determine to be followers of Jesus Christ. Some months before, these women had organized themselves, electing Srue as their president. Kat, who knew the English language best, having been a part of the missionary family, translated study and worship materials that Mrs. Snow gave them. The developing ability of these women to sing, and the enthusiasm they exuded as they led the other believers in songs of the Christian faith, brought much joy to their teachers.

As the *Morning Star* headed into the channel, it was towed toward the open sea by several large whaleboats, as was common in those days. A number of the ship's passengers, including Salpasr and Paitok, had joined the young men who strained against the oars. Finally, well beyond the reef, the boats were pulled alongside of the *Star,* and those who were passengers among the wet and winded oarsmen clambered aboard. The lines were dropped, and the boats made their way back to the harbor entrance.

Their period of heavy exertion over, Paitok and Salpasr stood on deck with the Snow family and trained their gaze toward the island, their thoughts many and complex. They were watching all that was familiar to them disappear. They were leaving their families and heading for destinations they could not imagine—Salpasr and his wife to Ebon, Paitok to Honolulu. Yet they were excited to be on their way. They trusted the man and woman who stood with them, and believed in the guidance of the One whose Word they eagerly studied.

The little group at the stern railing continued watching as, one by one, the escorting canoes dropped away and the distance between the *Star* and the island increased. The people in that beloved place were closed off in their own tiny world, but despite the agonies that racked Kosrae, the island community was alive, and in its heart the Gospel spark had indeed burst into flame. ✠

Notes - Chapter 3

1. Benjamin Snow, *The Missionary Herald*, 1856, pp. 313-314
2. Snow, personal correspondence to Ephraim Clark, Honolulu, Oct., 1855
3. Theodora Crosby Bliss, "Micronesia: Fifty Years In The Island World," 1906, p. 25
4. Snow, *The Friend*, Honolulu, July, 1857, p. 53
5. Snow, personal correspondence to E. Clark, March 18, 1857
6. James L. Lewis, "Kusaien Acculturation 1824-1948," 1948, p. 31
7. Snow, personal correspondence to E. Clark, March 18, 1857
8. Hiram Bingham, Jr., "Story of The *Morning Star*," 1907, pp. 33-34
9. Bliss, p. 22
10. Snow, personal correspondence to E. Clark, March 18, 1857
11. Snow, Annual Report 1860
12. Snow, personal correspondence to E. Clark, Feb. 17, 1859
13. Snow, "Primu Kusaie A Buk In Lutlut Ke Rid," HEA, Honolulu, 1860, p. 12
14. Lewis, p. 33
15. Snow, Annual Report 1860
16. Samuel C. Damon, "*Morning Star* Papers," *The Friend*, Honolulu, Oct. 1861, pp. 59-61
17. Snow, personal correspondence to E. Clark, Aug. 27, 1862
18. Ibid
19. Bingham, p. 62

NUNAK YOHK KE CHAPTER 4
1862-1867

Ke Mr. Snow ac Mrs. Snow eltal sun acn Ebon eltal srakna nunku ke acn Kosrae, ac nunku yohk ke mwet kawuk laltal we, pwanang eltal tiana sa in konokla mwet Marshall, ku etala kas Marshall. Orekma kunalos Ebon pa in liyaung church se ma oakwuki sel Dr. Pierson ac Pastu Doane. Sayen orekma inge, Mr. Snow ac Salpasr tuh orekma in lungasla Gospel lal Matthew nu ke kas Kosrae.

Ke June 1863, Mr. Snow el folokla nu Kosrae in liye lah fuka church we. Salpasr el arulana mas, na el ac mutan kial tuh welul Mr. Snow folok nu Kosrae. Len tolu tukun eltal oai Kosrae, Salpasr el misa. Mr. Snow el kitalik Gospel lal John nu sin mwet Kosrae—pa inge book se oemeet ke Bible ma lengla nu ke kas Kosrae. Ke sripen pus mwet Kosrae su lutlut ke Primu se Mr. Snow el orala, ouinge elos ku in riti Gospel lal John.

Meet liki Mr. Snow el sun acn Kosrae inge, oasr lokoalok se inmasrlon Tokosra Lupalik II ac mwet lun church, ke sripen mwet Christian elos tia insese nu sel lah el srakna akfulatye mwet tol lun Sinlaku. Tokosra el foloyak ac us mwet lal in eisla acn se ma itukyang lun church. Ke wik sacna, Tokosra Lupalik II el tiana mas a el misa. El tu putatla misa ke acn se el tuh eisla sin church inge. Ke Mr. Snow el sun acn Kosrae, mwet onngoul luo tuh siyuk in baptaisla. Inen tokosra ma oulul Lupalik II pa Salik II. Pa inge yac se u se pangpang Kolo Folfol elos tui ac tila orek alu. In pacl se inge oasr pac lohm alu musaiyuk sayen lohm alu Posral ac Sansrik: sie ke Utwe Mah, sie ke Mutunpal, ac sie ke acn Srampal. Tia paht toko mutawauk in filfilla mwet in musai lohm selos apkuran nu ke lohm alu inge. Pa sis mutawauk in oasr mura ke tuka lulap ah. Mr. Snow el engan in liye kapkapak lun church uh, tuh el arulana asor in liye lah srakna pukanten mwet misa ke sripen mas sasu ma tuku saya me.

Pacl se akluo ma Mr. Snow el foloko nu Kosrae pa ke January 1864, ac el us mutan kial ac tulik luo natul welul. Paitok el foloko Hawai'i me ke pacl se pacna inge, ac el sramsram ke ma puspis ma el oru ke el muta Honolulu yurin mwet Christian we. Mr. Snow el insewowo in liye lah Likiaksa el arulana karinganang acn Pisin wo. Likiaksa el payuk tari sel Tulpe Pisin, ac eltal kewa mwet Christian. Mr. ac Mrs. Snow eltal engan ma lulap lah Lupalikkun ac Kat Otnaur eltal payukyak, ac eltal kewa mwet orekma in church Lelu.

Mr. Snow el lut lah pus na mwet su oaoa in mwet Christian fin acn Lelu ac oayapa ke tuka lulap ah. Mwet kol lun Church Kosrae elos kena tuh Mr. Snow ac sou lal in mutana Kosrae. Na pa limekosr selos simusla kais sie leta nu sin mwet kol ke mission fin acn Hawai'i in fahkak enenu lalos inge. Mr. Snow el lungasla leta inge ac supwala. Mr. Snow ac sou lal ah folokla nu Ebon ke kapin February, ac eltal wisal Lupalikkun ac Kat eltal in sifilpa lutlut yoroltal.

Benjamin Snow el sifilpa som nu Kosrae ke September 1865. U se fin acn Hawai'i ma fosrngakin missionary elos supwalla Mr. J. S. Emmerson in welul. Ma se meet eltal oru pa eltal som wi alu in kisakin sie church sasu in acn Malem. Na eltal som nu Utwe, ac Tulensru, leum se we, el pwanultal nu ke lohm alu sasu se ma mwet Christian we elos srakna musai. Pa inge lohm alu se meet ma eka tufahlfal sang oru. Mr. Emmerson el arulana kaksakin mwet Christian Kosrae mweyen kutu selos ku in ngetla riti Gospel lal John nufon ke kas Kosrae! Oayapa kutu selos arulana oaru in lutlut ke kutu book ke Wuleang Matu ke kas English. Ac ke elos on, Mr. Snow el lohng lah pusralos arulana wo liki meet. Mr. Emmerson ac Mr. Snow eltal akilen kolyuk wowo lal Likiaksa ke church Lelu, ac kolyuk lal Kutuka ke church Sansrik. Tusruktu, Tokosra Salik II el insesrisrik seltal mweyen mwet uh insese nu seltal lukel.

In 1866, *Morning Star* tuh kukakinyukla, na wangin inkanek lal Mr. Snow in som nu Kosrae. Ouinge mwet kol lun mission in acn Hawai'i elos sapla nu yorol Mr. Kanoa, su orekma in acn Gilbert, tuh elan folokla nu Kosrae ac luti mwet we. Mr. Kanoa el arulana alken in fahkak kas ac luti mwet uh ke yac luo.

In 1867, Mr. Snow ac sou lal, oayapa Lupalikkun ac Kat, eltal sroang nu fin oakan fakfuk loat soko ma oai Ebon ac wela nu Kosrae. Elos lut na pwaye ke elos lohng lah Mr. Kanoa el tuh baptaisi mwet siofok limekosr. Church Utwe ac church Tafunsak elos alu in lohm ma musaiyukla ke eka tufahlfal. Mwet in church Lelu elos mutawauk in musai lohm alu sasu se fin acn Langosak. Lohm se inge orekla pac ke eka tufahlfal.

Mr. Snow el nunku mu pacl fal tuh elan mosrwela sie mwet Kosrae in mwet sropo nu sin church Kosrae. Mwet se el sulela pa Lupalikkun natul Tokosra Lupalik I. Tusruktu el enenu in pwapa meet yurin missionary wial in acn Micronesia.

– CHAPTER FOUR –

LEFT ON ITS OWN
1862-1867

ABOARD THE *MORNING STAR*

Kosrae had not yet disappeared from view when Benjamin Snow, aboard the *Morning Star*, began writing letters. Already he was planning his return:

I write this to solicit your attention in securing as early and frequent opportunities for our revisiting our old station in order to strengthen and encourage the little church and possibly to receive additions, or more sadly to confirm excommunications.

There was but one feeling, so far as I could learn, on the part of all Kusaie, in respect to our return—that we should visit them as often and remain as long as possible. Everyone who said anything about it urged our frequent return, to remain a month or two as we might be able. I shall not be surprised to learn that the good work is going forward quietly, steadily for a while at least. Though it can hardly be expected to go forward permanently without more means of grace than they can have among themselves.

I do earnestly hope, if the Morning Star or any other missionary craft which may come to us next season, that arrangements will be made for our visiting Kusaie while she goes on to Ponape, then returns to take us back to Ebon. It seems to me the Church owes this to the rich grace of God which has been shown to that dying people. But for the explicit orders from Boston received last year, it would have been very difficult for me to have made it look like duty to have left them so entirely unprovided for this year.[1]

THE SNOWS AT EBON

Both Benjamin and Lydia Snow had difficulty adjusting to life in the Marshall Islands. During their early months on Ebon [located 349 miles east of Kosrae] their hearts ached within them—their minds almost totally on the "little church and poor people" of Kosrae. This constant longing for Kosrae, of course, hindered them from becoming settled in their new assignment. Benjamin Snow, now in his mid-40s, wrote, "Mr. Doane will report me very backward in the Marshallese language. You know that Brother Bingham objected to my removal from Kusaie on account of my age. As my children are learning the language rapidly, it is possible that I may do something in my second childhood!"[2]

Their isolation seemed to bear heavily upon them. They were in the unfamiliar and confining surroundings of Ebon—a circle of small, flat islands enclosing a deep-water lagoon—among people they did not know. "It makes sad havoc with the social, if not with the spiritual part of our nature, to be and live so isolated. The tendency is to stoicism, if not to barbarism. I FEEL IT—and my wife I presume, feels it more than I. My children are ignorant of their situation comparatively, and so the greater their misfortune. I hope the experience of my associates differs widely from mine. Not that I am a perfect misanthrope yet. I feel that there is hope that I may yet do something for the heathen, though I may not do all that I should for my family and friends."[3]

Lydia wrote to Susan Sturges on Pohnpei of the "low spirits" she was experiencing on Ebon and how much she missed the Kosraean people. "I can't make society out of this people, as hard as I try!"[4] She was grateful for the companionship and assistance of Salpasr's wife.

Salpasr, Benjamin Snow's Bible translation assistant, proved to be very helpful. He worked diligently with the missionary to put the Gospel of Matthew into the Kosraean language and assisted with the printing of the Kosraean Gospel of John on a new hand press. He and his wife set a good example of Christian living among the people of Ebon, who respected and loved them. By the middle of 1863, however, Salpasr was seriously ill. In June, when the *Morning Star* arrived to take Mr. Snow—Lydia and the children remained on Ebon—back to Kosrae for his first visit, the young man was carried aboard to be returned to his home island, with his wife accompanying him.

DEATH OF SALPASR

By the time the little ship was nearing its destination, Salpasr was very weak. Mr. Snow leaned over him and asked where he wanted most to be, expecting him to say "Kusaie." "In heaven," he answered. Mr. Snow then asked who it was he most wanted to see, thinking that the answer would be, "My mother"—but it was "Jesus." Salpasr was reunited with his mother and other members of his family, but three days after reaching Kosrae, he died.[5] The passing of Salpasr cast a shadow over the reunion of Benjamin Snow and his friends, yet death was so common among them that no one was surprised. The fledgling church gratefully noted the young man's contribution and surrounded his sorrowing wife and other family members with love and attention.

After his first few days back at Kosrae, Benjamin Snow—who had been pessimistic about what he would find there—wrote to the mission secretary in Hawai'i: "You will be glad to learn that the Good Shepherd has been caring well for my 'poor Kusaiens.' Last Sabbath evening two more came out and declared themselves on the Lord's side, and one of them was Paitok's mother. She dates her awakening to the last message of Paitok to her from the boat in which he was helping tow out the *Morning Star*. The other was an older brother of Salpasr."[6]

GOSPEL OF JOHN IN KOSRAEAN

The missionary was able to give each Christian in the Lelu church, as well as those in the Sansrik group, a copy of the Gospel of John in their mother tongue. They already had small portions of the Scripture in Kosraean, received while the Snows were still living among them. This was the first book of the Bible, however, to be completed in its entirety in their language. Five years earlier, Benjamin and Lydia Snow—after initially balking at the idea—had finally taken on the monumental task of putting Kosraean into written form. Now, in the excitement generated by the new book, and with the help of their primer, people industriously continued the process of learning to recognize and read the words of their own language.

Mr. Snow also distributed second-hand clothing that Christians in Honolulu had collected and sent. "These garments proved very timely and very acceptable. Our people passed a unanimous vote of thanks to those friends who so kindly thought of their poverty."[7]

LUPALIK II STRUCK DOWN AND REPLACED BY SALIK II

King Lupalik II did not often dare to challenge the Christian cause in any overt manner while the Snows were living on Kosrae. Once they had departed for Ebon, however, the king began to revive and openly flaunt many of the ancient customs his predecessors had abolished. He placed much emphasis on the annual ceremony honoring the breadfruit goddess, Sinlaku. "Heathenish sings and dances" were reinstated to their former places of prominence. When the small band of 30 Christians, led by Kutuka and young Likiaksa, had asked King Lupalik to stop these, he was extremely annoyed at their effrontery. In retaliation he seized some land considered to be church property and destroyed the crops being cultivated there.

What happened next was later described to Benjamin Snow, who wrote in June 1863: "The following Wednesday, while he was at that place with his men, directing them how and where to cultivate for himself, the king fell down and died on the spot, with no previous sickness or any apparent cause of his death! One of the most marked cases of 'He that being often reproved and hardeneth his neck shall suddenly be destroyed and that without remedy' [Proverbs 29:1 KJV]."[8]

Startled and frightened, 62 people requested baptism during that first visit of Mr. Snow. Though not all of them passed his stringent requirements for church membership, a goodly number were received into the church, nearly doubling the number of communicants. The new king, Salik II [SIGH-lick], and others of Lelu's nobility, witnessed the baptisms in complete sympathy with what was taking place. Mr. Snow noted that the new Queen Sisra—a sister of Kat "Kittie" Otnaur—was already counted among the Christians, though her husband would not allow her to become a communicant member of the Church.

LAST OF THE BLUE SKINS

Among those baptized and receiving communion was a former priestess of high status. Her conversion marked the end of any public worship of Sinlaku. An oft-told myth recounts the departure of Sinlaku for Yap in 1863. According to this story, she had left Kosrae several years before—her presence incompatible with the work of the Christian missionaries—only to return when the Snows departed for the Marshall Islands. In 1863, she left in defeat, never to return. The ancient places of worship at Menke and Wiya were abandoned and, though ancestral spirits continued to dominate the imaginations of some people, the formal order of blue skin priests and priestesses disappeared.

CHURCHES BECOME CENTERS OF VILLAGE LIFE

There had been 57 administrative localities around the large island under the old monarchical system. With the decrease in population and with the church fast becoming the center of island life, villages were forming around the houses of worship in three locations on the large island: at Utwe on the west side of the harbor; at Mutunpal in Malem [MA, as in "mat" -lem, as in "lemon"]; and at Srampal, Tafunsak [TA, as in "tap"-fun-sak, as in "sack"]. Those con-nected to the land gave permission for people to build homes in the vicinity of the church buildings. A fourth community materialized near the meeting house at Sansrik. The fifth and original center for Christian worship was at Posral on Lelu Island.

Death from influenza and other introduced diseases continued unabated. In 1863 the high mortality rate actually drove a number of young men to leave Kosrae—most of them from Lelu's chiefly families. They enlisted as crew members aboard whalers, frightened to remain in a place surrounded by so much dying.[9] Even the recently elected King Salik II left. He stayed away only a few months; others, however, did not return for years, and a few never did.

PAITOK RETURNS FROM HAWAI'I

Only six months after his 1863 visit, Benjamin Snow returned—this time bringing Lydia, Carrie, and Freddy with him. The family stayed in their old Pisin home during January and most of February of 1864. There was much for which to rejoice.

Arriving with them, fresh from his Hawai'i sojourn, was Paitok. He had been cordially received into the Honolulu home and family of a Rev. L. Smith and quite impressed those who met him. Having experienced so many disappointments, Mr. Snow had worried about how Paitok might react to the trip. The missionary agonized over whether or not it had been wise for him to send the young man away in the first place. Would the unsophisticated youth turn out to be an embarrassment to him and to the tiny church on Kosrae? But with Paitok's return came glowing reports of his radiant testimony and humble demeanor, more than confirming Mr. Snow's initial faith in him. And Paitok, looking handsome in his new clothes, had many amazing, amusing, and hard-to-believe stories to share with his family and friends in Lelu. Both he and Mr. Snow pronounced the Hawai'i adventure a ringing success.

MORE REASONS FOR REJOICING

Other Kosraeans, too, were proving reliable. Mr. Snow was especially gratified by the trustworthiness and good judgment exhibited by Likiaksa. The conscientious manner in which he had cared for the Pisin property greatly impressed the missionary. Benjamin and Lydia both made note of Likiaksa's "Christian Spirit," and were delighted with his choice of a wife. Likiaksa had recently married Tulpe Pisin, a young Lelu woman who had been a valued helper in the missionaries' home while they lived at Kosrae and one of the first to commit herself wholeheartedly as a Christian.

And to their profound joy, the Snows found that their adopted son, Lupalikkun—the youngest son of their early friend and protector, Good King George—had returned to the church fold. In fact, Lupalikkun and the Snows' former house girl, Kat "Kittie" Otnaor, had married, and both were active members of the Lelu congregation. Overwhelmed with a sense of gratitude, relief, and utter happiness, Mr. Snow decided to give these two outstanding young people special training. When the Snows returned to Ebon in late February, Lupalikkun and Kat would go with them.

From Pisin, on January 7, 1864, Mr. Snow wrote to the directors of the mission, "You may be assured that it looked cheering last evening to see one hundred Kusaiens crowded into our large room for Wednesday evening prayer meeting—with many others in and about the doors—all with eyes, ears and mouths intent on catching every word of truth. Two young, responsible chiefs and their families were among them, giving their testimony to the truth as it is in Jesus. One of these chiefs is the son of old Sesa and the other the son of old Sikein. Verily this looks like the work of God. Glorious! Glorious! How truly was it written, 'Rejoice, thou barren that bearest not, break forth and cry, thou that travailest not; for the desolate hath many more children than she that hath an husband' [Isaiah 54:1 KJV]."[10]

On January 25, he wrote:

Yesterday was a high day for Kusaie. It was communion day for the little church. I received eleven new members to it—by profession of their faith and baptism—and those two young chiefs were among them, as well as the wife of one of them, Sisisa. She is the most beautiful looking young woman on the island. And her eager attention to the truth adds much to her loveliness. After I had baptized the parents, it was my privilege to baptize a darling little boy of theirs, only a few months old. There were one hundred fifty people present, including the King, and Sigrah with his wife. I have seldom if ever seen a more solemnly delicate propriety observed by any Christian audience.

But we will rejoice with a chastened joy; for it is not all light, not prosperity without adversity. We are pained to learn that four of the church members have fallen and been set aside. The discipline in each case was prompt and decisive. Some of those too who had professed themselves on the Lord's side have not maintained their fidelity. But none of them seem to have fallen entirely away, for they continue to associate with the Christian people and attend all the meetings.[11]

MORE MISCHIEF BY THE TOKOSRA AND KANKU

One of the newly converted chiefs protested to Mr. Snow that King Salik II, back from his travels, had seized his land after the baptisms had taken place. The king had justified his action by quoting a conversation he remembered having with Benjamin Snow some years before he became king. When the missionary had tried to persuade him to become a Christian, he had expressed his concern that if he did, the old king would confiscate his possessions. He remembered the missionary telling him that he would be "infinitely better off as a Christian even if he should lose everything, and even become a mere cook or lowest servant to the king, than to have possessions and not be a Christian."

Mr. Snow was aghast that King Salik had used his name and words to "prop up his wickedness." He privately reprimanded the king, and then did so publicly before a large Sunday congregation. The king restored the chief's land to him.

To become Christians, and then continue living in their neighborhoods and among their family members, was often very difficult for the new disciples. During this 1864 visit, Mr. Snow wrote:

The opposition shown by Kanku has taken so decided a course that not one of his subjects are among the converts. One of his stewards, a young man of much promise, knowing that he could not avail himself of any of the meetings or religious privileges of any kind in an open way, left Kanku and went to live with Kutuka. Kanku sent for him—and then went for him, finding him returning from a search for food. He caught him and beat him and kicked him so unmercifully that the poor fellow was unable to do anything for some time.

This seemed to strike such a terror to the rest of his people that none of them have ventured anything openly in the way of turning to God. We learned that Kanku subsequently went to the King and tried to get him to join with him in such high-handed and cruel opposition as to put an entire stop to the whole religious movement. But the King thought it not a wise policy and declined cooperation. In this we can see a very plain and kind answer to the prayers of the Christian people in regard to who should be king—this was their constant prayer when we were here before, till the present king was crowned. The honor properly belonged to Kanku, but he was so greedy in getting the old king's property when he died, that in order to make peace he yielded his claim to the kingship to Sipa, who became Salik II. Though he has not answered my hopes, he has done vastly better for the Christian people than Kanku would have done.[12]

POHNPEIAN MISSIONARY ON KOSRAE

Among the perplexities that Benjamin Snow faced during this visit was the matter of Narcissus, a Pohnpeian convert sent with his wife to Kosrae as an evangelist in 1863. Mr. Snow felt that his colleagues at Pohnpei had overstepped the bounds of their authority in doing this without having first discussed the matter with him. Though he felt that Narcissus had done well in exciting the common people and improving communication between them and the king and chiefs, Mr. Snow was upset. He expressed his concern in a letter to his superiors in Hawai'i:

From many things I see and hear, I cannot think that Brother Sturges did wisely in sending him so far from home before giving Narcissus more of a trial at Pingelap or some outpost on Ponape.

Narcissus did nothing whatever in the way of manual labor, except to make a little spout to the sink. He even rebuked Likiaksa very sharply for spending his time in getting food for them (when he was short of help), saying he ought to stay at home and help him on the language. And yet he used no Kusaien whatever in all his intercourse with the people. He wanted to know of Likiaksa and Kutuka if I had ever made missionaries of them. They told him that I had taught them the teachings of Jesus and what they must do to be Christians. "But I am more than that. Mr. Sturges made me a missionary."

His meetings sometimes were unmercifully long, wearying not only the uninterested but the Christians, too. Notwe said, one time they did not get home till daylight Monday morning! Finding that the King and the two chiefs next to him did not attend his meetings, he started and carried on a regular circuit of meetings with them at their own houses, thus adding these separate exercises to the regular Sabbath exercises. These were so successful that he (in playfulness perhaps) said "Who led Israel into Canaan? Joshua." "Who led the Kusaiens to the King? Narcissus."

From these things and many others which might be said, does it not seem that a little more should be done for Kusaie than an occasional flying visit of ours, even though the intervals be filled up with so good service as the "missionary" from the church on Ponape? "Sanctify them through thy truth" [John 17:17 KJV], was the prayer of Jesus. How can we hope for a sanctified people when they have so little truth and that but poorly understood? Is there no danger of trying to make the work of evangelizing Micronesia a thing too cheap? I greatly fear it.[13]

Narcissus was soon recalled to Pohnpei, much to Mr. Snow's relief.

BELIEVERS ON THE LARGE ISLAND INCREASE

Benjamin Snow described another prayer meeting in the Pisin home during this visit:

It was very rainy and squally, but there were about one hundred present, and two—one a young man and the other a middle-aged man from Utwe—declared themselves, for the first time, followers of Jesus. Their long and interested attention showed that it was no impulsive act. My tender emotions were quite moved to see several of the old Christians go, one after another, and sit down by those two and in a low tone of voice—they could scarcely be heard except by themselves—speak instructive and encouraging words to them. This is their practice with all the new recruits from the ranks of the enemy.

One of our hard old cases, whose wife is among the recent converts, wedged his way up as near as he could to hear the conversation. Mrs. Snow says that his wife seems like one raised from the dead. For when she last saw her she seemed in the last stages of disease, unable to talk only by a whisper. Her present appearance shows that in her younger days she must have possessed rare attractions of personal beauty, while her husband is one of the coarsest looking men on the island.

Tomorrow, January 26, I am expecting to go to Utwe to receive several others to the church. You may remember that this is the large village at South Harbor, the largest village on the large island. I go there to receive several, because there are two or three young women there who are so diseased and out of health as to make it quite impossible for them to come to Lelu. I spent a very interesting evening with them and several others at that place during my last visit from Ebon. A very precious work of grace has been going on at that place during the past few months.

One of the favorable indications is that twenty-one among them have learned to read almost without a teacher, so that they can spell their way along through the Gospel of John, which I brought them last year, quite intelligently. One of the young men from there came and sat down by the side of Mrs. Snow last evening after the meeting and told her of his great joy that two more of the people of Utwe had turned to God. "I have been praying and praying that God would help more of them to turn, and now here are two of my near relatives tonight who have spoken for Jesus." The wife of this young man was the wife of one of those Rotumans we took to Ponape in '57. She first spoke of her determination to serve God that evening I spent at Utwe referred to above. We shall probably receive them to the church with others during my expected visit tomorrow.[14]

KOSRAEAN CHURCH LEADERS APPEAL FOR SNOWS' RETURN

Just before the Snow family had arrived from Ebon that January, leaders of the Church on Kosrae had been talking among themselves about what they might be able to do to have the Snows permanently return to them. They realized that "because of their poverty" they would be unable to support the family themselves, so they decided to send a petition to Christian friends in America and the Hawaiian Islands. It is significant that a mere 12 years following the arrival of the missionaries, each of these men was able to express himself in writing in his own language.

Mr. Snow noted:

We learned of these things indirectly not long after we came. And as no particular encouragement was given to it by ourselves, it was dropped for awhile. During the week of preparation for the Lord's Supper, the subject came up again and they wanted my advice. I suggested, of course, that they choose several from among their number to get together and draw up such a document or expression of their thoughts as would meet their wishes, and then sign it and send it on. They chose five to do this work. But instead of coming together, each wrote for himself and then came together and found themselves unable to put their writings into one. They gave them to me for solution; and scanning them over, I thought as each of them seemed to have peculiarities of its own, and not being very long, I would translate each of them.

I will give you Kutuka's first:

"I say to you what I see now. I think it is the will of God for you to return to Kusaie. While I think so, the church and those who have turned to God think the same. I say to you, send word to all our friends to ask God to teach them to know what is the will or wish of God. While Mr. Snow was at Kusaie before, I did not truly smell the fragrance of Jesus. Now his smell is very precious to me. Do not think that I wish to turn to the groveling things of earth again, but rather to the things that belong to God. Yes, you understand what I say. It is good for you to pity me, as God is merciful to all. You knew me before when I desired not to do the will of God. Though God has blessed Kusaie, yet we are not able to hold up alone. I desire that father and mother return. (signed,) Kutuka."

The humiliating references to himself are characteristic of almost all his remarks and prayers, showing a penitent remembrance of his repeated falls.

The next is from Likiaksa, the young man who occupies Dove Island and has the care of my stock and things there. Take them all in all, I regard him and his wife the most humble, reliable and efficient members of the church on Kusaie.

"Our friends in every place: We desire you to think tenderly of us, and send Mr. Snow to Kusaie to teach us. We know not how to read. We do not know correctly the meaning of the Book. We all desire to learn, but there is no man to teach us. Others are turning to God, but there is no man to teach them. Because it is not good for those who are blind to teach those who are blind, we cannot be good. On this account, we desire that Mr. Snow come to Kusaie rather than another man. If another man comes, it will be a long time before he can learn the language in order to teach us. For these reasons we desire that our father and our mother should return to Kusaie. (signed,) Likiaksa."

The next letter is from Paitok, who was with you in Honolulu.

"Our American friends, we desire to write to you something which we, the people of Kusaie, think now. How can Kusaie become straight? Who cares for the sheep which belong to Jesus on Kusaie? Because Mr. Snow has gone to Ebon there is no man to teach us what is truth. Yes, we know that Jesus is able to teach us what he desires us to do. Another thing we wish to say to you at this time concerns who is able to lead men into the truth. On this account we desire that Mr. Snow should return to Kusaie to teach us the truth. For had he not come to us before, we could not possibly have known the words of Jesus. On this account, we the Church of Kusaie very greatly thank God that he has helped some of the people here to turn to God.

Now it is as though the Holy Spirit has come to us at this time on Kusaie because all the Christian people desire that Mr. Snow should return to Kusaie. This is our very strong desire. (signed,) Paitok."

The next is from our boy George, a young man now and we hope, a Christian.

"I thank God that he has helped the church of Kusaie to unite in thinking that it is good for Mr. Snow to return to us to teach us the truth. For we cannot possibly know what we should do. Jesus knows that we are weak. For this reason, we wish Mr. and Mrs. Snow to return to Kusaie to explain God to us, and teach us God's will. I wish to tell you what a great good God is doing for Kusaie now. I want to send my love to you, my own friends. (signed,) George [Lupalikkun]."

The next and last is from the young man who wrote before to Rev. E. W. Clark. His writing looks as though it was rather a hurried affair.

"I thank God that He has helped the church of Kusaie to come together to compose a letter to all the missionaries on the Sandwich Islands. I want to say to the Sandwich Islands Church at this time that it is good for you to unite in one work to return Mr. Snow again to Kusaie. For the Kusaien people know what Mr. Snow teaches or says. He too knows what the Kusaien people say. For all the Kusaien people are very strong in their love for Mr. Snow. The church women of Kusaie also desire that Mrs. Snow should again return to Kusaie to teach them. They very greatly wish this. It is the same with the men of the church. They wish Mr. Snow to teach them. (signed,) Kilafwa Nena."

There you have their thoughts very literally translated. It would be difficult to find a people more hungry for the truth than most of the Christian people here. During two weeks of our stay, I had a school three hours per day with something over ninety scholars in the Gospel of John. Nearly all the church members read it very readily. And yet it is surprising to see how much truth there is in that remark of Likiaksa's, "We do not know correctly the meaning of the Book." We can hardly appreciate their ignorance—mere children in knowledge as they are—next to no well-defined knowledge of Bible history, Bible geography, oriental and civilized customs, laws and manners—matters that we can hardly remember when we did not know.

While I tried to be diligent in instructing them during the years I was with them, yet you know how unsusceptible the gross mind of the heathen is to Bible truth till the grace of God softens the heart and prepares it for the seed of the kingdom. You know the hard work of regeneration on Kusaie is of recent date. There was no general movement until the year we left, so that the large majority of the converts are but poorly instructed in the written word. And now soon they may fall into errors and take up with practices not according to the gospel. We are already seeing plain evidences.[15]

LUPALIKKUN AND KAT ACCOMPANY
THE SNOWS TO EBON

In mid-February 1864, the Snow family returned once again to Ebon, this time with Lupalikkun and Kat—known to the Snow family as George and Kittie and both 22 years of age—accompanying them. Though Benjamin concentrated on his work among the Marshallese, he and Lydia took the time to instruct the young Kosraean couple. Thrilled to be back in the heart of their adopted family, Lupalikkun and Kat remained with the Snows on Ebon for more than three years, studying, working on translation, helping in the missionary home, and sharing their faith with the Marshallese people.

CONCERN FOR MISSIONARY CHILDREN

The Snows were also concerned about the education of their own children. Carrie, now 8 years old, and Freddy, 6, were growing up fast. Luther and Louisa Gulick, who had first traveled with the Snows to Micronesia in 1852, had been reassigned from Pohnpei to Honolulu, where Luther replaced Ephraim Clark as General Secretary of the Hawaii Evangelical Association. The Gulicks invited the Snow children to live with them in Hawai'i in order to go to school. Benjamin and Lydia seriously considered the offer, but decided not to send their children away.

Another missionary child was on their minds in 1864. Doreka Opunui had written from Hawai'i telling them of the death of her 11-year-old Galen. In May, Lydia reported to Susan Sturges on Pohnpei:

His mother wrote us how much little Galen had loved to read his Bible and to pray—and how much he thought of our instructions. He had hoped to be a missionary and go to Kusaie, but was happy when he died because he hoped to be with Jesus. The death of her boy appears to have been the means of bringing his mother back from her wanderings.

While at Kusaie the last time, the boy Palikkun, who had lived for some time with the Opunuis and afterwards in our family and learned the truth of God, for he could read the English Bible well, came to the conclusion to put away his sins and superstitions and accept the salvation of Christ. He has a wife who sympathizes with him in this. This last visit to Kusaie was one of deep interest to all of us Snows, and we have reason to think of profit to the people—for the Christians, of whom there are quite a number now, seemed so in earnest to make the most of it.[16]

SNOW FAMILY TRAVELS TO HAWAI'I

In the spring of 1865, the *Morning Star* took Gilbert Island missionary Hiram Bingham, Jr., who was very ill, back to Hawai'i. Benjamin Snow left his work at Ebon to assist in caring for Mr. Bingham during the long voyage. Lydia and the children accompanied him. This was the Snows' first trip beyond Micronesia since arriving in 1852. George and Kittie were left in charge of the Ebon station, including the mission school. Mr. Snow took with him his Kosraean translation of the Gospel of Matthew and the draft of a Kosraean hymnal to be printed in Hawai'i and then forwarded to Kosrae. His Ebon hand press had been destroyed in a fire the year before and had not been replaced. While in Honolulu he accepted another large presentation of clothing, a gift from Hawaiian Christians for "the nakedness of those poor disciples" on Kosrae.

As they returned to Micronesia in early August, Mr. Snow wrote, "Mrs. Snow is not so vigorous as we could wish. Thus we are in hopes that the quiet and rest of Micronesia life will bring back her usual vigor and elasticity. There is no want of cheerfulness, but want of strength. There are none other than the pleasantest feelings in view of being on our way to our field of labor in loved Micronesia. Our visit to civilization has only tended to quicken our interest in our life work among the heathen. The children seem unusually happy in each other, and pleasant in their plays."[17]

Instead of disembarking with his family when the *Morning Star* reached Ebon, Benjamin Snow stayed aboard to make his third visit to Kosrae since moving to the Marshall Islands. He planned to remain for six weeks while waiting for the missionary vessel to continue its usual itinerary to the west.

MISSION BOARD OFFICIAL VISITS KOSRAE

Traveling aboard the *Morning Star* on its round trip from Honolulu was Mr. J. S. Emmerson, making a general survey and report of the Micronesia Mission for the Hawaiian Evangelical Association. He wrote of the welcome extended to Mr. Snow when the *Star* reached Kosrae.

"On September 8 we arrived to leave Brother Snow with the people of his first love. We formed a very high opinion of their love for their teacher—their modest demeanor, their warm-hearted thanksgiving prayer and hymn at meeting with their pastor. But so quiet, so dignified, so subdued were all their exhibitions of joy, I could but give thanks in my heart, and say of a truth, the Lord is with this people!"[18]

During the few days the ship was in port, Mr. Emmerson accompanied Mr. Snow to the dedication of a new church building in Malem, at which Kutuka officiated. In Utwe they met the head chief, Tulensru, who had recently become a Christian. The chief proudly showed them where the first coral block church on Kosrae was in the process of being erected by his people. On the next Sunday, Mr. Emmerson went to church in Lelu with "Brother Snow and his interesting and hopeful people"—noting that the worshipers attended "in clean and comely attire."

This mission official from Hawai'i further described the Kosraean people as having "humble, industrious, thoughtful, inquiring, self-reliant and Christ-like spirits." Natural Kosraean attributes seemed to him enhanced by the Gospel. King Salik II told Mr. Emmerson that the Christians were his best subjects.[19]

Mr. Emmerson was impressed with the diligence with which the Christians studied their Kosraean language Scriptures. He wrote:

The Gospel of John, which they have had for a year or more, is committed entirely to memory by many of the adults and young people. Some, also, are search-ing the Old Testament in English, seeking for knowledge and understanding. One of them said to me, "What does 'firmament' mean?" and when the word was explained, he felt enriched.

The same man had a disagreement with his wife. It was on Saturday, and he was expected to teach the people on the Sabbath. Though the problem was resolved, he was troubled, and spent a sleepless night—was shut up and knew not what to say. He opened the Psalms and read the two words, "Rejoice always." His sadness was soon turned to rejoicing, and he was so greatly enlarged that Sabbath with joy in the Lord, that he was filled with rejoicing. That the Lord was with him that day, he had no doubt. That this people have simple, childlike confidence in God is so apparent that one cannot mistake it.

The King and the high chiefs are not numbered with the Christians. The people look to Jesus only as their guide and leader. The King and his brother have not yet allowed their wives to join the church, although they desire it. The people told us, as the first thing they had to communicate when we arrived, "The King has forsaken his old god of storms and seasons as a worthless dependence, and is now waiting for more light about the true God." That he, as well as the people, are seeking for light is very apparent.[20]

Mr. Snow himself was very gratified to see how well the Christians were progressing under the leadership of Kutuka and Likiaksa. Members of the church were working hard at learning to read with understanding the words of their own language as they pored over the passages of Scripture available to them. In his journal Mr. Snow wrote, "How interested in the Word, and the work of life they are. It is hard to keep my heart and emotions in their place when I see what God has wrought for this poor, benighted people."[21]

Benjamin Snow was impressed with how much better the Kosraeans could sing than during the years he and Lydia had lived among them. Tulpe Pisin, her sister Notwe Kras, and Sepe Naurpat were appreciated song leaders and teachers. They had learned well the "do-re-mi" Solfege System of writing and reading music that Mrs. Snow had taught them. They were experts at reading the triangles, circles, diamonds, and squares of the shaped notes, but their few sheets of printed hymns were now tattered and faint. The women were excited and grateful to hear from Mr. Snow that their own Kosraean hymnal was in the process of being printed in Hawai'i.

He also noted during this 1865 visit that the discipline of the church seemed to have been kept up with its usual fidelity—"two having been set aside and one restored."[22]

BENJAMIN SNOW DESCRIBES A TOUR OF KOSRAE

To the mission secretary in Honolulu, Benjamin Snow wrote:

My visit here has been very pleasant—never more so as far as the people are concerned. The only drawback has been the fact that my family are alone on Ebon and not with me. The people here have been very kind and have done all they could to make my stay comfortable. I never before made the tour of the island when I found so much to encourage and rejoice my heart.

I began my tour on September 25th, the day before having received twenty-one to the church in Lelu, and baptizing five children. I spent the first night in Malem where I had a deeply interesting evening service at the new church Kutuka has just dedicated. Some fifty or more were present, many of them listening with the delighted interest of young converts. The next day we had a church meeting and communion service with three being baptized into the church.

In Utwe or South Harbor that evening, four were examined and received to the church and three children were baptized. One of them was a little Ebon girl who was thrown away by her parents and left to die on the beach at the time that the large fleet came from the Marshall Islands when Dr. Pierson was here. She was picked up by one of our people and taken care of, and is now in the care of one of those I received to the church. She herself wanted that I should baptize her, which of course, I gladly did. I was told by one sitting by me that she leads a life of prayer with as much regularity and apparent devotion as those older. And this same one tells me that the change in her manner and in her life has been very marked. [The Marshallese girl was now 10 years old.] We had to have our communion service in one of their small houses, because two of the church members living in it were too diseased to be taken out. There were twenty-two communicants there—eleven male and eleven female, besides others in and about the doors. One of those received to the church was an old priestess.

The next morning we took an early start up that most charmingly beautiful lagoon on our way to Lissa, where we breakfasted and spent most of the day. Here we examined three more and received them to the church, and baptized one child. One of those received was so diseased that she had to be brought in to the place of meeting on boards. Another was unable to stand during the reading of the articles of faith and covenant, or even to kneel when baptized. You would go a long way before you would find a more interesting and pleasant face than the third one has. It was her little daughter that I baptized. I don't know that I ever administered the memorials of the Savior's sufferings and death with feelings so tenderly affected as on that occasion. And yet it is seldom administered in circumstances so uninviting to the eye as then and there. It was a puzzle to me how our Baptist brethren could have baptized those two young women.

We reached our next place several miles distant just at dark. I found that old woman who had previously prayed herself along to the female prayer meeting, very low and hardly able to speak. Yet she recognized me and seemed glad to know that I had come. She gave me the names of all her children and told me where they died. She referred to one little incident with a good deal of feeling, which I had entirely forgotten. It was that once when she called at my house, I gave her cloth for a dress. With considerable emotion she said that had made us firm friends. She had been so little instructed in the things of religion, and was so very feeble that I thought it not well to administer the sacraments. She was entirely blind and recognized her friends only by their voice. Here we met a little company from Lelu, and gathered together for our Wednesday evening prayer meeting.

But the incident of most interest at this place was at our morning worship the next day after our arrival. I had just finished reading the passage for the morning when one of the women, calling me by name, said "I thank God that he has helped me to turn to him." This is their usual form of expression when they turn and embrace the true God. She made a few other remarks and had hardly ceased speaking when another upon the other side of the house followed in the same way. It was so unexpected, earnest and artless that it took us all by surprise and several were melted to tears. Of course, I followed with words of encouragement to them and to all, urging others if they felt the same not to hesitate to confess the true God.

But I have noticed that no urging seems to move them at such times. If they have not decided beforehand, they will not go because the tide sets that way. I noticed while we were singing our hymn that the husband of the first one who spoke, who is a wild, reckless fellow, tried to join us in singing. But he soon gave up, for he had all he could do to keep back his tears, and conceal his emotions. I have seldom witnessed more manifest tokens of the Spirit's presence than at that little morning worship in that native cookhouse.

At one of the houses nearby, where I called afterward as I was leaving, I found *an old acquaintance sick, who had been indulging a hope for some time. After talking a little with him and praying, I noticed as I gave him the parting hand that his eyes were swimming with tears, which was all the reply he could make. His heart was too full to speak. The remainder of our way that day along the north coast was through the darkness of heathenism. At one place there had been cases of conversion, but they had died during my absence.*

At the place where we stopped during the following night, was an infirm old man, nearly blind. He has been an important character on that side of the island during his day—mostly in a religious way. His interest in the true God has been increasing for two or three years. He has had some of the sacred trees cut down to see what the effect would be. Somewhat recently, his son—a powerful man—has been declining and increasing in religious interest. I found on talking with the old gentleman that he was very anxious to know whether his son, Alik, was coming out that night on the Lord's side.

And in talking with the son, I found he was more anxious about his father than his father was about him. He talked with him several times before the meeting and got Kutuka to do the same. So in the evening, the old father spoke but the son was not ready. I wondered a good deal at that, for the son was evidently more intelligently interested than the father. I got Kutuka to ask him in the morning. It seemed that he felt his father was very old and feeble, and he feared he might die without confessing the true God. I should think the chances for dying was about an even balance. So delusive is sin and the Devil.[23]

Mr. Snow remained exceedingly cautious when it came to receiving individuals into the official membership of the church. During this visit in the fall of 1865 he examined more than 100 persons who were requesting baptism and decided to accept only 28 of them into full fellowship. The others were required to remain as students to await his next visit.

In an editorial, an official of the American Board in Boston wrote: "The remarkable progress of the Mission on Kusaie, without benefit of a missionary during Benjamin Snow's long absences, was one of the most striking things that has ever happened in the history of missions."[24]

LIKIAKSA AND KING SALIK II

While Kutuka's church responsibilities were primarily confined to the large island, Likiaksa's authority was increasing beyond the Pisin property to the church in Lelu. Conflict took place frequently between King Salik II and the two men, with Likiaksa bearing the brunt of the king's tirades. King Salik was pleasant enough during Benjamin Snow's visits, but when the missionary was absent, the king made trouble, especially for Likiaksa, who lived closer to Posral. He was prodded along in his mischief by two of the ranking chiefs. Powerless in the face of the continued decline in Kosrae's population, King Salik was provoked by the growing authority enjoyed by Likiaksa as more and more of Lelu's residents embraced Christianity.

King Salik was cautious about interfering too blatantly, however. He remembered clearly the strange and sudden death that took his predecessor, King Lupalik II, when he was interfering with the Christians. To satisfy the demands of the people, he appointed seven commoners—some of them Christians—from seven districts on the large island "to sit with him once a month to deliberate concerning civil affairs and to enact laws and regulations for the general welfare." But the king, exceedingly jealous of all encroachments on his power, was a very unpopular ruler. Increasingly, he took to drowning his frustrations in the liquor he received from the captains of visiting ships.

THE *MORNING STAR* IS SOLD

Benjamin Snow was upset, as were other members of the Micronesia Mission, when word reached the far-flung stations that the *Morning Star* had been sold in December 1865 without prior word to or from the missionaries. Earlier, Mr. Snow had complained that Capt. Charles Gelett was "trying to use the name and missionary character of the *Morning Star* to forward and promote his business affairs."[25] Though the regular schedule of the vessel was sometimes disrupted because of this, the directors had approved the captain's enterprises as a means of helping to defray the expense of operation. But as the months went by, the escalating costs of maintaining the aging ship brought the executives of the mission boards in Boston and Honolulu to a united conclusion. The vessel was sold. Since the little ship was truly their one link to one another and to the resources of the world beyond Micronesia—their "lifeline," they called it—the isolated missionary families felt deserted.

MISUNDERSTANDINGS AND RUMORS

Not only were the missionaries distressed about the sale of the mission ship and the fact that there was no scheduled replacement, there was growing dissension between them and the officials of the mission boards as to who had the final authority in policy making. Was it the American Board of Commissioners for Foreign Missions in Boston, or the Hawaiian Evangelical Association in Honolulu? How much authority did the personnel of the Micronesia Mission have—the men and women who were actually involved in the field?

Some time later, the Snows heard that there were to be no more general meetings of the Micronesia Mission within Micronesia—that future meetings would be held only in Honolulu, with the Hawaiian Board taking on many of the responsibilities formerly handled by the American Board. Benjamin Snow wrote to Luther Gulick, "My Lydia says that she has never felt so lonesome since she has been in Micronesia as she felt when learning what had been done in regard to our mission. Do you remember whether that is the first feeling after marriage, and if so, whether it usually lasts long? For I suppose we are married to Hawai'i whether or no. I have not been informed as to who is to be bride or who bridegroom, but rather suspect that as we are the weaker vessel our virtue is to be mostly passive. For the gospel is 'wives submit yourselves unto your own husbands' [Ephesians 5:22 KJV]. I used to think it took two to make a bargain. But in these last days and perilous times, it is hard telling what new order of things may turn up."[26]

It was a sham battle, for later they learned that the American Board had ordered a replacement for the old *Morning Star*, and that the missionaries in Micronesia would not only be permitted, but encouraged, to gather for the traditional, biennial Micronesia Mission meetings that were so important and valuable to them.

KANOA SENT TO KOSRAE

With the *Morning Star* sold and not yet replaced, Benjamin Snow was not to visit Kosrae during 1866. He was annoyed to learn that the Hawaiian Evangelical Association had reassigned one of its Hawaiian teachers in the Gilbert Islands—J. W. Kanoa, with his wife, Kaholo, and their six children—to Kosrae. The Hawaiian had served on Kosrae 10 years earlier, arriving with Dr. Pierson in 1855 and departing with him in 1857. Though he knew Kanoa well, Mr. Snow was angered that this assignment had been done without first consulting or even informing him. Kanoa had the reputation of being a zealous preacher, but he was not an ordained minister. Indeed, none of the Hawaiian missionaries in Micronesia during these early years were ordained, and unfortunately were often considered by their American colleagues on the field as unable to carry the responsibilities of being "full-fledged missionaries."

When—during the summer of 1867—a Capt. Baker offered free passage to the Snow family from Ebon to Kosrae aboard the whaleship *Washington*, his generous invitation was quickly accepted. At Kosrae, Benjamin Snow was astonished to learn that Kanoa, since his arrival, had admitted 105 new converts into the church.

Mr. Snow wrote, "I was not a little surprised that Kanoa should have received so many to the church. Though it is true that he has been here for some four to five months, his hope may be better than my caution. He needed less faith in receiving some than I should, not having known their former lives."[27] As always, Benjamin Snow was suspicious about receiving great numbers into church membership.

However, as he observed the dedicated efforts of Kanoa during the days and weeks that followed, Mr. Snow changed his mind about the Hawaiian evangelist. He concurred with the wishes of the Kosraean Church—and endorsed a petition of the king to the Hawai'i-based mission authorities—that Kanoa be permanently transferred to Kosrae. The petition was denied.

As his 1867 visit progressed, Benjamin Snow felt it necessary to discipline some of the older members of the church for falling back into "the habits of the island in regard to feasting at funerals." In spite of this, and those initial doubts concerning Kanoa's methods of outreach, Mr. Snow was quite encouraged by what he observed that year. He even came to admire Kanoa's diligence. There were 118 pupils of all ages attending Sunday School in Lelu, "sitting in little circles on the floor, some of the classes touching the backs of others, and yet with no disturbance or confusion."[28]

Some years later, after having worked with Kanoa in the Marshall Islands, Mr. Snow said of him, "As an enthusiastic and successful teacher, I am sure there has not been his equal among the Hawaiians in Micronesia. I miss him badly!"[29]

NEW CORAL BLOCK CHURCHES

The congregations in Utwe and Tafunsak were meeting in church buildings constructed of coral blocks, and the Lelu congregation was constructing one in their village—63 feet by 50 feet—on a prominent point of land known as "Langosak." Mr. Snow noted this was "quite a monument to the industry and skill of these people."[30]

Kanoa reported to his superiors in Hawai'i concerning the construction of the Lelu church, "We all joined in the building of the large church, everyone building with enthusiasm and joy. All three stone churches are good, with no superior ones in the Micronesian islands. This new church is on the island where the king lives. The king worked, as well as the chiefs, the common people, the seekers and the members. The work was light because of the unanimity of thought."[31]

Reassured, Mr. Snow felt that the time had come to ordain a Kosraean pastor to lead the multiplying flock. He chose Lupalikkun, his adopted son George, as the one most fit for ordination. The missionary approved of the young man's humble demeanor and fervent spirituality. He was also of the opinion that Lupalikkun's princely rank would make him more acceptable to the Kosraean people. Lupalikkun and Kat had returned with the Snows aboard the *Washington* following three years on Ebon. They were excited to be back among their own people, who gave them a hearty welcome. But the ordination plan was temporarily suspended when the *Morning Star II* arrived on its maiden voyage through Micronesia. ✦

Notes - Chapter 4

1. Benjamin Snow to Ephraim Clark, Sept. 1, 1862
2. B. Snow to E. Clark, July 30, 1863
3. B. Snow to E. Clark June 24, 1863
4. Lydia Snow to Susan Sturges, May 18, 1864
5. Hiram Bingham, Jr., "The Story of The *Morning Star*," 1907, p. 64
6. B. Snow, personal correspondence, June 24, 1863
7. Ibid
8. B. Snow, unpublished correspondence, June 27, 1863
9. "Kusaie In The Nineteenth Century," undated, p. 11
10. B. Snow to L. Gulick, Jan. 7, 1864
11. B. Snow to L. Gulick, Jan. 25, 1864
12. Ibid
13. B. Snow to L. Gulick, Feb. 1, 1864
14. B. Snow to L. Gulick, Jan. 25, 1864
15. B. Snow to L. Gulick, Feb. 1, 1864
16. L. Snow to Susan Sturges, May 18, 1864
17. B. Snow, personal correspondence, Aug. 5, 1865
18. J. S. Emmerson, *The Friend*, Jan. 1866
19. American Board cf Commissioners for Foreign Missions Yearbook, 1865
20. Emmerson, *The Friend*, Jan. 1866
21. B. Snow, journal entry, 1865
22. Ibid
23. B. Snow, personal correspondence, Oct. 9, 1865
24. ABCFM Annual Report, 1867
25. B. Snow, personal correspondence, June 24, 1863
26. B. Snow, personal correspondence to L. Gulick, Jan. 15, 1864
27. B. Snow to L. Gulick, 1867
28. Ibid
29. B. Snow, personal correspondence, 1875
30. B. Snow to L. Gulick, 1867
31. Kanoa to the HEA, Dec. 15, 1867, translated from Hawaiian

NUNAK YOHK KE CHAPTER 5
1867-1877

Ke September 1867, *Morning Star II* tuku Hawai'i me nu Kosrae, ac Mr. Snow ac sou lal ah srakna muta we. Oasr book sasu wi oak soko ah tuku, ma Mr. Snow el tuh lungasla nu ke kas Kosrae, na pressiyuki Hawai'i: Gospel lal Matthew, oayapa book in on se oemeet in kas Kosrae. Tukun pacl sac missionary nukewa ma orekma Micronesia elos toeni Pohnpei. Elos nunku mu sala in akmusrala Lupalikkun nu ke mwet sropo. Ouinge ke Mr. Snow el foloko nu Kosrae, el sulela tuh Lupalikkun elan deacon se oemeet lun acn Kosrae. Na tok kutu, Likiaksa ac Kutuka oayapa deaconla. Ke October 24, lohm alu se orekla ke eka tufahlfal tuh kisala Langosak. Mwet nukewa su wema *Morning Star II* Pohnpei me elos wi akfulatye alu in kisa lohm sasu sa.

Mr. Snow el sifil foloko nu Kosrae ke 1868, ke pacl se *Morning Star II* usla kutu kufwen mwe musa Hawai'i me in tuh sang orala lohm alu sasu in acn Malem. Mutan kial Salik II, Kasra Sra Nuarar, el wi alu Lelu ke Mr. Snow el muta we, oayapa mutan se ma matu oemeet fin acn Kosrae in pacl sac, el wi pac alu, el finne sie mwet tol fulat ke alu lun Sinlaku meet.

Ke tuku se lal Mr. Snow nu Kosrae in 1869, el akmusraella Lupalikkun tuh elan pastu se emeet lun mwet Kosrae, ouinge el pa mwet se oemeet in akmusra nu ke pastu in acn Micronesia nufon. Pastu Lupalikkun el yac 27 ke el akmusrala. Ke tuku se inge, Mr. Snow el kitalik Gospel lal Mark su el tuh lungasla. Mr. Pogue, sie mwet kol fulat ke mission board in acn Hawai'i su tuh welul Mr. Snow, el kaksakin kapkapak lun church Kosrae. El liye lah mwet uh finne munas in ikwa, a elos arulana moniyuk ke moul in kulansap lalos. Ke November 18, 1869, Mr. Snow ac sou lal nufon tuh wela *Morning Star II* in folok nu America in mongla ke yac se. Oak soko ah oayak liki molsron Lelu, na sa na sun sie asr na upa, pwanang oak ah musalla pe acn ah. Wo ouiya, wangin mwet misa. Elos soano malem tolu, na wela soko pacna oak nu Hawai'i, na sifilpa oayak in som nu United States. Tukun yac se, eltal folokla nu Honolulu ac tufah lohngak we lah Pastu Lupalikkun el misa, yac se tafu tukun el akmusrala. Ke ma inge eltal suwoslana nu Kosrae, tufa tuh eteyuk lah Deacon Kutuka el misa pac. Church Kosrae tuh fohsak ke mwet kol luo inge misa. Kutu mwet uh fulokla nu ke ouiyen alu lalos meet. In October 1871, Mr. Snow el akmusraella Likiaksa, su pastu se akluo lun mwet Kosrae.

Ke Mr. Snow el tuku nu Kosrae ke September 1872, el tuh us Gospel lal Luke in kas Kosrae ac kitalik nu sin mwet uh. Tukun lungasyukla Gospel akosr ah tari, Mr. Snow el lungasla book in Orekma, Sie John, Luo John ac Tolu John ke yac sac pacna. Ke kapin 1873 Mr. ac Mrs. Snow, oayapa Mr. ac Mrs. Whitney, luo pac missionary in acn Marshall, elos som nu Kosrae in kasru orekma lun church nwe ke February 1874, na elos folokla nu Ebon.

In pacl se inge puseni mwet ma tuku saya me ac muta Kosrae. Sie u ah tuku Ocean Island me mweyen sracl acn we. Sie u ah tuku Nauru me—elos kaingkin mweun ma orek we. Oasr aset onkosr wi u luo inge. Mwet sac inge kewa elos orek lokoalok yohk fin acn Kosrae. Sie mwet ingunyar America su arulana eteyuk in acn Pacific ke inkanek in pusrapasr ac anwuk lal, el oai Kosrae ke March 1874. Inen mwet se inge pa Bully Hayes. Tokosra Salik II el siyuk sel Bully Hayes elan usla mwet lokoalok inge liki acn Kosrae. Bully Hayes el pwapa yorolos ac elos sroang nu ke oak nes na lulap okoal, pangpang *Leonora*. Meet liki elos oayak liki molsron Utwe, paka se tuhme, na oak soko ah longyak ac musalla na. Tukun ma inge, Bully Hayes ac mwet fin oak ah elos weang mwet ma tuh orek lokoalok nu sin mwet Kosrae. Elos nimnim yohk, ac orek anwuk inmasrlolos sifacna ac oayapa yurin kutu mwet Kosrae.

Pastu Likiaksa el som nu Utwe ac suk lah mea el ku in oru in kasru mwet Kosrae we. Tokosra Salik el wi pac nimnim, pwanang wangin kasru lal nu sin mwet lal. In September 1874, Benjamin Snow el tuku nu Kosrae ac srike in kutongya ma orek inge. Oasr oakan mweun soko lun mwet England oai Kosrae, ac Mr. Snow el tukakin ma Bully Hayes ac mwet sac inge oru fin acn uh. Bully Hayes el tuh kaingla nu Pohnpei ke reoa soko, a pusiyen mwet lal ah wela oak England soko ah. Sie sin aset ah el tuh mutana Kosrae—inel pa Harry Skillings.

Mwet Christian fin acn Kosrae elos srunga na pwaye ouiyen moul lal Tokosra Salik II. Ke ma inge, Mr. Snow el tuh kasrelos in pangon sie meeting in lohm alu Lelu ke November 2, 1874. Mwet pukanten elos fahkak nunak lalos, na ma wotla yorolos pa in sisila Tokosra Salik II liki wal lal, ac siena mwet in aolul. Elos akwalyalak Sigrah, na el walkin Tokosra Sru IV. Pa inge pacl se oemeet mwet uh tuh wi mwet suksuk in sulela mwet se ma ac tokosra. Mr. Snow el oakla pisen mwet uh ke 1874: oasr mwet Kosrae 397, mwet Micronesia saya 98, mwet Polynesia 8, mwet America 6, ac mwet Europe 6—toeni orala mwet 515. Pisen mwet ma oaoa mwet lun Church pa mukul 54 ac mutan 38—toeni orala mwet 92.

Mr. ac Mrs. Snow eltal tuku nu Kosrae in September 1875, ac eltal kitalik Primu sasu se. Pa inge yac aklongoul tolu laltal in orekma Kosrae. Ma oakwuki in pulan pacl sac pa: alu in lotutang ke Sunday, su tafweyukla ke Sunday School ac mwet nukewa wi na; alu in "meeting" orek ke tafun len tok nu sin mwet ma baptaisla tari tuh elos in kusen siyuk ac sramsramkin sifen mwe lutlut ke alu meet ah. Oasr alu tafun len tok ke Wednesday; ac oasr alu in pre ac lutlut Bible tafun len tok ke Friday, ma nu sin mutan mukena. Kufwa Lun Leum orek pacl akosr ke yac se fin acn Lelu. Ke eku in Saturday meet liki Sunday akosr ah oasr alu in aknasnas orek. Kais sie Sunday in Kufwa Lun Leum pa pacl in baptais ac eis mwet sasu nu in church. Mr. Snow el oakiya tuh lotutang se emeet ke kais sie malem, in oasr alu in Malem Sasu. Len sac fin tuh Sunday se, na ac orek ke Monday. Pa inge pacl mwet in Church elos ac fahkak ma elos tafongla kac.

Mr. Snow el folok nu ke orekma lal in acn Ebon. El mas ke "stroke" se ke 1876 ke el yac 58 matwal. El kwafeang na in lungasla book lal Ruth, Philippi, Colossae, Sie Thessalonica ac Luo Thessalonica. Book limekosr inge sun acn Kosrae in September 1876. Book nukewa ma Mr. Snow el lungasla nu in kas Kosrae pa Primu luo, book in on se, ac book singoul tolu ke Bible.

In October 1877, Mr. ac Mrs. Snow eltal som liki acn Ebon ac folokla nu America. Mr. Snow el misa fin acn Robbinston, Maine ke May 1, 1880, ke el tuh yac 62.

– CHAPTER FIVE –

TURMOIL, CHANGE AND GROWTH
1867-1877

MORNING STAR II

Commanded by veteran missionary Hiram Bingham, Jr., the new *Morning Star II* sailed into Lelu Harbor on September 18, 1867.

Of that arrival, Capt. Bingham wrote, "We were welcomed by the Rev. Mr. Snow and Kanoa and their families. We saw much to cheer, as they were gathering in a more than golden harvest. On the day of our arrival quite a number of Kusaien children and their parents visited the *Morning Star* with an interest very similar to that shown by the children of Honolulu on her arrival from Boston. A song of welcome sung by them, as they gathered on the top of the afterhouse, will not soon be forgotten."[1]

GOSPEL OF MATTHEW AND
NEW HYMNAL REACH KOSRAE

Benjamin Snow was elated to find on board the *Star* printed copies of his Kosraean translation of the Gospel of Matthew as well as the first Kosraean hymn book. So eager were the Kosraeans for their new Scriptures and hymnal that he immediately began the process of distribution. He wrote of his great satisfaction in observing "groups of Christians hungry for the Word of Life, lying around their little jacket-lamps at night, working their way through the Gospel of Matthew and the new Kusaien hymn book."[2] American Board funds had been provided for the printing of Matthew, but Mr. Snow was especially grateful for the generosity of the "Honorable P. C. Jones" in Honolulu, who paid for the printing of the hymnal.

The Snow and Kanoa families boarded the *Morning Star II*, traveling to Pohnpei for a gathering of all members of the Micronesia Mission. During the meeting, Benjamin Snow's colleagues objected to his ordination plan for Lupalikkun as premature. Albert Sturges—now without either Luther Gulick or Berita Kaaikaula, originally his partners in the Pohnpei mission—worked in the midst of a much larger population spread over considerably more land area, and had experienced even more difficulty and frustration than Benjamin Snow.

It had been "eight years before Pastor Sturges had his first acceptable Ponapean convert."[3] He simply could not imagine any Micronesian being ready for ordination. He vetoed Pastor Snow's proposal.

KOSRAE'S FIRST DEACON

Benjamin Snow compromised. He decided it would be a good step forward in the development of the Church on Kosrae to select some of the best and more devoted members for the office of deacon. Deacons would have certain responsibilities in helping those who were sick and in spreading the faith in other ways. Also he thought it would be an excellent step toward ordination. So it was Lupalikkun, the Snows' Little George, who became the first deacon of the Kosrae Church.

Soon after, Rev. Snow also consecrated Kutuka and Likiaksa as deacons.

DEDICATION OF LELU'S NEW CHURCH

When the *Morning Star II* returned from Pohnpei to Kosrae on October 21, on board with the Snows were other missionaries serving in the Marshall and Gilbert Islands, who had also attended the biennial mission meeting. All of them were honored guests at the dedication of Lelu's new coral block church on the 24th.

Capt. Bingham wrote:

The dedication was an occasion of much interest to the people, and the many visitors from the Morning Star *will remember with pleasure the taste displayed in the decorations of the church with flowers and leaves. The audience of some two hundred were all finely dressed—and every stranger present, as he looked upon the walls of solid masonry, and heard the sweet singing, and marked the attentive eyes and listening ears, must have felt that the Gospel had "free course and been glorified" on this lovely isle of the Pacific.*

It was with much pleasure that upon the morning of the next Lord's day, we sat with some one hundred and fifty of these converted heathen (nine of whom were baptized that day) in the same place, at the Lord's table, to commemorate His dying love. On the following day, October 28th, we were to have sailed, but headwinds prevented our final departure until Saturday morning, the 2nd of November, when—assisted by six native canoes and the King's boat, besides our own two boats—we safely reached the open sea; though had we been ten minutes later, the headwind which sprung up would have greatly imperiled us.[4]

THE YOUNG DEACON'S WITNESS

One evening not long after he became deacon, Lupalikkun met a sailor on shore leave who was looking for some excitement. Deacon Lupalikkun, himself just 25 years old, took the young American to a prayer meeting in the church. The sailor was so moved and impressed that he made public confession of his sins, accepted the Lordship of Jesus Christ and then attended church regularly during the long period his ship was anchored in Lelu Harbor. His friend, Deacon Lupalikkun, was his interpreter, guide, and Bible teacher for the duration of his stay.

Benjamin Snow noticed with gratitude that a number of seamen on Kosrae, even some "old, tough specimens," were beginning to appear in church. This was in marked contrast to earlier years, when these men often tried to break up the work of the mission.

MRS. SNOW, CARRIE, AND FREDDY
TRAVEL TO AMERICA

The *Morning Star II* returned the Snow family to Ebon, then continued south to leave the Kanoa family at Butaritari, and other Hawaiian and American missionaries at their assigned posts in different parts of the Gilbert Islands. In late December the vessel sailed back to Ebon to pick up Lydia Snow, Carrie, and Freddy for the return trip to Honolulu—leaving Benjamin alone in the Marshall Islands. With the children, Mrs. Snow went on to the United States. She had been absent from her homeland for 16 years. The reunion with family and friends in New England was a wonderful boon to her, while Carrie, almost 11, and Freddie, 9, were overwhelmed by curious relatives and mind-expanding experiences.

A friend in Honolulu described Lydia Snow as she passed through on her way to America in 1867. She appeared an "almost gaunt figure, worn with the toils, privations and abstemious living of Micronesia, dressed much in the fashion of 1852." Following her sojourn in the United States, Mrs. Snow returned to Hawai'i in 1868 "a splendid, filled-out figure, with rosy cheeks, and in tasteful modern dress, full of health and animation. Her vivacity was always sparkling... She came back glowing with enthusiasm enkindled by working in the Woman's Boards of the U.S. She had gone from town to town, state to state, working with zeal and missionary fervor in meetings both of women alone and also in full-church assemblies."[5]

In two meetings with Honolulu women, Mrs. Snow's "earnest words and flowing tears" were recorded as being unforgettable. "...At a large missionary meeting in Fort Street Church, when several important men spoke at length, Mrs. Snow gave 'the choicest part of the evening' in a short address from the pulpit steps! ...This was the first time a woman had ever spoken extemporaneously from a foreign pulpit in Honolulu... Since the majority of the church held to the old doctrine 'Let your women keep silence in the church'... a concession was made that evening... to allow Mrs. Snow to SPEAK from the 'pulpit steps.' ...By her most womanly and appropriate address she laid the great wall of prejudice flat before her and made it a suitable and pleasant thing for a woman to address a mixed assembly."[6]

KUTUKA WRITES TO EDITOR DAMON

Benjamin Snow took advantage of the 1868 voyage of the *Morning Star II* to make still another visit to Kosrae. While there, he wrote the editor of *The Friend*, "Kutuka wishes me to tell you something of the good work on Kusaie. My present visit has been one of the most pleasant I have ever made. I have enjoyed the visit more from their cordial sympathy with me in my loneliness while my family is away from Micronesia. Even the children never seemed so affectionate, trusting and loving, and their sweet singing has been a great source of joy to me. At almost every turn I would have some sad, some touching or some loving remembrance of the past of our missionary life on this gem of the Pacific."[7]

At the same time, Mr. Snow forwarded a letter to Editor Damon from Kutuka. Mr. Damon explained and shared the letter in *The Friend*:

When we visited Kusaie in 1860, we became acquainted with a native Christian who spoke a little English. He is now a deacon of the church. Occasionally since that time, we have received letters from him. By the return of the Morning Star, *we received one, from which we copy as follows. It was written in the Kusaien dialect, but was translated by the Rev. Mr. Snow.*

"Now I send you my love, and to all your family, and to all our friends there. I want to tell you something about the good work of our Great Lord in heaven. The seed of God has grown up in all the villages on Kusaie. There is but little wanting, and the land will be filled with it. On this account, we believe that God has heard what you have asked for Kusaie, for no man is able to do such a work. It is God alone. I know Jesus will kindly brood his little chickens under his wings. This is all. I am Kutuka, Your brother in Christ." Such a letter indicates that the true Gospel leaven is at work.[8]

NEW CORAL BLOCK CHURCH FOR MALEM

Shipped from Honolulu on the *Morning Star II* in 1868 were materials to be used for the fourth coral block church to be built on Kosrae—this one in Malem. The editor reported in *The Friend*: "It will be recollected by some of our readers that about six months ago an effort was made to raise the small sum of a little over one hundred dollars to aid the Christians on Strong's Island in purchasing the materials for their new chapel. In addition to a collection of about $60 taken up in the Bethel congregation, we also received $40 from C. A. Williams, Esq., and $20 from H. A. P. Carter, Esq. By the return of the *Morning Star*, we learn that the materials forwarded were duly landed. At a meeting of the native church, a committee was appointed to acknowledge the donation, and a unanimous vote of thanks was passed. 'Every hand was up,' writes the Rev. Mr. Snow."[9]

Christianity was now the primary influence on Kosrae. Not only had most of the nobility on Lelu embraced the new religion, but many of the commoners on the large island—where three thriving congregations met in fine coral block church buildings—were also Christians. Among those participating in a testimony service while Benjamin Snow was present in September 1868 was Queen Sra Nuarar, the wife of King Salik II. The wife of another high chief, a woman who had held one of the most important ranks in the old priesthood and was the oldest woman living on the island, also participated.

Lydia, Carrie, and Freddy Snow returned to Micronesia at the end of 1868, bringing with them, right off the press in Hawai'i, Benjamin Snow's Kosraean translation of the Gospel of Mark.

ASSESSMENT OF MR. POGUE

J. F. Pogue, "Delegate of the Board" of the Hawaiian Evangelical Association, was on the *Morning Star II* when all four of the Snows boarded at Ebon to make their 1869 visit to Kosrae. They carried with them printed copies of the Gospel of Mark. Earlier that year, Mr. Snow had completed the Kosraean translation of the Book of Acts and the First, Second, and Third Letters of John. He planned to send them for printing in Hawai'i on the return trip of the *Star*.

Mr. Pogue, whose assignment was to survey the situation in the Micronesia Mission, wrote of being struck by the extreme beauty of the verdant mountains of Kosrae, in contrast to the flat coral islands he had been seeing as he traveled through the Gilberts and Marshalls. Even more striking to him was the appearance of those who gathered on the Lelu wharf to welcome the Snows.

"It was delightful to see old and young men, women and children, coming around and taking them by the hands and greeting them with warm salutations." He described the Kosraeans as being well dressed and commented that their faces were those of civilized people. "There are four church buildings on this island, and one of them has one hundred and fifty members. [This number includes both baptized members and those seeking baptism.] The people can all read and join in the songs of Zion."[10]

On a number of occasions, Mr. Pogue repeated his amazement with the vibrancy of Kosrae's churches in light of the poor health and small number of people who called Kosrae home.

LUPALIKKUN ORDAINED
THE FIRST KOSRAEAN PASTOR

During this visit, Mr. Snow ordained Lupalikkun, the youngest son of Good King George, as Kosrae's first pastor. How proud and pleased Benjamin Snow was! He had known Lupalikkun as a father knows a son since the young pastor was 10 years old—that "bright, active, good-looking lad" who had moved in with them at Pisin soon after they first arrived at Kosrae. Mr. Snow had educated him as an adolescent and then, after five years of misunderstanding and miscommunication between them had ended, had taken him to Ebon for serious training. It is true that Mr. Snow's sentimental attachment to Lupalikkun was very strong and certainly influenced his decision. Also, he felt that Lupalikkun's high chiefly rank made the young man more acceptable than Kutuka or Likiaksa as a leader of the people. Mr. Snow, who was not a frivolous man, nor one easy to please, had great confidence and trust in the ability and spiritual strength of Lupalikkun.

Pastor Lupalikkun, at age 27, became not only the first pastor of the Church on Kosrae, but also the first ordained indigenous minister in all of Micronesia. His congregation numbered 173 active communicant members, while the entire Kosraean population of some 475 persons was counted within the Christian community. Deacons Likiaksa and Kutuka served as Lupalikkun's primary assistants. The wives of the three men—Kat, Tulpe and Notwe—led the work among the women.

The Snows remained on Kosrae while the *Morning Star II*, with Mr. Pogue aboard, sailed on to Pohnpei. After the mission executive had reviewed the work of the mission there, and supplies were off-loaded, Albert and Susan Sturges, with their daughters, Harriet and Julia, boarded the ship for the return trip. The vessel stopped at Kosrae, where the Snows boarded. Both families were scheduled for furloughs in the United States.

WRECK OF THE *MORNING STAR II*

All were in buoyant spirits as the ship prepared to leave Kosrae for Honolulu on October 18. At evening prayer the missionary families and their children joined others on board in singing "Homeward Bound" as the ship weighed anchor and set sail from Lelu Harbor. But when Capt. Tengstrom went on deck after supper he found that the vessel had been working in towards the island and, caught in a strong current, was dangerously near the reef.

Hiram Bingham, Jr., who was also aboard, described what happened next: "Boats were lowered and began towing her off shore. An anchor was let go in twenty fathoms of water and held her till a severe squall came up. Preparations had been made to slip the cable, in case the wind should favor, and try to shoot out clear of the reef with the fore and aft sails. But in trying to effect this after the squall, instead of shooting ahead, she only sagged off and soon struck the reef, broadside on. The surf was heavy, the shore rocky, and all hope for the vessel was gone."[11]

It was an extremely frightening experience for the two missionary couples and their children, going suddenly from the excitement and joy of beginning eagerly anticipated vacation trips, to the horrors of being flung upon a jagged coral reef by a wild sea. Albert Sturges told colleagues later that he thought for sure they would all be crushed and drowned. Fortunately the small boats were freed and no passenger or crew member was lost. It was midnight when, soaked and frightened, they landed on shore. Their Kosraean friends, who had been witnessing the tragedy, were waiting to help. Within a few hours, the ship from which they had escaped was pounded to pieces.

It was three months before the *Star's* marooned passengers were finally able to take passage aboard the *Annie Porter*, which reached Honolulu February 8, 1870. The missionary families went on to San Francisco, and from there by train to the East Coast. The American Board recovered $18,000 in insurance money on the wreck of the *Morning Star II* and raised another $10,000—again from American Sunday School children—and the building of another *Star* was begun.

DEATH OF PASTOR LUPALIKKUN

As was true of a majority of his fellow Kosraeans during those years, young Pastor Lupalikkun was not of vigorous health. The Church on Kosrae was devastated when, early in 1871 (the specific date is unknown), at the age of 29, Lupalikkun died. His illness and death took place just a year and a half after his ordination, and during the time the Snows were away from Micronesia.

An article appeared in *The Friend* in July of 1871, celebrating the Kosraean church and its youthful pastor: "The Kusaiens are a Christian people. They fear God. They dwell in peace, are industrious, and as well clothed as Hawaiians. Four houses of worship are opened on the Sabbath, which are filled with those who delight to keep holy the Lord's day. One hundred fifty-nine persons are connected with the church under a pastor chosen from among themselves. This pastor is the son of Old King George, who took Mr. Snow under his protection when he landed upon the Island to instruct the people in the Christian religion. The Queen is a church member, and gives good evidence of being a humble Christian. The King is moral, intelligent, somewhat avaricious, not a church member, but does not oppose."

And then—appended to the article as though the distressful news had just reached his desk—the editor continued: "With deep sorrow we have to record the death of the pastor of this Church. He was a high chief, a humble Christian, a man of influence. Since his death there has been disaffection in the Church, but nothing serious. May the Lord raise up upon those islands, and from that once degraded people, a nation to illustrate the truth of his faithfulness in all generations."[12]

With the death of Pastor Lupalikkun, only two daughters from among Good King George's eight children were still living, Kenye Kitinwak and Sepe Awe. Soon after the young pastor died, his grieving sister, Sepe, gave birth to a son whom she named George in honor of her younger brother. [This George became the father of the extended George family of Fomseng.]

SNOWS RETURN TO THE ISLANDS
ABOARD *MORNING STAR III*

The *Morning Star III* sailed from Boston on February 27, 1871, bound for California, Honolulu, and Micronesia. Having spent a year in the United States, Benjamin and Lydia Snow boarded the *Star* in San Francisco on July 22 for their return to the islands, agreeing that the new missionary vessel was a marked improvement over the one it replaced.

For the first time the Snows were without their children. Fifteen-year-old Caroline and 13-year-old Fred remained in America to attend school in Massachusetts. This parting was exceptionally difficult for the Snow family— especially for the children whose entire lives up to this point had been inter-twined daily with that of their parents, and whose language and cultural outlook were much more Kosraean or Marshallese than American. Their homesickness during the first months of this separation was overwhelming. Acclimated to the warm sunshine and moist air of Micronesia, that first dry, dark, and exceedingly cold New England winter added greatly to their depression. The young teenagers clung tenaciously to each other for support.

Having received the heartbreaking news of Pastor Lupalikkun's death when they arrived in Honolulu, the Snows decided to bypass Ebon as they returned to Micronesia, continuing aboard the *Morning Star III* straight to Kosrae. There, they did what they could to comfort the grief-stricken church and, in particular Kat, the pastor's young widow. But their Kittie was not the only widow in need of comfort when they reached Kosrae. A second widow awaited them. The Snows had two months to adjust to the news of Pastor Lupalikkun's death, but when they learned upon disembarking at Kosrae that Deacon Kutuka, too, had died, it seemed almost more than they could bear.

DEATH OF KUTUKA

Benjamin Snow shared his grief in a letter to Samuel Damon in Honolulu:
Dear Brother: Accompanying this you will find a couple of notes from Kutuka's widow and daughter to you. You will probably be surprised, as we were, to learn of his death. No one has passed away from among this people whom we shall miss so much as Kutuka. He was always among the first to greet us on our yearly visits, and the last to say "Goodbye." He is the only one who has known and been with us through all the changes, trials and prosperities of our work on Kusaie. Now that he is no more with us, I was surprised to see how much I had leaned upon him. For days after our arrival it seemed as though he would drop in somewhere and we should hear his voice again either about our house or in our meetings.[13]

LIKIAKSA ORDAINED AS KOSRAE'S SECOND PASTOR

Deacon Likiaksa, the young caretaker of Pisin and the other protégée of Benjamin Snow, was ordained by the missionary in October 1871, to take Pastor Lupalikkun's place. Likiaksa, who was from Utwe, had joined the Snows' household as an adolescent. Like Lupalikkun, he had shared a close and loving relationship with the Snow family. Likiaksa—with his wife, Tulpe Pisin, beside him—proved himself daily to be worthy of the missionary's trust.

Pastor Likiaksa was recognized in *The Friend*:
After the death of the lamented Rev. George Snow [Pastor Lupalikkun], the Kusaie church and people were left without a spiritual guide. The Reverend Benjamin G. Snow, who had been in the habit of making an annual visit to the Island, being in the United States, the people became negligent, and some of the

church members forsook their first love, and engaged in practices not proper for those connected with the church. By the Morning Star, *Mr. and Mrs. Snow visited this, their first missionary home. They were very kindly received by the people of their former charge. A new pastor was chosen and ordained to the work of the ministry—Reverend Likiak Sa. Meetings were held, church members instructed, discipline enforced in the church, the wayward warned.*

These efforts were blessed by the Master. The people began again to realize their responsibilities. Many wanderers returned to duty. This people and their new pastor deserve, and should have our sympathy and prayers. The church numbers about one hundred sixty members who support their own pastor and contribute to the benevolent operations of the day.[14]

When the Snows—having remained at Kosrae for almost four months—left for Ebon aboard the *Morning Star III* in February 1872, the people appeared to them to be in a much better state than they had been for some time. Mr. Snow wrote to Editor Damon:

We found much to sadden us during this visit to Kusaie. Our long absence with no pastoral care for the church, and much of untoward influence from without, had led many of them to go astray, and eight at one time had been carried off by kidnappers! But their church discipline had been kept up with their usual fidelity.

Our visit as usual did much to strengthen the things that remain and tone up the Christian feeling all over the island. Nine were admitted to the church, ten children baptized, a pastor ordained to take the place of George [Lupalikkun] who, as you know, had died. One of those who had been a deacon was among those who was kidnapped. It is fearful to what extent slavery business is carried on in these seas.[15]

No one was exempt from church discipline. Not long after the Snows returned to the Marshall Islands, Queen Sra Nuarar, the wife of King Salik II, was expelled from church membership. Since the king was extremely jealous of his position, it is significant that the Lelu Church leaders were able to dismiss his wife without retaliation. The king did continue the quarrels with the newly ordained Pastor Likiaksa that had begun in 1863. One of these concerned the mission cattle. But when the young man refused to remove them from Lelu to the large island as the king insisted, King Salik II was unable to collect the fine he imposed.[16]

BIBLE TRANSLATION CONTINUES

In September 1872, Benjamin Snow was able to return to Kosrae and distribute copies of his translation of the Book of Luke, which he had completed the year before. All four Gospels, as well as the New Testament books of Acts, and First, Second, and Third John, were now available in the Kosraean language.

Mr. Snow struggled hard in his translation work. With his whole heart,

he wanted the Kosraeans to be able to read the Scriptures in their own language—and he had that same desire for the people of the Marshall Islands.
But the prerequisites and processes of translation were demanding. The
languages had to be mastered, as well as time found for concentration in
the midst of countless other responsibilities and a myriad of daily interruptions. And though he always had willing, loyal assistants—as Salpasr and
Lupalikkun were during earlier years—they had neither the educational nor
religious backgrounds to be of truly significant help.

In addition, there was the scrutiny of his missionary colleagues. For a
number of years, Benjamin Snow suffered criticism of his work by Edward
Doane—who, on one occasion, referred to Benjamin's Marshallese translation
of the first chapters of Matthew as "the mere work of an infant."[17] Mr. Snow
was greatly relieved when the task of translating the Marshallese Scriptures
could be turned over to an amicable and competent new American Board missionary, the Rev. Joel Whitney, who, with his wife Louisa, joined the Snows at
Ebon in 1872. Now Mr. Snow could concentrate on his Kosraean translation
projects.

In late 1873, Benjamin and Lydia Snow traveled from Ebon to Kosrae, this
time taking Joel and Louisa Whitney with them. Mrs. Snow and the Whitneys
remained at Kosrae while Mr. Snow continued aboard the *Morning Star III* to
Pohnpei and the Mortlock Islands. For more than two months, Lydia, Joel,
and Louisa engaged in teaching, counseling, and evangelistic work among the
Kosraeans while awaiting the return of Benjamin.

Joel Whitney reported in *The Friend*: "Kusaie is one of the most beauti-
ful of islands, and the Kusaiens are the most hospitable people, of all the
Pacific."[18] He was also much impressed by the competent leadership of the
youthful Pastor Likiaksa. But all four missionaries were distressed by some
Ocean Islanders, and a number of non-Micronesians, who had recently arrived
and were making themselves at home across Lelu Harbor in the Sansrik and
Mutunlik areas of the large island. Their boisterous presence also distressed
King Salik II and the Kosraean people, who seemed at a loss to know what to
do about them.

In February 1874, the *Morning Star III* returned the two missionary
couples to the Marshall Islands.

AN INFLUX OF FOREIGNERS

A series of events was beginning to occur on Kosrae that would have
lasting consequences. C. F. Wood, visiting the island in October 1873 on a
yachting trip through the Pacific, painted a word picture of the setting for

these occurrences:

Kusaie cannot but strike one with melancholy. Here are the relics of a fine race of people, utterly ruined by their contact with whites. The natives are more robust looking than those of Ponape, but they will soon be extinct. There are now not two hundred on this large and fertile island that used to hold its thousands. In the twelve months ending in December 1872, upwards of sixty died, and already this year twenty-six have succumbed.

I found on shore here natives of Ocean Island. Their country had been stricken with a famine, and some trading vessel had carried them here out of kindness. They now wanted me to take them home again, but I declined, out of respect to the laws of my country.[19]

Though visitor Wood's population figure was less than the actual 375 Kosraeans who were counted that year, he underscored the sad reality of life and death on the island. The whaling industry was now phasing out of the Pacific, but the diseases those sailors had inflicted upon the islanders continued to take their toll. Syphilis was the worst, but influenza, measles, and other diseases that in America were seldom fatal, continued to strike the Kosraeans with terrible results. Benjamin Snow sorrowfully commented that the Kosraeans kept burying many more than were being born.

Then, the dying Kosraean race received—certainly unwillingly in the beginning—several groups of people who married and settled into Kosraean society. In addition to the Ocean Islanders, some natives of Nauru appeared. They had been compelled to leave their home island because of tribal warfare. Ocean Island and Nauru, two isolated bits of Micronesia located along the equator west of the Gilbert Islands, were sometimes classified with the Gilberts. Ocean Island—or Banaba—is 40 miles south of the equator. Nauru, 160 miles west of Ocean, was known during the 19th century as Pleasant Island. Just 25 miles below the equator, Nauru is 426 miles south of Kosrae. [In the early 20th century, both islands would become valuable sources of phosphate, a bird-generated fertilizer that was mined by a series of companies and shipped off to the agricultural fields of New Zealand and Australia.]

In the 1870s, Ocean Island and Nauru were referred to by sea captains as being "happy hunting-grounds for beachcombers."[20] Two or three of these adventurers and runaway sailors set themselves up as traders, but most did very little physical work. Half a dozen of these renegades led the two groups, one fleeing famine and the other fleeing war, to take refuge on Kosrae.

Louis Becke, a young Australian seaman who was on Kosrae for six months in 1874, left descriptions of these six white men. Though he was prone to the liberties of poetic license, Mr. Becke did have firsthand experience with these eccentric fellows. He wrote that the group included Harry Terry, a jovial, white-haired British military man who had deserted his ship more than 50 years earlier. He had several island women and a number of children with him. There was Bob Ridley, a heavily tattooed ex-convict over 70 years of age. He was on Kosrae with his young wife, "the clever and beautiful Lalia," a native of Easter Island [Rapanui] who possessed "a regal manner and a strong veneer of civilization." Pleasant Island Bill, a "good-for-nothing with a warm heart and unlimited capacity for whisky," had his Gilbertese wife with him. Harry Skillings, originally from Portland, Maine, and known as "the Adonis of the South Seas," had "clear-cut features, long curly locks of dark hair, and a drooping mustache. With a blase manner, he simply laughed at wounds and death."[21] It was whispered that the three young Nauruan women who were with him were his wives. Seth, a young American who had run away from a whaling ship, and Dick Mills, another deserter, completed the roster of six.

These men and their confrontational Nauru and Ocean Island companions numbered close to 100 individuals and were an enormous disruption to village life. The mild Kosraeans were afraid of these ruffians. Each sea captain who came into one of Kosrae's harbors with his ship was entreated by King Salik II to transport these groups away from the island. The unwelcome visitors also sought passage on the various ships, but no captain wanted them aboard.

CAPT. "BULLY" HAYES

Then, during the first week of March 1874—just after the Snows and Whitneys had returned to Ebon—the notorious South Sea adventurer, Capt. William Henry Hayes of Cleveland, Ohio, sailed into Lelu Harbor in his magnificent 218-ton brig, the *Leonora*. The ship, luxuriously fitted and immaculately kept, was famous throughout the Pacific for its speed. This speed, and the *Leonora*'s four brass cannon, were needed on a vessel engaged in the dangerous business of kidnapping and station robbing. The Kosraeans were already acquainted with "Bully" Hayes. The swaggering seaman had sailed the *Leonora* into their island's harbors on a number of previous occasions. They found his nickname appropriate.

On his current voyage, Capt. Hayes was collecting coconut oil from various traders with whom he had connections in the Gilbert, Marshall, and Caroline Islands. Stopping at Kosrae in 1872, he had coerced King Salik II to begin preparing copra for the manufacture of valuable coconut oil. Now he had come to collect. The king immediately told Bully Hayes of his anxiety concerning the Nauru and Ocean islanders and their white leaders. After making sure that he had settled the coconut oil dealings, Capt. Hayes reassured the worried monarch by promising to take the troublemakers away in the already crowded *Leonora*. Eighteen-year-old Louis Becke, supercargo [officer in charge of cargo] on the *Leonora*, recounted this meeting with the Kosraean king, commenting that Salik II was a curious combination of "shrewdness, generosity, cant and immorality."

"A cripple from rheumatism, the Tokosra sat hunched up in his chair clad in European clothes, consisting of military white duck trousers and a black coat of the style known in New England as a claw-hammer. On one arm of his royal chair lay a huge Bible, whilst on the other was a long churchwarden's clay pipe. By the king's side leant Queen Sra, a pretty little woman with wavy black hair. Her podgy fingers were much bejewelled and two heavy gold earrings hung from her ears."[22]

The king's servants placed a banquet before Bully Hayes and Louis Becke consisting of an enormous roasted pig, and huge quantities of fish, taro, and yams, for which the king and queen bowed their heads to give thanks. Hayes presented a basket of liquor to the king, whose "worn, anxious face was soon wreathed in smiles." In his drunken haze, King Salik began mixing quotations from the Scripture with sailors' oaths while professing great friendship with Mr. Snow. He talked of the beauty of Kittie, Pastor Lupalikkun's young widow, who was living at Pisin with Pastor Likiaksa and Tulpe.

Bully Hayes agreed to take the Nauru party to Ujelang atoll and the Ocean Island group to Enewetak, for the amount of $1,000. They were then to sell Capt. Hayes all the oil they produced during the next five years. It was also arranged that the *Leonora* would transport the traders and their followers from Lelu Harbor to the south harbor at Utwe until Bully Hayes was ready to leave Kosrae.

WRECK OF THE *LEONORA*

When the *Leonora* reached Utwe Harbor, smaller and much more exposed than Lelu Harbor, Capt. Hayes found four whaleships inside. Two of them were getting underway. The *Leonora*'s skipper waited until the second one had slipped through the passage, then entered the narrow little harbor and dropped anchor between the remaining two ships and the dense belt of mangrove trees that hid the beach. Sailors began to tow cattle ashore, while young Becke traded goods for yams and taro with the Utwe Kosraeans. Pastor Likiaksa stood near to make sure that his people were not cheated. The date was March 15, 1874.

Some hours later, noticing a heavy cloud rising over the horizon to the southwest growing blacker and blacker, Bully Hayes called Capt. James Knowles of the *St. George* and Capt. E. C. Pulver of the *Camilla* to the deck of the *Leonora* for a conference.[23] With no time to put out to sea, the men discussed how best to brace for the storm. Capt. Knowles and Capt. Pulver reluctantly agreed to attach a line between their ships and Capt. Hayes' vessel, in an effort to keep it off the coral heads that lurked just beneath the surface between the *Leonora* and the mangrove swamp. As soon as the line was secure and the whaling skippers were over the side, Capt. Hayes began preparing for the ordeal. All decks were cleared of everything that could be placed below—including the crowd of passengers, now considerably increased by the traders and their Nauruan and Ocean Islander retinue.

It was late evening when the first gust hit the brig with a solid sheet of rain and spray. With the wind came the waves, rolling in through the harbor entrance. Recognizing a much more vicious storm than he had expected, Bully Hayes ordered the traders to take the women and children ashore in the ship's boats as quickly as possible. He sent Louis Becke below for the ship's papers and any small articles of value he could carry.

There was a grinding, shuddering thud as the ship's keel struck a large coral mushroom. Sailors aboard the *Camilla*, in an effort to save themselves, had severed the connecting line between the ships. The next gusts finished the *Leonora*. Later, Louis Becke reported that he was knocked unconscious by a piece of wreckage and would have drowned if Lalia and one of Harry Skillings' men had not dragged him to shore—and that the water was in a great state of commotion as sharks fought for the bodies of pigs washed overboard from the sinking brig.

The storm was ferocious in its intensity, but it was the *Leonora's* unfortunate position within the harbor that proved disastrous. Capt. Hayes had maneuvered his vessel into a position close to shore, a location advantageous to the off-loading of goods and animals. Anchoring there was ordinarily no problem, but with the sudden wind and wild sea—and the other two ships blocking an escape—the *Leonora* was doomed. By dawn's light the two whaleships sailed into a placid sea—the only sign of the *Leonora* was the main topmast showing above the surface of Utwe Harbor.

AFTERMATH OF THE WRECK

For a number of days there was pandemonium caused by the traders and others who stayed drunk on liquor salvaged from the ship, but Bully Hayes soon had the survivors organized into an encampment 200 yards down the beach from Utwe village. He busied himself collecting coconuts, and made an agreement with his former passengers to feed them if they would manufacture coconut oil for him.

The oil was to be obtained from 48,000 coconuts that Capt. Hayes coerced King Salik II into agreeing to pay as compensation for goods the *Leonora's* captain claimed had been taken by Kosraeans as it washed up on shore. The crew of the *Leonora*, together with most of the men from Nauru and Ocean Island, were kept busy in their boats pulling up and down the lagoon and mangrove channels as far as Okat Harbor collecting the coconuts. They worked alongside the rust-colored canoes of Kosraeans who were also employed by Bully Hayes in this work.

The inevitable reaction of Bully Hayes and his crew to the monumental disaster of losing their ship became an excruciating, on-going trauma for the Kosraean people. As weeks turned into months, quarrels erupted more and more frequently between stranded Capt. Hayes and his equally stranded passengers. There was so much fighting, drinking, and shooting that Pastor Likiaksa urged the villagers in Utwe to move to Lelu.

Leaders among the Kosraeans in Utwe got Louis Becke and Harry Skillings to go with them to demand that Bully Hayes put a stop to the fighting and the interference with their women. Capt. Hayes was so angry that he severed relations for a time with the two men, forcing them to live elsewhere. Mr. Becke moved to a settlement near Okat and Mr. Skillings moved to Mutunlik on the south side of the entrance to Lelu Harbor.

Much later, after he had cooled down, Bully Hayes asked Louis Becke to go to Lelu to try and make peace for him with the king. King Salik II was drunk during the interview, but Queen Sra entertained Mr. Becke by showing him some bound volumes of *Leslie's Illustrated Paper,* sent to her by Hawai'i's new queen, Emma. Louis Becke found that the tranquility of Lelu village, and particularly in the settlements on the south side of Lelu Harbor, was constantly broken by the Ocean Islanders and Nauruans, who had returned from Utwe to their original settlements and were continually fighting among themselves. Louis Becke also found Lalia living at Pisin with Kittie. Lalia remained there for a considerable length of time teaching the Kosraean women to weave hats, at which she was adept.[24]

Toward the end of the summer of 1874, Bully Hayes began to find his enforced confinement on Kosrae intolerable. He was not the beachcomber type, and began to make plans for leaving in the best of the *Leonora's* boats for either the Marshall Islands or Pohnpei. The king tried to keep Capt. Hayes from doing this, knowing that once he was gone, the reckless Ocean and Nauru islanders would be even more difficult to control.

Jealous and hungry for power, some of the white traders began scheming to kill Bully Hayes, Louis Becke and Harry Skillings. Kittie learned of the plot through Pastor Likiaksa and was able to warn the three of them in time to save their lives.

On September 15, in the midst of this plotting, a schooner sailed into Lelu Harbor. It was the *Matauto*, commanded by Edward Milne, an Englishman, but flying a German flag. There was a rush of the various conspirators to board the ship. Bully Hayes is said to have argued so violently with Capt. Milne that he challenged the English trader to a pistol duel the following morning. But by morning, the *Matauto* had slipped out to sea.

MR. SNOW ARRIVES ON THE SCENE

Four days later, the *Morning Star III* arrived from Ebon, bringing Benjamin Snow to Kosrae. He had heard about Capt. Hayes' shipwreck and came to see what he could do to help his Kosraean friends, who were finding themselves more and more at the mercy of this infamous buccaneer. Leaving Mr. Snow at Kosrae, the *Star* proceeded to Pohnpei, where Bully Hayes' disruptive presence at Kosrae was described to Capt. Dupois of the British warship, HMS *Rosario*.

During the next three days, Mr. Snow had a number of long conversations with Bully Hayes, who began making a pretense of praying before meals and insisted that his whole colony attend worship with him when Benjamin Snow was in Utwe.

When HMS *Rosario*, with a complement of 145 officers and men, arrived on September 22, Capt. Hayes had no idea that authorities on the ship had been on his track, sailing through the Marshalls, the Gilberts, and the Carolines inquiring about him. The captain conferred with Mr. Snow and Pastor Likiaksa, and at his request, Benjamin Snow wrote the following letter:

I am happy to comply with your request concerning a letter from me as an American citizen in regard to Captain W. H. Hayes, who is also a citizen of the United States of America.

I have known the said Hayes personally for a few years past, but have known much more of him by reports, which have almost invariably been greatly to his discredit, or, as you Englishmen would say, he has the reputation of being "a very clever rogue." I had hoped that a brighter phase might open up to his character from some source, but I have looked in vain.

Having heard that his vessel was wrecked on this island, the field of my earlier missionary labours, I availed myself of the earliest opportunity to getting here, that I might render such assistance by my presence and counsel as might be needed. The prospects of meeting you here in your man-of-war capacity was another very strong inducement for me to come at this time, feeling assured that you would feel only too glad in adjusting any matters that might need such force and authority as you have at your command. And I am sorry to find that your presence is very timely in the case of this Captain Hayes—"sorry," for I would fain have found such a state of things as might not require your aid.

Having been on this island a week, what I can learn of the said Hayes only confirms—yea, even strengthens—previous evil reports I have heard of him, so that I am constrained to say, in all sincerity, and in the interest of our common humanity, that you will be doing a most praiseworthy act by taking him on board the Rosario *and taking him to Sydney, where he may be brought under the cognizance and jurisdiction of civil law.*

I am fully aware of the difficulty and delicacy of your situation in thus proceeding with a citizen of a foreign Power, but I think I can assure you, as a citizen of the United States, that our Government would gladly make common cause with our cousins across the water in arresting and bringing to justice such outlaws as this said Captain Hayes has so long had the reputation of being. Of course I cannot speak officially, but my firm convictions are that the course you are contemplating in taking him to Sydney and delivering him up to the American authorities there will not only be approved, but applauded. It will certainly relieve our Micronesian seas of one of the greatest sources of annoyance we have had during the twenty and more years I have been a resident missionary on these islands…

Long live your noble Queen, and long may there exist peace and the most fraternal goodwill between our two national Governments. I remain, B. G. Snow, Missionary of the ABCFM, Kusaie, September 26, 1874.[25]

LAST DAYS OF CAPT. HAYES

Learning of the intent to take him prisoner, Bully Hayes and a companion put out to sea in a small boat, where they remained just below the horizon until HMS *Rosario* left Kosrae. Coming back to land, Capt. Hayes outfitted another small boat and sailed for Pohnpei. From Pohnpei he traveled by various means to Guam, Manila, and finally San Francisco. From there, he made his way back across the Pacific to Apia, Samoa, where his legal wife, Amelia—a white woman from New Zealand—lived, with their twin daughters, Leonora and Laurina, and son, Fred.

In January 1877, Capt. Hayes left Apia for the purpose of revisiting Kosrae, but he did not reach his destination. He is said to have been murdered by the cook on board the *Lotus*, to whom Bully Hayes had been especially cruel.

HMS *Rosario* had taken Louis Becke from Kosrae in October 1874, as well as others of the *Leonora's* crew. N. Nahnsen, the Danish first mate, was left in charge of Bully's property, and therefore did not sail with the *Rosario*, nor did Will Hicks, the half-Fijian second mate, who hid out and thus avoided arrest. One after another, the Nauru and Ocean Island traders found transportation and departed, until only Harry Skillings, who flew the American flag over his door, remained on Kosrae.

KING SALIK II DEPOSED AND THE SIGRAH ELECTED

On November 2, 1874, the Christian Kosraeans and their supporters deposed the drunken King Salik II. This deposition and the investiture of the Sigrah in his place as King Sru IV were recorded by Benjamin Snow and published the following year in *The Missionary Herald*.

The king and queen had both been going to the bad, and going it hard, for a long while. Last Saturday the idea got possession of some of the chiefs and more influential of the people, that they had a right if they chose to exercise it, to depose the old king and put a new man in his place. It was understood by certain ones that there would be a meeting on Monday in the Stone Church in Lelu, to consult upon the matter, and if thought best to put the thing through.

No public notice was given of the meeting, but the chiefs sent out their runners, and before noon all the chiefs and about one hundred men were gathered in the Lelu church. They sent for me to be present. Kanku presided, and the meeting was opened with prayer by the pastor, and (amusing to me) by singing "There is rest for the weary." I feared there might be some division of feeling as to who should be the new king, if they concluded to elect one.

But Kanku spoke first, and spoke well. According to the customs of the island the place belonged to him, but he, with great magnanimity, proposed Sigrah for the new king. Each of the chiefs in order spoke, then quite a number of the common people followed. I was surprised at the fearlessness and manliness with which many of them spoke. It came out that there was quite a feeling in favor of Kanku, but as he had proposed Sigrah, they yielded their preference and would go for Sigrah. One young man was strongly for Kanku, as being an older man and of more experience, and remarked that if Sigrah did not do well they could put in Kanku afterwards.

All had their say that wished to speak, even their old missionary among the rest. Then the vote was put: first, to depose the king. Every hand was up with a will. Second, shall Sigrah be his successor? This was carried, too, with equal unanimity and apparent heartiness. After attending to a few other little matters, at their request I led them in prayer, consecrating the newly elected king to his work. The meeting was then closed by all singing the thanksgiving hymn.[26]

The Sigrah—his given name was Tulensa—was now King Sru IV.

While this meeting was in progress, Salik II heard about his deposition and had packed his belongings and was ready to leave Posral. When the Kanku came to inform him officially about it, Salik stated the deposition was "a work of God for the prosperity of the island and for the good fortune of the church." That evening Benjamin Snow visited the deposed king in his new quarters and found the Kanku leading devotions.

"Quite a number of people were present and the place was as solemn as a house of mourning. It was hard for the people to get over the almost reverential feeling they had for their Tokosra, and humiliating in the extreme for the proud old fellow to have them address him by his common name. But no one dared to use the title of Tokosra toward him after it had been given to another."[27]

CENSUS OF 1874

Before leaving for Ebon on November 14, Benjamin Snow made another census of the island. He found 397 Kosraeans, 98 other Micronesians, 8 Polynesians, 6 Americans, and 6 Europeans, for a total of 515 persons living on Kosrae. Ninety-two persons were considered to be in good standing and thus enjoying full membership of the Church—54 men and 38 women. Mr. Snow was also able to complete the Kosraean drafts of Colossians, First and Second Thessalonians, and prepare them for the printers in Honolulu.

KING SRU IV

The new king, Sru IV—the younger brother of King Lupalik II—was considered an enthusiastic Christian. He was an ardent supporter of the church and held weekly meetings with "fallen" church members. Though only nine persons were added to the church rolls in 1875, the new king led the Lelu Christians in erecting a new and finer church building in their village on the Langosak point near Pisin. The *Bartholomew Gosrold* sprung a leak at Kosrae in August and was repaired with the cooperation of the Kosraeans. Everything had to be unloaded out of the ship, but not a single item was stolen. Capt. James Wallis wrote a letter of appreciation to King Sru IV and the Kosraean people for their kindness. He also left a letter for Mr. Snow, commending him for his work on the island, while applauding the honesty and hospitality of the Kosraeans.

CAPT. COLCORD'S WIFE DESCRIBES HER VISIT TO KOSRAE

On September 16, 1875, Benjamin and Lydia Snow and their colleagues, Joel and Louisa Whitney—with the Whitney's new baby, Johnny—left Ebon aboard the *Morning Star III* in the company of Capt. and Mrs. Andrew D. Colcord to travel to Pohnpei for a meeting of the Micronesia Mission. En route, the *Star* put in at Kosrae on Sunday, the 19th. The next day Mrs. Colcord, who was visiting Kosrae for the first time, recounted her impressions in her journal:

This has been a very happy day. About 4 o'clock Sabbath afternoon, we came in the lagoon. Kanku, who is next to the King in authority, came on board, and with him was Likiaksa, the pastor here. Kusaie is a delightful place. The land is high and mountainous, and covered with verdure. The harbor is small and the land seems near, so the eye can distinguish all the foliage. This is not a coral isle, but of volcanic formation.

Went ashore in the evening to prayer-meeting; several Kusaiens took part. Conlerler [Konlulu], who came as a passenger with us from Ebon with his wife and two children, talked, and Mr. and Mrs. Snow expressed great surprise that he could speak so well; said that he had outdone himself. His mother died while he was away. He has been cooking for the Snows at Ebon. All seemed glad to see the Morning Star. *They sang the* Morning Star *hymn and were very friendly.*

This morning as soon as breakfast was over, we went ashore with Mrs. Snow to her house where she used to live on Dove Island, which is at the extremity of the mainland where it runs out to a point in the harbor. Likiaksa met us at the landing; his house is back of Mr. Snow's and he takes care of the premises. There is just room for the two houses and a garden on the islet, which is connected with the mainland by a made walk. Mr. Snow's house has one very large room then a bedroom in one corner, storeroom opposite, and spare rooms in the other two corners. The walls are thin strips of wood or clapboard, tied together like some of our window-blinds. The posts are of mangrove... Where the roof fastens on to the large posts the cord is of two colors and put on much as rigging is done, close and even, in layers. The roof is thatched, and the walls are plastered inside and out with a plaster of lime made from shells, so the house looks as if it is painted white.

Soon the people began to come in and shake hands. The children sat down on the floor just inside the door and were busy looking over and reading a primer Mr. Snow has been printing. I went out for a walk; some of the children went with me, and we got several kinds of ferns and flowers that grow on the trees and rocks. Got some bright orange mimosa blossoms, and a fragrant herb—looks like pennyroyal—that some captains use for medicine for sailors, and call "spankerboom tea." There are bright scarlet hibiscus flowers on large trees, very showy.

Tokosra is King; the Queen's name is Srue. They are a very pleasant, pretty couple and quite genteel in appearance. The Queen called at Mrs. Snow's just as we were coming off to dinner, and brought trays of breadfruit all cooked, and taro and bananas. She also sent some aboard to Mrs. Whitney. As we were coming off, we invited her to come and take some dinner with us, which she did. She wore a pink-and-white brilliant dress and a white flannel sacque. Her hair was combed smoothly back and combed in a pug at the back of the head, and looked very neat. She has pleasant black eyes and comely features.

In the afternoon we all went up one of the rivers. Got a bunch of the "vegetable ivory" which grows there, and in shape is similar to the pandanus. Later we called at the King's. He has two houses; one seemed to be a dwelling house, the other a sort of Council House, it is so large. The floor is made of mangrove roots tied together close; makes a very smooth, nice floor. There were walks of the same extending all around the house. The fastenings of the frame were very pretty, laid in large patterns with two-colored cord, black and brown.

The King always sends a present of food of some kind after anyone has called upon him—Kusaie fashion! He sent plenty of bananas and coconuts, and also oranges, lemons, pineapples, mummy apples and sugar-cane, with taro and breadfruit.[28]

AN UPDATED KOSRAEAN PRIMER

As noted by Mrs. Colcord, the Kosraeans showed great interest in an expanded Kosraean language primer that Mr. Snow had written and printed for them on a new press at Ebon, and which he now delivered to them. This primer was an elaboration of the much simpler primer that Benjamin Snow had written and distributed in 1860 while still living on Kosrae. As a result of that earlier primer, and the impassioned determination of the Kosraeans to read, the entire adult population was now literate in their language. Now, Mr. Snow produced the new, augmented primer to help them teach their children.

In Hawai'i, the editor of *The Friend* praised the production of this primer in his publication:

Primu Kusaie—Buk in Lutlut ke Rid—[Kusaien Primer—A Book To Teach Reading—] Ebon Mission Press, 1875—The title of a book of eighty pages, written and printed under circumstances, difficulties and disadvantages which can hardly be appreciated. Mission labor cannot be fully represented. Books are written and printed in Europe and America with marvelous facility and rapidity, but how wide the contrast in the way that a similar result is accomplished in Micronesia.

In 1852 the Rev. and Mrs. Snow landed on Kusaie, or Strong's Island. For four years they labored to preach the gospel and teach the people in "pigeon-English," and discarded the vernacular language, but found the effort fruitless. They then cast aside all they had done, and commencing anew thoroughly mastered the vernacular of the islanders, and this little book is one of the results of their labor. Not only are they missionary linguists, but printers and book-binders.

Such results, combined with the benefits accruing to commerce and shipping in those remote seas, cannot be fully and fairly represented at Philadelphia. "Having had perfect understanding of all these things from the very first" [Luke 1:3 KJV], relating to the Micronesian mission and missionaries, Messrs. Snow, Sturges, Doane, Bingham, Whitney and others, we could wish we might do for them what the Evangelist Luke has done for Christ and His apostles, by writing His gospel and the "book of Acts." Our American missionaries in Micronesia are most worthy successors of those first Christian missionaries of the apostolic age. Small and insignificant as their contribution may appear, we intend that this little book shall, at the Great Centennial, represent the Micronesian missionaries.[29]

The Snows continued aboard the *Morning Star III* to Pohnpei where they attended the biennial meeting of the Micronesia Mission. Returning to Kosrae following the meeting, Benjamin and Lydia Snow disembarked and remained there through November in the heart of the Christian community. It would be Mr. Snow's final visit to Kosrae.

THE HARRY SKILLINGS FAMILY

It appears to have been during this prolonged stay of the Snows at Kosrae that Harry Skillings began his conversion to Christianity. His boyhood home had been Christian, and he and Benjamin Snow shared many similar memories and identical traditions—perhaps even some common acquaintances—as both men were from Maine. One of the Nauruan women who had accompanied Harry from Nauru—Sitoma, called "Jenny"—was the mother of Harry's son, Fred, and his daughters, Hattie, Louisa, and Nellie. Jenny's father, Kanapu, also lived with them on Kosrae. Two other Nauruan women, still in their early teens when they arrived with Harry, became the wives of Kosraeans. Tirime married Tolenoa, also known as "Captain," and Ingiter married Palik George. [Harry's descendants dropped the final "s" from "Skillings."]

FEATURES OF THE KOSRAEAN CHURCH IN 1875

Certain characteristics of the Church on Kosrae, now 23 years old, were firmly in place. The weekly Sunday morning worship service—at which all women and girls sat primly on the left side of a central aisle, and all men and boys sat erect and dignified on the right, all on woven mats—was followed by an hour of Sunday School for which all worshipers remained. On Sunday afternoon there was a prayer meeting. This Sunday afternoon service was a time for baptized church members only. They came together to ask questions and hear more from the missionary or pastor on the topic or text of that morning's sermon. Each of these three Sunday assemblies was never less than one hour in duration—each could, and often did, extend to two hours.

Other weekly gatherings of the young church included a prayer meeting on Wednesday afternoons for church members, and a prayer meeting and Bible study session on Friday afternoons for church women. When the Snows were in Lelu, the Friday service was always led by Lydia Snow.

The Lord's Supper was shared four times a year, on the first Sunday of each new quarter. For this service the four village congregations came together in Lelu. Baptisms and the reception of new members into the church took place at this service. On the afternoon of the Saturday before, members of the church would assemble for a "cleansing" service—a time of confession and self-preparation prior to partaking of the Holy Meal. Hymn singing had already become an important part of each of these services.

Another regular but unique service that had become a fixture of the church was the new-month service of public confession. It took place without fail on the morning of the first day of each new month—again, always in Lelu—unless the first day of the month was a Sunday, in which case the new-month service took place on Monday. At this service, individual members of the church, who had made a mistake or sinned since the last new-month service, were required to stand and tell the congregation what that sin or mistake was, and what he or she intended to do about it. The speaker could ask to rest—temporarily or permanently—from church membership, or seek to be forgiven. It was taken for granted that church members who did not attend this monthly service were thus asking to be dropped from membership. After a period of time, those who had been dismissed or released from the church, could return to a later new-month service and ask to be reinstated.

This was the discipline that Benjamin Snow insisted upon and to which he referred over and over in his letters, reports, and published articles. While on Kosrae, Mr. Snow made the judgments. After his departure this became the responsibility of the pastor and deacons, working together. This monthly service, with the processes involved in requiring confession and granting forgiveness, became a continuing part of the Church on Kosrae.

The no-work-on-Sunday rule was observed, not only by members of the church, but by most other Kosraeans as well. Saturday was now a day of preparation. Women made sure that the best clothing was washed and ready for members of the family to wear the next day. Men prepared the food that would be eaten between and after the Sunday services.

Another feature of Christian life had taken hold on Kosrae: It had become the custom for members of the church to gather in family units the first thing in the morning and the last thing in the evening for a period of Scripture reading, hymn singing, and prayer together. The heads of most families, even those outside official church membership, were rigorously faithful in leading this twice-daily ritual, with their wives and children gathered around them.

RETIREMENT AND DEATH OF BENJAMIN SNOW

Back on Ebon in December, Benjamin Snow, now 58 years old, suffered a minor stroke, which marked the beginning of the end of his great career. He made a noble effort to continue his work, though much of his old vigor was gone. During 1876, he managed to complete the Kosraean translations of the Old Testament book of Ruth and the New Testament book of Philippians, which—along with printed copies of Colossians, and First and Second Thessalonians—reached Kosrae on September 25 of that year in the care of Capt. Colcord aboard the *Morning Star III*.

On October 31, 1877, Benjamin and Lydia Snow reluctantly left Ebon aboard the *Morning Star III* and returned to the United States. In New England they were reunited with Caroline, now 21, and Fred, 19. It had been six years since the family had been together. Retiring with Lydia in Robbinston, Maine, Benjamin Snow died there May 1, 1880, at age 62.

Though celebrated as the man who planted the Church on Kosrae, Mr. Snow also had tremendous influence on the Church in the Marshall Islands, where he worked as the primary missionary from 1862 until 1877. Yet Kosrae remained close to his heart, as evidenced by his annual visits and his steady, conscientious efforts in translating the Scriptures into the Kosraean language. Throughout his active years—while on Kosrae and later from the Marshall Islands—Benjamin Snow led the Kosraean people in forming a mature, workable, Christian society while guiding them through one crisis after another. The chiefs and the common people alike responded to his strictness as well as to his love. These two attributes became the primary characteristics of their church.

Years later, Mr. Snow's daughter-in-law, Mary Hitchcock Snow, wrote, "He saw his work at Kosrae bear fruit in an intelligent and Christian population. And what great singers they were, Mr. Snow having taught them from the beginning to sing hymns."[30]

Several decades after Mr. Snow's death, a German doctor working in Micronesia, in commending Benjamin Snow's efforts to teach the Kosraean people, included this remark: "The Kosraeans are the healthiest of all of the island peoples."[31] How ironic—and what a tribute—after foreign diseases had caused so much suffering and death, for so many years, among Kosrae's people.

The American Board eulogized: "His influence lives after him in the changed lives and character of many immortal souls, who, but for him, might have lived and died without ever knowing the Savior's love."[32] ✙

Notes - Chapter 5

1. Hiram Bingham, Jr., *The Friend*, March, 1868
2. Benjamin Snow, American Board of Commissioners for Foreign Missions Annual Report, 1867
3. E. Theodora Crosby Bliss, "Micronesia: Fifty Years In The Island World," 1906, p. 24
4. Bingham, *The Friend*, March, 1868
5. Mary Dillingham Frear, from the diary of Martha Chamberlain, quoted in "Old Boards for New," Sixtieth Annual Report of the Woman's Board of Missions for the Pacific Islands, Honolulu, June 2, 1931
6. Ibid
7. B. Snow to S. C. Damon, Oct. 20, 1868, as quoted in *The Friend*, Jan. 6, 1869, p. 1
8. Samuel C. Damon, *The Friend*, Jan. 6, 1869, p. 5
9. Damon, *The Friend*, p. 1
10. J. F. Pogue, *The Friend*, July 1870
11. Bingham, pp. 77-78
12. *The Friend*, July 1871
13. B. Snow to S. Damon, Feb. 1872
14. *The Friend*, July 1872
15. B. Snow to S. Damon, Feb. 1872
16. James L. Lewis, "Kusaiean Acculturation 1824-1948," 1948, pp. 36-37
17. B. Snow to S. Damon, undated
18. Joel Whitney, *The Friend*, Feb. 1, 1875
19. C. F. Wood, quoted in Basil Lubbock's *Bully Hayes, South Seas Pirate*, 1931, p. 260
20. Albert F. Ellis, *Ocean Island and Nauru, Their Story*, 1935, p. 9
21. Ibid, p. 264
22. Ibid, p. 261
23. Francis X. Hezel, SJ, *Foreign Ships in Micronesia*, 1979, p. 108. (Lubbock's names for the two whaleships and their captains (*Europa*, Capt. Ed Fish, and *St. George*, Capt. Zachariah Grant, pp. 268-269) appear fictitious).
24. Lubbock, p. 282
25. Ibid, pp. 288-289
26. "Kusaie In The Nineteenth Century," undated, p. 14
27. Ibid, p. 15
28. Joanna C. Colcord, unpublished "Journal of Mrs. Andrew D. Colcord, Aboard the Missionary Brig *Morning Star* on a Voyage to Micronesia, 1875," New York
29. *The Friend*, March 1, 1876
30. Mary Hitchcock Snow, ed, "Incidents In The Life of Mrs. Benjamin G. Snow," Woman's Board of Missions for the Pacific Islands, Honolulu, 1931
31. Ibid
32. E. Theodora Crosby Bliss in Mary A. Marvin, "A History of Missionary Work in Micronesia, 1852-1910," p. 309

NUNAK YOHK KE CHAPTER 6
1877-1888

In pulan yac singoul sie inge oasr kapkapak wowo puspis yurin mwet Christian fin acn Kosrae. Missionary sasu elos use nunak sasu, oayapa mwet kol lun church Kosrae elos mutawauk in oakiya ouiyen mukuikui lalos sifacna, pwanang inkaiyen mwet Kosrae elos moulkin fasin sasu ac sisla fasin matu lalos.

Ke 1877 mwet kol in acn America ac Hawai'i su orek pwapa ke mukuikui lun missionary, elos akilen lah sufalla mwe mongo ac kof fin acn Marshall ac Gilbert. Pus pacl mwet missionary America su muta we elos mas, ac kutu selos misa. Pukanten mwe mongo ac yohk kof fin acn Kosrae, na pa elos sulela in mokle mission school lalos liki acn Marshall ac Gilbert nu Kosrae. Elos sap Dr. Edmund Pease, missionary se su orekma Ebon, in som nu Kosrae ke October 1878, ac suk sie acn ma lutlut luo inge ku in musa we. Tokosra Sru IV el usal Dr. Pease rauni acn Kosrae, ac eltal sulela sie ipin acn Walung pangpang Wot. Tokosra Sru el sang acn sac nu sin mission ke ku lal sifacna, ac wangin mani el eis kac. Tusruktu tuh oasr sramsram se srumunyuk inmasrlon mwet Kosrae lah Tokosra Sru el eis mani sin mission in sang molela acn Wot ac sruokya lal sifacna, ac wangin ma el sang nu sin mwet la acn ah. Sramsram se inge finne tia pwaye, oru itukla wal in tokosra sel Sru IV ke 1880. Kanku pa aolul, na el pa Tokosra Sru V.

Mwet Christian Kosrae elos insewowo lah ac oasr lutlut se lun mission fin acn Wot. Pastu Likiaksa ac mwet in church Kosrae tuh sang kuiyalos in sakunla acn se ma solla tuh lutlut se ma oan fin acn Marshall ah in oan we. Elos musaela kutu lohm fahsu tuh in nien muta lun tulik lutlut, oeyepa sie lohm lutlut ac lohm in mongo se. Lohm sin missionary fin acn Ebon ah tuh taltalla a utukla fin *Morning Star III* nu Kosrae in sifil musaiyukla fin acn Wot. Ouinge lutlut Marshall tuh tuyak fin acn Wot ke kapin 1879. Oasr tulik mukul Marshall 26, ac mwet luti lalos pa Edmund ac Harriet Pease, ac Joel ac Louisa Whitney. Mwet Kosrae elos kulang nu sin missionary sasu inge oayapa tulik lutlut Marshall. Elos tuh finsrak mu tulik natulos sifacnu ac mau ku in wi pac lutlut.

Pastu Likiaksa el pakiya pacl tuh mwet lun church in usla mongo ac kite missionary ac tulik lutlut fin acn Wot. Ke elos ac som nu we elos muta Insief. Oasr lohm se sel Tokosra Sru V ac sou lal, oayapa lohm se sel Pastu Likiaksa ac sou lal fin acn Insief. Ke Sunday nukewa mwet Kosrae su muta Insief elos ac som wi alu fin acn Wot.

Company German luo tuh oakiya orekma in kuka lalos fin acn Marshall, na in 1879 elos mutawauk in orekma fin acn Kosrae. Mr. Cole pa sifen company se pangpang Capelle, ac ma nukewa fahsr wo inmasrlon company se inge ac mwet Kosrae. Inen company se akluo pa Hersheim. Mwet orekma ke company sac elos tuh fuhlela mwet Kosrae in orek soemol, tusruk elos tia akkalemye nu sin mwet uh lah ac yokelik misa lalos elos fin tia sa in ela. Tukin malem singoul lupan misa lalos alukela ma elos ku in akfalye. Ke sripa se inge, Mr. Hersheim el sifacna tuku Marshall me in orekma kac. In pacl se inge acn Marshall oan inpoun mwet Germany, su pakiya tuh Mr. Hersheim in pah sifen government lalos we. El fahk mu ke sripen mwet uh tia ku in ela misa lalos ke molin khaki, na el ac eisla acn selos, su pa acn sin mwet suksuk wi pac molsron Lelu ac molsron Utwe, ac oayapa acn Pisin ac Yenyen. Pastu Likiaksa el tuh aol mwet suksuk lun acn Kosrae in simusla leta se nu sin mwet se ma fulat emeet sin mwet German in acn Pacific, su muta Samoa. Mwet fulat se inge el tuku nu Kosrae ke July 1881, in orek nununku ke fohsak se inge. El tuh tia lela Pastu Likiaksa in wi sramsram a el wotela mu Hersheim pa pwaye. Dr. Pease el tuh foloyak ac illa liki meeting sac ke sripen tiana suwohs oreyen nununku sac.

Lydia Snow el foloko nu Kosrae in September 1881 tuh elan sie mwet luti fin acn Wot. El yac 61 in pacl sac. Mwet Kosrae nukewa, oayapa tulik Marshall ma wi lutlut Wot, elos arulana engan in sifilpa liyal. Elos musaela lohm se sel ac arulana akfulatyal. Tia paht el masak ac enenu in folokla nu acn sel in acn Maine. Mrs. Snow el misa we in 1887.

Lillian Cathcart, su tuh welul Mrs. Snow tuku, pa mutan lolap se emeet ma orekma in missionary fin acn Kosrae. In pacl sac oasr tulik mukul Kosrae weang lutlut Wot.

In 1882 mission school fin acn Gilbert tuh mokuila liki Abaiang nu Wot. Mwet Christian Kosrae sifilpa kasru in sakunla acn lutlut se inge in oan we, ac oayapa musai lohm lutlut, lohm mongo, ac lohm sin tulik lutlut. Tulik mukul Gilbert 8 tuh wi lutlut se inge. Mwet luti lalos pa Alfred ac Lavinia Walkup.

Ke wik in pre in January 1884, Tokosru Sru V el sap in wanginla kutu ouiyen sunak ma elos pahla kac oemeet me. Kalmac pa elos tia enenu in orakrak ye mutun tokosra, ku mama ke elos sramsram nu sel, ku akfalye pacl in kitakat lalos nu sel. Tia enenu in orekmakinyuk kas in sunak nu sin tokosra, mwet suksuk ac oayapa in masrlon sou. Mwet Kosrae tuh arulana lut, tusruktu elos kaksakin oakwuk sasu lun Tokosra Sru V inge, mweyen pa inge ma fal nu ke moul lun mwet Christian. Mwet nukewa saok sin God ac elos nukewa oana sie ye mutal.

Ke February 1884 *Morning Star III* tuh musalla ke molsron Yela. Mwet Kosrae elos kasru in usak mwet nukewa fac nu finmes ah, a wangin mwet misa. *Morning Star IV* el steamer soko, ac el yohk liki *Morning Star* nukewa meet. El sun acn Kosrae in June 1885. Fred Snow, wen natul Mr. ac Mrs. Snow, el tuh sie sin mwet orekma fin oak ah. El yac 27 in pacl sa.

Mwet Spain elos mutawuak in leumi tuka nukewa ke Caroline Islands ke 1886. In yac sac pacna, lutlut se aktolu tuyak fin acn Wot. Tulensa L. Sigrah el sifen kamtu ma musai lohm twek se fin acn Yonrak. Tulik mutan Marshall 10, tulik mutan Gilbert 10, ac tulik mutan Kosrae 7 tuh muta we ac lutlut yorol Sarah Smith ac Mrs. Cole (katinmas kial Mr. Cole su tuh orekma ke Capelle Company fin acn Lelu).

– CHAPTER SIX –

THREE MISSION SCHOOLS AT WOT
1877-1888

CHANGE IN MISSION STRATEGY

With the departure of the pioneer missionaries, some fundamental changes began to take place, not only for the Micronesia Mission, but for the Church on Kosrae. Many of the original converts and leaders, who had first welcomed the Gospel, had passed from the scene. Fresh personnel within the mission organizations initiated a new emphasis that ironically increased the missionary presence on Kosrae while diminishing its control of the Church. At the same time, maturing members within the Kosraean Christian community began the unspoken process of making their Church Kosraean and their culture Christian.

The same voyage of the *Morning Star III* in 1877 that returned Benjamin and Lydia Snow to the United States brought Edmund M. and Harriet Sturtevant Pease to Ebon. During that year, Dr. Pease—a missionary trained in both medicine and theology—began seriously to question the advisability of American missionaries continuing to live on the low coral atolls and acting as evangelists. "Would it not be much better to preach the gospel through native lips than in our own brogue-tainted native?"[1] Why not transplant the existing mission schools from the "hot, unproductive Marshall and Gilbert Islands to rich, fertile Kusaie?"

Dr. Pease submitted this proposal to the Micronesia Mission. "We could obtain land from the king, and build houses for both missionaries and students. We could have a sort of family school, where all the pupils would be under our immediate supervision. The pupils would be away from the contaminating influence of their homes, and the interference of their chiefs. When the *Morning Star* makes her annual visit we could go around and locate our teachers and secure new scholars. If work grows, lady missionaries could come to Kusaie, and other missionaries would last longer in the healthier high island."[2]

His colleagues agreed, as did the directors of both the Boston- and Honolulu-based boards. A report of Dr. Pease's reconnaissance of Kosrae appeared in *The Friend*, in which he described the island and explained the new strategy.

Kusaie is a single island having a language of its own, different from that of any other island, high or low. Geographically it is classed as one of the Caroline Islands, but I don't see why it should have been considered one of a group at all, unless out of courtesy lest it feel lonesome. It doesn't look lonesome, every foot of it smiling with verdure from the sea to the mountain tops.

Vegetation is not content with covering the land only. It hangs from every cliff and crowds out into the sea. Acres of mangroves grow in the salt water on the surrounding reef. Vines and ferns and mosses and other parasitic plants cling to the trees and stumps, all struggling for room enough to live and be beautiful. I have seen trees so covered with various kinds of verdure that I had to study a little to make out which were the true leaves of the tree. The Kusaiens have a way of killing a tree here and there in order to have it dry for firewood, but the ferns and mosses that cover some of these make them even more beautiful than the living trees.

Kusaie will henceforth be considered the head station of the Marshall Islands, but if you want to have a clear idea of things, don't forget that it is not one of the Marshall Islands at all. The scholars who come here will be wholly separated from their own people and will but rarely have opportunity to communicate with them by letter. For the missionaries to make the tour of the Islands, as they do yearly on the Morning Star—it can be done from Kusaie as easily as from Ebon. It may take a week or two longer and may not, according to the wind. (I talk about the wind as if we always expected to depend upon that just as we have always done, but we are all hoping for steam to come to our aid in some form.)

There is both an advantage and disadvantage in being thus away from the people—advantage, in that our pupils cannot very well run away until the year is out—disadvantage, in having no way to get near the people and do them good DIRECTLY, except this handful of scholars.[3]

SNOWS ENDORSE NEW PLAN

In a letter to Dr. Pease from their home in Maine, Benjamin and Lydia Snow shared their warm approval of the new plan. From Benjamin: "It has long seemed to me that gem of the ocean, beautiful Kusaie, having been so long and so wonderfully preserved from foreign residents, must be designed for the Master's use, and I am rejoiced at the prospect of its being occupied for such a blessed purpose as that of training future laborers for Eastern Micronesia and the Gilbert Islands, no less than the Marshall Islands. True, it may be entered upon as an experiment, but there are some bright and very hopeful phases connected with it, at least sufficiently as to justify a beginning in that direction."[4]

Lydia, having penned her husband's words for him, wrote for herself: "Mr. Snow has…given his opinions so it will hardly be necessary for me to express mine, which are essentially the same—though I cannot allow this opportunity to pass without telling you how thankful I am that our dear Kusaie children may in that way be educated, a few of them at least, for mission work either on their own island or some other where their services may be called for. Unlike the low islanders, the Kusaiens are naturally adapt in the acquisition of the English....We were called away from Kusaie in '62, just at a time when they would have appreciated instruction. I wish you could know how highly they prized our instruction the few weeks we visited each year."[5]

KING SRU IV GIVES WOT TO MISSIONARIES

On October 12, 1878, Edmund and Harriet Pease arrived at Kosrae, commissioned by the American Board to locate an appropriate site for a mission school complex. He was 49 years old and she was 32.

King Sru IV toured the island with Dr. Pease and, together, they selected a large section of land in the northwest part of the island. The undeveloped property, known as Wot [pronounced wote, but spelled Mwot and pronounced mote—as in "oh"—by the missionaries], held many possibilities. On the lee side of Kosrae, Wot included a beach backed by a shallow swamp, with a steep mountain rising just beyond. Eventually the missionaries would build three schools on the sloping ridges that pointed toward the sea. The highest ridge—some 150 feet above sea level and commanding a magnificent view of the inland mountain range to the back and the lagoon, reef, and ocean to the front—would one day be the location of a school for girls. The first school to be built, however, would be for the Marshallese students on the west side of the property.

There were generous acres for planting, several springs, and a dashing mountain stream. The area was isolated from the more populated parts of the island, and Dr. Pease felt this was an added advantage. Though he found the Kosraeans "gentle and hospitable,"[6] he wanted the students away from any distracting influences of Kosrae's villages, far enough so that the island's residents could not upset the strict routine of school life.

The king gave Dr. Pease the entire Wot area of approximately 1,000 acres to use for the schools, exercising his power of eminent domain. The lease was officially signed in October 1879, but some of those in the original landowning families resented the king's action. There were rumors that instead of giving the land for mission use, King Sru had sold it to the missionaries and pocketed the money. This was not true, but the rumor continued to spread. In anger, a few in the landowners' families cut down food-bearing trees before leaving to settle in a neighboring district.

KING SRU IV DEPOSED AND SUCCEEDED
BY KING SRU V

As a result of King Sru IV's action, and the rumors and complaining that followed, his former popularity began to wane. In 1880 he was deposed and succeeded by the people's choice, the Kanku, as King Sru V. The new ruler was Sru IV's brother-in-law and also the son of King George's mother's brother.[7]

MARSHALL ISLANDS TRAINING SCHOOL

During 1879, Dr. Pease traveled through the Marshalls and gathered 26 students—all boys. They reached Kosrae aboard the *Morning Star III* on October 4, with several dismantled Ebon mission houses in the hold. Captain Isaiah Bray and his crew helped in the reconstruction of these buildings at the Wot site chosen for the Marshall Islands Training School, as did a large number of volunteers from among the Kosraean community.

When the mission ship arrived, those aboard found that the Kosraean Christians, led by Pastor Likiaksa, had already cleared and cleaned part of the Wot property and erected several island-style thatch buildings—including a dormitory, a classroom and a dining pavilion—in preparation for the establishment of the school. The anger of the people had been directed toward King Sru IV and what they perceived to be his arrogant and underhanded treatment of the landowning families—not toward the mission and the missionaries' desire for a place to build.

Indeed, members of the Church on Kosrae were excited and optimistic about the mission schools being located on their island. They missed the firm and loving direction of Benjamin Snow. In spite of a school plan that focused, not on the education of Kosraeans, but on that of low-islanders—they were hopeful that the missionary presence at Wot would benefit their Church and, more specifically, would be a boon to the Christian education of their own children and young people. The warmth of their welcome and the overwhelming generosity with which they supplied labor and materials to the arriving missionaries and their students was typically Kosraean—traits noticed and appreciated by all of the American, Hawaiian, and Japanese teachers who took their turns at Wot during the next 85 years.

Dr. Pease commented, "This is certainly the most lovely spot in all Micronesia, and our Kusaien neighbors, with their gentle ways and warm affection for us, supply an additional charm to this evergreen island, most justly styled: 'The Gem of the Pacific.'"[8]

Joel and Louisa Whitney, also arriving from Ebon, settled temporarily with their children in a house near the wharf being constructed at the edge of the Wot beach. While the Kosraeans of nearby Leap were helping to build a permanent home for them up at the site of the Peases' home and the Marshall Islands Training School buildings, an unusual high tide swept in, destroying all low-lying houses along the Walung coast, including the Whitneys' and those of their Leap neighbors.

Classes for the boys from the Marshall Islands were begun, with Edmund and Harriet Pease teaching English, Louisa Whitney teaching arithmetic, and Joel Whitney teaching Bible—though Mr. Whitney gave much of his time to continuing the translation of the Marshallese Bible. The Whitneys were proud that their son, Johnny, could soon speak in the Kosraean language as well as he did in Marshallese and English.

MRS. PEASE SHARES SOME OBSERVATIONS

On February 16, 1880, Harriet Pease described the school in her journal. "It was four months last Friday since the king gave us possession of this beautiful location. In the meantime, ten houses besides our own have been erected—the schoolhouse, five houses for the Marshall Island people, one for Mr. Whitney, a cookhouse for each family and a nice wood house for us... On Monday the schoolhouse was cleared of its accumulated rubbish, and on Tuesday we arranged the classes and made preparation to begin school in earnest the next day."

She continued on March 19: "A great wonder appeared in our midst this afternoon. The cow we have been expecting reached here in safety."[9]

The location of the Marshall Islands School, high on the cliff above Insief, was difficult to reach. Almost at once, Dr. Pease put the Marshallese boys to work building a suitable walkway between the school and the beach. His wife described the process: "It was hard work, involving much digging and lifting, for the cliff is quite steep; but now we have a good road from our front doorsteps to the beach, a distance of about forty rods. A house which had a foundation of stone has stood near where ours is now. These stones were disposed of by using them for the walk this side of the cliff. The church which the Kusaiens had commenced, and which we purchased, had a large number of stones roughly hewn from the coral reef for its foundation. The king came with seventy-five or a hundred men the other day, and moved the building near the foot of the hill for a boathouse and bathhouse."[10]

MRS. WHITNEY WRITES OF KOSRAE

Also in March 1880, Louisa Whitney wrote of their new home on the mountain side, and shared reflections of the current situation among the Kosraeans:

Our house is a compound of native and foreign building. We have windows from our house at Ebon, also four doors and a board floor for the sitting room and dining room. The rest of the floor is made of reeds tied together, covered with Ebon matting.

The sides of the house are thatched outside in addition to the roofs. Both together do not make a very tight wall, but it answers well enough. The roof jutting over on all sides keeps the rain from beating in. The Marshall Islands people thatch with pandanus leaf, but that is scarce here. The Kusaiens use instead the leaves of the vegetable ivory tree. The sides of our cookhouses are made of sticks of wild hibiscus peeled and split. This is the cheapest building material, as the island is overrun with it, and it is easy to cut. The reason we do not use it altogether is that it is soon eaten up by worms.

Our house, twenty-four by thirty-two feet, is divided into four rooms: sitting room, dining room, bed room, study and store room. We put the cookhouse, according to rule, on the west side supposing that would be the leeward. I have wondered how it would seem to be at the north pole and have every direction south. We have not got there quite, but we do seem to be in a spot where all sides are to the windward. The wind comes up the valley and at the north and west sides of the house more than the others, but often breaks over the hills and comes down in gusts, from the east and south. Our house really has no leeward.

It would be difficult to find a more fertile soil anywhere than that of this island. It rains more or less almost every day, though we had quite a dry spell in February.

The Kusaiens number about four hundred. They are a people noted for kindness, hospitality and honesty. We are feeling very sorry for them now on account of the way they have been treated by traders. There have been two traders on the island for over a year, belonging to the rival firms A. Capelle & Co., and Hersheim & Co., both headquartered in the Marshalls. Mr. Cole, the trader belonging to the former is, so far as we know, a respectable moral man. His wife is a white lady. Of the other the less said the better. They have both alike done the people wrong in letting them run into debt. The people were not blameless in this for they had been warned against debt by their missionaries.

Mr. Hersheim came here a few weeks ago, having lately been appointed German Consul of these islands. He took away the [Hersheim] trader to whom the people were indebted several hundred dollars, and imposed upon them a fine of more than the whole amount of the debt. The chiefs say they were afraid of him because he was a [German] consul. He drew up a paper which the king and chiefs were foolish enough to sign without knowing what was in it. They thus promised to pay 133,000 lbs of copra at the end of ten months. In case of failure to do so, he is to take possession of a part of the island. The land designated includes the homes of the chiefs, also the two best harbors (Weather and Lee) and the Mission premises at Lelu.

The fine imposed was for breaking a verbal agreement obtained under false pretenses. Copra sells here for one and a half cents per pound. The chiefs have appealed to the Consul General at Samoa for help. The island is not capable of producing the required number of coconuts in the time. The chiefs have been unwilling to sell any of their land to foreigners ever since an insurrection made by foreigners many years ago.[11]

AN UNFAIR INVESTIGATION

The Kosraeans somehow managed to produce the amount of copra demanded by Mr. Hersheim, but they could not pay for the trade goods, the price of which had been added to the fine. Pastor Likiaksa did his best to protest on behalf of his people. He penned a letter which the chiefs signed and sent to it to Samoa, the center of German operations in the Pacific. Though members of the German government had no official authority over Kosrae at this time, they were responsible for the actions of their countrymen who were traders throughout the area.

On July 2, 1881 Imperial Consul General Zempf arrived in Lelu, convening an investigation aboard his ship, the *Habieht*. He refused to hear the testimony of Pastor Likiaksa, who, in the estimation of the missionaries, was the only Kosraean who could speak English well enough to know what was going on—and English was the language used for the investigation. Incredibly, Consul General Zempf considered Pastor Likiaksa prejudiced, while condoning the obvious conflict of interest in Mr. Hersheim's duel role as consul and trader.

Dr. Pease, who was also present, left the ship in disgust when he saw how things were proceeding. Though the king and the chiefs had indeed signed the "mortgage," the missionaries were convinced that the nature of the agreement they were signing—particularly the preposterous rate of interest required—had never been sufficiently explained to them.[12]

WORSHIPING TOGETHER

That same month Harriet Pease wrote in her journal of the Marshall Islands School at Wot:

Our new airy church-schoolhouse combination was dedicated yesterday, the 17th. The Kusaien church was here in a body to partake of the sacrament with us. The frescoing would doubtless be considered rude, being only the native thatch; but with a clean floor for the people to sit on, and a bouquet of roses on the organ, we worshiped with thankful hearts, having no strings of conscience with regard to Romans 13:8.

It is twenty years since Mr. and Mrs. Snow left their flock here to go to Ebon; and so, of course, the young men and women of today have grown up with only the most elementary instruction. They are eager to learn, and we hope our coming will not be in vain, though we work directly for the Marshall Islanders.

The queen has been quite a regular attendant at school and our weekly woman's prayer meeting since May, and as she understands the Marshall Island language well, she can and does impart what instruction she gets to her own people. Pray that the remnant of the most amiable people in all the Pacific may be saved.[13]

FIRST SCHOOL YEAR CONCLUDES

August 5 was the closing day of the first school year at Wot. For the final recitations and ceremony the Marshallese boys all wore white shirts and pants. The Kosraean boys in the student body were dressed in white shirts and blue pants.

Mrs. Pease reported:

They all had on necklaces of a bright scarlet flower which grows abundantly here. The girls had sack-dresses alike and orange-colored flowers, with a bunch in each earlobe in place of earrings. It was their own idea and they all looked very prettily. The Ebonites quite outsung themselves. I am sure you would have enjoyed hearing the Kusaiens sing "Saviour, More Than Life to Me," and "There were Ninety and Nine." They have sweet, plaintive voices.

An event occurred after the ceremonies which quite astonished us. The Kusaien scholars all went down to their houses on the beach, and we thought nothing of it, as that is what they generally do. In a little while [Pastor] Likiaksa came in and remarked that some presents were coming for us. We looked out to see the men and boys coming in procession with baskets of cooked food; a whole pig dressed, ready to cut up, and some shells. Then followed the women and girls with tol [wide belts]—the native dress of both men and women in former times. They are made of banana-fiber, variously colored, and are woven on miniature looms at which the women sit on the floor. Some of these are quite pretty. Such an exhibition of gratitude was new, and quite overwhelming.[14]

MRS. SNOW RETURNS TO KOSRAE

Joel and Louisa Whitney, with their three children, returned to the United States the end of September 1881. The *Morning Star III* that took them away had arrived on September 24 with two American women eager to assist in the Marshallese school at Wot. One of them, Lillian Cathcart, was the first single woman to serve as a missionary on Kosrae.

Accompanying Miss Cathcart was Benjamin Snow's widow, Lydia, now 61 years old, returning to the island she and her husband had first made their home almost 30 years earlier. It was 16 months since her husband's death, and six years since she and Mr. Snow had last visited Kosrae. Mrs. Pease noted in her journal, "The Kusaiens would like to carry her off bodily; and the Marshall Islanders are so glad that one of them said on Sunday that he trembled all day, he was so full of joy."[15] Mrs. Snow's Kosraean and Marshallese "children" built a cottage for her near the school. From all over the island her Kosraean friends beat a path to her door, anxious to see her face and to hear her voice once more.

But the strain of the long trip and the demands of her life at Wot took their toll. On December 22, Lillian Cathcart wrote to friends in Hawai'i, "It is six months tomorrow since we sailed from your beautiful tropical city. I know you will all be very much grieved, though I presume not so very much surprised, to learn how very much our dear Mrs. Snow has failed since we left Honolulu. It has been a constant giving out in every respect. It would be almost impossible to give you any idea of how weak she is."[16]

Her failing health forced Mrs. Snow to leave Kosrae the next year and return to the United States, where she was cared for by her daughter, Caroline, who never married. Lydia Snow died in Maine five years later, in 1887, at age 67.

LILLIAN CATHCART DESCRIBES WOT SCHOOL

Miss Cathcart described the situation at Wot in an article for *The Friend*. "Imagine," she suggested,

...a school building upon a small island in mid-ocean, situated upon a grassy plateau, some sixty feet above sea level. Its walls are of poles about the size of one's wrist; the roof is of thatch; the floor, doors and windows imported. It is supplied with wall maps and globe. The view—from the one side lies the mighty deep, with its ever restless waves dashing upon the reef, breaking in beautiful foamy spray with constant music. Upon the other, rise the mountains, thickly wooded to their summits. In a cluster surrounding the school stand two neat board houses for the missionaries and eight or ten native houses for the pupils.

Seated within that school building, upon benches or the floor, are thirty or more children of the tropics. Among them are three or four babies, who lie upon their mats and sleep, cry or play, as suits their fancy. No more eager and persistent in the acquisition of knowledge are any of the pupils in the homeland—and no less of a pleasure do we find it to assist them.[17]

The pupils here are a very pleasant set of boys and are so neat, with sufficient clothing which they keep scrupulously clean, hair shingled. They are polite in every respect.

Mrs. Pease is one of the most cheerful, helpful and sympathetic persons I ever met. He is not so demonstrative but is, I think, no less earnest and kind, and a man of deep religious experience. They are both decidedly in favor of a girls' school, but there is not a strong enough teaching force here now to do it.[18]

GILBERT ISLANDS TRAINING SCHOOL MOVES TO KOSRAE

In the 1882 American Board yearbook it was noted:

Because of the deaths among American personnel of the Gilbert Islands mission it is no longer thought wise to station our missionaries on islets where the land, if that can be called land which will not grow civilized fruits and vegetables, is so nearly on a level with the ocean that if a wave ten feet high should suddenly sweep over the reefs, the island would be four feet under water. The Hawaiian missionaries do not suffer so much as Americans and will continue their work.

The training school is removed to Kusaie, a big and healthy island, where the scholars from the Gilberts can be well provided for. Our missionaries will be concentrated on Kusaie. Opportunity will be given by the visits of the mission vessel for a more careful oversight of the churches and for the work of the native laborers on the Gilbert Islands. Instructions were sent out by the Morning Star III *for removal of school buildings as are worth removing from Apaiang to Kusaie and the reestablishment of the Training School there.*[19]

It had been a sad season for the American Board's personnel in the Gilbert Islands. Missionary Horace Taylor lost his 21-year-old wife, Julia, to typhoid fever just six weeks after they arrived at Apaiang in 1874. In 1881, Mr. Taylor lost his second wife at Apaiang—Julia's sister, Jennie—of complications of childbirth. He was forced to relinquish his work at the Gilbert Islands school in 1882, to take his three children back to the United States.[20]

Dejected, apprehensive, and lonely, the Taylors' colleagues, Alfred and Margaret Lavinia Walkup, remained at Apaiang, but were instructed by the American Board to move with the school to Kosrae as soon as transportation was available.

As they had done three years earlier with buildings from the Marshall Islands mission at Ebon, Capt. Isaiah Bray and his crew loaded the dismantled mission houses and school from Apaiang on board the *Morning Star III*. The Rev. Mr. Alfred Walkup, a former boxer, with his wife and small son, John, were also aboard the *Star* when it reached Kosrae on August 13, 1882. With the eight Gilbertese boys who accompanied them, the Walkups would open the second planned school at Wot.

A location was chosen above and to the east of the beach that fronted the

Wot property—opposite the Marshall Islands school, which was above and to the west of the beach. The site was neatly cleared and prepared by a group of Kosraean church men, ready when the *Morning Star* arrived. The Walkup and Taylor houses from Apaiang were reassembled, but now they were placed one on top of the other to make a single two-story dwelling. A steep thatch roof covered the structure, with eaves that extended more than eight feet from the walls on all four sides, the outside edges supported by posts. Thus a large, covered veranda encircled the house. The Gilbert Islands' school building was erected nearby, and classes were begun.

TWO BOARDING SCHOOLS NOW OPERATING AT WOT

Just as when the schools were located on the low islands, attention was given to methods of conducting missionary work as well as to academic subjects and instruction in Bible. "The principal object of these schools is fitting young men for teaching and preaching the Gospel. Second, all pupils as they enter the schools shall distinctly understand that they come to study for the highest and noblest work in which any man can engage; namely, the preaching of the Gospel of God our Savior, and for no other purpose."[21] Activities also included other types of learning: Every pupil had to clean, cook, and wash, and spend at least an hour a day in farm and garden work.

The schools produced enough food for their own use, while also teaching improved farming methods and impressing upon the minds of the Marshallese and Gilbertese students the importance of a farm in an island economy. New crops were tried, and new animals and fowl introduced. A better variety of banana, the Brazilian, was brought from Hawai'i, as well as a larger and better coconut variety from Samoa. Papayas, mangoes, and other fruits, too, arrived in this way, plus new varieties of taro, sugarcane, and sweet potato.

Concerning both of the new schools, Edmund Pease reported, "The scholars are enthusiastic and diligent, always willing to work, and as far as we can judge, they have been steadily growing in their Christian life. The great embarrassment which the schools are likely to encounter is the impossibility of accommodating all who wish to come."[22]

Alfred Walkup reported in 1883 that his students made more progress at Kosrae in five weeks than they did at the Apaiang school during an entire year. "The climate, food, and competition help both intellectually and spiritually. There is more thoughtfulness and seriousness, more of higher resolves than I ever knew at Apaiang."[23]

The Peases and Lillian Cathcart spoke Marshallese with their students, and the Walkups used Gilbertese with theirs, but none of the five could easily converse in Kosraean. Also the distant location of the schools in relation to the more populated areas of Kosrae, and the preoccupation of the missionaries with their low-island charges—beyond Dr. Pease's occasional medical forays—left little opportunity to build ties between the Kosraean Church and the Wot Mission Schools. However the Kosraeans, under the leadership of Pastor Likiaksa, continued their hospitable ways toward the students and their missionary teachers—and were very grateful as, year by year, Kosraean boys in ever-increasing numbers were welcomed into the Marshallese school as day students.

IMPORTANCE OF THE *MORNING STAR*

It was during this period that the value of the missionary vessel became conspicuously clear. The *Morning Star III* was kept busy transporting personnel, supplies, and mail between Hawai'i and Micronesia and carrying students and the missionary teachers who recruited them between the various islands of the Marshall and Gilbert groups and Kosrae.

The *Star* was also called upon for humanitarian purposes when the need arose. In August 1883, the schooner *Staghound* was wrecked at Kosrae, stranding the surviving officers and crew members. Three months later the *Morning Star III* transported them to Pohnpei, where other transportation could be arranged.

At about this same time, the Japanese corvette *Ryujo*—with the entire 10th class of the Japanese Naval Academy aboard—stopped briefly at Kosrae during a cruise through the islands. This was the first Japanese warship to enter Micronesian waters.[24]

KING SRU V ABOLISHES SUNAK

The popularity of King Sru V had been declining, but when—at the urging of Dr. Pease and others of the missionaries—he got up in the Lelu church on January 11, 1884, and declared that he was abolishing "sunak," he won the gratitude of his people. Sunak was the system of strict etiquette that governed individual speech and behavior with reference to the king, the queen, various other members of the royal family, the chiefs, and their families—and even between sisters and brothers. This announcement astonished and delighted the Kosraeans. Once they had grasped the significance of the king's decree, they all, chiefs included, hurried to shake his hand—something they could never do before—and express their joy and gratitude.[25]

Mrs. Walkup wrote to her parents:

Most of the Kusaiens spent the Week of Prayer at Lelu on the other side of the island. They rejoice in the abolishment of "Sunak." We don't yet know all this means and probably never will. The king and queen and five different degrees of chiefs require homage from the people. The women must not stand in the presence of the queen, but crawl or hitch along till they get out of the house. They must sit in a certain position before their brothers—must not sit on his mat or eat food cooked by him. There are many foolish reasons why they shall not marry certain persons.

Many years have the missionaries been trying to get them to give up these customs, but never before would a king abolish it... Some of them attend Dr. Pease's school but we only see them when they come to bring us food. They are always dressed when they come near the mission, but at work they dress in native style, wearing the tol—a long sash woven from banana fiber on simple looms.

King and Queen are very kind and have been Christians for some years, though she has been put out of the church at times for lying. She likes to rule, but she wants to be on the right side of the missionaries and not do what will displease them. Some of the Kusaiens think she does not like the abolishment of "Sunak"![26]

Lillian Cathcart also thought the abolishment of sunak was a step forward for Kosrae. She wrote in her journal, "It is not only a relief, but a sign of progress toward social equality, to have the king issue this proclamation... From now on, no more crouching nor cringing."[27]

WRECK OF THE *MORNING STAR III*

On February 22, 1884—"having nearly finished her work in all the groups"—the *Morning Star III* was wrecked at the mouth of Kosrae's westside Yela Harbor, within sight of the mission schools at Wot, 15 years after the *Morning Star II* had sunk near the mouth of Lelu Harbor on the east side of the island.

The ship was under the temporary command of Capt. George F. Garland in the absence of Capt. Isaiah Bray, with whom he had worked as first mate aboard the *Morning Star II*. The trip to that point had been successful. Upon arriving at Kosrae, the *Star* turned in toward the harbor, but immediately met trouble: A very heavy swell and strong wind would not permit a normal entry.

Capt. Garland directed his sailors to attach a line to the first of the four stationary buoys that were used to help warp a vessel in or out of the channel. The *Star* was moving along slowly against wind and current toward the inner harbor as the captain tried to maneuver it into the pocket in the reef that formed a basin just big enough to hold the little brig. But suddenly the crew felt the line give, and the ship began to move toward the reef. The anchor was no longer holding and, in spite of all they could do, a heavy sea broke over the stern and the ship was tossed upon the reef and capsized. It was all over within five minutes. Passengers and crew were saved without injury: Most of the freight and some parts of the ship were salvaged; but the vessel itself had to be abandoned as a total loss.[28]

As they had done in 1869, the people of Kosrae helped rescue the survivors—including Pohnpei missionaries Annette Palmer, Frank and Carrie Rand, and their small daughter, who were housed by Wot missionaries while they waited for another ship. Six weeks went by and no ship appeared, so there was no way to send word to the outside world about the wreck.

Finally on April 17, the captain, Mr. Rand, and the second mate, Henry Worth, with one sailor, Tara, fitted up the ship's long boat with a sail and a stock of food and water for two months and set out for Pohnpei, 365 miles to the northwest. Astonishingly, Capt. Garland and his three companions made the hazardous journey in their small, open boat in nine days. A commercial vessel took the captain to Hong Kong where he was able to send a cable to the Boston headquarters of the mission. From Hong Kong, he traveled to San Francisco, then back to Hawaiʻi, finally arriving in Honolulu on August 8 to report on the loss of *Morning Star III* more than five months before.

The August issue of *The Friend* reported the wreck of the *Star* with no lives lost, concluding the article, "The vessel has wisely been kept fully insured. During the thirteen years of voyaging these dangerous waters, the vessel has many times been in peril, but by a kind providence has hitherto escaped without serious harm or loss."[29]

STEAM-POWERED *MORNING STAR*

Prior to having any knowledge of the wreck, but because they knew the vessel was old and would soon have to be replaced, the American Board in Boston had ordered a new ship for the Micronesia Mission. Actually the *Morning Star IV* was nearing completion when the wreck occurred and was sent on its way before the end of the year. "Thus they could say, 'Scarcely had one *Star* been quenched in the sea before another rose to carry on!'"[30]

The *Morning Star IV* was much larger than the previous vessel, having about four times the capacity of the one lost in February. It also had a steam auxiliary power unit that could be used to supplement sail power. The new *Star*—a packet of 450 tons—cost $45,000, almost twice as much as the others. It would take more to operate, but it would provide more service, and thus seemed worth the investment. Again, Congregational Sunday School children in America gave the money in the form of "shares" in the "business enterprise" of carrying God's Word to the people of Micronesia.

JUGGLING MISSIONARY PERSONNEL

To fill the gap between the wreck of the *Morning Star III* and the sailing of the *Morning Star IV*, a small schooner, the *Jennie Walker*, was chartered in Honolulu for a trip to Micronesia. Among other passengers, it carried in its cramped quarters Robert and Mary Logan and their daughter Beulah, returning to Chuuk [known then as "Ruk," and later as "Truk"]. It reached Kosrae on August 22, 1884. The arrival of the schooner found Edmund and Harriet Pease more than ready to leave on furlough, tired and worn out by the heavy responsibilities of the previous seven years. But there was deep concern at Wot. Dr. and Mrs. Pease had expected new missionaries aboard the *Star* to take their place in the Marshall Islands school. None had arrived. And the Walkups were alone at the Gilbert Islands Training School, having yet to welcome any replacement for Horace Taylor, who had been with them in the school at Apaiang.

The immediate problem was solved when Annette Palmer, headed for Pohnpei, agreed to remain temporarily to help Lillian Cathcart with the Marshallese school, where she had been assisting since the wreck of the *Morning Star III* six months earlier—though that arrangement would leave the women alone with the Marshallese. The two Wot schools were distinct and some distance separated them, but the two single teachers could request help from the Walkups if they needed it.

The *Jennie Walker* continued its trip west, taking Mrs. Rand and her daughter, who had been stranded on Kosrae since the wreck of the *Star*, to Pohnpei, and returning the Logan family to Chuuk. After servicing those mission outposts, the schooner returned to Kosrae in early November, where the Pease family boarded for the trip east to Hawai'i. From Honolulu, they continued to the United States. There, Dr. Pease, who had completed translation of the Marshallese New Testament, guided it through the printing process while he was on furlough.

The day after the Pease family left for the United States, Lillian Cathcart penned in her journal:

We are happy to occupy Dr. Pease's house this year and the cottages will remain empty. And this is how we are left: Miss Palmer is to take charge of the housekeeping; Kefwas is to remain to help with the cooking, cleaning and general housework; Na is to wash and iron; while Kenye is to come and sweep on Saturdays. Mrs. Pease has trained all three Kusaiens for the past three years and we feel that we are much favored in having such good help.

They are all among our best day scholars and use English very well, so Miss Palmer can talk with them without an interpreter–and they will be able to help her in that respect when she is trading with other Kusaiens, for she is also going to buy our native food.

Miss Palmer will teach most of the classes in English. I shall teach in Marshallese with the help of some of the best scholars who will teach some classes. Out of school I shall have charge of family worship with the school, Sabbath school, etc. The most advanced scholars will take turns preaching on Sabbath. [There were 21 Kosraean students in the Marshall Islands School during 1884.][31]

During the first seven days of January 1885, Miss Cathcart, Miss Palmer, and the Marshallese; the Walkups and the Gilbertese; and Pastor Likiaksa and the Kosraeans united for daily observances of the Week of Prayer.

A MISSIONARY SON RETURNS

The *Morning Star IV*, using its steam-powered engine to enter Lelu Harbor, arrived at Kosrae June 12, 1885. This *Star* was three-masted, with an iron smokestack as tall as the masts. Depending on calms and headwinds, the trip from Honolulu under sail usually required from 16 to 62 days. It took only 10 days for the new vessel to cover the distance from Hawai'i to Kosrae. The finely carved figurehead of the new mission ship intrigued the Kosraeans—a woman in a flowing white dress with high-button shoes, holding an open Bible in her hands.

At the railing of the ship stood a 27-year-old man who had signed on in Boston as chief engineer. It was Fred Snow. His feelings upon returning to the island of his birth can only be imagined. Certainly he thought of his parents—his father Benjamin, now deceased, and his mother, Lydia, being cared for in her home in Robbinston, Maine, by his sister. He remembered well his carefree childhood—much of it spent at Pisin—and began searching the faces of those Kosraeans who, standing on the old stone wharf, returned his gaze. How poignant was his reunion with Pastor Likiaksa—now in his mid-40s—who had been an older brother to him in the Dove Island family home.

But the young man could not spend much time visiting and reminiscing. Mail and provisions had to be off-loaded, and the ship's supplies of firewood, fresh food, and water replenished. The missionaries at other stations were waiting to be transported back to the annual meeting of the Micronesia Mission, which would be held this year at Kosrae. With its efficient crew, the *Morning Star IV* went on with the regular tour, doing all the necessary work in half the time required by former vessels. Its speed made it possible to make several trips from Honolulu each year, if needed.

SPAIN TAKES CONTROL OF CAROLINE ISLANDS

At the close of 1885, political trouble flared in Micronesia. There was a controversy between Germany and Spain over which country should control these "pinheads of creation," as one missionary called the islands.[32] Should it be Germany, because there were some German businessmen operating among them? Or should it be Spain, because of its interest in the nearby Philippines?

Officials of the American Board commented editorially: "It is difficult to imagine under what pretext Spain can claim any authority over these islands. For over thirty years the American Board has had missionaries in the Caroline, Gilbert and Marshall Islands. While a few German traders have had business houses on the Marshalls, there has been no attempt on the part of any European power to assert sovereign rights in any of these three groups. If it were the policy of the United States to annex territory in the Pacific, these islands would belong to our government on the grounds of the benefits conferred upon them by our citizens."[33]

Germany sent warships to raise the German flag on a number of the islands within the Caroline group. This action was taken to counteract Spanish attempts to regulate activities of German trading firms in the area. The Marshall Islands had already been annexed to the German Empire; administration of the islands was turned over to the Jaluit Gesellschaft, formed by the merger of several German trading companies.

Spain did not protest the seizure of the Marshalls, but bitterly opposed Germany's claim on the Carolines. The matter was submitted to Pope Leo XIII in Rome for arbitration. He declared in favor of Spain by right of discovery 250 years earlier, but Germany remained to administer the Marshall Islands and was given freedom of trade within the Spanish territory.

Spanish efforts to establish a government proceeded at a moderate pace. In 1886, a Spanish warship visited the eastern Carolines. Anchoring in Lelu Harbor during the last week of July, the captain sent for King Sru V, who was then living near the Wot mission schools. The king, accompanied by Alfred Walkup, hurried to Lelu, where the Spanish commander informed him that they had come to take possession of Kosrae in the name of Spain. He required King Sru V to sign a paper acknowledging Queen Doña Maria Christina as ruler of Kosrae! The next day, Kosraeans watched dumbfounded as the Spanish flag was unfurled above the king's dock in Lelu. The commander went around Kosrae in a steam launch, stopping at Wot for lunch with the missionaries. The Kosraeans feared that the island would soon be overrun with foreigners who, until this time, had been prevented from moving onto the island by King Salik II's decree of 1874.

Actually, Spanish rule was little noticed on Kosrae. Neighboring Pohnpei, where the Spanish established their headquarters, did not escape so easily. From the beginning of the Spanish occupation, missionaries on that island were harassed by pro-Catholic officials and the priests who had accompanied them. The missionaries on Kosrae, heartsick and frightened about happenings on Pohnpei, expected that they, too, would suffer this fate. But they were never molested.

MISSIONARY IMPRESSIONS

In 1886 one of the missionaries described the Kosraeans, "They are a quiet, gracious and friendly folk, so polite that they will never break your heart with a bad answer, but, regardless of the truth, will say what they think will best please you."[34]

MORE MISSIONARY WOMEN ARRIVE

When the *Morning Star IV* returned to Kosrae on September 1, 1886, it brought Edmund and Harriet Pease back, refreshed from their furlough. Three more young American women also arrived. Miss E. Theodora Crosby, age 22, was to help in the Marshall Islands Training School, while Miss Sarah L. Smith, 21, and Miss Lydia E. Hemmingway, 48, were to establish a new boarding school for girls. Unfortunately, Miss Hemmingway returned to the United States within a few months due to illness. Miss Palmer returned to her work with the girls' mission school on Pohnpei.

Theodora Crosby wrote of her arrival:

"Land Ho! Kusaie!" Such were the welcome words which greeted us at sunset one evening twenty-eight days out from Honolulu; twenty-eight days of water and sky, and sea birds, and bilge water, and sea food, and seasickness; twenty-eight days under a burning tropic sun, the glare on the water almost blistering our faces if we stayed on deck, whiling away the time by reading, playing on the organ, and sleeping, and making large plans, and sighing for terra firma.

We go to our staterooms at an early hour, sure that we shall not sleep a wink; whereupon I fall asleep at once, and awake at two o'clock in the morning to find my room flooded with moonlight, and a dark, shadowy something looming up outside my window. I scramble out of my berth and to the sofa, and there, within a mile of us, lies beautiful Kusaie, its hills rising like substantial ghosts in the moonlight; and here and there along the reef lights are moving—some folks are out fishing. You may be sure there is little sleep for me during the remaining hours of the night; it is hard for me to realize that the Kusaie of my waking and sleeping dreams is before me. "And so He bringeth them unto their desired haven" [Psalm 107:30 KJV].[35]

Sarah Smith wrote her family:

Soon after dinner we were called to see the cloud-obscured outline of the island dimly rising against the sky in the west. We watched as the suggestion of land took form and color. After seeing no land but the little low strips of coral for so long, it was a marvel to us—this high, irregular mass rising against the sky—and as we drew nearer, we could sympathize with Jeremiah in his enraptured exclamation, "The New Jerusalem!"

From end to end, about seven miles, the hills, deeply serrated, rise abruptly, and are clothed from base to summit with a dense green garment of tropical vegetation. We were landed on a strip of coral beach next to a group of black, basaltic rocks, where a great tree throws its spreading branches, with dense green foliage, far over the water at high tide.

A number of Kusaiens were there to greet us, and Mr. and Mrs. Walkup came along the beach to invite us to breakfast at their house. We first went up the steep hillside by a long, winding path set with irregular steps of white coral, to Dr. Pease's house. After taking a peep at the house, we followed a winding path against the side of the cliff to Mr. Walkup's.[36]

Of her first Sunday on Kosrae, Miss Smith wrote:

This morning Likiaksa, the Kusaien pastor, came with some of his people to service with us. Dr. Pease decided to have it in the sitting room—a large room opening upon the veranda by two doors and four windows. The Doctor rang the church bell at half past nine. This bell is one that was saved from the wreck of the Morning Star III, *and hangs in a tree a few feet in front of the house, with a cord running to the piazza. The Kusaiens came, filing up the path all in Sunday cleanness, and seated themselves upon the matted floor, while the king and queen* [Sru V and Sepe Awe] *looked dignified and majestic in chairs. We sat facing them on the opposite side of the room. Including our scholars, there were about forty present...*

In the afternoon we held a prayer meeting, conducted by Mr. Walkup. Several of our number spoke and prayed. Mrs. Walkup told, with considerable emotion, of discouragements and doubts as they looked, week after week, for the Star, *and of the renewed lesson of trust and hope that it had brought in the return of Dr. Pease and his family, and in the promise of a school for girls. Then Dr. Pease spoke of their joy in returning, and told of the way in which the girls' school had been secured, speaking warmly of the growth of woman's work in America.*[37]

That voyage of the *Star* brought two more cows for Dr. Pease, and the first coffee, avocado, pomegranate, and a new and sweeter orange, to be planted on Kosrae. There was also a variety of flowering plants—including roses, plumeria, bougainvillea, and pink Mexican creepers—plus a large shipment of lumber from Honolulu to be used in building the girls' school.

TRAINING SCHOOL FOR GIRLS

At recent meetings of the Micronesia Mission, the missionaries had discussed the need to train young island women in addition to the young men. Alfred Sturges had made the comment, "It is one of the strange things about our people that they do not pair off so as to have man and wife equal in age, sense, good looks, or anything else!"[38] The missionaries were anxious that their isolated male students find appropriate, similarly trained mates when the time came for them to return to their home areas.

In 1881 Edmund Pease had written to the American Board earnestly calling for a school for island girls:

There is an eligible site on the hill just inland from our Marshallese school, in full view and about five minutes walk therefrom. We desperately need an energetic married couple, or better, two single ladies.

I need not urge the necessity of providing wives for our graduates who are to be the pastors and teachers of the islands. No missionary work will ever abide unless it is rooted in Christian homes. Such homes will never be found until models are provided in the families of the spiritual guides. If the wife is an ignorant heathen, the home is impossible. Who will give first gifts for buildings—who will give themselves lovingly to the work?[39]

Now, with the arrival of the building materials, Dr. Pease would see the fulfillment of this dream. During 1886 Kosraean day students had been teaching two large, successful schools for children in Lelu and Malem. The students of these schools were asked to help transport the lumber up the hill, with a large contingent of Kosraean men and the Marshallese and Gilbertese boys assisting, under the direction of chief carpenter T. L. Sigrah,[40] formerly King Sru IV. Theodora Crosby described this process in an article published in Life and Light for Women, entitled "Thank Offerings in Micronesia."

For about two weeks the children and adults were there, toiling up the steep hillside with their heavy burdens—no light task in the heat and glare of the tropical sun. But I wish you could have seen their bright and happy faces! I wish you might have heard them sing as they worked! Theirs was a joyful service, because they offered willingly of their services—all that they had to offer—unto the Lord, as willingly and as joyfully as of old the people brought their offerings for the building of Solomon's Temple. These people are willing to do when they are given the opportunity. Their offerings come from hearts the more full of thankfulness because they have had so little in their lives for which to be grateful. At about this time, when the men were helping in this way, we attended the closing exercises of the two Kusaien schools on the island [in Lelu and in Malem]. After the services, Mrs. Pease took the opportunity to suggest that the women of the island do their share of the good work *by making tols—the native dress—to be sent to America and sold for the benefit of their own church. When she had finished speaking, she asked all who thought it a good thing to do to raise their hands. Much to our amusement every man in the room raised his hand; they thoroughly approved of the women doing their share. That the women also had willing hearts was proved by the result, a large number of tols being made and sent to us.*

That their expressions of thankfulness for their churches and schools, and of love and gratitude to those who are trying to help them, are sincere, is proved by their daily lives; by their striving to help the work in every way they can. They have little of this world's goods, but in their poverty they bring to us food for ourselves and for our school—they bring offerings of shells, mats, fans. "Such as they have" they gladly and prayerfully give unto the Lord.[41]

Dr. Pease reported the resulting school, which Tulensa L. Sigrah and his Kosraean crew constructed, "well built, commodious, and satisfactory in all respects." It stood on the highest and most desirable part of the Wot property, known as Yonrak [YON, as in "yawn"-rock].

THREE SCHOOLS AT WOT

By 1887 three mission schools were in full and active operation on Kosrae. There were 10 Marshallese, 10 Gilbertese and seven Kosraean girls enrolled in the Girls' Training School. Twenty young men from the Marshall Islands were students in the school conducted by Edmund and Harriet Pease and Theodora Crosby. Lillian Cathcart shared the work prior to her departure for the United States later that year. Alfred and Margaret Walkup instructed the 27 Gilbert Island youths on another part of the Wot campus. Some of the Marshallese and Gilbertese students who were young adults, had wives and small children with them.

 An American Board official commented on the role of Sarah Smith with the 27 Micronesian girls in the new school at the top of the hill: "We can imagine the difficulties that beset her path. Three sets of girls, speaking three totally dissimilar languages, to be cared for; a heavy burden to a young and untried missionary."[42]

But Miss Smith was not alone with the girls. She was assisted by Mrs. Cole, the generous and efficient American woman who had moved to Wot from Lelu some months earlier. Not a missionary, Mrs. Cole had come to Kosrae in late 1879 with her husband, who managed the A. Capelle & Co. business on the island. Approximately seven years later, Mr. Cole was shot and killed aboard a ship as he was returning to Kosrae from the Marshalls. He was buried at Mutunsrem. His young wife—with their children, Grace and Willie—remained on Kosrae. A Christian, Mrs. Cole offered her services to the missionaries at Wot, and soon became indispensable in the work of the schools there. Since the missionaries were concentrating on the Marshallese and Gilbertese languages, Mrs. Cole's knowledge of the Kosraean language was a great boon to them. Sarah Smith commented:

It would not have been possible for me to include the Kusaien girls had it not been that to Mrs. Cole, who has been with us from the beginning, the language is as familiar as English, after the years she has spent on the island. With her two children, we make a happy family of thirty-one. The house is wide and airy—planned more for use and comfort than for beauty. With open doors from our large, square sitting room which is furnished with four windows and a door upon the veranda, we can take advantage of any breeze that may be stirring. The girls' sleeping rooms above, five on each side of the hall, have been occupied, some by two, some by three girls; while the undivided attic may, in the future, help us in the enlargement of the school.[43]

Our life from week to week has been the same story of little things done in a scarcely varying routine—the daily practical house work in which each must be instructed afresh almost daily, the hours of school work, and the afternoons of sewing, study, work, and recreation, ending with the hour spent about the lamp after evening worship. Minds have been waking up, and are now, it may be, just ready for the earnest work in the school.[44]

Beside the boarding students at the Marshall Islands School, the number of day scholars from among the Kosraeans was increasing. From 20 to 30 boys and young men came from different parts of the island to live near the Wot mission so that they could have the advantage of instruction by the missionaries in Bible and the English language. These Kosraean day students lived with families in Insief and Leap and in small thatch houses along the Wot beach. The students in all three schools did their own cooking, washing, and sewing and took care of their dormitories, besides attending classes each morning and working on the farm each afternoon.

Dr. Pease wrote, "The school farm is of value, not only in training the scholars in habits of industry and giving them healthful exercise, but in furnishing a large quantity of food. We try to teach them how to work, how to live, and how to make Christian homes. And we always have this encouragement: These Micronesian people are all eager to learn, and there is nothing that they so much wish to know as the Word of God!"[45]

In July 1888, Alice C. Little, 23, arrived to assist the Walkups in the Gilbert Islands school.

CELEBRATING NATURE'S ABUNDANCE ON KOSRAE

The Americans at Wot knew that the prevalent impression in the United States was that the missionaries in Micronesia had many hardships and privations to endure. In an effort to correct that impression, at least so far as those who lived on Kosrae were concerned, Harriet Pease, in 1888, wrote for *Life and Light for Women:*

The productions of the Gilbert Islands are mostly confined to the fruits of the coconut and pandanus trees, neither of which white people eat to any great extent. The water in the wells is brackish, and that caught from a thatched roof is neither pure nor sparkling. There is little to look out upon but ocean—ocean or the lagoon. The days and nights are hot.

But what do we have in Kusaie? We are up on high ground—we have beautiful mountains and trees to rest our eyes upon—banks covered with ferns, ferns and mosses hanging from the branches of trees, greenness and beauty everywhere— nights that are almost always cool and comfortable for sleep—pasture for cows and goats, so that we have milk most of the time, eggs in abundance, ten or fifteen varieties of bananas, breadfruit, taro, yams, pineapples, limes, papaya, mangoes, water from a never-failing spring or direct from heaven—soil sufficiently fertile to grow roses, hibiscus, oleander, and various other flowering plants. In addition to these, we have all the foreign food that we need.[46]

To this, Sarah Smith added,

Isolation, absence from friends, the long intervals of silence, are not the trials of life in Micronesia that they seem to you, who are at a distance. Perched upon a spur of one of these broken hills, we have a wide outlook over the stretch of sea beyond, the reef in front, land behind, the long range of deeply serrated hills, fresh with their richness of verdure from January to December. No little wandering breeze can pass us without a message. When a person once reaches our nest, I think he would find it almost the pleasantest spot on the island.

I feel over and over, as I look out on the fresh beauty of our little world after an early morning shower, with a rainbow spanning the islet toward the west, and everything a-sparkle under the first rays of the sun, "Truly the lines have fallen to me in pleasant places."[47]

Then the mood shifted. ✠

Notes - Chapter 6

1. Edmund M. Pease, "A History of Missionary Work in Micronesia 1852-1910," Mary A. Marvin, ed, p. 345
2. E. Theodora Crosby Bliss, "Fifty Years in the Island World," p. 38
3. E. M. Pease to the Hawaiian Evangelical Association, Honolulu, 1877
4. Lydia V. Snow, unpublished correspondence, Robbinston, Maine, April 24, 1879
5. Ibid
6. E. M. Pease in Mary A. Marvin, p. 345
7. "Kusaie in the Nineteenth Century," undated, p. 15
8. Americal Board of Commissioners for Foreign Missions, Annual Report 1882
9. Harriet S. Pease in Marvin, p. 13
10. H. S. Pease in Marvin, p. 14
11. Louisa Whitney, personal correspondence, March 26, 1880
12. "Kusaie in the Nineteenth Century," p. 17
13. H. S. Pease in Marvin, p. 15
14. Ibid, p. 21
15. Ibid, p. 22
16. Lillian Cathcart, personal correspondence, Dec. 22, 1881
17. L. Cathcart, The Friend, March 1882
18. L. Cathcart, personal correspondence, Dec. 22, 1881
19. ABCFM, Annual Report 1882
20. Albertine Loomis, To All People, Hawaii Conference UCC, Honolulu, 1970, quoted by Donald J. Sevetson in "No One Left Out," Anacortes, Washington, Nov. 10, 2002
21. E. T. Crosby Bliss, p. 38
22. Ibid, p. 40
23. Ibid, p. 39
24. Mark R. Peattie, Nan'yo, The Rise and Fall of the Japanese in Micronesia, p. 7
25. "Kusaie in the Nineteenth Century, p. 17
26. Lavinia Barr Walkup, personal correspondence, Jan. 12, 1884
27. L. Cathcart, March 5, 1884
28. Albert S. Baker, "The Third Morning Star," The Friend, Honolulu, Sept. 1942
29. The Friend, Aug. 1884
30. David & Leona Crawford, Missionary Adventures in the South Pacific, p. 231
31. L. Cathcart in Marvin, pp. 32-33
32. Edward Doane, journal entry Oct. 13, 1885
33. The Missionary Herald, 1885, p. 380
34. Bliss, p. 8
35. Crosby [Bliss], "Land Ho! Kusaie!" in Marvin, pp. 309-310
36. Sarah Smith in Marvin, p. 49
37. Ibid, pp. 49-50
38. Bliss, p. 39
39. ABCFM, Annual Report 1881
40. John P. Sigrah, cornerstone papers, April 30, 1909, courtesy of Hashime Vicente
41. Bliss in Marvin, p. 95
42. ABCFM in Bliss, p. 41
43. Smith in Marvin, p. 53
44. Smith in T. C. Bliss, "Fifty Years in the Island World," pp. 41-42
45. E. M. Pease in Bliss, p. 43
46. H. S. Pease in Marvin, p. 56
47. Smith in Marvin, p. 57

NUNAK YOHK KE CHAPTER 7
1888-1894

Lavinia Walkup, mutan kial Alfred Walkup, el misa ke August 1888 ke el yac 33. El pukpuki Wot, acn ma lutlut Gilbert tuh oan we. Mr.Walkup el usla tulik tolu natultal ac folokla nu America. Sie pac missionary, John Forbes, el wi mutan kial fahsr in som orekma fin acn Pohnpei, tuh ke eltal tui Kosrae, Mr. Forbes el masak ac misa ke October 1889. El pukpuki Wot. Theodora Crosby, mutan se su tuh tuku nu Kosrae in kasru lutlut Marshall in 1886, tu masak ac el fulokla nu America in 1888.

Yurin mwet Kosrae, Tokosra Sru V el misa in 1888, ac mwet se ma aolul, Tokosra Lupalik III, el misa in August 1889. Mwet sefanna su mwet Kosrae pangon mu fal in aolul, el tuh som liki acn Kosrae in 1863 in wi selu fin oak in fakfuk loat. Mwet se inge, Tulensa, tuh fulokinyukme nu Kosrae liki acn Honolulu, na mosrweyukla el in January 1890. Wal lal pa Tokosra Sa II. Missionary ac mwet sac ma etal panglol "King Charley."

In 1889 missionary Protestant nukewa fin acn Pohnpei supweyukla liki acn we ke sripen government lun acn Spain we arulanu patok alu Catholic. Mwet Spain inge elos kunausla lohm sin missionary ac eisla acn lun mission ke ku. Kutu sin missionary su muta Pohnpei elos tuku nu Kosrae ac luti fin acn Wot. Louise Fletcher ac Annette Palmer eltal use tulik mutan singoul itkosr ma lutlut yoroltal Pohnpei, nu Pisin. Pastu Likiaksa, Deacon Konlulu ac mwet Lelu elos arulana kasrelos ke lusen yac luo ma elos muta we.

Pastu Irving Channon ac mutan kial, Mary, eltal tuku nu Kosrae in August 1890 in mwet luti ke lutlut Gilbert fin acn Wot. Jessie Hoppin el wi pac tuku nu Kosrae in weang mwet luti ke school lun tulik mutan fin acn Wot. Malem na onkosr tukun elos sun acn Kosrae, paka na upa se tuh sun acn we ke March 4 nu ke 7, 1891. Apkuran lohm nukewa fin acn Kosrae musalla. Fahsu ke lohm alu akosr ah sohkla, ac yohk acn musalla ke sinka ah kewa. Sak nukewa fin acn ah ikorla, pwanang wanginla fokinsak. Oasr kutu mwet misa ke paka sac, tusruktu pus mwet misa ke sripen sracl ac mas upa ma sikyak toko. Oasr tulik mutan Pohnpei limekosr ma lutlut fin acn Pisin wi misa, na mwet luti luo lalos elos usla tulik singoul luo lula nu Mokil.

In March 1892, mwet Christian fin acn Kosrae elos orala tukeni na yohk se in kaksakin God ke karinginyuk lal nu selos ke pacl in ongoiya lulap sac.

Lutlut tolu fin acn Wot tuh fahsr na, ac mwet nukewa we elos orekma in sifil musai acn we. In 1893 American Board tuh supwama kamtu se nu Wot. Inel pa Mr. George E. Bowker. El tuh use sak ac kufwen sroasr welul. Pukanten mukul Kosrae elos insewowo in welul Mr. Bowker orekma. Kutu selos tuh arulana etala kamtu sel. Lohm se emeet elos orala pa lohm twek se ke school lun mutan ah. Oasr acn in lutlut, acn in mongo, acn in muta lun tulik lutlut oayapa acn in muta lun missionary, ac nien filma se.

Oasr pacl missionary su muta fin acn Wot ac us kutu tulik lutlut in som wi alu Lelu, ku oayapa church tolu saya. Ke pacl lutlut uh mongla, na missionary elos ac som pac mongla Pisin. Ke missionary inge nukewa ac sim leta nu sin mwet kawuk lalos ac sou lalos, elos fahkak lupan kulang lun mwet in church akosr fin acn Kosrae. Finne srikla mongo tukun paka sac, mwet uh ac sa na sang kutena mwe mongo ma oasr yorolos in kasru missionary ac tulik lutlut Wot. Pacl puspis elos ac sim kacl Pastu Likiaksa lah el sie mwet arulana alken ac inse pusisel. Kutu pac mwet ma elos sramsram kac ac kaksakin in leta lalos pa Tulpe Pisin, mutan kial Pastu Likiaksa; Deacon Konlulu ac Wa Inkoeya, mutan kial Konlulu; Deacon Alik, su kunla muta, ac Kilafwakun, wen natul; Kephas ac Kenye su muta Pilyuul; Na, mwet luti se Malem, ac Sra mutan kial; Tulen ac mutan kial fin acn Insief. Missionary nukewa elos arulana insewowo ke elos akilen lupan kulang ac kwafeang lun mwet Christian Kosrae.

In 1894, Dr. Pease ac sou lal ah elos som liki acn Kosrae. Elos tuh orekma yac singoul onkosr fin acn Wot. Mrs. Forbes ac tulik mutan se natul eltal wi pac folokla nu America. Dr. Clinton Rife ac mutan kial, Isadore, eltal tuku in aolul Dr. ac Mrs. Pease. Miss Theodora Crosby el kela ac welultal foloko, ac mwet luti ke lutlut lun tulik Marshall. Oasr tulik lutlut Marshall tolngoul tolu ke pacl sac. Oasr pac mutan fusr luo wi pac tuku in kasru Jessie Hoppin, Annette Palmer ac Alice Little ke lutlut lun tulik mutan. Ineltal pa Annie Abell ac Louise Wilson. Pastu ac Mrs. Channon eltal srakna mwet luti ke lutlut Gilbert. Pisen tulik lutlut laltal pa tulik angngaul tolu. Pukanteni tulik mukul Kosrae tuh weang lutlut Marshall, ac tulik mutan Kosrae ekasr tu weang lutlut lun tulik mutan.

In pacl se inge, oasr mwet Kosrae su wi orekma ke school tolu fin acn Wot. Kutu selos mwet kamtu, kutu orekma ke ima, kutu orekma luin lohm sin missionary, kutu karinganang tulik mutan. Oayapa pusiyen selu fin *Morning Star* elos mukul Kosrae.

Pastu Likiaksa el kol mwet Christian Kosrae in sifilpa musaela lohm alu akosr ma tuh musalla ke paka se in 1891. Lohm alu inge nukewa safla ke 1894.

CHAPTER SEVEN

DOMAIN OF THE *MORNING STARS*
1888-1894

ILLNESS AND DEATH AMONG THE MISSIONARIES

Late in 1888 the Micronesia Mission fell into a "slough of despond"[1]—the Wot community in particular. On August 16, at the age of 33, Margaret Lavinia Walkup died in her home at the Gilbert Islands Training School on Kosrae

Harriet Pease, her colleague at the Marshall Islands Training School, wrote in her journal on the 17th:

One week ago last Sunday Mrs. Walkup worshiped with us at our English meeting, and yesterday morning she went away and left us. A complication of difficulties, for which human remedies were of no avail, caused her death. All night we watched her life ebbing away, and a quarter before five she was gone. Wednesday night three little children—the oldest not yet seven, the youngest less than two—went to sleep knowing they had a mother; in the morning they awoke to find that she had left them.

We lined the sides of the coffin with a beautiful vine that grows on her porch, and added white flowers and ferns. She was dressed as she was when the children had last seen her before she was taken ill. We sang "One Sweetly Solemn Thought," and "The Lord is My Shepherd." Dr. Pease read the beautiful Episcopal burial service, and after the Kusaien, Gilbert and Marshall people had seen her, we laid her away in a pleasant spot near a wild banyan tree. The afternoon was rainy, but brightened as we started for the grave. Just as the grave was covered the sun set in splendor, and a beautiful double rainbow appeared. Our hearts go out in deepest sympathy for Mr. Walkup and his three motherless children.[2]

The American Board sent an impressive obelisk-style headstone which marks the grave at the site of the school in which she taught. In addition to her name and dates of birth and death, Revelation 14:13b is written out in both English and Gilbertese.

In April 1889, classes were suspended at the Gilbert Islands Training School while Alfred Walkup escorted his three children—John, Eleanor, and William, the latter two having been born at Wot—to the United States, where they would be cared for at the Tank Missionary Home in Oberlin, Ohio. Tain, one of the outstanding Gilbertese students, accompanied the family as far as Hawai'i, where Mr. Walkup enrolled him in a mission boarding school. Two older students at Wot, Taramarawa and his wife, Neimaiu, were left in charge of the Gilbert campus and remaining students until new missionary teachers arrived the following year. [Two years later Alfred Walkup returned to Micronesia as captain of a new mission ship, the *Hiram Bingham*, which sailed between the Gilbert Islands, the southern Marshalls, and Kosrae.]

The Rev. and Mrs. John Forbes, appointed to the Pohnpei mission, were aboard the *Star* when it made its scheduled stop at Kosrae October 18. Rachel Forbes was experiencing a difficult pregnancy, and the couple disembarked so she could have the care of Dr. Pease. But John Forbes himself became ill and died of dysentery two weeks after their arrival. He was 29 years old. So the missionaries buried a second colleague at Wot just a year after they had buried the first. Rachel Forbes, John's 22-year-old widow, and her daughter, Anna, born the following March, remained for the next four years. After a reasonable time, Mrs. Forbes was assigned to teach with Sarah Smith and Alice Little—the latter having been transferred from the Gilbert School when Mrs. Walkup died—at the Girls' Training School at the top of the hill.

In the December issue of *The Friend*, editor S. E. Bishop wrote:

The Morning Star *came into port* [at Honolulu] *most unexpectedly Monday afternoon, November 18, about three o'clock. As she steamed steadily onward it was evident that no damage to the vessel had interrupted the voyage. She was not expected to be back in Honolulu before the first of May 1890. Those who went out to meet her, and saw the missionary ladies, Miss Crosby and Miss Ingersoll* [of the Pohnpei Mission], *sitting on the deck, wan and weak, did not need to ask why the Star has been sent back. The ladies were speedily taken ashore, medical examination made, and it was a relief to learn that while Miss Ingersoll might find it advantageous to remain in Honolulu a little time before going on to the States, Miss Crosby's illness was not so serious as to prevent her taking the steamer* Australia *on the succeeding Friday, and getting into a more invigorating climate as soon as possible.*

Both of the missionary ladies were suffering from nervous troubles. The constant rainfall on both Ponape and Kusaie, with the intense heat of the tropic sun, is most debilitating, even to vigorous constitutions. Miss Smith, who came up from Kosrae to care for the invalids on the voyage, will return to her work in the girls' school, on the return trip of the Star.

This interruption of the voyage is a serious matter in view of the impossibility of accomplishing the missionary work that must be done, as well as the large expense involved. It costs about fifty dollars a day to run the Star, *and ten months barely suffice to take the vessel down and through the various groups of islands and back again to Honolulu in season to refit for the next year's trip. The* Star *sails nearly 11,000 miles each year, and to accomplish this distance in time, must steam about one-fifth of the ten months allotted.*

Dr. Pease and wife on Kusaie were somewhat fatigued from the incessant care they had taken for months, night and day, of Miss Crosby. Miss Little, left alone with twenty-eight girls to look after, will gladly welcome back Miss Smith, associated with her in care of the school.[3]

Earlier, Dr. Pease had reported 33 Marshall Islanders—men, women, and children—in his Wot school in 1889. "Every one of the boys during the year declared his purpose to serve the Lord."[4]

SPANISH PERSECUTION OF MISSIONARIES ON POHNPEI

Circumstances for missionaries on Pohnpei continued to deteriorate. They were driven from their stations by the anti-Protestant sentiments of the Spanish, and their schools and churches were either seized and destroyed or bombarded from the sea and burned. Missionary Edward Doane was taken for a time to Manila, where he was kept under house arrest. In May 1890, having finally reached Honolulu, Mr. Doane died, worn out by all he had endured.

The situation of those missionaries remaining at Pohnpei was extremely volatile, but the *Morning Star*—forbidden by the Spanish to sail near the island—could not go to their aid. In response to a letter Annette Palmer smuggled out to the American consul in Manila, she and the other American Board missionaries on the island—Estelle Fletcher and Frank Rand—were finally rescued by the United States Navy. Carrie Rand and Ida Foss, who was Mrs. Rand's sister, were already "in exile" on Kosrae.

Under the protection of Cmdr. H. C. Taylor, the missionaries were taken aboard the naval ship *Alliance* when it reached Pohnpei October 16, 1889, and transported to Kosrae. Mrs. Cole, who had been helping at the Pohnpei girls' school, was also rescued with her children. The Spanish administration vigorously objected to any of the mission students leaving Pohnpei, but 17 girls managed to accompany their teachers. They reached Kosrae November 6.[5]

Though Miss Little at the Wot Girls' School invited the Pohnpeian girls and their teachers to share the facilities on the Yonrak hill, Miss Fletcher and Miss Palmer felt it best to keep the groups separate. They went to Lelu and set up their school at Pisin. Mrs. Cole was with them and, after some months, Miss Foss went to relieve Miss Palmer, who returned to Wot. The school remained at Pisin for two years, receiving a great deal of aid and attention from Pastor Likiaksa and members of the Lelu church, who had initiated their welcome by re-thatching the Pisin house for them. Deacon Konlulu was of particular help to the missionaries and their Pohnpeian students in supplying various daily needs.

A FUNERAL

On New Year's Day, 1890, a Kosraean neighbor of the missionaries died. Mrs. Pease wrote:

Tulen heard of Christ from Mr. Snow, accepted him and no one knows that he ever turned aside from the right path. His wife died while we were in America in 1885. He has said every time we have gone away to the Marshall Islands that he should die before we returned; but had been able to come to see us occasionally until within the past two or three months. He died of old age—his mind clear to the last. When asked if he was afraid to die, he said, "Oh, no; my Jesus is with me." And if asked if he prayed, he answered, "I can't forget to pray."

Wonderful change, from a thatched hovel to a heavenly mansion! How I should have enjoyed watching him as the glories of heaven dawned upon him. His own canoe was used as his coffin, a piece having been taken off each end, and the openings closed with the ends of his own chest. Pastor Likiaksa came round, and we all went to the little church just below us [in Insief]. He read the fourth chapter of First Thessalonians, and it was interesting to hear him point his people to Christ, and exhort them to follow in the footsteps of their neighbor who is gone.[6]

DEATHS OF KING SRU V AND KING LUPALIK III

There had been other deaths. As within the missionary community, the Kosraean community was going through a lengthy period of mourning and adjustment. In 1888 King Sru V died. The Sesa, who was considered the most qualified candidate to succeed him, refused to be made king, so the son of King Salik II was installed as Lupalik III. He was a favorite with the people, but lived less than a year after becoming king, dying in August 1889. The Sesa again refused the office.

KING SA II

The only other Kosraean considered eligible to be king was the Suwarku, a chief who had been working as a sailor—with his home port in Honolulu—since 1863. That was the year a number of Kosrae's young men, disheartened by so much illness and death, had chosen to leave their home island. His name was Tulensa, but among his shipmates and friends in Hawai'i, he was known as "Charley." His grandmother and King George's mother were sisters, and his father and King Oa were brothers.

At the request of the Kosraean people, Tulensa returned to Kosrae, traveling from Honolulu aboard the *Morning Star IV*, to become King Sa II.[7] Formally inaugurated on January 20, 1890, the new ruler—known to the missionaries and other foreigners as "King Charley"—had never officially married. Sometime after becoming Kosrae's king, he married Srue Nueliki. Though they had no children of their own, they adopted several from among their relatives. King Sa [SA, as in sad] had a very difficult time adjusting to life back on Kosrae. He had become so accustomed to the life of a bachelor sailor that he found the restrictions placed upon him by his rank, as well as what was expected of him by the Church, to be frustrating and confining. During the early years of his kingship he drank heavily and, much of the time, found himself at odds with the missionaries at Wot.

OBSERVATIONS OF MR. DEWAR

In July 1890, Mr. J. C. Dewar, aboard his yacht the *Nyanza*, visited Lelu and commented in his journal: "The island of Kusaie is a great Protestant missionary stronghold, and the people appear to be painfully good. None of them dared to drink or smoke, and when I offered the local trader a newspaper, he piously replied that he never read anything but the Bible. Notwithstanding all these fine professions, the missionaries have not succeeded in inducing the King to stop his grog and tobacco, if he can get a chance of enjoying himself in this manner in secret."[8]

ARRIVAL OF THE CHANNON FAMILY

In August 1890, Wot Mission personnel and students were encouraged by the arrival of three new missionaries. Irving Monroe Channon, age 28, and his wife, Mary Long Goldsbury Channon, 25, came to take the place of the Walkups at the Gilbertese school. With them were their two small children, Paul and Lillian. Jessie R. Hoppin, also 25, arrived to teach in the Girls' School. She had just completed two years on the faculty of the Kawaiahaʻo Seminary in Honolulu.

The Channon family had left their home in Oberlin, Ohio, June 11, traveling by train to San Francisco, then aboard the steamer *Alameda* to Hawaiʻi. They left Honolulu aboard the *Morning Star IV* July 12. More than five weeks later, weary from the many weeks of travel and the seasickness she had constantly battled since leaving California—and with two young children to watch over—Mrs. Channon wrote in her journal:

We sighted Kusaie early Monday morning, August 18. It looked like two great blue peaks rising out of the water. After awhile, they joined hands—and soon we were near enough to see the shore line and then the trees. It was not until five o'clock that we were near enough to sight the mission—Dr. Pease's house and the Girls'

School. Our house was hidden by the foliage. With the glass we could see the girls at their school looking at us. We all stood on deck so that they could see what a company there was of us! We had visits from some of the islanders that evening, and amongst them was King Charley. That night I had such a restful feeling. To think we were at our journey's end. The very mountains seemed to have a peaceful look. The white birds flying against the beautiful green foliage made a beautiful sight.[9]

"A DAY IN KUSAIE, MICRONESIA"

Theodora Crosby wrote a story describing life at Wot—a portion of it in the form of a skit—that proved to be very popular among American Sunday School children. Published in Boston by the Committee on Junior Work in 1891 and distributed to Congregational churches throughout the United States, it was entitled "A Day In Kusaie, Micronesia." The story began:

You will please consider yourself transported to an island in the South Pacific Ocean, 2,500 miles from everywhere, one might truly say. A beautiful little island, only eighteen miles in circumference, but with mountains 2,100 feet high, covered to the very summits with a dense tropical foliage, and broken into mountain chains by beautiful valleys, through which wind, like silver threads, little rivers of fresh water—an island so beautiful, it is rightly called "The Gem of the Pacific," where there is not a road, or a store, shop, post office, railroad, horse or carriage, or anything which tells of civilization.[10]

In some detail, Miss Crosby then described Wot and what life was like at the Marshall Islands School, writing in a way that appealed to children and inspired the adults who taught them. Christian educators used the story and skit to great effect, combining them with stories of the *Morning Star* missionary vessels, for which American children in Congregational churches throughout the U.S. had developed a strong and sentimental sense of ownership.

TYPHOON SLAMS INTO KOSRAE

The Channons and Miss Hoppin had been settled in their new homes at Wot for only six months when a typhoon of "unusual force and duration" hit Kosrae March 4, 1891, lasting for three days. Mary Channon wrote of the terrifying experience of having to flee with her family from their home at the Gilbertese school—exposed on an elevated point of land—to the Marshallese school, more protected by the mountain.

It rained hard all day Monday, then on Tuesday morning it began to blow, and it was so dark we had to have lamps. Irving came up to get his woolen clothes as it was so cool, and after lunch—in the midst of the drenching rain and increasing wind—he went up on the house to fasten the roof. But the storm was growing worse and worse, the house creaking and straining. When we heard the timbers breaking and the iron roof and shingles began flying in every direction, we put on gossamers [heavy raincoats] and wrapped the children in blankets and mats. We contemplated going down around by the beach instead of along the narrow path on the side of the hill—and just then all our boys appeared.

A boy each took Paul and Lillian, and I rushed out with three month old Willie in my arms. Irving pulled me back as a heavy piece of iron roofing fell where I was rushing to. We staggered out against the rain again and Irving held me on the inside and three boys braced me on the outer side toward the precipice to keep me from being blown off the path, all the quarter of a mile around to the other mission houses. We were fleeing for our lives. Before I had reached any distance I was drenched through to the skin, the poor baby could hardly get his breath and cried, but did not get very wet.

Finally we reached the Snow Cottage where the Rands and Miss Foss were staying. They had already begun to worry about the strength of their house. Still the storm raged furiously. Soon the houses down on the beach were all down and the Kusaiens came up to take shelter in Dr. Pease's empty Marshall houses. Once we saw some Kusaien women rushing to take shelter in a Marshall house and a moment after they passed part of a tree fell in their path.

Harriet Pease remained in their house doing her best to keep things dry while Theodora Crosby and Annette Palmer were with the Marshallese families attempting to help and reassure them. Jessie Hoppin and Sarah Smith were huddled with the frightened girls at the top of the hill. We feared all Tuesday night and all day Wednesday. Wednesday evening at six o'clock, Mr. and Mrs. Rand, Miss Foss, Irving and I gathered in one room and prayed and prayed—then sang "My Faith Looks Up to Thee," and others, but the storm seemed to rage worse.

After our prayers, a Kusaien came over to say that Mrs. Pease, with her sons and little Anna Forbes, were coming over because their house was leaking everywhere and the floors were so wet they could not stay. The Kusaien and Mr. Rand both had to holler as they stood side by side, the storm was so loud. It was hardly safe to venture outdoors and we knew Mrs. Pease would only come under extreme necessity with delicate Anna Forbes. Mrs. Pease did not come, however, for someone suggested boring holes in the floors to let the water off. It blew constantly and with increasing intensity. That night I feared that we might be driven out of the house if it fell, and that the children would perish in the storm.

The children cheered us a good deal for they were unconscious of the danger. Wednesday night was another sleepless night, but we succeeded in taking short naps. Four Gilbert boys sat up and watched, ready to waken us if the house seemed to be falling, ready to assist us. I never in my life passed such fearful nights as Tuesday and Wednesday nights, March 4 and 5.[11]

Jessie Hoppin described the girls crowding in with her and Sarah Smith in the dining room of their building during the first part of the storm. Windows blew in, walls shuddered and they were wet, but they were together in one place. At noon on Wednesday, when the eye of the storm brought a lull in the wind, Miss Hoppin "went down the hill to get the milk, but there was no such article to be had. Our little mountain stream had swelled into a huge river and all the cows were on the other side of it. On my way up I found two little kids, made motherless the night before by the falling of a tree upon their fond parent. These I brought home, one under each arm, and immediately named them 'Tornado' and 'Typhoon'."[12]

At three o'clock that afternoon the wind rose again. Miss Hoppin wrote:

At four it raged. Great trees went crashing down, flinging their great branches through the air. Our veranda posts stood out in mid-air, and still the wind rose steadily. Three Gilbert boys came to help us. They were wet and cold, and after having some hot drink, they clothed themselves in some of my dresses, and funny enough the tall fellows looked in them. The boys worked wiping up water and carrying out buckets-full all night. The girls stayed with us in the schoolroom and we prayed, singing songs to counteract the winds, while a row of girls was perched upon a table placed against the folding doors between the sitting room and schoolroom to keep the doors from blowing open. Still the wind rose, lighting flashed, the sea roared, and rain fell in torrents. We watched for morning.

Morning always does come and it did that time, and with it such a picture of desolation as it had never been my lot to see before. What few trees were left were leafless and broken, and the wind sounded dry and wintry through them. The coconut trees stood with their heads off. All the breadfruit, limes, bananas and things of that kind were on the ground. The island looked as if a great fire had overspread it. Not a church was left standing, most of the native houses were down, and no thatch plants were left with which to build.[13]

As was true for everyone on the island, Miss Fletcher, Mrs. Cole, and the Pohnpeian girls at Pisin had been, at first, unaware of the approaching typhoon. Estelle Fletcher wrote,

Tuesday morning a strong wind commenced blowing. We did not think it more than a trade wind, but it blew stronger and stronger till it reached a gale. The first warning we had that there might be danger, our trees commenced blowing down. Soon after this we saw our house was not going to stand long. We only had time to get the girls together, and had not been out of the house more than twenty minutes when the roof fell. The storm raged all night. Wednesday morning the Kusaien house where we had taken shelter began to go, so we passed on up to the king's place. Trees were falling in every direction. Mrs. Cole and I, with two Kusaiens, took advantage

of a lull in the storm to return to our house and see how things were. What a wreck!
All, everything absolutely ruined![14]

Harriet Pease continued the story of devastation:

We are so sorry for our poor Kusaiens. At Lelu seven houses only are reported as
habitable, and these were only kept so by constant propping. At South Harbor every
house is down but one, and that has no roof. Malem very few houses are down, but
the waves were so high and furious that the water came into them, so that the people
had to hang around the sides of the houses in order to keep out of it.

At two places the hurricane has thrown up a wall of rocks on the reef for some
distance, so high that the breakers cannot be seen above it. This makes a smooth
passage for canoes between the shore and it, which sometimes used to be very rough.
The oldest people on the island remember hearing others tell of just such another
hurricane eighty or ninety years ago, which lasted but one day and night.

I told the Kusaiens that I would pay them if they would take turns and work all
night during the storm. But when it was over and I handed them their pay, Nena said,
"I can't take any pay. We should have died if you hadn't taken care of us these three
days when our houses were blown down. If we work afterwards we will take pay."

Now we wait, and hope, and pray that this hurricane may not have sent our dear
ones on the Star *to a watery grave.[15]*

AFTERMATH

Edmund Pease with some of the Marshallese families and students, and
Alice Little, Rachel Forbes, and a few of the Marshallese girls, were aboard the
Morning Star IV touring the mission outposts in the Marshalls when the typhoon
hit. They returned safely to Kosrae March 28. Mrs. Forbes tearfully embraced
her daughter, Anna, a frail child who had just turned one. Dr. Pease was grateful
to be reunited with his wife, Harriet, and their sons, Ned and Frank, but profoundly discouraged to find one of his special projects utterly destroyed by the
storm. For many months he had been painstakingly copying lyrics and music
for a Marshallese hymnal. Most of those pages had disappeared in the wind,
while those that remained had been completely ruined in the deluge of rain.

When the *Morning Star IV* left Kosrae to return to Hawai'i in April, it carried
a hurriedly scribbled note from Irving Channon to the director of the Hawaiian
Evangelical Association. In spite of the horrendous experience he had just been
through and the daunting challenge of recovery ahead, his letter reflects a faith-
generated optimism.

The storm blew down all my school buildings as well as unroofed my house. It
will take at least $150 to repair, lumber and labor. I don't know just where the money
is to come from. I have written to Boston my needs but perhaps it would be best for

*the Hawaiian Board to recommend it and ask also for it. Food is also very scarce and
I must order more rice than usual.*

*I hope the Board will grant me the salary you recommend as the storm has badly
damaged my furniture and ruined much, and for several years we will be replacing
it. But we don't care about our things. We are thankful to the Lord that our lives are
safe. And we have good health. I never was better in my life in spite of all the work,
and Mrs. Channon and the little ones are also all well. We are very happy in our
work and are looking forward to the time when we will have a quiet time with only
our regular work to do.*[16]

Part of the folklore of the Christian era at Kosrae dates from this typhoon in
1891. Pastor Likiaksa and his family were in their Utwe home when the winds
began to blow. One after another the houses of the village were partially or
totally destroyed as the hours and the days of the storm continued—even the
roof of Utwe's stone church was lifted off and carried away. But, it is said, the
small, poor house of the pastor, its woven walls and thatch roof unfazed by the
blasts of the gale and the deluge of rain, sheltered in safety the holy man and
his family!

In truth, the Kosraean community was sick and disheartened. Most of their
homes and all of their churches were either considerably damaged or completely
gone, and their crops were destroyed or blown away—though the Channons
were impressed with how quickly the Kosraeans found and began planting
sweet potatoes, a fast-growing crop. There had been only a few deaths among
them as a direct result of the typhoon, but the sicknesses and famine during the
weeks following the storm took many Kosraean lives.

There was sadness among the missionaries, too. Ailing, Sarah Smith was
taken to Honolulu aboard the *Morning Star IV* on the April voyage, with Mrs.
Rand and Miss Palmer accompanying her. Over the next few months at Pisin,
five of the 17 Pohnpeian girls with Miss Fletcher and Mrs. Cole were stricken
with dysentery and died.

"Regular work" for everyone on Kosrae was seriously interrupted. The missionaries, their students, and the Kosraean people were all forced to wait for
building materials to be replenished, either by nature or by ship. And though
there was some rice for the residents at Wot, most people who survived did so
on fish and wild roots and, after a time, sweet potatoes.

CIRCLE TOUR OF KOSRAE

In a description of an October 1891 tour of Kosrae that included a visit to
the ruins of Lelu's ancient enclosures, Harriet Pease shared information and
insight concerning the island's recovery from the typhoon that had enveloped

them six months earlier.

Mrs. Cole went with us to the wonderful walls which have been so often described. The legend given by the old, old people is that King Awane Sakow lost a little girl about twelve years old, and so great was his grief that he could not endure the sight of any other girls of her age. He issued an order that every one of them on the island be killed. He is talked of as the cross king. He had a large enclosure made of immense stones, which it is hard to see how human hands could have lifted, and into this he moved his family. It used to be the custom to keep their dead unburied until nothing but the bones was left. Then these were thrown into a deep place in the water. A big stone is pointed out on which he used to sit and mourn.

There are several openings or gateways in this high, wide wall, and there is a winding passage up which canoes could come at high tide, and the natives deposited food for their king at the several gateways. The royal family had a special bathing place enclosed by walls. In it are three stone tubs, or oblong, hollow places of three different sizes. To bathe where the king had bathed was strictly forbidden, as the person so doing might become king.

The queen used to be kept entirely out of sight of the common people. Old customs are not easily rooted out. The other day when the present queen [Srue Nueliki] went out in a canoe and paddled it herself, some of her subjects were horrified. No queen was ever known to do such a thing before.

We went back to Dove Island to wait for the tide. At four o'clock the boys brought up the canoes, and we started for Malem, which is a ride of an hour or more from Lelu. Pastor Likiaksa accompanied us. At Pilyuul we called for a minute to see Mrs. Snow's Kephas and Kenye. Ever so many people were having a "bee" to build them a new house. They seemed very glad to see us, and immediately took down a bunch of nice cooking bananas, the first I had seen since the storm, as an expression of their joy. When they found we were going to sleep at Malem, they said they were all going too, so we went on our way. When our canoes were spied at Malem there was a great commotion, as our visit had not been heralded. One woman seized the midrib of a coconut leaf, and the way the rubbish flew from the front of her door toward the ocean was funny.

By the time we reached the shore a crowd had gathered, and Na the teacher, who lived with us several years, led off in the hand-shaking. We were ushered into the building now used for a church, the stone church having lost its roof during the hurricane. This was clean, having a board floor in the center, and a reed floor around that. A rocking-chair and three other chairs, two bunks with mats, a sheet for each one, and some pillows were brought in. A boat sail was used for a partition at one end of the church, and I was furnished with a room "fit for a queen," especially if she were on a picnic.

I announced that we had just eaten at Lelu, so they need not think about food for us. The struggle for subsistence makes it impossible for them to think of much else just now. When everybody had donned their "best bib and tucker" they assembled in the church for evening worship, after which our boys sang for them their temperance songs and recited the temperance catechism. They sang for us. To close we all sang together, "Wonderful Words of Life," and then laid us down to rest.

Next morning we had a breakfast of chicken, taro, bananas, fish, pasruk—a wild root which they have to eat more than anything else just now—and sugar-cane. The canoes had been taken early to Musral, the mouth of a river. We said our goodbyes, and started on a long, hot walk to the beach where the canoes were, Sra, Na's wife, accompanying us. We called at Yesing, where was a house or two, and of course we should not have been hospitably treated if they had not given us food; so more sugarcane, pasruk, and a chicken were given us.

At last we reached the river, which is only wide enough for one canoe. Mangrove roots line it on either side, and the trees all the way are straighter than those by the river on the north side. At Taf we came out into a wide opening where there are a few houses. The people were glad to see us, but were so sorry we had not sent them word, so that they might have treated us more generously. But we were glad they had not known, for they would have had to be hungrier than they are for a few days after.

A brisk shower lengthened our call somewhat, then a few minutes' ride across South Harbor brought us to houses occupied by some sick and feeble old people, one of whom was totally blind, but who preaches the Word on the Sabbath as best he can. More regrets were expressed, which ended in one woman's going out and seizing a hen, tying its leg, and giving it to us. Another found three fresh eggs. I did not like to take from them, but it would have hurt their feelings if I had not, so I gave presents in return. I told them I came to see them and not to get food. Yes, they knew that, but they wanted to express their love to us.

As soon as the tide would allow we entered another and wider river homeward bound. At just six o'clock we darkened our own door once more, having been absent fifty hours.[17]

THANKSGIVING CELEBRATION

Included in a letter written by Miss Hoppin in February 1892 was this paragraph: "It is a year ago next week Thursday since the hurricane, and the Kusaiens are going to have a feast in celebration—not of the hurricane, but of their deliverance from it—and to express their thankfulness for the increase of food on the island as well as to 'eat, drink, and be merry.' The food does increase and the Kusaiens begin to bring it in again in small quantities to assist the school. Years it will be before the fallen trees will be replaced by new ones, but each month brings more food. Probably the days of hard famine for the

Kusaiens are over, unless another storm comes–but we do not expect it."[18]

MISSIONARIES STRUGGLE TO CONTINUE THE SCHOOLS

Because of the scarcity of food on Kosrae—particularly at their Pisin school in Lelu—Estelle Fletcher and Ida Foss decided early in 1892 to move with the 12 remaining Pohnpeian girls to Mokil, a small atoll located some 80 miles southeast of Pohnpei, there to await the resolution of the Pohnpei situation. Frank and Carrie Rand accompanied them aboard the *Morning Star IV*. Miss Foss returned to Kosrae two years later to continue assisting at the Girls' School, where she remained until 1896.

Trying to make adjustments for illnesses, synchronize furloughs and compensate for departures meant that the missionaries at Wot seldom felt that their schedules were normal or that the number of classroom teachers was adequate. It seemed that they were always in need of replacements or in the midst of some sort of upheaval.

Even when food was plentiful, the problems at the Girls' Training School were always many. There were the three languages and a balance to be maintained between the Marshallese, Gilbertese, and Kosraean students. Great diversity in the ages of the girls also generated complications. Sarah Smith, the school's founder, had left mission employ to marry Capt. George Garland of the *Morning Star IV*. With Alice Little again assisting at the Gilbert school, Jessie Hoppin was left to be principal and sole missionary teacher at the Girls' School. Executives of the mission boards and her associates, however, considered her eminently qualified to carry the responsibility.

In case she needed to call for help from her colleagues in the other two schools, Irving Channon had cleverly installed a network of telephones that connected his house at the Gilbert School to the Pease house among the Marshallese, and to Jessie Hoppin's room at the Girls' School. This system became a much-used and appreciated means of communication between the missionaries in the three locations.

Irving Channon reported in March 1892 that there were 16 boys, eight married couples and seven children at the Gilbert Islands Training School. In 1893 that total had increased by one child. There were 20 girls with Miss Hoppin at the top of the hill[19] and, by this time, Annette Palmer had returned to Kosrae from furlough to assist her with them. Edmund and Harriet Pease were holding their own with the Marshall Islands Training School, despite Theodora Crosby's departure when ill health forced her to leave Micronesia following the typhoon.

On February 3 of that year Miss Alice Little returned to the United States.

The lady with the "sparkling eyes" had been a popular teacher and a favorite of colleagues since her arrival in 1888. The Wot community bade her a reluctant farewell. Then, on July 3, Louise E. Wilson, 24, arrived from California and, "with rare devotion and self-sacrificing love, won her way into the hearts of the girls."[20] [In April, the missionaries had been gratified to hear that the Snows' daughter, Carrie—born at Pisin 37 years earlier—was now teaching in a Chinese school in Honolulu.]

VISITORS AND OTHER DIVERSIONS

During 1893 the American Board sent lumber and other materials aboard the *Morning Star IV* to repair or replace classroom, dormitory, and chapel facilities that had been damaged or destroyed during the typhoon—including mission houses and the Girls' School building. The board hired George E. Bowker, a 33-year-old American carpenter living on Pohnpei, to go to Kosrae and do the work. Mary Channon wrote of him, "He was a Christian in every true sense of the word."[21] Mr. Bowker's Pohnpeian wife did not accompany him, but he had his young son, Rensalaer, along. The two of them were house guests of the Channons for several months. Then Mr. Bowker sent for his wife and small daughter, Lucy, who came to join him and his boy in a small house he had built for his family. The carpenter took his turn leading worship, for both student groups and missionaries when they gathered for English-language services. He proved to be an invaluable instructor to the students as they assisted him, and to the Kosraean men, who—out of curiosity as well as a desire to help—flocked to Wot during his stay.

The girls' building at the crest of Yonrak that resulted from Mr. Bowker's work with his enthusiastic labor force was a fine New England-style structure three stories high, with a covered veranda on three sides of the first floor. The first floor, from three to eight feet above the ground on the sloping hillside, consisted of a large parlor or common room, a dining room, a kitchen, two schoolrooms and two storerooms. The parlor and dining room could be joined by opening a large door in the wall between them. On the second floor were two bedrooms for the missionary women and six smaller rooms for the girls, connected by a wide hallway. The third floor, or more properly, the attic, was used for storage. The glass windows at the back and sides of the building provided views of the mountains and valleys, and from the front windows the students could look out over the lagoon, the reef, and the ocean. To the northwest they could clearly see Okat Harbor. The upper front windows became a favorite lookout, not only in their perennial watching for the *Morning Star*, but for canoes as they approached from the villages to the north and east.

At Miss Hoppin's request, Mr. Bowker and the Gilbertese boys erected a flag pole on Yonrak near the new building—"a nice straight and long mangrove tree which 'Morning Star Alik' found for us. We repaired Mr. Channon's old flag, and it was raised. All the schools were here. The missionaries sang 'Rally Round the Flag,' the girls joining in the chorus. We shall use a white flag on the pole probably more than the American flag. A white flag on the hill means, when seen from the returning *Star*, that all is well among the missionaries on Kusaie."[22]

Mary Channon wrote of another diversion that year. She and her husband escorted the staff and student body of the Gilbert Islands School on an excursion.

We went from Mwot to Mutunte, about three and one half miles from here. From there we followed one of the rivers about two and one half miles back from the beach and saw some most beautiful scenery. The mountains seem to be cut asunder by the river which flows through a deep gorge about three hundred feet high—rising with perpendicular sides.

We followed this gorge, walking in the narrow river and climbing over stones, wading through water waist deep, until we reached the place where the river falls in two cataracts not far apart. One is about sixty feet high and the other must be almost twice as high. It was a wonderful sight and of great interest to our scholars who, for the most part, knew of no other scenery than of coral reef before they came here.[23]

The missionaries and their students continued their practice of getting aboard the Wot canoes and traveling to Lelu occasionally—to share in special services with the Kosraean Christians, or just to take a vacation. Years later Mrs. Channon recalled "the great generosity and kindness the Kusaiens showed us when any of our schools or scholars or missionaries stayed at Pigeon [Pisin]— that little island apart from Lelu—bringing us food, cooked so wonderfully in their native ovens."[24]

EXCURSIONS FOR THE GIRLS

Sometimes the students of the Girls' School—much more restricted than the boys in the other two schools—were escorted by their teachers on walks along the beach at Insief and beyond. The girls delighted in these outings.

On one of these excursions, Miss Hoppin was with the girls in a secluded place when one of them asked her if she was allowed to do anything she pleased. Miss Hoppin was not sure how she should answer, but said "Yes," whereupon the girl cartwheeled and began walking on her hands![25]

On another such stroll in 1893, the girls and their teachers "called" at the house that King Sa maintained in the area.

His wife [Srue Nueliki] met us at the door. She is very nice looking. It is said that the Kusaiean women are the best looking of any of the Micronesians. The king was not at home. His wife brought forward two rocking-chairs, while the girls sat qui-etly on the sand outside. She could not talk English and we only stayed long enough to see what the house was like. It was made of native material, with the exception of the glass windows. The floor was covered with native matting. One side of the wall was all pasted up with pictures cut from newspapers and some advertisement cards. On a little shelf were a few porcelain mugs; a table in the middle of the room and a clock on the wall completed the furnishings. We met the king as we were leaving. He had been out in his canoe.[26]

When word was received at Wot that the Sigrah had died on March 3, 1893, both Mr. Channon and Dr. Rife hurried to Lelu to pay their respects and to participate with Pastor Likiaksa in the funeral and burial services. During the weeks following the death, Sigrah's wife, Srue, and two of their daughters spent time at Insief to be near the missionaries.[27] [Sigrah had been Tokosra Sru IV until deposed in 1880.]

EASTER SUNDAY AT WOT

While the *Morning Star IV* was in Micronesian waters, Capt. Garland's bride, the former Sarah Smith, was aboard with him. She enjoyed visiting with her friends at Wot—both missionaries and students. She was there for Easter on April 2, 1893, and described the combined service:

Our Easter was a very happy day to remember, and one which I think our scholars will look back upon pleasantly for a long time. At eleven o'clock the three schools and many Kusaiens were gathered in the Gilbert Church, which had been ingeniously decorated by the boys with flowers, ferns, and coconut leaves, and great branches of delicate Pride of India, with its feathery foliage and lavender-tinted, fra-grant blossoms. From the beams overhead hung festoons of green, and others were stretched from side to side on coconut cord. A table filled with dishes of roses and hibiscus stood by the organ.

The Gilbert scholars on one side and the Marshall scholars on the other sat fac-ing each other in the body of the church, leaving a wide aisle in the center. At the back of the church were Kusaiens, with the missionaries in a wide crescent at the front. All the girls were in white, and as we entered the church after all were seated, and the breeze ran through before us stirring all the fresh green things overhead and all about, the picture was a very lovely one for an Easter morning.

The Easter exercise which had been especially prepared—"The King of Love," with singing of carols and hymns, responsive readings and recitations by the scholars (all but the Scripture in English)—came first, and was followed by the communion. Two of our girls, Kaka and Teria, taking the names Bathsheba and Rebecca, were received into the church, and then sweet little Mary Goldsbury Channon was bap-

tized. Very lovely she and her mother looked, all in white; the baby is so beautiful! Altogether the morning was very full of glad things.[28]

ANOTHER TRIP TO THE VILLAGES

Life and Light for Women published an account by Jessie Hoppin of a trip around Kosrae. Mrs. Pease's similar tour two years earlier had taken 50 hours. This one lasted six days.

We have been talking for some time about making the circuit of this island. We asked Doctor's advice about it, and he approved; then we asked Pastor Likiaksa. He seemed pleased and invited us to stop at his house at Lelu, and said he would help us find canoes. And now tonight Mr. Channon has telephoned up to say that he will not only lend us his two big canoes, but will go himself as far as Lelu and furnish boys for the two canoes. What could we want more?

May 26, 1893—We were all up by five o'clock this morning, baking bread and packing and doing last things about the house. Kefwas and Nena came to help about tying up mats and covering them with leaves to keep them from getting wet. Mr. Channon also came to offer his service. At eleven o'clock we started from the shore, where all the missionaries and scholars from the other schools were gathered to see us off. You should have seen the nine canoes, each bright with the many colored dresses of the girls, each trying to outrun the others. Nearly all the girls helped pole. I stood and poled all the way to Mutunte, a distance of more than two miles. The boys said that was the reason our canoe came in ahead...

At Mutunte our Banaba friends, Gilbert-speaking people, had lunch prepared for us—cocoanuts, taro and breadfruit. Knowing how scarce food really was with them, we gave them the lunch we had brought, mostly bread.

We had ordered our canoes sent ahead to the "carry" [Insrefusr], as a canoe would float there some two hours after it was low tide on the reef. They were not there, but a very long distance ahead, at another Banaba settlement. Rather footsore, tired and warm, we still had no other resort but to press on to our canoes. The result of it all was that it was candlelight when we reached Pisin, the island where we were to stay. We found a crowd of Kusaiens on the shore to meet us—Pastor Likiaksa and wife, and many more. We were not a little surprised to find supper all ready, and set out on a table with tablecloth, water pitcher and glasses, a duck, all cooked—even if it was not of tender years—breadfruit, taro, and tea.

Kefwas established himself as our cook and steward. Pastor Likiaksa and Tulenkun brought in a food cupboard, a sofa, and two beds. It was very funny to see Pastor Likiaksa, with his gray hair, and the rather stout Tulenkun, making up the beds, as they insisted on doing, with their own pillows and bedding. When I said, "But, you see, we brought our own things," Pastor Likiaksa replied, with a twinkle in his eye, "Put it right on top; it will make it softer." We had forgotten our lanterns, but they brought their own lamps. The girls spread down their mats, and began to feel quite at home.

May 27—The king sent in food to us this morning, as did many others. Pastor Likiaksa furnishes us with milk, and all the Kusaiens are kind. We went calling today on the king and chief families. After we reached home, Pastor Likiaksa sent us in a whole pig all cooked, and taro, yams, and breadfruit. After supper we went to a spring a long distance away, taking a large container for drinking water.

May 28—We all attended church this morning. The Kusaiens have not rebuilt their church here in Lelu since the storm, and their temporary place of worship is scarcely a shelter from the wind and rain.Pastor Likiaksa preached what seemed like a very earnest sermon from the text, "Search the Scriptures." The Kusaien singing is very sweet compared with either Marshall or Gilbert. At the close of the service he asked our girls to sing, which they did.

After church I took one of the girls and went down to see Deacon Alik. He is one of Mr. Snow's old pupils. He has been blind for a long time, and now he has had a stroke of paralysis. There were only two ways of reaching his house. Our usual one was on the shore, but high tide blocked up that path. The other was through the bush, which way we tried to take. We ended up making our way to the shore, and wading, shoes in hand, while a number of hungry-looking dogs stood on the stone wall and barked their disapproval at us. At last we came to the right house. We found Deacon Alik very weak and unable to talk, but his face lighted up, and he seemed pleased that we had come to see him. His son offered to take us home in his canoe, and we gladly accepted the offer.

We all went again to the Sunday afternoon meeting. It lasted from three until five o'clock. It was a prayer meeting, and a great many took part. We had our own Sunday School, prayer meeting, and evening prayers all in one in the evening. Then the girls put on their sleeping dresses, and lay down on their mats. When they were all quiet and the light turned down, we let them sing, as they do at Wot Sunday evening…

May 29—Got up early this morning and took a walk over to Deacon Alik's place. Kilafwakun, his son, offered to pilot us in a trip around Lelu Island. He took us to the cave and a number of interesting places. It was very pleasant to have Kilafwakun with us, aside from the real service he rendered us. He is very pleasant, polite, and talks very good English. He seems very much devoted to his father, and scarcely ever leaves him. We called on people along the road, and sat down and rested in one or two places along the way, also visiting Sigrah's grave. We reached [Pisin] by noon, having been clear around the island; so you see it is not a large one by any means.

May 30—After breakfast we began to pack our goods, preparatory to proceeding on our journey. We measured out the rice and bread which we had not used, because the Kusaiens had brought us so much food, and left it with them because we knew that food was low with them. It is neither taro nor breadfruit season, and they hunt the mountains for wild yams. We had many callers on this our last morning at Lelu. About noon we were all ready to push off from the shore.

I stayed till all the other canoes had gone ahead, and was left with rather small girls, who could not paddle much to cross the bay, which was quite rough. Pastor Likiaksa took in the situation at once, and came running down to the shore, jumped in and took a paddle. I supposed he was simply going as far as the other side, but not so. He went clear on to Malem, and walked all the way back that same night, dear old white-haired man. He reflects many of the qualities I have heard attributed to Mr. Snow. He has a great many little graceful and polite, thoughtful ways about him…

Pastor Likiaksa had sent word on ahead that we were coming and we were feted along the way and when we reached Malem. I had never seen Malem before and was very much taken with the place. Most of the houses were neatly built with grass growing in the yards. The people there see less of the outside world than the Lelu people, and they seemed greatly pleased to see us, and entertained us royally. When we returned from our bath, we found supper all ready for us, laid out on a table improvised from boxes and boards. Right after prayers we began to prepare for bed; that is, to sleep on the floor in the schoolhouse, as there was no other room big enough to hold us all. Na, the teacher, would not hear to our sleeping on our mats on the floor, and in a little while they had brought in three Kusaien beds and made them up with sheets and pillows.

May 31—We were up by three o'clock, all packed up and ready to start. Then we had to wait until nearly light, because the waves were so high. The ride from Malem onward was very picturesque. We did not stop at Utwe, lest we should have trouble passing a shallow place in the river farther on. We rode for a long distance in a salt-water river, the widest and having the most variety of all the Kusaien rivers. When we emerged from the shelter of the mangrove trees which grew along either side of the river, we found ourselves at the mouth of our old familiar river about two miles down the beach from Mwot.[29]

COWS, SHEEP, AND GOATS

Not only did Pastor Likiaksa have a herd of cows, so did King Sa II. There were also at least eight milk-cows at Wot—the missionaries, their children, and others enjoying fresh milk each morning and evening. The king had five sheep that ran loose in Lelu. "They have never had their [wool] cut or washed and they are really quite a frightful sight—and sometimes quite dangerous!"[30] Many people owned goats, called "nani" [pronounced "nanny," as introduced from America], and there were wild goats in the mountains hunted for their meat in much the same way that wild pigs were hunted.

LETTER TO STOCKHOLDERS OF THE *MORNING STAR*

A mission letter was distributed among American Sunday School children during 1893, entitled "Some Days on the *Morning Star.*" Written by Dr. Pease, it read in part:

Dear Stockholders of the Morning Star: *I have been asked to write you of your old love, the* Morning Star IV. *All our lives and work while among the islands are bound up in her. The mission is called 'The Morning Star Mission.' Events are often dated by the missionaries as so long before or after her coming. When she arrives with letters, books, food, clothing, newspapers, and other things, the great busy world in which you live comes down to this remote corner of creation and we feel that after all we haven't been dropped out or forgotten…*

By means of this vessel we carry to our people (on the little, narrow, low, flat, three-cornered sand banks) teachers, books, take back our scholars to their homes and get others for our training school, we look after our little churches and schools, we supply the wants of our teachers and preachers, we collect their contribution to the Board, we rebuke, exhort, and comfort and help those who need as best we may.

If for any cause the Star fails to appear at the islands, the Christians feel as if they had been forgotten or deserted, while their enemies triumph. When she comes, the good people thank God and take courage, while the Philistines hold their peace.

I would like to take you on board your vessel as she is about to leave Kusaie for one of her trips to the Marshall Islands. She is anchored two miles or more from the station, but you can get into a canoe and the boys will paddle you out to her. Are you afraid? Don't you see the outrigger? That will keep the canoe steady. As we move rapidly along out of the boat passage between the breakers, just look down at the bottom of the ocean, which is not very deep just here. For a quarter of a mile you float above a sapphire and emerald floor, gorgeous beyond description, while fish of various sizes and shapes, red and blue and black and white and spotted, move lazily about. It would seem that nothing could be more beautiful.

But we must hasten on to the vessel, for the flag is up, and she will soon be off. As you go up the ladder and come on deck you are at first surprised to see so many people and so much activity in this quietest of all spots. A large part of the Kusaiens seem to have collected to give the vessel a good send-off and to sell her a few more bunches of taro and bananas and chickens (you didn't know before that chickens come in bunches, did you? But they do.) There are the missionaries and their families and helpers—native men and women and children from the schools, boys also, and young men, the girls and young women of the girls' school, with a teacher in charge. Then there are the ship's company—two engineers, officers, sailors, cook, and stew-

ard, seventy or eighty in all—with their things. And on your vessel passengers are not limited to 150 or 250 pounds luggage as on steamships in America. Everyone takes all he wishes, for the vessel is large, the voyage is long.

Oh, the bananas! Bunches big and little, all about the deck and between decks, tied up to the rigging, hanging from every available nail or peg or hook, and stowed away in safe corners. I'm afraid you think the Morning Star *is in the banana trade.*

Will you stay on board? Do not mind the long swell that begins to play with your Star, *tossing it up and down as if it were only a straw. Soon you will see green and beautiful Kusaie, the "emerald gem of the Pacific," beginning to grow smaller in the distance while her groves of cocoa palms and breadfruit trees seem to wave you a reluctant farewell and bid you come back again as soon as ever you can. You see the bits of mist rising from the deep valleys, the clouds hanging around the steep mountain sides, which are covered with verdure to their very tops, the hazy, dreamy atmosphere, the white birds which the sailors call "bosuns" soaring aloft here and there, the lines of surf breaking with its everlasting murmur on the coral reef which fringes the shore—it is all a matchless picture which one who has once seen can never forget. Who that has once lived on this almost enchanted isle but always longs to return? And the polite, affectionate people there! But I shall get too homesick…*[31]

Dr. Pease, when he wrote this children's letter, was aware that his own days on Kosrae were coming to a close.

NEED FOR REINFORCEMENTS

In January 1894 Dr. Channon wrote to his mission superintendent:

I am glad to report us all as in good health, though somewhat tired. Our greatest sorrow is that Dr. Pease must return and leave no one to fill his place. Miss Hoppin heroically tries to hold things together in the Marshall Islands School with the hope that someone is on his way. This plan weakens the force in the Girls School and Miss Palmer is in a bad state nervously, while it is also a great strain on Miss Hoppin to keep house alone and have a boys school. Who is coming to the help of the Lord?

I am glad to report my school in good condition. We sent out our first lot of teachers this year and hope to keep it up hereafter. We are, of course, greatly pleased with the coming of the new Gilbertese Bibles amongst us. They are beauties. What a monument to Mr. Bingham's faithful, painstaking labor.[32]

Mrs. Channon expressed her feelings. "We have been praying very earnestly for the Holy Spirit the past year. At times it has seemed that He was not with us, for our trials have been so numerous and each one harder than the last. But we have had great grace and wisdom, which although we did not see at the time—yet trusting that we were being led—we feel that it was truly God-given wisdom."[33]

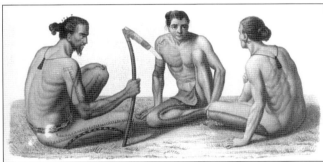

Above: Houses and People of Kosrae, 1824. "Habitation Dans L'ile Ualan"—Postiles and Kittlitz, artists aboard the French ship *Coquille* that visited Kosrae June 3-13, 1824, preserved many incredible images of early Kosrae and its people. (*Coquille* expedition)

Center: Men of Kosrae, 1824. "Habitants de L'ile Oualan."

Below: Women of Kosrae, 1824 "Femmes de L'ile Oualan." (*Coquille* expedition)

The Rev. and Mrs. Benjamin G. Snow.
Benjamin and Lydia Snow, with David and Doreka Opunui,
were the first Christian missionaries on Kosrae, arriving
August 21, 1852. The Snows posed for a photographer
in Honolulu during their 1870-1871 furlough.
(Buck collection)

Pastor Likiaksa and his wife, Kenye, 1890.
Likiaksa, Kosrae's second pastor (1871-1905), married
Kenye after the death of his first wife, Tulpe Pisin.
(The Hawaiian Historical Society)

Above: Interior of the Lelu Church, circa 1895. (The Hawaiian Historical Society)

Center: Interior of a Kosraean cookhouse, circa 1895. (The Channon Collection, courtesy of Maeva Hipps)

Below: Wot Mission Campus, circa 1895. Wharf house, extreme left; Gilbert Islands School, above the beach left; Marshall Islands School, right; Girls' School, upper right. Today's Walung Elementary School stands where the Marshall Islands School was located. (The Hawaiian Historical Society)

Above: Wot beach and wharf, 1896. (The Hawaiian Historical Society, Irving Channon photo)

Center: Mission House, Marshall Islands School, Wot. Home of the Pease family, 1878-1894, and the Rife family, 1894-1906. (The Hawaiian Historical Society)

Below: The Gilbert Islands School, Wot, circa 1895. At right, the home of the Walkup family, 1882-1889, and the Channon family, 1890-1905. All that remains today is the coral-stone walkway and Mrs. Walkup's grave marker. (The Hawaiian Historical Society)

Above: *Morning Star III* lies on the reef at the mouth of Yelu Harbor, February 22, 1884. (The Channon Collection, courtesy of Maeva Hipps)

Below: *Morning Star IV* in Okat Harbor, 1896. A series of ships, each bearing the name *Morning Star*, served the Micronesia Mission from 1856 through 1905, carrying passengers and freight to and from Hawai'i and between the islands. *Morning Star IV* was in service the longest — operating from 1884 to 1900. Many Kosraean men worked as sailors aboard these vessels. (The Channon Collection, courtesy of Maeva Hipps)

Above: The Rev. Irving M. Channon and his wife, Mary Goldsbury Channon, were in charge of the Gilbert Islands School at Wot from 1890 to 1905. (The Channon Collection, courtesy of Maeva Hipps)

Below: The first seven Kosraean girls to be enrolled in the Wot Girls' School pose with their teacher, Mrs. Cole, in 1887. (The Hawaiian Mission Children's Society Library)

Above: Girls' School, Wot, May 1893. Erected in 1886, and repaired after sustaining heavy damage in the typhoon of 1891, this building was destroyed in the typhoon of 1905. (The Hawaiian Historical Society)

Center: Arriving at the Wot wharf, circa 1895. Mrs. Channon is seated center, with several of her children. (The Channon Collection, courtesy of Maeva Hipps)

Below: Kosraean men carry four large "hump-head" parrotfish for the Marshall Islands School, Wot, 1895. (The Channon Collection, courtesy of Maeva Hipps)

Above: American Board Missionaries at Wot, Kosrae, pose with their children in front of the Girls' School in July 1895. From left, standing: Miss Louise Wilson, Miss Ida Foss, Mr. Irving Channon, Miss Theodora Crosby, Miss Annette Palmer, Dr. Clinton Rife and Mrs. Isadore Rife. Seated: Mrs. Sarah Smith Garland holding Dorothea Garland, Paul Channon (standing), Dr. Edmund Pease holding Ruth Garland, Lillian Channon (standing) and Willie Channon (seated on grass), Mrs. Mary Channon holding Hiram Channon, and Mary Channon (standing). (The Channon Collection, courtesy of Maeva Hipps)

Below: Pastor Irving Channon with his senior Gilbert students, Wot, circa 1900. (The Channon Collection, courtesy of Maeva Hipps)

Above: Tulensa Sigrah, deposed as Kosrae's King Sru IV in 1881, with his family in 1886. Beside him in white is his wife, Tulpe Srue, known as Fititi. Between them is their oldest daughter, Sepe Awe Siminlik. She and her second husband, Kun Miswan, were the parents of sons Nana, Nena, Shiro, and Aaron Sigrah, and daughters Sra Ule Kilafwa

Palik and Ruth Simeon Sigrah. Sepe's third husband was Pastor Fred Skilling. Tulensa Sigrah's other two daughters are Kasralap and Srue Sarom. The boy standing behind his father is 11-year-old John Paliknoa Sigrah, who grew up to be Kosrae's last king and seventh pastor. (Hawaiian Mission Children's Society)

Below: Students of the Girls' School, Wot, circa 1900. Kosraean girls, with girls from the Marshall and Gilbert islands, were trained to be pastors' wives and teachers by a series of missionary women from 1886 to 1911. The school was located on the Yorrak ridge, highest point on the Wot campus. (Hawaiian Mission Children's Society)

Above: Christian Training School at Wot, circa 1935. Girls' classroom & dormitory building at Wot, with the Baldwin house, left. This school building stood from 1909 to 1942. It was dismantled, and the lumber carried to Malem, by the Japanese military. The concrete foundation and steps still stand. (The Channon Collection, courtesy of Maeva Hipps)

Below: Elizabeth Baldwin (seated) and Jane DuBois Baldwin, circa 1936, before the front doors of their home at Wot. The Baldwin sisters were in charge of the Christian Training School at Wot for 25 years, 1911 to 1936. In 1926, Elizabeth Baldwin completed the first translation of the Kosraean-language Bible. (Buck collection)

Above: The eastern tip of Kosrae, including Lelu Island and Lelu Harbor, photographed during World War II, February 26, 1944, from a Navy reconnaissance plane. (U. S. Navy)

Center: Japanese ambulatory malnutrition patients stand before the Japanese military hospital in Malem, September 1945. The scarcity of food during the last two years of World War II resulted in much suffering among both the Kosraeans and Japanese. (George D. Olds III)

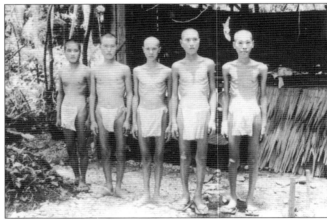

Below: Aliksa Kanku house at Katem, Lelu, September 1945. Used as a clinic by the American military, this was the only building left standing in Lelu at the end of World War II. (George D. Olds III)

Above: Tafunsak and Malem villagers watch as the American flag is raised at Inkoeya on September 15, 1945. (George D. Olds III)

Center: Pastor Palik Kefwas and his wife, Sarah, with their children: Mitchigo, Charity, Tulpe, and Misima—Pisin 1950. (Mary Ruth Hanlin)

Below: Marshallese and Kosraean students with Palik Asher (second from left) and Palik Kefwas (center back, in white)—Wot 1954. (Alice Hanlin Buck)

Above: Sixteen-year-old
Mary Alice Hanlin at Wot,
1949. (Mary Ruth Hanlin)

Center: Mrs. Mary Ruth
Hanlin and her children,
Alice, Ruth Ann and John,
on the Wot wharf, 1949.
(Buck collection)

Below: The Rev. Dr. Harold
Hanlin and Miss Lucy
Lanktree, Pisin, 1954.
(Mary Ruth Hanlin)

Above: A new church is built in Tafunsak, 1950. (Mary Ruth Hanlin)

Center: Utwe Church, 1950. (Mary Ruth Hanlin)

Below: A new church is built in Malem, 1950. (Mary Ruth Hanlin)

216

Above: The Rev. Eleanor Wilson at Kwajalein, June 12, 1961. She served at Wot from 1936 to 1941, and was the first missionary to return to Kosrae following World War II. (Kentron Hawaii Ltd.)

Center: At the ordination of Elden Buck. The Rev. Clarence F. McCall (Kosrae 1936-1940), Alice and Elden Buck, First Christian Church, Fullerton, California, August 14, 1958. (*Fullerton Tribune*)

Below: Erafe Tosie with Lauren & Lisa Buck, Pisin, 1961. (Alice Hanlin Buck)

The American Board appealed for a successor for Edmund Pease: "In the Marshall Islands is a work ably maintained by Dr. Pease long after the time of his retirement has come. He has conducted the Training School, directed the evangelistic work, industrial work, and, in the rare intervals of rest, translated the Scriptures and many hymns. It is a high privilege to take up the work so grandly begun."[34] Their entreaty was not in vain.

PRAYERS ARE ANSWERED

Dr. Pease, age 66, his wife, Harriet, and their sons, Ned and Frank, returned to America in 1894, along with Rachel Forbes and her daughter, Anna. [In 1917 Anna Forbes and Frank Pease, both born on Kosrae, were married.] Those remaining at Wot were given a great boost as three new recruits and one return-ee arrived to relieve the personnel shortages at the schools. Annie Abell, 31 and completing a two-year assignment with the mission at Chuuk, was asked to help in the Girls' School. Also arriving was Clinton F. Rife, a 28-year-old pastor and medical doctor who took charge of the Marshall Islands Training School. He was accompanied by his wife, Isadore Rote Rife, 26. Theodora Crosby, now 30, returned to assist them after an absence of five years.

SCHOOL ROUTINE

There were now 33 Marshallese and 43 Gilbertese young men studying at Wot, in addition to the Kosraean boys who attended the Marshall Islands School as day students—and growing numbers of Marshallese, Gilbertese, and Kosraean girls in the school on Yonrak ridge.

The three schools settled into a routine with not much variation: six weeks of school, then two weeks of vacation—an eight-week schedule that was repeated throughout the year. Though there were no class assignments during vacation weeks, rest was not available to either the students or their teachers. House and farm work continued for the students, while for the missionaries, it was catch-up time—and the students were constantly in need of supervision. And whether school time or vacation, gathering for morning and evening prayers took place every Monday through Saturday, with church services morning, afternoon, and evening each Sunday, for all residents at Wot.

During one of the vacation periods, Mary Channon wrote of planning some diversion "to entertain our scholars, and I think it has done them good and us, too."

Miss Hoppin had our boys spend the evening at her house on Monday where they played games... It was a very rainy night and as I retired, I heard one of the boys sing-

ing at the top of his voice. It was a cheering sound through the pouring rain and wind.

The following night, instead of the three schools gathering to sing, we opened up our partition in the school house, lighted it up with lanterns and gave over to time for them to enjoy themselves. We assisted in suggesting the games. A sheet was hung, and the girls on one side and the boys on the other, guessed the shadows. A sack race was very amusing, "roll the platter," and putting a finger through a hole blindfolded caused a great deal of fun. We put no restraints on their noise, and they did not care to. I think the purpose of the evening was fully carried out. Our banana house being overfull, containing about fifty bunches, we served bananas.[35]

CHURCHES REBUILT

Life was improving for the Kosraean community. During 1894 members of the church, under Pastor Likiaksa's leadership, were able to complete the rebuilding of all four of the coral block churches—each of them having been extensively damaged in the 1891 typhoon. The building in Lelu was completed in July. Mrs. Channon described it: "The thick plastered walls are made of coral rock, and a new roof of iron was put on. The doors and windows have Gothic arches. The church is large and very pleasant. There are a few seats or pews across near the back of the church. The king has a box [an enclosed seating area with a gate at the front of the sanctuary] which is papered with the same paper as his house."[36]

Reporting the rebuilt church to his mission board superiors, Irving Channon wrote, "It required the labors of all the people on the island for several weeks, and at the dedication service the people, of course, attended en masse. The king seems to be holding fast to his profession of faith, and under his rule no liquor is to be had on the island."[37]

Several months later, each of the other three church buildings was dedicated within the same week. Mrs. Channon commented, "Malem on Tuesday, Tafunsak on Thursday, and Utwe on Friday! Our students attended the service on Friday and I took the children. Irving and Dr. Rife went to all three, and Dr. Pease to the last."[38]

KOSRAEAN INVOLVEMENT AT WOT

Because they were available and trustworthy, the missionaries were using more and more individuals from among the Kosraean community in various capacities at the school—indeed, Kosraeans had worked extensively at Wot since the very beginning—as builders, farm workers and domestic helpers. They had provided canoes for the mission schools all through the years—sometimes ordered by the missionaries and paid for, but more commonly, presented as gifts. Kosraeans had also become the preferred sailors aboard the *Morning Star* missionary vessels. Their devotion as Christians, their smiling eagerness, and their unlimited energy more than compensated for their lack of formal education. ✛

Notes - Chapter 7

1. William E. Strong, *The Story of the American Board*, Boston, 1910, p. 448
2. Harriet Pease in Mary A. Marvin, "A History of Missionary Work in Micronesia 1852-1910," p. 60
3. S. E. Bishop, *The Friend*, Dec. 1889
4. Edmund M. Pease, *The Friend*, May 1889
5. H. Pease in Marvin, p. 69
6. H. Pease in Marvin, p. 70
7. "Kusaie in the Nineteenth Century," undated, p 18.
8. J. C. Dewar as quoted in F. W. Christian, *The Caroline Islands*, p. 156
9. Mary Long Goldsbury Channon, journal notes, 1890, p. 7
10. E. Theodora Crosby [Bliss], "A Day in Kusaie, Micronesia," p. 1
11. M. L. G. Channon, personal correspondence, March 13, 1891
12. Jessie Hoppin in Marvin, p. 90
13. Ibid
14. Estelle Fletcher in Marvin, pp. 89-90
15. H. Pease in Marvin, p. 94
16. Irving Channon to J. S. Emmerson, Hawaiian Evangelical Association, April 1, 1891
17. H. Pease in Marvin, pp. 96-98
18. J. Hoppin in Marvin, p. 101
19. I. M. Channon, personal correspondence, March 4, 1892 & Jan. 16, 1893
20. E. T. Crosby Bliss, "Fifty Years in the Island World," p. 55
21. M. L. G. Channon, "Black Sheep," unpublished paper, courtesy of Maeva Hipps
22. J. Hoppin in Marvin, p. 141
23. M. L. G. Channon. unpublished paper, courtesy of M. Hipps
24. M. L. G. Channon. personal correspondence, May 2, 1893
25. M. L. G. Channon, unpublished, undated "Memories of Kusaie, 1890-1905"
26. Louise Wilson in Marvin, p. 284
27. M. L. G. Channon, journal: July 1892-November 1895, Kosrae, p. 80 and p. 85, courtesy of M. Hipps
28. Sarah Smith Garland in Marvin, p. 151
29. J. Hoppin in Marvin, pp. 141-145
30. M. L. G. Channon, "Kusaie," March 11, 1895, p. 9, courtesy of M. Hipps
31. E. M. Pease, "Some Days on the *Morning Star,* 1893"
32. I. M. Channon, personal correspondence, Jan. 10, 1894
33. M. L. G. Channon, personal correspondence, 1895
34. E. T. Crosby Bliss, "Fifty Years in the Island World," p. 53
35. M. L. G. Channon, personal correspondence, 1895
36. M. L G. Channon, personal papers, courtesy of M. Hipps
37. I. M. Channon, in *Life and Light for Women* as quoted in Marvin, p. 380
38. M. L. G. Channon, personal papers, courtesy of M. Hipps.

NUNAK YOHK KE CHAPTER 8
1894-1901

Sie sin mwet Kosrae su weang lutlut Wot oemeet pa mwet fusr Insief se. Inel pa Alik, tuh mwet uh elos panglol Kefwas. Nina kial pa Limanro Kamat, ac papa tumal uh el mwet Jamaica su sie mwet fakfuk loat. Kefwas el arulana sroalsroal mweyen el kwa papa sac. Missionary fin acn Wot elos liye lah Kefwas el lalmwetmet ac alken. Meet liki el weang lutlut Wot el tuh orekma fin oak ekin sie selu. Ke el weang lutlut Wot el wi school lun tulik Marshall. El mukul na wo sifa se ke lutlut ah. Ke safla lutlut lal, arulana yohk kasru lal nu sin missionary, mweyen el pa tafweang nunak lalos nu sin mwet Kosrae, oayapa nunak lun mwet Kosrae nu sin missionary uh. Tok el tuh sie mwet luti ke lutlut Marshall fin acn Wot. Mutan kial pa Kenye Liokas. Na tok el sie deacon lun Church Kosrae.

Ke May 1894 Mr. Channon ac mwet kol lun Church Kosrae elos akmus-raella Deacon Konlulu, na el pastu se aktolu lun mwet Kosrae.

Ke 1894 Irving Channon el tuh orala sie Bible class nu sin mukul in Church Kosrae, su arulana engan in wi class sac. Elos ac kal som nu Wot wik nukewa ke lusen pacl lutlut sac orek. Tokosra Sa II el sie sin mwet ma wi class sac. In 1895 mukul Sialat in acn Tafunsak elos orala oak lulap Kosrae soko ac sang in ma lun lutlut Gilbert fin acn Wot.

Sie mwet luti pwengpeng fin acn England el tuku nu Kosrae in 1896. Inel pa F. W. Christian. El tuh kaksakin ke el liye lah mukul Lelu pukanten fahsr wi alu, ac nukum nuknuk na wowo. Mutan uh elos wi pac nukum nuknuk kato, ac sracsra nacna fin sifelos. Kutu selos sunya surafraf otwot ma oasr robin kac orekla ke sropon usr, pangpang "kusus." Tokosra Sa II el usal Mr. Christian mutwata ke pot lulap Lelu. Mr. Christian el som pac nu yorol Pastu Likiaksa, ac el akilen lah el sie mwet lalmwetmet ac moniyuk ke orekma. Mr. Christian el tuh kaksakinul pac Kefwas ke sripen el tuh simusla kas English pukanten ac lungasla ke kas Kosrae, ac sang nu sel. Mr. Christian el som pac nu Wot in liye lutlut tolu we. Ke el osun nu sin Dr. Rife ac Mr. Channon el akilen lah mukul luo inge eltal mwet na fas ke orekma ac lalmwetmet.

Ke 1896 Mr. Channon ac tulik mukul Gilbert elos tafwela wharf Wot ah tuh in sun acn loal inkof ah. Elos oayapa orala inkanek soko ke eot eka, mutawauk ke wharf ah nwe ke sun school Gilbert elucng ah. Innek soko inge srakna oan nwe misenge.

Mwet luti sasu luo tuku pac in orekma ke school lun mutan in 1897. Ineltal pa Jenny Olin, mutan Sweden se, ac Emma Kane, mutan Hawai'i se. Tulik mutan Gilbert longoul luo, tulik mutan Marshall longoul sie ac tulik mutan Kosrae limekosr tuh wi lutlut lun mutan fin acn Wot ke 1898. Sie sin tulik mutan Kosrae su tuh wi lutlut pa Louisa Skilling. Papa tumal ah, Harry Skillings, el sie mwet America su muta Kosrae, na el tuh orekma in kamtu fin acn Wot in akfalye molin lutlut lal Louisa. Sie pac tulik mutan Kosrae we pa Rebecca Tulenkun [Palikkun]—ac sie pac, el an natul Kilafwakun, su ma natul Deacon Alik Lelu. Tulik mutan ma matu elos lutlut ke kais sie book in Bible. Tulik ma srik lukelos elos lutlut ke sramsram in Bible. Elos nukewa lutlut tuta, orek mongo, aknasnas, orek ima, oayapa otwot kupwes ac surafraf.

Mukul Kosrae 120 tuh som muta Wot ke wik se in 1899 in musai sie lohm lutlut lun tulik mutan. U se inge kolyuk sin Tokosra Sa II, Pastu Likiaksa, ac Paliknoa John Sigrah, sie mwet suksuk fusr. Mwet Kosrae inge sifacna use sak ac fasu nu ke lohm sac, ac Dr. Rife el kasru ke kufwen sroasr. Ke elos us sak toasr inge utyak nu Yonrak, oasr mwet srital ke mwe on welulosyak fahsr in akpwaryalos ac in akkeyalos. Orekelik mwet orekma ah nu ke u akosr, na ke sripen yohk pwar lalos oru arulana mui orekma lalos. Lohm sac fit 35 lusa ac fit 20 sralap, na elos awia ke fuh ac kwalla fasu kac ke len sifanna. Ke lotutang in len tok elos orala sinka ah. Ke infulwen len akluo, tulik lutlut ac mwet luti lalos orala sie kufwa nu sin mwet orekma nukewa. Meet liki elos mongo, Pastu Likiaksa el eis pacl lal in kaksakin God ac in fahk lupan engan lalos in kasru orekma lun mission. Tukun mwet nukewa elos yuk on soko, na Pastu Konlulu el pre, ac mwet nukewa mutawauk mongo.

Sie mukul fusr Germany, su inel pah Philipp De la Porte sie mwet luti in acn Gilbert, tuh supweyukme nu Kosrae in lutlut yurol Irving Channon fin acn Wot. Tukun yac luo, Dr. Rife, Pastu Channon, Pastu Likiaksa ac Pastu Konlulu elos mosrwella in pastu ke September 1899. Pastu De la Porte ac mutan kial eltal som nu Nauru ac missionary we ke yac puspis.

Ke 1899 government lun acn Germany tuh molela Caroline Islands sin government lun acn Spain. Wangin mwe lokwalok Mwet Germany elos oru nu sin Church Kosrae ku nu ke lutlut fin acn Wot.

American Board tuh kukakunla Morning Star IV ke May 1900. Victor Melander el sie mwet America su orala company in kuka lal fin acn Kosrae. El tuh payuk sin Neneus, sie mutan Kosrae, ke 1890. Oasr oak soko okoal pangpang Tulenkun, ac el arulana kasru missionary ke el kalkal in masrlon acn Kosrae, Pohnpei, ac kutu pac tuka in acn Micronesia. Sie kamtu lal fin oak soko ah el payuk sin Tiokwe, mutan Nukuoro se. Ke Tiokwe el muta Kosrae el aengani yurin mutan Christian we, ac tia paht el baptaisla. Tiokwe el mwet se oemeet in fahkak Wosasu nu sin mwet Nukuoro.

Ke sun 1900 oasr orekma lun mission ke acn lumngaul akosr in acn Marshall, Gilbert, Kosrae, Pohnpei, Mortlock ac Chuuk. Kutu missionary America ac Hawai'i elos orekma fin acn ingan, tusruktu inkaiyen mwet su oru in arulana sa puseni mwet Christian fin acn Micronesia, elos mwet Micronesia sifacna. Apkuran mwet kol inge nukewa elos tuh lutlut Wot.

CHAPTER EIGHT

MISSIONARIES COME AND GO
1894-1901

ALIK KEFWAS

After 15 years, the missionary teachers were seeing the wisdom of having welcomed from the start a few Kosraean young people into the schools as students. Among the earliest of these was one who had taken advantage of his home's proximity to Wot. His name was Alik, but he was also known by the Bible name chosen for him, Caiaphas—or, as he spelled it, Kefwas. Though he competed in a classroom where Marshallese was used as the primary language, he excelled, and the missionaries soon singled him out for special tutoring. Dr. Pease worked with him one on one, teaching him to read and write English and giving him religious instruction.

Kefwas stood out as an intelligent and industrious scholar, and he stood out in another way also. His skin was significantly darker than that of his classmates. His nickname among the Kosraeans was "Black Kefwas." His father was a Jamaican whaler whose ship had anchored for several weeks in Utwe Harbor during the height of the whaling industry. Kefwas was born of a tryst that sailor had with Limanro Kamat, a young woman of Insief.[1]

After spending several years of his youth traveling as a sailor himself, Alik Kefwas had returned to Kosrae and to his mother's family—the primary landowning family of the Wot property—just about the time Dr. Pease and King Sru IV were selecting the site for the mission schools. Not only was he an excellent student, but the missionaries began relying on Kefwas as an appreciated and respected aide. He cooked for them; acted as their major Kosraean language interpreter; was liaison between them and the Kosraean community; accompanied them on their forays into the villages. As the years went by, the missionaries used him as a teacher and still later as a Bible translator. Members of the Kosraean Church also began turning to him for insight and advice. He married Kenye Liokas, developed into a serious, capable Bible scholar, and was selected to be a deacon of the Church. His gentle, congenial nature made him easily available to anyone who sought him out. By 1894 Alik Kefwas was approximately 45 years old.

MR. CHANNON CONDUCTS
TRAINING CLASSES FOR KOSRAEAN LAYMEN

The missionaries at Wot continued to assist in the development of the Church on Kosrae. During 1894 Irving Channon conducted a series of weekly training classes at his Gilbertese school for Kosraean church men. The study course was popular and successful. Many of the men walked from five to 15 miles from their villages, and paddled another four miles down the lagoon to the school, in order to participate. It was reported that King Sa II, who could be notoriously difficult and had long resisted efforts to convert him—after getting comfortable with another lifestyle during his 27 years in and around Hawai'i— attended regularly and "showed by his life that he was a changed man."[2]

KONLULU ORDAINED AS KOSRAE'S THIRD PASTOR

It became apparent to Irving Channon that Pastor Likiaksa, the vener- ated leader of the Church on Kosrae, was losing some of his stamina. With the Pastor's blessing and the approval of other Church leaders, Mr. Channon offici- ated at the ordination of Deacon Konlulu as Kosrae's third indigenous pastor on May 20, 1894. This action was of great benefit to the Church as well as to Pastor Likiaksa during his declining years.

The new Pastor Konlulu was a veteran member of the Church on Kosrae. As a young man, he and his wife, Kenye Wa, and the first two of their six children, Peter and Abraham, lived for several years on Ebon where Konlulu served as cook for the Snow household. When Konlulu returned to Kosrae with his family in 1875, it was obvious that he had made great strides in his Christian life. He quickly became an important part of the Church leadership. Kenye Wa Inkoeya, Pastor Konlulu's wife, was one of the six women celebrated as being among Kosrae's first converts.

Mary Channon wrote of the new pastor: "Konlulu is a good-looking man and a very fine man, too. I wish [you in America] could see some of our faith- ful Christian men. I think you would be many times surprised to see what fine looking earnest people they are."[3]

A VISIT TO UTWE

The day after Pastor Konlulu's ordination, Mr. Channon took his family, and the Gilbertese student body, to Utwe to help the men of that village pull from the forest the new canoe he had ordered from them. The log had been hollowed out sufficiently to be drawn to the water, where the work on it would be finished. Mrs. Channon described the trip in a letter to her parents on May 22, 1894:

At two places on the way, all the boys had to get out and help draw the canoes, and in one place all the women but myself and little ones walked. One place was like a narrow river and the water so low that the outrigger had to be carried, those who carried it having to walk in the deep black mud...

After about three-fourths of a mile through the narrow stagnant river, we came to a wide place like a lake... We sighted Utwe, a hamlet of native houses on a rocky islet. We found only women at home, as the men were away across the bay working on the canoe, so as soon as the women and bundles were put ashore at Alik's house, Irving and the [Gilbertese] boys departed to help on the canoe. Sra, Alik's wife, a little short woman, received us very kindly into her home. The other women of Utwe also welcomed us gladly...

During the afternoon I went out to visit the old and blind people in the few little houses. One woman looked as though she might be 70 years old; she sat in a doorway and received us. She was quite blind in one eye and her dress had no sleeves. Sra told us that she was very poor, and having no relatives whatever, she lived on the kindness of others there. There was one man who had just a hole in his face below his eyes, no mouth or nose. He was putting thatch on a house. Further on I saw an old blind man, a half caste, also a sick man. The old woman gave me a number of small shells which she had cleaned. [These tragically disfigured individuals bore the ravages of the venereal diseases which had been introduced to Kosrae by the whalers.]

Soon after our return the men also returned. They had had very hard work pulling out the canoe. Had our school not helped, they would have been two days about it. Two men were hurt by falling and the canoe's grazing them. While supper was prepared I visited the cookhouse, and saw some men preparing breadfruit, breaking it up into small pieces. The cookhouse is built like all other houses except that the floor is built all around a large square center for a fireplace. This is about 8 X 13 feet square. After supper, we all gathered in the front room of Alik's house for prayers. I think there must have been fifty in all, including the Kusaiens there.

After prayers, the beds were assigned. The married people, fifteen in number, were to sleep in the cookhouse; the boys, eighteen in number, in the front room of Alik's house. The missionary and his four children occupied one small room at the back of this large one, and Alik and his wife occupied the other.

On rising we found that Alik and Sra had spent the greater part of the night fishing so that in the morning we were feasted with fine fish from the harbor. At breakfast, the fish, taro, and bananas were served in dishes woven from the coconut leaf. The moist food is usually served in a long, flat boat about the length of the width of a dining table. It has a rim about the edge. We embarked at about ten o'clock and reached home not far from two o'clock.[4]

LAUNCHING CANOES AND POUNDING FAFA

In early 1895 Pastor Channon commissioned the building of yet another new canoe for the use of the mission. It was being fashioned by the men of Sialat, Tafunsak. February 16 was the day the great rough-hewn log was to be brought from the forest to the lagoon and launched. Theodora Crosby, invited to the launching, described the day and its festivities:

We left Mwot shortly after three o'clock in the morning. It was a glorious night, the moon being full, and it was so light one could see to read without difficulty. Two canoe loads of Gilbert boys went on ahead of us, and our canoe was also well filled. We were so sleepy during the first hour or so that we were very quiet. Just as the sun was fairly beaming down upon us in the morning freshness we came to Sialat, where we received a cordial welcome from the assembled people and from Pastor Likiaksa, who was master of ceremonies.

There were two houses—in one, great preparations were in progress for the feast, but the other, the one nearest the sea, was for the missionaries. Both houses were merely thatched roofs extending to within three feet of the ground and open on all four sides. The one we occupied had fresh mats laid on the ground, so it was nice and clean. After we had greeted the people we went over to the other house where they were making fafa, which is the "summum bonum" of a Kusaien feast.

There were four young men, the principal operators, while some half a dozen others were assisting. Before each of them was a large flat stone, perhaps two feet in diameter. On this they pounded the taro, taking the roots after they had been baked in the um, or native oven, on hot stones, and pounding them till it was one solid mass, spongy, like dough. When this process was completed it was put in a clean breadfruit or banana leaf and passed on to other workers who placed it on the stones in front of them and added baked bananas to it, kneading them in till they were thoroughly incorporated with the mass. Then it passed into other hands; one man was adding the juice from the sugarcane to a part of it, another added coconut milk—and this, by the way, is not the water in the nut. They grate or scrape the meat very fine, then strain it through a mass of coconut fiber. It comes out thick and creamy. Then several others place it in sections of banana leaves. A last worker squeezes coconut milk and the grated coconut on the top like frosting, and the fafa is done. It is delicious!

By and by, Pastor Likiaksa brought us some breakfast. They gave us pigeons, breadfruit, bananas, fish and fafa—and apologized for the meagerness of the meal! We were very hungry, as we had been up six hours, and canoe riding four hours had given us keen appetites.

About eleven o'clock the men all went back into the woods to bring the canoe down to the water, and when they were ready one of the boys came and told us. A rough path had been made by cutting down small trees and bushes—on either side a real tropical jungle. At length we came out on a little clearing where the new canoe lay. So far it consisted only of the trunk of a tree, hollowed out, and roughly shaped on the outside. The finishing was to be done later, after it reached the mission.

One of the oldest Kusaiens now stepped forward and—after they had fastened a heavy cable to the canoe and placed rollers under it and for some distance on the road seaward—placed the men at regular intervals, holding the large rope. Then he stood by the canoe and harangued them for perhaps five minutes. He gave a cry—very much like a college yell—which was answered by the men; then they gave a long pull, a strong pull, and a pull all together, which started the canoe and gave it such an impetus that they ran with it some distance. When they paused, the yell was repeated, and the answering cry from the men. The simultaneous pulling got the heavy canoe over the ground with a rapidity that astonished me. At the last rush it floated on the sea, and their task was ended.

The ride home was delightful; the sun was setting, a cool breeze blowing from the mountains, and there was just enough motion to rest one, almost a lullaby. The moon was rising as we swept round the last point and drew up on the beach at Mwot.[5]

FACULTY AT WOT SCHOOLS FINALLY ADEQUATE

There were nine American missionaries teaching at Wot during the 1895 school year, and the missionaries reveled in having sufficient personnel to share the work load. Irving and Mary Channon were at the head of the Gilbertese school; Clinton and Isadore Rife and Theodora Crosby were with the Marshallese—though Miss Crosby would leave in March of the next year, again because of ill health. Annie Abell, Ida Foss, Annette Palmer, and Louise Wilson were at the top of the hill, their Girls' School now the largest of the mission's three training centers. Jessie Hoppin was on furlough.

Everyone was delighted when Dr. Pease returned to Wot from his retirement home in Claremont, California, to stay for more than a year. He was still in the process of translating the Bible into the Marshallese language and wanted, once more, to be close to his language informants.

SPANISH MAN-OF-WAR

In August 1895, a Spanish man-of-war brought Governor Pidal from Pohnpei to Kosrae. King Sa II and the people of Lelu hosted a huge feast to honor the Spanish governor, the ship's captain, and officers, on the evening of the 9th, and the next day participated in a meeting with the governor to which all Kosraeans were invited. Among other topics, the governor discussed various industries, such as hat making, that the Spanish authorities might assist the

Kosraeans in starting.

The man-of-war was the one that had intercepted the *Morning Star* in 1889 in Pohnpeian waters, when the *Star* had been refused permission to approach that island. That particular incident, and the treatment of Pohnpei's Protestant missionaries by the Spanish, were much in the thoughts and conversations of the missionaries at Wot. But accompanying Governor Pidal was Henry Nanpei, a young Pohnpeian leader who was known to the missionaries as an important friend of the Protestant cause. Seeing Henry in the governor's entourage, Dr. Rife—in Lelu for the meeting and festivities—decided to extend an invitation to the governor and the crew of the man-of-war to visit Wot before returning to Pohnpei.

Sure enough, on Monday morning, August 12, the Spanish ship appeared in the waters off the reef at Wot. Mary Channon described the visit of the Spanish governor in her journal:

The Governor came ashore, visited the schools, heard the singing and then had a long talk about various matters. He seemed pleased to see the islanders so intelligent and Irving put in a word about how it used to be at Ponape. There was no priest on board as we thought there might be, and we saw that they were interested to see our work was to help the natives to an education. The Governor said he regretted very much not letting the Star *go to Ponape, but such were his orders from Madrid. He and the officers were certainly very gracious. Nanpei came also. We were rather surprised that they should let him. He went up to see Miss Palmer who wanted to learn all she could about Ponape people. They all left about noon, and sailed away at five o'clock while we raised our Spanish flag and bade them farewell.*[6]

BRITISH SCHOLAR'S ACCOUNT
OF HIS VISIT TO KOSRAE

On May 2, 1896, F. W. Christian, a British scholar, sailed from Pohnpei with Capt. Melander aboard the trader's schooner, the *Tulenkun*. "Captain M., an American subject, offered me a passage by her to Kusaie, his headquarters," wrote Christian. After stops at Mokil and Pingelap they sighted Kosrae on the 9th.

Towards sundown, after a spell of miserable weather, the clouds lifted a little and disclosed the sharp and angular outline of Kusaie standing out clearly defined under a pall of inky blackness, the tops of the mountains hidden in bank upon bank of cloud haze and smoky wreaths of teeming vapor.

Late at night we pass the twinkling lights of the missionary settlement of Mwot, high up on the hill slopes, flashing out a greeting as it were through the dense gloom... In the early morning, May 10th, on rounding the promontory, the island of Lelu with its spacious harbor on the far side, comes in sight… The main island reminds one of Rarotonga, with the bizarre features a little softened down. The altitude of the highest peak is about the same. In the middle are two needle shaped peaks set close together.

We are now close up to the settlement with the King's new lumber and shingle house standing forward prominently amongst many humbler abodes, under the shade of a noble Callophyllum tree. Right in front of us lies Captain M.'s dwelling, his storehouse and copra shed flanked by white-walled outhouses. Seaward extends the wharf built up sturdily of blocks and lumps of coral and basalt fragments, with a topping of black and white pebbles and sea-shells. There we anchored about ten o'clock.

Numbers of natives are passing and repassing on the road beyond, for it is Sunday and church time is nigh, and defaulters run the risk of censure. Everyone seemed greatly interested in our arrival, and many thronged the landing place to welcome us on shore.

The men were neatly dressed in European garb, the women in loose graceful gowns. Most of them wore flowers in their hair, and for head-gear broad low hats of Pandanus-leaf trimmed with tasteful ribbons of banana fibre, in tinting which delicate fibre they excel. Pink, white and red roses, crimson hibiscus and the amber and purple tassels of the Barringtonia flower, form so many bright touches in a pretty picture of rich and subdued tones of color happily blended. Thus we landed on the shore of Kusaie.

The King bade us heartily welcome, and introduced us to his wife and household who seemed thoroughly pleasant people, and made one feel quite at home from the very first. The afternoon passed rapidly away in conversation, the King apparently taking a lively interest in the proposed exploration of the ruins on his island, and promising, without any hesitation, his hearty aid and cooperation.

Whilst these preparations were going forward we paid a visit to Pastor Likiaksa, the aged teacher, a keen, alert, wiry old man, with an indefinable air of mingled wisdom, shrewdness and benevolence. Then we visited the other end of the village to call upon Kefwas, the intelligent school-teacher, named after Caiaphas, the High Priest, of evil fame. We persuaded him and Likiaksa to share our evening meal, and ere long roast fowl, fried fish, eggs, turtle, and taro were disappearing with fearful rapidity. Our dessert consisted of a mixture of taro, yam, coconut cream and ripe bananas mashed up together into a pudding, and steamed in leaves underground.

The two holy men refused wine and beer, contenting themselves with drinking huge mugs of scalding black tea, sweetened with tablespoonfuls of brown sugar. Soon after the meal was ended Likiaksa left, and Kefwas remained behind. Kefwas had compiled a small English-Kusaien list of words which he undertook to go through with me…

Some days later, after a comprehensive study of the Lelu ruins, F. W. Christian continued:

The king suggested an excursion along the coast to see something of the country, and visit the settlement and schoolhouse of the Boston Mission, offering to accompany me part of the way, but when pressed to introduce me to the missionaries he excused himself, saying that he was not very well pleased with them, and considered that they were unfairly usurping the power which properly belonged to him alone, but declining at the same time to more expressly state the grounds of his grievance.

Accordingly we started on our walk across the tidal plane between Lelu and the mainland. We hailed in passing the venerable Likiaksa hard at work on his little island of Yenyen weeding and digging amongst his sweet potato beds. He is devising traps and snares for the rats which have evidently been very busy amongst his cherished tubers… The King promised him a fine yellow Tom on the first opportunity, and we left the holy man somewhat comforted, delving and grubbing away with an energy astonishing for a man of his years.

After exploring the area of the Yekela waterfall with the king, as well as other parts of Tafunsak, the visiting Englishman boarded the *Tulenkun* for the trip on around to Wot.

Entering a little sandy cove we run alongside the wharf built of coral fragments and, climbing the winding stairway hewn in the hillside, find ourselves in the little settlement which forms quite a township—the headquarters of the mission. Like Caesar's Gaul it lies in three parts.

Each of these centers round its schoolhouse. The first establishment is allotted to the education of youths and boys from the Marshall Islands, in which archipelago the Germans, under certain restrictions, have granted the missionaries leave to establish stations for their propaganda. Dr. Rife is in charge. The second, under the Rev. Mr. Channon, is for the instruction of Gilbert Island boys, and the third, highest up on the mountain side, is occupied by the girls' school, where a mixed bevy of Gilbert, Marshall and Kusaie lasses live under the aegis of the ladies of the mission.

We strolled about the little settlement. Altogether the community wore an air of quiet prosperity and contentment. The students, some one hundred and forty in all, appeared on their very best behavior. The lads gave us a sample of their powers as choristers. The reader will perhaps be surprised to learn that part-singing is a very popular institution among Pacific Islanders.

The boys are taught various useful trades, such as carpentry and joinery, and the girls are instructed in the use of the needle and all manner of housewifely duties. It is a miniature copy of the Kamehameha School for native boys and girls at Kalihi in Honolulu, and doubtless the native in time will be the gainer for the gradual formation of settled habits of industry.

Of the kindly and hospitable people in charge of the Mission Station of course

there can be but one opinion. They believe genuinely in their work, and devote them-
selves with single-hearted zeal to what seems an unpromising and thankless task.
With those who frankly differ from them in their ways or methods they can argue
without bitterness or lack of charity, as all seekers after truth should surely do.

At sunset we went down to the Channon family's pretty little house to a spread of
native and imported dainties, and a most interesting evening's talk ensued. My host
proves an exceedingly well informed and liberal minded specimen of the professional
man of brain and action that Yale, Harvard, Princeton, and their sister universities
are turning out year after year to enrich Young America.[7]

Several days later Mr. Christian departed Kosrae on the *Tulenkun* with
Capt. Melander. King Sa II traveled with him to Pohnpei to pay his respects to
the Spanish governor, Sr. Pidal, who was scheduled to return home to Madrid.
Of King Sa, Mr. Christian commented, "He speaks English correctly and even
elegantly, and has proved a valuable assistant."[8]

GILBERTESE STUDENTS EXTEND WOT WHARF

During one of the two-week vacations in 1896, Irving Channon began
the "arduous task" of lengthening the Wot wharf so that it would extend into
deeper water. A stream, fed by an active spring in the swamp behind the beach,
was depositing sand in the landing area. The Gilbertese boys were divided into
two groups—one working mornings and the other afternoons—to bring stones
from the reef the school's two largest canoes. The missionary, with several helpers, did the piling and placing of the stones. At the same time, Mr. Channon
constructed an enclosed pond in the wharf, where he and the boys could keep
live turtles available for feasts.

When the job on the wharf was completed, the students and their teacher
began "paving the trail" from the beach up the mountain to the Gilbert school.
This was on the opposite end of the Wot beach from the steps that led up to
the Marshall Islands school. The Gilbertese boys constructed their trail using
porous coral stones which they chopped into blocks with axes. This fine walkway lifted those on the trail up out of the mud, and became a lasting monument
to the industry of the Gilbertese students.

MISSIONARY TEACHERS COME AND GO

In 1897 the *Morning Star IV* brought Jenny Olin and Emma Kane to teach
at the Wot Girls' School. Miss Olin, 30, originally from Sweden, was sent by
the American Board, and Miss Kane [caw-neh], a graduate of the Kamehameha
Girls' School in Honolulu, by the Hawaiian Evangelical Association.

The same voyage of the *Star* took the Channon family—now numbering six children—back to the United States. The four youngest—Willie, Mary, Hiram, and Stephen—had all been born at Wot. It was Mr. and Mrs. Channon's first furlough, and they spent it, primarily, with friends and family in Minneapolis, Minnesota. Also traveling aboard the *Morning Star IV*, from Pohnpei to San Francisco, was George Bowker, the missionaries' favorite carpenter, with his Pohnpeian wife and their children, now numbering three. Mr. Bowker had decided to move to California, where he "started a fruit farm in Fresno."[9]

When the Channons were ready to return to Micronesia the following year, the *Morning Star IV* was in dry dock in San Francisco for maintenance. Those who worked on the vessel did so reluctantly because of the many large centipedes that kept crawling out of the hull!

The missionaries were given passage from California on a privately owned sailing vessel, the *Queen of the Isles*, a "two-masted bald-headed schooner, one hundred feet long with a twenty-four foot beam."[10] In addition to the captain, first mate, engineer and cook, there were four Kosraean crew members who had worked aboard the *Morning Star IV* and were returning home.

VOYAGE OF THE *QUEEN OF THE ISLES*

The departure on August 26, 1898, was particularly poignant for Irving and Mary Channon, as they were leaving three of their children, the oldest only 10—in the United States. Paul, Lillian, and Mary were in a home for missionary children in Oberlin, Ohio. Mrs. Channon wept as they sailed through the Golden Gate and out into the Pacific. She noted her feelings in her diary: "One has rather a peculiar sensation as the shore of the native land grows dim in the distance, perhaps it can be described by what Mr. Channon says of the way he is affected when he thinks of the children left behind, as 'a funny feeling in the throat.' Yet we rejoice that the hour has come when we can go forth with the glad tidings of great joy, and with a prayer that God will abundantly bless our native land and our loved ones there. We go forth to those who are still in the darkness and bondage of sin."[11]

Four other Channon children—Willie, Hiram, Stephen, and baby Estella, who was born during the furlough year—were accompanying their parents back to Kosrae. Also with the family was "Queenie," Mr. Channon's great Dane.

Four other passengers, also American Board missionaries, shared the cramped quarters aboard the *Queen of the Isles*. Mr. Martin Stimson and his wife, Emily Hall Stimson, and Miss Elizabeth Baldwin and her sister, Miss Jane Baldwin, were traveling to Micronesia for the first time. The four of them were assigned to the mission endeavor at Chuuk.

Though the missionaries had hoped to put into Honolulu to visit colleagues and check for mail—and Jane Baldwin had looked forward to a few days of recuperation from constant seasickness—the captain decided to bypass the Hawaiian Islands. All they saw were the distant peaks of Mauna Loa and Mauna Kea above the clouds on the 16th day out of San Francisco. Fifteen more days passed before the little ship reached Jaluit in the Marshall Islands.

ELIZABETH AND JANE BALDWIN VISIT WOT

After two weeks at Jaluit, the ship continued west. It was the third Sunday of October when they sighted Kosrae. While the island tantalized them with its nearness, the ocean was so calm that it took another day and night to reach it. When those at Wot spied the vessel, Alfred Walkup—who had returned to Kosrae to cover for the Channons at the Gilbert school while they were away— paddled out beyond the reef with some of the students to meet it. He piloted the schooner into tiny Yela Harbor—or Morning Star Harbor, as the missionaries knew it.

As soon as the anchor was dropped the little *Queen of the Isles* was swarming with Marshallese and Gilbertese students, as well as Kosraeans, all of whom wanted to shake hands with everyone on board. Passengers and boxes were loaded into boats and canoes for the short trip to the mission wharf. The Channons were pleased to be home again, and their students were excited and grateful to see them. Since the men who moved the freight from ship to shore could work only when the tide was high enough to float their canoes and the school dinghy over the reef shelf, the ship would be at Kosrae for at least three days while the 35 tons of supplies for the mission were unloaded and carried to shore.

A cordial invitation was extended to the Baldwins by Jenny Olin at the Girls' Training School to be her guests while the ship was in port. The sisters were relieved to have a few nights of rest on land. They found it a breath-taking climb, past the Gilbertese school, to the place on the side of the mountain where the Girls' School was situated. According to custom, some of the students greeted Elizabeth and Jane by placing braided circlets of fresh flowers on their heads.

Little did the Baldwins, who decided to wear the lovingly prepared head leis "to please the girls," or the Kosraeans who wove them to welcome the sisters, realize how intricately their lives would be intertwined in the years ahead. These two women, who would be transferred by the American Board from Chuuk to Kosrae 14 years later, were destined to have more influence on the Kosraean Church and culture than any other missionaries except for Benjamin Snow.

After two days of rest, the Baldwin sisters bade farewell to the Wot missionaries—as well as to their new and future Kosraean friends—and continued aboard the *Queen of the Isles* to Chuuk.

MISSIONARY WOMEN WRITE A PETITION

During the years that the three schools had been located on Kosrae, there was a constant struggle between the resident missionaries and the Hawaiian Evangelical Association concerning when missionary visits from Kosrae should take place among the Marshall and Gilbert Islands and who should make those visits—when students would be gathered from those islands and when the trained students would be returned to serve. When trips of the *Morning Stars* did take place, restrictions were often made by the captain or traveling officials that hampered and irritated the mission teachers.

And there was growing dissatisfaction among the teachers in the Girls' School over the perceived second-rate service that the crew of the *Morning Star* was giving to their students, as opposed to courtesies extended to students of the boys' schools! There had also been complaints that some of the girls had been bothered by some of the younger males among the German passengers who were sometimes carried aboard the *Star*.

In December 1898, the five women who were currently teaching at the Girls' School signed a quickly penned petition when the students they planned to send home were denied passage on the *Morning Star IV* for lack of space. The women sent the petition aboard the *Star* to the Hawaiian Evangelical Association. It was entitled "Protest of the Lady Teachers of Kusaie Girls School in being Restricted from taking Passengers on the *Morning Star* among the Islands of Micronesia."

WHEREAS it has been recently called to our notice that the missionary ship, Morning Star, *in carrying on the work of touring necessary for the continuance of our training schools at Kusaie, is breaking the laws of the United States by carrying a larger number of passengers than her permit from the government allows, thereby jeopardizing the lives of the passengers, the liberty of the Commander and the honor and reputation of the American Board; and*

WHEREAS our work for the present year has been already seriously restricted; and

WHEREAS such restrictions continued would result in the final and total disbanding of our school;

THEREFORE resolved that the American Board of Commissioners for Foreign Missions and the Hawaiian Board be respectfully petitioned to take this matter into immediate consideration and to bring about such changes as shall make it possible to obtain a permit and carry as many passengers as the demand of the work requires;

RESOLVED that a copy of the above be sent to each of the above mentioned boards.

(signed,) Jessie R. Hoppin, Annette A. Palmer, Louise E. Wilson, Jenny Olin, Emma Kane—Girls' School, Kusaie, Micronesia, December 28th, 1898.[12]

The rush to get this petition written while the *Morning Star* was there underscored a perennial problem experienced by the missionaries. Mrs. Channon expressed it well. "We missionaries can only scan our mail while the *Star* is in port for there are so many, many things to do. Boxes to open, always more or less company to entertain, and orders to check, besides looking about and after things whenever the ship's boats land. Of course, classes come to a halt!"[13]

GIRLS' TRAINING SCHOOL REPORT FOR 1898

Miss Hoppin submitted a detailed report of the Girls' Training School to the Hawaiian Evangelical Association for that same year. There had been a total of 22 Gilbertese girls, 21 Marshallese girls, and five Kosraean girls during the year. Weddings between students of the girls' and boys' schools were not uncommon, but carefully regulated—and sometimes suggested and arranged—by the missionaries.

Ten new girls from six different Marshall islands have joined us. One of these is from Kwajalein, an island from which we had never had a representative before. These girls vary in age—the two youngest being about six years old and the oldest perhaps sixteen. One of them a child of six, is the grandchild of a trained teacher. Her grandmother, Emily, was one of the most thoroughly Christian women these islands have ever known. The child's father and mother and an uncle and aunt have been trained in the training schools and are doing active work as teachers.

On January tenth, we took into school a half-white girl, Louisa Skillings by name. Her father is an American and her mother a native of Nauru. We took her in partly because she is a very attractive girl and would be among the first to suffer at the hands of the Spanish officers who have visited us during the year and who say they are coming again; partly because she possesses those qualities which make her a desirable member of our school, and partly because our funds are low and her father is willing to work on the repairs on our building as pay for her tuition. Our school then numbers at present forty-eight.

There is another Kusaien girl whose father has asked to have her taken into our school. She is almost the only Kusaien girl among the older girls on the island, who has always had a clear record. Her grandfather was Deacon Alik, one of the salt of the earth, faithful from the time of his conversion until his death a few years ago. The only objection to taking her into school is that our building is so small for the number of girls already in school. The food and clothing of the Kusaien girls are furnished by their parents.

We are asking our Honolulu friends to aid us in erecting an addition to our building, for an assembly room—which we need very much—for a dormitory, and a bedroom which can be used for a sick room when needed for the girls. The material for such a building could probably be bought for $500 and we think that with Mr. Skillings' help and native workers, the building could be put up without sending for a carpenter. Dr. Rife kindly offers to oversee the work.

The older girls are studying specific books of the Bible, such as Ephesians and Galatians while the younger girls study Bible stories. They are studying missions in India and Turkey, and all students are members of the King's Daughters organization. All learn house work, table setting, cooking, sewing, etc., and work in the gardens and cutting the extensive lawn, the making of handcraft—baskets and hats.

Miss Wilson oversees the garden work and Miss Palmer the sewing. There are three prayer meetings a week—one on Sunday afternoon attended also by Kusaien women from outside our schools—one on Wednesday, conducted by the girls and designed to give them training for this kind of service when they go out to do more direct Christian work—and Friday.

Miss Olin's services are appreciated. She is learning the Marshall Island language. Miss Kane is proving herself valuable as a teacher. We have to thank the Hawaiian Board and the Kamehameha Girls' School for making it possible for us to have her with us. Her influence in the school is good, and she has been increasingly helpful in all departments of work—she has been teaching the girls music—and is a great comfort to us all.

We have worked together very harmoniously and happily and have enjoyed each other's companionship to a degree only to be appreciated by those who have been left in a foreign land with a limited number of companionable people of their own tongue. We have great reason to thank God for His blessing on our work and to go on with courage which is born of the conviction that this work is our trust from Him and that He is using this school-home to advance His Kingdom in the world. Respectfully Submitted, Jessie Rebecca Hoppin.[14]

DEATH OF HARRY SKILLINGS

After spending much of 1898 working at Wot—partially to work off tuition expenses for his daughter, Louisa, by doing carpentry—Harry Skillings, still in his mid-40s, died on October 19 and was buried on the 20th. Originally from Portland, Maine, he had arrived on Kosrae from Nauru in 1874, surrounded by his Nauruan family and retainers. As the months went by, Harry had exchanged a wild, self-serving youth for a calm and productive life among the Kosraeans, his adopted people. During the 1880s he had managed a trading company in Lelu. He served four of Kosrae's kings as interpreter and advisor. He also worked from time to time on the *Morning Star*. He was frequently in the company of King Sa II when the latter visited Wot during the 1890s.

Harry Skillings' wife, Jenny, continued living in their fine, "plastered" Sansrik home on the edge of Lelu Harbor. Wot's missionary women frequently visited her when they were in Lelu. Two of Harry and Jenny's children died in their youth, but the other two grew to be respected, productive adults: Fred— who had sometimes worked with his father on the *Morning Star*—became Kosrae's fifth pastor, and Hattie was Kosrae's last queen as the wife of King John Paliknoa Sigrah.

KOSRAEAN BUILDING PROJECT

The additional building that the teachers at the Girls' School had been wanting became a reality in July 1899 when Jessie Hoppin came up with another of her many unique ideas and plans. Sadie Smith Garland reported:

Miss Hoppin's thoughts on the subject crystalized into a conversation with Paliknoa [John Sigrah]. It had not seemed best for the mission to afford a new house just now, so Paliknoa was sounded to find out whether the Kusaiens would be willing to aid us by putting up a native house on this Kusaien plan—giving their work and material and being feasted at the end. Paliknoa—himself a former Kusaien student in the Marshalls school—seemed much pleased with the idea, and quite sure that the Kusaiens would be glad to accept the proposal.

And so it proved, for even the king, who is not disposed to be friendly to the missionaries, smiled upon the undertaking. Word was sent around the island, and last week the Kusaiens brought up most of the sticks, thatch and ridgepoles needed for the work.

At about nine o'clock on the announced day the sound of music was heard in the land. Much excited running hither and thither among the girls followed, and the watchers on the brow of the hill called back their bulletins to the groups on lawn and veranda: "Now they're marching along the beach. Oh, what a long procession!" "Now they're coming up the Channon way—No, they're going around the hill to Dr. Rife's path." "Here they come!"

And they came, led on by a much-traveled gentleman who for years lived in foreign parts, who roared forth his "Left! Right!" Then came the band, followed by twenty men, bearing on their shoulders the last great timber for the house, and marching in quickstep. Following them in single file was a motley procession, big and little, in a lengthening line, almost all of whom tried to respond to the "Left! Right!" of the leader.

The band? First Paliknoa, with an accordion which he tunefully plays. Paliknoa holds his head with a proud lift, which recalls his worthy father, Sigrah, and wears shoes. Next Alik, who used to be a sailor on the Star, with a policeman's whistle, which he shrilly and persistently blows. Then Joseph, with a triangular water-tank from the wrecked Horatio. This is the big brass drum which he rhythmically and energetically bangs. Then came Frank, with cymbals—two large iron spoons, the backs of the bowls beating in time to the music. Last came another with a small drum—an inverted milk pan of goodly size.

As the procession neared the spot where the house was to be erected, a halt was ordered and Paliknoa maneuvered the timber-bearers. They marked time, marched forward, marched backward; they changed the huge stick from right shoulder to left, from left to right, with marvelous precision, and as lightly as though it had been but a feather's weight. At last it was put down, and the procession resumed its line of march up to the main house, while the eagerly interested girls crowded the verandas, where the teachers also stood. All bore gifts of food—coconuts, bananas, pineapples, taro, breadfruit—and each deposited his share on the grass at the foot of the steps, until there was a goodly heap. Three or four old men, wishing to share in the good work, tried to carry off the lively march step with the sprightliness of youth, but with joints stiffened with rheumatism.

The king, who brought up the rear of the procession, was in a most genial mood, and fairly beamed upon us all. A little time was spent in resting and in greetings, while the men were served by the girls with a drink made from the fresh sap of the coconut bud called sakaru—donated by the boys in the Gilbert School and carried about in buckets, with cups from which to drink.

Then we were aware of a sudden pause in the merry noise, though we had heard no signal. All heads were bared and bowed, and our eyes were drawn to the white-haired old minister, Likiaksa, who stood at some distance under a breadfruit tree on the site of the house-to-be with his face uplifted in prayer. No word reached us, but a hush fell over the whole place.

The house is thirty-five by twenty; the workers number one hundred and twenty-one, and are divided into four parties, each under a leader and each assuming one corner of the house—one quarter—as its share. One who has not seen a native house in process of erection cannot conceive of the amount of work involved. No nails are used. The sticks, as they are brought into position, are rudely held in place with strips of strong bark, and at last tied with coconut cord, which is put on with great accuracy and firmness, and made, in the winding, into fancy patterns with various colors, so that the tying is really artistic when well done. If the sticks and timbers (all native, of course) are not straight and true, the house is poor looking and has less stability. But all the sticks brought for this house are as nearly perfect as can be, and the building is splendidly put together.

Dr. Rife furnished tools—spades, saws, level, hammer, axes, hatchets—and has had an eye on the work today, but found little to correct. The men had agreed not to race, as they sometimes do, for fear of shoddy work. But as the frame rose higher, the enthusiasm and jollity grew apace until there was a continuous uproar, with lighter intervals now and then when the girls passed about with their buckets of cooling drink—molasses and water, limeade or sakaru—for the heat was great and the men worked hard.

It was a sight to remember. The frame swarmed with active figures who, with agile movements, slipped from place to place tying, winding, sawing, hacking, passing the heavy sticks lightly upward, where they were as lightly caught by half a dozen hands and swung into place. At times we counted upward of seventy men upon the frame in every imaginable attitude of activity—a very good test of the strength of the frame.

Now it is time for the thatching to begin. The thatch, all prepared, lies waiting in great heaps in pieces six feet long. The leaf is doubled over a reed in rows and sewed through, each piece being fastened to the roof structure with coconut cord in three places, and the pieces set so close one above another as to widely overlap and leave no chance for a leak. On each side of the roof stand twenty men. The pieces of thatch are thrown lightly upward by others standing on the ground, and with wonderful speed are fastened into place, so that there seems to be no pause in the throwing and catching as the men work steadily upward.

Faster and faster the men worked, and at last found themselves racing as the final rows of thatch went on—but really, one could scarcely blame them. Their excitement was infectious. We gazed, fascinated, at the mushroom house growing under our eyes in a day. In just forty-five minutes from the first tying, the thatch was complete, even to the finishing touch. Both Dr. Rife and Mr. Channon agree that it is finely done.

And now the feast! Preparations were almost completed. The Kusaiens had come early the next day and worked vigorously on the siding of the house, which was finished about noon. The long tables were spread with seats for one hundred and twenty-seven. The hour set for the feast was two in the afternoon. Most of the white folks came up to witness the festivities. The rooms in our house were worth seeing, and as it turned out it was very fortunate that the plan was to have the dinner in the house, for there was a Kusaien downpour of rain nearly all day.

The front room seated about thirty, the middle room over forty, the large school-room more than fifty. The double doors connecting the three rooms were thrown open, and as Tokosra sat at the small table especially prepared for him, at the head of a long table in the front room, he could look down through the rooms to the back veranda. Ferns and flowers were everywhere; Japanese lanterns were hung in all the doorways. We could not put up the American flag and would not put up the Spanish, but the greenery was ample decoration.

But how to get the guests properly seated! The Kusaiens make very much of rank. In the first place the table had to be so arranged as to avoid any one sitting with back to Tokosra. I think it took half an hour to seat the guests. Despairing of making any headway, I called a council of Tokosra, Paliknoa and Pastor Likiaksa. All of any rank were singled out and places assigned them, but still they stood back and waited. "What is the matter?" "O, Sikein has not been found yet. We cannot go on till he comes."

Pastor Likiaksa assured me that he could not by any means sit near Tokosra— he must sit out in the other room with the majority of the people. I appealed to Tokosra, reminding him that while he was the leader in temporal affairs, Pastor Likiaksa was their spiritual leader and should sit in a prominent place, as he was to open the feast. Tokosra responded very heartily and insisted that Pastor Likiaksa sit at his left, with Paliknoa at his right. Then arose a new difficulty. No one would sit on the inner side of the second table because that would present their backs to some of their chiefs! So I went to Tokosra again and begged him to call by name those who should sit in those seats.

At last all were seated, and silence fell as Pastor Likiaksa rose and spoke. He reminded them what a privilege it is to the Kusaiens to have the schools here, and how much good had come to them, directly and indirectly, through the missionaries. He said that the teachers, in asking the Kusaiens to put up the house, had conferred a favor upon them, and that the work had been very small beside what had been given in return. This, he said, was a great day for Kusaie, when teachers and natives, chiefs and common people, were all gathered together to help each other with interest in a common cause. He spoke of God's goodness in giving them these friends, and continued that the most appropriate way to recognize it was by a prayer and hymn of thanksgiving. His prayer was very earnest, and at its close Na II, who is possessed of a very sweet voice, started the hymn. It swelled to a full male chorus in all the parts, and the volume of harmonious sound was noble.

At the close of the hymn Pastor Likiaksa called on Pastor Konlulu to speak and pray, and he responded briefly in the same vein as Pastor Likiaksa. At the close of his prayer, I expressed thanks to the Kusaiens in the name of the teachers and girls. The girls who had been chosen as waiters now stepped forward in their bright dresses and the feast began.

As the feast drew to a close the girls gathered on the veranda where the organ was and sang a little greeting. Then a dozen of them sang the Carpenter's Song from Miss Blow's book, "Busy is the Carpenter," imitating in the refrain the sound of the plane and hammer. The whole school then sang the Canoe Song, from Mrs. Frear's Kindergarten Songs, followed by vigorous applause from all. Then the tables in the front room having been put back, the Kusaien children who have been taught up here *stood in a row before the dignitaries. As many of the Kusaiens as could find a place looked in, and Miss Kane led the little folks in their kindergarten songs.*

I could see over the top of the organ how Tokosra was shaking with laughter over the motions of the little hands. At the close we all joined in the gospel hymn, "My Jesus, I love thee," which we knew to be a favorite with the Kusaiens. I wish I might have listened to it from a distance; it must have been very beautiful, for the Kusaiens are natural singers, and the girls were in their very best singing mood. A number from the other schools had come to look on at the feast, so we had a grand chorus of two hundred![15]

RULES OF CHURCH MEMBERSHIP

An observation of Louise Wilson concerning membership in the Church on Kosrae appeared in an issue of *Life and Light for Women*:

The Kusaiens seem to be steadfastly advancing in the right way. They have some peculiar ideas about some things. One is about people joining the church. They only take in the married people. This we think is a mistake, and have told them so. There was no doubt a reason for it in the early days, but now there is none.

I had been conversing with the friends from Lelu, and after I came in the house one of the girls inquired, "Is there any news?" "Yes," I said; "I have good news for you. Your brother Nena has decided to be a Christian."

A few evenings after, the sister came to me and said, "Mother Wilson, you told me Nena had repented?" I said, "Well, hasn't he?" Her answer was, "He hasn't said so in the church, has he?" I said I did not know anything about that, but I knew that he had told Mr. Channon that from henceforth he intended to lead a Christian life, and that to my way of thinking he was a Christian as soon as he gave his heart to Christ, without waiting to speak in the prayer meeting.

But the Kusaien way of thinking is, if a person should profess to be a Christian and not make an open confession with his mouth in prayer meeting, he or she is not a Christian at all.[16]

APPRENTICESHIP OF PHILIPP DE LA PORTE

A young German missionary, Philipp Adams De la Porte, had been sent by the Peniel Mission of Los Angeles, California, to teach in the Gilbert Islands in 1895. His dedication and determination, as well as his eagerness to cooperate, impressed the American Board missionaries who sent him to Kosrae to study the Gilbertese language with Irving Channon. The goal was to transfer Mr. De la Porte to the Hawaiian Evangelical Association and then send him to Nauru as a missionary, along with William, a student at Kosrae's Gilbert Islands Training

School, and Kenye, William's Kosraean bride. Since Mr. De la Porte spoke and taught the German language, the German governor of the Marshalls readily agreed, as Nauru was then considered to be a part of the Marshall Islands.

For almost two years Mr. De la Porte studied and assisted at Wot. He also used the time to visit and encourage the Kosraean churches, who were attracted by his youth and enthusiasm. In 1897 he returned to California to officially transfer from his mission—and then traveled on to Germany where he married. In 1899 the Wot missionaries and the Kosraean church leaders welcomed him back with his wife and their new baby, Augusta.

KOSRAEAN CHURCH ASSISTS IN ORDAINING MR. DE LA PORTE

In his 1899 report to the Hawaiian mission board, Irving Channon included, "Just before the *Star* left for the Marshall Islands, a council was organized at the call of the Mission Church. The Kusaien churches and pastors assisted, and Mr. De la Porte was ordained to the ministry. It was an occasion which deeply impressed the Kusaiens as well as one of great rejoicing to us as we looked forward to the opening of Nauru again."[17]

In a letter written on September 28 aboard the *Morning Star IV* en route to Nauru, Mr. De la Porte shared details of his ordination service:

September 19th was an eventful day in my life, for on that day I was ordained to the office of the Gospel Ministry. In compliance with the wish of the mission at Kusaie, an Ecclesiastical Council met on that day for the above mentioned purpose. There were present Rev. I. M. Channon of the Gilbert Islands Mission, Rev. C. F. Rife of the Kusaie and Marshall Islands Mission, and Reverends Likiaksa and Konlulu, Pastors of the Kusaien Church.

The Council was opened by singing the hymn, "The Morning Light is Breaking," followed by prayer by Rev. C. F. Rife. Rev. Channon was chosen Moderator, and Rev. Rife Scribe. I responded to a request by Rev. Channon and gave a sketch of my conversion and call to the Ministry, and also made a confession of faith. After answering a number of questions satisfactorily, the Council decided to proceed with the Ordination.

The Ordination Charge was given in a most impressive manner by Rev. Channon, the Right Hand of Fellowship by Rev. Rife, M.D. Rev. Likiaksa read the Scriptures and Rev. Konlulu offered the Ordaining Prayer. May I always be faithful in doing the duties of a true Minister of the Gospel of Christ.[18]

Twelve years later the Rev. Philipp De la Porte was still ministering at Nauru. He reported to the Hawaiian Evangelical Association that he was holding church services for the Kosraeans who were working there in the Pacific

Phosphate Company, Ltd, as well as for Pingelapese, Mokilese, Pohnpean, Chuukese and Mortlockese workers.

GERMANY BUYS CAROLINE ISLANDS FROM SPAIN

At the end of the Spanish-American War in 1898, the American missionaries on Kosrae, Pohnpei, and Chuuk had hoped that the United States would take over that entire area of the Pacific. America did annex Guam, but concerning the other islands, insisted only that Spain dispose of all remaining possessions. On September 30, 1899, Germany paid 25 million pesetas for the Caroline Islands and the northern Marianas.

Germany moved quickly. In October, Governor Rudolph von Brennigsten, on the ship *Kudat*, stopped briefly at Kosrae on his way to Pohnpei. As in Spanish times, Pohnpei was made the administrative center for the eastern part of the Carolines. German administration of the islands was a great improvement over the haphazard and sometimes ruthless government of the Spanish. Buying and selling alcohol or firearms were prohibited, but other trade was encouraged. The production of copra increased rapidly.

Not long after arriving at his post at Pohnpei, the German governor was informed that Marshallese young people were being educated at the schools on Kosrae and then returned to the Marshalls to be teachers and church workers. Though there was more freedom of movement during the German era than during the Spanish, the Governor questioned the training of Marshallese at Kosrae. He decided to look into it, and news of his plan to visit reached Wot.

WOT STUDENTS LEARN THE GERMAN NATIONAL ANTHEM

Mary Channon and Jenny Olin hurriedly taught the students to sing the current German national anthem in its original language. The women had learned the anthem from Philipp De la Porte. The governor and his entourage arrived one morning unannounced, and when they were escorted into the assembly room the governor was surprised and delighted to hear "Die Wacht Am Rhein" ["Keeping Watch on the Rhein"] sung with great spirit by the students. He complimented them highly and, as he left, told Mr. Channon that the missionaries could bring all the students they wanted from the Marshall Islands.

To his government he reported: "I hardly know a place that surpasses Kusaie in picturesque charm and natural beauty… The natives show a higher grade of cultivation than those of Jaluit, which may well be ascribed to the influence of the American Mission. It must be acknowledged that with the help of the magnificent natural advantages of Kusaie, the leaders of the Mission have done everything to make the stay of their pupils and their education pleasant. The instruction, too, is given in an earnest, judicious manner. The neat dresses of the pupils, their unconstrained joyousness and their healthy appearance, show that careful attention is paid to their physical well being."[19]

The Germans made no more effort to interfere with the missionaries. The new administration was satisfied, too, to allow Kosraean church leaders to handle problems that ordinarily would be taken care of by the courts, since Pastor Likiaksa, Pastor Konlulu and the other church leaders were already doing this with considerable success. This freed the Germans from having to establish a government bureaucracy on Kosrae, though they did insist on there being a king through whom they could communicate to the Kosraean community. They recognized Sa II in this traditional position. Actually, like the Spanish before them, the Germans had little effect on Kosrae—though the Kosraeans and the missionaries at Wot were told that they should no longer celebrate the Fourth of July.

The missionaries liked to tell the story of the first time the SS *Germania*, subsidized by the German government for Gesellschaft, the trading company, arrived in Lelu Harbor. It was early morning and the captain immediately sent for men to unload and load the steamer. But King Sa II told him emphatically that since it was the Sabbath, the Kosraeans would be resting and attending church. There was nothing the captain could do to influence the king to change his mind.[20]

CAPT. MELANDER ASSISTS THE MISSION

Though the Jaluit Gesellschaft now had a trading monopoly in the Eastern Carolines as it did in the Marshall Islands, it was unsuccessful on Kosrae where Capt. Victor Melander, an independent Swedish-American trader, was operating. Capt. Melander—whose wife was Neneus, a Kosraean woman—had purchased the Lelu trading company, previously owned by Harry Skillings, in September 1892. By now he was firmly established on Kosrae and was a friend and supporter of the missionaries. With his ship, the *Tulenkun*, he made frequent trips to Pohnpei, as well as to the Mortlocks and Chuuk, often carrying mission personnel, mail, and food orders between the various mission stations. Occasionally he traveled all the way to San Francisco for supplies and trade goods, carrying mail for the missionaries in both directions. Capt. Melander was much relied upon and greatly appreciated by members of the Micronesia Mission.

He was also indirectly responsible for the Christian message first being shared on one of Micronesia's two Polynesian atolls, Nukuoro, south of Pohnpei.

Tiokwe, a woman of that island, became the wife of the carpenter who traveled with Capt. Melander as part of his crew. Impressed and influenced by the women of Kosrae's Christian community, Tiokwe became a Christian herself and was successful in introducing Christianity to her people on Nukuoro. Her inspiring story appeared in a small pamphlet published by the American Board.[21]

CONCERN FOR THE GILBERT ISLANDS

Because of the strictures imposed by the Spanish-American War, and later the need for repairs, the *Morning Star* was out of service, and because Capt. Melander did not travel to the Gilberts, communication was nonexistent between the mission at Kosrae and those islands during 1899 and 1900.

Irving Channon complained that, even with a chartered vessel while the *Star* was unavailable, the Gilbertese work was being neglected: "It will cost too much and the effect will be very serious. The teachers must be paid, they must be counseled (they are but children), new teachers must be located—we have seven ready to go—and we need recruits in order to keep the work up with no diminution of teachers in the years to come. We can get along as far as food is concerned, but to cripple the work... 'I pray not that thou shouldst take them out of the world, but that thou shouldst keep them from the evil one' [John 17:15 KJV]."[22]

The missionaries were further stymied when word was received that the American Board had decided that the cost of repairs to the *Morning Star IV* was more than the mission ship was worth. In May of that year it was sold in San Francisco, and there was no plan for a replacement.

KOSRAE SUFFERS DROUGHT AND INFLUENZA

In August 1900, Louise Wilson wrote:

There has been less rain this year than any since I first came here. The Kusaiens say they cannot remember having had a year like it before. We think it was owing to the lack of rain during the months of March and April that we had so much sickness in our school. We had two serious cases of dysentery in the girls' school. One, after a long illness, recovered. The other died inside of a week. A number of others might have proved serious if they had not been taken in hand when the first symptoms appeared. Those were anxious days, especially as we knew we did not have suffi- cient medicine of the proper kind in the mission to hold the disease in check if many more were afflicted with it. Three children belonging to the married people in Mr. Channon's school died about the same time.

The influenza has begun amongst the Kusaiens, and the only thing to expect is that we will have it here in a few days. Our storeroom is beginning to look very bare, and would look more so if we had not bought some extra provisions of the Rifes' before they went on furlough. We are using our last tin of kerosene, and last week we began on our last fifty pounds of flour, but we will still get along for a few weeks and not be hungry. If the ship holds off for a month longer it will be rather serious for our school—with so many mouths to feed and only a small number of demijohns of rice left in the house in way of food for them.[23]

Among the Kosraeans who died during the influenza epidemic was Queen Srue Nueliki on October 3. The conversion of King Sa II was further confirmed by his Christian demeanor at the time of his wife's death. A friend of the king's, Mr. Thompson—a survivor of the 1899 shipwreck of the American whaler *Horatio*, Capt. E. L. West[24]—was also a new convert. He was married to Srue Katin Alokoa on Christmas Day, 1900, in Malem, where he was encouraged by "the interest of the people" in the school he had established for them.[25] He and Srue had one daughter, Evelyn, before he left Kosrae. Evelyn later married Basi Siba. [This sailor is not connected to Kosrae's Thomson family.]

HAWAIIAN EVANGELICAL ASSOCIATION RELINQUISHES ITS ROLE IN MICRONESIA

By the turn of the century there were 54 stations and out-stations of the Micronesia Mission in the Marshalls, Gilberts, Mortlocks, at Chuuk, Pohnpei, and Kosrae. Though a number of American and Hawaiian missionaries were appointed to key posts across eastern Micronesia, the majority of workers overseeing the swiftly increasing numbers of Micronesian Christians were themselves members of the island communities—most of them graduates of one of the three mission schools at Wot, Kosrae.

In 1901 Annie Abell, having served at Wot for six years, returned to the United States. That same year the Hawaiian Evangelical Association relinquished its official part in the Micronesia Mission. The Boston-based American Board of Commissioners for Foreign Missions continued its historic ties with the churches, missionaries, and schools of the Gilberts, the Marshalls, and the Caroline Islands. ✠

Notes - Chapter 8

1. Tulensru Tupak, personal conversations, June 20, 2001
2. E. Theodora Crosby Bliss, *Fifty Years in the Island World*, p. 55
3. Mary Long Goldsbury Channon, "Kusaie," March 11, 1895, p. 9, courtesy of Maeva Hipps
4. M. L. G. Channon, "Our Trip to Utwe," unpublished paper, courtesy of M. Hipps
5. E. T. Bliss in Mary A. Marvin, *A History of Missionary Work in Micronesia 1852-1910*, pp. 136-137
6. M. L. G. Channon, "The Spanish Man-o-war," unpublished paper, courtesy of M. Hipps
7. F. W. Christian, *The Caroline Islands*, p. 150ff
8. Ibid, p. 168
9. M. L. G. Channon, "Black Sheep," unpublished paper, courtesy of M. Hipps
10. Eleanor Wilson, "Too Old?" p. 6
11. Ibid
12. Jesse Hoppin to Hawaiian Evangelical Association, Dec. 28, 1898
13. M. L. G. Channon, "My Trip to Ruk," 1892, p. 21
14. J. Hoppin to HEA, Feb., 1898
15. Sarah Smith Garland in Marvin, pp. 245-247
16. Louise Wilson in Marvin, p. 283
17. Irvin Channon report to HEA, 1900
18. Philipp De la Porte to HEA, Sept. 28, 1899
19. E. T. Bliss, p. 55
20. Ibid, p. 35
21. M. L. G. Channon, "Memories of Kusaie, 1890-1905," pp. 5-6
22. I. Channon, personal correspondence, 1899
23. L. Wilson in Marvin, p. 260
24. Rodrigue Levesque, *Ships Through Micronesia 1521-1991*, p. 71
25. M. L. G. Channon, journal entry, Feb. 10, 1901, courtesy of M. Hipps

NUNAK YOHK KE CHAPTER 9
1901-1911

D r. Clinton Rife el akilen lah mwet fusr su aksafye lutlut lalos fin acn Wot, ac fulokla nu ke yen selos, elos supwar mweyen mwet matu ke church lalos elos tia lungse lohng nunak lalos. Mwet matu Kosrae elos pahla in nunku mu mwet fusr enenu na in inse pusisel ac porongo na kas lun mwet matu. Dr. Rife el tuh oakiya sie un mwet Etawi fin acn Wot ke February 2, 1901 nu sin tulik lutlut ke school tolu, ac oayapa mwet fusr Insief ac Leap. Elos sulella Alik Kefwas in president se emeet lalos. Mwet fusr nukewa arulana engan lah oasr u se lalos sifacna.

Dr. Rife ac Pastu Channon finne kafofo ke school Marshall ac school Gilbert fin acn Wot, eltal suk pac inkanek in kasru Church Kosrae. Oasr pacl eltal som nu in kais sie mura in muta yurin mwet kol lun Church, ac topuk mwe siyuk lalos ac luti ke Bible. Dr. Rife el oayapa srike in kasru mwet mas. Pastu Channon, Alik Kefwas, ac John Mackwelung, eltal lungasla kutu Psalm ac kutu leta lal Paul nu ke kas Kosrae.

In April 1901, Mr. Channon el tuh kasrel Tokosra Sa II in konauk acn fal tuh soko inkanek in musalla Okat lac nu Lelu. Inkanek soko inge arulana eneneyuk, yokna nu ke pacl wangin along. In 1902, Mr. Channon ac tulik lutlut Gilbert tuh kasru mwet Lelu in musai sie tower ke lohm alu Langosak tuh in nien tapweng. Tapweng se inge supweyukme sin mwet kawuk lal Miss Hoppin fin acn America tuh in sie mwe esmakunul Louisa Skilling su tuh misa ke el srakna wi lutlut Wot. Mwet Christian Kosrae elos musaela pac lohm na wowo se fin acn Pisin in 1902, mweyen missionary elos ac som muta Lelu ke pacl oak Germany soko ma kasrusr inmasrlon Australia ac Hong Kong ac oai Kosrae. In July 1902, Miss Olin ac Rebecca Tulenkun eltal oakiya elementary school se lun acn Lelu. Eltal oayapa orala sie oakwuk sasu ke Sunday School lun tulik fin acn Lelu ac Malem. Ma kunaltal in akoo mwe lutlut nu sin mwet luti inge kewa.

Yac aklumngaul tukun missionary elos sun acn Kosrae, mwet in Church elos akfulatye Jubilee lalos ke August 21, 1902. Apkuran in mwet Kosrae nuke-wa tuh wi toeni ke len sac. Elos arulana engan in lohng sramsram lun mwet matu tolu su akkalemye ouiyen moul lun mwet Kosrae meet liki Mr. Snow el tuh sun acn Kosrae. Pastu Likiaksa ac Pastu Konlulu eltal takunla pac sramsram ke mwet Christian Kosrae oemeet.

Arulana pukanten mwet tuh weang Church Kosrae ke malem ekasr tukun pacl in Jubilee sa. Mwet kol lun church elos tuh som nu ke lohm nukewa in sramsram yurin sou nukewa. Mwet matu nukewa ma soenna mwet Christian elos tuh auliyak ac siyuk elos in weang Church. Sie pac ma yohk sripa in pacl sac pa oakwuki lun Un Mwet Etawi fin acn Kosrae nufon ke February 1903. President se oemeet lun Etawi Kosrae pa Fred Skilling. El tuh yac 29. Benjamin ac Joseph, wen luo natul Pastu Likiaksa ac Tulpe Pisin, eltal wi pac mwet kol ke pacl se Etawi Kosrae tuyak. Pastu Konlulu el misa in 1903. Pastu akakosr Kosrae pa Likiaksa Yal. El akmusrala ke November 18, 1903.

Ke 1905 mwet kol lun Church Kosrae elos tuh siyuk American Board in fuhlela tuh Church Kosrae in sifacna lac, ac in tia sifil ma lun mission. American Board elos insese nu ke nunak se inge, ac mwet nukewa arulana insewowo ke oakwuk sasu se inge.

Sie pac paka na upa tuh kunausla acn Kosrae ke April 19, 1905. Mwet Kosrae limekosr misa ke paka se inge, ac tulik mutan Marshall se tuh misa pac fin acn Wot. Wanginla fahsu ke lohm alu akosr Kosrae, ac sie lohm alu ah musalla na pwaye. Lohm sin mwet uh wi pac arulana musalla. Fokinsak nukewa wanginla. Ke June 23, malem luo tukun paka sac, Pastu Likiaksa el misa. El tuh pastu Kosrae yac tolngoul akosr. Ke el misa, Pastu Likiaksa Yal el mukena pastu fin acn Kosrae.

Ke sripen lohm nukewa ac ima nukewa kunausyukla ke paka sac, missionary fin acn Wot elos wotela mu tulik lutlut ke school Marshall in folokla nu Marshall, oayapa tulik Gilbert in folokla pac nu Gilbert. In May 1905 sou lal Channon elos folokla nu America, ac mwet lutlut Gilbert ac sou lalos elos folokla nu Gilbert. Ke May 1906 sou lal Rife ac mwet lutlut Marshall tuh som nu Marshall. Lutlut lun tulik mutan pa lula fin acn Wot. Mwet luti lalos pa Louise Wilson, Jennie Olin ac Jessie Hoppin. Tia paht na Miss Wilson el fulokla nu America ac Miss Marion Wells el tuku aolul.

Ke 1907 mwet Kosrae elos mutawauk in sifilpa musai lohm alu Langosak. Elos tufahlla eot ke eka in sang orala falful kac, ac elos ayaol fahsu ke tin. Tufahna orekmakinyuk tin ke sie lohm alu Kosrae. Elos moli lam nuk na kato nu ke lohm alu sac. Sak na wowo Kosrae pa sang orala srungul oayapa patun ke winto ah. Lohm se inge kisakinyukla ke April 1908. Ke oak lulap Germany ac oai Lelu, pukanten mwet tuh srola in som intoein lohm alu ah. Elos arulana kaksakin lah mwet Kosrae pa sifacna musai lohm na yohk ac kato se inge.

Tulik mutan Kosrae oayapa mutan Marshall ac Gilbert srakna fahsr wi lutlut Wot. Ke sripen school luo lun tulik mukul ah tuh kauli, school lun mutan ah tuh kwaco ke wangin mukul in oru orekma toasr. Papa ac nina Kosrae elos kena tuh tulik mukul natulos in ku in wi lutlut, ouinge wotla tuh tulik mukul Kosrae ku in wi lutlut. Pa inge pacl se emeet missionary ac mwet kol lun Church

Kosrae elos tukeni pwapa ke acn Wot. In 1909 American Board tuh sifilpa supwalma Mr. George Bowker in musai loom lutlut sasu se fin acn Wot. Lohm se inge apkuran in oanu lohm se el tuh musai in 1893. Mukul Kosrae 137 tuh kasrel Mr. Bowker musai lohm lulap se inge fin acn Yonrak.

Ke Tokosra Sa II el misa in 1910, mwet Kosrae elos pangon mu elos tia enenu in oasr tokosra sasu se lalos. Tusruktu, mwet Germany elos sap mwet Kosrae in sulela sie mwet nu ke wal lun tokosra. Mwet se elos sulella pa John Paliknoa Sigrah. Sifen government lun mwet Germany su muta Pohnpei el sim nu sel Tokosra Paliknoa ac fahk lah sie tokosra el tia ku in mwet kol ke church. Tusruktu Tokosra Paliknoa el srakna moniyuk in kulansap ke Church.

CHAPTER NINE

CATASTROPHE AND INDEPENDENCE
1901-1911

FIRST CHRISTIAN ENDEAVOR SOCIETY ON KOSRAE

Early in 1901 Dr. Rife organized a Christian Endeavor Society among the Marshallese, Gilbertese, and Kosraean young people who were studying and working at Wot. He included in the organization those who lived in Insief, Leap, and other nearby settlements along the Walung coast.

The initial meeting took place on February 2, with Alik Kefwas elected president of the new group. Though he was now in his late 40s, it was unanimously felt by both young people and missionaries that Kefwas was the one to lead the newly organized group. C. E., as the society came to be known in the United States, had been started for the youth of the Williston Congregational Church in Portland, Maine, exactly 20 years earlier—on February 2, 1881—by their pastor, the Rev. Francis E. Clark.

Mr. Clark had been searching for something that would keep the young people of his church families from straying away. Other than Sunday School classes for children, the church was geared to adults and run by adults. As a consequence, the youth were bored and floundering, not only from a lack of interest, but also because they were being lured by activities in the community beyond the church—activities that often conflicted not only with the church schedule, but with the teachings of the church. Pastor Clark wanted his teenagers and older youth to have an association that was truly their own, yet one that would keep them in the heart of the congregation.

The result of his searching, planning, and praying was Christian Endeavor. The new organization gave the Williston youth a voice within their church, while providing an opportunity for them to learn the roles and rules they would need as they grew older and stepped into positions of church leadership. Above all, it was the means of youth-sponsored outreach—a way for the young people themselves to bring their neighborhood friends and comrades at school into the church.

Pastor Clark's Christian Endeavor Society proved so popular and effective among the young people of the Williston Church that the idea went from local to national to international—from denominational to interdenominational—

within a very few years.

Still a young man, Clinton Rife himself had been nurtured in Christian Endeavor. Now, after six years as a missionary on Kosrae, he began to notice a growing disinterest in the church among the young people. Aging leaders held tightly to the reins of control and more or less ignored the youth—or took for granted that they would follow simply because that was what was expected of them. Young men were being trained for church leadership at Wot, but often—after graduating and returning to their home villages—their efforts were discounted or minimized by older church members. They were accused by their elders of being presumptuous and "uppity." This was especially true at Kosrae where subservience rather than personal initiative was considered proper for teens and young adults.

Dr. Rife felt certain that Christian Endeavor, which had meant so much to him in his own development as a Christian, could do the same for the students at Wot as well as for Kosrae's youth. Their discouragement could be turned around as they became involved in their own organization within the church. He was right. Like the American young people in Williston, the Kosraean and other Micronesian young people at Wot were very enthusiastic about their new Christian Endeavor Society. C. E. meetings were held each Sunday following the afternoon Prayer Meeting in the Marshall Islands Training School church and classroom building. As many as 80 teenagers and young adults could be counted on to be present.

JOHN PALIKNOA SIGRAH

One of the young men who participated was 26-year-old Paliknoa Sigrah, who had just become a member of the church on January 1. Though they had known and appreciated him since his earliest student days with them, the missionaries found themselves more and more impressed with him as he matured. Paliknoa was the son of Tulensa Sigrah, King Sru IV, and his wife Tulpe Srue, known as Fititi. He had married another Wot student, Hattie Harry Skillings, and their family of children was growing. *Life and Light for Women* published a paragraph about him written by Louise Wilson:

A bright and influential young man on Kusaie is Paliknoa, a high chief and a nephew of the present king whom he will succeed some day. He is attending the Marshall Training School, so he and his family live on this side of the island. His house is the abiding place for most of the children who come here to the day school. He asked if the number of children was to be limited. When told "No," he said he could take care of fifty without very much trouble.

Now his mother begins to find fault with him for allowing common children to mingle with his chiefish children; but while he is always kind and courteous to her, as a son should be, yet he does not let her chiefish notions interfere with what he believes to be a good work, and to all appearances he treats all the children alike. One is no better than another when it comes to a case of discipline.[1]

A ROAD FROM OKAT TO LELU—
AND AN ARGUMENT

In April 1901, Mrs. Channon wrote: "The Kusaiens are en masse cutting a path from Lelu to Okat Harbor. The king has taken it up in earnest. Miss Hoppin has been back and forth over it both ways twice this week, having some business in Lelu. The tides are poor and this will be useful at such times. It is two and one-half hours walk, and it is not a sidewalk by any means, but in emergencies it will be useful."[2]

During the construction of this road, which Mr. Channon helped the king to engineer—following in some places an ancient trail—an argument broke out between King Sa's men and the chief Sikein, who was dissatisfied over the distribution of food. The king declared that if Sikein continued to quarrel about it, the food would all be thrown away. Miss Wilson wrote about what followed:

Sikein did not cool down. He tried to load his gun but was so nervous and excited he could not get the cartridges in. The people were trying to coax him to give up the gun, but they had to take it by force—then Sikein fainted. When he came to himself, he realized what a fool he had been and how much harm he might have done. He sent a message to the king saying he was ashamed of himself and wished to beg his pardon. The king, who has a mixed record concerning his relationship with the Church, actually committed himself to church membership the last communion Sunday. He sent word back that he forgave Sikein freely, and would not remember what he had done.

Mr. Channon happened around there that same evening after the trouble. The king in talking to him about it said, "I was so glad I was a Christian! Why, any other time before this I would have been so angry that I would not have gotten over it for a week; but when I saw how angry Sikein was, and what he did, I went back into my house and sat down and thought. I said to myself, 'He is so angry, he does not know what he is doing, so I will not remember what he has done. I will forgive Sikein.' Then I felt so happy! I am so glad I am a Christian!"

They said none of them would have blamed the king if he had lost his temper, too, for he had great provocation. But no; he was tested and tried, and God gave him the victory. Mr. Channon remained with them over Sunday, and preached to them on "Brotherly love." At the afternoon prayer meeting, Sikein asked the king and all the people to forgive him for the way he had acted.

*From all we see and can learn, the ones concerned did forgive one another, and
are good friends today.*[3]

MISSIONARIES ASSIST KOSRAEAN CHURCH

The Marshallese and Gilbertese boys' schools at Wot were the primary
responsibilities of Clinton Rife and Irving Channon, but both men took great
interest in the life of the Church on Kosrae—indeed, part of Dr. Rife's job description as outlined by the American Board included oversight of the Kosraean
Church. Alone or together, the men often traveled to Lelu, as well as to other parts
of Kosrae, preaching, leading training sessions and Bible studies, answering questions and making recommendations. Dr. Rife also presided over occasional clin-
ics, which were always appreciated. At times their families or groups of students
would accompany the missionary men, to the delight of the villagers.

In 1901 and 1902, Irving Channon, in the midst of his other duties, supervised a Bible translation team that was putting a few more of the Apostle Paul's
letters and some of the Psalms into the Kosraean language. Those primarily
involved in assisting Mr. Channon with this project were Alik Kefwas and John
Mackwelung. John, known commonly as Mackwelung, was another of Kosrae's
young leaders who had attended Wot's Marshall Islands Training School. Mr.
Channon was also meeting regularly with those Kosraeans assigned to preach
in the villages on Sundays. He shared various lessons with them and assisted
them in their preparations. Though ordinarily this involved only four men at a
time, others would join the sessions in their eagerness to learn. Pastor Konlulu
would often be present as well.

The king's conversion and the subsequent life changes he made—plus
the earnest preparations of the Church for the approaching jubilee celebration—generated an excitement among some of Kosrae's prominent young men.
Pastor Likiaksa's sons Joseph and Benjamin (Galen, the youngest, had died the
year before), along with Fred Skilling, Dan, South Harbor Sru, and others got
to their feet during a first-of-the-month prayer service to "make a stand for
Christ" and express their desire to become members of the island congregation.
Other young men followed their example. It was a good time in the life of the
Kosraean church.

BELL TOWER FOR LELU CHURCH

Yet another of Irving Channon's activities with the Kosraean Church during 1902 was designing and supervising the construction of a bell tower at the
front, waterside corner of the Lelu Church building at Langosak. Jessie Hoppin

had spearheaded a fund drive to purchase a large bell as a memorial to Louisa Skilling, Harry's daughter and Fred's sister, who had died following a short illness while a student at Wot. She had been an intelligent, beautiful young woman—a favorite of the missionaries and the pride of her family.

Mrs. Channon wrote, "Louisa Skilling was taken sick, and after about four weeks she died of peritonitis. Her loss is deeply felt. She was becoming an important help among the girls in the Girls' School. Her death was a beautiful one—the words she spoke to her family, friends and others were very thoughtful and touching. She sang much at the last. It was a great blow to Miss Hoppin, as she had grown to love her very much."[4] Friends of Jessie Hoppin in the United States responded generously to her request and a large, handsome bell was purchased and shipped to Kosrae.

On two different occasions Mr. Channon took the Gilbertese boys from Wot to help the church members gather the coral stone used in constructing the tower. The church carpenters were very impressed with the sturdy scaffolding he and his students built and from which the Kosraean masons worked to lay the stones of the tower higher and higher. This picturesque, whitewashed tower, with its belfry arches and domed roof, became the dominant landmark of Kosrae's famed Lelu Harbor.

"What an event," Mrs. Channon wrote, "when the bell was hoisted into the new tower and it began ringing for Sunday services. It could be heard all around the bay and up in the mountains."[5]

NEW HOUSE FOR PISIN

German steamers now traveled between Sydney and Hong Kong—making the round trip every four months and calling at Jaluit, Kosrae, Pohnpei, and Chuuk on both north and south voyages. This was a great boon to the people of Kosrae, who began looking forward to the food and other materials that were being brought in by the traders. It was also a valued help to the missionaries—there had been no *Morning Star* since May 1900—giving them direct and frequent communication with the outside world.

After completing the bell tower, the church leadership—with King Sa II and his nephew, John Paliknoa, taking charge—volunteered to build a new house at Pisin. It would be a place where the missionaries could be comfortable in Lelu while they attended to the business that accumulated when the steamer was in port. The missionaries had been accustomed to off-loading freight from the *Morning Star* in Okat or Yela harbors, which were nearer to Wot on Kosrae's northwest side. The steamers, being much larger ships, required the facilities at Lelu. Louise Wilson wrote:

Since the steamers come every two months, and some of us must be at the harbor when they arrive, it is so nice to have a quiet house where we can go and call it our own. The house is a few minutes' walk from Lelu village and right on the edge of the water.

Miss Hoppin and I, with twenty-eight girls, are spending a vacation here to show them that we appreciate it by living in it for a few weeks. It is built on the American Board property, in the exact spot where Mr. Snow's house was built fifty years ago when he and his wife came to Kusaie as their first missionaries. The Kusaiens are planning to have a celebration during this jubilee year in honor of Mr. Snow's arrival amongst them. They are so kind to us. They bring us food enough every day to feed all our girls, and keep this going as long as we stay.

The king calls on us every day to see if there is anything he can do for us or get for us that would in any way make us more comfortable. His nephew was asked to get us a large stone for a doorstep. He saw a nice flat one in the king's wall in the ruins, and what did he do but go and take that, and leave an opening in the wall! The king only laughed about it, and thought it was all right for the young man to take it as he did, without permission, seeing it was for the missionaries. We enjoy being amongst the people. They are very kind hearted. I admire them especially for the way they care for the old people. They are very kind to them. I asked who a certain old lady was. They said, "She is Frank's adopted mother." So she lived with him and he took care of her. Everybody is adopted by some one on whom they have no real claim, but on this island it means as much as if they were really related.

I remarked to one of the older men who brought some of the food, as we shook hands, "We are glad to know that the missionaries and Kusaiens are such good friends." "Yes," he said. "That is what we are always praying for—that we will all love one another."[5]

JENNY OLIN'S LELU SCHOOLS

In July of 1902 Miss Olin was at Pisin assisting with a school for the Lelu children. She wrote:

Rebecca Tulenkun, a native of Lelu, has been with me to teach in the village school, and I have also had one other girl here. We have lived in our house here on Pisin, and the Lelu people have been very kind to us. We had seventy scholars, their ages ranging from four to forty years or over, and nearly all of them attended school every day. Our term closed last Friday night.

My work with the Sunday School has been very interesting, as well. The classes have been rearranged and a teachers' meeting organized. While I have been here they have met with me, and by using an interpreter I have been able to help them. The teachers for the infant classes have at the same time met with Rebecca to study their lesson. Every week from thirty to thirty-five persons would be present at these meetings.

They are very eager to learn. They have so small a portion of the Bible in their own language, and even of such portions as they have, they do not have nearly enough copies. I have also reorganized their Sunday school, electing a superintendent and secretary. I visited their school a couple of weeks ago, and to judge from the interest shown by the different classes and the readiness by which the superintendent's questions were answered, I should say they were doing good work.[7]

WAITING FOR ANSWERS

In spite of the good rapport between the Kosraeans and the missionaries, and the positive signs in the life of the Kosraean Church, there was some cause for discouragement—a discouragement that the Kosraeans and the missionaries shared.

Many months had passed since the last word had been received from American Board officials in Boston and—as had happened in the past—during times of no communication, rumors took on lives of their own. Word had been received by the missionaries from Hiram Bingham in Hawai'i that the American Board was considering turning over their schools in Micronesia to the Germans and the British.

Louise Wilson agonized on behalf of her colleagues:

Of course we do not agree that the time has come for us to take our departure from these islands, but, again, if we cannot have a vessel at least as large as the old Morning Star *so as to do our work properly, we feel it would be wrong for us to stay here and have the work less than half done, the way it has been the past three years. I was talking with a Kusaien a few weeks ago about the possibility of our leaving here, and he said he would not believe it. "I don't want you to go! I don't want you to go!" He went away feeling very much cast down.*

Another picture comes before me. White-headed Likiaksa, who has been in the work for almost fifty years, although bent almost double with rheumatism, has always had a cheery word of welcome for us whenever we have entered his house, but this last time when we called, his face was clouded. All the old-time sparkle and wit seemed to have left his being. Was it because he was suffering more bodily pain than usual? No; but it was not long before we found out the cause of all this sadness.

With downcast eyes and almost as if he was talking to himself, he said, "I do not think it is right for the American Board to give up the work down here. What made them ever start it if they did not mean to keep it going?" How we hope it will not have to be given up! Three years is a long time to wait for them to come to a decision, yet perhaps this very waiting means that the very best will be done for us in the end.[8]

THE CHURCH CELEBRATES ITS JUBILEE

In August, 1902, the Kosraean Church marked its jubilee with a great celebration. It had been 50 years since Benjamin and Lydia Snow and Daniel and Doreka Opunui had arrived to plant the Gospel seed. There was scarcely a man or woman on the entire island who did not attend the festivities. The Lelu church, with its gleaming new tower, was decorated with "four banners of white cloth with the names of a half dozen of the first Christians sewed on in red."[9] For almost four hours the people listened as Pastor Likiaksa, Pastor Konlulu, and others recounted the coming of the *Caroline* with those first missionaries. They gave rapt attention to stories of Good King George, his son Lupalikkun, the first Kosraean pastor—and stories of Deacon Kutuka and his wife Notwe, of Salpasr and Paitok, and of the other early heros of the faith.

Louise Wilson wrote:

The Kusaiens invited everyone at our mission to be present at the celebration of this jubilee. Everyone on the island, with the exception of a few old people, gathered at the Lelu church. Their program was a lengthy one. The most interesting part to the Kusaiens was narratives given by three old men, of how things were fifty years ago. They with one accord agreed that Christian living was far above what they had before the missionaries came to them. A recess was taken to partake of the food prepared for the occasion. In the afternoon a prayer meeting was held, at which many expressed their joy that the light of the gospel had been brought to them. It was a day of rejoicing for both the missionary and the Kusaien. From that time on many others have come out on the Lord's side, and we hope before long it may be said that every person on the island is a Christian. Some of the young men are very earnest in working to bring souls to Christ.[10]

Some who lately had fallen into sin repented publicly, with such obvious sincerity that a local trader remarked that he supposed the tobacco he had on hand would now be a total loss.[11]

Mr. Channon wrote: "The Jubilee Anniversary of the coming of Mr. and Mrs. Snow, and the Hawaiian Opunui and his wife, proved a blessed as well as a pleasant occasion. There was an extended program, in which the old customs and conditions of natives were compared with the present ones. At the evening service, an earnest appeal was made for all to begin the second half-century on the side of Christ."[12]

Under the guidance of Mr. Channon, and as a consequence of the great jubilee celebration, an amazing revival swept the Kosraean Church during the remaining months of 1902 and the early months of 1903. Irving Channon noted, "A movement, perhaps the most remarkable since the beginning of the work here, has been constantly gaining force, until now less than a score of

Kusaiens over fourteen years of age remain who have not made a profession of Christ."[13] Church leaders systematically visited each household on the island. Through their counsel and encouragement, every adult who was not yet a member of the church made "open confession of Christ." The new converts numbered almost 150.

WOT'S FIRST PRINTING PRESS

Toward the end of 1902 and well into 1903, Philip De la Porte and his family were at Wot, where Mr. Channon helped him by printing several books of the Bible and a small hymnal which Mr. De la Porte had translated into the Nauruan language. Irving Channon had gotten a hand press several years earlier which he used to print scripture passages and lesson-helps in Gilbertese—as well as in Marshallese and Kosraean. The fonts of type were limited, and he would often have to "manufacture" additional letters. Mrs. Channon reported that several of the Gilbertese boys had become expert printers and book binders.[14]

ALL-ISLAND CHRISTIAN ENDEAVOR FOUNDED

A significant reason for the continuing revival among the Kosraeans was the enthusiasm generated by the new, all-island Christian Endeavor Society. This organization was established within the church in February 1903 with the help of Dr. Rife, after leaders of the church had noted the benefits of Christian Endeavor among the Kosraean young people and other students at Wot, where it had been initiated two years earlier. Twenty-nine-year-old Fred Skilling, the son of American Harry Skillings, was elected its first president. With his sisters, Hattie, Louisa, and Nellie, he had attended school at Wot and was well regarded by both the missionaries and his fellow Kosraeans.

Of the new island-wide organization, which met in Lelu following Meeting each Sunday afternoon, Mr. Channon reported: "The Christian Endeavor Society has a regular attendance of over one hundred, with forty active members. No doubt some of their converts are less earnest than others, and some may have been only following the example of others, but the most skeptical observer would admit that the Spirit of God is working mightily among the Kusaiens."[15]

And Mrs. Channon added her observation: "The Christian Endeavor Society has been started with much success. It is a new era in Kusaien history, as they have never admitted any unmarried person to church, nor considered that they could be Christian. If there was ever a Christian worker, it is the king these days!"[16]

DEATH OF PASTOR KONLULU

In the midst of the new fervor and progress of the church, sadness descended in 1903 when Pastor Konlulu died. He had been a pastor for nine years. Surviving him were five sons and one daughter: Peter Fikil, Abraham, Asher, George, Likiak and Kenye Niatking Wakap.

DEACON LIKIAKSA YAL ORDAINED
AS KOSRAE'S FOURTH PASTOR

On November 18, 1903, with the leaders of the church consenting, missionaries Irving Channon and Clinton Rife ordained Deacon Likiaksa Yal as the fourth pastor of the Kosraean church. "Yal"—the place-name of the new pastor's home area in Lelu—was used in conjunction with his given name to distinguish him from the first Pastor Likiaksa, who was still living. Pastor Likiaksa Yal would serve for the next 22 years.

THE *CARRIE AND ANNIE* AND THE *VINE*

With no *Morning Star* in service, a small schooner, the *Carrie and Annie*, was purchased by mission officials in Hawai'i to make a trip to Micronesia in 1903. The schooner was not large enough to do all that was necessary, but the missionaries were grateful at least to receive their mail. When it left Kosrae it carried Alfred Walkup—who had been helping temporarily at the Gilbert Islands school—and Louise Wilson back to the United States for furlough. Also aboard for the 4,700-mile trip was 12-year-old Willie Channon, sent by his parents to attend school in Minneapolis. It was more than six months before his family at Wot received news of him. Willie made his family proud by becoming a pastor when he reached adulthood.

A second small schooner, the *Vine*, sailed for the Micronesia Mission late that same year. On a tour of the Marshalls with the Wot missionaries and some of the Marshallese students, it scraped over a reef. Returning to Kosrae, Capt. O. Anderson ordered it hauled onto its side next to the Lelu wharf to see what repairs were necessary. Astonishingly, he forgot about the incoming tide, and the schooner sank alongside the wharf! Irving Channon and Clinton Rife went to Lelu and, after looking over the situation, suggested the *Vine* be pumped out, refloated, repaired, and allowed to dry out.

Having missed several anticipated trips to the Gilberts, Mr. Channon announced that he was going to travel there aboard the *Vine*. Hearing this, Mrs. Channon said that if he was going, she was going, too—with the five children! So, with Irving Channon as first mate—his watch the chronometer, as the one belonging to the ship had been ruined in salt water—and with John Mackwelung as second mate, they departed for the Gilberts. Their crew was Kosraean because the American and Hawaiian crew refused to sail again with the *Vine's* discredited Capt. Anderson. The *Vine* successfully visited the various mission stations in the Gilberts—including some which were now operated by the London Missionary Society in the southern islands—returning safely to Kosrae two months later.[17]

GOOD NEWS

In 1904 both the *Carrie and Annie* and the *Vine* were sold when the *Morning Star V* was launched in June. The news of this launching brought great relief and joy to the Kosraeans and to the missionaries at Wot. American Board officials, after much deliberation, had come to the conclusion that they would maintain the work in the islands, since the British and German mission societies were not ready to assume the financial responsibilities necessary to become involved.[18] This meant that a new mission ship was needed. The plan was this:

Instead of having a vessel like the old Morning Star, *which made an annual voyage from Honolulu through the groups in Micronesia, returning to Honolulu after ten or twelve months, it is proposed to build a vessel of wood, not to exceed 300 tons burden, with auxiliary power to remain in Micronesian waters.*

There are now German steamship lines in the Caroline and Marshall groups, and in this way all supplies can be forwarded, giving to the stations much better provision than they obtained in former days by the Morning Star. *The missionary vessel need not come each year to Honolulu or San Francisco, but can make Kusaie or Ponape its home port and can easily make two trips a year through the several groups. This will be a distinct gain over the service of previous years.*[19]

CENSUS OF 1905

A slow increase in the island's population was registered in the census of 1905. There were now 516 Kosraeans.

DR. RIFE ENGINEERS THE INSREFUSR CHANNEL

King Sa II—encouraged by the German administration, which was always anxious for more copra—decided that the Lelu mangrove channel should be opened to the lagoon at Insrefusr, making it possible for farmers to transport their copra by canoe at high tide all the way from Tafunsak to Lelu. The king promised to do away with the "coconut tax"—called kweb—and allow people to own their own land, if they would open the channel.²⁰ With this incentive, men, women, and children, in happy competition and with very few tools, dug the opening. Dr. Rife served as engineer for the project. This new waterway was a boon to all travel to and from Lelu, Tafunsak and beyond. Until now, canoes had to be carried over the land barrier that stood between the Lelu mangrove channel and the waters of the lagoon.

CHURCH IS GRANTED INDEPENDENCE
FROM THE MISSION BOARD

For the Kosraean Church, the year 1905 was of particular significance. Invigorated by the success of the revival two years earlier, and inspired by the dedication of their youth in Christian Endeavor, Pastor Likiaksa, Pastor Likiaksa Yal, and other leaders of the church petitioned the American Board for independence from the mission. Their request was granted.

Thus, 53 years after the arrival of the first missionaries, the Kosrae Congregational Church became autonomous. There was some skepticism and reticence among the resident missionaries, but they agreed to relinquish official supervision of the island church. They continued in charge of the schools at Wot. Kosrae's church leaders—as well as the entire membership—were pleased and grateful, though some of them too, had their misgivings about proceeding on their own.

MORNING STAR V

The American missionaries and their Christian training schools were now being serviced by the new Morning Star V, which had traveled east from Massachusetts to Micronesia through the Suez Canal. A small steamer of 403 tons, it was the first vessel to bear the Morning Star name that was not outfitted with sails. The well appointed cabins and ample cargo space impressed the missionaries and islanders alike—and everyone was amazed by how swiftly the vessel moved from island to island. The captain was their old friend George Garland, who had served on the Morning Stars III and IV.

SHOULD THE SCHOOLS MOVE BACK
TO THE LOW ISLANDS?

Yet, in spite of the advantages provided by the new vessel, transportation remained sporadic and difficult. Mission personnel became more and more convinced that better and more permanent results for the Christian cause in the Marshalls and the Gilberts would materialize if the missionaries in charge of those areas were to reside there permanently instead of on distant Kosrae.

So the pendulum of opinion was swinging back to the way the mission had been operated prior to 1879 when the low-island schools were transferred to Kosrae. Now it was felt that the churches in the Gilbert and Marshall Islands were suffering because of the infrequent visits of their leaders. The training schools might be used to help bring more consistent oversight if they could be moved from Kosrae back into their home areas.

A natural catastrophe brought about these moves sooner than had been anticipated.

ANOTHER DEVASTATING TYPHOON

On April 14, 1905, the *Morning Star V* had anchored in Yela Harbor on the lee side of Kosrae, after returning from a tour of the Marshall Islands. Accompanying Capt. Garland on board were his wife, the former Sarah Smith, and their daughters, Dorothy and Ruth. Mrs. Garland wrote:

A terrific cyclone swept over the island on the 19th of April. The fury of the elements was terrible. About 7:30 a.m. the ship was driven across the harbor, dragging her anchors, and remained lodged against the rocks, scraping and bumping incessantly. The duration of the storm was about seven hours. But although so much shorter than the hurricane of fourteen years ago, which lasted three days, the work of destruction was in the present case more complete.

We lay that night on the sandy reef, but the next morning, with the help of kedge anchors and lines, the ship was pulled off, and we were soon at our usual anchorage. Thousands of dead fish floated by, whipped to death on the coral, doubtless—and poor, bewildered birds wheeled and fluttered all about us and over the stricken swamp crying and calling.[21]

OTHERS DESCRIBE THE CATASTROPHE

Jessie Hoppin described the scene at the Girls' School:

The storm was a cyclone and struck us first from the northeast. Then there was a dead calm, perfectly breathless, when the center passed, and then it came in double fury from the southwest. It picked up the whole house and carried it some five feet bodily, setting it down with a crash on to the stones, which broke through the floor and I fully expected we would all be buried alive then and there. All the doors and windows stood on the bias. The lamps shattered on the floor, and the heavy bookcase in the dining room fell on its face. And then the old house halted and waited until

Miss Wilson and I had gotten our sixty-one girls out into the storm.

Our good Mackwelung was there and a number of the Marshall and Gilbert boys. The air was black with flying things. A number of the boys laid hold of me, and we all started down the path going before the wind. Something struck the whole back of my head, and things looked black for a minute. Then the wind lifted me off my feet, and I had to sit down on the ground to keep from being carried quite away. The boys, dear brave fellows, never let go their hold on me, and I knew they were trying so to surround me that things flying in the air should strike them and not me...[22]

Louise Wilson continued the story:

The boys said that the little workshop belonging to Dr. Rife was still standing; if we could reach that they thought they could hold it from going to pieces as it was small and in a more sheltered place, and give us a refuge. We had not been outside very many minutes before everyone had to go down on the ground to be kept from being carried off their feet. Two boys with me said, "Ruth is dead." I could see her stretched out on the ground a few feet away from me, but could not reach her, for about the time she was struck on the head with a flying stick, a hardwood stick came whizzing through the air and struck me in the back, leaving me helpless.

It seemed as if my back was broken, but it was nothing as severe as that. The stick had struck three of my ribs. The German doctor here says my hurt is not a dangerous one, but poor little Ruth! He shakes his head and says, "Very dangerous." She is a small Marshallese girl about twelve years old. The stick struck her in the head fracturing her skull very badly. The cut is a deep one, a piece of bone an inch long was broken right out of the skull. It seems as if it will be a miracle if she gets well. She is so good and patient through it all... [Ruth died of her injury six weeks after the typhoon].[23]

WHAT TO DO?

Making a quick assessment immediately in the aftermath of the typhoon, the missionaries decided to accept Capt. Garland's invitation to sail with him to Pohnpei. That island had escaped the typhoon fourteen years earlier when Kosrae had been so severely damaged. "We took sixty girls of our boarding school on the *Morning Star*, hoping to find shelter there until other arrangements could be made. As we drew near to the island we saw it was one mass of destruction, so the girls were carried back to Kusaie to live as best they can."[24]

Back on Kosrae Jessie Hoppin described the girls and their teachers crowding into Mr Channon's woodshed, one of the few buildings that could be sufficiently repaired for temporary use. A month later she wrote: "We are having a new house put up on Yonrak, our old place. Palikkun, a young Kusaien, has married our Rebecca. He put up first a small place for our kitchen where he and Rebecca live while he puts up the main part. This 'main part' will have three rooms, one for us, one for the girls down below, and a low sleeping apartment upstairs. If the lumber holds out there will be a wide veranda on two sides where we can dine and a narrower veranda on another side. I am much pleased with Palikkun and we are very happy over the prospect of a place of our very own."[25]

On May 6, Clinton Rife included in his annual report to the American Board:

You will have been informed by cable of the destruction of our mission property on Kusaie by storm. It happened on April 19th, and lasted only about four or five hours in its severity but it perfectly devastated the island. We are living in my workshop. Five of the Kusaiens were killed. All houses were blown down—most personal property damaged or lost.

The churches were all unroofed, one of them entirely destroyed, and two others have the walls seriously damaged. The people will not be able to erect houses until a new crop of thatch leaves can grow and mature. This will probably require more than a year. Their food trees are perfectly bare, beheaded and uprooted by the thousands. Happily they do not depend entirely on food which grows above the ground and so will be able to subsist until coconuts, bananas, and breadfruit begin to bear again. The beauty of the island is gone, and it will require years for it to reach its former splendor.[26]

In her journal, Mary Channon wrote that one of those killed in Tafunsak was the daughter of Kilafwakun, a brother of Mackwelung. She also noted how prominent the great stone walls of the Lelu ruins were after the typhoon. They stood lofty and stark above the landscape as all the trees were down. Yet the freakish wind had taken only two sheets of iron roofing from the frame house built at Pisin three years earlier.[27]

DEATH OF PASTOR LIKIAKSA

On June 23, 1905—in the midst of the devastation and sadness caused by the typhoon—the Kosraeans suffered the loss of their revered Pastor Likiaksa. He had served the Church faithfully as spiritual leader and guide for almost 34 years. As his mentor, Benjamin Snow, had so often done, Pastor Likiaksa championed the cause of his people against those unprincipled foreigners who found their way to Kosrae, and he was unafraid to stand up to the kings when their self-interest was hindering the purposes and progress of the Church. His Christian humility and unswerving devotion were clearly apparent and conscientiously imitated by the members of his congregation.

Clinton Rife's announcement of the death appeared in *The Missionary Herald*, "I am sorry to report the death, on June 23, of Likiaksa, the pastor here on Kusaie, who was the elder of their two ordained men. He was ordained in 1871, and has always been faithful. I think he was as ready to administer reproof when needed by any one in his flock as was any one I know in these islands. His death is a great loss to the people. And so those who were living when the first missionaries came here, fifty-three years ago, are passing away."[28]

Pastor Likiaksa had been a gracious friend to the missionaries. In retirement, Mary Channon fondly remembered his frequent visits to her family at Wot. "He would often send us a piece of meat or a plate of the pounded taro delicacy, fafa, before he came up from Insief. The children dearly loved that fafa and looked forward to receiving it."[29]

Also dear to Mrs. Channon was a story that had circulated among the missionaries for many years. It spoke of both the faithfulness and the good humor that characterized Pastor Likiaksa's life. One day, as was his custom, he took food out to a whaling vessel that had just anchored in Utwe Harbor. In reciprocating the Pastor's kindness, the captain offered him beer, which Likiaksa refused. The captain insisted and the pastor persisted. Finally, out of patience, the captain said, "Look, if you don't drink it, I'm going to throw you overboard!" Pastor Likiaksa smiled and replied, "Beer hurt, water no hurt!"[30]

Pastor Likiaksa and his first wife, Tulpe Pisin, were among the very first of Kosrae's Christians. He was survived by five of their seven children: Benjamin, Joseph, Mary Tosie, Martha Siba, and Lydia Simeon. His youngest daughter Elizabeth had died as a young adult. His son Galen [named for Benjamin Galen Snow, a name commonly spelled "Killin" by the Kosraeans] had died in 1901. Approximately 63 years of age when he died, Pastor Likiaksa was also survived by his second wife, Kenye.

Pastor Likiaksa Yal carried on as leader of the Church on Kosrae.

WOT BOYS' SCHOOLS DISBAND

At least one of the Micronesia missionaries saw in the typhoon a blessing. Mr. Walkup commented that the destruction of the old houses at Wot meant that "surely the work will go to the low islands now, as requested two years ago." And so the work of disbanding the boys' schools was begun. Goodbyes shared between missionary colleagues, classmates, teachers and students, and the Kosraeans and their Wot friends were heartfelt and somber.

The first to leave were Irving and Mary Channon, who had been in charge of the Gilbertese school for 15 years. They departed in May, a month before the death of Pastor Likiaksa, as the *Morning Star V* returned to Honolulu. Traveling with them to the United States were their five youngest children—Hiram, Steve, Stella, Grace, and Irving, Jr.—the latter two born at Wot since the Channons'

1898 furlough. This industrious, vibrant, and cheerful family would be missed by their many Kosraeans friends. [From 1908 through 1912 the Channons continued to work with the Gilbertese on Ocean Island (Banaba). Between 1919 and 1932, they lived in the Philippine Islands where Mr. Channon served as dean of the Silliman Bible Institute in Dumagete, later Silliman University.]

All but two of the Gilbertese boys left Kosrae as the Channons left, to return to their low-island homes, some of them long before they had expected to. Almost all of them would become teachers. The two who remained at Wot did so temporarily "to assist the girls' school over the hard places."

The next to leave was Jessie Hoppin—in September, for furlough in Ceres, California—as Jenny Olin returned to Kosrae from her furlough. In March 1906, Isadore Rife left for the United States with her three children—John, Frances, and little Margaret, all three of them born on Kosrae. Then in May, a year after the typhoon, Clinton Rife and 27 Marshallese boys departed for Jaluit. Dr. Rife was an energetic principal and conscientious teacher during his 12 years on Kosrae, and his medical gifts had been gratefully received by missionaries and students at Wot, and by men, women, and children in all parts of the island. Now he would share these gifts in the Marshall Islands. Mrs. Rife, with their children, joined her husband at Jaluit in July 1907.

With the departure of Dr. Rife and the Marshallese boys, Louise Wilson wrote, "This leaves Miss Olin and myself alone on Kusaie, with forty girls. We shall be perfectly safe in staying alone, as everyone on the island is a friend to us and will help us in any way they can. The Kusaiens are certainly a very accommodating people."[31]

GIRLS' SCHOOL CONTINUES

After much soul-searching and prayer, the missionaries had decided to continue the operation of the Wot school for island girls, at least for the near future. They did not consider it expedient to enroll girls in the schools for boys now being reorganized on the low islands. There were also some Marshallese and Gilbertese parents among the church leaders in those areas—particularly those who themselves had studied at Wot—who implored the missionaries to continue making it possible for their daughters to be instructed by missionary women at Wot. So, with some trepidation, it was decided that the doors of the Girls' School would remain open.

One of the major concerns was shared by the Kosraeans, as well as Miss Wilson and Miss Olin. Just how long could the Girls' School continue operating outside the framework of support that had been provided by the two boys' schools? Classes were continued—"Bible, Bible history, German, English (for the Gilbertese girls only) [The German government would not allow English to be taught to the Kosraean and Marshallese students], physiology, geography, singing, arithmetic, writing, and a new study for the older girls from a book titled 'Self and Sex'." Without the boys, however, the girls had to do considerably more outdoor work than in former years.[32]

MORNING STAR V SOLD

There was more confusion and distress in 1906 as word drifted through Micronesia that *Morning Star V*, the handsome steamer that had made both the missionaries and the island Christians so proud, had been sold after having been in service less than two years. It was impossible to secure the coal necessary to operate the ship among the islands. There was no coal in Micronesia.

END OF A REMARKABLE ERA

For the Micronesia Mission, a significant era had come to a close. Mission ships of the future would be much smaller vessels confined within island regions, and there would not be another called the *Morning Star* until 1948.

And though the boys' training schools were beginning again on a small scale in both the Marshall and Gilbert islands, it would be many decades before the Micronesia Mission would have a program of Christian education that came close to duplicating what had transpired during those 26 years on the three-school campus at Wot.

RECOVERY AT KOSRAE

The two missionary women at Wot were touched and grateful when Rebecca's husband, Palikkun, his friend, Alokoa, and some of their Insief neighbors volunteered to construct various native-style buildings for the Girls' School, to replace, at least temporarily, a few of the buildings lost in the typhoon. For them, this act was a splendid example of the remarkable optimism and selfless generosity that had come to characterize Kosraean Christians.

The entire population of the island had suffered the loss of their homes, their churches, and many of their food sources in the typhoon. There was no way to hurry the process of rebuilding and replanting, but faith was strong, and the people encouraged one another by repeating the Psalmist's words, "Weeping may linger for the night, but joy comes with the morning" [Psalm 30:5b].

In spite of the hardships, the Kosraeans were proud of their newly independent church. They found hope as they watched their young people rally and develop in the increasingly active and popular all-island Christian Endeavor Society. And in true Kosraean fashion, they banded together to assist one another through the lean, long months of rehabilitation.

Slowly, the island and its people recovered.

REBUILDING OF LELU CHURCH BEGINS

A brief notice appeared in the September 1907 issue of *Life and Light for Women* with some encouraging news: "Some months ago the Kusaiens began working to get the lumber ready for their church building in Lelu. Since the cyclone they have worshiped in an open shed, but now they intend restoring their church, and all able-bodied men are giving almost all their time to the work. They had not been able to do it before, for lack of food, as it took nearly all their time to hunt or provide food for their families."[33]

THE VILLAGE SCHOOLS

Early that year Jenny Olin attended one of the new-month church meetings in Lelu. She wrote:

The village schools were not very well maintained last year, owing partly to the rebuilding of the Lelu church and partly to a general lack of initiative. Now that the church is almost finished and the monthly meeting would be the most convenient time to see a large number of them together, I wished to stir them up to do better. After their business was finished I told them my thoughts on the subject. They listened attentively, and when I had finished they appointed teachers for each of the five principal villages, including Insief.

Two of the teachers began the next Monday, and the rest the week following. The great drawback is that they have nothing to work with—no books, slates, pencils nor anything else. It makes it very much harder for the teacher where he has to provide everything from his own mind. Some of those appointed to teach objected because they were not fitted to be teachers. It is really true, but they are the best we have, and they can at least teach the children to read and write, even if they do not do much more.

Later in the day I was talking over things with a number of them. When they complained of having no educated people to be teachers, I said, jokingly, "I will have to take in some boys in the girls' school and teach them." "Yes, do that," was the immediate answer, rather to my surprise, for I had not imagined them to be so ready to give up their sons for this work. Later, Rebecca told me that her husband said I could have their son Ralph, born last February, for our school; or, if it would take too long for Ralph to grow up, he would send his own little brother instead.

There are a large number of boys, from ten to fourteen years of age, who would make an ideal boys' school, if one only had the time to give to them. Sometimes I wish I could do this work. By taking them young enough and teaching them, they might be saved from some of the moral pitfalls which are in their way and cause so many of them to stumble in their early young manhood. The Junior Christian Endeavor Society is doing something toward this.[34]

JUNIOR CHRISTIAN ENDEAVOR

Just four years after the inauguration of the Christian Endeavor organization for their teenagers and young adults, Kosrae's church leaders concluded that it was time to do something for those in their families who were even younger. From the earliest years they had made the effort, with varying degrees of success, to maintain Sunday Schools in each village congregation for their children. Both the Snows had vigorously insisted that this be done. But Sunday School for adults and children alike followed the morning worship service. Now, on Sunday afternoons, children were gathering around the buildings where their older brothers and sisters were meeting for Christian Endeavor. The curiosity as well as the distraction needed to be addressed.

So began the Junior Christian Endeavor Society on Kosrae—inaugurated on the first Sunday in February 1907. The outbuildings that had sprung up beside each of the churches were now being used—not only on Sunday morning for Sunday School—but on Sunday afternoon for a Christian Endeavor group for children. These groups were carefully staffed by those appointed from among the adult members of the church—and just as the young people's group was popular, so the children's group proved very popular. As with the older group, singing became a significant part of Junior Christian Endeavor. By 1908 both of these C. E. Societies were flourishing in all four village churches.

RECONSTRUCTED LELU CHURCH DEDICATED

In April, 1908, Louise Wilson described the new Lelu church building in a letter to friends:

The Kusaiens have just finished rebuilding their large stone church which was so badly wrecked in the storm three years ago. It is really a very nice building. Strangers coming ashore from the steamer for a few hours almost always stop and go in to look at this building. They marvel that the Kusaiens have done the work all themselves.

They have hewn out from trees large pillars of light wood, shaped and smoothly planed. But the wood of the door and window casings is what takes a stranger's eye. It is almost the color of walnut and the grain of the wood is beautiful. It would take a fine polish if they knew how to do it. This wood only grows at one place on the island, and is not at all plentiful. They have spent days, weeks and months hewing, sawing and planing.

When it came to make the floor they did not know just what to do but solved the problem by going out on the reef and cutting out blocks of stone. These are all cut evenly and fitted in and cemented together. The roof is of galvanized iron, bought of the trader who donated fifty dollars toward the church. They really have a church building to be proud of. They will dedicate it Easter Sunday, and we are planning to take all our household the ten miles to attend.[35]

Jennie Olin was at Pisin for two weeks before Easter, waiting for the steamer. She wrote:

The people were busy doing the last things in and about the church, and practicing for the dedication. The women helped to white-wash the walls of the church, inside and out, and in cleaning away the rubbish, rebuilding the stone wall surrounding the church yard, etc. They also brought gravel and sand for the yard and paths. Everything looked nice and clean.

No one, however, knew how to dedicate a church, so they left the arrangement of that to me. I did not know much more about it than they did, but happened upon a dedication service which Mrs. Pease had sent me some time ago with some other papers. I took that for my model, translating parts, and adapting the rest to the attainments of the people in singing.

April 17th Miss Wilson and the girls came, and on Sunday we celebrated Easter and communion in the morning, and dedicated the church in the afternoon. Everything went on pleasantly, and everybody seemed pleased with themselves and with one another. The new lamps for the church were much admired, and they certainly were an improvement on anything they ever had there within my recollection.

On Monday a big feast was prepared, and at 5 p. m. the bell rang to call everybody to the feast. One cow, one large turtle, and I do not know how many pigs, had been sacrificed for the occasion. It had been a hot, dry day so we could assemble out of doors. The food was divided into portions, one for us of the girls' school, one for the king, one for the trader here, and one each for the different villages. Then we were called to come and sit in our places. The gravel of the churchyard furnished a nice, clean table, as well as seats for most of the people. We foreigners had a bench to sit on. When all was ready, Tokosra's nephew Paliknoa made a speech, thanking the people and the chiefs for the help given toward the building. Then the blessing was asked and people were invited to partake. [King Sa II was too ill to attend.]

Our portion of the feast furnished food enough for all our girls for two days, so you can imagine the size of it. It is the expected thing to carry home whatever one cannot eat, at a feast or any other time. It took all the girls and several men to carry home to Pisin the remains of our portion. Early the next morning I took most of the girls home to Wot, leaving Miss Wilson to await the steamer.[36]

KOSRAEAN CHURCH UNDERGIRDS
REMAINING WOT SCHOOL

The Kosraeans had been disturbed by the closing of the Marshallese and Gilbertese schools and saddened by the subsequent departure of most of the missionaries. The schools, with their American educators, had existed on the island since 1879 and 1882. Everyone was anxious that the Girls' School at the top of the hill, with its remaining small but dedicated corps of teachers, would not disappear as well. Education had become an important priority for the Kosraean people.

A sense of ownership for the remaining Wot school began to develop that coincided with an unprecedented willingness on the part of the missionaries to welcome opinions from Kosraean church leaders in planning and policy development at Wot. With the missionaries and the Kosraeans agreeing, it was decided that the Girls' Training School would become co-educational.

This decision was welcomed by Kosraean parents who were eager to have their sons educated, but agreed to with trepidation by the missionaries. How could they handle adolescent students of both sexes in the same school? But reality compelled the missionaries to concede—they needed the manpower! Certainly the young women were capable of gardening, raising chickens and doing certain types of fishing. But feeding the pigs and milking the cows, climbing trees for coconuts and breadfruit, cleaning away the wild foliage in the banana patches, cutting firewood and then carrying the food and the wood to the school kitchen—this was all considered man's work. Building fires in the ground ovens and handling the hot rocks used to cook the food were also the responsibility of men. Kosraean parents considered the missionaries' offer to exchange schooling for farm work and other types of assistance to be generous—and their sons were certainly willing.

The boys would be cautiously chosen and carefully segregated from the girls—how else could the day-to-day operation of an isolated boarding school be handled?—but it was felt that the experiment was worth a try. So in 1909 there were 43 students at the Wot school: 26 Marshallese girls, 10 Gilbertese girls, four Kosraean girls, and three brave and fortunate Kosraean boys! The four girls were Notwe Mackwelung [Isaiah Benjamin], Srue Mackwelung [Frank Skilling], Louise Palikkun [Irving Mackwelung], and Ellen Skilling [Alokoa Tol]. The boys were Palikkun Tulensru, Isaiah Benjamin, and James A. Sesa.[37]

AMERICAN BOARD SENDS AN OLD FRIEND TO WOT

On October 5, when the steamer *Germania* entered Lelu Harbor on one of its scheduled stops, not only was there material on board for a large, two-story structure to be erected at Wot—the culmination of much prayer and planning both in Boston and on Kosrae—but a master carpenter was along to build it. Their friend and mentor, George Bowker, all the way from California this time, had once again been hired by the American Board to supervise construction at the mission school. It was an exciting time for the residents at Wot, many of whom remembered Mr. Bowker from his profitable visit in 1893 when the Girls' School building—so badly damaged in the typhoon of 1891—had been extensively repaired. Kosraeans had learned much from working with him, and they eagerly welcomed him now. Things were looking up!

For the month of October and on into November, the cement, lumber, and iron roofing were moved from Lelu to Wot by a volunteer crew of 137 Kosraean men, led by Pastor Likiaksa Yal. Their names were recorded for posterity and sealed in a bottle that was buried in the concrete foundation of the new school. It was not found until more than 60 years later.

A team made up of Joseph, Miswan, Na, Moses, Tosie, Oasruka, Sabino, Tala, Songrasru, Dan—and John Paliknoa Sigrah, now a deacon—brought the sand and gravel up the hill, mixed the cement and served as carpenters. Palikkun and John Mackwelung worked as assistants to Mr. Bowker.[38] With such willing, earnest help, the work proceeded quickly. The result was an imposing structure with a first-floor veranda on three sides, the lower floor containing class rooms, the upper floor, the girls' dormitory. There was a large, accessible attic to use for storage. It stood near the crest of the Yonrak ridge where its 1893-built predecessor had stood, and could be seen from miles away.

The number of missionaries remained at two that year. Louise Wilson departed for California in 1909, but Jessie Hoppin was back from her furlough to rejoin Jenny Olin. The following year their number rose to three as Marion Wells, age 26, became part of the Wot team of teachers.

LOSS OF THE *HIRAM BINGHAM II* AND DEATH OF ALFRED WALKUP

Sixteen years earlier, the American Board had provided a small, 30-ton ship, the *Hiram Bingham*, to carry missionaries, students, and freight in the Marshall and Gilbert Islands. Alfred Walkup, the boxer-turned-missionary, became the much-admired captain of this little schooner. With his knowledge of the languages, the customs, and the people of both island groups, Capt. Walkup proved to be of great value to the work. By 1907 the constantly used ship had worn out. In 1908, the year veteran missionary and Bible translator Dr. Hiram Bingham, Jr., died, Capt. Walkup took possession of the *Hiram Bingham II.*

The new ship was built in San Francisco to Capt. Walkup's specifications, somewhat larger than its predecessor with a newly designed gasoline engine. Capt. Walkup's young-adult children—John, 28, Eleanor, 26, and Alfred, 23 (the latter two born at Kosrae)—sailed with him on an uneventful voyage straight from San Francisco to Banaba (Ocean Island). From there, Capt. Walkup sent his children back to the United States in the company of his American crew. At Banaba he hired a crew from that island and departed for Butaritari in the Gilbert Islands.

Tragedy struck May 4, 1909—just two weeks before the missionary's 60th birthday. Forty miles from Butaritari a sudden squall struck the ship, instantly capsizing her. After struggling in the water for five or six hours, Capt. Walkup and those with him could not right the schooner. In addition to the captain, there were five crew members, and an eight-year-old girl who was the sister of a crew member on her way to the mission school at Butaritari. In a small dinghy they salvaged, the seven drifted for 28 days before they were found by fishermen in the vicinity of Ebon.[39]

Alfred Walkup, weak from hunger, thirst, and exposure, died a few days after being carefully transported to that atoll.[40] Tenderly nourished by Ebon Christians, the others survived. Capt. Walkup was buried in a well-marked grave near the church at Rube, Ebon. Mt. Wakap, Kosrae's third highest mountain peak at 1,608 feet—looming over the Wot property and his wife's grave—was named by the Kosraeans in his memory.

GILBERT ISLANDS COME UNDER BRITISH RULE

Partly because of the loss of Alfred Walkup and the *Hiram Bingham II,* the American Board in 1910 agreed to relinquish part of the work in the Gilbert Islands—on those atolls below the equator—to the London Missionary Society. The Gilberts had come under British rule in 1892 and, though "cutting the ties" was difficult for the personnel of the Micronesia Mission, it made sense that an organization in Britain now oversee the work there.

Members of the Church on Kosrae, the Wot community, and Irving and Mary Channon were all rejuvenated by a two-month visit the Channons made to Kosrae during 1910. At the time, Mr. and Mrs. Channon were in charge of the Bingham Institute, a mission school located on Banaba between Nauru and the Gilberts. It had been five years since the missionary family had departed Kosrae.

DEATH OF KING SA II AND ELECTION
OF KING JOHN SIGRAH

With the domination of Kosraean society by the Church and the increasing-ly important roles of the pastor and other leaders, the Kosraean king no longer had much influence. King Sa II neglected to appoint new chiefs when old ones passed away. People gradually discontinued paying tribute to him. When he died in 1910 public opinion was in favor of not electing another king. But again, the German officials wanted someone at the head of the Kosrae government to act as liaison with the administration in Pohnpei. A hasty election was held.

Thirty-five-year-old John Paliknoa Sigrah, a prominent member of the Church—son of King Sru IV and nephew of the late King Sa II—was chosen. In 1911 the new king, perhaps feeling a bit heady from his elevation, toyed with the idea of restoring some of the royal privileges, and a few people—out of both respect and fear—began bringing traditional offerings to him which he did not discourage. Two of Kosrae's church leaders wrote a letter to Governor Kerstung, the German magistrate at Pohnpei, critical of the new king. King John was reprimanded by the governor, who also wrote to Miss Hoppin requesting that she make sure that the king understood the nature of his errors and would not repeat them.

King John was given specific procedures to follow. He was also permitted to keep one-third of the three-mark head tax and two days' service per year from each man. But in order to keep the church and government functions separate, he was told that he could not hold an official church office.[41] He continued, however, to serve as a lay preacher and deacon. As years went by, John Sigrah was increasingly admired by many, both within the Kosraean Church and com-munity and the Pacific world beyond Kosraean shores, as an astute and devoted leader. ✠

Notes - Chapter 9

1. Louise Wilson in Mary A. Marvin, "A History of Missionary Work in Micronesia 1852-1910," p. 283
2. Mary Long Goldsbury Channon in Marvin, p. 270
3. L. Wilson in Marvin, p. 284
4. M. L. G. Channon in Marvin, p. 289
5. M. L. G. Channon, unpublished "Memories of Kusaie, 1890-1905," p. 3
6. L. Wilson in Marvin, p. 285, p. 288, p. 291
7. Jenny Olin in Marvin, p. 297
8. L. Wilson in Marvin, p. 288
9. Clinton Rife in Marvin, p. 281
10. L. Wilson in Marvin, p. 292
11. Albertine Loomis, *To All People*, p. 939
12. Irving M. Channon in Marvin, p. 298
13. I. M. Channon in Marvin, pp. 287-298
14. M. L. G. Channon in Marvin, p. 298
15. I. M. Channon in Marvin, p. 298
16. M. L. G. Channon in Marvin, p. 290
17. M. L. G. Channon, "Memories of Kusaie, 1890-1905," p. 2
18. Mary A. Marvin, p. 302
19. *Life and Light for Women*, in Marvin, p. 302
20. Harvey Gordon Segal, *Kosrae, The Sleeping Lady Awakens*, 1989, p. 120
21. Sarah Smith Garland, *The Friend*, Aug. 1905
22. Jesse Hoppin in Marvin, pp. 332-333
23. L. Wilson in Marvin, pp. 330-331
24. *The Missionary Herald* in Marvin, p. 321
25. J. Hoppin in Marvin, p. 333
26. C. Rife, Americal Board of Commissioners for Foreign Missions Annual Report, 1906
27. M. L. G. Channon, personal papers, courtesy of M. Hipps
28. C. Rife in Marvin, p. 325
29. M. L. G. Channon, personal correspondence, undated
30. M. L. G. Channon, "Memories of Kusaie, 1890-1905," p. 5
31. L. Wilson in Marvin, p. 339
32. J. Olin in Marvin, p. 353
33. Ibid, p. 361
34. Ibid, p. 368
35. L. Wilson in Marvin, p. 369
36. J. Olin in Marvin, p. 368
37. John P. Sigrah, cornerstone papers, April 30, 1909, courtesy of Hashime Vicente
38. Ibid
39. I. M. Channon, personal correspondence to T. Murray MacCallum, Jan. 2, 1934, courtesy of M. Hipps
40. William E. Strong, *The Story of the American Board*, Boston, 1910, p. 454
41. John L. Fischer, "The Eastern Carolines," p. 58

NUNAK YOHK KE CHAPTER 10
1911-1922

Elizabeth ac Jane Baldwin eltal missionary fin acn Chuuk yac singoul tolu meet liki supweyukla eltal nu Kosrae tuh eltal in mwet luti fin acn Wot. Tamtael se inge sun acn Kosrae ke September 6, 1911. Miss Elizabeth el yac 52, ac Miss Jane el yac 48. Missionary sefanna srakna muta Wot in pacl sac, pa Miss Hoppin. Miss Wells el tuh som orekma fin acn Banaba (Ocean Island). Miss Olin el tuh masak ac som nu Australia in ono, na el misa we ke September 2, 1911 ke el yac 44. Ke 1912, Miss Hoppin el som liki acn Wot in muta Pisin ac orekma yurin mwet kol Sunday School Kosrae. Oasr pacl el tuh som nu Jaluit ac kasru lutlut lun mission we.

Miss Elizabeth ac Miss Jane tuh tia pwar lah oasr tulik mukul wi tulik mutan lutlut. Na pa eltal sraclik mukul liki mutan ke pacl in lutlut, pacl in orekma, ac pacl in mongo. Pacl in alu mukena pa elos toeni. Ke 1914, pisen tulik lutlut fin acn Wot pa tulik ongoul limekosr. Kutu sin tulik inge mutan Marshall. Oasr pacl tuh sufalla mani ma supweyuk sin American Board nu ke lutlut ah, na Miss Baldwin luo inge eltal sang mani laltal sifacna in akfalye ma eneneyuk. Ke lusen pacl eltal muta Wot, wangin tulik lutlut enenu in moli kutena ma, ke sripen kulang lun Miss Elizabeth ac Miss Jane. Mwet Kosrae elos pangon Miss Elizabeth "Mother Baldwin" ac Miss Jane "Mother DuBois."

Sayen orekma puspis laltal ke school Wot, mutan luo inge eltal lungasla Kas In Kol lun Etawi nu ke kas Chuuk, kas Marshall, ac kas Kosrae. Tulik lutlut elos printi Kas In Kol inge ke kitin press se ma oasr Wot, na kitakatelik nu ke kais sie tuka ke yac nukewa. Mwet Kosrae elos orekmakin pac Kas In Kol inge ke alu in lotutang ac eku in sou lalos.

Ke World War I tuh srola ke 1914, mwet Japan elos eis lalos tuka nukewa ma oan inpoun mwet Germany. In pacl sac, oasr Intermediate School sefanna ke tuka inge, pa school se fin acn Wot.

Ke pacl mweun sac orek (August 1914 nu ke May 1918) wanginna oak tuku saya me in use mwe mongo ac mwe kuka. Ouinge mwet nukewa fin acn Kosrae elos sun moul na upa ac ongoiya. American Board tia ku in supwama mwe kasru nu sin Miss Baldwin luo, oayapa mutan luo ah tia ku in supwala leta lalos nu sin American Board, ku nu sin sou lalos. Meet liki mweun ah, Miss Hoppin ac Rose, kitin tulik mutan Gilbert se el nutella, eltal tuh mutana Jaluit, meyen wangin inkanek laltal in folokla nu Kosrae. Arulana upa nu seltal mweyen apkuran in wangin mongo we. Mwet Christian fin acn Jaluit elos kasreltal ke kitin mongo ma oasr yorolos, oanu ke mwet Christian Kosrae tuh kite Miss Baldwin luo wi tulik ac mwet matu ma welultal fin acn Wot.

In pacl se inge tia sun book longoul ke Bible ma lungasyukla nu in kas Kosrae. Mr. Snow ac mwet kasru lal ah tuh lungasla book in Matthew, Mark, Luke, John, Orekma, Ruth, ac itkosr sin leta lal Paul. Mr. Channon ac mwet kasru lal ah tuh lungasla pac kutu leta lal Paul, ac oayapa kutu Psalm. In 1914, Miss Elizabeth Baldwin el tuh mutawauk in lungasla book nukewa ma soenna lengla nu in kas Kosrae. Mwet se ma welul ke leng uh pa Alik Kefwas.

Ke safla World War I, u sasu se tuyak, pangpang "League of Nations" (Un Mwet Pwapa Lun Mutunfacl Lulap Faclu). U se inge insese tuh mwet Japan in nununku Mariana Islands, Caroline Islands, ac Marshall Islands. Oak lulap Japan kasrusrsrusr inmasrlon Japan ac tuka inge ke wik onkosr nukewa. Ke 1919 arulana fusrasr mwet uh in eis mwe mongo, nuknuk, kerosene ac kufwa in musa lohm Japan me. Miss Elizabeth ac Miss Jane tuh arulana engan ke eltal ku in sifil eis leta ac sim leta nu sin sou laltal oayapa nu sin American Board. In 1920 eltal orekmakin mani laltal sifacna in eis kufwa nu ke sie lohm sasu seltal fin acn Wot. Ipinsak kac uh onola in mau tia kasrla. Tamtael se inge tuh insewowo ma lulap ke lohm se seltal inge.

Japan tiana mutunfacl Christian se, tusruktu "League of Nations" tuh sap mwet Japan in fuhlela orekma lun missionary Catholic oayapa missionary Protestant fin acn Micronesia in fahsr na. Sayen ma inge, sie un mwet Christian in acn Japan pangpang "Nan'yo Dendo Dan" tuh supwama missionary lalos sifacna ke 1920 in orekma Chuuk ac Pohnpei.

Pastu Likiaksa Yal el matuoh, na mwet kol ke Church Kosrae elos sulella Fred Skilling in pastu se aklimekosr lun Church Kosrae. Elos akmusraella ke 1921.

In 1922 Miss Hoppin ac Rose, tulik mutan se natul, eltal som nu United States in mongla. Ke Miss Hoppin el foloko in sifil orekma Kosrae ac Jaluit, Rose el mutana California in lutlut we. El yac 11 in pacl sac.

– CHAPTER TEN –

AN ERA OF ISOLATION
1911-1922

BALDWIN SISTERS REACH WOT

It was summertime 1911 when the Baldwin sisters said goodbye once again to their family in New Jersey and began the long trip back to Micronesia. While they were away for their furlough year, the American Board had turned over the work in Chuuk to the Liebenzell Mission of Germany. The sisters were reassigned to what they understood was a Christian training school for girls at Kosrae.

When they arrived on September 16, 1911, the school at Wot was given new life. Some among the Kosraeans remembered meeting them when the Baldwins had briefly visited the mission school—and the sisters certainly remembered that visit in 1898 as they were on their way to Chuuk. They recalled the invigorating climb from the dock up to the school with its magnificent view, and they remembered the hospitality of Jenny Olin. They were sad to learn that several months prior to their arrival, Miss Olin had been taken to Australia due to illness. What they did not know at the time was that Jenny Olin had died in a Sydney hospital on September 2. She was only 44 years old and had served at Wot for 14 years.

Marion Wells had been reassigned to work with the Channons at Ocean Island (Banaba), where she married the Rev. Frank Woodward in March 1912. Only Jessie Hoppin remained to assist Elizabeth and Jane Baldwin in getting acquainted and settled in their new place of service.

EARLY YEARS OF ELIZABETH AND JANE BALDWIN

Life in the islands was completely different from what the two sisters had imagined before they had first reached Micronesia. Born into a well-to-do New Jersey family—Elizabeth on April 11, 1859, and Jane on June 9, 1863—they were the youngest of the four children of Samuel A. and Mary Addis Baldwin. Known as "Lizzy" and "Jenny" to their parents and siblings, the sisters were faithful members of Newark's First Presbyterian Church. At an early age they felt "called to take the Good News to those living in darkness,"[1] but also believed that they should honor their father and mother by caring for them as long as the parents were living.

It was not until 1898 that both Samuel and Mary Baldwin had died, and the two women were free to apply for work in the "foreign field." However, when an official of the Presbyterian Board learned that Elizabeth was already 39 years old and Jane was 35, he told them that the time had passed for them to begin work in another country or learn a strange language and try to adjust to life in a far-off land.

Instead of letting the rejection discourage them, the sisters offered themselves to the board of the Congregational Church—the American Board of Commissioners for Foreign Missions—in Boston. When this board secretary asked where they wanted to work, the Baldwin sisters replied, "Where no one else wants to go." Their devotion and willingness so impressed the board's leaders that they swiftly assigned the sisters to Chuuk in Micronesia. Elizabeth and Jane had never heard of that place, but they knew their prayers had been answered. By November 1898, the Baldwin sisters were at Chuuk.

BALDWINS AT CHUUK

Their lives at Chuuk had been anything but monotonous. The sisters were responsible for the 25 boarding students and, night or day, when the girls were in their dormitory, one or both of the sisters were there with them. There were also a number of day students who were married, including the wives of some of the young men enrolled in the nearby Boys' Training School.

On weekday mornings after the Baldwins taught several classes each, they spent an hour giving the students music lessons, at which the girls were very good, and they led them in calisthenics. In the afternoons they supervised work assignments and play hours. In addition, the sisters led morning and evening devotional services, ordered supplies, wrote reports, managed the mission's finances, took care of first aid, and operated a kindergarten with an enrollment of 50. All of this but the kindergarten they would do at Kosrae.[2]

When the *Morning Star V* reached Chuuk in late November 1905, it was the first visit of the vessel in more than five years. The Baldwins were again able to send out reports and receive mail and supplies. In addition, the *Star* gave them the opportunity to make field trips—Elizabeth to the Mortlock Islands south of Chuuk and Jane north to the Hall Islands—to recruit girls for their school and encourage former students who had already returned to their homes. They also gave counsel and shared materials to help the teachers who labored on those isolated outposts.

In expressing her appreciation for the *Morning Star V*, Elizabeth wrote, "The people here are greatly delighted with her speed and accommodations, and who can measure her influence for good as she goes among them bringing assistance in their times of difficulty, temptation and discouragement, and those who will instruct them in the ways of the Lord?"[3]

After serving at Chuuk for more than 11 years without a break, the sisters took their first and only furlough beginning in 1909. Since ships had begun traveling between Micronesia and Germany, the Baldwins decided to return to America by way of Turkey to visit their half-brother Theodore and his wife Matilda, who were missionaries there. In the United States they stayed with another brother Wilmer and his family in East Orange, New Jersey. They did not get much rest, as they were kept busy speaking in different churches about the mission work in Chuuk.

BALDWINS SETTLE AT WOT AND
MISS HOPPIN MOVES TO LELU

As they had been deeply involved in their work at the American Board Girls' School in Kutchua village on the island of Dublon [Tonoas] at Chuuk, so Elizabeth and Jane Baldwin now immersed themselves in their work with the school at Wot, Kosrae.

After several months, it was decided that Miss Hoppin would move to Pisin to work with the church leaders and assist the Sunday School teachers. Her move was an ideal solution to the escalating distress that the conservative Baldwin sisters were having as they tried to work with the more progressive Miss Hoppin. Their differences were particularly apparent in areas of student discipline and dress. Though Miss Hoppin left Wot with some sadness—she had taught there for more than 20 years—she was excited about being near her many former students in Lelu on the other side of the island. The generosity of her decision gave Miss Elizabeth and Miss Jane an opportunity to develop their own program at Wot, and the move pleased the members of Kosrae's Church. Kosraeans had always been attracted to Miss Hoppin's enthusiasm, and some of them had even been willing to consider her innovative ideas.

So by 1912 the Baldwin sisters were on their own. They both spoke Chuukese, but that language did not help now. They decided that Elizabeth would learn the Kosraean and Gilbertese languages, while Jane concentrated on Marshallese and Gilbertese. In that way one or the other would be able to communicate with all of their new charges. They had already proven one skeptical mission executive wrong when—at 39 and 35 years of age—they had learned the language of Chuuk. Now, Miss Elizabeth was 52 and Miss Jane was 48, but learn the new languages they did!

To distinguish between the sisters, Miss Elizabeth became "Mother Baldwin" to the students and to most Kosraeans, while Miss Jane was known as "Mother DuBois"—DuBois, a family name, being her middle name. "Baldwin" was not difficult for the students to pronounce, but "DuBois" caused a few problems. They had been amused when one of their graduates later wrote to Miss Jane, addressing her as "Mother Two Boys."[4]

WHAT ABOUT THE BOYS?

The sisters were dismayed by the presence of boys at their new post. They had arrived believing that the school was, as it had been before, for girls only. At Chuuk, much of their energy had been spent in trying to keep their girls from having any contact with boys—not only those from nearby "heathen" villages, but those attending the boys' mission school next door. They were not at all certain that boys and girls could be together in a single school. Having never taught boys, their experience at Chuuk convinced them that they would rather not try.

But the experiment at Wot was now almost three years old and, for better or for worse, it appeared that the boys were there to stay. The original three who had become part of the student body in 1909 had been joined by four times that number. After all, it took considerable energy and muscle to carry those 100-pound bags of rice from the wharf-house up the mountain to the kitchen storeroom. The young men had proven their worth as hard workers, and several of them excelled as students.

There was another part to the story. In spite of the fact that those in charge of the Micronesia Mission had decided that it was expedient to train the low-island students in their home areas, many Marshallese and Gilbertese parents, as well as pastors, disagreed. This was especially true of those who had themselves studied in the schools at Kosrae and continued to consider Wot the ideal place for their children. It was difficult for Gilbertese students to travel to Wot now that their home islands were administered by the British and there was no *Morning Star* in service, though a few did manage to get to the school. It was much easier for young people from the Marshall Islands to travel to Wot as German ships made regular trips between Jaluit, headquarters for the German administration in the Marshalls, and Kosrae. So when low-island girls arrived, accompanied by a few boys, the Baldwins accommodated the young men as well as the girls. How could they send them away? And as more Kosraean families offered their sons to help at the mission, Miss Elizabeth and Miss Jane found it increasingly difficult to say "No." Consequently as the months went by, more and more boys were incorporated into the student body.

A SCHOOL FOR GIRLS—A SCHOOL FOR BOYS

The inevitable happened. A school for boys was established alongside the Girls' School in 1913. The boys had always had their own classes, but it did not seem right to the sisters that both sexes be included in a school still often referred to in the homes and churches of Micronesia as the Girls' Training School at Kosrae. Though not separate the way the Wot boys' schools had been separated in years past, during this early period at least, the Baldwins began referring to their "two schools."

Before and immediately after the sisters arrived, boys at Wot slept in island-style thatched-roof buildings along the beach near the wharf-house. Now a new dormitory was built for them part way up the hill near the area which had been occupied by the Marshall Islands Training School before it was disbanded eight years earlier—an acceptable distance from the girls' dormitory located at the top of the Yonrak hill. The Baldwins were not only adamant that the boys and girls be kept apart in the evenings, at night, and in their class periods, but also that the boys have their own kitchen and dining room. These minimal facilities were erected and maintained by the boys in the vicinity of their dormitory. The sisters finally considered the arrangement acceptable, but they had created a double work load for themselves.

The school day began with morning devotions, which the sisters led. Surprisingly, this was the one activity of the day that students of both schools were allowed to attend together—though the girls sat on one side of the room and the boys on the other. Naïvely, the sisters felt that the hanky-panky they were so concerned might happen during meals and class time surely could not happen during worship periods. To the Baldwins the nature of these devotional services, and the fact that they were always attended by all staff members and various Wot neighbors, made them safe.

But the students found ways to communicate without their teachers knowing, as have students the world over before and since. Generously, the girls offered their hymnals for the boys to use, and sure enough, the boys would find notes tucked between the pages. Later, as the girls cleaned the chapel, they would look for and often find notes left for them beneath the corners of the mats on which the boys had been sitting.

After morning devotions, the students would divide for breakfast and then attend their separate classes to study math, English, Bible, music, and geography. In the afternoons, while the boys took care of the animals and worked at planting and gathering food, the girls received training in different aspects of homemaking, which included gardening. The girls were closely supervised.

Evening bath time for the boys took place in the Wot River, while the girls made do with buckets in a bath house built around a rain-filled cistern immediately next door to their dormitory. The Baldwins had their own cistern, but were not much concerned with comfort. Despite the heat and humidity, the sisters always wore conservative, high-collared dresses with skirts that reached the floor and sleeves that stretched to below their wrists. Every night the two of them went to bed fully clothed in order to be instantly available for any emergency that might arise.

As time passed, new buildings were erected. By 1913 the Wot campus consisted of 13 buildings of varying sizes—four foreign and nine native—the largest being the two-and-a-half-story classroom and dormitory building that had been erected for the Girls' School in 1909. These buildings were primarily located at Yonrak on the top of the hill. The boys' dormitory, kitchen, and playing field in the old Marshallese school area were lower on the hill to the south. The site of the Gilbert Islands School down the hill toward the north had been abandoned to the jungle—though Mrs. Walkup's grave in the school cemetery was well kept, and its monument easily seen on a bluff above the steep, coral-stone walkway the Gilbertese boys had constructed between their school and the wharf. The grassy path from the Girls' School higher up the mountain connected with that coral walk as it wended its way down to the beach. Though this "Gilbertese" trail was easier to maneuver than the steeper "Marshallese" trail, some individuals when alone refused to use it because of its proximity to the graves.

GENEROSITY AND STRICTNESS

When mission funds ran low, as they frequently did, the Baldwins relied on the availability of their own family money. The students had work assignments that helped support the school, but none of them paid a tuition or used money for any other expense while living and studying at Wot during the years that Mother Baldwin and Mother DuBois were in charge. All student expenses, as well as most construction costs, were paid for by the Baldwins.

Gradually, but inexorably, the indelible stamp of the Baldwin sisters came to rest on the two schools. Earlier missionaries at Wot had been conscientious and strict, but none had approached the almost fanatical ways reflected by the two women from New Jersey. A rigid inflexibility went hand-in-hand with their selfless generosity. This was particularly true in their insistence that the dresses they provided for the girls free of charge must cover the entire body, including arms, legs, and neck—not only for attending morning and evening worship services and all classes, but while working in the gardens as well. The boys were required to wear long-sleeved shirts at all times, work periods included.

TOPICS FOR SUNDAY SCHOOL AND CHRISTIAN ENDEAVOR

Slowly the Baldwins learned to appreciate their adult Kosraean colleagues and began to trust them to watch over the girls. This policing of the girls was of utmost importance to the Baldwin sisters, and it was some time before they allowed themselves to accept the assistance of others in doing it. But now the sisters—relieved at least partially of that tedious responsibility and becoming increasingly familiar with the new languages—began spending more and more of their afternoons translating. They translated daily Christian Endeavor topics and weekly Sunday School lessons into Chuukese and Marshallese as well as Kosraean. They would often spend considerable time trying to find an appropriate scripture text for some of those topics and lessons since only portions of the Bible had been translated into those three languages.

After the topics and lessons had been translated, they were given to some of the girls who had been taught to set type. When the type was set, the boys did the printing on a small hand-press that had been sent to the school, Mr. Channon's press having long before disintegrated. For the Kosraean Church these topics and lesson plans were much relied upon. For many years the daily Christian Endeavor topics had been faithfully followed for morning and evening family worship in homes around the island and were the primary calendar used by the people.

FROM THE GERMANS TO THE JAPANESE

German administrators in Micronesia knew very little of the rumblings of war, and the islanders knew nothing—but on August 4, 1914, when German troops crossed the border into Belgium, World War I became a fact. On the 15th of that same month, Japan issued an ultimatum to Germany demanding withdrawal of the German fleet from the Far East. When no reply was received, Japan declared war on Germany August 23, 1914.

On October 5, the First South Seas Squadron of the Japanese navy anchored off Kosrae—sending a small contingent ashore on Lelu Island to raise the Japanese flag, making Kosrae a detachment of their Pohnpei garrison. This was one of a "series of swift and bloodless occupations of German Micronesia."[5] By the end of that month the Japanese naval forces had seized all of the Marshall Islands, the Carolines, and the Marianas—with the exception of Guam—from the Germans. [Since the end of the Spanish-American War in 1898, Guam had been considered a possession of the United States. The Gilbert Islands had become a British protectorate in 1892.]

German schools were closed and Japanese schools opened. German officials were imprisoned. The trade language for the islands was changed once again, this time from German to Japanese. Encouraged by their government, a few Japanese colonists began moving into various parts of Micronesia, though with the exception of one or two businessmen and four or five fishermen, they did not settle on Kosrae.

The only secondary school in Micronesia during the early years of the Japanese administration was the school at Wot, where Elizabeth and Jane Baldwin maintained classes for 65 young women and men in their two schools. As the student body—primarily Kosraeans—increased, so did the staff of islanders who assisted the Baldwin sisters. Most of the workers were assigned from the Kosraean Church, but a few were Marshallese and Gilbertese who had been students at Wot and had either been chosen or had asked to remain. Some of them had married Kosraeans.

ELIZABETH BALDWIN BEGINS BIBLE TRANSLATION PROJECT

The Kosraeans were increasingly eager to have the complete Bible in their own language. Benjamin Snow had translated the four Gospels, the book of Acts, and seven of the Apostle Paul's letters, plus the Old Testament book of Ruth. Assisting Mr. Snow were, among others, Salpasr and Lupalikkun. Mr. Channon, with the help of Alik Kefwas, Fred Skilling, and John Mackwelung, had added several more of Paul's letters and a few of the Psalms to the existing Scriptures in Kosraean. The balance of the New Testament and the bulk of the Old Testament had yet to be translated. The Baldwins understood the need and shared the desire of the Kosraean people that the entire Bible be available in the vernacular of that island.

In 1914 Elizabeth Baldwin began the arduous and lengthy task of translating the remaining books of the Bible into Kosraean. Though her other responsibilities continued unabated, the translation project became her priority and remained so for the next 12 years.

Hiram Bingham, Jr., one of the early American Board missionaries in the Gilbert Islands, had first created a written version of Gilbertese and had then translated the entire Bible into it. It was considered an exceptionally skillful piece of work. Mother Baldwin, having learned the language of the Gilberts to use with those Gilbertese who were at Wot, used Mr. Bingham's translation, as well as the American Standard Version of 1901, as the basis of her work. Her assistant throughout the Kosraean translation project was Alik Kefwas.

REPERCUSSIONS OF WORLD WAR I

By 1915, communication between the Baldwin sisters at Wot and the executives of the American Board in Boston was practically nonexistent, with the resources and attention of the board directed elsewhere. With Germany and the United States absorbed in a war being fought on the Atlantic Ocean and the

European continent, the islands of Micronesia were left alone and nearly forgotten. Economic help and postal and travel assistance vanished. People living in the islands had to fend for themselves; missionaries and their schools were on their own.

Jessie Hoppin, who for several years had been commuting between Kosrae and the Marshall Islands, was forced to remain at Jaluit when the war began. German ships were no longer available to provide transportation. There were other inconveniences and hardships for her as well, but her Marshallese associates and neighbors were considerate and kind, generously sharing what little they had with their respected teacher and friend.

At Wot, the Baldwin sisters were confined to the mission school campus. There was little reason to visit Lelu, since Victor Melander's trading company was without foreign goods. It would have helped relieve conditions a bit if the Marshallese students could have been returned to their families, but there was no way to send them home. So the students and teachers at Wot relied on food grown on the mission plantation. Salt, as in days gone by, was boiled from sea water. Though the students were accustomed to the flour and rice that were no longer available, a diet of only island-grown foods was not much of a hardship for them. But for the Baldwins—who were used to supplementing native foods with American canned goods shipped in to them—preparing palatable, satisfying meals became a challenge.

Both women had always enjoyed their daily cups of tea and coffee, but neither of these beverages were obtainable. The priorities of the women, however, were strong. If any sugar managed to find its way to Wot, it was used for making rollers for their press, not for sweetening drinks. They might not be eating well, but their production of materials for the class room and Church went forward as usual. Nothing could be sent to Chuuk or to the Marshalls, but they continued to produce materials in those languages, stocking them until some means of conveyance appeared. Meanwhile, the lessons that Mother Baldwin and Mother DuBois wrote for Kosrae's Sunday School and Christian Endeavor came off the active little press at the same regular intervals and were much used and appreciated by the people of that island.

SOME PROGRESS DURING BLEAK YEARS

In addition to these dated lessons and the recently undertaken project of rendering the remaining books of the Bible into Kosraean, the missionary sisters were busy with several other major projects. Also being translated and printed during 1915 and 1916 were a simplified "Life of Christ," an abridged edition of *Pilgrim's Progress*, and an arithmetic book—each produced in the Kosraean,

Marshallese, and Chuukese languages.

Still, the years 1915, 1916, and 1917 were, in many ways, bleak and difficult for those at Wot. The school's class, work, and worship routines were faithfully maintained, but the students had to work extra shifts in the plantation gardens to produce what was needed to feed everyone. The students of both schools, as well as their teachers, were grateful, therefore, for the kindness of the Kosraean Church. Members of the congregations in Lelu, Tafunsak, Malem, and Utwe— with Pastor Likiaksa Yal confidently in the lead—consistently took their turns to provide food and labor to assist the mission throughout these trying years. These gifts, sincerely shared, included the considerable time that was always involved in gathering and preparation and in traveling the distance to and from their homes to the Wot community, so removed and alone.

As nothing was being delivered to Kosrae, clothing deteriorated. The heat and humidity, the heavy rains and dampness, and the traditional method of washing—beating clothing with heavy sticks on rocks at the river—took their toll. The total lack of new yardage and thread was particularly trying for the Baldwin sisters, who were unwavering in their insistence that the students—the girls in particular—be properly and neatly covered from head to toe at all times. As the war years followed one after the other, the two Baldwins, as well as their female helpers, became very clever and innovative with the needle.

ROYAL BOND

During these Spartan years, the pair of sisters from New Jersey formed an unbreakable bond with Kosrae's royal pair that would last the rest of their lives.

Now in their prime, King John and Queen Hattie took it upon themselves to draw the two American women under their wings and into their care. Sometimes in the company of a few of their children, sometimes just the two of them, the king and queen would appear at the Wot wharf, their canoe loaded with all manner of Kosraean produce, plus fish, chicken, and pork, to share with Miss Elizabeth and Miss Jane. How the sisters enjoyed and looked forward to these visits! They would listen eagerly as King John told them of events and circumstances on the other side of the island—while Queen Hattie sat on the floor before one and then the other, massaging the aching muscles of their weary legs.

AMERICAN BOARD RELINQUISHES ITS WORK IN THE GILBERTS

In 1910 the southern part of the Gilbert Islands had been turned over to the London Missionary Society by the American Board. Negotiations slowly continued and, on July 1, 1917, the remaining work of the American Board in the Gilberts was finally given to the board's venerable British counterpart. The Gilbert Islands had been under British rule for 25 years, so sentimental possessiveness and nostalgia were replaced by what seemed to be common sense and ecumenical wisdom. The few girls who had continued to find their way to the school at Wot to join their Marshallese and Kosraean sisters there, no longer came.

LEAGUE OF NATIONS MANDATES JAPANESE RULE

At the conclusion of the war, on May 7, 1918, the Supreme Council of the League of Nations officially assigned to Japan the islands north of the equator that had formerly been administered by Germany. This League of Nations agreement with Japan was referred to as "The Mandate." The Japanese controlled the islands of Micronesia through their South Seas Government or Nan'yo-cho. "The major maritime enterprise in the opening of Micronesia to Japanese development was the Nippon Yusen Kaisha (Japan Mail Steamship Company), or NYK, the largest steamship line" in Japan.[6] Ships began steaming out of Kobe Harbor every six weeks with foodstuffs, building materials, machinery, coal, and sundries—along with a few passengers, mostly government officials and business people. One of the two main routes led to British North Borneo by way of Yap, Palau, Angaur, Davao in the Philippines, and Manado in the Celebes. The other route took the ships to Saipan, Chuuk, Pohnpei, Kosrae, and Jaluit. The ships returned to Japan "loaded with copra, sugar, Manila hemp, charcoal, coconut oil, and assorted marine products, along with a handful of passengers—officials on leave, a copra broker or two, and maybe a few missionaries."[7]

NEW MISSION HOUSE AT WOT

As the Japanese administration took hold, the Baldwin sisters began to realize relative ease in ordering and procuring goods for themselves and their school. By 1919, food and materials ordered via the NYK arrived with such convenience that—when compared to the previous five years—the process seemed miraculous! Their letters to the American Board and to their families, now dispatched through Japan, were filled with words of gratitude.

The sisters were so buoyed by the new possibilities that they began making specific plans for the house they had long wanted to build for themselves at Wot. Finally they would be able to leave their small corner apartment in the girls' dormitory. Using their own family funds—and the advice of Capt. Melander and the Japanese administrative officers in Lelu—termite-treated lumber, sheets of iron roofing, glass windows, and screen were ordered from Japan. The shipment arrived in 1920 and, after it had been transported to Wot, the actual building was begun by a sizable contingent of accommodating carpenters from the Kosraean Church. Led by Pastor Likiaksa Yal and King John Sigrah, these Kosraean men talked of feeling honored and grateful to be able to assist their missionary teachers in this significant way. They were assisted by Wot's lively group of male students, while the female students often entertained with songs as they distributed refreshing drinks.

Facing west, the house was raised on concrete pilings on the east edge of the Yonrak ridge, immediately next door to the large classroom and dormitory building. A screened veranda enclosed two sides at the front of the house, opening into a large sitting room with an office at the south end. This room was separated from the sitting room by a handsome wall of varnished, woven reeds and connected by an arched doorway.

To the back was an enclosed sleeping porch, lined on the south and east with sliding glass windows. A tiny bathroom, which hung over the east side of the house, boasted the first indoor toilet facility on the island. This luxury, flushed with water dipped by bucket from a rain-filled barrel, was connected to a cesspool. As the sleeping area and bathroom were on the downhill side of the house, the sisters' privacy was insured. The windows there were a good 12 feet above the jungle floor that dropped quickly away toward the Wot River.

To the right of the sitting room was the kitchen, which soon proved to be too small for the sisters' needs. Sometime later, a much larger kitchen was added to the north side of the house. Like the bathroom, it was actually a separate building connected to the main house by a narrow, enclosed passage. It was dominated by an enormous wood stove. As this room, too, was high above the slope of the hill, the windows on three sides offered incredible views of the campus, the mountains, the lagoon, and the ocean beyond. The area beneath the kitchen was enclosed and became the "press room" where the on-going translation projects of the busy sisters were type-set and printed.

Above the sitting room—and reached from that room by a well-built stairway—was a spacious, secure attic with a sturdy floor. It was used by the Baldwins for storage. There was only one outside door in this fine new house, and the two residents held the only keys to its lock. From that door, the sisters stepped out onto a concrete slab. Only three feet away were the steps that led up to the encircling veranda of their school.

By this time the sisters had ceased saying that they had "two schools" at Wot. Though the young men and women continued to be carefully segregated from one another for most activities, it was a matter of reason to begin referring to the existence of a single mission school, which the two Miss Baldwins called "The Kusaie Training School."

NAN'YO DENDO DAN

Under terms of the Mandate, Japan's South Seas Government was obliged to permit Christian missionary activity in Micronesia. German missionaries—both Catholic and Protestant—had been expelled as enemy nationals by the Japanese navy within a year of the Japanese takeover, but "Christian evangelism was quickly reestablished in Micronesia after the war."[8]

Though Japan was not a Christian nation, the Japanese government actually subsidized the efforts of Japanese Christian missionaries for most of the 30-year period of Japanese rule. The government was eager, however, for Japanese missionaries to take over the work that had been going on in Micronesia. This was particularly true of the work begun and maintained by the German Liebenzell missionaries in and around Chuuk, but it included as well American Board work in the Caroline and Marshall Islands.[9] In the official Japanese view, the attempts of the missionaries to "civilize" the Micronesians complemented the efforts of the Japanese government to do so.[10]

When the Japanese Kumiai Mission Board rejected a proposal made by Dr. J. L. Barton of the American Board that the Kumiai churches assume responsibility for work in Micronesia and, at the same time, did not answer the call of its own government to do so, it was proposed that Dr. Hiromichi Kozaki, pastor of the Reinanzaka Kumiai Church in Tokyo, organize the mission with the help of other Japanese Christian leaders. In 1920, the Nan'yo Dendo Dan, or "South Seas Evangelical Group"—a small, independent group formed by Dr. Kozaki—began sending workers, first to Pohnpei and Chuuk, later to the Marshalls, and almost 20 years later, to Kosrae. Priests of Buddhism and Tenri-kyo, a Shinto sect, did serve Japanese immigrants throughout the mandated area,[11] but there was no attempt to convert Micronesians.

THOSE INDOMITABLE SISTERS

The Baldwins on Kosrae slipped quite comfortably into a routine that used the Japanese administration and its amenities to bolster their work at Wot. It had never been so easy and convenient to place and receive orders of food and materials, even during the days of the *Morning Stars* and Germany's steamships. True, there were newly introduced foods and manufactured goods that bore little resemblance to their American equivalents—but still, after having gotten by with so little, adjusting to these changes was almost pleasant. Some of their lists of needs, routed through Japan, went all the way to American Board headquarters in Boston, Massachusetts, and to family members in Newark, New Jersey, to be filled.

Miss Jane did the ordering and maintained inventory of all that now lined the shelves of the dry, secure, and commodious attic in their new home—while Miss Elizabeth, with the unflagging assistance of Kefwas, stuck with great persistence to her translation work. They were a team, these two women. Elizabeth Baldwin was the "major"—and Jane her faithful "sergeant," responding to every suggestion of her superior officer. Miss Jane did very few things without first consulting her older sister. One of the things she liked least to do was go to Lelu on errands without Elizabeth. Jane once commented that when she was in Lelu without her sister, she would "stand facing the mountain on the other side of which was Wot," thinking of Elizabeth and wondering what she was doing and how she was managing. Much later, recalling those years, Miss Jane commented, "We were like a pair of scissors. One blade could not work without the other."[12]

Now that transportation was available, officials of the American Board in Boston and family members in Newark urged the two women to take a vacation. They had been on Kosrae for nine years, and Board officers knew that the period of the war had been especially grueling for them. For a time Elizabeth and Jane considered that option. They decided that if the Board could find workers to come to Kosrae to take their places at the school while they were away in the United States, they would consider a furlough. However, the Board, unable to find new volunteers, wrote back, "Close the school and come home." To the Baldwins, there was no choice. How could they leave their students? They were convinced that if the young people and children currently studying at Wot were to go home to await the sisters' return, they would never come back. For these two devoted women, a furlough was just out of the question.[13]

There were other reasons for rejecting the idea of a furlough. After surviving the lean war years, the sisters were excited by the way things were finally progressing for them and their beloved school. They were in the midst of the Kosraean Bible translation project, new students were once again arriving from the Marshall Islands and even, occasionally, from Pohnpei and Chuuk; supplies were available; and, frankly, they were enjoying their new house. In their opinion there was simply no time nor reason for a vacation.

MISS HOPPIN'S DISTRESS

The situation was different for Jessie Hoppin at Jaluit. She had suffered more than the Baldwins during the war years, just barely surviving on the slim local diet that had been available to her in the Marshall Islands. Complicating her state of affairs was her adoption of a Gilbertese child. Miss Hoppin had fallen in love with a darling, 3-year-old girl, the daughter of a Gilbertese couple who had studied at Wot during the years Miss Hoppin had taught there. The students had married and returned to the Gilbert Islands to teach and preach. It was in the Gilberts that their Rose Kaumaip was born in 1912. When her parents took her to Jaluit in 1915 to visit their former teacher, it was arranged for Miss Hoppin to adopt the little girl. This adoption had taken place when World War I was beginning, and it was partially because of Miss Hoppin's concern for her new daughter that things had been so difficult for her. She had neglected her own needs in order to feed Rose.

Though Miss Hoppin now tried valiantly to return to the hectic schedule she had been accustomed to before the war, she found that recovering from the malnourishment she had suffered was a very slow process.

INTRODUCING CARL HEINE

A close colleague of Jessie Hoppin at Jaluit during the war years and immediately after was Pastor Carl Heine. He and his family had done what they could to assist Miss Hoppin and ease her situation, but there was very little food to go around. Everyone was on the brink of starvation.

Carl Heine had first arrived in the Marshall Islands during the early 1890s as a sailor aboard a whaling ship. A German immigrant to Australia, Mr. Heine had deserted his ship at Namdrik Atoll, disillusioned with life at sea. At Namdrik, he fell in love with and married Arbella, a Marshallese woman whose family had welcomed the sailor into their home. The Christian demeanor and practices of Arbella and her relatives so inspired the lonely young man that he converted to their faith. Sadly, Arbella died giving birth to their only child, Claude. Carl later married Arabella's younger sister, Nengij, who had been blind from birth. Together, the two of them raised Claude and a large family of their own.[14]

As years went by, Carl Heine developed into such a dedicated Christian that he became a leader in the Marshall Islands Church. His unique status as an "adopted Marshallese," his commitment as a Christian, and his fluency in the Marshallese, German, and English languages brought him to the attention of the missionaries, who first used him as a teacher and later ordained him as a pastor. He was so diligent in all his endeavors that Dr. Clinton Rife, acting on behalf of the American Board in approximately 1910, installed him as one of the Board's missionaries in the Marshall Islands. [The Rife family returned from the Marshall Islands to the United States prior to World War I.]

CHURCH OFFICIAL FROM HAWAI'I VISITS JALUIT

Visiting Jessie Hoppin at Jaluit in 1920, George P. Castle of the Church in Hawai'i was appalled at the condition in which he found her. It had been more than 10 years since her last furlough and the deprivations of the war years had left their mark. Mr. Castle felt that Miss Hoppin was greatly in need of a vacation. He wrote an angry letter to Frank F. Bell of the American Board in Boston, dated November 20 of that year.

"Miss Hoppin needs a furlough!" shouted his letter. Carl Heine could act as "special agent to assume duties on the very day that Miss Hoppin leaves the field," he continued, as Pastor Heine already did this during those periods Miss Hoppin was on Kosrae. Mr. Castle suggested that Miss Hoppin's feelings had been "deeply hurt" by the Board which, she suspected, was trying to "dismiss her."[15]

Responding in early 1921, Mr. Bell assured Mr. Castle that this was not the case. He expressed his appreciation for George Castle's concern for the isolated missionary, as well as for the support of Elizabeth and Jane Baldwin, who had also written a strong letter to the Board in Miss Hoppin's defense.

ALL-ISLAND CHRISTIAN ENDEAVOR DIVIDES, TWICE

On Kosrae in 1921, officers of the all-island Christian Endeavor Society finally voted to divide their organization into four separate entities.

Following the establishment of Christian Endeavor in 1903, all members gathered in Lelu each Sunday afternoon. This placed the burden of travel on C. E. members who lived in Tafunsak, Malem, and Utwe. A few people walked, but most of them went to Lelu and returned by canoe. By 1905, the people of Tafunsak were using the Insrefusr entry into the Lelu mangrove channel, and the channel between Mutunlik, Malem, and Utwe was well-used. But, depending on the tides, those who did not live in Lelu were often away from their homes for three days at a time.

Then, three or four years after Christian Endeavor had been established, the leaders made a decision that was not unanimous. Responding to the pleas of their non-Lelu members, the officers decided on a unique plan. Tafunsak members would still be expected to travel to Lelu for C. E. meetings. But members in Malem would join with those in Utwe. As Utwe village was still located across the south harbor, Malem villagers would go by canoe through the channel, across the open harbor, straight to "Utwe Ma." People of Malem benefitted least by this plan. Traveling to Utwe by canoe took even longer than the canoe trip to Lelu. In spite of this, the two groups in their separate locations thrived. On special days, of course, they were all expected in Lelu.

In 1921, approximately 14 years after the first separation, another separation was initiated. The all-island committee agreed that it was finally time to allow four separate Christian Endeavor groups to meet in their own villages, no travel involved. Relief was great among the people of Tafunsak and Malem, and each group flourished. Interest in Christian Endeavor and the Church was given a needed boost, and membership increased. Partially as a result of new-found enthusiasm, the Tafunsak church broke ground for a new building on October 17, 1921.

FRED SKILLING ORDAINED KOSRAE'S FIFTH PASTOR

Members of the Church on Kosrae were anxious about their aging pastor, Likiaksa Yal. Though he remained alert and willing, it became increasingly difficult physically for him to handle the pastoral responsibilities of his congregation, worshiping as they did on most Sundays in four separate locations on the island. It was decided that the Church should have a second pastor to relieve the older man's burden.

In 1921, Miss Hoppin and the two Miss Baldwins enthusiastically joined the leadership of the Church in choosing and then ordaining 47-year-old Fred Skilling, an industrious and admired member of the Church and community, to the Christian ministry. Since his student days at Wot and his apprenticeship as the first and long-time president of the all-island Christian Endeavor Society, Fred had been groomed for many years—at least from the missionaries' point of view—as a potential pastor. The only son of American Harry Skillings and his Nauruan wife, Sitoma, Pastor Fred was in every other way thoroughly Kosraean.

A DECISION SPARKS A DREAM

In 1922, Jessie Hoppin made a personal decision that had great consequences for generations of Kosrae's children. This decision was the spark that ignited the process from which Kosrae's public school system developed. Miss Hoppin decided that her adopted daughter, Rose, should be educated in the United States—and when Rose, as an educated young woman, returned to Micronesia and Kosrae, she became the primary force in getting Kosrae's public schools organized.

After World War I had ended, Rose began attending school on Jaluit, and visiting Kosrae when her adoptive mother traveled there. She became fluent in both Kosraean and Marshallese, and—to the delight of her mother—was a quick-witted, eager student.

Rose accompanied Miss Hoppin in 1922 on the missionary's long-awaited furlough, which had finally been approved and arranged by the American Board. Together, traveling by train, they visited relatives and churches in different regions of the United States. Then, when it was time for Jessie Hoppin to return to her responsibilities in Micronesia, Rose remained to attend school in California. Though she was only 11 years old, Rose announced, after only a few weeks in her new school, that she wanted one day to return to Micronesia as a teacher. She held to that dream during her 13 years in the United States, even when her advisors, sensing her intellect and observing her talents, strongly urged her to remain in the U.S. and study nursing.[16] ⚶

Notes - Chapter 10

1. Eleanor Wilson, "Too Old?" p. 4
2. Ibid, pp. 22-23
3. Ibid, p. 26
4. Ibid, p. 28
5. Mark R. Peattie, *Nan'yo, The Rise and Fall of the Japanese in Micronesia*, pp. 62-64
6. Ibid, p. 144
7. Ibid, p. 148
8. Ibid, p. 840
9. Wynn C. Fairfield, "Christians from Boston," 1944, p. 2
10. Peattie, p. 840
11. Tadao Yanaihara, *Pacific Islands under Japanese Mandate*, Oxford, 1940, p. 238
12. Wilson, pp. 30-31
13. Ibid, p. 3
14. Mary Lanwi, personal conversations, July 26, 2001
15. George P. Castle, personal correspondence to Enoch F. Bell, ABCFM, Nov. 20, 1920
16. Kosrae Department of Education, Rose Mackwelung Library Dedication, Jan. 7, 1994

NUNAK YOHK KE CHAPTER 11
1922-1930

Ke 1922 oasr mwet Japan ekasr muta Kosrae—mwet inge mwet kuka ac mwet patur. Mwet Kosrae elos insewowo ke puseni mwe kuka ma wi oak Japan tuku. Tok oasr taktu Japan se tuku muta Lelu.

Governor Japan se su muta Pohnpei el supwala police sergeant se in mwet tutafpo lal fin acn Kosrae. Oasr pac mukul Japan welul in mwet kasru lal. Elos nukewa muta Lelu. Sergeant se inge el orek funmwet nu sin mwet Kosrae, ac pukanten pacl el sulallal nu selos. Ma sap lal uh arulana upa, ac mwet fin tia akfalye, na el sap in sringsring elos, pwanang kwaseyuk sergeant sac ac mwet lal uh. Mwet Kosrae elos supah ke mwet Japan inge lungse na susar, oayapa ke elos isis mano misa. Missionary elos fahk lah ouiya inge ma lun mwet pegan. Ke ma inge mwet Kosrae elos tiana akfulatye sergeant sac, a elos pangon mu mwet kol na pwaye lalos pa Tokosra Paliknoa, oayapa pastu luo lalos. Fin oasr alein ke acn, ku akukuin inmasrlon sou, mwet kol lun church pa ac orekma kac.

Ke 1923 mwet Japan elos mutawauk in srikeya acn nukewa ac oakiya masrol ke acn lun kais sie sou. Elos eisla acn na lulap inmasrlon inging uh tuh in ma lun government Japan. Mwet matu Kosrae elos lain oakwuk se inge, mweyen kitakatelik tari acn nukewa tuh in ma lun mwet. Tusruktu mwet Japan elos srunga lohngolos. Ke sripa se inge, oasr fohsak lulap inmasrlon mwet Japan ac mwet Kosrae, oayapa inmasrlon mwet Kosrae sifacna.

Miss Elizabeth Baldwin ac Alik Kefwas eltal kwafeang na in lungasla book nukewa ma lula ke Bible. Sie press sasu, su arulana yohk liki press se meet ah, tuh supweyuk nu Kosrae ke 1923. Mukul Marshall se ma tuh lutlut Wot el arulana etala orekma ke press se meet ah. Inel pa Jonah Metwarik, ouinge el na pa orekma yohk ke press sasu sac. Tulik mutan lutlut pa takunla leta nukewa ke kais sie sra book meet liki ac pressiyuki. Glass lal Miss Elizabeth tuh musalla in 1924, na el supwala nu England in orekla. Mutal ne munasla a el tia tui in orekma ke leng uh.

Pastu Likiaksa Yal el misa in November 1925, yac 22 tukun el tuh akmusrala, na Pastu Fred Skilling el mukena pastu lun acn Kosrae.

Orekma in leng uh safla ke 1926. Ke tari ah, kunla na pwaye mutal Miss Elizabeth. Jonah ac tulik lutlut Wot elos orekma na in printi sra book lula ke Bible. Ke tari, elos ac orani ac twani ac sang pac kolo na kac. Bible luo ku tolu na pa ku in orekla ke len se. Pastu Fred ac deacon lun Church elos us book nukewa ma tari ac kitalik nu sin mwet Kosrae. Mwet nukewa elos saokkin Bible natulos yohk liki kutena ma lalos saya.

George ac Eleanor Lockwood eltal missionary in acn Marshall, na ke 1928 American Board supwaltalla nu Kosrae in kasru Miss Elizabeth ac Miss Jane fin acn Wot. Miss Elizabeth el yac 69, ac Miss Jane el yac 65 in pacl sac. Mr. Lockwood el luti class ke lotutang ac ke tafunlen tok el wi tulik mukul orekma ke ima. Mrs. Lockwood el wi pac luti class, ac sang orekma kunen tulik mutan. El arulana sumat ke luti on, oayapa el kasru Miss Baldwin luo in aksasuye Book in On Kosrae. Oasr tulik mutan srisrik luo natin Pastu ac Mrs. Lockwood: Althea ac Winifred.

Mwet kol in pacl se Etawi tuh tufahna tuyak fin acn Kosrae ke 1903, elos srakna kol Etawi ke 1929, na pa mwet fusr in pacl se inge elos tia pulaik ku pwar in weang. Ke Mr. Lockwood el siyuk in oasr Etawi lun mwet fusr sifacna, mwet kol lun Etawi tiana insese nu kac.

Ke Sepe Intara, su mutan kial Pastu Fred Skilling, el tuh misa, Pastu Fred el sifilpa payuk sel Sepe Awe Siminlik, su ma wial Tokosra Paliknoa.

– CHAPTER ELEVEN –

A BIBLE IN KOSRAEAN
1922-1930

JAPANESE ADMINISTRATION ON KOSRAE

The Pohnpei branch office of the Japanese Nan'yo-cho [South Seas Government] was represented on Kosrae by a single police sergeant and several underlings who were stationed with him in Lelu. The sergeant disliked Kosraeans, and the feeling was mutual. He frequently ordered beatings, which were administered either by him or by one of his men. Due to his belief that corporal punishment was a quick, efficient way of getting at the truth, he sometimes beat both parties when a disagreement came to his attention. One method he occasionally used to get a confession was to have the man he suspected squat with a stick inserted horizontally behind his bent knees. After four hours of this, the man being punished was temporarily unable to walk[1]—and inclined to say what the sergeant wanted to hear!

Sometimes the police sergeant made impossible demands concerning a work project just to see what objections might be voiced. When the Kosraean workers accepted his orders without objection, whether it was possible to comply or not, the sergeant was all the more irritated. He described the Kosraeans as the worst group of "yes-men" he had ever seen. When the governor made his annual inspection tour from Pohnpei, the Kosraeans hesitated to register their complaints because they had learned that the sergeant was quick to retaliate after the governor left. So he continued to play his cruel cat and mouse game with his workers. Young adult and middle-aged males, especially, experienced first-hand the sergeant's unfair treatment, as they were all routinely conscripted to work under his direction at various projects in road building, dock improvement, and jungle clearing.

Paliknoa Sigrah—King John—was Kosrae's "high chief," and each of the four villages had their own chiefs, but even the relatively minor matters that these local leaders were permitted to handle had to be reported to the sergeant. Still, the people looked to their king as their authority—certainly not the Japanese police sergeant.

The Church on Kosrae continued to deal with the kinds of secular affairs that ordinarily would have been handled by a local court. Either the sergeant was oblivious of the extent to which the Church was handling land quarrels and other disputes between individuals, or he preferred to ignore Kosraean affairs as long as they did not conflict with Japanese regulations. It could be that he was unaware of many of the Church's activities since the people avoided contact with him and his office as much as possible. Though there was some dissatisfaction among the people with decisions that the Church Committee made, it was not great enough to overcome the distrust the people felt for the Japanese.[2] No problem among the Kosraeans themselves was ever taken to the police sergeant for resolution.

The animosity Kosraeans felt toward the Japanese police sergeant and his henchmen made it easier for them to complain among themselves about certain obvious and annoying cultural differences. They were especially repulsed by the Japanese practice of cremation. Also, Kosraeans were very uncomfortable with the Japanese indifference to nudity. The newcomers often worked with their shirts off and would strip down to their loincloths when they were fishing. Bathing commonly took place in private, but if there were Kosraeans in the vicinity, the Japanese made no effort to cover their nude bodies. It did not matter where they were or who saw them. Most Kosraean men—and certainly all of those who were related to the Church—wore long-sleeved shirts and long pants for all activities, including hard work. Bathing was done in the dark, or within an enclosed area. When others were near, bathers adhered to strict rules of modesty. Though by this time Kosraeans had long been eating rice—first introduced to them by the Wot missionaries, who imported it aboard the *Morning Stars* for their students—they disliked much of the other food that the Japanese ate, some of which was now being sold in their stores.

But the most fundamental difference between the Kosraeans and the Japanese was religious. As Christians, Kosraeans reflected the attitudes of their missionary teachers who considered the Japanese heathen. Though Church leaders were unable to overtly oppose Japanese authority, they did offer passive resistance and showed their discomfort with Japanese ways. For example, Church officials refused to recognize anyone as truly married if the ceremony was performed in the police office by the sergeant—and this rarely happened.

The Japanese made efforts to increase their influence. Prominent Kosraeans, along with other Micronesians, were taken on tours to Japan. Badges of merit were given to various individuals. The prosperity that gradually developed during the Japanese regime was popular, and people were able to buy foreign goods on a far more extensive scale than ever before. Still, general prosperity and Japanese indoctrination did not win the esteem or loyalty of the Kosraeans.[3]

LAND MATTERS

Confusion arose over the Japanese approach to land ownership. Japan's South Seas Government considered the control and allocation of land to be a major administrative function. They had encountered a patchwork of landowning systems in Micronesia—clan or communal property, feudal claims, and private ownership. In 1923 the Japanese began land surveys and registration programs to identify ownership, measure boundaries, and confirm land titles throughout the mandate. It was unilaterally decided that all unused or uncultivated communal land was the property of the new government.

"On Kosrae, large tracts of the interior were understood by the Japanese to be unused communal land and were consequently counted as government territory. In fact, these lands had passed some years before into private Micronesian owner-ship, but Kosraeans were too intimidated to contradict the surveyors."[4]

NEW PRINTING PRESS

In 1923, the arduous Bible translation project was given a great boost. To celebrate the 25th anniversary of the Baldwins' arrival in Micronesia, friends in America sent them a foot-powered press that was much larger and far superior to their hand press. When it arrived, it was carefully balanced on a canoe and transported from the dock in Lelu to Wot, where the boys carried the heavy crate up the steep trail to the site of the school. The new and cherished machine was installed on a concrete pedestal in the small, protected "press room" below the mission house kitchen. It did not take long for Jonah Metwarik, the missionary sisters' bright young Marshallese assistant, to master the new machine.

Jonah, born on Aur Atoll in the Marshall Islands, was a mission school stu-dent at Jaluit by the time he was 12 years old. He was almost 16 in 1914 when he was sent to study at Wot. His industry, dexterity, and accommodating nature brought him quickly to the attention of the Baldwin sisters, and he soon became a favorite. Miss Jane taught him how to use the hand press, and in a very short time he could operate it better than his teacher.

By the time the foot-powered press arrived, Jonah had become a competent printer. But he and the wonderful new machine could produce only what had already been translated. That process continued daily in Miss Elizabeth's study on the floor above the press room, as the missionary and her faithful assistant, Alik Kefwas, labored on. With so much else constantly going on at the school, there were not enough daylight hours to dedicate to the Bible project—so Miss Elizabeth continued the work in the evenings by the pale light of a kerosene lamp. In 1924, when her glasses broke, she sent the prescription to England to have another pair made—a process that took more than a year. But she could not wait. She felt compelled to finish the work.

As pages, chapters, and books of the Bible were completed, the handwritten manuscript was carried from Miss Elizabeth's desk to another area of the mission house. There, girls who had been trained to set type carefully assembled each page, letter by letter, within the frame of the plate. The plate was then taken down to Jonah, who secured it to the press for printing. Next, the newly printed page was taken to Miss Elizabeth to be proofread. When errors were found, the page had to be reset and reprinted, which then required another reading.

Books of the Bible which previously had been translated through the efforts of Benjamin Snow and Irving Channon were also painstakingly checked, set, and printed so they could be included in the current project.

The press room had no space for the finished pages, so these were stored in an array of racks lined up in the Baldwins' living room, leaving the sisters barely inches to move about. The entire process was tedious and slow. Miss Elizabeth knew that her eyesight was failing, but she was convinced that only she could do the work, so—in spite of her sister Jane's pleading and her own growing awareness that what she was doing was permanently damaging her eyes—she continued translating, polishing her work, and reading the proofs, with Alik Kefwas conscientiously working beside her.

JONAH AND HELMET MARRY

Early in 1925, Pastor Likiaksa Yal officiated at a festive Wot wedding when Jonah Metwarik married Helmet Kapinwere. This marriage delighted the Baldwins—some said that it was the result of their own careful planning. The 18-year-old bride was a student from Ailinglaplap Atoll in the Marshalls. The 25-year-old groom had become so essential to the Baldwin sisters that when he graduated some years earlier, they had asked him to remain as their personal assistant, as well as a printer.

The young couple moved into the typhoon house, a structure nestled against the Yonrak hill just below the Baldwin residence. Since Helmet already knew how to set type, she and Jonah soon became an indispensable team in the press room—sometimes with students assisting, sometimes not.[5] They also worked upstairs doing chores for the missionary sisters, who were very much like mothers to the newlyweds.

DEATH OF PASTOR LIKIAKSA YAL

Along with all Kosraeans, those in the mission community at Wot took time to mourn the loss of Pastor Likiaksa Yal, who died November 25, 1925. He was survived by his wife Tulpe "Handkerchief," and two stepsons, Freddy and Sru. For 22 years he had served as the respected leader of the Kosrae Congregational Church. After the much-loved old pastor was laid to his rest, the Misses Baldwin, Miss Hoppin, and members of the Church and community rallied in support around Pastor Fred Skilling, now Kosrae's only pastor.

KOSRAEAN BIBLE COMPLETED

The enormous task of producing a Kosraean-language Bible had been accomplished by the end of 1926. The Kosraeans had yet to receive their books, but Elizabeth Baldwin, now totally blind, was content. Against enormous odds, she and Alik Kefwas had completed their work. For the first time the people of Kosrae would be able to read for themselves all parts of God's Word in their own language.

The books were manufactured right there at the mission school. Under Jonah's supervision, the Wot boys continued the printing while Jonah and three helpers bound the pages. Doing the sewing by hand, each of the four young men was able to complete two or three of the large, thick volumes per day, if there were no interruptions. It was several years before supply met demand. The island's people, who for many years had been 100 percent literate in their own language, were immensely grateful for their new Bibles.

As was the practice of the Baldwin sisters for all materials that came off the press at Wot, the new Bibles were distributed at no cost. With Pastor Fred and the deacons assisting, the books were delivered to Church families as quickly as they were bound. At once, the Kosraean Bible became the most valued possession of each family.

The translating, printing, and binding of the Kosraean Bible—every aspect of the monumental project carried out at Wot—was an astonishing feat. This accomplishment remains an exhilarating testimony to the dedication of each individual who was involved in it, beginning with Elizabeth Baldwin and Alik Kefwas.

KOSRAEAN DICTIONARY

At the time that Miss Elizabeth was finishing the translation of the Kosraean Bible, Miss Jane was completing another project. During the translation process, Jane Baldwin and Alik Kefwas compiled two carefully arranged lists which contained all the words used in the translation, including the various forms of those words. In one list, the words were written alphabetically in Kosraean, with meanings in English; in the other, words were noted in English with definitions in Kosraean. Painstakingly, Miss Jane wrote these words and definitions in two leather-bound notebooks. The orthography she used was, of course, the orthography that Miss Elizabeth had used, and—with only minor adjustments—was the one originally settled upon by Benjamin Snow in the late 1850s and consistently used by him in his primers and in those parts of the Bible that he had translated into Kosraean. Though they were never printed and distributed in book form, the Baldwin dictionaries were a valuable asset to both sisters in their translating and teaching, as well as to the missionaries who followed them to Kosrae. They remain a physical link to the two women and a vivid example of their commitment.

JANE BALDWIN SUMMARIZES THEIR WORK

Years later, and in answer to questions posed to her by a grandniece who was then a student at Vassar College in New York, Miss Jane outlined the work she and Miss Elizabeth did at Wot:

We were in full charge of the Kusaie Training School, but the work was not alone to train and teach these native children, translating many of their lessons in the native tongue. We also cared for the sick in our school and all the natives on the island. There were colds, fevers, whooping cough, babies nearly choking to death, and bad burns. One boy had the Achilles cord cut by the boy behind him who was slashing his long knife recklessly through the tall grass. A man, while hunting wild pigs, fell on his spear, which went through the muscles of the upper leg leaving ugly sores. One year we gave out over a thousand doses of medicine. When dysentery was raging, a physician was sent to Kusaie, and we were indeed glad to resign this part of the work.

There was no arithmetic [text] in the Kusaien tongue, so my dear Lizzie translated one. This book was printed on a tiny hand press and bound. Then my dear Lizzie was requested to translate the Bible. She took as helper a man knowledgeable in the Kusaien language. School could not be closed, so she arose very early to begin the day with translating, then returned to it after school and worked until darkness settled. Although she applied herself strenuously to the task, it required twelve years to complete the Bible.

Then the matter of publishing had to be considered and later the binding. The Board sent us a little dummy book to enable the boys to study the hand sewing of books. It then required two years for four boys to sew all the books. Our students did all of the work, the girls distributed the type and set it up, while the boys printed. It was impossible to employ skilled labor, in fact, there was none on the island and in addition there was no money to pay their wages. All the work was a willing offering to the Lord.

In addition, an abridged edition of Pilgrim's Progress *was translated and printed in three languages. Yearly the C.E. topics with daily readings were translated and printed for the people. In the school work the effort was made to train these boys and girls to return to their islands or villages as preachers and teachers to their own people. We had the joy of hearing that one [Marshallese] boy, who married one of our school girls, preached fine sermons. Think not that we were satisfied with the work accomplished. Gladly would we have labored on, had eyesight and physical strengths been equal to the task. We can only commit the little accomplished to the Master and pray that He will bless and increase it to the salvation of many precious souls.*[6]

ANOTHER BUSY MISSIONARY

By 1927 more than 20 years had passed since the last *Morning Star* had plied the waters of Micronesia. The few remaining missionaries, however, benefitted from regular voyages of Japanese ships that linked the mandated islands to the motherland. The vessels were old but seaworthy; the officers and crews who operated them were courteous and efficient; accommodations were clean—and for the most part, the ships ran on schedule. Correspondence that took place between the missionaries and officials of the American Board was funneled through the dependable Japanese postal system.

Jessie Hoppin, in her 37th year in Micronesia—and still hardy in her early 60s—traveled comfortably and frequently between Jaluit and Kosrae. She had long been fluent in both the Marshallese and Kosraean languages. In the Marshall Islands, she represented the American Board as the principal and primary teacher at the Christian training school on the island of Jabwor in Jaluit Atoll. She was also the administrator and chief counselor for the 22 Congregational churches scattered across those coral atolls.

"Traveling comfortably" did not characterize her trips to visit those distant congregations. Miss Hoppin was often required to travel aboard one of the large, ocean-going outrigger canoes made by the Marshallese, relying on the navigational skills of those expert sailors. If the sea was calm, the going was easy—but she had many a harrowing trip when the vessel in which she was riding was tossed about like the proverbial cork, and she literally had to hang on for dear life! Her remote congregants, some of whom were former Wot students, were always grateful to receive her. They shared their food and at night would spread a mat for her on the coral gravel floor of their open-air church pavilion, often singing to her as she fell asleep.

To assist Miss Hoppin and those far-flung congregations, the American Board assigned an American couple to the Marshall Islands Mission in 1927. These two—the Rev. George and Mrs. Eleanor Lockwood, ages 32 and 29—did much to ease the load on Jessie Hoppin, especially at the Jaluit school. But it was still Miss

Hoppin who, with the help of Carl Heine and the Marshallese pastors—many of whom, along with their wives, had also been her students at Kosrae—selected the young people who would be sent to the Wot school.

When she was on Kosrae, Jessie Hoppin made her headquarters at Pisin. She was a popular and appreciated Bible teacher. She also maintained close ties to those Kosraean women who had been with her at the Girls' Training School at Wot 20 and 30 years earlier. When she was in residence at Pisin, these women were constantly coming and going. And it was not only the women who came—Lelu's children visited Miss Hoppin individually and in groups. The children enjoyed being with her, and she thoroughly enjoyed them. They were welcome in her home not only to hear Bible stories but to share homemade cookies.

Miss Hoppin was especially busy with the Lelu children at Christmas time, when she taught them songs and skits appropriate not only to the season but to their age level. The children loved Christmas as Miss Hoppin explained it to them, and their parents delighted in watching their children perform in the church on Christmas Day.

Adults, too, came to Miss Hoppin when preparing for Christmas, eager for their own new songs. It had become a popular custom for groups representing the four village churches to gather in Lelu on Christmas Day to perform for one another and most other Kosraeans as well—unless Christmas fell on a Sunday, in which case the celebration would take place on Monday. Leaders of the church considered the Christmas festivities too raucous to be presented in church on the Lord's Day. It was also unthinkable that any portion of the Sunday schedule of services be adjusted to accommodate activity not regularly a part of that day's prescribed agenda.

In addition to handling the steady stream of visitors at Pisin and managing the activities she initiated and led, Jessie Hoppin was a close friend and advisor to the king, John Paliknoa Sigrah, and to Pastor Fred Skilling. Also, she functioned as liaison between the Baldwin sisters and the Japanese administration and between the sisters and Capt. Victor Melander's nephew, Arthur Herman, who had come from Oakland, California, to help his aging uncle.

The relationship between the Baldwin sisters and Jessie Hoppin was support-ive, but the three women found it difficult to work in close proximity with one another. Miss Hoppin, long the principal teacher at the girls' training school, had been disconcerted when the sisters first arrived in 1911. The Presbyterian tradi-tion that had nurtured Miss Elizabeth and Miss Jane was much more conservative than the Congregational tradition that had nurtured Miss Hoppin. Sixteen years after the Baldwin sisters arrived at the school at Wot, they maintained a daily schedule that had varied little over their long tenure. The personalities of the calm, opinionated women from New Jersey clashed with the more spontaneous traits of the little woman from Wisconsin. But the Church in Micronesia, and particularly at Kosrae, benefitted from the complementary ways of service that these three devout Christian women developed during their years in the islands and so conscientiously performed.

OTHER MISSIONARIES

Christians in the Marshall Islands, as well as those on Kosrae, considered the three American women at Kosrae to be their missionaries. Many of them had been trained at Wot by the Baldwins, and the leadership of the Marshallese Church looked to Miss Hoppin as their "mother," guide, and primary advisor.

As time went by and the dynamics of the Micronesia Mission shifted, there was not much exchange between the Chuuk and Pohnpei churches and those at Kosrae. Before they were transferred to Kosrae, the Baldwin sisters had worked almost 12 years at Chuuk. The passing years and the distance gradually diminished their influence there, but the Christian Church was growing at both Pohnpei and Chuuk, just as it was at Kosrae and in the Marshall Islands. In 1927 the Japanese administration permitted missionaries of the Liebenzell Mission of Germany to return to Chuuk. There were no German missionaries assigned at Pohnpei, but the energetic missionaries of Japan's Nan'yo Dendo Dan were working there, as well as at Chuuk.

THE CHURCH OF KOSRAE AT 75

August 1927 marked the 75th anniversary of the arrival at Kosrae of the first missionaries with the Good News of Christianity. Sweeping changes had taken place within the Kosraean community during the intervening years. Vast improvements reflected the accuracy of King Kamehameha III's letter to Good King George. The force of barbaric cruelty had been replaced by the strength of Christian gentleness. People had been freed from an overwhelming fear of evil spirits that were once felt to infest everything around them. The bonds of ancient taboos which, prior to the arrival of the gospel, had greatly handicapped their freedom of movement and thought, had disappeared.

With their liberation from hampering superstitions, Kosraeans were realizing an improvement in health—and with the casting off of certain hobbling and demeaning requirements of a repressive class system, individuals experienced a new-found mental well-being. Education, even at the elementary level of the day, was generating confidence and self-respect that had been absent before. Love, rather than fear or hate, characterized their feelings toward neighbors. Their respect and love for God, as well as their consistent, unencumbered worship, gave them an appreciation of Christian values that bound the community together and influenced the entirety of their lives.

The people of Kosrae had developed a conscience which took for granted that each person's needs were the needs of the group. Problems common to the widow and the orphan in more "civilized" countries of the world were unknown on Kosrae. A vital, workable Christianity was firmly rooted in the belief that they were to be Christ-like. In a remarkable way, the Church on Kosrae had preserved the spirit of first-century Christians.

But within the structure of the Church, problems had arisen. Because of the rigid set of rules controlling Church membership and the usual struggle and contention between generations, an inherent mistrust of youth persisted among the leaders of the Kosraean Church. The idea was prevalent that young people had no other course but to "sow their wild oats" before they were acceptable to the Church. Even when they were finally received as Church members, young people were looked upon with misgiving.

Under penalty of extreme criticism, the pattern of worship was expected to follow an exact form for every sort of service on any occasion. Leadership was concentrated in the hands of a few, and it was their word that was followed. No one was allowed the freedom of Christian activity without first being instructed by the proper authority to take action. For instance, a Church group going to sing for someone who was sick without being specifically sent, or a person cleaning the church yard without being assigned to do so, would be criticized by the leadership. There was much discussion in the lengthy meetings of the leaders of the Church concerning mistakes of individual church members. Those castigated were asked to "rest" for at least a year, during which time no responsibility was delegated to them.

There was also the matter of a Victorian morality and code of conduct in dress, which had been intensified by the well-known position of the Baldwin sisters. Women's dresses in particular had to be "sewed to requirement"—not only for Sunday worship, but for everyday wear as well. The men were expected to wear shirts while working in the mud of their gardens, fishing on the reef, or thatching their houses. Long-sleeved shirts were obligatory for worship.

Along with the firm denunciation of dancing, smoking, and drinking, strict rules for outward appearances tended to produce a false morality among church members who were lax in their consideration of what might be called a "higher righteousness." There was little discussion critical of hurtful gossip or false pride, and no discussion that condemned the abuse of wives by their husbands—though all three, unfortunately, were very common among Kosraeans.

SUNDAY SCHEDULE DOES NOT VARY

The form of worship was tightly set, with the Baldwin sisters concurring with a format that—to a considerable extent—had been instituted by Benjamin Snow. Congregational worship took place at 10 o'clock every Sunday morning in each of the four villages and at Wot. Church bells were rung at 9:30 for the benefit of communities with few clocks and no wristwatches, and then a second ringing took place at 9:55. In actuality the exact moment when a bell rope should be pulled was only the best guess of the bell ringer.

As the months and years went by, a few simple benches were built and placed on the right side toward the back of the church to accommodate older male worshipers. Along the right wall at the front of the church was a bench reserved for the king, the pastor, the deacon, and any foreign male dignitary who might be present. In fact, from the very first Sunday in which Mr. Snow led services on Kosrae, the king and high-ranking chiefs were elevated on benches or chairs to the right of the pulpit or worship table. The queen, pastors' wives, female missionaries, and other foreign ladies were seated along the wall at the left front—either on benches or on mats on the floor. All other worshipers sat on the floor.

Sunday School followed the morning service, with most of the congregation remaining in place. There were Sunday School classes for the children, who left with their teachers to go to their own gathering places in buildings and pavilions around the church. Adult Sunday School was a bit less formal than the service which preceded it, but with a given order from which leaders did not deviate. The memorizing of "Golden Text" Scripture verses, begun years before as a teaching aid for children, was a technique now used in the adult setting, as was the asking and answering of Bible- and lesson-related questions.

When Sunday School was over, members of the congregations walked to their homes, or to the Lelu church guest houses if they were from other villages. A simple, cold lunch, which had been prepared the day before, was eaten, sometimes communally and at other times individually. At Wot on Sundays, the Baldwins refused to eat or drink anything that had been heated. These and other Sunday "rules" kept by the missionary sisters were adhered to by many Kosraeans as well.

The two o'clock bell called people back to the churches for "Meeting"—the name had been abbreviated from "prayer meeting," the term Mr. Snow had used. At Meeting, the text of the morning service was discussed, with members of the congregation asking questions. Mostly, however, this service had evolved into a time of sharing verses of Scripture and selecting hymns to be sung, all related to the morning's theme. Then it was time for Christian Endeavor.

Sunday evenings were frequently used for visitations by Church leaders to the ill or those who were otherwise unable to leave their homes.

KOSRAE'S EVANGELISTS

By 1927 Christian Endeavor had become highly organized, with the membership in each of the village church societies divided into committees. These committees were very active, accepting with utmost seriousness the responsibilities assigned to them. The five primary standing committees were Worship, Outreach, Arrangements, Finance, and Service. Though each of these groups were vital to the smooth functioning of Christian Endeavor, it was the Outreach Committee whose obligation it was to bring in new members—or to "win new converts."

In Kosraean, the name used for "outreach" literally means to "go," or to "travel"—and this is exactly what they did, four times a year. The Lelu Outreach Committee traveled to Malem, for instance, and the Malem committee traveled to Lelu, while the Utwe group went to Tafunsak and the Tafunsak group to Utwe. Names of those contemplating membership and of backsliders—individuals who had never committed themselves to Christ—were given to the visitors by the local committee. Members of the visiting committee then divided themselves into groups of two or three to go to the homes of those on the local list to counsel, pray, and invite them to the Sunday afternoon Christian Endeavor service, urging them to become part of the society.

This proved to be an excellent method for bringing in new members. That the visitors were from another village and probably unrelated to the ones they visited, plus the effort they expended in traveling a distance to share their witness and concern, combined to produce an attractive and effective means of outreach. The people who were recipients of these types of visits almost always responded in the affirmative, making their way to participate in that Sunday's Christian Endeavor service in their village church—most of them publically committing themselves to Christ and becoming an active part of the group.

Seventy-five years later, this is still the way it is done.

KOSRAE'S FIRST HOSPITAL

One project of the Japanese administration for which the Kosraeans were sincerely grateful was the branch of the Pohnpei hospital that was opened in Lelu in 1927. Almost three decades earlier, Kosraeans had experienced the benefits of foreign medicines and medical practices when Dr. Edmund Pease and Dr. Clinton Rife had worked among them, and some of their grandparents had described the assistance of Dr. George Pierson during the 1850s. Also, the Baldwin sisters had reached out to help in emergencies. But medical assistance had always been sporadic and limited.

Now, for the first time, medical help became available on a daily basis to everyone. Kosrae's hospital, staffed by a fully trained physician, a nurse, and a pharmacist, was much used by the islanders.[7]

LIFE AND DEATH OF CAPT. MELANDER

On January 12, 1928, the Baldwin sisters, Miss Hoppin, and the people of Kosrae lost a long-time friend and champion when death came to Victor Melander just five days before his 83rd birthday. Of Swedish descent, he has emigrated with his family to the United States and settled in Oakland, California. As a boy, Victor had been enthralled listening to tales spun by sailors who converged on the docks of the towns and cities developing along the shores of San Francisco Bay. The possibilities for adventure and fortune-hunting among the islands of the Pacific intrigued Victor, and, while still a teenager, he signed on aboard a ship sailing for the South Seas.

But young Mr. Melander was too ambitious to remain for long as a mere sailor under the command of another. He visited several locations looking for a place to establish a trading company. In the mid-1880s he found Kosrae, where King Sru V gave the industrious Swedish-Californian permission to set up his business. As his dreamed-for enterprise flourished, the island became home for him. In 1890—the year Jesse Hoppin arrived to teach at Wot—Victor married Neneus, a woman of Kosrae. The couple had no children of their own, but Victor later adopted Neneus' son, John.

Using hired Kosraean laborers, Victor Melander developed a profitable copra business on land purchased from King Sa II in the Pukusrik and Tofol areas of the main island. With his trading business prospering, he purchased a ship—christening it the *Tulenkun* [a common Kosraean name]—to carry merchandise between Kosrae, Pohnpei, the Mortlocks, and Chuuk. He was a help to missionaries in each of these locations, as well as to government officials, who found him efficient and reliable in carrying mail, personnel, and freight. Though he used some Kosraean sailors, most of those who worked on the *Tulenkun* were Chuukese. Several of them eventually married Kosraean women. One of his primary assistants, however, was Lakimis, a man from the Marshall Islands whose son, Nelson, later married Florence Esau Tilfas.

As his business grew, Capt. Melander, as he came to be known, built a small schooner which he named the *Palangu*. In the Kosraean language, "palangu!" is an exclamation similar to the English "For goodness sake!" Tradition has it that as Capt. Melander constructed the vessel, those who watched the process uttered "Palangu!" over and over again. "So THAT'S how it's done!" Thus the captain had a name for his new little ship.[8] He used the *Palangu* to transport passengers and freight around Kosrae between the harbors of Utwe, Lelu, Okat, Yela, and Wot. Trips of the *Palangu* between Lelu and Wot were especially beneficial to that mission community on "the other side" of the island.

After Neneus died, Victor married Srue Intakuntin, who was also known as Srue Kir. He and Srue had no children of their own, but in 1918 they adopted the son of a Leap woman who had died after giving him birth. They did this with the consent of the child's natural father, Philip. Already in his 70s, Victor was very pleased with the tiny boy and named him Hilton. Both Victor and Srue lavished their love on the boy.

In the early 1920s, Capt. Melander recruited his sister's son, Arthur Herman, to travel from the family home in Oakland to assist him in his trading and copra businesses. Young Arthur savored Kosrae and, as his uncle had done, took a Kosraean wife. Also like his uncle, Arthur was energetic and capable. In fact, the two men were so similar that they soon began to get on each other's nerves. Shortly before Victor died, the uncle and his nephew parted company in anger, though they both remained on Kosrae.

Capt. Victor Melander was buried in a well-marked grave on a Pukusrik hillside where he had built a house with a commanding view of Lelu Harbor. Arthur Herman inherited his uncle's trading business, but was dismayed to learn that the old man, in his last weeks of life, had deeded his land to his wife Srue Kir and their son Hilton. What could be done to get possession of that valuable and productive Pukusrik and Tofol land? To everyone's dismay, Arthur returned his young wife to her father and took Srue as his wife! This was an enormous insult to an innocent young woman, an act so blatantly selfish that it engulfed not only her and her family in shame, sadness, and puzzlement, but the entire Kosraean community as well. There was a loud protest from the Church which in no way could sanction such behavior, so Arthur and Srue were married by the Japanese police sergeant, who had quickly provided Arthur his divorce.[9]

LOCKWOODS ASKED TO HELP AT KOSRAE

The strict but pleasant routine that the Baldwin sisters had created for themselves at Wot was about to be interrupted. They were advancing in years—Miss Elizabeth was 69 and Miss Jane, 65. Elizabeth's blindness meant that Jane ran the errands and did most of the supervising at the school. Though they were not complainers, the sisters needed help. Jonah and Helmet were of great assistance to them around their home, but the two women were in need of significant relief in operating the school. All aspects of administration and teaching were still in their hands and the pressures were taking their toll. The health of both women was failing.

In 1928, after the Baldwins had made enumerable requests for additional missionary personnel at their school, the American Board asked George and Eleanor Lockwood to divide their time between their responsibilities in the Marshall Islands and the needs on Kosrae. Willing and congenial, the Lockwoods did their best to fit into the Wot routine during their extended stays on that campus. They found their newly acquired knowledge of Marshallese a major help as they worked with the Marshallese students and staff at Wot.

George Lockwood taught and took over management of the plantation gardens and livestock, supervising the boys and arranging their work assignments. He had studied tropical agriculture and was anxious to share new patterns and methods of planting and cultivation with his students. The boys, in turn, were curious and eager to learn. Their months with George Lockwood at Wot were profitable ones.

Eleanor Lockwood also taught and helped with the oversight of female students, while caring for their young daughters, Althea, 3, and Winifred, not yet a year old. Eleanor was particularly appreciated as a music teacher.[10] Though it was sometimes difficult for the young couple to please the Baldwins, the elderly sisters were grateful for Eleanor's help in choosing and preparing hymns for an enlarged edition of the Kosraean hymnal they were working to complete. [This Baldwin edition, built on the hymnal compiled by Mr. Snow in 1865 and received by the Kosraeans in 1867, is still in use.]

By 1929 Miss Elizabeth and Miss Jane were not as actively involved around the campus as in earlier years, but their house remained "command central" for the Wot school.

A SUGGESTION CONCERNING CHRISTIAN ENDEAVOR

During 1929, Mr. Lockwood made a concerted effort to reach out to the leadership of the Kosraean Church. He was courteously received and always welcome in their midst. His humble demeanor was attractive to them, but his ideas and suggestions were sometimes viewed with suspicion when they seemed to depart from those of the Baldwins. Sometimes his ideas had never even been contemplated by the sisters, much less negated, but this was enough to cause skepticism. The Baldwin sisters exerted an immense influence over Kosraean Christians through their former students, who were moving into positions of authority in all of the island's churches. Their uncompromising rigidity seemed to resonate with Kosrae's traditionally authoritarian culture. In Church matters, pronouncements by Elizabeth and Jane Baldwin were the law.

George Lockwood's criticism of the form Christian Endeavor had taken was one matter that caused misunderstanding between him and the leaders of the Church. Christian Endeavor was now almost 26 years old on Kosrae. It had been initiated at Wot in 1901 by Dr. Clinton Rife for the expressed purpose of training young people in Church polity and leadership, and as an evangelistic tool for welcoming unchurched youth. Alik Kefwas had been first president of the Wot Christian Endeavor. Two years later leaders of the Church—recognizing the positive effect C.E. was having on the young people at Wot—approved the inauguration of an island-wide Christian Endeavor Society, with young Fred Skilling elected president. Now, in 1929, Deacon Alik Kefwas was an elderly man and Pastor Fred Skilling was 55. The other youth, who had been charter members when the organizations were new, were also middle-aged and older adults. Christian Endeavor had proven so immensely popular with the Kosraeans that when members reached adulthood, no one ever "graduated" out of C.E., as had been originally intended by the Rev. Mr. Francis E. Clarke when he founded the society for Congregational Church youth in 1881.

It was obvious that the active Junior Christian Endeavor Society was serving an important purpose for Kosraean children. The singing of those Sunday afternoon groups practically lifted the thatch right off the outbuildings where the children regularly gathered. Teenagers and young adults, however, were expected to fit unobtrusively into the adult Christian Endeavor. It was almost as though those in the 15- to 30-year-old category simply did not exist.

But when Mr. Lockwood suggested that it might be a good idea for adult members of Christian Endeavor to step aside and allow the current group of Kosraean young people to have their turn, the recommendation could hardly be comprehended, much less accepted. Though many of the island young people attended the Sunday afternoon Christian Endeavor service and were even welcomed as members, all aspects of leadership remained in the hands of older persons. New officers were elected annually, as had been the practice from the beginning, but those elected were mature adults.

The suggestion of the well-intentioned missionary was dismissed and Kosrae's Christian Endeavor Society remained predominately an adult organization for another 35 years.

HAJIME HIRATA

The Reverend and Mrs. Hajime Hirata, a dedicated Japanese Christian missionary couple assigned by the Nan'yo Dendo Dan, arrived in the Marshall Islands in 1930. Mr. Hirata and his wife, Fumie, quickly became much appreciated additions to the mission staff at Jaluit. Mr. Hirata taught with Carl Heine in the mission school and helped with the oversight of the Marshalls' far-flung churches. He was especially useful during those months that George Lockwood was away on Kosrae—and his presence also meant that Claude Heine, Carl's eldest son, was freed to work full-time with Miss Hoppin as she concentrated on translating more of the Bible into the Marshallese language.

With Elizabeth and Jane Baldwin still active at Wot, assisted by George and Eleanor Lockwood, and with Jessie Hoppin spending half of her time in Lelu, traveling easily between the Marshall Islands and Kosrae, the Nan'yo Dendo Dan was under no pressure to appoint missionary personnel to Kosrae.

A WEDDING FOR THE PASTOR

It was during this time that Pastor Fred Skilling, a widower, married his second wife, with Pastor George Lockwood presiding over the festive occasion in the Lelu church.

Fred, the son of the American Harry Skillings and his Nauruan wife, Sitoma, had married while still a teenager. His wife, Sepe Intara, was the daughter of Sampa, the oldest son of Notwe Kras, who was one of Kosrae's very first Christians. Fred and Sepe became the parents of five sons: Frank, Henry, Joseph, Simeon, and Norman; and six daughters: Ellen [Alokoa Tol], Lilly [Robert Aliksa], Lucy [Elijah Tosie], Mary [Paliksru Kun Miswan], Hannah [Alik Isaac Andrew], and Nellie [Clinton Benjamin]. Not long after the birth of their youngest child, Norman, Sepe died.

It was natural and expected when Pastor Fred, still in midlife, chose another wife. His choice brought together two of Kosrae's primary families. Sepe Awe Siminlik was the daughter of Tulensa Sigrah, King Sru IV, and his wife, Queen Tulpe Srue, known by the nickname "Fititi." With her brother, Paliknoa—the current King John Sigrah—"Princess" Sepe, with her two younger sisters, had enjoyed a pampered childhood, surrounded by servants. She, too, had married young. Her first husband was Kilafwa "Jacob" Lonno, by whom she had a son, Soarku, and two daughters, Sepe Intaluo and Rebecca, who died as a young woman while in Rabaul.

Sepe Awe Siminlik's husband Jacob also died young, whereupon the still-youthful widow took as her second husband Kun Miswan, whose father was from Rotoma [a lone island north of the Fiji group]. Sepe and Kun became the parents of four sons, all of whom took the name "Sigrah"—the chiefly title inherited from their mother and conferred upon their father—as their second name: Nana Sigrah, Nena Sigrah, Shiro Sigrah and Aaron Sigrah; and two daughters: Sra "Ule" [Kilafwa Palik George] and Ruth [Simeon Fred Skilling].

With his marriage to Sepe Awe Siminlik, Pastor Fred became the brother-in-law of the king, who was just one year his junior. They were friends who had studied together at Wot and then worked together for many years as the preeminent leaders of the Kosraean community. The children and stepchildren of the two men were now teenagers and young adults, a number of them already married and starting families of their own, and most of them having also studied at Wot.

SMALL BUT CONSPICUOUS JAPANESE PRESENCE

Though much smaller than Japanese communities in the Marshalls and on Pohnpei, Chuuk, Yap, and Palau, the Japanese presence on Kosrae was now solidly ensconced. In his book *Nan'yo, The Rise and Fall of the Japanese in Micronesia, 1885-1945*, Mark R. Peattie describes "the only significant colonial settlement at Kusaie" as "not more than a hundred Japanese, mostly Okinawan fishermen and a handfull of traders" who had built "a tiny community of houses and stores, which added to the existing church, hospital, police station, and the NBK [the Japanese South Seas government—Nan'yo-cho] branch office."[11]

ALIK KEFWAS HELPS WITH MARSHALLESE BIBLE

Jessie Hoppin and Claude Heine spent long hours in her Jabwor, Jaluit, home, working on the translation of the Bible into the Marshallese language. Often Alik Kefwas, fluent in Marshallese, would join them in this endeavor. Scheduled Japanese freighters and passenger ships continued to make travel between Kosrae and the Marshalls relatively easy.

When Alik Kefwas first began visiting Jaluit, Marshallese children would run and hide when they saw him. The story had circulated among the children that he would eat them! Alik knew that they were frightened by his unusually dark skin. Gently, he would say to them in Marshallese: "I don't eat people. I love God and I love you. Come! Share this food with me." It was not long before the children of Jabwor were all his friends.[12]

A BOND WITH THE MARSHALLESE

A strong connection between Kosrae and the Marshall Islands had gradually developed through the years, as several generations of Marshallese leaders studied at the mission schools at Wot. Some of these students stayed on to teach following graduation, and a few married Kosraean schoolmates. There were also a number of Kosraean women living in the Marshall Islands as wives of Marshallese pastors and teachers. In addition, Jessie Hoppin—working as she did with Christians of both language groups—did much to make the relationship between Marshallese and Kosraeans a dynamic and beneficial one.

Most of the atolls that make up the Marshalls group lie east and northeast of Kosrae, within easy sailing distance of that island and each other. Enewetak, on the other hand, is isolated from the rest of the Marshall Islands in the distant northwest, 259 miles due north of Kosrae. It was difficult to find anyone willing to live and teach on that distant outpost, so the missionaries and students at Wot took on Enewetak as a special project. They commissioned John Mackwelung to go to Enewetak as teacher and evangelist. He had learned the language while studying with Marshallese students at Wot, where he had remained after graduation to teach. He took with him to Enewetak his second wife, Sepe Insopus, and some of their children. Some time after his arrival he was ordained as pastor by the grateful leaders of the Marshallese Church, who were pleased to have him working with the people of that remote location. ✛

Notes - Chapter 11

1. James L. Lewis, "Kusaiean Acculturation 1824-1948," pp. 43-44
2. Ibid, p. 44
3. Ibid
4. Mark R. Peattie, *Nan'yo, The Rise and Fall of the Japanese in Micronesia, 1885-1945*, pp. 97-98
5. Donald Jonah, personal conversation, Kosrae, Aug. 29, 2001
6. Jane D. Baldwin, personal correspondence to Carol Tompkins, Orange, New Jersey, April 29, 1941, courtesy of Irving L. Selvage
7. Peattie, p. 87
8. E. J. Kahn, Jr., *A Reporter in Micronesia*, p. 164
9. Salik Cornelius, personal conversation, Kosrae, Aug. 1, 2001
10. Mary Lanwi, personal conversations, July 26, 2001
11. Peattie, p. 184
12. M. Lanwi, personal conversation, May 16, 2002

NUNAK YOHK KE CHAPTER 12
1930-1941

Pastu Fred Skilling pa sifen Church Kosrae in pacl se inge, ac Tokosra Paliknoa pa sifen government. Tusruktu kutu pacl uh Pastu Fred pa ac akiwala mwet ma akukuin ke acn ac oayapa pacl oasr lokwalok saya sikyak. Na ke sripen Tokosra Paliknoa el deacon, mwet uh elos akfulatyal ac soano kas lal ke pacl oasr fohsak ke mukuikui lun Church. Inkaiyen pacl uh mwet kol luo inge insese ac akasrui ke ma kunaltal. A kutu mwet Kosrae orekma lun government elos tiana insewowo ke ouiyen kolyuk lal Tokosra Paliknoa— elos pangon upala sap lal.

Oasr kupasr na ku se inmasrlon mwet Kosrae ac mwet Marshall ke sripen pus mwet Marshall tuh wi lutlut Wot. Mutan Kosrae ma payukyak nu sin mukul Marshall elos wi mukul tumalos orekma fin acn Marshall, ac mutan Marshall ma payuk nu sin mukul Kosrae, elos mwet Kosraela. Claude Heine, mukul Marshall se ma kasrel Miss Hoppin ke leng Bible in kas Marshall, el use sou lal ah nu Kosrae tuh elan fototo nu yurol Miss Hoppin. John Mackwelung el tuh sie mwet luti Kosrae fin acn Wot, na el us sou lal som nu Enewetak in kasru Church we. Mwet Marshall elos arulana engan ke orekma lal yorolos, oru elos akmusraella tuh elan sie pastu. Tok, Frank Skilling ac mutan kial, Srue, eltal som pac in kasru Church Enewetak.

Ke John Mackwelung ac sou lal ah folok nu Kosrae, mwet kol lun Church Kosrae elos akukuin inmasrlolos sifacna lah John el ac pastu pac lalos ku tia. Tukun kutu malem, elos wotela in sifilpa akmusraella John Mackwelung nu ke pastu lun Church Kosrae, in kasrel Pastu Fred Skilling.

Oasr mwet America luo su rauni acn Micronesia in tuni moul lun mwet we, na tok kais sie seltal simusla book ke ma eltal tuh liye. In 1934 Paul Clyde el sim ac fahk lah Miss Baldwin luo eltal toanya mwet Kosrae, pwanang mwet uh tia ku in eis kutena mwe lutlut sasu sayen ma missionary luo ah lotelos. El mu mwet kol lun Church Kosrae elos oru oapana. In 1935 Willard Price el srumun lah arulana wo orekma lun missionary oayapa church fin acn Kosrae. El fahk lah Miss Elizabeth ac Miss Jane eltal arulana insianaung, ac ke sripen elah Christian lun mwet Kosrae, acn we arulana misla ac wangin mwe lokoalok yohk sikyak we. Kalem lah mwet sim luo inge tia nunak se ke ma eltal tuh liye.

Miss Elizabeth ac Miss Jane Baldwin eltal matuoh na eltal mongla liki orekma laltal fin acn Wot ke 1936. Eltal tia lungse folok nu America, na pa eltal som muta Kalung, Lelu, ac Tokosra Paliknoa el musai kitin lohm seltal we. Jonah ac Helmet eltal muta ke lohm se oan sisken lohm seltal, eltal in mu ku in tafwela kasru laltal nu sin nina matu luo inge. Inkaiyen mwet kol lun Church in pacl sac elos tuh wi lutlut Wot, oru fususna pacl elos fasr mutwata yorol Miss Elizabeth ac Miss Jane.

Mwet kol lun American Board elos supwama missionary sasu tolu in mwet luti ke school Wot ke June 1936. Ineltal pa Clarence ac Cora McCall, ac Eleanor Wilson. Yokna kapkapak lun school ke sripen orekma wo lalos, tusruktu oasr pacl Mr. McCall ac Miss Wilson arulana akukuin ke ma eltal nunku mu fal in orek. Mr. McCall el arulana etu orekma ke ima ac ke karinginyen pig, cow, ac won. Tulik mukul Wot elos pwar in welul orekma. In pacl se inge mukul Marshall luo, Pastu Alexander ac Pastu Caleb, eltal mwet luti pac ke lutlut Wot. Sie mutan Christian Japan, Miss Yamada, el tuku wi mwet luti fin acn Wot ke 1937.

Miss Hoppin el tuh arulana nunku ke acn Yenyen, mweyen el sensen lah mwet Japan ac eisla ac orekmakin nu ke lungse lalos sifacna, ke sripen acn Pisin ac Yenyen ma lun American Board. Daniel Opunui ac kutu sin tulik Marshall ac Gilbert ma lutlut Wot elos pukpuki fin acn Yenyen. Ke ma inge Miss Hoppin el nunku mu wo in orekla sie acn mwesas ac kato we, tuh in mwe esmakin mwet somla meet. El nunku mu sahp Miss Elizabeth ac Miss Jane ac pukpuki pac we. El sim pac fahk lah ac wo in musaeyuk sie lohm fin acn Yenyen tuh in nien mongla lun mwet mutwata nu Kosrae.

Ke 1938 Miss Eleanor Wilson el srukak nunak lal ke pacl in muta lun mwet kol ke Church lah fal in oasr deaconess in wi deacon orekma. Miss Elizabeth, Miss Jane ac Miss Hoppin eltal wi akkeye nunak se inge. Church Committee elos sramsram kac paht na, ke sripen kutu selos tia lungse. Tusruktu tok, pastu ac mwet kol lun church elos insesela in srisrngiyuki kutu mutan kulansap oaru ac wo elah in deaconess. Tia kalem lah mutan ekasr ku su inelos.

In 1939 Miss Hoppin el som nu United States in tuh mongla ke malem ekasr. Ke el akola in foloko, government lun acn Japan tia lela elan foloko, na Miss Hoppin el arulana supwarla kac. In yac sac pacna, sie pac mutan Japan el tuku in wi mwet luti fin acn Wot. Inel pa Miss Ren Suzuki. Ke October 31, 1939, Miss Elizabeth Baldwin el misa fin acn Lelu. El pukpuki Pukusrik, sisken na kulyuk lal Captain Victor Melander. Tulik Marshall luo ma aksafye lutlut Wot, eltal payukyak ac wi mwet luti ke school we. Ineltal pa Isaac Lanwi ac Mary natul Claude Heine.

Miss Jane Baldwin el tuh sifacna akilen lah sie pac mweun lulap inmasrlon mutunfaclu ac sikyak. Ouinge el sulela elan folokla nu America. Meet liki el som el pwapa yorol William Mongkeya in moli sie ipin acn Inkoeya tuh Jonah ac sou lal in muta we. Miss Jane el orekmakin mani lal sifacna oayapa mani ma mwet Christian Kosrae tuh wi pac sang.

Miss Jane el yac 75 ke el som liki acn Kosrae ke February 17, 1941. Miss Wilson el welul in liyalang ac kasrel. Eltal oayak nu Japan, na toko nu United States. Eltal som nu New Jersey nu yurin sou lal Miss Jane. Miss Jane Baldwin el muta we yac oalkosr, ac el misa we ke July 5, 1949.

CHAPTER TWELVE

UNDER JAPANESE CONTROL
1930-1941

PASTOR FRED AND KING JOHN SHARE LEADERSHIP

Nine years after his ordination, Pastor Fred Skilling was firmly established at the helm of the Church on Kosrae. His relationship with his brother-in-law, King John Paliknoa Sigrah, was mostly cordial. They complemented one another in their roles as leader of the Kosraean Church and indigenous leader of the island government under the Japanese administration. Sometimes, however, their roles crossed. It was not uncommon for Pastor Fred to be called upon to mediate land problems or other conflicts in the community. In fact, it had long been the tradition for the pastor to act as liaison or even judge when confrontations arose between neighborhood groups or individual citizens. On the other hand, as the island's leading layman, King John had a prominent part in making church decisions. The two men were close and enjoyed an amiable association. This could not be said, however, for the relationship of King John and some of the younger men who were chosen to serve with him in Kosrae's government. Though they were courteous and respectful when with him, as custom required, these men often complained in private that the King was demanding and unreasonable in what he required of his workers. All of them—King, chiefs, and commoners—continued to be disheartened and frequently angry at the way they were treated by Japanese authorities. Unwilling to risk the wrath of these overlords by voicing their discontent, they lashed out in frustration among themselves.

GREAT DEPRESSION AFFECTS MISSION

By 1931 the United States, as well as the rest of the industrialized world, was struggling in the Great Depression. As had happened during World War I, most of the sources of money used to support the mission endeavors of American churches evaporated.

In 1932 George and Eleanor Lockwood were recalled from the islands when the American Board could no longer afford to keep them there. The Baldwin sisters remained, continuing to be responsible for their own support.

The work of the Micronesia Mission was further diminished in 1933 when, for lack of funds, the Nan'yo Dendo Dan was forced to recall the popular and accommodating Pastor Hajime Hirata and his wife to Japan.

More than ever, Pastor Carl Heine was the mainstay of the Church in the Marshall Islands—especially during the second half of 1932 and the first half of 1933, when Jessie Hoppin was away on her final furlough as an active missionary. As she had always done on her furloughs, Miss Hoppin traveled widely among churches in the United States, describing the devotion of island Christians and generating concern for the work in the Marshalls and at Kosrae—though this time it was primarily prayer that was offered. There was little money. Miss Hoppin did enjoy a visit with her daughter, Rose, now a young woman of 22 and close to completing her studies in California. When Miss Hoppin returned to Kosrae in October 1933, she did so as a retired missionary. She was 68 years old, but felt that there was still a great deal that she could do, both at Kosrae and at Jaluit. She was especially determined to complete more of her Marshallese Bible translation project.

CLAUDE HEINE MOVES FAMILY TO KOSRAE

Though various missionaries, including Benjamin Snow, had worked at translating the Bible into Marshallese, the Christians of those islands were still without many of the Bible's books. Claude Heine was Miss Hoppin's chief translation assistant, and his home was conveniently close to the mission house at Jabwor, Jaluit, where he was available when Miss Hoppin was there. But since her return from furlough she was spending most of her time on Kosrae, and Alik Kefwas—busy with his own Bible teaching efforts among the Kosraeans—was not always free to assist her.

At Miss Hoppin's request, Claude Heine moved his family to Kosrae, where they took up residence in a two-story house on Pisin next door to the house occupied by Jessie Hoppin. With Claude and his wife, Grace, were their five children: Dwight, Katherine, Mary, Elizabeth, and John. Almost immediately, Mrs. Heine noticed that her daughters' dresses did not quite meet the standards of modesty evident in the Sunday wear preferred by Kosraean women and girls. The family missed church their first Sunday on Kosrae because Grace Heine had not finished lengthening the sleeves of her daughters' dresses. The young Marshallese family, however, was warmly welcomed by the Kosraeans—and it was not long before the older Heine children were enrolled as students at Wot.[1]

VISIT OF PROFESSOR CLYDE

The year 1934 brought a rare visitor to Kosrae: The American Paul H. Clyde, who had been invited by the Japanese government to make an extended voyage through the mandate. Japan had withdrawn from the League of Nations in 1933, and the U.S. government was growing more and more uneasy about rumors of a military buildup in the islands, something specifically forbidden by the terms of the mandate. Permission for Paul Clyde to tour the Japanese-controlled area was granted in part to appease the Americans.

A professor at the University of Kentucky, Dr. Clyde kept a scholarly record of his inspection tour. He was quite critical of some of the Protestant missionaries he met in the islands, who, he felt, had been "isolated too long from every tendency in modern religious thought." Those of "broad, intelligent and sympathetic purpose," he wrote, were "sadly outnumbered by those whose chief weapons of propaganda are ritual, fundamentalism and the horde of superstitions which still pass even in some parts of the west for religion."[2]

Dr. Clyde noted that Christianity had been "a major influence in the life of these islands for many years." In the Caroline Islands, with a population estimated at 36,000, "the Catholics number 12,828 and the Protestants 11,390. The latter are members of churches maintained both by the American Board and by a Protestant mission from Japan." In the Marshall Islands, where the native population was almost 10,000, the Catholics numbered some 600, and the Protestants 3,000—with the Protestants claiming a large additional number of nominal Christians.[3] Dr. Clyde continued:

Christian proselyting, curious as it may seem, has tended to increase in the years since Japan assumed a mandate over the islands. This is significant in itself. But far more striking is the fact that in 1932 the Imperial Japanese government (heathen, be it noted) contributed Yen 30,000 (about $10,000) to Christian missions throughout the mandated islands. Of this sum Yen 7,000 was given to the Roman Catholic mission and Yen 23,000 to the Protestant mission of Japan. A Japanese Buddhist mission received Yen 700. The striking character of this friendly attitude on the part of the Japanese government toward Christianity in its mandate could perhaps be better understood by Americans if the Government in Washington, D. C., were discovered in the act of subsidizing Japanese Buddhist missions in the Philippines...

Legally, the attitude of the Japanese government may be traced of course to Article 2 of the Mandate itself, which stipulates that "the Mandatory shall promote to the utmost the material and moral well-being and the social progress of the inhabitants." Since Christianity, of a sort at least, was widely disseminated through the islands when Japan assumed the mandate, it was convenient to continue using it as one of the props supporting native morality. At all events it is there, and, after a fashion, prospering with the official, not to say financial support, of the Japanese government.[4]

Describing the missionaries themselves, the chief problem for Paul Clyde—particularly on Kosrae—seemed to be the missionaries' stand on chastity. Of the Baldwin sisters he wrote:

Consider the methods by which native young men and women are trained in a rigid code of sexual morality in a native mission school. It is conducted by two American maiden ladies who have both outlived the allotted span of threescore years and ten. For thirty-five years, interrupted only by one trip to America in 1910, they have struggled with the task of keeping the island Christian. Their only contacts with the outside world are the religious magazines and a few newspapers brought by the occasional vessel from Yokohama. It is a conservative statement to say that they are living in their recollections of a Nineteenth Century world.

The native village [Lelu] of this particular island is almost a model of municipal morality, for one will look there in vain for a dance hall, bar or brothel (the most conspicuous structure being the village church); yet it was considered far too worldly a place by these maiden ladies in which to nurture the spiritual life of these young wards. Hence their school, where youth are instructed in the ways of a rigorous fundamentalism, is hidden far in the jungle, twelve miles from the meager temptations of the village. Yet even these protective measures avail but little.[5]

The Baldwin sisters had nothing to do with the selection of Wot as the site for the mission school. That decision had been made 56 years earlier—33 years before Elizabeth and Jane were assigned to Kosrae. It is also of interest to note that, in addition to their religious periodicals, the Baldwins subscribed through the years to *The Literary Digest*. Though information about the world beyond Kosrae was often late in reaching them, they made a conscious effort to keep themselves abreast of the times. During their visit to the United States in 1910 the Baldwins had been surprised to discover that many of the women they met did not know as much about world affairs as they themselves did.[6]

Paul Clyde continued his analysis:

What the spinster missionary fails to realize is that the problem is social and economic as well as moral. Native youth is not beset by the economic problems of the American college graduate. There is no unemployment problem, for everyone is unemployed, most of the time. Work is an unnecessary luxury indulged in by only those who ape foreign and western ways. A simple thatched cottage and perhaps an outrigger canoe are the native's capital. Nature does the rest. In the words of an American trader, many years in the islands, the native has only three things to do: eating, sleeping and loving. The first is no problem, for nature provides bountifully; the second remains as a natural consequence; and so all his energies must remain for the last.

*Recall the scenes that have been painted so often on the pages of the South Sea
fiction (they are more real than the average westerner is apt to believe): a tropical
island floating on a blue ocean; the sun sinking into the western sea; a few moments
only of twilight and then that softest of all lights—a tropical moon. Pale shadows of
palm leaves sway langorously in rhythm to the distant murmur of the coral surf. Two
dusky figures pass silently in the amber light, the native girl and her lover.*

*For eighty years and more in the islands, the missionary has struggled against it.
He has preached the holiness of Christian wedlock, and that without it, fulfillment of
love is a sin. The native girl listens, and for a week, perhaps a month, she conforms.
She is a Christian and rather proud of it. But always beating against these codes of a
so-called civilized world comes the murmur of the surf, the light of that amber moon,
and then, the voice of her lover.*[7]

Professor Clyde added that the Catholics dealt with this dilemma, "if not
effectively, at least quietly," through private confession. Protestants suspend
from the church. Protestantism, he suggested, was more difficult to teach than
Catholicism because it discarded outward symbols and "had fewer trinkets
to offer." In desperation, the islander turns to "a brand of fundamentalism
which offers golden streets and harps to the virtuous, and damnation to the
depraved."[8]

REPORT OF A JOURNALIST

In 1935, posing as an absent-minded professor of botany, an American
freelance reporter, Willard Price, traveled extensively through Micronesia with
his wife, aboard the *Yokohama Maru*. His discerning observations were subsequently published in the *National Geographic Magazine*, *Harper's Magazine*, the
London Daily Herald, and a number of other publications—and became the basis
for several books. Mr. Price's account of the few days he and Mrs. Price were on
Kosrae painted a vivid picture of the people and the place.

*Here at last is the tropic paradise of one's dreams. We cast anchor at dawn in the
snug harbor of Kusaie. In its still morning beauty the small island of Lelu looks like
a model in wax for exhibition purposes rather than a real island. Hospitable-looking
thatch homes nestle in its groves. Canoes line its shore. Yonder on a little point stands
a white church, as primly as if cut out of cardboard.*

*The captain is cursing, of course, forsaking the Japanese language to do it. One
must go to English for choice epithets. This is no dream world to him. He wants stevedores. "Sunday morning," he growls. "Everybody will be going to church!" as if that
were the greatest crime in the calendar. "We have to sit here and twiddle our thumbs
until they get done with their psalm singing." He glared as if it were my fault. And it
was—or that of my compatriots.*

For eighty-three years missionaries of the American Board of Boston have been at work in Kusaie. Let us go ashore and see the results. We are taken off by Arthur Herman, lone American planter, the first American we have met in all the Japanese islands. Evidently Kusaie agrees with him—he is portly and jovial. On the copra-scented pier we meet Mrs. Herman, a native of Kusaie, more jovial and more portly. One look at her beaming and enlightened countenance and we conclude that the missionaries have done a good job.

Her face is not unusual. We walk down the village street through a sea of seraphic smiles. There are low bows and soft good mornings. All the inhabitants are in long white robes as in the realms of the blest. Houses are so neat that they ache. Music drifts about—whistled, hummed, twanged—hymn tunes familiar in New England churches.

"I've arranged for you to stay with Miss Hoppin," says Mr. Herman, "because you wrote you wanted to see something of the natives. Around my house you wouldn't see anybody but Japanese. But the natives are at Miss Hoppin's all the time. I suppose you've heard of her—white goddess of the South Seas, they call her. She's just about God to them, and no mistake. Her slightest wish is law. If I want anything of the natives I have to work to get it and pay well for it. Anything she wants she has only to mention. They would do anything in the world for her. So would I for that matter—I'd give my right hand for her."

When you catch a tough old planter ready to give his right hand for a missionary, that missionary has something. Who is this paragon? If we were expecting to meet a looming, booming personality we are mistaken. A cunning little old lady, as neat and bright as a new pin, her gray hair encompassed in a coronet of snow-white shells, awaits us on a bit of an islet just big enough for her and her house in an enchanting grove of palms, mangoes, papayas, banana trees, breadfruit, scarlet hibiscus and lavender bougainvillea. This world of loveliness is not two hundred feet from shore to shore. It is connected with the island of Lelu by a grass grown causeway. Over that causeway stream the natives day and night; coming to bring coconuts, or coming to get medicine, or just coming.

A snatch of breakfast, and it is time to go to church. We find the white church on the shore of Lelu already occupied by a thousand people. The king leads the singing. The most blasé visitor must feel a tingle run along his ribs as these thousand trained voices take to the air. The volume and beauty of it is so great that one would not be surprised to see the sheet-iron roof go sailing off into space. Then the native minister [Pastor Fred Skilling], in high-collared white drill suit and bare feet, preaches. Through the open windows we can see the ship, waiting for stevedores. The stevedores are all in church. The service is long. When the last prayer is finished and we make to rise, the king, who sits beside us, whispers, "Now, Sunday school."

No one leaves. It is not until nearly one o'clock, after three hours of services, that we pass out and some of the men answer the insistent whistle of the steamer. But they must work fast, for there is another service at three and another at five. Double pay cannot induce them to miss a service.

There seems to be nothing fanatical about Miss Hoppin. In fact her creed appears to be solidly grounded in gastronomics, long recognized as one of the foundation stones of religion. Jesus fed the multitude. Every native who comes to Miss Hoppin's house gets fed. Incidentally, he always brings something to feed Miss Hoppin—so it works both ways. She is their champion against all injustice. Several petty officials have been discharged because of her complaints of their harshness toward the natives. One, sent back to Japan, committed suicide. Since then she has complained no more. "They do the best they can," she admits. So, instead of lodging complaints against them, she feeds them too.

Two other extraordinary American ladies of Kusaie are the Misses Baldwin, large, strong-faced women whose fortitude belies their ages of seventy-five and seventy-one. They are in charge of the mission school where eighty-eight young men and women ranging from thirteen to twenty years in age are being taught reading, writing and religion. We paddled the eight miles to see them.

The school is a dingy barn of a place perched on a hilltop with a magnificent view of lagoon and sea. It has the feeling of being completely removed from the world and all its wiles. Magazines do come from America but all pictures of women in low-necked or close-fitting gowns are clipped out before the journals are allowed to reach the eyes of island youths. The cult of the throttle-necked and ankle-length Mother Hubbard prevails. The missionaries have not been off the island in twenty-four years. In 1911 they went to America and got a dress pattern; the dresses of the girls have been cut from it ever since.

My wife asked, "How much material does it take for one of the girl's dresses?"

"Six yards," replied the elder Miss Baldwin.

"Oh, that must be expensive. One of my dresses takes only three yards."

Miss Baldwin stiffened. "It is never expensive to cover the body," she said.

Two hundred and fifty phonograph records of the lighter sort were sent by well-meaning friends in America. The missionaries took them to an upper room, locked the door, removed the horn from the phonograph so that no sound might escape from the room, and played the records through. Then they dispatched them by boat to a point far outside the reef where bottom is said to be a good mile down, quite beyond the reach of the best native diver, and consigned them to the deeps.

The ladies have been won over by the mysterious island silences to the conviction that the second coming of the Lord is close at hand. In a world of increasing wickedness, they see all the prophecies being fulfilled. "Apart from the world on this little island, we feel that perhaps we can see such things more clearly than those who are in the midst of the false teachings."

Far be it from us to cavil at their beliefs. They may be terribly right. The folk of Sodom and Gomorrah scoffed, and were sorry for it. I do not seek to caricature but only to portray these two remarkable personalities—and to make a truthful portrait there are some important strokes of the brush still to be added.

One is that both these devoted women have given their lives for Kusaie, and the elder has given her eyes as well. She translated the entire Bible in the Kusaie language. She broke her glasses and sent the prescription to England to be refilled. In the meantime, the proofs were ready to read. She felt that the natives must not be made to wait for their Bible. So she read the proofs—and went blind.

But the great work was completed and the Kusaiens have their Bible. The blind translator places her hand upon the great three-inch-thick volume, her monument, and in her peaceful, unseeing face there is no regret. She goes on translating—arithmetics, grammars, Bible helps. Her sister reads aloud the English version and she dictates the Kusaie. Of course in addition to these cloistered tasks there is the schoolwork to supervise—the daily guidance of eighty-eight inquiring minds. The curriculum may be lopsided, the pedagogy faulty, but the devotion is superb. A flaming object lesson for the Japanese official, or for any other official for that matter who is supposed to exist for the good of the people.

What have been the achievements of this mission school and other missionary work in Kusaie in the last half century? Once an island dreaded for its savagery and brutality, where American whalers murdered and were murdered, where American ships were sunk in the harbor, where disease and violent death reduced the population from two thousand to two hundred, Kusaie is now an unbelievable isle of twelve hundred healthy and happy angels.

In olden times murders sometimes scored one or two hundred a year. "How many murders a year now?" I asked the king.

He smiled, "There has not been a native murder in my lifetime," he said. The king is sixty years old.

"How about minor offenses? How many cases of detention in your jail in a year?"

"Jail!" exclaimed the king. "But there is no jail!"

"Well," I said, "whatever you call it. You must at least have some place to put the tipsy ones until they sober up." In all islands that I had visited infraction of the liquor law was the most common offense and the jails were always well patronized by alcoholic convalescents.

"But there is no drinking on Kusaie."

I thought he meant relatively none, only a few cases a month. But he went on to explain that no native has been known to taste alcohol in the past thirty years.

"I myself drank and smoked when I was a young man," he said, "but not since. If anyone drank now, every man's hand would be against him."

"And smoking is under the ban too?"

"Tobacco does not sell well here, although I am sorry to say that a few of the young men smoke. I have told my sons that if they smoke I will throw them out of the family." He said it with a broad smile expressing his easy assurance that it would never be necessary for him to carry out his vow.

Marriage is a sacred institution on Kusaie. Divorces are unknown. I am speaking of course of the natives, not of the newcomers. There is no house of ill fame. There is practically no disease. There are no native medicine men, no charms or other superstitious devices to ward off illness, and the Japanese doctor goes fishing. Native physique is splendid. Poling develops the arm muscles; and standing braced in the canoe, the leg muscles. When the Japanese came, wrestling matches were staged between Japanese and Kusaiens. Such matches are now forbidden, for the native men always win and the rulers lose face.

Service is exchanged for service. I build your house and you deliver my child. I do your fishing as well as my own and you do your farming plus mine. Poverty is not allowed. Those who have give to those who have not when typhoon wipes out a plantation or accident deprives a family of its providers. Orphans are promptly absorbed into other homes…

The population of Kusaie is twelve hundred, of whom only thirty are Japanese. Several times these administrators applied torture to wring "confessions" from recalcitrant natives, but in each case a threatened uprising made them back down. The king refused to allow his people to work for their Japanese masters on Sunday. Japanese officials argued with him in vain. One Saturday they undertook to wring consent from him by force. He was detained all day in the government office and subjected to "questioning" which was accompanied by the liberal use of burning cigarettes applied to the flesh. The natives gathered outside the office and were about to rush the place when an official came out on the porch, saw the crowd, and hastily reported to his superiors. The king was released. His people still went to church on Sunday…

Anyone who wishes to take a few lessons on how to do the right thing upon every occasion should visit and study King John of Kusaie. We saw him three times a day at least, for he dined with us in the thatch house on the two-hundred-foot isle along with Miss Hoppin, [Pastor] Fred Skillings, shark-hunter [Pastor] John Mackwelung and old Caiaphas [Kefwas] who was an improvement upon the high priest after whom he was named. The king was at home on any subject. It is the office of a king in these islands to be able to do everything superlatively well. King John, although sixty years old, was powerful, broad of chest, and could swim, spear, paddle, with the best.

The king clung to the old ways, with one exception. He had a pocketful of calling cards and delighted in handing them out. He gave me one. On it was printed, "K. J. Sigrah." Sigrah was his family name. I asked him what the K. J. stood for.

"King John," was the answer![9]

America at the time of the settlement after the Spanish-American War offered Spain a million dollars for Kusaie, thinking to use it as a base and cable station. The deal fell through, but in another sense America has now captured Kusaie. In time the American missionaries will doubtless be supplanted by Japanese. But for the time being the officials are well content with the work of the missionaries and the missionaries vastly prefer Japanese control in the island to either German or Spanish. And it is very appropriate that the nationality which devastated Kusaie should have redeemed it. Whether this redemption was due more to the peculiar merits of the Christian faith or to the sacrificial devotion of its representatives, who shall say? At any rate, no one who takes the trouble to look through the superficial idiosyncrasies of the genus missionary can fail to agree with [Robert Louis] *Stevenson:*

"Those who have a taste for hearing missions, Catholic or Protestant, decried, must seek their pleasure elsewhere than in my pages. Whether Catholic or Protestant, with all their gross blots, with all their deficiency of candor, of humor, and of common sense, the missionaries are the best and most useful whites in the Pacific."[10]

BALDWIN SISTERS MOVE TO LELU

Five months later, on April 16, 1936, Elizabeth and Jane Baldwin retired. They moved from their large, comfortable home and unrelenting responsibilities at Wot to Lelu. At Kalung, close to his home near the Lelu dock, King John supervised the building of a small house for them. Baldwin family money provided the materials, while the labor was lovingly donated by the sisters' Kosraean friends, led by King John and Pastor Fred.

There were only three rooms in the house—the kitchen; the living room, which served also as dining room; and the bedroom. A tiny bathroom "the size of a clothes closet" was attached to the bedroom. Across the front of the house was a porch they enjoyed at evening time, but on which they seldom sat during the day. Bright sunlight was hard on Miss Jane. Her eyes, which had long been doing the seeing for both sisters, were deteriorating.

Shortly before they moved from Wot, Miss Elizabeth suffered an accident that permanently impaired her health. She and Miss Jane were on the school's large canoe taking some students and their baggage to Lelu when a large wave tipped the canoe over, dumping everyone and everything into the lagoon. As they struggled for breath and for footing in the relatively shallow water, a heavy box of books fell on Miss Elizabeth's back. From that time on she was not very well, though as usual, she refused to complain.[11]

Jane and Kenye, two girls from the Wot student body who had been part of the sisters' household for several years, moved with them to Lelu to assist with cooking and house cleaning. Companions as well as helpers, the girls slept on the floor in the sisters' bedroom. Jane was the daughter of Caleb Kojerik, one of the Marshallese pastors teaching at Wot. Kenye, the daughter of Palik George, later became the wife of Aliksa Wesley.

Jonah and Helmet also moved with the sisters to Lelu and were provided their own small house next door to the Baldwins. Their family now included a daughter, Linda, and a son, Donald—both born at Wot. A third child, Elizabeth, was born there at Kalung. As far as Miss Elizabeth and Miss Jane Baldwin were concerned, Jonah and Helmet were irreplaceable. The teachers at Wot continued the production of Christian Endeavor topics and Sunday School helps for the Kosraeans without Jonah's expertise, with students he had taught to operate the press.

The Baldwin sisters were relieved to be settled at Kalung, and, in many ways, life there in Lelu was pleasant for them. Mail and supplies were received without the long round-trip by canoe from Wot. Their "children" often dropped in to visit, or came by to seek help in preparing a Sunday School lesson or a talk for a meeting. New babies were shown off and held by Miss Jane, who always had a present—often a can of milk—for each infant.

The Baldwins had seldom ventured into the four village churches, but their influence on those churches could hardly be calculated as almost all of the current Kosraean church leaders had been carefully trained by the sisters in the school at Wot. Feeling deeply indebted, these grateful students now reciprocated with affectionate concern for the two elderly women who had no intention of ever leaving Kosrae.

All Kosraeans, no matter their age, considered Elizabeth and Jane Baldwin as their mothers. The sisters' generosity, their strictness, their modesty, and their devout Christian faith paralleled the virtues that Benjamin and Lydia Snow had demonstrated—though values of generosity, strictness, and modesty were also integral parts of the existing Kosraean culture prior to 1852. Indeed, the existence of these characteristics among the Kosraeans, and their recognition of them in Mr. Snow, brought the Kosraeans with relative speed into the Christian fold. The lessons that the Church on Kosrae had received during the several decades in between—when missionaries representing a more liberal interpretation of Scripture and a more relaxed lifestyle had lived among them—were forgotten during the years that Kosrae was isolated from America and dominated by the uncompromising stance of the two authority figures at Wot. No one doubted or questioned the Baldwin sisters—rather, the Kosraeans obeyed them and loved them.

PROGRESS UNDER THE JAPANESE

The Baldwins, along with everyone else on Kosrae, were benefitting from the infrastructure that had emerged under Japanese leadership. In addition to the police station [there had been great relief when the original police sergeant had finally been recalled to Japan], a well-run clinic-hospital, and a post office, there was now an elementary school in Lelu. An important function of this school "was to teach the Japanese language and in general develop respect for Japanese culture."[12]

There were several Japanese-operated retail outlets, as well as the trading company operated by planters Arthur Herman and his young nephew, Jack Youngstrom. Jack had come to join his uncle from the family home in Oakland, California, just as Arthur had joined his uncle, Victor Melander, at Kosrae almost two decades earlier.

Vegetable gardening was encouraged by the administration. It not only provided a new source of income for industrious farmers, but introduced vegetables into the Kosraean diet. Miss Elizabeth and Miss Jane had almost forgotten the taste of some of the vegetables that now graced their Kalung table.

ARRIVAL OF THE McCALLS AND MISS WILSON

In mid-May 1936 a small Japanese steamer brought three new missionaries to Kosrae: Clarence and Cora McCall and Eleanor Wilson. Miss Wilson, age 45—born and raised in Massachusetts—had been sent by the American Board to Japan in 1925 where she taught for eight years at the Kobe Theological Seminary. In 1933 she was called back to the United States to serve in the American Board offices in Boston. One of her responsibilities was to find a Japanese-speaking missionary couple to replace the Baldwin sisters at the Kosrae Christian Training School at Wot—but when she found that couple, the wife was hesitant to go to so remote a place where there would be no other American woman.

Miss Wilson wrote, "I heard the accusing voice of my New England conscience. How could I ask her to go where I was unwilling to go myself? The depression had cut heavily into the Board's resources and there was not enough money to send another missionary. I found that the fare by Japanese freighter was within my means. Careful inquiry led me to believe that I could live for one year on Kusaie for $150. I decided to go. So with my ticket and with this sum of money, I set off by Japanese freighter from Boston to Yokohama where I could catch a smaller Japanese boat, the only transportation to Kusaie in these Japanese Mandated Islands."[13]

The Rev. Clarence McCall was age 54 when he reached Kosrae. His wife, Cora Campbell McCall, was 57. They had raised a son and a daughter in Japan (two other sons died there as children) where the McCalls served for 22 years as missionaries of the Christian Church/Disciples of Christ, and then for six more years with the American Board. Now they were responding to Miss Wilson's request for teachers at the Kosrae mission school. They joined Eleanor Wilson in Yokohama and embarked with her on the long trip through the mandated islands. When the small ship finally steamed into Lelu Harbor, it was surrounded by outrigger canoes before the anchor could be dropped.

Eleanor described their arrival: "When formalities with the harbor master had been concluded, two fine-looking men wearing white suits with high collars fastened under their chins in the fashion of Japanese officials, climbed aboard to welcome us. One was the much respected and loved pastor, Fred Skilling, and the other the king of the island, John Sigrah."[14]

"HOME SWEET HOME"

That same evening, the McCalls and Eleanor Wilson were invited to dinner at the Lelu home of Elizabeth and Jane Baldwin. Miss Wilson later reminisced:

Dinner was served on their narrow porch as the additional persons could not be seated together in their small living-dining room. As the meal progressed, I marveled how two Victorian ladies had ever adjusted themselves so perfectly to the life of this tropical island. They seemed as much at home as King John and Queen Hattie, or Pastor Skilling and his wife, Sepe.

As the meal ended, I saw a little cavalcade coming down the white coral road. It was the Lelu village band and its members were proudly bearing their instruments. They stopped by the steps of the Baldwins' house and struck up a familiar tune. It was "Home Sweet Home." Did they intend that I should feel at home on Kusaie or did they want me to realize they were sympathizing with me, because I was so far away from my home in America? I could not look into the future and see that one day Kusaie, perhaps the most beautiful island in the whole world, would be home to me.[15]

The party broke up after evening prayers—reverently led by Pastor Fred, with Pastor McCall assisting—at the conclusion of the meal and the concert.

Following those first days among the Kosraeans, Miss Wilson found herself in total agreement with Willard Price, who had visited the year before: "The early missionaries had transformed Kusaie into an island paradise where going to church and smiling seemed to be the chief industries."[16]

With considerable optimism, the three new missionaries continued on to Wot where they settled into their assignments at the Kosrae Christian Training School. The McCalls moved into the mission house so recently vacated by Elizabeth and Jane Baldwin, while Miss Wilson occupied a two-room apartment in the three-story school building next door. Though the life was entirely new to them, they were determined to walk faithfully in the footsteps of the many others who had preceded them up that steep mountain trail to the Yonrak campus.

Eleanor Wilson later wrote that in addition to the students, who spoke two different island languages [Marshallese and Kosraean] while learning English, "we have cows, pigs, and chickens at the school. Coconuts, bananas, and breadfruit grow on the school land. The students study in the mornings and work at their tasks in the afternoons. We set out a plantation of pineapples that grow readily in the soil of this high island. My $150 lasted me all through the year."[17]

One student who quickly endeared himself to all three of the new missionaries was Palik Kefwas, the 17-year-old adopted son of the respected Bible teacher and Wot landowner, Alik Kefwas. The boy's eagerness in class, his perfect attendance record, and his willingness to do what was asked of him—along with the impressive way he had of anticipating their requests—served to bring him to the attention of his teachers.

YENYEN QUESTION

In 1936, from Jabwor, Jaluit, Miss Hoppin wrote to Mrs. Mary Hitchcock Snow—the widow of Benjamin and Lydia Snow's son, Fred—about a memorial she wanted to see built on Yenyen, the islet near Pisin that Benjamin Snow and Daniel Opunui had purchased in 1852 as the site for their gardens. Among the missionaries who had served at Kosrae since that time, Miss Hoppin was perhaps the most prolific writer. She was constantly sending letters to a vast number of individuals and congregations in Hawai'i and the United States sharing her dreams for the islands she loved and making specific requests for help with the innumerable projects that her active mind constantly generated.

The next year, still anxious about what was to become of Yenyen, she wrote on June 16, 1937, to the Rev. Wynn C. Fairfield of the American Board in Boston:

I wish in particular to speak about the little island of Yenyen which belongs to the American Board. I believe it is about three acres in size. I learned from a friend that Yenyen was for sale, and that Mr. McCall was contemplating asking Mr. Hata, our government official on Kusaie, whether Yenyen could be sold legally.

Now this Mr. Hata is the official who put a leper on Yenyen in 1934 and told the Mission to move their goods away from there! I had and have good reason to know that should such a question be put to this official, he would say that if the Mission did not longer need Yenyen the government would take it by sale or otherwise, probably otherwise. So I went at once to Mwot and asked Mr. McCall to give me the first chance to buy Yenyen if it is to be sold, and not by any chance to ask Mr. Hata about the legality of selling it. So Mr. McCall promised me he would wait. This is the first time there has been an opportunity for writing you a letter that I feel sure will not be censored.

For anyone living on the Mission land at Pisin for any length of time, Yenyen is very important. I have spent many months at a time at Pisin. We got firewood, coconuts, material for building and many other things at Yenyen. Pisin is most beautiful, but without many natural resources. Also, Yenyen is too near to Pisin and to Lelu for it to be a desirable place for post houses for the government. Moreover, on Yenyen is the Mission cemetery. There the body of one of the first Hawaiian missionaries is buried, and of others—among whom are students from the Training School at Mwot.

I presume that by this time you know that the Baldwin sisters expect to end their earthly days on Kusaie. It seems to me that with all their self-sacrificing gifts to the American Board, the Board should try to make it SURE that their dear "earthly tabernacles" are not left where any common Japanese official can dig them up for any reason.

Of course, we all know that these two women have given their services through many years to the Board, that is, have paid their own salaries. Perhaps you may not know that they "went almost in rags" during the World War in order to help support the Kusaie Training School and to repair and paint the mission houses. They have given their fine house, that cost them thousands of dollars, to the Board—and have built a smaller, uncomfortable house [in Lelu] for themselves, much inferior to their house at Mwot. They also paid all the expenses of the school for the first months of 1936, up to the arrival of Mr. McCall and the new missionaries. I have never heard any word of complaint from these two dear people.

Now after all this peroration, I have arrived at my idea. It is this—If the Board feel they must sell Yenyen, please give me the first chance to buy it. That means of course, give me time to raise the money for it among my friends. But as a necessary means of security, let the Board hold the title in trust forever, the ownership of the land being understood in the American Board only, and there put on record. If, however, the Board decides to keep the property, that is not to sell it, I humbly suggest, as a lifelong friend of the Board, that they consecrate it as a Memorial Park, NEVER, NEVER to be sold or molested.

"Park" is a much more beautiful name than "cemetery," and Yenyen, by nature very beautiful, could be made a very beautiful memorial park—"Snow Memorial Park" or "Baldwin Memorial Park" or a combination of both would call out the deepest affection of the Kusaien people. Or "American Board Memorial Park"! It would always be kept in order by the love of the island people.

If the Board decides to let me buy Yenyen, please say in your letter to me simply, "Your request regarding Yenyen is granted." Then I will understand. If, however, the

Board decides not to sell Yenyen but to keep it for a permanent Memorial Park, as suggested earlier in this letter, then please write fully about it in the regular mail and make it also as public as possible by any other normal means. I do not care to use Yenyen for myself, dead or alive, but I would delight being on a committee to make it a most beautiful memorial for the dear departed…

Just a word more about cemeteries. Mrs. Walkup and Mr. Forbes, former missionaries of the Board, are buried on the Mission land at Mwot. Should the Board ever discontinue their work on Kusaie, the deeds say the land reverts to the natives. The surveyors said it reverted to the government according to present land methods on Kusaie. I presume the Mwot property is not so very secure, unless the Board has mercy on the natives and holds it. The Pisin and Yenyen and Lelu real estate come under a different form of deed. They are registered as ABCFM property, I believe. So returning to the cemetery problem, if by any chance the Mwot property is lost to the Mission, the bodies of the two missionaries at Mwot could be removed to Yenyen.

By this mail I am writing to a friend who some time ago inquired about donating a memorial building to be erected perhaps on Yenyen. I have suggested to her that she write you to find out if you have decided to make Yenyen a Memorial Park, that is if she still feels like making this gift. There is a very good location for a house on Yenyen, quite separate from the part where the cemetery is. A guest house is greatly needed at or near Lelu.

Either Jaluit or Kusaie address will always reach me. Jessie Rebecca Hoppin.[18]

Miss Hoppin did not have to buy Yenyen to rescue it from the Japanese—and neither did it become the Memorial Park she had hoped for. The small island remained the property of the American Board of Commissioners for Foreign Missions, as did its tiny neighbor, Pisin.

JAPANESE TEACHER FOR WOT

Students and teachers alike were enamored of a vivacious Japanese woman, Miss Yamada—not yet 30 years old when she arrived in mid-1937—sent by the Tokyo-based Nan'yo Dendo Dan, to teach at Wot. Very quickly she become an integral member of the mission school family.

CENSUS OF 1937

The 1937 census counted 1,332 persons living on Kosrae.

Chamorro men: 1	Chamorro women: 6	total: 7
Japanese men: 31	Japanese women: 9	total: 40
American men: 3	American women: 5	total: 8
Kosraean men/boys: 645	Kosraean women/girls: 622	total: 1,267

Though there were some Marshallese, Gilbertese, and other Micronesians included in the "Kosraean" total, this was the first time since 1855 that there were more than one thousand Kosraeans. Over the previous 30 years, the population had more than doubled.

NEW TEAM GUIDES MISSION SCHOOL

Mr. McCall was well-suited for his assignment at Kosrae. He was a conscientious principal and classroom teacher, and, too, he was truly enthusiastic in his desire to make the Wot plantation productive. During the afternoons he worked alongside his students, determined that the school's farm and gardens should not only adequately feed the student body and staff, but also provide enough extra to generate some cash to pay for other school needs. His diligent work habits gave rise to gossip among the Kosraeans that he sometimes worked on Sunday, and his fluent Japanese caused some idle chatter about the possibility of his being a Japanese spy. Neither piece of hearsay was true, but it was true that Mr. McCall was able to converse with government officials in Lelu in the Japanese language. as both his wife and Miss Wilson did also.

Elizabeth and Jane Baldwin, in retirement in Lelu, were disturbed when they began hearing stories of some of Mr. McCall's "modern methods" and of his theology, which they were certain was more liberal than theirs. They grumbled, too, when they heard rumors that he had relaxed some of their cherished rules of conduct for the Wot students. Eleanor Wilson found herself caught in the uncomfortable middle: trying to support and assist Clarence McCall in what he was doing at Wot, and, at the same time, trying to calm and reassure the elderly sisters, whom she respected and loved.

CONFLICTS AMONG MISSIONARIES

But the Baldwins were in distant Lelu, while Miss Wilson and Mr. McCall struggled to operate a school together at Wot. Eleanor was in her mid-40s and Clarence was already in his 50s, both long accustomed to their own ways of getting things done. The two missionaries often found themselves at odds with each other, and as the months went by and 1938 dawned, their efforts to get along became increasingly difficult. The extreme isolation of the school exacerbated their problems. Both were committed Christians and determined to do a good job at Wot, and they were sad and frustrated by their situation.

The Kosraeans—not only those who worked in close proximity to the missionaries, but others as well—were quite aware of the differences of opinion between the two American teachers. The islanders noticed these conflicts between missionary colleagues from the very first, and they would continue to see them in the future. These clashes of personality and conviction—sometimes concerning procedure, sometimes over a matter of discipline, sometimes a simple misunderstanding blown out of proportion by loneliness and overwork—gave the Kosraeans insight into the New Testament stories of Paul's criticism of Peter [Galatians 2:11-14], and the rift between Paul and Barnabas [Acts 15:36-40], and were the source of some relief when they, themselves, had difficulty working together.

Clarence McCall was extremely frugal. He regularly stopped at the school kitchen, located on the path between Wot's farm animals and the school buildings, to insist that everything he considered eatable be used in preparing the students' meals. This included the dry remains of coconut meat from which the oil had been squeezed, a material the Kosraeans ordinarily fed to chickens. Eleanor Wilson objected to what she considered to be his dictatorial, autocratic style and his lack of sympathy for the students whose menus she helped plan.

Cora McCall kept to herself in what had been the Baldwin's house. She trained the girls who helped her there, but did no classroom teaching. She, as well as Eleanor, suffered frequent illnesses, which added to Clarence's work-load. As they came to know and utilize the gifts of Miss Yamada, both the McCalls and Miss Wilson found it refreshing to have her on the faculty. They were also grateful for the consistent and conscientious help of the two dedicated Marshallese pastors, Alexander Milne and Caleb Kojerik, who served with them as class room teachers, and for the ever-faithful members of the Kosraean staff.[19]

KOSRAE'S FIRST DEACONESSES CHOSEN

In a tribute to Elizabeth and Jane Baldwin and Jessie Hoppin—and a sign of the high esteem in which the officers of the Church held these missionary teachers, as well as other women who had been a part of the Wot family in years past—the Kosrae Church Committee accepted a major innovation in 1938 that they would not have considered but for the urging of these respected American women. Since the beginning days of the Church on Kosrae there had been deacons—the earliest of them selected by Benjamin Snow. Now, for the first time, deaconesses were chosen to work alongside the deacons.

At first, the idea was not unanimously approved. Committee members were guided through their arguments and other aspects of the decision-making process by Eleanor Wilson. It took several months of explanation and rationale shared by Miss Wilson, including discussions of the New Testament reference to Phoebe [Romans 16:1], plus the acknowledgment of a cultural preference for keeping men and women separated during worship, before the all-male committee finally agreed.

The primary responsibility for these first deaconesses, one to represent each of the four villages, was to serve Holy Communion to the female congregants. This relieved the deacons of having to walk with the communion trays among the women, who were often seated so closely together on the floor of the church that it was impossible to move among them without touching them. Later, the deaconesses were assigned to gather the elements of communion, as well as to do preparation and clean-up. In addition, these women became members of the All-Island Church Committee, joining the pastors and deacons in the governing body of the Church on Kosrae.

The new deaconesses were not necessarily wives of deacons. Each one was selected for her own godly character and Christian reputation, not because she was someone's wife. This was an impressive step for a society in which a woman's standing in the community merely reflected that of her husband.

NEW MISSIONARIES FOR ENEWETAK AND NEW PASTOR FOR KOSRAE

When Pastor John Mackwelung and his family returned to Kosrae after eight years on the Marshallese atoll of Enewetak, John's daughter, Srue, and her husband, Frank Skilling, went to Enewetak in their place. Both Frank and Srue had the advantage of exceptionally nurturing childhoods. Frank was the oldest son of Pastor Fred Skilling, while Srue was raised by her adoptive father, Alik Kefwas, the revered deacon, Bible teacher, and translator. Frank and Srue had been outstanding students at Wot and had stayed on as instructors following their graduation and marriage. Now, in 1938, they traveled to minister to the people of Enewetak, taking with them their youngest son, Roger Misio, who was four years old.

Meanwhile, leaders of the Church on Kosrae were divided concerning John Mackwelung's position among them. Should they recognize him as a pastor when they had not been involved in his ordination? There were prolonged and heated arguments, and months went by before the decision was finally made to reconsecrate John as the sixth pastor of the Kosraean Church. Eleanor Wilson and Clarence McCall officiated, with Elizabeth and Jane Baldwin concurring. Years earlier, John had been an appreciated and faithful helper for the sisters at Wot.

During this time John Mackwelung became a widower for the second time when his wife, Sepe Insopus, died. She was the mother of five of his eight children: Irving, Kenye, Palik, Jaboar, and Tulensa. Allen, Srue [Frank Skilling] and Notwe [Isaiah Benjamin] were the children of his first wife, Sra Niarlang. One child from both sets of children—his daughter Srue and his son Palik—were adopted by Deacon Alik Kefwas who had married Pastor Mackwelung's sister, Kenye Liokas. John Mackwelung subsequently married his third wife, Tulpe Insurufofo.

DEATH OF ELIZABETH BALDWIN

From time to time, Elizabeth Baldwin was confined to her bed, but would then rally. On her 80th birthday, April 11, 1939, she was able to receive her friends and treat them to doughnuts, as was her custom when she had visitors. Food, however, no longer appealed to her. She wanted only ice cream made with no flavoring and not much sugar. After moving to Lelu, Miss Elizabeth and Miss Jane had purchased a kerosene-burning refrigerator and enjoyed having ice cream on hand.

Early in October, a fall put Miss Baldwin in bed. She was in great pain but seemed not to have broken any bones. She refused to have a "heathen" doctor called, but as she grew weaker and weaker, she realized that an autopsy would be performed if she died without having been seen by the Japanese doctor. Reluctantly, she permitted him to come to her bedside. He could do nothing more than to give her a sedative, which she refused to take. The doctor left with the request that he be summoned again if needed.[20]

Two weeks later he was called once more, this time to sign her death certificate. Elizabeth Baldwin died on October 31, 1939, in the bedroom of her Lelu cottage. She was buried on the bluff at Pukusrik, just a few feet from the grave of Capt. Victor Melander, on land donated to the sisters by Arthur Herman. The grave site was high above the mangrove channel that wended its way toward Tafunsak—and Wot. Mother Baldwin had lived courageously, giving herself unstintingly to the work of the Micronesia Mission for 40 years. Her outstanding accomplishment was the Kosraean Bible.

Jane Baldwin was certain that she could not live for more than six weeks without Elizabeth. She ordered a gravestone for her sister and herself. It was engraved with all the data about them both—with the exception of Jane's death date—and set in place. King John and Queen Hattie moved right in with her, using the living room of the little house at Kalung as their sleeping quarters. Three meals a day were prepared for them to share. Miss Jane ate and she lived.

SECOND JAPANESE TEACHER FOR WOT

After Miss Yamada was recalled to Japan in 1939, Eleanor Wilson sent word through the American Board to the Nan'yo Dendo Dan that another Japanese teacher was needed at Wot. In 1940, Miss Ren Suzuki—an experienced educator in her early 40s—arrived, and was soon made assistant principal of the school. As both Eleanor Wilson and Clarence McCall had served in Japan and spoke the Japanese language, and since the island was administered by the Japanese government, it seemed not only logical but important to have a Japanese teacher on the mission school staff. The Japanese language was now a part of the curriculum.

As Miss Yamada had been, Miss Suzuki was a dedicated Christian and a conscientious classroom teacher who adjusted quickly to the rigors of life at Wot.

MISSION SCHOOL THRIVES

It was a productive and satisfactory year for the school community. There were 60 Marshallese students and 30 Kosraean students studying at Wot, plus three Pohnpeians: Peter, Masao, and Sigmund. The problems between Miss Wilson and Mr. McCall had eased as they learned to work together and as others joined them to share the considerable workload.

Subjects of study as well as teaching techniques rejected by the Baldwins or unknown to them were incorporated and used by a competent group of teachers. The faculty included Miss Suzuki, Miss Wilson, Mr. McCall, Pastor Caleb, Pastor Alexander, and also Srue and Frank Skilling, recently returned from Enewetak. Rose Kaumaip Hoppin, now 28 years old, had returned from her studies in California in 1935. She, too, was teaching at Wot.

Through the diligence of Mr. McCall and plantation foreman Frank Skilling, the mission gardens and animals were providing ample food for the boarding students and staff. The Japanese government's regularly scheduled ships carried in supplies and brought and returned students from the Marshall Islands with considerable convenience.

MARSHALLESE MARRIAGES

As in years past, the Wot school continued to be the ideal spot for Christian young people to find what the Church in both the Marshall Islands and at Kosrae considered to be appropriate marriage partners. This Kosrae campus was ideal for Marshallese students—who gathered at Wot from many different atolls—to meet and marry.

On April 2, 1940, encouraged by her grandfather, missionary Carl Heine, and her father, Claude, Mary Heine became the wife of Isaac Lanwi in yet another Wot wedding. The service was happily performed by Mr. McCall, who recognized great potential in the young couple. Both Mary and Isaac had been gifted students and now, upon graduating and marrying, they became part of the mission school's faculty. Isaac, 22 years old, went on to become a respected doctor of ophthalmology. Mary, 20 years old at the time of her marriage, subsequently became a much-admired spokesperson for women's issues, not only in the Marshall Islands, but throughout Micronesia and the Pacific.

JESSIE HOPPIN AND McCALLS LEAVE MICRONESIA

When Miss Hoppin left for the United States in 1939 for what she anticipated would be a brief vacation, the Japanese administration, without explanation, refused to grant her a visa to return to Micronesia in 1940.[21] She was greatly distressed, having expected to live out her life near her daughter and among her island friends. She made a home for herself in Ashland, Wisconsin, where she experienced emotional distress during World War II because she could not communicate with Rose or her friends in Micronesia. Jessie Hoppin died in Ashland on January 14, 1949, age 84, having been able to reconnect by letter with her daughter after the war was over.

Though in 1939 Japanese officials on Kosrae denied the rumors of pending war, the missionaries were increasingly uneasy about their situation. In mid-1940, after more than four years on Kosrae, and not long after the Lanwi-Heine wedding, Clarence and Cora McCall left for the United States. They traveled through Japan without incident. For the next 10 years, Mr. McCall ministered to congregations in Ashland, Oregon, and Spearfish, South Dakota. In May 1950 he and Cora retired to Pilgrim Place in Claremont, California, where he died in 1962, age 80, and she in 1966, age 87. [On September 14, 1958, Pastor McCall took part in the service of ordination for Elden Buck in Fullerton, California.]

JANE BALDWIN DECIDES TO RETURN TO NEW JERSEY

With the McCalls gone, Eleanor Wilson was left in charge of the school at Wot. Visiting Miss Jane one day in October 1940, she was startled to hear the veteran missionary—so determined to die on Kosrae and be buried beside her sister—suddenly say, "I don't want to live out here through another war. I lived during the World War on native foods but I am now too old to do that again."[22]

Miss Wilson did not think a war was imminent, but told Miss Baldwin that if she wished to return to the United States, she would escort her. Jane Baldwin was now 75 years old and, with a bad leg and impaired eyesight, could not travel alone. She was reluctant to take Eleanor away from Wot, but the elderly missionary had definitely made up her mind to leave Micronesia. A radio message was sent to the American Board treasurer to make travel arrangements for the two women.

A HOME FOR JONAH'S FAMILY

As she prepared to leave, Jane Baldwin was worried about what would become of Jonah, Helmet, and their children. Though they had visited family members in the Marshall Islands from time to time during the 1930s, their chosen home was Kosrae. Miss Jane shared her concern with Pastor Fred, King John, and others. Soon offers of land for Jonah were being received from people in all four of Kosrae's villages who remembered with sincere appreciation the integral part he had played in the production of their Bible. Miss Jane, with her foreboding about the possibility of war, felt that the offer of William Mongkeya in Tafunsak would provide the safest, most peaceful place for the little family to settle.

Supplemented by the generous gifts of Kosraean Christians, money from the Baldwin family was used to purchase the desirable piece of property at Inkoeya, Tafunsak. King John Sigrah, Pastor Fred Skilling, and trader Arthur Herman signed the deed as witnesses to the sale. Miss Jane was greatly relieved, as Jonah and Helmet—giving voice to their keen awareness of this great blessing received through God's people—began the process of moving to their new home. At Inkoeya, during the years ahead, three more children were born to them: Christopher, Julian, and Alden. The entire family became intricately involved in the life of the Tafunsak congregation and community, into which they were welcomed.

DEPARTURE ABOARD THE *PALAU MARU*

A dispatch was finally received by the two women stating that they would have passage on the *Palau Maru* traveling from Jaluit back to Japan in February 1941. Miss Wilson packed her belongings and bid the students and staff members at Wot an emotional farewell. She was relieved by the fact that the spirited Miss Yamada had just returned from Japan and could take her place on the faculty. The boys carefully transported Miss Wilson's boxes to Lelu where King John, Jonah, and others were working hard to crate the freight that Miss Baldwin had chosen to take with her.

Eleanor Wilson narrates the day of departure, February 17, 1941:

Determined as Miss Baldwin was to leave, nevertheless it was a very sad occasion for her. She was not only leaving her sister's grave, but also the place which had been her home for almost thirty years. She knew every person living in Kusaie. She had named many of them. They were her "children" and she was leaving Kusaie never to return.

She sat on her deck chair as one after another of her friends came to shake her hand and say "goodbye." When Jonah, her assistant of many years, came he dropped to his knees and prayed for a safe journey for this woman who for so long had been like a real mother to him. The whistle blew, the folks scurried down the gangplank onto their canoes. A bevy of outriggers loaded with people waving and singing followed the ship until we steamed out of that little harbor. One young man, to show his feelings, took off his shirt, swung it over his head a few times and let it fly as far as it could before landing on the water.[23]

Jane Baldwin and Eleanor Wilson traveled aboard the *Palau Maru* through Micronesia and up to Yokohama, Japan. From Tokyo they traveled across the Pacific Ocean to San Francisco aboard the *Tatsuta Maru*. Transiting the United States by train, Miss Wilson went to her family in Massachusetts while Miss Baldwin was reunited with her niece, Anna Baldwin, in Orange, New Jersey, where she lived for the next eight years. Jane Baldwin died in her 86th year, on July 5, 1949, 10 years after the death of her sister, Elizabeth, and six months after the death of Jessie Hoppin. ✛

Notes - Chapter 12

1.   Mary Lanwi, personal conversations, Majuro, July 26-27, 2001
2.   Paul Clyde, *Japan's Pacific Mandate*, pp. 124-126
3.   Clyde quoting Japan's "Annual Report to the League of Nations, 1932," p. 89 & p. 171
4.   Clyde, pp. 120-122
5.   Ibid, pp. 124-125
6.   Eleanor Wilson,"Too Old?" p. 27
7.   Clyde, pp. 125-126
8.   Ibid, p. 124
9.   Willard Price, *Pacific Adventure*, pp. 269-287
10. Price, *Japan's Islands of Mystery*, pp. 211-223
11. Maribelle Cormack, *The Lady Was a Skipper*, p. 11
12. John L. & Ann M. Fischer, *The Eastern Carolines*, Pacific Science Board, New Haven, 1957, p. 61
13. Wilson, p. 30
14. Cormack, p. 11
15. Ibid, p. 12
16. Price, *National Geographic Magazine*, April 1936
17. Cormack, p. 13
18. Jesse Hoppin to Wynn C. Fairfield - ABCFM, June, 16, 1937
19. Lanwi, July 26-27, 2001
20. Wilson, p. 31
21. Price, *Japan's Islands of Mystery*, p. 220
22. Wilson, p. 33
23. Ibid, p. 35

NUNAK YOHK KE CHAPTER 13
1941-1948

Ke Miss Eleanor Wilson el som liki acn Wot, Miss Suzuki el principalla lun school se inge. Mwet luti sayal pa Frank ac Srue Skilling, Isaac ac Mary Lanwi, Miss Yamada, Pastu Alexander, ac Pastu Caleb.

Mwet Japan elos pakutangiya acn Pearl Harbor, Hawai'i ke December 7, 1941. Ke mwet Kosrae elos lohng ke pweng se inge elos tiana etu lupan ma upa ac mau sikyak nu selos ac nu sin mutunfahl saya. Mwet mweun lun acn Japan mutawauk in elma nu fin acn Kosrae, wi pac mwet sac puspis ma utuku in tuh mwet nimpu lun mwet mweun inge. Mwet Japan elos sulela in oakwuki fin acn Malem, oru ke June 6, 1942 elos sapkin mwet Malem nukewa in mokuiyak ac som muta Inkoeya. Pisen mwet Malem in pacl sac oasr ke 312. Elos arulana asor in sisla acn selos ac ima lalos. Elos tuleya lohm alu selos ac usla musaela Inkoeya. Yohk kasru lal William Mongkeya, Joe Kasrlung, Sam, ac Musrasruk Tinteru ke elos sun acn sasu selos.

Sap soko tuku Jaluit me tuh tulik lutlut Marshall Wot in folokla nu Marshall. Pastu Alexander ac Pastu Caleb eltal welulos som. Miss Suzuki el folokla nu Japan, na Isaac Lanwi el principalla. El ac Mary, Frank ac Srue tuh mutana Wot nwe ke tari mweun ah. Mwet mweun Japan elos som nu Wot ac eisla lohm twek sin missionary ac tuh in iwen mongla lun mwet fulat lalos. Lohm nukewa saya elos tuleya sak, tin ac winto ka ac usla nu Malem. Elos nunku mu Miss Yamada el spy se lun mwet America, oru elos usalla ac kalilya Putuk, na tok elos folokunulla nu Japan.

Moul lun mwet Kosrae in pacl se inge tuh arulana upa. Mukul nukewa ma yac singoulyak nu ke mwet matu enenuna in orekma nu sin mwet Japan. Pisen mwet sac nukewa fin acn Kosrae alukela mwet 6,000, a pisen mwet Kosrae tia sun 2,000. Oasr ma sap orekla ma enenu lah mongo nukewa in utukla nun mwet Japan, pwanang in arulana sufalla mongo nun mwet Kosrae sifacna.

Mwet America elos mutawauk in pakutangi acn Kosrae ke January 18, 1943. Pukanten mwet Japan misa wi mwet Kosrae tolu. Sie bomb ah sonol Evelyn Basi ke el kaing liki lohm sel fin acn Inkoanong, Lelu. Namie, sie sin tulik srisrik luo ma el kafis inpaol, el misa ke kutu wik toko ke sripen yohk kinet kacl. Alfred Kinere el misa pac ke sie bomb ah kunausla oak okoal in lulu Lelu. Ke fong sacna mwet Lelu nukewa elos som liki acn selos in wikla ke ima lalos fin acn wan. Mwet Utwe elos som nu Koasr ac nu fineol ah. Mwet Malem elos som liki acn Inkoeya, ac wikwik Yekurak, Pukusrik ac Mutun Eol. Mwet Tafunsak elos som nu ke acn se pangpang Yopa.

Mwet Japan elos tuh orekmakin lohm alu akosr fin acn Kosrae inge kewa, nu ke lohm in motul lun mwet orekma tuku saya me, oayapa mwe nien kufwen sroasr ac kufwen mweun. Oaksohk America fahsrna ac pakutangi acn uh. Lohm alu nukewa lun mwet Kosrae tuh wi pac musalla. Ke pacl ma mwet Kosrae tia ku in tukeni alu in lohm alu lalos, elos tia sisla in tukeni pre in sou lalos yen elos muta we.

Mwet fulat ke U. S. Navy elos som sramsram yurin missionary su tuh muta Micronesia meet liki mweun ah. Eleanor Wilson, Jane Baldwin, Jessie Hoppin, Alice Little, ac George Garland (captain fin *Morning Star III, IV,* ac *V*) elos tuh akkalemye ma elos etu ke ouiyen molsron ac inyoa Kosrae. Elos fahkak pac inen mwet ma mwet America inge ku in lulalfongi in kasrelos elos fin mau oai Kosrae.

Ke September 6, 1945 oaksohk America sohk sun acn Kosrae in sisi pwepu in akalemye nu sin mwet Japan we lah mweun ah tari, na elos in akoo sie mwe akul in fahkak lah elos ac srasra po nu sin mwet America. Mwet Japan elos akfalyela sap se inge. Ke September 8 oak lukwe lun U. S. Navy oai ke molsron Lelu. Mwet kol nukewa lun un mwet mweun Japan elos naweyukla ac takla tu Sansrik. Tukun elos saini pwepu in oakwuk sasu, flag lun acn America srip-sripyak. Ke mwet mweun America elos osun nu sin mwet Kosrae elos sa na in akilen lah elos mwet Christian. Fin acn Kosrae, oeyepa in acn Micronesia nufon, pus mwet Christian tuh arulana kulang ac sang kasru yok nu selos, oru elos arulana lut.

Pastu Fred Skilling el arulana engan lah el moul liye ke safla mweun uh. El misa ke September 15, 1945. Pastu John Mackwelung el siyuk elan mongla liki orekma in pastu, na oru wangin pastu fin acn Kosrae ke yac luo. Finne ouinge, mwet in church elos mutawauk in sifil musai lohm alu lalos. Mwet Lelu elos musa lohm fahsu na lulap se fin acn Fukil. Mwet Malem elos musai lohm alu lalos Sungankuta. Mwet Utwe musai lohm alu lalos ke acn sasu se, ke acn Inposral. Mwet Tafunsak elos sifil musai lohm alu lalos ke acn se na oan we meet, fin acn Srampal.

Eleanor Wilson pa missionary se oemeet in sun acn Kosrae tukun mweun ah. El tuku in January 1947, ac el akmusraela pastu sasu luo: John Paliknoa Sigrah ac Palik Kefwas. Kais sie mura elos sulela deacon ac deaconess sasu: Isaac Andrew ac Srue Frank, Lelu; Alokoa Tol ac Helmet Jonah, Tafunsak; Tara Tebuke ac Kenye Mira, Malem; Tulen Lorena Tilfas ac Sra Violet Kun Tilfas, Utwe. Tia paht toko Sepe Lupalik Palsis el aolul Helmet in acn Tafunsak. Miss Wilson el akkeye Church Kosrae in supalla Nelson Sigrah ac Isaiah Benjamin in missionary nu sin mwet in acn Puluwat.

Oak sasu soko, *Morning Star VI,* tuh oai Kosrae ke February 1948. Sie mwet fusr Hawai'i, Daniel Akaka, el sie sin selu fac—tok el sie sin senator lun mwet Hawai'i nu ke U. S. Congress.

Pisen mwet Kosrae ke 1948 pa mwet 1,775. American Board elos supwama sie missionary sasu in sifil musai mission school fin acn Wot. Inel pa Dr. Harold Hanlin, ac mutan kial pa Mary Ruth. Tulik tolu natultal pa Alice, John ac Ruth Ann. Sou se inge sun acn Kosrae ke April 1948. Mwet kol lun Church Kosrae tuh sulela mwet kamtu ac kutu mwet orekma saya in akoela acn Wot tuh in ku in sifil oasr lutlut we.

– CHAPTER THIRTEEN –

RAVAGES OF WAR
1941-1948

SITUATION AT WOT

The staff at the Wot school did their best to cope with the departures of the McCalls and Miss Wilson. Ren Suzuki was left in charge, with Isaac Lanwi serving as her assistant. Mary Lanwi, Miss Yamada, Frank and Srue Skilling, and the two Marshallese pastor-teachers, Alexander and Caleb, remained as teachers. Rose Hoppin had departed for Pohnpei with her new husband, Tulensa Mackwelung, the son of Pastor John Mackwelung and Sepe Insopus. The plantation gardens and farm were still producing, and the ships were operating on schedule between Japan and Kosrae, and Kosrae and the Marshall Islands. Morale had been low when the American missionaries left. When it became apparent that the remaining staff was managing fine, morale picked up.

News of the Japanese attack at Pearl Harbor on December 7, 1941, reached Kosrae, but details were sketchy. A baffling question would plague everyone on Kosrae for the next four years, including the Japanese: Which of the many rumors they were hearing were true, and which were not? Students and staff at Wot, along with the entire Kosraean population, were certainly aware that the number of Japanese on Kosrae was increasing rapidly, but for the time being, mission school personnel were left mostly to themselves, and life at the school continued as usual, even after Miss Suzuki was recalled to Japan during the course of the 1942 school year. Shipping schedules were maintained and, during the school break in the middle of that year, Isaac and Mary Lanwi—now with two small sons—made their third visit to Jaluit since their marriage in April 1940 and returned safely to Kosrae.

PEOPLE OF MALEM FORCED TO RELOCATE

Then the realities of World War II began to cause major upheavals in the lives of the Kosraean people. In April, the citizens of Malem were told that they had to leave their homes, gardens, and church to relocate to the north side of the island. They were given until early June to complete their move. Japanese authorities had decided to build their primary military installation along the southeast coast of Kosrae, an area which included the village of Malem.

It was a heartbreaking time, as well as a backbreaking one. Houses that could be dismantled were taken apart and the pieces carried to Inkoeya—the area of Tafunsak to which the village had been assigned. Back and forth the people walked the three miles between Malem and Sansrik, carrying what they could. Occasionally they had the help of some of the Japanese and Korean laborers working in the area, along with the use of several Japanese trucks, if the drivers were so inclined. From Sansrik to Inkoeya they transported their possessions by canoe—first across Lelu Harbor and then through the mangrove channel to Insrefusr and on to Inkoeya.

The Malem villagers were aware that what they left behind would be demolished. They were distressed to be leaving the graves of their loved ones, particularly those who had recently died. Confused and sad, the villagers gathered for a last Sunday in their beloved church, led by chief Paul Ittu and his wife, Srue; Nena Charley and his wife, Sarah; Songrasru Alokoa and his wife, Kenye. The next day the men of Malem took their wood-frame Sunday School building down piece by piece and carried it all to Inkoeya, where it was reassembled as their church. The church bell, too, was carried to Inkoeya and rehung in a makeshift scaffolding beside their temporary church building. By June 6, 1942—the deadline given them—all 312 men, women, and children of Malem had moved.

The first weeks at Inkoeya were profoundly difficult.Though some of the families had been able to erect houses of sorts from materials carried from Malem, there were no gardens they could call their own. They were grateful for the sympathetic assistance and generosity of Inkoeya land-owners—William Mongkeya, Joe Kasrlung, and others—who were not compensated by the Japanese for the conscription of their land for use by the people of Malem. Brothers Sam and Musrasrik Tinteru of neighboring Pukusrik also helped ease the food shortage for the newcomers. In fact, the entire community of Tafunsak—the village least disturbed by the movements of the Japanese military—rallied to assist the Malem refugees.

OTHER DISRUPTIONS

Early in 1943, a radio dispatch from Japanese authorities at Jaluit was delivered to Isaac Lanwi, now leader of the Wot community, with the names of Marshallese students, most of them teenagers, to be returned to the Marshall Islands. They left on the next ship for Jaluit with Pastor Alexander and Pastor Caleb accompanying them.

It now became impossible to maintain class and work routines. Most of the Kosraean girls, and some of the boys, were returned to their families. Japanese workers arrived to dismantle the classroom, chapel, and dormitory buildings, requiring the boys and men who were there to help. All lumber, roofing, and windows were transported to Japanese construction sites in Malem. Thatched structures were left alone, but only the Baldwin house among the foreign-style buildings was left intact. The Japanese chose to keep the house as it was for their own purposes.

As the staff and student body who remained viewed their mangled campus, they shared a collective numbness. Under the leadership of Isaac and Mary Lanwi, however, they regrouped, counted their blessings, and agreed on some plans. They would try not to antagonize the military leaders, who appeared at Wot with increasing frequency, bearing ever-new directives. The staff tried to help as the Japanese relaxed in the mission house, which they had designated as an officers' retreat. It was unpleasant for the people at Wot to see the building where their Bible had been translated, printed, and assembled being used as a kind of clubhouse or bar, but they kept their silence.

As their Japanese masters grew to trust them, those living at Wot were treated reasonably well. One of the Japanese officers seemed drawn in friendship to Isaac and Mary Lanwi, and the young Marshallese couple tried to reciprocate. When Mary gave birth to their third son, the officer gave the baby his name, Makato, meaning "honesty" in Japanese. Indeed, all of the Japanese officers seemed to enjoy their visits to Wot, as Isaac, Mary, and the others did their best to be courteous and to do what was being required of them.

JAPANESE BUILD-UP AND ENTRENCHMENT

Change was coming fast, not only at Wot, but in all parts of Kosrae. Ships deposited so many Japanese soldiers and civilian workers on the island that their numbers soared to more than 6,000. An additional thousand laborers were brought from Pohnpei, Ocean Island, and Kiribati to work on roads, build gun emplacements and concrete bunkers, chop away the jungle, and level the ground for the airstrip being constructed between Malem and Utwe. Inexplicably, Kosraean men were taken away at this same time for road building, hangar construction, and other war-related work on Pohnpei.

Both Pohnpei and Kosrae were strategically valuable to the Japanese. Each of the islands had "several reasonably good anchorages, but more important, their rugged interiors offered excellent defensive possibilities, particularly in the positioning of coast defense artillery."[1] Consequently, many caves and a labyrinth of tunnels were dug in Lelu's hill—newly named "Mt. Boro"—as well as in Kosrae's southeast mountains. Across the harbor from Lelu Island, large camps for foreign workers were built at Tafweyat and Tofol.

Japanese authorities, increasingly tense over events of the war and paranoid about the possibility of allied spies on Kosrae, decided that Miss Yamada should leave Wot. They were irritated by what they considered to be her American ways and suspicious of her use of English. She was arrested and taken to Lelu, and for some weeks was jailed at Putuk in a makeshift cell not far from those occupied by the American planter, Arthur Herman, and his nephew, Jack Youngstrom. Late in the year Miss Yamada was returned to Japan. [Fifteen years later, while attending the Pan Pacific and Southeast Asian Women's Conference in Tokyo, Mary Lanwi and Rose Mackwelung were reunited with Miss Yamada. They found their Japanese colleague in financial need and gave her the money they had with them, plus some of their clothing. They also located and visited with Miss Suzuki, who was comfortably situated.]

At Miss Yamada's request, Isaac Lanwi and Frank Skilling had hidden her personal possessions in a hole they dug at Wot, but later it was discovered by Japanese officers who confiscated everything in it. At this same time, soldiers smashed the large foot-operated press that had served Kosrae so well over the previous 20 years, and scattered the tiny pieces of type across the jungle floor. No American propaganda would be produced there!

Arthur Herman and Jack Youngstrom remained imprisoned. While there was still food available, the Japanese assigned Palikkun Web to feed the two men. Palikkun was severely beaten one day when a breadfruit he dropped from a tree hit the metal roof of the house of a Japanese officer who mistook it for a bomb! Later in the war, when food was very difficult to find, the two Americans nearly starved. It was against the law for family members or friends to feed prisoners, but people risked their lives to slip them something to eat. Japanese guards chopped several fingers off the right hand of Tom Tilfas, one of these friends, who was discovered giving prisoners food.

U. S. BOMBS KOSRAE

On January 18, 1944, as those at the mission school were organizing a meager celebration to honor Frank Skilling on his 54th birthday, the first American bombing raid on Kosrae took place. Wot was not bombed, but for those in other areas of the island—particularly in Lelu—the experiences of that day were horrifying.

Running from her home at Inkoanong, Lelu, with both a 2-year-old child and an infant in her arms, Evelyn Basi was killed on her front steps. The child, Maruko, survived. Tiny Namie lived for some weeks, but eventually succumbed to her wounds. Alfred Kinere—crossing Lelu Harbor in a canoe with several others—died when a bomb hit and sank a nearby Japanese ship. Only these three deaths among the Kosraeans were directly attributed to American bombs. There are no records of the many Japanese casualties.

The air strikes by American planes continued on January 20, 22, and 24.[2] Even Wot did not escape these later raids. During one of them the Baldwin mission house and the typhoon house next door, home to the Lanwi family, were strafed. Amazingly, no one was injured. [Two Japanese ships were sunk in Lelu Harbor, and a small freighter, the *Sunsang Maru*, was run aground at Pisin where it stays as a reminder of the war.]

In the villages, reaction to the bombing was swift. Immediately after the airplanes had disappeared in the eastern sky on the 18th, there was a mass exodus from Lelu Island. The people paddled, swam, and walked away from their homes to hide themselves and their children in the foliage on their farmlands across the harbor. They made temporary shelters for themselves at Fomseng, Lukaf, Limes, Finpal, Sitkaf, and Putuk. In Utwe, those still living at Melok on the west side of Utwe Harbor quickly joined their fellow villagers ensconced at Koasr, where their dismantled church had already been reconstructed. Others climbed into mountain areas at Isra, Selmeoa, Yemulil, and Saolung. The people of Malem left their temporary homes in Inkoeya, scrambling up to hide at Yekurak, Pukusrik, and Mutun Eol. Tafunsak residents, too, retreated to the mountains above their village—most of them clustering in the area of Yopa.

MISERIES OF WAR INTENSIFY

For the next 19 months the people of Kosrae lived in their mountain hideouts. The more fortunate among them erected tiny sleeping shacks from pieces of lumber they managed to carry with them. Others made lean-tos of palm leaves and tree branches, or found caves in which to huddle. The women did what they could to feed their children as surreptitiously as possible, since the Japanese military was demanding all food caught, raised, found, or picked. All able-bodied Kosraean men, including older boys, were forced to work for the Japanese. The men left their families each day to work as the authorities demanded—fishing, gathering land crabs, gardening, preparing coconut oil, building, making charcoal or salt, cutting mangrove logs—whatever they were told to do. A number of teenage and young adult males worked as waiters, kitchen help, and dormitory stewards in the Japanese military camp and headquarters in Malem.

As the months went by, food became increasingly scarce. Due to the efficiency of U. S. submarines, supply ships were no longer reaching Kosrae. As in other areas of the island, Wot's supply of rice and flour dwindled and disappeared. The school's cattle, pigs, and chickens had been taken away months before to feed the soldiers. Coconuts and garden produce had to be turned over as soon as they were ready or ripe. It became a kind of grim game for those at Wot, trying to hide from the ever-suspicious and nosy Japanese authorities a portion of the food they were producing in order to feed themselves.

PRAYER BECOMES THE MAINSTAY

Kosraean families continued the custom of morning and evening Bible reading and prayer, sometimes joining with nearby families. The Malem villagers constructed a thatch-roofed open pavilion to use as a church in the mountains at Yekurak. Some of the Lelu people worshiped in a small church erected at the Fomseng home of George Kanku and others gathered in a little church at the Putuk home of Likiak Mike.

There were no group activities of Kosrae's congregations during these months. The Japanese requirement that they bow to the Emperor at the beginning of any public gathering was considered a grievous insult that the Kosraeans refused to observe.[3] Prayer meetings were frequent—the celebration of the Lord's Supper infrequent. Contributions were nonexistent, as there was neither money nor produce, but there was daily thanksgiving for God's protection and care. As the son of an American father, Pastor Fred Skilling was forced to keep himself in hiding during the height of the war. Baptisms and weddings were postponed. Funerals were handled by local church elders. Japanese military leaders were aware of some church services. At times, they permitted them—at other times they would disrupt a service, demanding that it be discontinued. Sometimes they purposely desecrated a worship area by smoking or having loud and lewd conversations there.

The four stone village churches had been taken from the worshipers early in the war because—as the finest and largest buildings on Kosrae—they were quickly put to use as offices, dormitories, warehouses, or arsenals. The churches were destroyed in American air raids because it was known that they were being used by the enemy. There was great sadness among the Kosraeans—first, because of the ways their cherished houses of worship were being used, and later when they were destroyed—but they were sustained by a deep and vital faith that was not dependent on buildings.

QUEEN HATTIE'S MIRACLE STORY

One of the stories from these war years that has found its way into Kosraean folklore concerns the people's experience with the severe famine caused by the unavailability of food. Queen Hattie began leading the women living near her in nightly fishing expeditions. Village women traditionally fished together whenever the tide was right, night or day. Women fishing in groups was not unusual. But now it was different as they had to be very careful that they were not observed by the Japanese. The queen would gather the women and girls on the beach, and in the darkness, they shared a period of prayer. Then, filing into the lagoon, they dipped their nets under the surface.

In the shallow waters, there appeared a multitude of strange little black fish. Easy to catch, they were a new species that the Kosraeans had never seen before. Nets were re-woven with smaller mesh in order to hold the bite-sized fish. Back in their humble houses, huts and caves, the mothers would feed their hungry children—and then, a few nights later, repeat the process. Following the war this type of fish was never seen again. Did the bombs disturb some ancient feeding ground? Had ocean currents altered to drive a new species of fish into the waters of Kosrae's lagoon?

"We were fed by the hand of God," was Queen Hattie's explanation. "It was manna" [Ex. 16:35].[4]

CONTEMPLATED ATROCITIES

In mid-1945, because of the acute lack of food (more than 300 of the Japanese garrison had died of malnutrition, disease, or outright starvation[5]), some desperate Japanese officers decided on a gruesome course of action. The Kosraeans would be exterminated—machine-gunned and buried in tunnels that the men of Lelu had been forced to dig in the mountains above their Fomseng houses. When the digging was complete, there were actually drills enacted to see how fast the men could get their families up into the tunnels, leading the villagers to believe that they had made bomb shelters. There were similar diabolical plans for the people of Utwe, Malem, and Tafunsak.

In another scenario, Lelu residents were told to assemble for canoe races in the mangrove channel facing Yalup, Finpal, and Putuk. After they had gathered, machine guns hidden in the underbrush were to be fired on them. But friends of Kosraeans among the Japanese soldiers in Lelu learned of the intent of their superiors, put on their uniforms, and mixed themselves among the people, thwarting what otherwise would have been another of the unthinkable tragedies of that war. Before the perpetrators could regroup and proceed with their evil intentions, the end of fighting was announced.

Other island communities in Micronesia faced similar plans at the hands of the Japanese military, and on at least one, the evil scheme was carried out. On Ocean Island [Banaba] all but one of the 200 people remaining there were slaughtered.[6] On Jaluit, 74-year-old Carl Heine was beheaded by the Japanese. Before the war he had told Eleanor Wilson that he wore a goatee because he wanted to look like Uncle Sam! He paid with his life for his love of all things American.[7] His son, Claude Heine, and Claude's wife, Grace—the parents of Katherine Hilton and Mary Lanwi—were also assassinated by the Japanese because of their ties—both real and imagined—with the United States.[8]

THE WAR ENDS

At Wot, Carl Heine's granddaughter, Mary Lanwi, was startled to see the Japanese officer most familiar to them come running up the Yonrak ridge. They understood him to be the third-ranking military officer on Kosrae. Now, as on many previous occasions, he was looking for Mary's husband, Isaac, the leader of the Wot community. Mary feared that his arrival meant yet another harsh requirement. Isaac, who spoke fluent Japanese, took the officer into the typhoon house where he broke into tears as he reported to Isaac America's victory over Japan. In friendship, Isaac cried with him.[9]

The months and years of living in constant fear, unremitting hardship, and enforced servitude came to an end for the Kosraean people. In their isolation, the end seemed to come so suddenly that it took some time to process the truth. On September 6, 1945, American planes dropped leaflets on the unused Kosrae airfield, instructing the Japanese to surrender, and to indicate peaceable capitulation by placing a white sheet marked with a red cross on the field. The next day it was there.[10]

Two American Navy destroyers steamed into Lelu Harbor on September 8—the USS *Hyman* and the USS *Soley*. The Japanese Command was waiting —in uniform and at attention—at Sansrik. What happened was described by a war correspondent who filed his report through U. S. Pacific Fleet Advance Headquarters in Guam:

Kusaie Island in the Carolines, September 8th, 1945—The American flag finally was raised over this Pacific island today, fulfilling a 47-year-old petition addressed to Congress begging the United States to annex it. Commodore Ben H. Wyatt, USN, San Jose, California, Commander of the Kwajalein Naval Air Base, received the surrender of Japanese Lieutenant General Yoshikazu Harada aboard the destroyer USS Hyman a few hours before the flag raising. Commodore Wyatt was acting for Rear Admiral J. K. Harrill, USN, Commander Marshall & Gilbert area.

Raising the flag and American occupation of this island brought tears of happiness to the Kusaiens who could get down from the hills in time for the ceremony. Years of activity by Congregationalist missionaries had fostered a love for the United States that caused them to petition during the Spanish-American War to come under the American Flag.

An honor guard from the two destroyers present, the Hyman *and* Soley, *took part in the ceremony.*[11]

U.S. NAVY'S SECRET LIST OF PARTISANS

A part of the Japanese Empire for more than two decades before the war, Micronesia had been out of bounds to foreign travelers. The movements of the few who had gotten in were highly curtailed. As a result, strategic planners in the American military had not known what to expect when U. S. Armed Forces arrived in these islands. There had been heavy fighting with great loss of life at Tarawa in the Gilbert Islands and at Kwajalein in the Marshall Islands as American troops pushed the Japanese westward. What could the Americans anticipate when they landed on Kosrae? Military surveillance proved that the enemy was deeply entrenched on the island. Would there be those among the Kosraeans they could actually trust who might come forward to help them?

A restricted 1944 U.S. Navy publication, "Civil Affairs Handbook on the East Caroline Islands"—covering such topics as geography, history, customs, the Japanese government, health, education, communications, and economics—also included succinct profiles of 16 individuals on Kosrae. Much of the information was gathered by Naval Intelligence from missionary Eleanor Wilson.

The U.S. Navy sought additional information from other missionaries who had worked at Kosrae. Jessie Hoppin who, after 49 years in Micronesia was living in Ashland, Wisconsin, and Alice Little, who had taught at Wot from 1885 to 1892 and was now living in Oberlin, Ohio, both shared details concerning the culture of Kosrae. George Garland, who had been captain of several of the *Morning Star* missionary vessels in the 1890s and early 1900s, was also living in Oberlin and was able to discuss specific problems of navigation among the coral reefs of Chuuk, Pohnpei, Kosrae, and the Marshall Islands with personnel from military intelligence.[12] From her home in Orange, New Jersey, and in her 80th year, Jane Baldwin sketched a chart of the Chuuk lagoon for the U. S. Navy![13]

During the war, Adm. Chester W. Nimitz had written, "We have seen the enduring evidence of the *Morning Star* missionaries. They have planted a seed of faith which the cruel strain of enemy conquest could not wither. We are proud to follow their trails, only sorry that we cannot do so with their weapons."[14]

AMERICAN SERVICEMEN DISCOVER CHRISTIAN FRIENDS

As it turned out, the Americans took Kosrae without a fight. The surrender was peaceful, and subsequent weeks were quiet as, under the direction of the U.S. Navy, the Japanese prepared to leave the island. Tidings of the Japanese surrender and American victory were posted on Japanese-built bulletin boards around the island, in both Kosraean and English. Though still having difficulty believing that the war was actually over, more and more Kosraeans summoned the courage to come out of hiding. Tentatively, they smiled their welcome to the Americans they met.

One of these youthful Americans included his impressions in a letter to his family:

The work of the missionaries was outstanding and is evident wherever we go. In the first place, the Kusaien people are reputedly 100% literate. They cannot all speak English, but they all read and write their own language, thanks to the missionaries. The latter may have introduced Christianity and clothes, and have banned liquor and smoking, but they did not attempt to make the Kusaiens over into Americans. Rather did they strive to help the Kusaiens become better Kusaiens. They brought a printing press which they let the Kusaiens use to print their own books for teaching in their own schools. As a result of the mission teachings, the natives hold regular prayer meetings and church services on Sunday, which is a day of rest. Their standards of behavior are remarkably pleasing—they are courteous, honest and extremely thoughtful.[15]

Henry P. Van Dusen of New York's Union Theological Seminary wrote of the similar experiences and impressions of hundreds of American service men who found themselves in Micronesia and other parts of the Pacific during and immediately following the war. To the surprise and delight of these young Americans so far from home, they were welcomed in these islands by Christian brothers and sisters. Appropriately, Dr. Van Dusen gave his book the title, *They Found the Church There.*

Writing of this same phenomenon in the *National Geographic*, Robert Moore remarked on the many Micronesians who spoke English and mingled freely with the American G.I.s. Always, when questioned as to where they had learned English, the islanders would give the same answer: they had learned English in mission schools. A heavy-print caption in Mr. Moore's article reads: "Missionaries made friends for America"—and in the article, he tells something of the history and accomplishments of the missionary movement in the Marshall Islands.

The Japanese knew that unless they could stop the movement, they could never lead the natives to their side, and so they sent many islanders to advanced Japanese schools on Jaluit, Pohnpei, and even in Japan. However, the Marshallese gained most of their training through native evangelists and teachers who had attended the mission schools on Kusaie, in the Caroline Islands. In the villages now you will see these preachers and instructors still at work and in the meeting-houses. Those who know English have also started conducting elementary classes in the language. Old and young attend. All want to learn to talk with the Americans.[16]

Perhaps the ultimate compliment and most succinct observation came from Admiral Nimitz himself, who, after touring the area immediately following the Japanese surrender, commented, "I cannot get away from the idea that if mankind were foolish enough to have another war and wipe out western civilization…it might be that right in these islands would be found the roots of a new civilization that will be better than what we have been able to build up to now."[17]

KOSRAEANS WELCOME MEMBERS OF THE U.S. COAST GUARD

Two days after the Japanese surrendered aboard the *USS Hyman* in Lelu Harbor, with the *USS Soley* standing by, a third American ship arrived at Kosrae: The *USS Ricketts* of the United States Coast Guard. Orders for the officers and crew of the *USS Ricketts*, U. H. Leach, Jr., Commanding Officer, were to "participate in the occupation and government of Kusaie Island, Caroline Islands, from 10 September, 1945 to 13 October 1945, and in the transportation of Ponapean natives on Kusaie back to Ponape and Kusaien natives on Ponape back to Kusaie."[18]

Sailors from the *Soley* and the *Ricketts*—the *Hyman* had embarked for Pohnpei the same day the surrender was signed—were given strict rules of conduct by their commanding officers for their times ashore, whether on duty or for recreation. Memories of both the Kosraeans and the American servicemen confirm that contacts with the Kosraean people were appreciated and enjoyed.

One sailor noted, "Everywhere we went the Kusaiens gathered, happy and smiling, and bowing in gratitude, offering us food and homemade baskets or other symbols of Kusaien appreciation. Because bowing was a trait they had been forced to acquire by the Japanese, one of us suggested they forget that and either shake hands, wave, or tip their oddly shaped straw hats. This they took up quickly. Soon, wherever we walked, the Kusaiens were tipping their hats to us in greeting!"[19]

A FLAG RAISING

On September 15, two officers—lieutenants Bushman and Woodhouse—and several crew members from the *USS Ricketts* were transported by canoe to the Malem village at Inkoeya, where the two men officiated at an American flag-raising ceremony. Prior to the ceremony, however, the Americans were hosted by Chief Paul and his wife, Srue, to a surprisingly elaborate feast, considering their impoverishment.

Lt. Woodhouse later explained to his fellow officer, Lt. Olds, what happened next: "After dinner at the Malem village, the American flag raising ceremony took place…the Spanish, the Germans, the Japanese and now the Americans. The ceremony was not noisy or gaudy as with bands playing and flags waving. Rather different from the neat alignment of military ranks, the nondescript group of approximately 400 young and old people in every type of costume, made up in sentiment what they lacked in appearance. These folks did not remember the whalers; they did remember their real friends, the missionaries from the United States. Perhaps they would soon return. And then as the flag reached the top of its papaya mast, a small group of Kusaiens started to sing—in English—'My Country 'Tis of Thee.' No one spoke, no one stirred, until the first and last verses were completed. Then many smiles and many cheers. Better days were here again!"[20]

DEATH OF PASTOR FRED SKILLING

On the way back to Lelu their hosts stopped with them at the funeral of Pastor Fred Skilling. Lt. Woodhouse described the occasion:

Fred Skilling was dead at 71. This man had eleven children and, counting his great grandchildren, his heirs numbered over one hundred. The Kusaiens have a funeral service similar to the Irish "wake." Large quantities of food, consisting of coconuts, baked breadfruit, bananas, roast pig, papayas, smoked fish and other island delicacies, were piled outside the deceased's home. There were at least two hundred people present, all in mourning, for Mr. Skilling had been the preacher for the whole island. Many women were gathered in his home alongside the coffin which was beautiful in a primitive sort of way. It was a plain wooden box covered with sheets to which ferns had been sewn; he was laid out in white with ferns sewn to his garments.

Pastor Skilling had lived to see his dreams come true with the American occupation of his island. The day the Japanese surrendered, they say he arose from his bed to witness the jubilant celebration—and was able to stand throughout the entire affair. Then he went to bed and never rose again. He died happy that the Japanese had lost and the Americans were in control of the island.

Now the people paid their respects to their spiritual leader by entering the low doorway of his home on hands and knees. The coffin was just inside and as the entire group of mourners had to crawl in they were already in a kneeling position when they drew alongside the body. Finally, after each person had paid respects, the coffin

was raised and Pastor Skilling began his last trip, up the muddy trail to the grave.
Pastor Mackwelung, the deceased's assistant, said the last words; then three hymns
were sung by all present. During the singing several women broke down completely.
They were allowed to have the last view of the remains.

After the coffin had been lowered into the grave, matting and rocks were piled
upon it, and finally with the coming of dusk, a small wooden cross was placed on
top. Then came the feast back at the Pastor's family home. But we were due to return
to the ship. Bidding farewell to host and hostess, the canoes quietly slipped through
the water until the bow-wake made more sound than the voices back at the Pastor's
compound.[21]

Ill for some months before the end of the war, Pastor Fred Skilling had been
house-bound in his family home at Finpal. He had served conscientiously as
pastor of the Church on Kosrae for 24 years.

REBUILDING HOMES AND CHURCHES

By September 20 all Japanese personnel, plus a Japanese military hospital, had been moved from Lelu. Following that date, citizens of Lelu began to
rebuild their village. A clinic for Kosraean men, women and children was set
up by the Americans in the only house left standing on Lelu Island—the Aliksa
Kanku house at Katem.

Citizens of Utwe voted to rebuild their village—not at its prewar location
on the west side of their harbor, but at Utwe Taf, with its convenient land connection to the rest of the large island.

It was early October, after the Japanese had completed U.S. requirements
for stripping weapons, dumping ammunition, and stacking all equipment by
the Sansrik docks, that a Malem contingent was allowed to investigate their old
village site and make preparations for the return of their people from Inkoeya.
Quite a few Japanese buildings remained in the area, which now became the
property of the returning landowners. Their temporary church was once again
dismantled and moved back to Malem. The church bell was also returned, but it
had cracked and was later replaced. The bones of some who had died at Inkoeya
and Yekurak were tenderly carried by family members to be re-interred in
Malem, while others were left where they had been buried. Japanese hardware,
tools, and kitchen utensils were scattered everywhere. Malem families spent days
gathering knives, dishes, pieces of furniture and other items for their own use.
Another benefit for Malem villagers returning to their land, proved, ironically, to
be the gardens the Japanese had planted. As the war ended, these gardens were
not yet producing, but by the time the people of Malem returned to their home
area there were acres of tapioca, bananas, and potatoes ready to gather.[22]

Slowly—very slowly at first—the Kosraeans rebuilt their villages. But as the reality of their freedom took hold, the most difficult of tasks seemed light. Former gardens were eagerly reclaimed. Fishing expeditions were fun, and the catch was their own. Best of all, Sundays were as they had been before the war. Almost everyone gathered for public, shared worship on the first day of each week—albeit in buildings humbler than those appropriated by the Japanese—and the singing soared!

Erecting these temporary church buildings was the first community effort in each of the villages. Though getting individual homes restored was frequently disheartening and took time, the work of preparing places of worship was swiftly completed. Almost immediately Malem villagers were meeting in their reassembled frame church building, which they decided to place across the Malem River at Sungankuta instead of at the old Mutunpal site.

After demolishing what was left of their original church at Srampal, members of the Tafunsak congregation erected their building on that same site. The people of the Utwe congregation built their first post-war church building at Inposral in the heart of their new village at Utwe Taf. The citizens of Lelu raised their new church building at Fukil. True, the roof was thatch and the floor was sand, but they were thrilled to be worshiping openly, together again as a congregation in their own village. It would take awhile to build a permanent church structure at the former Langosak location. Just removing the rubble of their bomb-destroyed pre-war church would take considerable effort and time.

While each village church was being rebuilt—at least temporarily—the mission school campus at Wot was left as it was with a small staff of caretakers. Isaac and Mary Lanwi with their three little boys, Nijima, Kojima, and Makato, plus a number of other Marshallese who had been stranded on Kosrae during the war years, were returned by U.S. military ship to Kwajalein, and from there on other ships to their various home atolls.

PROGRESS AS WELL AS DISCOURAGEMENTS

One development marred the otherwise encouraging revival of church life. For personal reasons, Pastor John Mackwelung felt it necessary to remove himself from active status, so by the beginning of 1946 the Church on Kosrae was without pastoral leadership. As missionaries had always been involved with the ordination of pastors on Kosrae, church leaders did not feel that, on their own, they could choose and ordain someone as pastor. Yet the fervor and devotion of the membership continued strong, and King John Paliknoa Sigrah—already recognized as head deacon—was its undisputed leader.

Christians of all four villages began again to gather in Lelu the first day of each month for their new-month service of confession. Sunday morning worship services and Sunday afternoon Christian Endeavor meetings were also frequently shared during this period, with people coming together on foot and by canoe from all areas of the island—many arriving in Lelu village on Saturday and returning home Monday.

The year 1946 was one of mixed emotions. The end of the war brought with it euphoria that pervaded all of Kosrae. Food was still scarce, but people were exultant to be free of their oppressors. Churches were open and again the center of community life. The absence of an active ordained pastor, however, had a hobbling effect, and many within the membership were reluctant to move too quickly. That Deacon John Sigrah did not hesitate to make certain decisions was alarming to a few, and there was some discord. "When will our missionary friends come back to assist in our recovery?" the people asked.

SEARCH FOR MISSIONARIES

The missionaries were closer to returning than the Kosraeans realized. As officials of the U.S. Navy, which was now administering the islands under the direction of Rear Adm. Carleton H. Wright, traveled across Micronesia trying to assess needs and prioritize relief efforts, they were told repeatedly—on island after island, in village after village—that what the people wanted was to have their missionaries back. In the face of so much war-induced devastation, this seemed a startling request to Navy personnel.

To their credit, the Navy Administration heard and acted. While helping to restore property; improve health, sanitation, and agriculture; and establish civil government, medical facilities, and schools, emissaries were sent to those Catholic and Protestant mission agencies which had been established in the area prior to the war. Executives of the American Board of Commissioners for Foreign Missions in Boston, Massachusetts, were contacted and urged by the Navy to send their missionaries back to Micronesia. The International Missionary Council joined to entreat the American Board to resume its historic work.

The American Board needed no prodding. Plans had already been made to continue and further mission endeavors among the islanders of Micronesia, once again in cooperation with the Hawaiian Evangelical Association, as in the first 50 years of the Micronesia Mission.

The only missionary who had worked in the islands prior to the war and was still physically able to return was Eleanor Wilson, now 55 years old. The Board, grateful for her willingness to go back to Micronesia, assisted in getting her ready. By the end of 1945 she was in Hawai'i awaiting her military orders—papers granting her permission from the U.S. Navy to enter their restricted area—and transportation to her new assignment in the Marshall Islands. While in Honolulu she was ordained a pastor by the Hawaiian Evangelical Association in renowned Kawaiaha'o Church.

The Rev. Harold Hackett of the American Board went to Micronesia to survey the situation. On Kwajalein he met Navy chaplain, the Rev. Dr. Harold F. Hanlin, who had been assigned to the Naval Air Station there in November 1945. Mr. Hackett asked Lt. Hanlin if he would be interested in returning to Micronesia as a missionary after he had been released from Navy duty.

Harold Hanlin was intrigued and inspired by the Marshallese Christians. During his year as Kwajalein's chaplain, he helped distribute editions of newly reprinted Marshallese-language Bibles and hymnals, which had come from the mission board through Navy supply channels. He visited a number of their villages and worshiped in their churches, not only in Kwajalein Atoll, but at Majuro and Enewetak. He witnessed the stirring welcome that the Marshallese had given to the Rev. Eleanor Wilson when she finally arrived from Hawai'i in August, 1946, and was able to assist her as she began her work. Chaplain Hanlin told Mr. Hackett that he was definitely interested in the American Board's invitation, but would have to discuss such a major decision with his wife before making a commitment.

During a family leave in Indianapolis, Dr. Hanlin, age 41, and his wife, Mary Ruth Martin Hanlin, age 38, decided to accept the Board's proposal to become career missionaries in Micronesia. Once separated from the Navy, he and his family began to prepare for their departure from the United States. [An ordained minister, Harold Hanlin had earned his Th.D. as a young man and was thus "Dr. Hanlin" to his students of Greek at Butler University, where he was teaching before World War II took him into the Navy chaplaincy. Subsequently, he was "Dr. Hanlin" to his colleagues as well as to the islanders throughout his years in Micronesia.]

ELEANOR WILSON RETURNS TO KOSRAE

Miss Wilson reached Kosrae in January 1947—the first visit to that island of a mission representative since the end of the war 16 months earlier. Having heard that she would be coming, King John assigned men from each of the four villages to build one quarter of a house for her at Pisin to replace the one destroyed in the war. Each wall was carried to Pisin from a different village, complete with openings for windows and doors. The pieces were lashed together so perfectly that Miss Wilson, delighted and grateful, stated that no one would have guessed how the house had been constructed.

Miss Wilson was pleased to renew her friendship with King John and Queen

Hattie. She held both of them in the highest esteem, considering them giants of the Faith, and her opinion was justified. Always referred to by the Kosraeans as "Kasra" [Queen], Hattie Sigrah was a respected midwife. Once, when called upon to deliver a child that was a breech presentation, she explained her method to Eleanor. "First I prayed to the Lord, and then I washed my hands in Listerine."[23]

Of the king, Miss Wilson observed, "He was a magnificent man of great warmth of heart, strength of mind, and that mysterious force which the Polynesians call 'mana.' He had some source of inward strength that nothing external could alter. Even the Japanese conquerors became aware of this quality in the Kusaien king."[24]

GETTING EVEN

A poignant conversation Eleanor Wilson had with the king was later recorded in a book celebrating her life as a missionary and the lives of those with whom she worked.

"I heard that a Japanese official treated you very harshly during the war," Eleanor said regretfully.

King John nodded gravely. "Yes, he did," he admitted, but then added brightly, "But I got even with him!"

Eleanor was astonished to hear the King say this for she had thought the saintly old man incapable of malice or of a desire for revenge. "What did you do?" she asked curiously.

King John smiled. "When he was hungry, I sent him food!" [Romans 12:20]

She might have known! King John was a doer as well as a hearer of the word! And it had worked, as the good man never doubted it would. The astonished Japanese officer had come to him and asked humbly about the religion the King practiced.[25]

THE KOSRAE ISLAND COUNCIL

Under the new American Trusteeship, the Kosraeans elected an island council, which greatly pleased the aging king. The council functioned as a local legislative and advisory body and also in an advisory capacity to the Pohnpei District Administrator.

The Kosrae Island Council was composed of the four village magistrates and secretaries, each of whom was elected to office for two years by popular vote. In addition, a chief magistrate of the entire island and an all-island secretary were elected for terms of two years. The council considered problems of an island-wide nature and acted as liaison between the inhabitants and the district administrator's representative when he accompanied field-trip parties to the island.[26] [For administrative purposes, Kosrae was considered a part of the Pohnpei District.]

One of the first and most difficult problems these village councils had to address concerned the allocations of land as handled by the Japanese adminis- tration. American officials of the Trust Territory found it next to impossible to make sense of local land tenure, with Kosraean landowners disputing practi- cally every acre that had been appropriated by the Japanese in the days when the verdict of the Japanese land surveyor had been supreme.[27]

TWO NEW PASTORS ORDAINED

During new-month service on the first day of April 1947, Eleanor Wilson— with the endorsement of the Kosraean Church leadership—ordained King John Paliknoa Sigrah as a pastor. Since he was already 71 years old, she ordained at the same time a younger man to serve beside him. Thirty-year-old Palik Kefwas was the adopted son and protegé of Deacon Alik Kefwas, the revered Bible teacher, who was now in his 90s. Miss Wilson had known Palik well as a conscientious student at the mission training school during his teens. Now a respected Bible teacher in his own right, Palik was the obvious and welcome choice to stand and serve beside John. The two became the seventh and eighth pastors in the 95-year history of the Church on Kosrae.

It is a mark of the genuine humility of the older man and of the dedication and confidence of the other—whose wife, Sarah, was the king's granddaugh- ter—that any feelings of intimidation the younger man might have felt were overcome as the two pledged before the congregation to work together. Palik Kefwas had established Bible classes in each of the villages, where young par- ents sought and appreciated his counsel. It was expected that some of Pastor Palik's responsibility would be with a rejuvenated Christian training school at Wot—he was already the confidant of many of Kosrae's young people. Pastor John would continue to advise and teach the Church's laymen, as he had already been doing as senior deacon. There was a spirit of exuberance and high expecta- tion among all who were present in Lelu's church at Fukil that day, as the two men were consecrated as the first post-war pastors. And none was more grateful than John Sigrah himself, who had often said that he would rather be pastor than king. Though his people continued to refer to him as Tokosra, it saddened him. "Do not call me Tokosra," he would say gently, "for I am no longer king. You must not forget that now we are a democracy, and I am something much better than a king. I am a pastor!"[28]

NEW DEACONS AND DEACONESSES CONSECRATED

As part of the new day dawning for the Kosraean Church, Eleanor Wilson assisted in choosing a deacon and deaconess for each of the four village congregations. From the very beginning of the Church on Kosrae, the pastors and deacons—and much later, the deaconesses—were considered to represent and serve the entire island. Though these persons were often from Lelu, technically they functioned for the whole Church. After all, went the reasoning, there was really only one Kosraean Church, though it did have four meeting places. New-month services of confession were always held in Lelu, however, as were the services and celebrations on Christmas, Easter, and other special days. But in many ways each of the four congregations was unique, and during her 1947 visit, Miss Wilson helped Church leaders see that having a deacon and deaconess from and for each of the villages was logical and would be of great benefit to each of these congregations. The appropriate persons were selected and consecrated: For Lelu, Deacon Isaac Andrew and Deaconess Srue Frank Skilling; for Tafunsak, Deacon Alokoa Tol and Deaconess Helmet Jonah, later replaced by Deaconess Sepe Lupalik Palsis; for Malem, Deacon Tara Tebuke and Deaconess Kenye Mira; and for Utwe, Deacon Tulen Lorena Tilfas and Deaconess Sra Violet Kun Tilfas.

Following Miss Wilson's suggestion, the new deacons and deaconesses were chosen to serve for a period of two years. This term limit did not fit traditional patterns, and the assumption soon became prevalent that men and women designated by the Church to be deacons and deaconesses, would hold those positions for the rest of their lives, or until debilities required them to step down.

KOSRAEAN MISSIONARIES SENT TO PULUWAT

In this 1947 period of revitalization for the Church on Kosrae, there was another piece of business that Eleanor Wilson and the leadership cooperated in accomplishing. Actually, what they did was an amazing illustration of the resurrected vibrancy of the Kosraean Church, which had been quiet during the challenging war years, but hardly lifeless. Nelson Sigrah—one of King John's sons and a graduate of the mission school at Wot—was commissioned by leaders of the Church on Kosrae to represent them as a missionary to the Puluwat Islands, two atolls located between Chuuk and Yap, a thousand miles west of Kosrae. A man who had been struggling to find an appropriate place to serve, Nelson was delighted with the challenge. A widower, he was accompanied by his teenage son, Alokoa.

The following year, the Church sent Isaiah Benjamin to join Nelson in the

Kosraean mission effort in the Puluwats. Isaiah was accompanied by his wife, Notwe—a daughter of John Mackwelung—and their 12-year-old son, Gordon. Isaiah and Notwe were also graduates of the Mission Training School at Wot. They remained in Puluwat teaching and preaching for two years.

HANLIN FAMILY TRAVELS TO MICRONESIA

The Hanlins spent a month in Honolulu awaiting transportation to Micronesia. While there, they were commissioned in the Makiki Christian Church of Honolulu. The service made a lasting impression on 14-year-old Alice who, with her brother, age 12, and sister, age 8, was called forward to stand with her parents—all of them thus commissioned together as missionaries to Micronesia.

After long voyages aboard a Navy troop transport from Hawai'i, and a blunt-nosed landing craft from Guam, the Hanlins arrived at Chuuk just before Christmas 1947. They were welcomed by Anna Dederer, formerly of the German Liebenzell Mission, now assigned to the Girls' Training School at Kutchua, Dublon—the same school that the Baldwin sisters had served from 1898 to 1910. She was a cheerful woman with a self-deprecating sense of humor. Also there to welcome the Hanlins were Dr. Clarence Gillette, on temporary loan to the Micronesia Mission from the American Board's work in Japan, and veteran missionary Miss Eleanor Wilson.

Due to an epidemic of sleeping sickness in Pohnpei, the Navy detained Mrs. Hanlin and her children at Chuuk, although Dr. Hanlin and Miss Wilson were given permission to travel to Kosrae via Pohnpei in January 1948 aboard a Navy vessel. During their additional three and a half months at Chuuk, Mrs. Hanlin, Alice, John, and Ruth Ann remained as guests at the Girls' School, where they were able to observe and participate in the day-to-day activities of that busy mission. They were especially pleased when Nelson Sigrah visited from his post in nearby Puluwat. It was exciting to meet a Kosraean and begin elementary language lessons with him.

CENSUS OF 1948

In the 1948 census, 1,775 Kosraeans were counted—a sizeable increase over the 1,267 counted in the 1937 census.

MORNING STAR VI ARRIVES

When Eleanor Wilson and Harold Hanlin reached Kosrae on February 4, they were enthusiastically greeted by Pastor John Sigrah, Pastor Palik Kefwas, other church leaders, and many of the members. A house had been built for the Hanlins at Pisin, next door to Miss Wilson's. As Dr. Hanlin walked into his new home he found a multitude of tropical flowers decorating the interior, inserted between the plaits of the woven reed walls.

Two weeks later Miss Wilson and Dr. Hanlin were among the many who stood on Lelu's shore to welcome the *Morning Star VI* on its maiden voyage to Micronesia. Built at Boothbay in Maine as the yacht *Norseman*, the vessel was a two-masted schooner 63.5 feet in length, with a three-cylinder diesel motor. Capt. Price Lewis and his crew had sailed from Boston aboard the re-christened *Morning Star VI* on July 27, 1947. They passed through the Panama Canal— where they picked up Henrietta, the ship's cat—and into the Pacific. Once again there was a *Star* to link the mission stations from Jaluit to Chuuk.

Miss Wilson wrote of the arrival. "After forty-two years without a *Star*, *Morning Star VI* was welcomed to Kusaie on Sunday afternoon, February 22. Old and young rushed out of the church building to the edge of the water where they watched the white schooner tie up to the buoy in Lelu Harbor. The Queen and I had jumped into a canoe and had guided the *Star* to its anchorage, and then over the side of the ship we went to welcome the crew of five bearded young men." Among them was Daniel Akaka, a Hawaiian youth who would later become one of Hawai'i's senators in the United States Congress.

Eleanor Wilson continued, "I would have given a good deal to have been able to snap the King's expression when Captain Lewis handed him a Kusaien New Testament with 'King John Sigrah' written in gold on the cover. No one could have doubted his pleasure as he accepted the gift, saying, 'But I am no longer King.'"[29]

DR. HANLIN WORKS TO REOPEN MISSION SCHOOL

After a grand celebration, with most of Kosrae's people participating, and a restocking of provisions, a rested crew sailed the *Morning Star VI* on toward Pohnpei and Chuuk. Miss Wilson continued to work with Kosrae's church leaders as she awaited the return of the *Star* to transport her to her post in the Marshall Islands. Harold Hanlin began working to get the former Baldwin house ready for his family and to prepare for a new group of students at the site of the old mission school.

He wrote of the challenges he faced at Wot:

The wharf was partially demolished, the large stones having been taken away during the war. The plantation was completely overgrown with tropical vines and ferns—banana plants and young coconut trees were being choked by the vines which encircled and almost covered them. The walkways up to the school proper had been hastily cleared before I arrived, but in many places wild pigs had rooted up the sod and spoiled the grass. Only foundation stones, cement steps and tall concrete columns remained of the three-story school building and the two-story chapel building—they had been torn down and carried away during the war. The few buildings which were left were in a sorry state.

The Baldwin house, the principal dwelling, was still standing—it had been used by Japanese officers during the war and changed to suit their purposes. It was riddled with bullet holes which testified to the accuracy of the strafing fire of allied planes. It plainly showed the effects of long neglect in its broken windows, sagging doors, weatherbeaten and faded paint, and in its crudely altered interior. A two-room house was also left—it had been built for protection during typhoons but would not afford much protection even in a rainstorm, for its roof, too, was full of bullet holes.

I looked at all the desolation and devastation and thought of the constructive work of some seventy years of missionary activity torn down by war and wasted through neglect—it was a discouraging thought. Then I remembered all the people who have studied in this place and then gone out to lead the churches of Micronesia. I thought of all the people here in these islands, in Hawai'i and in America, who are interested in having this school rebuilt—and who are praying and giving to that end. I was encouraged and began to plan for the repair of our house and to visualize all that needed to be done to reopen this school.[30]

Once again the Kosraean Church sprang into action for the cause of the school at Wot. From the Lelu congregation came six carpenters to help Dr. Hanlin erect the buildings, with Likiak Rufweni as chief carpenter. Those working with Likiak were Basi Siba, Jesse Wakup, Kilafwa Irang Aliklof, Kilafwa Palik, and Joshua Abraham. Jacob Aliklof, and later Boas Abraham, were assigned to get some of the plantation cleared and gardens planted. Norman Skilling was there as the new missionary's language teacher and translator. Forty men from two of the villages went to Wot and, in two days, put up a new wharf house. Men from the other two villages began making a large canoe for the mission school. Everyone was exhilarated as they anticipated the reopening of the school, and, with Dr. Hanlin, were eager for the arrival of his family.

FROM CHUUK TO KOSRAE ABOARD *MORNING STAR VI*

Woven palm-frond baskets filled with island produce, stalks of bananas, and tethered live chickens lined the deck of the *Morning Star VI* as it pulled away from the Moen dock. It was Monday afternoon, March 22, and Mrs. Hanlin and her children, relaxing on deck after the final hectic hours of packing and farewells, were elated to be on their way to Kosrae at long last. They talked animatedly with each other as the *Star* crossed Chuuk lagoon and headed through a pass in the encircling reef out into the open ocean. Immediately, enormous swells broke over the bow of the little ship, sweeping most of the produce and all of chickens into the sea and sending the passengers scrambling below deck for protection.

As the *Star* was tossed, twisted, and slammed, the passengers braced themselves on their bunks, sick to their stomachs and not just a bit apprehensive. There were eight people in the aft cabin, which was designed to accommodate four. Mrs. Hanlin, Alice, John, and Ruth Ann shared the tiny, 6- by 12-foot space with a young Marshallese family—Pastor Barton Buttenga; his wife, Likimen; and their two small daughters, Helping and Dorcas. They were all seasick. A ninth passenger, Dr. Clarence Gillette, clung to his bunk in the galley, grateful that he did not have to move to make way for dinner preparation—Albert the cook was sick, as were several others of the crew. Only Capt. Lewis and Danny Akaka seemed unaffected by the wild, erratic movements of the tiny vessel.

By the third day, as the sea calmed down, so did stomachs. But there was disappointment when the Captain announced that, though they had traveled 600 miles, they were only 60 miles from Chuuk! By the fourth day Mary Ruth was able to write in her diary, "Alice combed her hair, I washed my teeth, but no fresh water to wash our hands or faces."[31] Someone had left the faucet open and most of the ship's supply of fresh water had been lost during the night. Alice wrote, "I was envious of the *Star's* mascot, Henrietta. She could wash her face without water and was the calmest one on the ship!"[32]

Despite their discomfort, the passengers sang together in their cabin that evening, joined by Danny and the captain. The calm demeanor and thoughtful concern of these two were gratefully noted by the Hanlins, an Indiana family who found themselves bobbing in the middle of the vast Pacific.

In the wee hours of the fifth night, Mary Ruth Hanlin was awakened by the sharp sound of an ominous crack. Eight feet of the main mast had broken off. Though no one was injured, there was much shouting and confusion as the crew struggled to save what they could of the main sail and rigging. The tiny auxiliary engine, usually kept in reserve to help get into and out of harbors, was started, and the *Star* began making better time.

The sixth day dawned, and with it a bit of rain, giving the three Hanlin children the luxury of brushing their teeth for the first time since leaving Chuuk. It was, after all, Easter Sunday! They joined the others gathered in the cockpit for a worship service led by Dr. Gillette. Later, Danny Akaka continued teaching the Hanlin children how to play the 'ukulele. The sea was calmer, and there was plenty of time to practice.

On March 29, day seven, Pohnpei appeared on the horizon, and by evening the ship had anchored in the placid waters of Kolonia's harbor. Their time ashore among U.S. Navy families and Pohnpeian Christians was a welcome respite for the dizzy passengers. Somewhat mended and patched, and with water and fuel tanks refilled, the *Star* left Pohnpei the evening of April 1.

Alice continued the story:

Our hopes for a short conclusion to our trip didn't last very long. Something took the wind out of our sails! We drifted until the Captain decided to use the auxiliary engine again. After a short time the engine broke down, and we drifted some more. For five days, we drifted most of the time, sailing only now and then when a breeze came along. During that time the Captain and First Mate worked practically day and night, first trying to discover what was wrong with the engine and then trying to fix it.

Enough breezes came along to bring us within sight of Kusaie at last, but not enough to get us into the harbor. So near and yet so far! Again we drifted, wishing for a strong wind to come up. But none came. On the next day, after the engine had been temporarily repaired, it brought us safely into the harbor at Lelu and all the unpleasant memories of a difficult voyage were overcome by the joy and happiness of the welcome which the Christian people of Kusaie gave us.[33] ✚

Notes - Chapter 13

1.   Mark R. Peattie, *Nan'yo, The Rise and Fall of the Japanese in Micronesia*, p. 231
2.   Harvey Gordon Segal, *Kosrae, the Sleeping Lady Awakens*, p. 151
3.   Mary Alice Hanlin [Buck], conversation with Lise Sam, personal diary, Nov. 19, 1954, p. 48
4.   Maribelle Cormack, *The Lady Was a Skipper*, p. 204
5.   Peattie, p. 304
6.   Segal, p. 153
7.   Cormack, p. 104
8.   Mary Lanwi, personal conversations, Majuro, July 26-27, 2001
9.   Lanwi, personal conversation, Kosrae, May 16, 2002
10. George D. Olds, III, "A Letter From Kusaie," unpublished manuscript, Nov. 26, 1945, p. 23

11. Segal, p. 162

12. Wynn C. Fairfield, "Christians From Boston," Oct. 30, 1944, p. 7a

13. Irving L. Selvage, personal correspondence, Sept. 18, 2001

14. Chester W. Nimitz quoted in Clarence W. Hall's "She Is Skipper of the *Morning Star*," *Reader's Digest*, Nov. 1957, p. 2

15. Olds, p. 11

16. Robert W. Moore, "Our New Military Wards in the Pacific," *National Geographic*, Sept. 1956, p. 33

17. Nimitz quoted in "Our Christian World Mission" position paper, American Board of Commissioners for Foreign Missions, Boston 1952, p. 3

18. Olds, p. 1

19. Ibid, p. 8

20. Ibid, p. 18

21. Ibid, pp. 18-19

22. Salik Cornelius, personal conversation, Malem, Oct. 3, 2001

23. Cormack, p. 203

24. Ibid, p. 200

25. Ibid

26. Trust Territory of the Pacific Islands, "13th Annual Report," Dept. of State publication 7183, May 1961, pp. 23-24

27. Peattie, p. 100

28. Cormack, p. 200

29. Eleanor Wilson, "From Kusaie," unpublished manuscript, Aug. 1948, p. 11

30. Harold Hanlin, "Mission Letter," ABCFM, Boston, May 15, 1948

31. Mary Ruth Hanlin, unpublished "Five Year Diary," March 26, 1948

32. M. A. Hanlin [Buck], "From Truk to Kusaie on the *Morning Star VI*—A Few Memories," *The Friend*, Honolulu, Aug. 1948, p. 10

33. Ibid

NUNAK YOHK KE CHAPTER 14
1948-1952

Harold Hanlin el oai Kosrae in February 1948, malem luo meet liki sou lal ah tuku. El tuh wi alu pacl luo in kais sie mura meet liki mutan kial ac tulik natul sun acn Kosrae in April. El finsrak pac mu sou lal uh in ku pac in osun yurin mwet Kosrae nukewa. Ouinge ke Sunday se oemeet lalos fin acn Kosrae elos wi alu Lelu, ke Sunday akluo elos alu Malem, Sunday aktolu Utwe, Sunday akakosr Tafunsak. Mwet matu ac oayapa tulik elos arulana pwar in lohng ac liye ke tulik tolu in sou se inge ku in mukena tuyak ac on. Ke Sunday se elos wi alu Malem ah, falful ke acn sin tulik mukul nguri, na tulik mukul nukewa putatla nu infohk ah.

Mwet Christian fin acn Kosrae elos akoo arulana yok tuku lun missionary sasu inge. Elos akoo on oayapa mwe lung in sang nu selos meyen elos nunku mu mwet inge ac sun acn Kosrae ke Christmas ke yac sac 1947. Tusruktu ke sou sac tuh oai e ke April 1948, mwet kol lun Church elos sulela tuh program se ma elos tuh akoo nu ke Christmas, ac fah orekla na ke May 3. Mwet nukewa tuh fah tukeni fin acn Lelu ke len sac. Elos tulokunak sak in Christmas soko ke sie lohm fahsu fin acn Pisin, ac sap missionary uh in muta siska. Mwet in church ke kais sie mura elos eis pacl lalos in mahs ac on utyak ke inkanek nu Pisin, ac us mwe sang lalos. Missionary sasu inge elos tiana ku in mulkunla Christmas wowo se ma orek nu selos in May inge.

Dr. Hanlin ac sou lal elos muta ke lohm sin Miss Baldwin luo ah fin acn Wot ah. Mwet kol lun Church Kosrae elos sulella Palik Asher ac mutan kial, Sepe Fransilia, in som muta Wot ac kasru missionary sasu inge. Falyang lah matwen tulik natul Palik ac Fransilia tuh oapana matwen tulik ke sou aset se inge. Eltal tukeni lutlut forfor fin acn Wot, oayapa yen fototo nu Wot. Eltal kewa kawakyak: Alice, Almeda, John, Asher, Lucy, Ruth Ann, Spencer ac Kenye. Tia paht tok na tulik natul Dr. Hanlin eltal etalla kas Kosrae. Ke kutu malem tok, Alice ac John kasru papa ac nina kialtal in leng.

Mwet kamtu onkosr Lelu tuh solla in kasrel Dr. Hanlin in sifil musaela lohm lutlut fin acn Wot. Likiak Rufweni pa sifen u se inge, ac mwet welul pa Basi Siba, Jesse Wakup, Kilafwa Aliklof, Kilafwa Palik ac Joshua Abraham. Jacob Aliklof ac Boas Abraham tuh som kasrel Palik Asher in orekma ke ima, ac Norman Skilling el orekma yurol Dr. Hanlin in lotel kas Kosrae. Mwet orekma inge ac tulik nukewa tuh toeni in lohm sin missionary ke lotutang ac eku, in alu ac aetuila ke orekma kunalos. Dr. Hanlin el orala sie pwapa tuh pastu fin acn Marshall in tuku nu Kosrae ac lutlut ke Bible, oayapa ke orekma lun pastu, ac in kasru pac akoo acn Wot tuh in sifil mutawauk lutlut we. Pastu longoul luo tuku, ac elos lutlut ac orekma we malem onkosr.

Deacon Alik Kefwas el misa ke September 9, 1948. El yac 100 matwa. Dr. Hanlin ac Pastu John Paliknoa Sigrah pa oru alu in pukmas ke church Tafunsak. Deacon Kefwas el pukpuki fin acn sel Insief.

Ke mutun 1949, captain lun *Morning Star VI* el folokla nu America, na American Board sapla nu yorol Dr. Hanlin tuh elan aolul ac captain fin *Morning Star*. Sripa se inge oru Mrs. Hanlin pa karingin orekma fin acn Wot. Pastu Palik Kefwas el usla sou lal liki acn Tafunsak, tuh elan kasrel Mrs. Hanlin ke pacl ma Dr. Hanlin el wangin. Mrs. Hanlin, Pastu Palik, ac oayapa Alice, tuh orala conference singoul ke summer sac nu sin mwet fusr Kosrae. Mwet fusr 254 pa wi conference ekasr inge.

Tulik lutlut elos mutawauk in tuku nu Wot ke August 1949. Lutlut ah mutawauk ke November. Oasr tulik Kosrae singoul tolu, tulik Marshall singoul eu, tulik Pohnpei tolu ac tulik Pingelap tolu. Mwet luti lalos pa Mrs. Hanlin, Pastu Palik, Frank ac Srue Skilling, Flora Aliksa, ac Alice Hanlin. Oasr pac mwet luti luo Marshall me: Keju Johnny ac mutan kial, Charlotte.

Ke sripen papa ac nina kial Mrs. Hanlin eltal munasla, ouinge Mrs. Hanlin el enenu in folokla nu yoroltal in March 1950 mweyen el mukefanna natultal. Dr. Hanlin el tuh filiya *Morning Star VI* yorol Eleanor Wilson in acn Marshall, ac foloko nu Kosrae in liyaung lutlut Wot. Ke May 1950 el ac tulik natul tuh folokla in mongla United States. Alice el tuh asor ke sripen el ac mau tia wi sou lal foloko, meyen el ac enenu in weang lutlut college. Pastu Palik Kefwas el tuh sang kas in kasru nu sel mu elan som ac lutlut ke inen acn Kosrae. Pastu John Sigrah el oayapa akkeyel Alice elan mau foloko nu Kosrae tukun tari lutlut lal uh.

In pacl se inge Pastu Palik el principal ke lutlut Wot. Tulik sasu elos tuku nu Wot ke September 1950. Pisen tulik lutlut oasr we, tulik eungoul eu. Lutlut ah fahsr wona ke 1950 ac 1951. Tusruktu mwet fin acn Wot tuh arulana supwar ke elos lohngak lah Dr. ac Mrs. Hanlin ac tia foloko nu Kosrae, a ako-eyuk in supweyukla eltal in som orekma Chuuk. Tok kutu, in July 1952, elos enganak ke Miss Lucy Lanktree el sun acn Kosrae in orekma Wot. El tuh sie missionary meet nu in acn China.

Mwet Christian Kosrae elos srakna kasru lutlut Wot in us mwe mongo ac som orekma pac we. Sayen ma inge, elos arulana kafofo ke musaiyen lohm alu sasu se Langosak, ke acn se na tuh oan we meet liki mweun ah. Dr. Hanlin el tuh lumahla petsa nu ke lohm alu se inge ke el srakna muta Kosrae. Mwet uh elos kena aksafyela meet liki August 1952 mweyen pa inge pacl in akfulatye tuku lun Wosasu nu Kosrae ke yac siofok somla. Ke sripen elos soano mwet fulat lun American Board in sun acn Kosrae, eneneyuk in kokola len in kisa, ac alu in akfulat, nwe ke November. Missionary ac mwet kol lun Church in acn Marshall, Pohnpei, Chuuk, Hawai'i ac Boston tuh tuku nu ke len lulap se inge. Apkuran mwet Kosrae nukewa in eis kunalos ke on ac oayapa ke kufwa na lulap in akpwarye mwet nukewa su tukeni ke len sac.

CHAPTER FOURTEEN

REBUILDING AND COMMEMORATING
1948-1952

NEW MISSIONARY FAMILY FOR KOSRAE

It was a Sunday when the new missionaries arrived, repeating what had happened so often in the past. The April 11 afternoon church services had just been concluded when the *Morning Star VI* limped into Lelu Harbor with its relieved passengers.

From Alice's perspective on the deck of the *Star*, the large crowd of colorfully clad worshipers who flowed from their church building at Fukil were like technicolor ants—especially when, suddenly spotting the *Star*, they began to scatter, running toward the canoes that lined Lelu's shore. Almost immediately the missionary vessel was surrounded by a happy jumble of people in bouncing canoes that jostled for space beside the little ship. John, whose 13th birthday had passed five days earlier aboard the *Star* as it drifted in the doldrums between Pohnpei and Kosrae, quickly responded to the timid but friendly invitation of a Kosraean boy, and scrambled down into the boy's canoe. Off the two of them went toward shore.

Dr. Hanlin was at Wot, having received no word about the *Morning Star* or his family, but Eleanor Wilson welcomed Mrs. Hanlin and the two girls into her canoe, and the young men in the bow and stern paddled the four Americans to Pisin. Alice marveled at the pulsating movement of the canoe as the expertly handled paddles pushed them forward through the water with synchronized precision. Many friendly people followed with the other passengers and members of the crew in a procession of canoes that reached from the *Star* to the landing at Mr. Snow's Dove Island. The yard was full of children, young people, men, and women—each one eager to shake hands with all of the newcomers.

But movement and talking ceased and the crowd stood transfixed when Alice, John, and Ruth Ann—prompted by their mother—stood in the doorway of one of Pisin's thatch houses and, in close, three-part harmony, began to sing:

Over the sea, over the sea,
Jesus Savior, pilot me.
Over the sea, over the sea,
Savior, pilot me.

Over and over, like a mighty sea,
Comes the love of Jesus
Rolling over me.

GETTING SETTLED AND ACQUAINTED

For the Hanlins, the next weeks consisted of a happy flurry of new experiences, new friends, and getting settled in a new home. Dr. Hanlin assigned
work to keep the carpenters busy while he helped get his family settled—first
in the typhoon house, and later in the repainted, re-roofed, and newly screened
Baldwin mission house.

Before his family arrived, Dr. Hanlin had twice preached in each of Kosrae's
four villages. Now he was anxious to introduce his wife and children to these
congregations, and members of these congregations were eager to meet the new
missionary family. It was decided that their first four Sundays on the island
would be devoted to visiting the churches. This meant a great deal of lengthy
canoe travel back and forth from Wot, but everyone cheerfully agreed to the plan.

On April 18 the five Hanlins worshiped with the Lelu congregation in the
large, thatched open-air church at Fukil. Alice, John, and Ruth Ann sang three
songs, to everyone's delight. The Hanlin children, on the other hand, were
intrigued by the fact that the Lelu children, if they chose, could entertain themselves during worship by playing in the sand of the church floor on which they
sat. During that weekend Pastor John Sigrah and his wife, Hattie—still referred
to as Tokosra and Kasra [king and queen]—were the Hanlin's gracious hosts,
as they were on each of the consecutive weekends when the missionary family
was at Pisin.

The Hanlins were in Malem on April 25. The church was crowded with the
entire community, especially curious to see and hear the three American children. The people were particularly captivated by Ruth Ann's light blond hair. The
Hanlins were amazed when the Malem children stood and enthusiastically sang
"Over the sea, Over the sea, Jesus Savior, Pilot me." Their teacher, Lise Sam, had
asked Alice for the words that first evening at Pisin, and during the intervening
two weeks had taught the song to Malem's Sunday School children.

There were so many children in the Malem church that Sunday that during
the service a section of floor at the left front of the sanctuary on which the small
boys were sitting suddenly collapsed out from under them, dropping with them
two feet to the ground below. No one was hurt—everyone was startled, especially the children experiencing the abrupt drop—but no one thought it was
funny except the three Hanlin children, who found it difficult to suppress their
giggles. After church the five visitors were served a delectable dinner proudly

prepared by chief cook Gideon.

For Sunday services on May 2 the family traveled to Utwe. As they had done on the prior Sunday—after crossing Lelu Harbor by canoe—they walked part of the way from Sansrik and part of the way they rode in a dilapidated but service-able Japanese truck. On May 9 they were with the congregation in Tafunsak. But the most joyful of these get-acquainted visits took place in Lelu on Monday, May 3, when everyone gathered for the new-month meeting.

CHRISTMAS IN MAY

That day was described in a newsletter penned by Harold Hanlin:

Last year when the people of Kusaie heard that a missionary family was on its way from America, they joyfully set about preparing to welcome them with gifts at Christmas time, for they confidently expected that we would be here by that time. But Christmas [1947] came and went, and we were still waiting in Truk for some way to get on to Kusaie.

In February Miss Wilson and I were able to get through on a Navy ship, and in April Mrs. Hanlin and our three children arrived aboard the Morning Star VI. *So the Kusaien people said, "We will get ready and give our Christmas presents now." On the third of May, the Christian people came together at Lelu, the principal village, for their regular monthly Malem Sasu meeting. The people of Lelu had brought their gifts some time before that, so those from the other three villages came now with gifts of handicraft for Miss Wilson, Captain Lewis of the* Morning Star, *and our family which they presented to us at our temporary home at Pisin, a small island joined to Lelu by a short causeway.*

On the Lelu side of that causeway a large group of people had gathered and were stirring about as some few were getting them organized. Then all the people from Utwe formed into an orderly procession and started toward Pisin, singing as they came. As the procession neared the living room, they broke into single file and came in, still singing, came to the table and placed their gifts on, around, and under it and then went outside again. This was repeated twice, as the Malem people and then the Tafunsak people also came in smiling, singing processions.

How the gifts did accumulate—beautiful hand-woven baskets, pretty fans, fancy shell head-bands, sturdy canoe paddles and many small sitting mats. Following the gift-giving, the three village groups sang several Christmas songs to us, standing in our front yard. After we had expressed our gratitude, the leader asked to hear our children sing, so they sang a few American choruses, a Trukese song, and even stumbled through a Kusaien hymn, much to the delight of our Kusaien friends. While this was going on, three men, representing the three congregations, were separating the gifts into three groups—for Captain Lewis, for Miss Wilson, and for ourselves.

After considerable handshaking all around, our visitors said "Muta" (Goodbye) and started on the long canoe journey to their homes.

We had no snow, no reindeer, no fancy decorations, but all could feel the true "Christmas Spirit" of that joyous occasion in May when the Kusaiens came to assure us of their welcome.[1]

SCHEDULES AND ADJUSTMENTS

In late April a ship had arrived with the Hanlins' household goods—17 crates in all—which the carpenters and other Lelu men carefully transported to Wot by canoe. The last to be carried up the hill contained a kerosene-burning refrigerator. Also in the freight shipment were the first lessons of the correspondence courses Alice, John, and Ruth Ann would be working through during their time on Kosrae. The plan was for Mrs. Hanlin to tutor John and Ruth Ann from the intermediate and elementary level Calvert School texts, while Dr. Hanlin would be responsible for guiding Alice through Chicago's American School high school courses. There were good intentions as study space was designated and books were opened.

But there was so much to be learned beyond the correspondence courses. A Kosraean family had been designated by Church leaders to assist the American family at Wot. Palik Asher, a Tafunsak layman and grandson of Pastor Konlulu, was assigned as mission plantation foreman. His wife, Sepe Fransilia, would help Mrs. Hanlin in the mission house. The ages of some of Palik and Francilia's children matched the ages of the missionary children. Almeda and Alice quickly became friends. From day one Asher and John were inseparable cohorts on many an escapade around the vast Wot campus and beyond. Kenye, Lucy, and Ruth Ann played together daily. The eldest Palik son, Elmer, was with relatives in Tafunsak, and son Spencer—between Lucy and Kenye in age—sometimes tagged along with John and Asher, and sometimes just pestered the little girls.

As they interacted with their new friends, the Hanlin children were immersed from the beginning in various aspects of the Kosraean culture—and the Kosraean language came readily to them. John and Ruth Ann picked it up at play, while Alice concentrated on learning it during morning and evening prayers and Sunday services by comparing the verses of Scripture in the Kosraean and English Bibles. As the chapel had yet to be rebuilt, these worship periods took place in the Hanlin living room. By September Alice was able to tell her father that sometimes words and phrases in his sermons and talks were being misinterpreted. His response: "Perhaps you should interpret for me." And so she did.

The language came slower for the parents. In the midst of responsibilities and the interruptions that seemed to sabotage each day, Mary Ruth studied Kosraean with Fransilia and Srue Frank, while Harold studied with Norman Skilling. At the same time, Harold was learning Marshallese from Barton. The Marshallese pastor had been asked to remain at Kosrae with his family for the specific purpose of teaching his language to the new missionary.

As the family got settled at Wot through the months of May, June, and July, the carpenters continued working to prepare the campus for students. The Kosraean-style school dining room and kitchen were completed, as were a tool house and a thatched dwelling for two teachers. Two dormitories for boys were reconstructed on pre-war foundations. Various church groups came to lend a hand on these building projects and to help Palik Asher and Frank Skilling clean and cultivate areas for bananas, taro, tapioca, and sweet potatoes.

REFRESHER COURSE FOR MARSHALLESE PASTORS

Since it would be some months before the Christian Training School was capable of housing and feeding the teenage students for whom it was designed, Dr. Hanlin and Miss Wilson, with the ready concurrence of pastors John Sigrah and Palik Kefwas, invited the pastors of the Marshall Islands to Kosrae for what was called "a short refresher course." In late August a U.S. Navy ship deposited eight Marshallese pastors in Lelu; in early September 10 more arrived on the *Morning Star VI*; and a few days later four more came on another Navy ship. All 22 were excited and grateful for the invitation.

The older men among them had studied with former missionaries—some in the Marshall Islands and a few right there at Wot. The younger men had previously studied with their own Marshallese Christian leaders as instructors. Pastor Palik Kefwas, who spoke Marshallese, joined the group for their studies, anxious to get all the training he could. They were an enthusiastic band of men, who dug not only into their studies but also into the work of rebuilding the Wot campus, knowing that some of the students attending the school would be their own children.

In the mornings Harold Hanlin taught Bible and pastoral courses, with Mary Ruth Hanlin helping with English and introducing new gospel songs and hymns. Rose Hoppin Mackwelung came once a week from Lelu to teach American history and music. The afternoons were devoted to various work projects. Participants were invigorated and inspired.

Dr. Hanlin wrote, "They are eager students who are very grateful for all they can learn. We use the dormitory for most of the class sessions, but a few are held in the living room of our home. We are also sending the Marshallese men two at a time to visit and preach in the Kusaien villages each Sunday. We think that this fellowship will be mutually beneficial to the Marshallese preachers and to the Kusaien Christians. We feel that this whole experience will be a mental and spiritual stimulus to them which will enrich all the rest of their ministry."[2]

DEATH OF ALIK KEFWAS

On September 9, 1948, Alik Kefwas died in Tafunsak. One of Wot's principal landowners, he had been a deacon, Bible translator, and a life-long supporter of the missionaries. *The Friend* carried Harold Hanlin's description of Kefwas and his funeral:

The oldest church member and the oldest resident of Kusaie has died and been buried. No one knows just how old Kefwas really was—but all agree that he was near the century mark, some saying that he was less and others saying that he was more than one hundred years old. For some years he has been inactive, although his general health was fairly good.

Kefwas was one of the large clan which occupied valuable property here at Kusaie when the missionaries first came to Micronesia. By the time the Christian work had developed to the point where a school was needed for these islands, the other leaders of the clan had died and Kefwas was the head. He had cooperated with the missionaries and had been their first outstanding pupil. Hence he became the first Kusaien Christian teacher for this island. His service did not lie in the pastoral field, however, but more strictly in the educational field, and the older men today tell about his work as the first "public school" teacher of Kusaie.

Since the site preferred by the missionaries for a school was on the property of Kefwas and his family, the clan relinquished its rights to the large plantation which has been used by the mission school ever since. They moved to Insief, a small community at one side of the mission plantation. At times the school ran into difficulties with its food supply. Usually Kefwas was the first and most generous in furnishing food for the students from his own property. He would come and ask the missionary for some boys to go with him to his home—they would return laden with taro, breadfruit, pasruk [mashed taro and bananas, baked in leaf-packages], bananas, and other types of native food.

Kefwas died on the evening of September 9th. The next day I conducted a funeral service for him in the church building at Tafunsak, the village where he had spent his last months in the home of relatives who cared for him most faithfully. The older of the two Kusaien pastors, the former King John, assisted me in the ceremony and spoke feelingly about the service Kefwas had rendered to the Kusaiens during his lifetime. The younger pastor had no part in the program because he was sitting with the mourners—he is Kefwas' adopted son.

After the ceremony, Kefwas' body in its neat home-made coffin was placed on a large outrigger canoe and taken to his own property adjacent to our mission school. Members of the family and friends followed in other canoes. When we drove our canoes up on the sand at Kefwas' beach we found others in which friends of Kefwas had come from the village of Utwe. Since they could not get to Tafunsak for the funeral they had come to Insief for the burial.

The heavy coffin was carried on the shoulders of several strong men up a steep, rocky path to the family burial ground on the side of a mountain overlooking the broad expanse of the blue waters of the Pacific Ocean. There Kefwas' body was interred, to lie at rest in the place where he labored for so many years in the service of the Lord and his fellow men.

As I went home afterwards, I wondered, "Who will take Kefwas' place as friend of the Training School?" My question was answered a few weeks later when Palik, Kefwas' adopted son, said to me one day, "Dr. Hanlin, do you know what I have been thinking?" When I replied negatively, he said, "I think I want to be a friend of the School, like Papa Kefwas. I will take his place." When I told him that we would all appreciate his helpfulness, and that the School would certainly profit by having another friend like Papa Kefwas, he humbly added, "I can not do as much as Kefwas, but I can do my best."

So our old friends pass along, and new friends take their place—the work of the Lord goes on, supported by His people.[3]

CHAPEL "PILLAR PLACING"

The day finally came to begin work on the chapel. Harold Hanlin had designed a two-story building with a wraparound first-floor veranda. Though the walls on either end of the large worship area would be solid, walls on the two sides would be only four feet high to insure good ventilation in Kosrae's tropical climate. There would be a room for storage at the back of the worship area. A private room for the housemother would also be there, located beneath the stairs leading up to the girls' dormitory, which would occupy the second floor.

In order to help get the building started, the men of the four village congregations volunteered to supplement the work of the six Wot carpenters by providing the lumber. Each village prepared a suggested amount of timber which was taken to the sawmill to be cut and then transported by canoe, or floated in the lagoon to Wot. Some of the larger pieces of timber were hewn by hand. After the lumber and logs had been deposited on the school wharf, they were carried on the shoulders of the men up the hill to the place of construction. In reporting this, Dr. Hanlin wrote, "One of the joys of the work here is the willing cooperation which the Kusaien Christians are giving us in this great task."[4]

It was 11:30 Wednesday morning, October 27, when members of the Wot community gathered at the site near the top of the Yonrak campus—the same site that had been occupied by the chapel dismantled by the Japanese military almost six years earlier. Instead of a ground-breaking ceremony, they were there for what had been announced as "a pillar-placing ceremony." There were Kosraean hymns and special songs by the Marshallese pastors' group. Both Dr. Hanlin and Pastor Palik offered prayers of thanksgiving and shared comments concerning the significance of the day. Then, to the applause of the people, the carpenters lifted a hand-hewn corner pillar and braced it in place.

PLANS MADE TO REBUILD LELU CHURCH

Describing himself as "a theologically trained preacher trying to make like an architect,"[5] Dr. Hanlin found his newly honed skills as a designer-of-buildings sought by the leaders of the Church. They were anxious to begin construction of a permanent church building on the old Langosak site in Lelu. The missionary met with the two pastors, the deacons, and other leaders to hear and discuss ideas. They hoped for a few innovations, such as electric wiring, but they all agreed that they wanted the new building to resemble the old structure they had loved. The bell tower in particular was to appear as much as possible like the one Mr. Channon had created for them in 1901, 47 years earlier. The bell had been rescued from the rubble. Several faded photographs were perused and memories were probed—Harold Hanlin then drew up a set of plans and presented it to the church leaders.

Everyone understood that the building they so eagerly anticipated was still several years from becoming reality. Much work had to be done in preparing the site, gathering materials, assigning responsibilities, and raising the necessary funds to buy windows, roofing, fixtures, and other items needed to complete the project. But they were relieved to have their ideas committed to paper by Dr. Hanlin—and especially pleased to have a drawing of the front elevation of the church building that Alice made from her father's floor plan. This gave them a picture of how the finished structure would look. By December 1948, work on the site had begun.

NEW CAPTAIN FOR *MORNING STAR VI*

When the *Morning Star VI* arrived to return the Marshallese leaders to their islands, it brought an appeal from Eleanor Wilson for Harold Hanlin to return with them in order to visit the churches in the northern atolls of the Marshall Islands. The Navy would not allow a woman to travel on their small ships to the outer areas, so she was asking him to go in her place. He left Kosrae with the

Marshallese group aboard the *Star* on January 18, 1949.

After he had fulfilled Miss Wilson's request, but while still in the Marshalls, Dr. Hanlin received a considerable jolt. Price Lewis, the young ex-naval officer who served as captain of the *Morning Star VI*, was suddenly recalled, and the American Board asked Dr. Hanlin to take his place. As he remembered his surprise at receiving this directive, Harold Hanlin later wrote, "ME—a landlubber from Oklahoma who hadn't even seen the ocean before I became a Navy chaplain! And the Navy's chaplaincy orientation course had not taught me anything about celestial navigation or the duties of a sailing ship captain. Nevertheless I decided to go along with the Board's request."[6]

It was common during those days to hear the islanders talk nostalgically about the pre-war days when the Japanese trading ships could be counted on to arrive frequently and on schedule. The U.S. Navy, currently responsible for the former Japanese Mandate, carried some civilian freight and passengers aboard their ships, but there was no set schedule and it could be several months between visits. For these and other reasons, having the *Morning Star VI* sailing between the islands seemed logical and timely—especially since it was the intention of the Micronesia Mission once again to welcome Marshallese students to the "Kusaie Christian Training School," or KCTS.

Returning aboard the *Star* to his family and friends at Kosrae on March 25 with the news that he was now captain of the mission vessel brought the expected reactions. The Kosraeans were dismayed and disappointed to be losing the on-island assistance of Dr. Hanlin—something they had come to rely upon and for which they were very grateful—just a year after his arrival among them. His wife was flabbergasted! This meant that Mary Ruth Hanlin would have to carry on as head of the mission operation at Wot—as principal of the school, worship leader and preacher, supervisor of both carpenters and plantation workers, all while maintaining her own household and tutoring her children.

On April 1 the *Morning Star VI*, with the new skipper on board, departed Kosrae with its Marshallese crew for Pohnpei and Chuuk. Meanwhile, Pastor Palik—feeling a great deal of empathy for Mrs. Hanlin because of the heavy responsibilities suddenly placed upon her—moved his family from Tafunsak to Insief to be close to Wot and thus able to assist her on a daily basis. His gracious act was much appreciated by Mrs. Hanlin, and the two became close allies and friends.

YOUTH CONFERENCES AT WOT

A series of 10 one-week conferences was in progress at Wot for the youth of Kosrae's village churches, "to encourage them in Christian living." Mrs. Hanlin decided to continue these conferences after her husband left as they were a project very close to her heart. She was greatly relieved to have Pastor Palik beside her to share leadership responsibilities. She wrote:

These people are devoted Christians—so isolated from the world, yet such a real part of the great family of God—and they are so eager to know more about the will of God for their lives. But like most of us, they have suffered in recent years from lack of teaching and from the inspiration that comes from gathering together for fellowship and study. Pastor Palik and I offered classes in "Stories of Jesus," "Meaning of Church Membership," "Gospels," "History of Christianity on Kusaie," and "Music." Alice, our oldest girl, led one devotional period each week in the Kusaien language. Over 250 people attended—and some 50 others came to help with the cooking. These people brought their own food and helped in the afternoons with the rebuilding or with work on the plantation.[7]

For three months enthusiastic groups of mostly young adults invaded Wot from all parts of Kosrae at the times designated for them. The conferences proved extremely popular, remembered by the participants with deep appreciation long after the week's activities had been completed and its lessons absorbed. Mrs. Hanlin was impressed that, with no visible sources of cash, these young people left a combined total of $75.52 in offerings for the mission, given during closing services.[8]

WAITING AND WORKING

Dr. Hanlin returned aboard the *Morning Star VI* on June 21 with many a hair-raising tale of his experiences at the helm of "God's Little White Ship." By July 27 he was off again, this time to the Marshall Islands to round up the students who would be attending KCTS. John and Ruth Ann accompanied him, leaving Mary Ruth at the helm of the Wot campus, with Alice there to help her.

Mother and daughter continued to be grateful for the presence, generosity, and kind assistance of Pastor Palik Kefwas. They enjoyed getting to know his wife, Sarah, and their children—Mitchigo, Misima, and Tulpe—as the young family often joined in morning and evening prayers in the mission house with the rest of those at Wot. When Palik and Sarah's fourth child was born on July 24, they asked Mrs. Hanlin to name her. Pleased to be so honored, she gave the little girl the name "Charity" as a tribute to a special friend in the United States.

Instead of church leaders gathering weekly with Pastor Palik in Lelu, they now traveled to study with him at Wot in preparation for leading Sunday services in the villages. Mrs. Hanlin had been overjoyed when the pastor reported to her that, following her suggestion, he had given a "Best Sportsmanship" award at the July 5 island-wide track and field competition in Lelu. It had been presented to Roland Stephen George of Malem, who had stopped in the middle of a race he was running to assist a competitor who had fallen and injured himself.[9]

"Overjoyed" was not the feeling that Mrs. Hanlin experienced when, several weeks later, she received a dispatch from her husband, sent through the U.S. Navy. Due to innumerable difficulties with the vessel, the return of the *Morning Star* would be delayed. The anticipated absence of her husband and two younger children for six weeks turned into three months. It was October 27 when "Sail Ho" rang out across the Wot campus. The *Star* had safely—and in many ways, miraculously—returned.

SCHOOL FINALLY BEGINS

Accompanying Dr. Hanlin aboard the *Morning Star VI* were 14 of the Marshallese young people chosen by Miss Wilson and leaders of the Jarin Rarik Dron—the organization of Marshallese Congregational Churches—to attend the Wot school. Each of the potential students was required to have completed the public school curriculum set up by the U.S. Navy, and be a member of the Church. These young people immediately joined the informal classes that Mrs. Hanlin and Alice had initiated for the four Kosraean young men—Edison Robert, Erafe Tosie, Gustin Charley, and Lister Philip—who had been welcomed to the campus in August. In early September they had been joined by three young men from Pohnpei, and later by three from Pingelap. By the time the rest of the Marshallese students arrived via Navy ship, and the other Kosraean students had come from their villages, there were 24 boys and 14 girls attending KCTS: 13 Kosraeans, 19 Marshallese, three Pohnpeians, and three Pingelapese—a total of 38 young people.

Following a convocation service on November 13, classes were formally started. Sharing the teaching load were Mary Ruth Hanlin, Alice Hanlin, Pastor Palik Kefwas, Srue Frank Skilling, Flora Aliksa, and two pre-war Wot students who had returned to Kosrae from the Marshall Islands, Keju Johnny and his wife Charlotte.

Officially in session at last, the school was doing what the mission board had intended—preparing young people for Christian service across eastern Micronesia. And among the students in this first post-World War II class were 12 future Church leaders who were to have considerable influence in Micronesia and beyond.

CHAPEL DEDICATED

The new chapel and dormitory building was completed by the end of November. The girls moved into their second-floor area, and Flora Aliksa took her place in the housemother's room beneath the stairway. As it had been from the time of the Baldwin sisters, the one door leading up to the girls' dormitory was padlocked on the outside every night—the only key stayed on a chain around the neck of the housemother. Parents of the girls insisted on this arrangement, and there was no fire-warden on Kosrae to protest. The lock was snapped closed at lights-out, and not opened again—except in an emergency— until dawn the next morning.

Each member of the student body and staff helped to prepare the first-floor chapel for dedication day. The carpenters finished the pulpit and altar furniture that Dr. Hanlin had designed, and the boys varnished the beautiful, native Kosraean woods used for the furniture and walls. While Mrs. Hanlin and the girls sewed the altar hanging, village church women wove the large sitting mats for the chapel floor. Decorations of palm fronds and flowers were hung on pillars and walls.

On Thursday, December 8, Dr. Hanlin and Pastor Palik led a triumphant service of dedication attended by the Wot students and staff and many others who had come to join them. Tokosra and Kasra with their son, Paul, were present, as were Jack and Erwine Youngstrom, Rose Mackwelung, leaders of the Church, the carpenters and their families, many of Wot's neighbors, and individuals from across the island. Also attending were Albert Hicking and his family. He was the Gilbertese doctor who became famous in the Pacific during World War II for finding that he could use green coconuts for intervenous feeding. The dedication was a great day of celebration and thanksgiving.

Mrs. Hanlin wrote, "In the three weeks since school started, the students had learned 'I Love Thy Kingdom, Lord' in English and sang it from memory as a special song for the occasion. For several weeks, also, I had been working with the carpenter group, whenever we had time, on 'My God and I.' They sang that in both English and Kusaien. Each church group sang several songs. Not only did we have a feast of songs and sermons and spiritual things that day, but the church people brought food for the students and themselves so that everyone enjoyed a feast of good things to eat as well."[10]

BACK TO THE ROUTINE, BRIEFLY

Classes resumed as the missionary family sent Harold off again to the Marshall Islands. He embarked December 16 aboard the *Morning Star VI*. The following week, members of the Wot community, with their neighbors joining them, celebrated Christmas there on the campus.

During the first seven days of 1950, Kosrae's Christians observed the Annual Week of Prayer, as had been their custom for many years. At the conclusion of the Wot observance, Jesse Lorok, Jude Samson, and Edison Robert were elected officers of the school's Christian Endeavor Society for the new year. On the 19th, Mrs. Hanlin was at the dock in Lelu with Kosrae's Church leaders as Nelson Sigrah and Isaiah Benjamin left to return to the Puluwat Islands, after a vacation with their families. The two men had visited Wot, sharing experiences of their missionary work with the intrigued students.

When in Lelu, Mary Ruth and Alice enjoyed visiting in the home of Jack and Erwine Youngstrom. Erwine was the adopted daughter of Frank and Srue Skilling. She and Alice had become good friends. It was early in 1950 that Jack's uncle, Arthur Herman, left Kosrae to seek medical treatment on Pohnpei for diabetes and its complications. As his condition did not improve, he made the decision to travel to his boyhood home in Oakland, California, where he later died among members of his family. His wife, Srue Kir, remained on Kosrae. Jack Youngstrom, who had inherited Arthur Herman's trading business, continued to assist with orders for Wot mission supplies, as his uncle and great uncle had done before him.

MRS. HANLIN DEPARTS

At Kwajalein in early March, where repairs were being made on the *Star*, Harold Hanlin received a distressing message from mission board authorities: Mary Ruth Hanlin's mother and father were both ill and seriously in need. As the only child of her parents, it was felt that Mrs. Hanlin should return to them as promptly as possible. The board appealed to the U.S. Navy for assistance in getting word to Mrs. Hanlin at Kosrae and providing transportation for her out of Micronesia. The Navy generously agreed to help.

Dr. Hanlin sent a radio message to Eleanor Wilson, who was teaching in the mission school at Rongrong, Majuro, informing her that there was no alternative at the moment but for her to travel to Kwajalein to take over as captain of the *Morning Star VI*. He bid farewell to the crew and boarded the small ship the Navy provided to take him to Kosrae. Arriving there the afternoon of March 8, he went immediately to Wot to share the upsetting news for the first time with his family—and then to help his wife prepare to leave 48 hours later. Departing Kosrae on the 10th aboard the Navy ship that had waited for her, Mary Ruth Hanlin was taken to Kwajalein, where she was put aboard a Military Air Transport Service flight for Honolulu. By March 16 she was with her parents in Oklahoma City.

In a letter circulated through the mission board, Harold Hanlin commended his wife and oldest daughter on their work at Kosrae the previous months while he had been away, on the *Star*:

Alice made a visitation tour of the villages of Kusaie, accompanied and chaperoned by a Kusaien matron. She traveled by outrigger canoe, on foot, and in a pre-war Japanese truck, and was graciously received and lavishly entertained at each village.

Mary Ruth had to supervise the activities of the students who began arriving before I brought the Marshallese group. She had also the problems which were brought frequently by our plantation laborers and carpenters. After the school program began she had more problems to work out—the Kusaien teachers of Bible and Music needed help and encouragement, the student work program had to be supervised, and she took the English class while Alice taught arithmetic. Mary Ruth did a grand job with all these things and truly is ready for the rest which a furlough provides. I hope she does not find additional burdens upon her arrival in Oklahoma.[11]

REMAINING HANLINS PREPARE FOR FURLOUGH

Dr. Hanlin stepped into his role as principal at Wot, reassigning some of the instructors and teaching some of the classes to compensate for Mrs. Hanlin's absence. He also began making preparations for his own departure with the three children. As Alice was 17 and John, 15, it was understood that the two of them would remain in the United States following furlough to attend high school and college.

Alice in particular was distressed by her imminent departure. On a day in late May as she walked barefoot through Tafunsak toward Lelu and the ship that would carry her and her family away, Pastor Palik walked beside her. He had become not only a close friend, but in many ways her spiritual mentor. She greatly respected him and admired deeply his own commitment to Christ and the Church. She was crying as they walked. How could God use her intense feelings for this lovely island and its beautiful people while the unknowns of the future were pulling her away?

Later, remembering those feelings and that walk, she wrote:

Pastor Palik seemed to know exactly what I was thinking, for he said,

"Alice, you must not cry because you are leaving Kusaie, but be happy because you are going to America where there is much knowledge and where you can learn many wonderful things. There is none of this on Kusaie. How I wish I were going so that I might bring some back. Please remember us as you study over there. Perhaps we will never know these things if you do not go and learn them for us."

What a challenge! I would not merely be going to attend school, but rather to learn for the Kusaien people. With this goal in mind everything would have a conse-crated purpose: I could help these people I love, even while away from them.[12]

On the dock in Lelu, Dr. Hanlin and his children mingled in the heart of a large group of friends who were now like brothers and sisters. As they awaited the "All aboard," John Paliknoa Sigrah, the older pastor and former king, shook Alice's hand. "Please come back to us," he said—and she promised him that she would.

ANOTHER MISSION MEETING

After a brief stop at Pohnpei, the Hanlins continued by ship to Chuuk, accompanied by new Pohnpei missionaries Chester and Margery Williams Terpstra, to attend a week-long meeting of the Micronesia Mission. Gathered for the first time with the American missionaries were some of the German missionaries of the Liebenzell Board. In order to remain in Micronesia—an area still under tight military control—Liebenzell personnel were beginning the process of becoming American citizens as required by the U.S. Navy. In 1949 the American Board had agreed to bring the work of the Liebenzell Mission in Palau, Yap, and Chuuk under joint planning and supervision, with the American Board giving partial financial support to the German missionaries, fulfilling yet another requirement.[13]

SECOND WAVE OF POST-WAR STUDENTS

Before leaving Kosrae, the Hanlins had been able to complete the freshman year of study with the 37 young people who were members of that first class to gather at Wot after the rebuilding of the campus—a school year which began in November 1949 and was completed in May 1950. In the fall of that year the new freshman class arrived. In this new class, which also included some of the future's brightest leaders, were 12 Marshallese men, seven Marshallese women, 21 Kosraean men, and 21 Kosraean women. These 61 additional students joined those who were already there at Wot, making a total of 98 young people to house, feed, and teach.

The 1950-1951 school year was not an easy one for the students or for their teachers. Pastor Palik Kefwas, Frank and Srue Skilling, Keju and Charlotte Johnny, and Flora Aliksa did their best to adhere to the schedule and maintain discipline and morale. The Christians of Kosrae continued their practice of sharing both food and labor with the mission school, but the large increase in numbers meant that food was sometimes scarce. However, as the months went by and the new students joined efforts with the original class, there was an upsurge in the productivity of the Wot gardens and in fishing expeditions. Gradually, the food situation improved.

THE LADY WAS A SKIPPER

From March 1950 until June 1951, the Rev. Eleanor Wilson—taking over for Dr. Hanlin—served as captain of the *Morning Star VI*. Her experiences that year were recounted in absorbing detail by author Maribelle Cormack in *The Lady Was a Skipper*. The book was condensed in *The Reader's Digest* after Miss Wilson was featured in the same magazine in an article by Clarence W. Hall. Both the article and the book were widely read and brought a level of publicity to the islands of Micronesia and to the Micronesia Mission that had never before been generated.

CAPT. WILSON SAILS TO KOSRAE

Shortly before turning over command of the *Star* to the new captain, Creston Ketchum, a Canadian who had been working in Okinawa, Miss Wilson visited Kosrae. She was returning to the Marshalls aboard the missionary vessel from a meeting of the Micronesia Mission at Pohnpei. Visiting Wot, she was impressed with the fine work that Pastor Palik Kefwas was doing with the large student body during the absence of the missionaries. He, in turn, expressed to her his appreciation for the faithfulness of each of those who were assisting as teachers.

Back at Pisin, Eleanor was astonished to see Pastor John Sigrah's son Nelson walk across the causeway toward her, accompanied by a small man who wore scant clothing. Nelson explained that he had returned to Kosrae for another visit—this time, for a very special reason. He introduced the missionary to the man beside him as the King of Puluwat.

"'Are you pleased to have a missionary on your island?' she asked the king.

"'Everybody very happy!' he beamed. 'Nelson, he taught us to smile, to sing. Once we did not know how!'"[14]

The king's wife and daughter, "very properly clad in print dresses and Japanese zories," stood shyly behind the king. Miss Wilson shook hands with them, as Nelson explained that his son, Alokoa, was now the husband of Lief, the daughter of the King of Puluwat, thus uniting "two kingly families." Proudly, Nelson also explained to the missionary that he had translated some of the Kosraean hymns into the Puluwat language, and that they wanted to sing for her. So, together, Nelson, Alokoa, Lief, and the king and queen of Puluwat sang a hymn for Miss Wilson in a language that had yet to be written. She was very impressed.[15]

Later, Eleanor Wilson visited Pastor John Sigrah and his wife, Hattie. She noticed that the king and queen had aged since her last visit to Kosrae. Hattie was no longer able to leave their home at Kalung, but she was sitting up on her sleeping mat to welcome Eleanor. Pleased to see her missionary friend, she apologized for not being able to prepare food for her with her own hands. Her nearby children, however, had fixed a very fine meal for the elderly couple to share with their visitor. It was Eleanor's last evening with Kasra Hattie. The old queen died on June 14, 1951, just a few weeks after Miss Wilson departed.

ALICE'S ASSIGNMENTS

At this same time, Alice Hanlin completed high school and began a summer odyssey that was so successful it was repeated the following two summers. The Speaker's Bureau of the American Board sent Alice as their representative from church camp to retreat to conference across middle America and on the East Coast. Her enthusiasm for Kosrae and its people, and her genuine concern for the Church and its leadership, won enumerable friends for the Micronesia Mission.

Alice was also asked to proofread a bilingual edition of the New Testament with parallel columns in English and Kosraean. The American Bible Society could find no one else in the United States who was capable of doing this. In an article published for Congregational Church youth, 18-year-old Alice explained: "Earlier missionaries had translated the Scriptures into the Kusaien language, but nearly all the books had been destroyed or damaged during the war. What a privilege to help send new Bibles to these people who longed for them so much. My work included correcting spelling, checking typographical errors, watching word order, seeing that no verse was printed twice and that none were left out; also noting punctuation, spacing, and hyphenated words. It required hours and hours of concentrated, word-by-word reading, and the fact that I was in my first year of college and wanted to stay on the honor roll extended the time considerably. In all, it took me thirteen months, but every page was a labor of love and every hour a part of my goal!"[16]

Meanwhile, Dr. Hanlin, as newly appointed superintendent of the Micronesia Mission—now including the work of both the American and Liebenzell Boards—was reassigned to Chuuk, where he arrived October 15, 1951. Mrs. Hanlin remained for some months in Oklahoma City to care for her father. Her mother had died some months earlier.

Above: "Land Ho!" From approximately 35 miles at sea, Kosrae's silhouette appears on the horizon of the sun-drenched Pacific. Its location 2,400 miles southwest of Hawai'i and 1,500 miles southeast of Guam makes it one of the most isolated islands in the world. (Elden Buck)

Center: Photographed from Pisin, June 1962, Kosrae's famed "Sleeping Lady" mountain range outlines the southwest part of the harbor. Mt. Finkol, left, is the highest peak at 2,064 feet. In the foreground is the wreck of a small Japanese trading vessel run aground during World War II. (Elden Buck)

Bottom: Lelu Harbor from Mt. Finkol. Lelu Island, with Yenyen Island and the causeway visible, left, and the harbor entrance, right —photographed January 6, 1962. (Elden Buck)

394

Above: Lelu Congregational Church as seen from Pisin, October 1960. The tidal area between the church and Pisin was filled during 1999 and 2000, and is now a parking lot accommodating the vehicles that crowd it during choir rehearsals, meetings and Sunday services. (Elden Buck)

Below: Palik Kefwas (pastor 1947-1952) and John Paliknoa Sigrah (king 1910-1947, pastor 1947-1957) at the time of the Church's centenial, Pisin, November 1952. (Harold Hanlin)

Above: Wot campus as seen from the lagoon, 1962. The wharf-house stands at the left end of the beach. On the mountain side above is the Yonrak portion of the campus where the mission house and classroom building stand. One of the boys' dormitories is visible between Yonrak and the canoe house, lower right. (Elden Buck)

Center: Wot campus from the air, 1963. Far left, the beach and wharf-house—center, the classroom building, mission house, chapel & girls' dormitory, and the thatched dining room. Left, below the school building, are the boys dormitories. The clearing, lower left, was the location of the Marshall Islands School from 1879 to 1905, an area later used as an athletic field. Today the Walung Elementary School stands there. (Elden Buck)

Below: Kosrae Christian Training School campus, 1962. Left, the mission house; center, the chapel (with girls' dormitory on the second floor). Right, the library end of the school building completed in 1961. (Elden Buck)

396

Above: The mission school canoe, *Kawak*, glides out of the Lelu mangrove channel at Insrefusr on its way to Wot, 1954. (Alice Hanlin Buck)

Center: Children at Wot, December 1954. Front row, from left: Tetsuko Jacob Taulung, Rosa Isaiah, Sra Jacob Taulung, Lerina Jack Musrasrik, Lucy Sam Musrasrik. Middle: Qulick Fredrick Aliksa; back row: Richard Aliksru Tolenoa, Johnson Jacob Taulung, Lupalik Luke, Emerson Kilafwa Nathan. (Alice Hanlin Buck)

Below: Wot students prepare for a fishing expedition, 1954. From left: staff member Lise Sam Musrasrik, Kenye Nena Aliksa, Tulpe Aliksru Tolenoa, Mita Anton Saelus, Mumeko Josse Charley, and Lucinda Nena Livai. Filing into the shallow lagoon, women surrounded schools of fish, snagging the fish in the large butterfly nets spread out between them. The catch was divided among participants. This traditional type of fishing is no longer practiced. (Alice Hanlin Buck)

Above: KCTS girls in Utwe, March 24, 1959. Standing at the mouth of the Finkol River, from left: Rinah Salik, Elvinia Nena, Kenye Nipi David, Simako Milton, Sanahe Kun Aaron, Akusta Likiaklik, Connie Alik, Sra Aliksru, Srue Palikoa, Magrina Tulenkun, Aklina Matthew and Hiroko Alik. Brian Alik Isaac is the boy at far left. (Elden Buck)

Below: KCTS boys in Utwe. With their teacher at the Utwe Church dedication, February 4, 1960, front row, from left: Elden Buck, Nena Kilafwasru, Kun Joe, Noel Tulensru; back row: Kemwel Tilfas, Hadley Alik, Marston Nena, Kasuo Leander, Paul Tilfas and Iwao Justus Mongkeya. (Alice Hanlin Buck)

Above: Utwe Church, 1962. (Elden Buck)

Below: January 27, 1962—two of Kosrae's last citizens known by their traditional chiefly titles Sikein and Sinikein at the edge of Lelu Harbor—Aliklof and his wife, Kenye, were faithful members of the Lelu congregation. (Elden Buck)

Above: The mission house at Wot was built for Elizabeth & Jane Baldwin. It was used by them from 1920 to 1936, by Clarence & Cora McCall 1936-1940, by the Japanese military as an officers' retreat 1942-1945, by Harold & Mary Ruth Hanlin and children 1948-1950, by Lucy Lanktree 1952-1954 & Alice Hanlin 1953-1955, and by Elden & Alice Hanlin Buck and daughters 1959-1962. The house, built of termite-treated lumber from Japan, was still in good condition when dismantled by the Wot landowners in 1980. (Elden Buck)

Center: KCTS student council, 1961-1962—front row, from left: Yosimi George, Mitchigo Skilling, Takae Joseph, Richard Tolenoa; back row: John Mike, Kasuo Isisaki, Natchuo Mongkeya, Kemwel Tilfas. (Elden Buck)

Below: KCTS classroom and library building built on the Yonrak ridge at Wot 1960-1961 by groups from the Tafunsak, Lelu, Malem and Utwe congregations, Erafe Tosie as chief carpenter— with three classrooms on the upper level; a storeroom, office and library were on the lower level. It was used only through 1965. The property reverted to the original landowning families in 1992. (Elden Buck)

Above: Harrison George &
Yamada Simeon Skilling at
Wot following their marriage
in October 1960. (Elden
Buck)

Below: May 13, 1962—Erafe
Tosie, left (pastor 1970-1999)
and Joshua Phillip (pastor
1981-1990), while teachers
at Wot. (Elden Buck)

Above: The spectacular north view from the Wot campus, April 1959. Kiel Island on the reef at the mouth of Okat Harbor can be seen in the distance. Today, jet aircraft touch down very near Kiel at Kosrae's modern airport, completed in 1983. (Elden Buck)

Below: On graduation day, May 18, 1962, KCTS students gather on the lawn at Wot for a farewell song and prayer together. (Elden Buck)

Above: February 1964—these girls are part of the last student body to study at Wot. Front row, from left: Alice Sru Jerry, Eleanor Franklin James, Emma Joseph Nelson, Salome Kun Tulenna; second row: Hatie Paul Sigrah, Sepe Sru Tulenna, Marisa Likiak Isaiah, Sepe Killion Abraham, Millerina Moses Lonno; third row: Tirime Aliksru Tolenoa, Kenye Palokoa Joe, Clara Tosie Thompson, Marsina Ezra Nena; fourth row: house-mother Tulpe Palikkun George, Sepe Seymore Caleb, Tesina Fredick Klingkun, Louisa Joshua Abraham, Ellen Freddy Likiaksa, Clara Nemia Tulensru, Kate Kilafwa Sikein. (Elden Buck)

Center: Tafunsak Church, 1962. (Elden Buck)

Below: Aliksru Tolenoa (pastor 1961-1988) with his wife, Sepe, in Tafunsak, March 2, 1964. (Elden Buck)

Above: January 8, 1977—
Srue Frank sits with children
on the grass at Pisin. Raised
by her adoptive father,
Deacon Alik Kefwas, Srue
attended the mission school
at Wot where she later
taught. Her husband, Frank
Skilling, was Kosrae's 10th
pastor. After his death, Srue
continued her service to the
church, and in particular to
the children of Lelu among
whom she worked as a devoted song leader and Bible-sto-
ryteller, until her own death
on November 26, 1984—six
weeks into her 90th year.
(Elden Buck)

Below: Anna Dederer,
Kosrae's last missionary,
served on the island from
1964 to 1970, making her
home at Pisin. (Elden Buck)

Above: Harrison George (pastor 1967-1987) officiates at a dedication of children in the Lelu church on Sunday morning, January 9, 1977. (Elden Buck)

Below: Alik Isaac (pastor 1954-1995) in the pulpit of the Lelu Congregational Church on Sunday morning, January 9, 1977. (Elden Buck)

Above: Delegates to the SHINE! Workshop in August 1984 head toward the tiny reef island, Kiel, to enjoy a day of picnicking together. Kosrae's jet airstrip now covers this area. (Alice Hanlin Buck)

Below: Aaron Sigrah (pastor 1979-1991) and his wife, Ruth, with their two youngest children, Rose and Leonard, in January 1977. An older son, the Honorable Rensley A. Sigrah, is Kosrae's current governor. (Elden Buck)

406

Above: Members of the Editorial Committee gather in the Lelu church library with Dr. Stephen Hre Kio, Bible Society consultant, and Alice Buck, project coordinator, April 29, 2000. Seated, from left: Pastor Salik Cornelius, Dr. Hre Kio, Mrs. Buck, Pastor Kun Sigrah. Standing, from left: Pastor Lyndon Abraham, Pastor Kun Caleb, Pastor Asher Palik, Pastor Takeo Likiaksa (Chairman, Church Council), Pastor Nena T. Kilafwasru, Pastor Walton Palik and Pastor Natchuo Andrew. After a process covering a period of ten years, the new translation of the Bible in Kosraean was completed on August 9, 2002. (Elden Buck)

Below: A choir sings on Easter Sunday, April 23, 2000, in the Malem church sanctuary. Pastors and deacons sit along the left wall, front. Pastors' wives and deaconesses sit along the right wall. With ceramic tile covering the entire 88 by 58 feet of floor space—with its handsome windows and comfortable seating—the sanctuary is unique on Kosrae. Most of the labor was volunteer, and $313,856 to cover the cost of materials was donated by members of the congregation, by Kosrae's other churches, and by many individuals. Everything had been paid for by December 23, 1999, when the building was dedicated. (Elden Buck)

Above: People of Lelu take their turn working at the construction site of the new church building in Utwe, September 22, 2001. (Elden Buck)

Center: The Honorable Rensley A. Sigrah, Governor of Kosrae State and a lay minister of the Lelu Congregational Church (left), congratulates his brother, Pastor Tadasy A. Sigrah, on the occasion of the latter's ordination in the Lelu church on May 1, 2002. (Alice Hanlin Buck)

Below: Lelu Congregational Church. On sesquicentennial Sunday, August 18, 2002, Kosraeans and their off-island guests leave the service of remembering and thanksgiving that inaugurated a week of festivities around the island, commemorating the arrival of the Gospel. (Elden Buck)

408

Above: Members of a Lelu choir sing from a pavilion outside the Lelu church as part of the celebration on August 21, 2002—marking the 150th anniversary of the Church. (Alice Hanlin Buck)

Below: Yosimi Idosi (left), Deaconess Hattie Conrad and Deaconess Alwina Aruo welcome Alice Buck back to Kosrae on January 22, 2003. (Elden Buck)

DR. HANLIN RETURNS TEMPORARILY TO KOSRAE

At the end of November, Harold Hanlin went to Kosrae to pack and ship the family's household gear from Wot to Kutchua, Dublon, Chuuk. Like Miss Wilson, who had visited KCTS in May, and Dr. Terpstra, the new missionary at Pohnpei who had visited three months earlier, Dr. Hanlin was impressed with the job Pastor Palik Kefwas was doing as school administrator. In the midst of his packing—a job he did not relish because he had to decide by himself what to leave, what to take, and what to throw away—Dr. Hanlin took his turn leading chapel services, counseling both staff and students, and teaching classes in English and algebra.

Not only was Harold Hanlin frustrated by the packing process, he was stymied and irritated by the unpredictability of the shipping schedule. The United States Navy's jurisdiction of the islands had been an emergency measure in the immediate aftermath of World War II. Now the reins of power were in the hands of an entity called the United States Trust Territory of the Pacific Islands, which governed the former Japanese Mandate through the U.S. Department of the Interior on behalf of the United Nations. One of the most horrendous problems faced by the new administration was trying to regularize the movement of ships—called "field trips"—between the islands of Micronesia. A delay of months was not uncommon.

Of Christmas 1951, Harold wrote to his wife:

We really had a good Christmas season here. Tafunsak and Utwe sent feast food a few days before Christmas. We took all the students and went to Lelu for Christmas Day. All the people seemed to enjoy the special songs and scripture verses regardless of interruptions and interferences of all kinds. The ushers kept walking up to the Christmas tree with packages of assorted sizes all during the program—climbing over children and trying to shoo them out of the way as they went back and forth. Somebody who apparently didn't want to bother the ushers just pitched several packages through the nearest window so they landed on the pile under the tree![17]

PREPARATIONS FOR THE CENTENNIAL

Dr. Hanlin had expected to depart Kosrae for Pohnpei and Chuuk aboard a U. S. Trust Territory ship in early January 1952, but was delayed until the ship finally arrived on February 12. While in Lelu during that month of waiting, he was able to watch the work proceeding on the new church building at Langosak just across the Pisin causeway. He answered questions concerning his drawings and offered advice as the work progressed. Prominent among the carpenters working on the project were the men who had helped him three years earlier during the rebuilding process at Wot. Other Lelu hands, as well as the hands of many from the neighboring villages, were also contributing to this work. The men came in teams on specific days, assigned to particular parts of the building.

Sometimes Dr. Hanlin would stand at the construction site with Pastor John Paliknoa Sigrah, now 76 years of age, and listen as the old man reminisced, recalling the unique personalities of his predecessors and describing the buildings that had stood on this spot in years gone by. Reminiscing came easy during this centennial year.

In Oberlin, Ohio, a friend and mentor from Pastor John Sigrah's youth was also reminiscing as time for the anniversary approached. In the process of her reverie, 87-year-old Mary Goldsbury Channon carefully wrapped a banner she had saved for 50 years and mailed it to Pastor John so that it could have a place of honor at the centennial celebration. It was one of the white banners that had decorated the interior of the Lelu church at the time of the jubilee in 1902. On it—emblazoned in red—were the names of some of Kosrae's first Christians.

Leaders of the Church on Kosrae were especially anxious to complete the new building in time for the August 21 event. It would be 100 years since the arrival of Benjamin and Lydia Snow, and Daniel and Doreka Opunui, aboard the *Caroline*. Church leaders were anxious for Dr. Hanlin to extend their invitation to other missionaries, to the leaders of churches throughout Micronesia, and to the advisors and directors of the mission organizations in Boston and Honolulu. The centennial was the ideal time to dedicate their new church, and they wanted as many friends and colleagues as possible to celebrate with them.

But the ship which arrived February 12 brought urgent letters from Eleanor Wilson, who was on furlough in the United States, and from Alice Cary, the American Board's Pacific Area Secretary in Boston, asking that the celebration be postponed from August until November so that both Miss Wilson and Miss Cary could attend.

Dr. Hanlin noted in a letter to his family, "I'll have to talk to Pastor Palik Kefwas and see if church and Christian Endeavor officials will reconsider the matter and adjust their plans accordingly. The principal difficulty is that breadfruit is very scarce here in November so the people will have a hard time getting together enough food for the feasting involved in such an occasion."[18]

The Kosraean leadership agreed to the postponement. Though some people grumbled, others were relieved to have the additional time to complete the building and prepare for the festivities.

NEW MISSIONARY FOR WOT

Miss Lucy Lanktree and Miss Louise Meebold had been American Board missionaries in China for many years but, with other missionaries, they had been driven from that country by the revolutionary communist government. Since neither was quite ready for retirement, the American Board decided to use them in Micronesia. In June 1952, Louise Meebold was sent to the Marshall Islands to work with Eleanor Wilson, and Lucy Lanktree was assigned to Kosrae to assist Pastor Palik Kefwas with school responsibilities at Wot. After several false starts from Pohnpei aboard the malfunctioning *Morning Star VI* , Miss Lanktree finally reached Kosrae in mid-July aboard a field-trip ship.

MORNING STAR VI LOST AT SEA

Capt. Chris Ketchum had skippered the *Morning Star* safely for six months when it was decided that the ship was no longer fit. In late October, the little vessel was being towed from Pohnpei to the Marshall Islands to be sold, when a storm "battered her weakened hull and broke her towline. The pumps could not save her. Aboard was Capt. Ketchum and one crewman. They knew the ship was doomed. It was impossible to launch a boat—there was nothing to do but for the two men to swim to the *Torry*, the towing vessel, which was standing by."[19] Fortunately this all came to its dismal climax one morning during daylight. From the *Torry* they watched as the *Star* began to break up and then sank quickly in 2,200 fathoms, just 80 miles from Majuro.[20]

CENSUS OF 1952

The 2,060 Kosraeans counted in the census of 1952 reflected the continuing growth of the island's population.

WALKWAY TO LELU

For years, Kosraeans had talked of creating a land-link between Lelu and the large island. Though the common way to travel between the two islands was by canoe, it had always been possible at low tide to walk across the tideland from the north side of Lelu to Finpikal, toward Tafunsak. But it was not an easy walk—how much more convenient it would be to have a walkway lifted up out of the shallow water and away from the whims of the tides. And that is exactly what the island council decided it was time to do.

The introduction of the gospel on Kosrae had resulted in an inclusive society that was incompatible with the traditional chiefly system that had kept Lelu Island off-limits to most of Kosrae's inhabitants in years past. What better way to extol Kosrae's Christian democracy at the time of the centennial than with a literal reminder of the tie that binds people together, replacing old patterns that kept people apart? The two islands would be linked by a causeway!

Large groups of men from each of the four villages were assigned portions along the length of the anticipated roadway. Wot students took time off and joined the work force. Women and children carried rocks, passed woven coconut-frond baskets of dirt, and toted teapots of drinking water. There were few shovels available, so workers used the cupped ends of coconut fronds—the part that clasps the tree. Coral rocks were brought one by one from all over the lagoon and harbor. As had always been true of any project jointly undertaken, laughter and camaraderie made heavy work light. The work was swiftly accomplished in an atmosphere of friendly competition. In some places as high as 15 feet above the reef, the causeway—almost half a mile in length—became a reality in just two weeks. Finished, it was wide enough to accommodate the one or two decrepit vehicles that the ingenuity of several apprentice mechanics kept in operating condition.

CONFLICT OVER A CROSS

As work on the Lelu church neared completion and a remnant of the construction crew was finishing detailed painting and decorating, groups of three or four frequently gathered in front of the building to discuss yet again the three-foot cross that stood at the pinnacle of the tower's dome. The discussions, often heated, had been going on since the day the chief carpenter, following Harold Hanlin's design, had secured the white concrete symbol in its lofty place.

For some of the older members of the church it was inconceivable that a symbol that commonly identified Catholic churches in Micronesia should stand atop their own new building. The anti-Catholic stance of earlier Wot missionaries whose colleagues had been so unfairly and harshly treated by the militantly pro-Catholic Spanish officials and their priests at Pohnpei in the 1890s had been set firmly in their minds.

But, responded others among the church leadership who tended to be younger, the cross was a Christian symbol. Catholics did not have a monopoly on the cross. It was true that no cross had graced the tower of earlier buildings, but during the war so recently ended, Protestant Christians on some islands in Micronesia had painted crosses on the roofs of their churches and American airmen, recognizing the symbol, had refrained from bombing them. Their own beloved church in Lelu, which had been contemptuously used by the Japanese as a dormitory for

Chinese laborers during the war, had no such symbol, and it had been completely destroyed. Was it not proper to mark the new building as Christian? So it was decided by a small majority that the cross should remain on the tower.

But the arguing continued and bad feelings festered. In the middle of the night, just hours before the arrival of their off-island guests, several Lelu churchmen took the matter into their own hands. Determined that what they were doing was right, they instructed a reticent carpenter to climb to the top of the tower. They directed from below as the cross, with some effort, was pried loose from its base and then tossed into the dark waters of Lelu Harbor just a few feet away.

This deliberate act of defiance on the part of a few was quickly noted and became an immediate topic of whispered conversation. Pastor Palik Kefwas was particularly dismayed. Not only had the warped notion of a few disgruntled persons counteracted a decision of the All-Church Committee and defaced the handsome new building on the eve of its dedication, but his role as an ordained leader of Kosrae's church was being challenged in what he considered to be an ominous manner. What could he do? The ship bringing their friends had already been sighted.

CENTENNIAL AND CHURCH DEDICATION

Pastor Palik's heavy heart was lightened as he stood on the dock with Pastor John Sigrah and most of Lelu's citizens and noted with pleasure the honored guests who lined the ship's railing. Missionaries Harold Hanlin and Eleanor Wilson smiled in recognition. With Miss Wilson stood Louise Meebold, Lucy Lanktree's former China colleague. The American Board's Miss Alice Cary, secretary of the Micronesian work in the Boston offices, stood beside Mrs. G. A. Johnson Ross, who represented the Hawaiian Evangelical Association. There were 10 island church leaders from Chuuk, Pohnpei, and the Marshall Islands, plus nine Marshallese students arriving to enroll at Wot. Within minutes, all of these new arrivals were engulfed in the warm reception of their Kosraean hosts.

On November 16, 1952, an exuberant explosion of praise took place on Kosrae. A huge congregation, including most of Kosrae's 2,000 residents, plus Lucy Lanktree and the Wot students, as well as the special guests, crowded into the new church building at Langosak. The service that began at 4 a.m. was solemn and sincere, yet joy-filled, interrupted only by short intervals for meals. Under the cherished white flag that Mary Channon had so lovingly mailed to her old friend, John Paliknoa Sigrah, and surrounded by decorations of fresh flowers and palm branches, the story was told and retold, both spoken and sung, until after 9 p.m.

Ten small children had been appointed to carry to the altar the many letters of greeting that had reached Kosrae from churches and Christian friends in America and other parts of the world. More than 50 other children wanted to take part. Several visitors reported that the resulting procession of children into the church was the most moving part of the day.

Miss Cary presented a silver baptismal bowl on behalf of the American Board. Eleanor Wilson presented a bronze vase. After graciously receiving these, Pastor Palik announced that the Kosraeans, too, had "a gift." It appeared that every person, every family, walked forward in an orderly, affectionate parade to place upon the table and platform gifts of baskets, hats, fans, belts, mats, shells, leis, headbands, model canoes, carved containers, and many other articles representing countless hours of labor and love. "This is the first time our people have had a chance to express themselves directly to an American Board representative," young Pastor Palik explained.[21]

Louise Meebold, so recently assigned by the Mission Board to Micronesia, commented, "Surely the Lord was in this place, and we all knew it!"[22]

Dr. Hanlin described the Centennial in a letter distributed by the Missions Council in Boston:

In November I had an all-too-short visit at Kusaie for the Centennial Celebration there and the dedication of their fine new church building at Lelu. That building is now our finest church building in Micronesia, and although we helped the Kusaiens with a gift of money, they have put a tremendous amount into it—both in money and volunteer labor—so that it is now a beautiful witness to the interest and devotion of the Christian people there.

The Centennial celebration was as well attended by folk from other islands as the transportation facilities out here would permit. The Kusaiens were disappointed because the brevity of our stay did not permit them to do many of the things they had planned. Five choirs had been rehearsing for months on a total of forty new songs—and we were able to hear only a few of them! The Celebration had to be held on a Monday—hence the people could not prepare the elaborate feast which they wanted to have, for it is their custom to forego as much work as possible on Sundays. But all in all, it was a very fine celebration.[23] ☦

Notes - Chapter 14

1.   Harold F. Hanlin, "Christmas in May," unpublished manuscript, Kosrae, May 23, 1948
2.   H. F. Hanlin, "Kusaie Christian Training School," *The Friend*, Dec. 1948, pp. 17-18
3.   H. F. Hanlin, "The Passing of Kefwas," *The Friend*, Dec. 1948, p. 18
4.   H. F. Hanlin, "Kusaie Christian Training School," pp. 17-18
5.   H. F. Hanlin, unpublished "My Autobiography—Harold Francis Hanlin," Claremont, June 4, 1985, p. 11
6.   H. F. Hanlin, unpublished "Autobiography—Harold Francis Hanlin," Claremont, Feb. 3, 1986, p. 20
7.   Mary Ruth Hanlin, unpublished "Kusaie Christian Training School," May 10, 1950
8.   M. R. Hanlin, "Five Year Diary," Feb.-May 1949
9.   Ibid, July 5, 1949
10. M. R. Hanlin, "Kusaie Christian Training School, " May 10, 1950
11. H. F. Hanlin, newsletter of March 11, 1950, Missions Council, Boston, p. 2
12. Mary Alice Hanlin [Buck], "Alice in Wonderland—Today," *The Bible Society Record*, 1953, pp. 20-21
13. American Board of Commissioners for Foreign Missions, "Our Christian World Mission" position paper, Boston, 1952, p. 4
14. Maribelle Cormack. *The Lady Was a Skipper*, 1956, pp. 216-217
15. Ibid, pp. 216-217
16. M. A. Hanlin [Buck], "Alice in Wonderland—Today," 1953, p. 21
17. H. F. Hanlin, personal correspondence, Kosrae, Jan. 3, 1952
18. Ibid, Feb. 12, 1952
19. Cormack, p. 16
20. Creston Donald Ketchum, *His Path Is in the Water*, p. 179
21. ABCFM, Annual Report 1953
22. Irvin Raymond Lindemuth, "Micronesia Missions: Proving Grounds of Christianity," unpublished thesis, Bangor Theological Seminary, Bangor, Maine, 1957, p. 282
23. H. F. Hanlin, Missions Council letter, Boston, January 15, 1953

NUNAK YOHK KE CHAPTER 15
1952-1959

Malem se tukun akfulatyeyuk tuku lun Wosasu, ac oayapa alu in kisa ke lohm alu sasu Langosak, Pastu Palik Kefwas el tuh masak ac tia paht el misa ke December 19, 1952. Meet liki kisa se inge tuh oasr akukuin inmasrlon mwet kol lun Church ke sripen kutu selos lungse in oasr sakseng soko fin tower ah, a kutu srunga. Elos vote kac, a sulala ma in oasr. Tusruktu fong se meet liki len in kisa ah, u se ma tuh lain ah sap sie mukul in fanyak ac esya sakseng soko ah, ac sisla nu in kof. Arulana yohk asor lal Pastu Palik lah u se ma supus inge in tuh lain oakwuk ma inkaiyen mwet uh tuh insese nu kac. Ke el sa na misa tukun fohs se inge, sou lal ah nunku mu pa oru el misa. Arulana yohk nunkeyen ma se inge sel. El yac na 35 ke el misa.

Alice Hanlin el srakna lutlut ke college, na ke el lohngak lah Pastu Palik el misa, el sifacna siyuk sin American Board elan folokla nu Wot in kasru lutlut we. Elos insese in supwalla in orekma yac luo. El tuh yac 20 ke el sun acn Kosrae in September 1953. Ke sripen el etu kas Kosrae, el pulakin mu yohk ma el ku in oru in sang kasrel Miss Lanktree oayapa tulik lutlut we ah. Tusruktu Miss Lanktree el nunku siena. El tia lungse Alice elan kas Kosrae, oayapa el mu wangin sripa in oasr pacl in aetui ac pwapa lun mwet luti ac mwet orekma ah. Ma pus fohsak in pacl sac. Alice el liye lah twang in neinyuk kof nukewa wohn, ac ima uh tiana karinginyuk wo. El liye pac lah tulik lutlut uh supwar ac kutu selos tiala pac wi class. Tok Alice el orala sie schedule sasu ac Miss Lanktree el insese kac, na tufah wola kutu.

Erafe Tosie el welul Alice lungasla Kas in Kol lun Etawi in akola nu ke 1954. Alice el tuh wi Malem Sasu ke November 1953, ke mwet elos vote in akmusraella Deacon Ernest Sigrah tuh elan kasrel Pastu John Sigrah, papa tumal, su yac 78. Tusruktu pusla inen mwet touyak nu ke vote sac oru arulana fohsak, pwanang pukanten mwet tia insese nu kac. In January, Committee lun Church sifil srukak mwet luo mwet uh in sifilpa vote kac. Vote se inge orekla ke Malem Sasu, February 1954. Alik Isaac el sulosolla in pastu se akeu lun Church Kosrae. Dr. Chester Terpstra el tuku ac akmusraella. Mukul in church Lelu ac Tafunsak elos pakiya sak ka na lulap soko Yela, ac taflela in orala soko oak. Mukul in church Malem ac Utwe elos aksafyela ac sang mangsrasr ac em nu kac, ac sroalela. Elos kulukin ac som nu Wot in sang okan lutlut ah. Lusen oak soko inge oasr ke fit 45. Tuh aluiyukla oak soko inge ke February 19, 1954, ac itukyang ine *Kawuk*. Mwet nukewa fin acn Wot tuh arulana engankin oak soko inge.

Ke August 1954 oasr conference luo orekla fin acn Wot nu sin mwet fusr Kosrae ma tia wi lutlut. Church Malem ac Utwe supwala mwet fusr tolngoul tolu in wi conference se meet, ac church Lelu ac Tafunsak supwala mwet fusr longoul oalkosr in wi conference akluo. Miss Lanktree el som liki acn Kosrae ke August 22 in luti ke school fin acn Rongrong, Majuro. Na Mrs. Hanlin el tuku Chuuk me nu Kosrae in kasrel Alice ke school Wot.

Alice ac Mrs. Hanlin eltal mutawauk in osun yurin mwet ke kais sie mura in sramsramkin lah ac ku in akiya Etawi lun mwet fusr. Eltal akkalemye lah ma in sang kasru mwet fusr in kapkapak ke elahn mwet Christian, oayapa akpulaikyalos in eis kunelos ke pacl in alu. Oasr sensen lun mwet matu ke nunak se inge, tusruktu church Tafunsak elos wotela in oasr Etawi Fusr we. Alice ac nina kial wi alu Tafunsak ke November 14, 1954, su ke pacl se inge akwuki tari Etawi Fusr fin acn we. President se emeet lun Etawi Fusr Tafunsak pa Daniel Seymour.

Ke May 24, 1955, Alice ac Mrs. Hanlin, mokuila liki acn Kosrae. Mrs. Hanlin el folokla nu Chuuk, acn el ac Dr. Hanlin luti we. Alice el som nu California, ac el tuh payuk nu sel Elden Buck we, su ma welul lutlut ke college.

In April 19, 1957, Pastu John Sigrah el misa ke el yac 81 matwa. Yokna ma kunal nu sin mwet Kosrae nukewa, mweyen ke ip lun government el pa tokosra safla lalos, ac ke ip lun church el tuh pastu se lalos. El tuh fahk nu sel Miss Eleanor Wilson ke 1947 lah el engan in pastu ke Church Kosrae liki na in tokosra lun acn Kosrae. Wal lun tokosra safla yorol. Eteyuk el yurin mwet Japan, mwet America, ac mwet puspis saya su forfor nu Kosrae. In December 1957, Deacon Frank Skilling el akmusrala—el pa pastu aksingoul lun Church Kosrae.

Oasr sie ouiya sasu sikyak Kosrae ke pacl se inge. Pus sin mwet America su orekma ke Trust Territory tuh tuku nu Kosrae. Elos tia mwet in church. Elos sismok ac lungse nimnim. Mwet fusr Kosrae su welulos orekma mutawauk in etawelos. Fahsr nwe apkuran mwet orekma nukewa lun government in tia mwet in church, ac mwet in church in tia wi orekma lun government.

In January 1959, Alice ac mukul tumal, Pastu Elden Buck, eltal sun acn Kosrae wi tulik srisrik luo natultal, Lisa ac Lauren. Supweyukla eltal sin American Board in mwet luti ke mission school Wot. Tulik mukul singoul eu ac tulik mutan singoul luo muta Wot soaneltal—tulik inge kewa tulik Kosrae. Ke yac itngoul eu somla, tufahna in wangin tulik tuku saya me in lutlut Wot. Erafe Tosie ac Alik Palsis tuh mwet luti pac we.

Wik se meet liki Easter 1959, mwet kol ac tulik lutlut Wot som nu ke kais sie mura in orek drama ac oayapa yuk on in Easter lalos. Ke len in Easter, March 29, pus liki mwet 900 tuh wi alu Lelu. Pastu Elden pa fahkak kas ke Sunday sac, Alice el kol Sunday School, ac tulik lutlut Wot elos on. Mwet Kosrae inge tuh arulana lungse program ke wik sac nu fon.

– CHAPTER FIFTEEN –

CHALLENGES AND CONFLICTS
1952-1959

DEATH OF PASTOR PALIK

Less than a month after the centennial celebration, an epidemic of influenza and meningitis swept over Kosrae. Among the nine who died was Pastor Palik Kefwas, one of the two ordained pastors and a Christian leader of extraordinary promise. He was 35 years old.

Pastor Palik had been the person ultimately responsible for the centennial celebration, including the dedication of the new church building. Pastor John Sigrah, now 77 years old and still revered as the primary leader of the Church on Kosrae, was no longer physically able to be involved in the nitty-gritty of preparation—but he did let people know what he wanted, and his wishes were usually followed. Separated by a wide generation gap—Pastor Palik was Pastor John's grandson-in-law—the two had very little in common beyond their commitment as Christians as they struggled to work together at the head of the Church. After the Hanlins left, Pastor Palik had remained at Wot where he was especially needed. But as the centennial approached, the young pastor left the oversight of KCTS to Lucy Lanktree and moved with his family to Lelu for the weeks leading up to the festivities. A number of the Wot students were assigned to him at Pisin to be of assistance as the day drew near.

By the time the ceremonies, feasting, and cleanup had been completed, Pastor Palik was physically and emotionally drained. The controversy over the church tower cross was unresolved; it had been a festering undercurrent during centennial activities. Discouraged, the pastor returned to Wot with his family, Miss Lanktree, and the students. Within days he fell ill. As his fever climbed, his frightened wife and colleagues took him by canoe to the hospital at Metais, Lelu, where his condition continued to deteriorate. Two nights later, on December 19, 1952, he died.

The Wot student body and the entire Kosraean community were stunned by this turn of events. Pastor Palik's family was convinced that he had died of a broken heart. The Church plunged into mourning and also into a period of solemn introspection. Among those particularly distraught was John Sigrah, who was left as the island's only pastor. The two leaders had not been able to communicate well, but as when a child dies before a parent, the death of the older man's grandson-in-law fell outside the natural order, and Pastor John was deeply saddened.

As the news of Pastor Palik's death spread beyond Kosrae, Dr. Hanlin wrote from Chuuk to friends in America in March 1953: "I have received the sad news of the sudden and unexpected death of Rev. Palik Kefwas, an outstanding, dependable leader who was largely responsible for much of the Christian development at Kusaie since the war. This is a serious blow to the effectiveness of our work at Kusaie. His loss will be keenly felt both in the church and in the school at Mwot."[1]

STRUGGLING FORWARD

The primary teacher and preacher for Kosrae's Church was gone. The one who, almost single-handedly, had continued the work at Wot following the departure of the Hanlins had been taken away. Pastor John Sigrah came out of semi-retirement and did his utmost to fill the void left by the death of his young colleague. He taught and otherwise assisted the lay-preachers as they prepared for each Sunday's assignment. When he could, he traveled to Wot to encourage the students and staff there.

When graduation day arrived in May, Pastor John gave the commencement address for the 36 KCTS students at the mid-morning ceremony. That afternoon he officiated at the weddings of three young Kosraean women as they married Marshallese classmates: Almeda Palik Asher to Anrube Rilometo, Myra Aliksa Kanku to Naphtali Langinbelik, and Marina Jorem to Lainej Lakatak.

Both Anrube and Naphtali became pastors in the Marshall Islands, as did their fellow-graduate, Harry Rakin. Graduate Jude Samson also became a pastor and for 35 years-and-counting has been president of Jarin Rarik Dron—the United Church of Christ in the Marshall Islands. Upon returning to the Marshalls, Jude married his classmate, Dinah Gaius, who has faithfully worked beside him through the years. Dinah became a dynamic leader in her own right, guiding the vibrant Drolul in Rarik Dron—the Christian Women's Fellowship—with its hundreds of members scattered across 24 atolls.

Three others in that graduating class were destined to be pastors: Calwin Edwin and Danny Leopold of Pohnpei and Kosrae's own Erafe Tosie.

MISSIONARY DAUGHTER VOLUNTEERS

Alice Hanlin, who was a sophomore at Phillips University in Enid, Oklahoma, was sad and bewildered upon hearing of Pastor Palik's death.

He was her Christian example, her spiritual mentor. His outgoing, though thoughtful, Christ-like nature had been her inspiration. The days went by and Alice's sorrow moved into a profound concern for the students at KCTS who were suddenly without their dynamic leader. She felt a strong empathy for Lucy Lanktree, who was now alone with the responsibilities of a school whose primary language the missionary did not speak. Alice had taken Pastor Palik's words seriously when they parted—she felt that she had been studying for him. Could she fill at least a part of his place at the school during this crisis?

She mulled the perplexity in a newsletter: "How I longed to go help, but being just 20 years old and having not yet finished college, it was impossible to think about—or was it? Kingdom building is accomplished by acting, not wishful thinking. I volunteered to go as a student helper if they would see fit to send me."[2]

Alice Cary, Pacific area secretary of the American Board—aware of Alice's knowledge of the Kosraean language and the level of her commitment—responded in the affirmative on behalf of the Board: they would send Alice to the school at Kosrae for a "short-term assignment" of two years as a student teacher. In a Missions Council newsletter, Alice wrote:

At 5:30 a.m., September 29th, the little ship with me aboard pulled majestically into Lelu Harbor, Kusaie—just one month after I left home in Oklahoma City. How beautiful it looked in its early morning splendor! At last I had reached my dear friends here and the welcome began even before I had stepped ashore. After shaking hands with those standing closest by, I saw old King John coming forward. He was dressed in his best white suit and had his familiar coconut fiber hat set square on his head. He shook my hand and thanked God for my safe arrival. Then with a broad smile he presented me with two miniature king's beds which he had made, and said joyously, "And a Merry Christmas to you!" (Any day can be Christmas in this generous man's heart.) Turning to those standing around he began a hymn of praise and thanksgiving and all joined in.

At Mwot the students' welcomed me with gay marching, special songs, and colorful headbands, beautifully conveying their love. I was here at last! I had one free week before starting classes, and in it I relaxed and unpacked. I have my same room (Heidi that I am) upstairs under the eaves, and can enjoy the same inspiring scenery that I did before.

However, along with this luxury goes a pretty busy schedule. My day begins between 5:30 and 6:00 a.m. and ends about 9:30 p.m. I teach four classes—Bible, hygiene, geography, and art—lead chapel one morning a week, and preach once a month. Extracurricular activities include translating the Sunday School lessons for the four village superintendents and their teachers, preparing lessons, grading papers, leading active games on Friday evenings, helping with the music and cook-

ing, and interpreting. Then there are those exciting unexpected things every day or two just to round out the program.[3]

CHALLENGES AND CONFLICTS

Almost immediately, Alice realized that all was not as it should be at Wot. For her own reasons, Miss Lanktree had decided that meeting with the school's Kosraean staff was not necessary. The absence of planning sessions grated on Alice—especially after the older missionary made it plain to her that she was not to have any conversations in the Kosraean language with members of the Wot staff. "The language of Wot is English!" And neither was Alice welcome to converse with Miss Lanktree about the school situation. Miss Lanktree would make the decisions and personally instruct individual staff members. Yet decisions were not made, much to Alice's frustration.

The absence of clearly articulated plans for the school, lacking since the death of Pastor Palik more than nine months earlier, had resulted in a low level of morale among members of the Wot staff who were not sure how to proceed. These staff members included Frank Skilling, work foreman, and his wife, Srue, a teacher; Sam Musrasrik and his wife, Lise, cooks; and Flora Aliksa, housemother. Morale was even lower among the students, who were continually tardy for chapel services and classes. Absences were common in the student body of 62 young people. Classes had no seating charts and attendance was seldom taken. A lackadaisical atmosphere pervaded the entire campus.

There were other consequences of the low morale. Food production on the superb farm-land that comprises a major part of the mission property was practically at a stand-still. Reliance on purchased food had consumed most of the school budget. Six days after she arrived, Alice wrote in her diary: "Starvation is slowly creeping up on us here in the midst of tropical abundance… Every day the cooks come at least once saying 'We have no food for the next meal,' and we hand over some rice. Students go off on their own to borrow and beg food from our neighbors! Everyone blames everyone else for this sad state of affairs. Aunt Lucy sees no solution, and fifteen new students arrived today!"[4]

Even worse was the lack of water in an area of the island that received an average annual rainfall of more than two hundred inches. All cisterns for rain-water catchment leaked—they needed to be cleaned and patched. Most of the gutters leading from the roofs to the cisterns had fallen away. Continuing her diary during that first week at Wot, Alice wrote, "This water situation is TERRIBLE! Today our one and only drum had less than an inch of water in it and it would only come out in drips—no stream at all. G-r-r-r!"[5]

Miss Lanktree did not want to discuss the problems. If Alice mentioned them, she was made to feel like an upstart or whiner. After Lucy complained to Alice that Frank was more willing to work for her than he was for Lucy, Alice decided to concentrate on her lesson plans in her attic bedroom and on preparing the meals for Lucy and herself. But when the older missionary left for Lelu to have the doctor check the open sores on her legs, Srue and Lise filled Alice's ears with their displeasure and grievances. In her journal Alice wrote, "How I miss Palik—How we NEED him!"[6] Alice also missed her family. So much was different without them there. She was on her own in a very difficult situation.

One poignant memory recorded by Alice was the baptism in the Wot chapel on October 29, 1953, of Robina, the youngest child of Pastor Palik, born after her father's death. "Everyone wept throughout the entire service."[7]

Gradually—very gradually—some things got better. A class schedule that Alice was finally allowed to introduce was being followed, but Miss Lanktree agreed to take only one class. Alice was given responsibility for all classes involving the most advanced students, some of whom were now in their fourth year at Wot. She was teaching geography, English, arithmetic, art, hygiene, and Bible. The bell—an empty propane tank hanging from a tree branch and hit with a piece of pipe—began ringing more or less on time. Though staff members hinted that planning sessions would be beneficial and appreciated, Lucy continued to balk at convening such meetings. "We can find out what we need to know and tell them what they need to do, individually."[8]

The food situation also got better with the considerable help of traders Jack Youngstrom in Lelu and the Carlos Etscheit family on Pohnpei.

A "BIRTH"-DAY CELEBRATION

Alice joined the girls in their dormitory above the chapel on the evening of November 7 to celebrate the birthday of Lise, cook Sam Musrasrik's wife. "They had her lie down on mats, then surrounded her with pillows—these they encircled with lighted lanterns. Then they began to march, around and around, singing as they placed gifts on the floor beside her. The symbolism was as if she had just been born!"[9]

NEW PASTOR CHOSEN

At the November 1953 new-month meeting, small pieces of paper were distributed to all present in the Lelu church so that they could select a new pastor. They were instructed to write the name of any person they wished to choose. The papers were collected in someone's hat and the names were read aloud and written on a blackboard. Many different names were read. After the counting was completed, it was Pastor John Sigrah's eldest son, Deacon Ernest, who had received the most votes. But during the next two months, so much dissatisfaction and dissension was voiced, that by January 1954, the ordination had been put on hold. Many felt that the voting was incorrectly done—that the leaders were remiss in not suggesting appropriate pastoral candidates for the membership to consider. Others felt that the election of Ernest had been a knee-jerk reaction of people long accustomed to choosing chiefly members of their society for positions of leadership. It was also the first time in the history of the Church that a pastor was being chosen without the active participation of a senior missionary. The Church membership was in the process of discovery and learning.

Finally the Church committee decided to void the November vote and organize a new election to take place at the new-month meeting on February 1. There were 377 members representing the four congregations present in the Lelu church. Two names were submitted for consideration by the church leadership: Ernest Sigrah and Alik Isaac. When the votes were counted, Alik had won with 210 votes to 120 for Ernest. There were 47 abstentions.[10]

So 46-year-old Alik Isaac, president of the island's Christian Endeavor Society, was chosen to be the ninth pastor of the Church on Kosrae. Not everyone was pleased with the decision—or with what some saw as manipulation by powerful individuals. Understandably, the family of Ernest Sigrah was particularly unhappy. On several occasions, Deacon Ernest and his wife, Rose, shared their hurt with Alice at Pisin—and the three of them prayed together for a sense of God's guidance through the turmoil. [One answer to those prayers occurred in the next generation when a son of Deacon Ernest was successfully treated during a serious illness by the doctor-son of Pastor Alik.]

Alik's ordination was delayed until July 12th, when Dr. Chet Terpstra arrived to officiate. The new pastor accompanied the missionary back to Pohnpei to study for several months at the Pastors & Teachers Training School at Ohwa. Pastor Alik took his new assignment very seriously, serving with dignity and devotion for the next 41 years.

KAWUK LAUNCHED

February 19 was an exciting day for the staff and students at Wot. Members of the Church on Kosrae were presenting a large canoe to KCTS. The men of Lelu and Tafunsak had felled a great ka [terminalia] tree from the rain forest above Yela, hewed it out, and carved the hull. The men of Malem and Utwe had sculpted the surfaces, added the large, impressive bow-piece and the outrigger, installed the seats, and painted it. Then it had been taken to Wot and was to be christened. Alice Hanlin, after mulling various possibilities, chose the name

Kawuk (friend) for the canoe. She wrote: "Our friends have made it for us. The name will be a continual reminder of the friendship between us at the school and the people of Kosrae's churches. The name reminds us also of Our Friend who is with us always—whether we are on the water or on the land—the One who is our anchor." [The word "kawuk" is also the word for "anchor" in the Kosraean language.]

Alice continued her account of that day: "After classes and a hurried lunch, we rang the bell signaling everyone to go down to the water's edge. There, after the men had lifted the huge canoe part way up onto the beach, we surrounded it and sang a hymn. I touched the bow and spoke its name, made a short speech, then asked Paul [Sigrah] to pray. Frank [Skilling] said a few words, and Deacon Joel [Wakuk] from Utwe as well—then another song was sung and they heave-ho'ed to put it into the canoe house, but it was too long. Aunt Lucy measured it—45 feet! Oh! It is beautiful!"[11]

DISHEARTENING INTERPRETATION OF A JOY-FILLED PLAN

It could be that in the periphery of Alice's mind there had been another thought in naming the new canoe *Kawuk*, a name which, incidently, proved to be very popular with islanders and students alike. Just before leaving the United States for Kosrae the year before, Alice became engaged to Elden Buck, a seminary student she had met in the King's Messengers Club, an organization of students at Phillips University who had dedicated themselves to missionary service. She shared her happiness with the Wot students and staff, many of whom had been her friends three years earlier when she lived there with her family, and some of them had seen his photograph.

But when two of the girls at Wot became pregnant—obviously an unaccept-able circumstance at the mission school—Miss Lanktree accused Alice of start-ing a trend toward engagements, "island-style!" "They see you and they want to be like you. You're engaged—they're going to do the same."

"I don't know when anything has cut me so deeply," Alice wrote in her journal. "How could she? Pregnancy is not synonymous with being engaged. In self-defense I said, 'This surely hasn't just started since I've been here.'

"'Well, a big part of it has—they're following your example.'

"I just wanted to lie down and bawl, but I went on preparing the salad, silently..."[12]

One positive consequence of the students' hurrying to become engaged was that these happenings precipitated the re-introduction of staff meetings at Wot. Everyone was relieved to be discussing problems as well as possible solutions, out in the open, together!

U.S. AIR FORCE AT KOSRAE

During most of 1954, a small group of Air Force personnel was stationed at Kosrae to monitor from that location the on-going nuclear tests that the United States government was conducting at Bikini and Enewetak atolls in the Marshall Islands. Several aluminum buildings, used as offices, dormitory, lounge, and mess hall, were erected at Finsrael beside the dock in Lelu. Seaplanes came and went with some regularity—often one or two a week touching down and taking off from the waters of Lelu Harbor. It became common to see low-flying planes over Wot. Most of the flights originated at Kwajalein in the Marshall Islands, but if planes were routed through Pohnpei, mail for Kosrae was sometimes put aboard, greatly pleasing recipients.

Occasionally Air Force men would visit Wot—almost always unannounced—and schedules and food budgets would be thrown out of whack. But when Alice or Lucy and students were in Lelu, the Air Force reciprocated with generous donations of prepared and unprepared food carried over from their Finsrael kitchen to Pisin.

JUGHEAD

Before dawn on May 5, those living on the western, northern, and eastern shores of Kosrae were awakened. Wot's cook exclaimed to Alice, "The sun was rising an hour too early—and in the north!" The entire northern "sky was lit from east to west with white light. It lasted for a few minutes and then faded, turning all the clouds red like a brilliant sunset. It was beautiful. We are 359 miles due south of Enewetak. Approximately 30 minutes later came the two reverberating booms that blew through the trees and shook the whole house for a couple of seconds—the blasts of *Jughead*, the final H-bomb test of the current series…"[13]

The United States government conducted 67 of these atomic and hydrogen tests between 1946 and 1958. The largest of these was detonated over Bikini Atoll—200 miles east of Enewetak—on March 1, 1954, two months prior to *Jughead*. Nicknamed *Bravo*, the Bikini test released a thousand times the destructive force of the bombs dropped on Nagasaki and Hiroshima. These tests turned the atolls of Enewetak, Bikini, and Rongelap in the northwest sector of the Marshall Islands into nuclear wastelands and set in motion an appalling, decades-long period of confusion, upheaval, misery—and often death—which continues today. This is true not only for the people of those three specific atolls and their descendants, but also for people throughout the Marshall Islands and other parts of Micronesia who suffer serious social repercussions and painful, on-going consequences.

SUMMER ACTIVITIES

When the end of the spring term arrived, Kosraean students returned to their homes. Unannounced visits to Wot by Lelu's U.S. Air Force personnel continued to distract, but were also welcomed, as the young men were now bringing generous gifts of food to share. Other visitors included the Finale family, an American couple with two small children who were on Kosrae for one year as part of the government's new public school program. The Trust Territory's Chief Justice Edward Furber and his wife, Ruth, also visited Wot several times that summer.

In addition to her other responsibilities during June, July, and August, Alice was asked to be part of a group of Kosraean educators who were meeting regularly to discuss the possibility of producing a uniform orthography for the Kosraean language—one that would be acceptable to the diverse facets of their island society. The group met every two weeks during that summer, but was unable to reach a consensus. Members of the committee did, however, appreciate the process they had begun and anticipated continuing their discussions the following summer.

Alice also visited the four villages during the early part of the summer, meeting with Church leaders to select a new class of students for the fall term. She met with the young people in each of the villages, inviting those who were interested to one of the two-week conferences the mission school staff planned to conduct in August.

The conferences proved to be a beneficial experience for the young people, as well as an encouragement for the staff at Wot. The Malem and Utwe churches sent 33 young people to the first conference, which began on August 2; and 28 Lelu and Tafunsak youth arrived August 17 to participate in the second conference. The Marshallese students, who had remained at the school for the summer, attended both events.

Earlier in the year Alice had been inspired reading *The Robe*, Lloyd C. Douglas' fictionalized account of the earliest Christians. She hit on the idea of serializing the book to share during the 10 available evenings at each of the conferences. Alice's animated narration in the Kosraean language and Douglas' wonderful story combined to intrigue the conferees who found it difficult to wait from one evening to the next. Years later, some from among those who had listened on the mats in the lamplight of Wot's chapel commented to Alice on their vivid memories of Marcellus, Diana, and Demetrius, and of the deep commitment of those first century Christians.

FACULTY TURNOVER

It is a wonder that Alice was able to concentrate on her story-telling during that second conference. On August 19 her mother arrived, having been sent to replace Lucy Lanktree, at least temporarily, at the Wot school. Lucy, who left on the 22nd, was reassigned by the Micronesia Mission to the Marshall Islands school at Rongrong, where Louise Meebold was also serving.

PROBLEMS WITH THE BOYS

Alice suddenly found herself at the helm of the mission school. She had been accustomed to deferring to Lucy Lanktree and masking her dismay when problems remained unsolved because they were not addressed. Now it was her turn. Her mother tried to be supportive but was so overwhelmed by the school's disarray that she was at a loss to know how best to help. Pastor Alik, back from his weeks of training in Pohnpei, and Deacon Aliksru Tolenoa of Tafunsak, served as willing advisors. Their responsibilities in other parts of the island, however, did not allow them much time at Wot.

One of the major difficulties involved the work assignments of the boys. There were still unresolved feelings of anger and sadness over the death of Herton Ernest the year before. The boys had been working in a particularly swampy area, and Herton—a student from Pingelap—had slipped and fallen from the log he was walking on, severely injuring himself in the groin. In a manner typical of Micronesian men, he had hidden his injury. By the time it became apparent that he was badly hurt and was transported to the doctor in Lelu, it was too late. He was buried in the little Wot cemetery near the grave of Mrs. Walkup. After being notified of his death, his parents—who were separated—came to Kosrae. Their heartbreaking visits, individually, to his grave at Wot were exceedingly traumatic for them, as well as for their son's friends and classmates who accompanied them.[14]

The Marshallese boys—unused to the rugged terrain of a high island—were often unhappy with their work assignments. They did not get along with their staff leader, Frank Skilling, who went ahead and did his own work, expecting that others would do likewise. This trusting attitude left him open to becoming the brunt of boyish shenanigans. One prank, repeated on several occasions, resulted from Frank's practice of gathering his young laborers at the beginning of the work period to give them their assignments, and then having prayer with them before they were dismissed to do their jobs. They may not have been eager workers but the boys did have a talent for concocting delay tactics. When Frank asked different ones of them to say the prayer before work began, each would try to make his prayer longer than the prayer the day before, thus chopping off ever-increasing minutes from the work period.

TAFUNSAK CHURCH INAUGURATES YOUNG PEOPLE'S C. E.

One joyous event of far-reaching consequence took place during November 1954 that far outweighed the dismal atmosphere at Wot. During the year, Alice had been meeting with individuals and groups of Kosrae's church youth in their home settings. In one or two of the villages there was actually a church youth organization of sorts—though the church leadership tended to be suspicious and very controlling of these.

As in years past, the young people were asking to have their own Christian Endeavor Society. And also, as in years past, the adults were less than enthusiastic about such a proposition. Though there were some among the leaders of the church who in private expressed their approval of giving the youth their own organization, they were unwilling to express that opinion openly in a gathering of their peers. Alice, herself only 21 years old, attempted to plead the cause for the young people before the church committee, but the rebuttal was always the same. In essence, "You are an American. Our young people are different. Kosraeans are still thinking like little children when they are your age. There is no way they can handle their own group."

When Mrs. Hanlin arrived, she agreed with those who felt that such an organization would be a great boon to the island's young people. While Alice's words might have been discounted because of her age, Mary Ruth's prestige as a respected adult missionary gave credence to her reasoning. Both women attended the October and November new-month church gatherings in Lelu. The leaders were at least willing to listen as the mother and daughter expressed themselves on behalf of Kosrae's disheartened young people, explaining their belief that such a group would nurture the youth in the Christian life while giving them the opportunity to develop leadership skills.

Members of three of the churches decided that they needed more time to consider the possible outcome of such a major innovation. In Tafunsak, however, the congregation courageously voted to organize a young people's Christian Endeavor Society. Alice and Mary Ruth were both present in the Tafunsak church for the first meeting of that organization on November 14, 1954. Daniel Seymour was elected the first president. That November Sunday was a proud and memorable one for the youth of Tafunsak—and a day that later came to have a great impact upon the entire population of Kosrae.

HANGING ON

The leadership of the Church decided to recall all Kosraean staff members from KCTS in November—a decision that was disturbing to Alice. The reported pregnancies at Wot earlier in the year were still the source of anxiety among church members. Indeed, the matter had been raised as one of the specific concerns during discussions regarding the suitability of organizing young people's Christian Endeavor groups on the island. The Kosraean adults at Wot were being held accountable, though each of them had been dismayed by what had taken place. To Alice's disappointment she was given no choice but to bid farewell to teachers Frank and Srue Skilling, cooks Sam and Lise Musrasrik, and housemother Flora Aliksa. She especially missed Srue, whose calm, wise counsel had been a great source of strength for her.

Conditions at Wot actually began to improve. Alice found the new school cooks, Malem's Tulpe and Robert Songrasru, very pleasant—and helpful beyond their kitchen assignments. Additionally, Alice and her mother began to settle into an effective working relationship. The two of them spent long hours trying to guide the school community into a semblance of order and compatibility. There were long talks in the girls' dormitory—and the boys were rounded up for their share of reprimands and counseling.

In a newsletter dated November 17, Alice was optimistic:

Because of the unfortunate food shortage, lack of school equipment and inadequate dormitory space, we decided that the school needed a temporary "work camp" program. The thirty-five boys were divided into four teams, which they enthusiastically named the Pirates, Eagles, Indians and Cowboys. Now, after only two weeks, they have built a new goat shelter and a huge pig pen; cleaned the coconut tree area and dried 1,700 coconuts to sell for copra; cleaned a large taro patch and banana area; and have begun landscaping the whole campus, with a fresh-water fountain at a spring near the beach. The villagers have caught the spirit, too. One hundred and seventeen men came and completely built a thatch house in one day, providing all the materials (except for four hinges) and donated all the labor.

And how's this for "diversion?" To get the day started in a spirit of unity and zest, I lead the fellows in exercises at 6:15 every morning. Mother and I have taken several excursions with one or more guides to look for new garden plots, inspect the pig pen, rejoice over the progress of the boys' cleaning, examine the buildings and advise on new projects.

Evenings are spent in conversational English with the students, and in happy singing. Yesterday, however, we had a near tragedy. While the boys were playing ball, one of them threw his bat which hit a boy on the sidelines in the head and knocked him out. Four boys hurried him to the dispensary in Lelu as the tide was just in.[15]

The injured boy was 20-year-old Roger Skilling, who lay unconscious for almost one month in the hospital at Metais. The first thing he remembered hearing as he was waking up, was the "Amen" of Alice's prayer as she and her mother visited his bedside.[16]

By the dawn of 1955, there was an atmosphere of cooperation and activity that had not been apparent at Wot for many months. Throughout the spring term, conditions and attitudes continued to improve, but the school year had not been an easy one for either the students or their teachers. As she completed her short-term assignment with the American Board and prepared to leave, Alice scribbled in the margin of her journal, "What really gets me, is wondering if these students will remember anything good about all of this? I pray that God will keep this precious group strong in His service!"[17]

Alice's prayer was answered. A surprisingly large number of those students left Wot to become committed teachers and leaders of Kosrae and the Marshall Islands. Hansen Lalimo, Jori Lokboj—who married his classmate, Keta Samson—Onesimus Anjorlok, and Tuadrik Latdrik all became pastors in the Marshall Islands. A Kosraean classmate, Tulpe Aliksru Tolenoa, became Tuadrik's wife and went to the Marshalls with him. Future Kosraean pastors in the class of 1955 were Harrison George, Asher Palik—who married classmate Mitchigo Palik Kefwas—and Joshua Phillip, who later married 1953 KCTS graduate Katherine Alik Isaac.

On May 24, Alice and her mother left Kosrae—Mary Ruth to return to Harold at Dublon, Chuuk, and Alice to Fullerton, California, to marry Elden Buck.

PASTOR ALIK ISAAC

Alik Isaac was not a large man but was nonetheless capable of carrying a very big load. At the time of Alik's ordination, Pastor John Sigrah was 79 years old and more or less confined to his home—though he did attend services there in Lelu when he was able. For the next three and a half years, Pastor Alik was the only active pastor for Kosrae's Christian community. Obviously he could not be in Utwe, Malem, Lelu, Tafunsak, and Wot all on the same Sunday. Fortunately there were consecrated deacons and diligent lay leaders who could conduct services and take care of the churches' daily needs. But only the ordained pastor could preside at the Lord's Table, officiate at marriages, pronounce benedictions, and take care of the other responsibilities for which he had been "set apart." One of Pastor Alik's main tasks was to train those whom he had chosen to lead the services in the four locations where he would be unable personally to preside. These men came together at his home or at Pisin early in each week to be told what the lesson would be for the following Sunday. Each congregation would then hear the same sermon, filtered through the understanding of five different preachers—one a pastor, and the other four, laymen.

Pastor Alik was diligent in his work, conscientiously carrying out his obligations as the island's spiritual leader. His headquarters was his home at Tenwak, a mile beyond Sansrik across the harbor from Lelu. From there the new pastor walked—no matter what weather conditions—with his devoted wife, Hannah, a daughter of Pastor Fred Skilling, always at his side. Each carried a small bundle containing a change of clothing, their Bibles, hymnals, and booklets of daily C. E. topics and texts, plus his notes. Sometimes one or two of their smaller children would accompany them.

If the pastor was required to be in Malem, they walked the two miles there, and then the two miles back again. If he was needed in Utwe, the round trip from Tenwak was 14 miles on foot. If he was expected in Lelu, they walked to Sansrik—then crossed the harbor by canoe, Pastor Alik paddling and Hannah bailing. If the meeting was in Tafunsak, they guided their canoe the two miles beyond Lelu Harbor through the winding mangrove channel, then skimmed over the reef for another three miles to their destination. If the tide was too low, they walked the distance along the sandy road that skirted the water's edge. It was another four miles of paddling, poling, and bailing to reach the mission school. If the tide was out, there was no traveling to Wot until it came in again—which was as often in the early hours of the morning as it was in the middle of the day.

Less than a year after his ordination, the administration of the school at Wot was added to Pastor Alik's duties. By 1956 he had moved his family of growing children to Wot—it was too time consuming to be going back and forth constantly. His weekly sessions with the Sunday lay leaders took place at Wot, which meant quite a lengthy canoe trip for each man, always accompanied by his wife, though individuals designated to lead worship changed from week to week.

Twenty girls from Kosrae's villages were assembled at Wot for informal study. In addition to morning and evening prayers, Pastor Alik taught Bible classes for them. The girls worked at keeping the area around the dormitory, and the winding path to the dock, free of weeds and foliage from the perpetually infringing jungle. The girls also maintained several small gardens in the Yonrak area. They spent their evenings singing.

CENSUS OF 1956

There were 2,220 Kosraeans counted in the census of 1956.

DEATH OF PASTOR JOHN SIGRAH

On the morning of April 19, 1957, Pastor John Paliknoa Sigrah was sitting in his yard making coconut twine. He complained of being dizzy and was taken to the hospital at Metais, where he died peacefully that evening, just two months short of his 82nd birthday. The former king was buried next to his beloved Hattie, who had preceded him in death by six years, beside their Kalung home in Lelu. It had been 10 years since he told Eleanor Wilson that he would rather be pastor than king, and was then ordained, the culmination of a life-long dream.

At the insistence of the German administration, he had become king in 1910 when he was 35 years old. He had been reticent at first to step into his hereditary role, but he served his people with distinction. Willard Price, the American journalist who met him in 1935 during a time when King John was forced to answer to Japanese overlords, wrote of him: "The king's blood was truly royal. For centuries his family had provided the people with kings. The result was an inherited poise and manner, a regal gentlemanliness, in contrast to the brisk, brusque ways of some foreign petty officials of common family who had been trained but not bred. The fact that the king is able to adjust himself with dignity to this situation of ruling and being ruled is a tribute to his kingliness."[18]

"There will be no more kings of Kosrae," John Sigrah had told his sons—and they abided by his word, making Kosrae the first and only area of the Caroline and Marshall islands to discontinue the custom of promoting hereditary kings and paramount chiefs. The government of the Marshall Islands maintains its House of Iroij [chiefs], not unlike the British system. The Kosraean governmental system is very American, and John Sigrah is the one most responsible for that.

But there is a part of the Kosraean system which is explicitly not American, and John Sigrah is responsible for that as well. While Americans sometimes employ exaggerated ways to avoid church-state mixing, Kosrae has developed a unique and workable blending of church and government. The manner in which King John comfortably bridged these two entities paved the way for what was to come.

NEGATIVE AMERICAN INFLUENCE

Most of the Americans who came to work for the Trust Territory government as teachers and administrative advisors were not church oriented. Some of them undoubtedly grew up attending Sunday School in their home towns in the United States, but like the American whalers a hundred years before them, when they were away from home, they exhibited a worldly indifference toward the church. Also, many of these men, and women, too, smoked. Some of them were heavy drinkers, and a few of them, alcoholics. Kosraean Christians did not consider smoking and drinking to be appropriate activities for members of the Church.

Young adults on the island were assigned to work with the newcomers. Initially these youthful Kosraeans—most of whom had just returned from stimulating experiences in other parts of Micronesia or in Hawai'i—felt a loosening of societal restraints. An unfortunate pattern developed suggesting that the American way was innately better than the Kosraean way. Just look at all the "things" Americans had! And were they not the teachers? The new generation of Kosraean leaders considered their friendly, recently-arrived colleagues educated and cultured, and they eagerly emulated them.

There had always been a few young men on the fringes of the community who tested the limits—who partied on Saturday night and slept all day Sunday. But by 1957 a division had appeared among the Kosraeans that had not been there before. Anyone who worked for the government, including those in the budding school system, almost automatically, did not belong to the church. Those who was active in the church and Christian Endeavor did not work for the government.

FRANK SKILLING ORDAINED PASTOR

On the second day of December 1957, Deacon Frank Skilling—the oldest son of Pastor Fred Skilling—was ordained as Kosrae's 10th indigenous pastor. He was 67 years old. Frank and his wife, Srue, had been associated with the church and with the school at Wot all of their adult lives. In the 1930s they had served for several years as missionaries to the people of Enewetak. Essentially, Deacon Frank was a farmer and fisherman, but now someone was needed to assist Pastor Alik, so Frank was rewarded for his lengthy and consistent Christian witness.

So another pattern was established. Through the years, younger men were always chosen to lead the Church of Kosrae as pastors. The first two, Pastor Lupalikkun and Pastor Likiaksa, were both in their 20s when they were ordained by Mr. Snow. The pastors who followed them were also young or middle-aged adults. It was not until John Sigrah was ordained that a new pastor was beyond 60 years of age. Pastor Palik, who was ordained with him, was only 30, while Pastor Alik Isaac was 47 at the time of his ordination. Beginning with Pastor Frank, a trend of ordaining only older men was begun. It lasted for the next decade. The position of pastor came to be considered the crowning achievement of a long life faithfully lived, instead of one for a dedicated younger person who could serve the people with energy and enthusiasm.

WORKING AND WAITING AT WOT

In late 1957, a group of strong and eager young men were chosen to go to Wot, not only to study, but also to maintain and improve the school's gardens. They cleaned vast areas of the plantation and planted new crops. Their female schoolmates—some having arrived the year before—continued to work hard keeping portions of the campus in the immediate vicinity of the mission house, chapel building, and dining room trimmed and neat.

Pastor Alik Isaac and Alik Palsis—recently returned to Kosrae from the Pacific Islands Teachers Training School at Chuuk, known as PITTS—conducted morning classes for these students, as well as morning and evening devotional services. All of them anticipated the arrival of new missionary teachers, as word was received that a young couple had been assigned by the American Board to administer KCTS. The newly appointed missionaries were expected toward the end of 1958. By this time 36 young people were ensconced in the dormitories at Wot: Seven boys and four girls from Lelu, six boys and five girls from Tafunsak, seven boys and three girls from Malem, and two boys and two girls from Utwe. It would be the first time in the 79-year history of the Wot mission that only Kosraean students were enrolled.

Excitement swept over all of Kosrae as word spread that half of the new missionary couple was not new to Kosrae at all, but rather someone familiar and loved. Alice Hanlin Buck, now 26, was returning to Kosrae with her husband of three years, the Rev. Elden Buck, age 27, and their two small daughters, Lisa and Lauren. The Buck family reached Pohnpei in November, but had to wait almost two months for a ship to Kosrae. While at Ohwa Elden worked with Joshua Phillip, one of the Kosraean students attending the Pastors & Teachers Training School, to write and produce Kosrae's Christian Endeavor topics and accompanying texts for 1959.

YET ANOTHER MISSIONARY RECORDS HIS ARRIVAL

The Bucks' arrival was described in a newsletter distributed by the Missions Council of Congregational Christian Churches.

Looking from our portholes on the M/V Kaselehlia at 9:30 on the morning of Wednesday, January 14, we saw it! Looming on the horizon was the island we had waited so long to see together. It is difficult to explain adequately our sensations, as Alice thrilled at coming home and I was overwhelmed by the fact that at last I was actually seeing this island I had grown to know so well "in absentia." It looked very large, jagged, and mysterious—the whole mountain range a grey silhouette against a bright horizon. Together we prayed a prayer of thanksgiving for the safe and sure leading of God.

We spent the morning on deck watching the island approach—eagerly trying to distinguish landmarks. The first to become apparent were the aluminum roofs of the mission buildings at Mwot. Again, an inexpressible sensation swept over me as I thought of the tremendous part this place has played in the history of the American Board in Micronesia—indeed, in the effective spreading of the Gospel of Christ throughout this part of the Pacific world. That we were privileged to join in this great heritage was a humbling thought.

At 1:30 that afternoon we rounded the northeast point of land and entered the small, secluded harbor which was once so popular with whalers and pirates alike. The mountains rose steeply on three sides with that lush, "dripping" tropical foliage climbing to the very tops of the highest peaks. The beautiful Lelu church became visible through the trees and then the harbor village itself.

Now, all along the beach, we could see men, women, girls, and boys running toward the dock area. By the time we were close enough to hear sounds from shore, the dock and its surroundings were jammed with people, and they were singing— softly it seemed at first—and then their voices swelled together. The ship was a good half-hour easing up to the tiny, rickety dock. We stood at the railing, each holding a daughter, drinking in the moment and glad it could last long for memory's sake. Lisa and Lauren both seemed to sense the thrill of the occasion and watched intently the many children gathering in the foreground.

As we drew closer, Alice was able to recognize many, but no one waved. They just stood there singing with one voice, their gaze steadily upon us, tears as well as smiles on many faces. We both had a difficult time seeing through misty eyes! There was no yelling from sailors or dockhands. Their work was done quickly and quietly in securing the ship.

Before we had stopped moving, the two Kusaien pastors had jumped the railing to greet us, and we were helped ashore before the gangplank could be put in place. Immediately we were engulfed in a sea of smiles and outstretched hands. I don't know who took Lisa and Lauren, but we all four made our way through the dense crowd separately—finding each other at the outer edge. The little girls, though wondering, were both smiling broadly. The boys who were to be our students at the Christian Training School were on the spot to unload our freight. This they did swiftly—almost tenderly.

The mission proper is on the other side of the island from Lelu, but a small home, built of bamboo, reeds, and thatch, is maintained for us at the harbor village—on Benjamin and Lydia Snow's Pisin. All afternoon and evening this house and the tiny island on which it is located, were full of people—many laden with gifts of food and flowers—eager to make us welcome. The singing which continued into the night, though done with the typical almost-expressionless faces, was full of deep feeling. We sat for several hours after darkness had fallen to listen as groups from the different churches and Sunday Schools took turns sharing the songs especially prepared for this occasion. It seemed a true climax for this memorable day as, with these brothers and sisters in Christ, we lifted our hearts in grateful prayer to our Heavenly Father for making this reunion possible.[19]

"WE PASSAGES" PROCEED

[Author's note: In the New Testament book of Acts, which is the history of the Early Church, Luke's narrative is written in the third person unless he is describing events in which he personally participated. Some biblical scholars refer to these as the "We Passages." I am grateful to be able to write a bit of the history of Kosrae's Church in the first person.]

With Pastor Alik, Pastor Frank, their wives and other church leaders, all 19 of the boys from the mission school were on the dock to greet us. Under the direction of Milton Timothy, Alik Palsis, and Erafe Tosie—and with many of the Lelu men assisting—our luggage and freight from the ship were quickly transferred to Pisin. By late afternoon as the tide came in, the boys took their positions along the length of *Kawuk*. They stood with their bare feet balanced on the canoe's narrow edges, bending as they began to pole in rhythm, pushing away from Pisin's stone retaining wall. We watched as the sleek 45-foot craft, now laden with our belongings, slipped across the lagoon and disappeared into the mangrove channel to begin the trip to Wot.

We remained in Lelu for the next day and a half getting mail ready for the return trip of the M/V *Kaselehlia*, planning with church leaders, working with Jack Youngstrom on some orders and visiting with the many friends of Alice who came to Pisin, anxious to meet her husband and see her children. Among these was Alice's former student, Deckla Skilling. We arranged with Deckla and her parents, Joseph and Ruth, to take her with us to help with our two little girls. She packed her things and was ready when we were, to travel to Wot.

On the afternoon tide of January 16, we boarded *Kawuk*, accompanied by the boys who had returned the canoe in the wee hours of the night before in order to take us "home." How clearly I remember the stillness as we wound through the narrow mangrove channel—the trees entwined above our heads with their assorted bouquets of ferns hanging from the branches, their 20-foot-long strands folding onto the mirror-smooth surface of the water. We were intrigued by the birds, flashing their white, black, purple, and red through the leaves. Occasionally one or two of the boys would jump in to help maneuver the large canoe through a tight curve.

It was almost an hour later that the scenery changed. Easing beneath the coconut log bridge at Insrefusr and out onto the rolling surface of the lagoon, we found ourselves in another pristine setting of nature's stunning beauty. The silence was gone. A hundred yards out, the ocean was thundering onto the reef and erupting into sparkling clouds of foam and spray. The swells rolling past beneath us made it necessary to hang on—and I noticed the boys watching the outrigger to make sure it remained on the surface. I was captivated by that graceful outrigger, six feet to the right of us, as it cut through the water making its own bow-split and wake.

For an hour we were propelled past the houses of Tafunsak, located just beyond the immaculate beaches where they nestled among the coconut palms and the breadfruit trees, all in the shadows of the majestic mountains behind them. These houses were separated far enough to maintain privacy, yet close enough for neighbors to visit without having to walk too far. Many of the buildings had thatch roofs, some had rusting corrugated iron roofs, and a few had roofs of shiny aluminum. People waved from among canoes pulled up on the sand, and children ran for distances, following us along the beach. Lisa in my lap, Lauren in Alice's, were wide-eyed—savoring the experience in their own little-girl ways.

On beyond Tafunsak, it was still two hours to go—skirting the mangrove swamps and crossing the harbors of Okat and Yela. It was dusk when the boys poled us up to the rock wharf at Wot, built 60 years before by Mr. Channon and his Gilbertese students. Lisa and Lauren were sound asleep—but they woke as we climbed the trail of hewn-coral stone with them in our arms, up the hill toward the gradually increasing sound of music. With their housemother, the girls were standing in the dim, late evening light on the prow of the Yonrak hill singing their welcome. We had arrived.

SCHOOL BEGINS

Alice and I had looked forward to several weeks of unpacking, settling in, and getting everything arranged for classes. That is not the way it happened. Everyone except the two of us—staff and students alike—was ready to get started. They had been waiting, literally for months. Why wait any longer? Almost overnight, we created a daily schedule and assigned ourselves, Alik Palsis, and Erafe Tosie—back from the Pastors & Teachers Training School at Pohnpei—to classes for 31 students. (Because of the needs of their families, five of the students had returned to their homes before our arrival.) Milton Timothy was already supervising the plantation work and Kenye Taulung was with the girls as housemother. Palokoa Joe and his wife, Selma, and Caleb Jackson and his wife, Srue, were the cooks. Everything seemed to say, "We're all set! Let's ring the bell and begin." And we did!

We designated KCTS to be, in American terms, an Intermediate School. The level of our students was roughly equivalent to the 8th grade. The young people at Wot, however, were older than the average American 8th grader. Most of them had been born during the bleak days of World War II, and thus were late in beginning elementary school. Understandably, those first post-war elementary schools—with inadequately trained teachers, ill-equipped class rooms and meager supplies—struggled to be in existence at all. Our youngest students were 17 years old, while most of them were 19 or 20, with a few who were even older. All of them had been longing for an opportunity to study.

The young men were housed in three dormitories—known as Pease, Channon and Rife—located halfway down the hill to the southwest, and the young women were settled in their dormitory on the second floor of the chapel at the top of Yonrak. Their eagerness, not only to learn, but also to cooperate with every detail of the admittedly full, non-Kosraean schedule I foisted upon them, was truly inspiring. They were happy to be at Wot. They were willing to work hard. They exhibited a desire for spiritual growth. We began classes with 19 young men and 13 young women.

In between our many new responsibilities, Alice and I unpacked and made ourselves comfortable in the 39-year-old Baldwin mission house. There were some bullet holes in the walls from the strafing by U. S. planes, but the building was as solid as when it was first erected. The termite-proofed lumber had cost the sisters extra dollars, but it was a wise expenditure. It was indeed a special house—and it was already home to Alice. Erafe and the boys helped me build a shower area below the existing mission house bathroom. It just fit—with a narrow, enclosed stairway that led from the sleeping porch above. We no longer had to hike down the steep trail behind the house to the Wot River to bathe—though doing that was certainly one more of the novel experiences we were having.

We sent Erafe Tosie off to California for nine months to attend a series of church-related work-camps under the supervision of my pastor-father, Dr. Carlton C. Buck, in Fullerton. Alice, while teaching her classes, supervising the girl students, and maintaining our home, organized a pre-school program for Lisa and Lauren. Deckla was a wonderful help with them and they were both jabbering Kosraean almost before we realized it. I arranged time for language lessons with Alik Palsis. Since my wife was already fluent in Kosraean, my masculine pride helped push me forward.

FASCINATING CUSTOMS

In getting acquainted with the students, I jotted down in my diary several customs that I found especially interesting:

The girls wore modest cotton dresses during the week—dresses that always had sleeves, with skirts that hung well below the knees. The design of the dresses that they wore on Sunday was the same, but the material was not. The cotton fabric of week-day dresses was replaced on Sunday by stiff, nylon tulle that easily revealed the colorful crewel-style embroidery on bodices and elaborately crocheted four to six inch hems on the slips that they wore beneath. Known simply as minini keke ["thin and stiff"], these dresses were considered the height of fashion on Kosrae in 1960.

Whatever the day of the week, all Kosraean women let their slips show. Why create the lovely crocheted or tatted border that decorated every woman's slip, and then keep it covered? Slips always hung two, three, or four inches below a dress's hemline—an obvious and pleasant fashion statement of the time. The art of creating these beautiful, often exquisite, lengths of crocheted lace was originally introduced by Wot's women missionaries as a proper way for young ladies to use their leisure time. Kosraean women, young and old, became experts at needle-craft.

I was intrigued by the fact that the strapping young men of KCTS were so comfortable with themselves that they could wear flowers in their hair and behind their ears on just about any occasion. There was no finger-pointing or teasing—it was just an accepted and fun thing to do. And Wot had lots of bright flowers, especially hibiscus in many varieties. Something else I noticed was how tenderly these boys treated small children and babies. I was not accustomed to seeing teenage American boys handling babies, especially not in front of their peers. It was obviously different on Kosrae. In spite of the strict division of labor between the sexes on the island, teenage boys carried babies around almost as much as teenage girls, apparently enjoying it.

There was a lot of teasing and horse-play. Out on the campus, if a student tripped or made some kind of small social faux pas, someone nearby would invariably call out the name or nickname of a grandparent or some other older persons in the family of the one being teased. At that, everyone in the vicinity—to the embarrassment of the one who was the brunt of the joke—dissolved into gales of laughter.

BEGINNING OF A RIVALRY IN SPORTS

The U. S. Trust Territory-sponsored secondary school at Yekula in Tafunsak opened just a few months before our arrival at Kosrae—and on March 6, our Wot mission school students participated in their first sporting event with students from that government school. It was a natural rivalry. We accepted the challenge for a volleyball tournament—and we lost all seven games! But the adrenalin was high, and there was nothing wrong with our enthusiasm. We knew there would be another chance at victory.

Sure enough, the very next month, on April 10 and 11, the Yekula students joined us at Wot for a series of baseball games: The Wot boys won four—the Yekula boys won three.

ENTIRE WOT FAMILY CIRCUMNAVIGATES KOSRAE

We were anxious to see Kosrae, but even more, we wanted Kosraeans to be able to see their mission school students active, well cared for, and learning. We spent much non-class time during our first two months at Wot preparing for a trip to the four villages. I worked up an Easter drama with the students and Alice taught them some spirited new songs—both the drama and the songs in the Kosraean language. The young people were very excited and did a superb job learning their dramatic roles and the words of the songs. As with all Kosraeans, the ability to harmonize was inborn, and so was a perfect sense of rhythm.

On the early morning tide of March 24—in *Kawuk* and several canoes borrowed from neighbors—we traveled west, then south, through the narrow mangrove channels and along the wider waterways to Utwe. In 1959, Utwe's shore was still lined with small, thatch-roofed houses. The villagers—led by Deacon Joel Wakuk and another of their church leaders, Edmond Tulenkun—waded out from between the houses to meet us, warmly receiving our group of 40. People laughed pleasantly, pointing at their own children among us, and little brothers and sisters ran up for their hugs. Pastor Alik and Hannah were there. They, and all of Utwe with them, did a superb job hosting us—and the students outdid themselves that night in a church packed with adults and children. Faces filled all the windows. It was the first time they had experienced the story of Easter so vividly presented.

And so it was in each of the villages—Malem on the 25th, Lelu on the 26th, and Tafunsak on the 27th. There was lots of walking—Alice and the girls rode in an old truck from Utwe to Malem, and from Malem to Sansrik. [Roland Stephen in Malem and Otniel Edmond in Utwe each maintained serviceable trucks during this period.] The boys and I walked. We all walked from Lelu to Tafunsak, and then back to Pisin to prepare for Easter. March 29 was Easter Sunday, with more than 900 in the morning service there in Lelu. I preached, the students sang, and Alice led the combined Sunday School session. The trip was a rousing success—and all of us were pleased and relieved when we walked up the mountain trail to our dormitories and houses at Wot on Monday.

COMPLETING THE FIRST SEMESTER

We took the time on April 15 to hike up the Wot River with the entire student body to the spectacular series of three waterfalls where we enjoyed swimming in the deep pools at the bottom of each. And on May 25, we all went to Kiel for fishing and a picnic under the trees on that tiny reef island at the mouth of Okat Harbor. Otherwise we continued with classes—which took place in the chapel and in the typhoon house, with the students sitting on the floor on mats—and before we knew it, the semester was over.

The students left to spend three vacation months with their families. They had continued to amaze and inspire us with their eagerness to learn and cooperate. They had studied hard, worked hard, played hard, and had exhibited the seriousness of their desire to live lives pleasing to God. We looked forward to their return in September.

OUR SITUATION

In July, I wrote to our American friends and supporting churches:

Our home and school facilities are, for the most part, in good condition, and we want for very little. The six water-storage tanks are continually full following our daily rains, and the mission plantation is supplying the necessary food above and beyond that provided by a U.S. government surplus food program.

If we had a complaint, it might be the mail service. Some of you may wonder at the space between letters. This is because mail arrives at and leaves Kusaie on the Trust Territory field-trip ships, which call here approximately once every two months. At times they come oftener but once already we waited over three months before hearing any word from "the outside world." Also, if some of you are missing replies to letters written around the last of March, it is because the weekly plane between Guam and Ponape developed engine trouble one week and dumped all mail into the ocean! Discounting this incident, air mail is by far the best way to write us even though it is grounded at Ponape to wait for a ship to bring it to Kusaie. It takes surface mail sometimes five months to reach us. Keep the letters coming.

And keep praying, too. God is blessing our work and we know that your interest and prayers on our behalf are largely responsible. Thank you.[20]

LESSON FROM DARIUS

My own attitudes had been continually challenged by those of our students. From among countless stories is one that features Darius.

When the field-trip arrived that May, Darius received a gorgeous Hawaiian-print shirt from his brother who was a sailor on the ship. Our students had very few clothes—perhaps only two changes, one they wore while the other was being washed. Darius caused quite a sensation when he wore his colorful new shirt around the Wot campus. But several days after he had received his shirt, I was surprised to see another student wearing it. Since parents had asked that we help the young people take care of their limited supply of clothing, I called Darius into my office to inquire what was going on.

"Hadley only had one shirt," Darius explained to me. "I already had three shirts, so I gave the new one to him!"

I had given away many shirts, but they were all old shirts that I no longer needed or wanted to wear. I had never given away a new shirt I had just received![21] ✛

Notes - Chapter 15

1. Harold F. Hanlin, Missions Council letter, Boston, March 17, 1953
2. Mary Alice Hanlin [Buck], "Alice in Wonderland—Today," 1953, p. 22
3. M. A. Hanlin, Missions Council letter, Dec. 7, 1953
4. M. A. Hanlin, personal diary, Oct. 9, 1953, p. 9
5. Ibid, Oct. 7, 1953, p. 7
6. Ibid, Oct. 18, 1953, p. 18
7. Ibid, Oct. 25, 1953, p. 25
8. Ibid, Oct. 31, 1953, p. 31
9. Ibid, Nov. 7, 1953, p. 38
10. Ibid, Feb. 1, 1954, p. 104
11. Ibid, Feb. 19, 1954, p. 108
12. Ibid, March 9, 1954. pp. 117-118
13. Ibid, May 5, 1954, p. 139
14. Roger Skilling, personal conversation, Kosrae, March 13, 2003
15. M. A. Hanlin, newsletter, Kosrae, Nov. 17, 1954
16. R. Skilling, personal conversation, Kosrae, Sept. 25, 2004
17. M. A. Hanlin, personal diary, May 1955, p. 189
18. Willard Price, *Japan's Islands of Mystery*, p. 221
19. Elden M. Buck, Kosrae Newsletter, The Missions Council, Feb. 8, 1959
20. E. M. Buck, Kosrae Newsletter, The Missions Council, July 14, 1959
21. The chronology and events recorded in this chapter for the year 1959 are verified in the daily entries of the author's personal journals kept during the 1959-1962 period of his residency on Kosrae.

NUNAK YOHK KE CHAPTER 16
1959-1961

Finne malem ma lutlut ah mongla ke 1959, Pastu Elden ac Alice oru pac kunelos in akfasrye conference akosr fin acn Wot. Conference se meet ma nu sin mukul fusr ke kais sie mura. Ma se akluo ah ma nu sin mutan fusr. Conference se aktolu ah ma nu sin mwet matu, ac ma se akakosr ah ma nu sin committee lun church Kosrae, wi mutan kialos. Mwet inge kewa tuh arulana engan in som nu fin acn Wot, ke sripen acn we sriyukla tuh kas lun God in luti-yuk we, oayapa aengani lalos we mwe akkeye lulalfongi lalos.

Lutluta tuh sifilpa mutawauk ke September, na oasr tulik onngoul luo weang ke yac sa. Harrison George el tufahna foloko liki Maunaolu College Maui, na el welulang Alik Palsis, Pastu Elden ac Alice in mwet luti Wot ke 1959. Erafe Tosie el tuh som nu California ac wi conference lun mwet Christian su elos tukeni musaella lohm Sunday School in kasru church sasu ekasr. El foloko ke December.

Ke sripen wangin na elya akilenyuk tokin akwuki Etawi Fusr in acn Tafunsak, ac wi pac yok kasru lal Pastu Elden ac Alice, oru mwet kol lun Etawi Kosrae elos wotela in akwuki pac Etawi Fusr fin acn Lelu, Malem, ac Utwe. Etawi Fusr fin acn inge tu srokakinyukla ke Sunday, November 6, 1959.

Mwet Kosrae nukewa elos tuh kasru mwet Utwe in musai sie lohm alu sasu, su kisakinyukla ke February 4, 1960. Onkosr sin mwet kol lun acn Wot, wi tulik Utwe ma lutlut Wot, tuh wi som in eis kunelos ke alu in kisa se inge. Tukun alu ah, kufwa na yok se tuh orek in akinsewowye mwet na pukanten ma toeni ke len sac.

Pastu Elden el siyuk sin Committee lun church in srakak mwet akosr nu ke School Board lun acn Wot—inelos pa Zakias George, Tafunsak; Sru Likiaksa, Lelu; Kephas Charley, Malem; ac Harold Edmond, Utwe. U se inge tuh otela in oasr sie lohm lutlut sasu musaiyuk Yonrak. Lohm lutlut meet ah tuh musaiyuk oe ke 1909, na mwet Japan elos tuleya ke 1942 ac usla nu Malem. Pastu Elden el lumala srikasrak ac aten nu ke lohm sac: classroom tolu, office se, storeroom se, ac library se. Ke February 25, 1960, tuh oasr alu in akinsewowoyela acn se ma lohm sasu se inge ac musaiyuk we. Pastu Alik Isaac, Pastu Frank, Pastu Elden, Harrison ac Erafe pah tuh kol alu sac, ac tulik lutlut elos on. Chief Magistrate Paul Sigrah, Mwet Nununku Linus George, Superintendent ke lutlut Kosrae

Florian Nena, ac mwet kol ke lutlut Yekula Royal Gifford, wi mwet puspis saya, tuh som nu Wot wi alu se inge. Erafe Tosie pah tuh chief carpenter, ac mwet Kosrae nukewa wi eis kunalos pac ke orekma na lulap se inge.

Sie pac len akilenyuk fin acn Wot ah pah June 2, 1960, len se ma tulik longoul akosr tuh srola ke lutlut lalos. Shiro Timothy pa valedictorian ac Holdon Musrasrik pa salutatorian. Pukanten mwet som akfulatye tulik srola inge. Ke lutlut ah tuh sifil mutawauk in September, Joshua Phillip el sie mwet luti sasu Wot. El tufahnu srola liki Pastors & Teachers Training School fin acn Pohnpei. Pisen tulik lutlut ke yac se inge oasr ke itngoul tolu.

Pastu Frank Skilling el misa ke December 2, 1960.

Tulik lutlut Wot elos pwar in srital wi tulik lutlut Yekula ke volleyball, yakyu ac kasrusr. Tusruktu sie pacl ma elos yokyu fin acn Wot ke March 1961, oasr suparla lun tulik inge ke sripen karinginyen srital ah tiana orek wo. Kutu wik toko, tulik lutlut Wot elos som wi alu Tafunsak ac elos oru program in Easter lalos ke eku sac. Tukun alu ah, tuh oasr lokwalok inmasrlon kutu tulik lutlut Yekula ac Wot. Len se tok ah, Principal Shrew Jonas ac Pastu Elden eltal suli tulik mukul akosr ke kais sie school tuh elos in tukeni sramsram ac suk ma ac ku in akmisyela inmasrlon tulik ke school luo inge. Elos tuh otela mu tulik Yekula ac tulik Wot in tukeni oru sie program ke Sunday in Easter in lohm alu Lelu. Ouinge tulik lutlut Yekula elos wi tulik lutlut Wot tukeni fin acn Pisin in luti on ma akoeyukla sin mission school in ako program se inge. Ke Sunday in Easter, tulik ke school luo inge tukeni orala program in Easter na wowo se. Tausin se oalfoko mwet tuh wi alu ke Sunday sac in liye ac lohng on lalos.

Ke November 1, 1961, Deacon Esau Tilfas ac Deacon Aliksru Tolenoa eltal akmusrala—ouinge eltal pa pastu aksingoul sie ac aksingoul luo lun Church Kosrae.

Ke November 23, lohm lutlut sasu fin acn Wot kisaiyukla. Lusen lohm sac pa fit siofok angngaul onkosr. Kitakatelik infukil onkosr ac sawalsrisr ah nu ke ip akosr, su tuh ngisreyuk kais sie church akosr fin acn Kosrae in musai kais sie ip. Pus na mwet som wi tulik lutlut ac mwet kol Wot in akfulatye safla lun orekma sac.

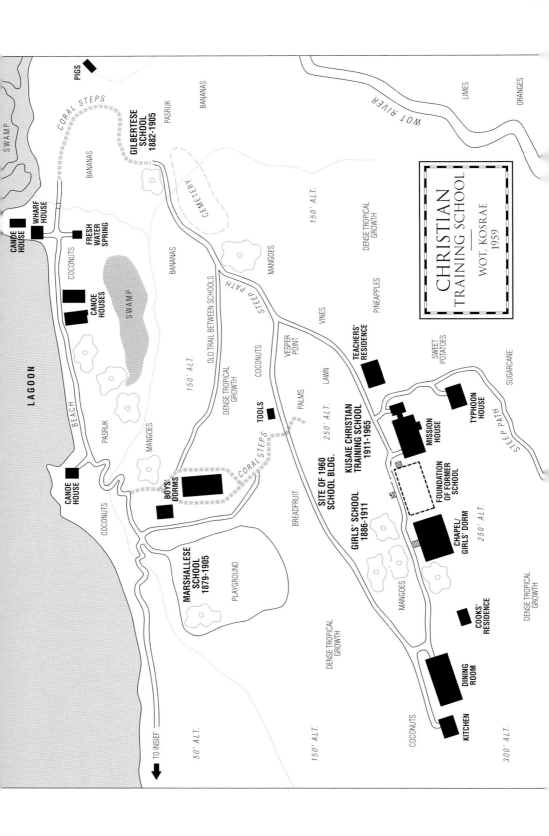

CHRISTIAN TRAINING SCHOOL
WOT, KOSRAE
1959

PIGS

CORAL STEPS

GILBERTESE SCHOOL 1882-1905

PASRUK

BANANAS

BANANAS

WOT RIVER

LIMES

ORANGES

SWAMP

WHARF HOUSE

CANOE HOUSE

FRESH WATER SPRING

COCONUTS

CEMETERY

150' ALT.

DENSE TROPICAL GROWTH

BANANAS

MANGOES

CANOE HOUSES

SWAMP

OLD TRAIL BETWEEN SCHOOLS

150' ALT.

STEEP PATH

DENSE TROPICAL GROWTH

COCONUTS

VESPER POINT

VINES

PINEAPPLES

TEACHERS' RESIDENCE

SWEET POTATOES

LAGOON

BEACH

PASRUK

MANGOES

CORAL STEPS

TOOLS

PALMS

250' ALT.

LAWN

MISSION HOUSE

TYPHOON HOUSE

SUGARCANE

CANOE HOUSE

COCONUTS

BOYS' DORMS

KUSAIE CHRISTIAN TRAINING SCHOOL 1911-1965

SITE OF 1960 SCHOOL BLDG.

BREADFRUIT

GIRLS' SCHOOL 1886-1911

FOUNDATION OF FORMER SCHOOL

STEEP PATH

MARSHALLESE SCHOOL 1879-1905

PLAYGROUND

CHAPEL/ GIRLS' DORM

250' ALT.

MANGOES

COOKS' RESIDENCE

DENSE TROPICAL GROWTH

TO INSIEF

50' ALT.

150' ALT.

DINING ROOM

DENSE TROPICAL GROWTH

COCONUTS

KITCHEN

300' ALT.

CHAPTER SIXTEEN

KOSRAE CHRISTIAN TRAINING SCHOOL
1959-1961

CONFERENCE TIME

It is difficult to imagine a more inspirational setting for a church camp, summer conference, or retreat than the campus at Wot, Kosrae. Its isolation from the rest of the island, the time and effort expended to get there, and the fact that it is a mountaintop where, cliché that it is, a person feels just a bit closer to God—these are all parts of the equation.

Consider the breathtaking views. Standing on the Yonrak lawn, there is the vast deep blueness of the ocean stretching out to the horizon, where it meets the lighter blue of the sky. Underlining this great expanse is the eloquently eternal action of the waves breaking over the long, frothy span of reef. Turn around and the senses are bombarded by the myriad greens on the sharp and rugged mountains that form Yonrak's magnificent natural backdrop. The words of Scripture come easily to mind now, as they have for those who have had the privilege of standing here throughout the decades: "I lift up my eyes to the hills—from where will my help come? My help comes from the Lord who made heaven and earth." [Psalm 121:1 NRSV]

Twenty-two canoes with 72 teenage boys aboard arrived on June 22 for the Bible study, work, and recreation we had organized for them. A high spiritual tone developed during their two weeks at Wot. Though it was not customary on Kosrae for people to express themselves personally during worship, almost half of them voluntarily spoke at our closing consecration service of new experiences with God during the conference and of their desire to follow Christ more closely in their lives. After returning to their villages, some of them got together to sing for worship services and to visit and help at the hospital. A group of those boys came with a huge supply of food they had collected for the conference that followed theirs.

Fifty-five teenage girls experienced Wot, sharing rich fellowship, singing, and study, from July 6 to 17. Kosraean adults were with us for Bible classes and worship from July 27 to August 7 and the church leaders, from August 31 to September 5 for planning and renewal. In the afternoons the women wove new mats for the chapel and mission house floors, and the men re-thatched the school's dining room. Then, for 10 days of the summer, Alice and I sent the staff for a respite in their village homes and enjoyed the campus by ourselves.

NEW HOUSE FOR PISIN

The two thatch-roofed houses at Pisin, the oldest having been built for Eleanor Wilson in 1947, were inadequate and deteriorating. In July, I designed a new house for Pisin which members of the four congregations agreed to help build—the first on that islet to have a concrete floor. The bottom four feet of the exterior walls were also concrete, with screening above, and an aluminum roof. Interior walls were of woven reed. A veranda stretched across the front, adding space. An existing concrete cistern was patched and incorporated into the back of the house to form a bath area, while the old outhouse on the far edge of the little island continued to serve its purpose.

The new house was dedicated November 13, at which time the church women presented new mats to cover the floors of the four tiny rooms. The little house proved to be a convenient and pleasant home-away-from-home.

NEW STUDENTS AND STAFF

Twice as many students as we could handle were asking to enroll at Wot that September. Alice and I had the depressing task of pruning the number to 65—the maximum our dormitories, food supply, and staff of workers could handle. We began the new semester on September 10 with 62 students. All but one of the previous year's students had returned, and the new class totaled 32, 17 boys and 15 girls new to KCTS.

Harrison George had just returned from Maunaolu Bible College on Maui where he enrolled after completing his course at Pohnpei's Pastors & Teachers Training School. He joined Alik Palsis, Alice, and me on the teaching staff. Shiro Milton Timothy was elected president of the student body and Yukiwo Tara, president of the Christian Endeavor Society. All students were members of Christian Endeavor, making our group the second active young people's Endeavor on Kosrae.

PRAYER ON A BEACH

I took my Lisa with me on some errands to Lelu in late September. When we were ready to return to Wot, the tide was too low to float the canoe, so she and I walked from Pisin to the bridge at Insrefusr—a distance of two and a half miles. There, we waited for the boys to pull the canoe through the channel that twisted among the mangroves. They would join us where the waterway flowed into the lagoon from under that coconut log bridge. I had a miserable headache so intense I was sick to my stomach. I lay on the beach trying to wish it away. Lisa, just two weeks beyond her 3rd birthday, played quietly in the sand beside me, aware that I was not feeling well.

My eyes were closed when I felt her put her hand on me and heard her say, "Daddy, let's pray," which she proceeded to do all on her own.

My years on Kosrae deepened my appreciation for prayer. When doctors, medicines, and other so-called conveniences of civilization were not available, prayer took on a new and powerful significance. To my considerable surprise, I found that trying to discern God's purpose for my life was a thought-provoking, frightening process when trusting God seemed to be my only option. Listening to the honest, simple prayer of a concerned and loving little girl gave me much more than another sentimental memory. I was ushered into the reality of God's presence.

The prayers of Kosraean Christians also did this for me. When praying, they included very few requests of a personal nature. Their prayers were filled, rather, with praise for God's greatness and for the authenticity of God's guidance. Their prayers were eloquent yet humble expressions of their desire to live in God's will. It was difficult for me to assign to the will of God some of the life experiences that my Kosraean colleagues credited to God's will—but as I listened, I had to admit that it often seemed that I could hear the voice of God. Similarly, Lisa prayed with such innocent, absolute trust, I was enveloped with a strong sense of God's closeness.

The more I became familiar with the language of the island, the more it was apparent just how profound the prayers of the people were. I strained to hear, for when they prayed in public, Kosraeans dropped their voices almost to a whisper. This pattern of behavior matched the manner in which their forebears had addressed the old kings—faces turned away, words mumbled. Even in church, the prayers of those leading a service were barely audible. I found that my compulsion to make my own voice clearly heard at all times when conducting public worship did not fit. When I was brazen enough to ask a pastor-friend why he whispered his prayers, he answered, "I'm not addressing the people—I'm talking to God."

MORE YOUNG PEOPLE'S CHRISTIAN ENDEAVOR SOCIETIES

At the invitation of the officers of the all-island adult Christian Endeavor Society, Alice and I joined them in their meetings on several occasions during the fall of 1959 to discuss the possibility of starting Christian Endeavor groups for youth in these villages that were still without them. The young people's C.

E. in Tafunsak had proven to be popular with the youth there, and the membership of the Tafunsak church was growing as a result. Church leaders in Lelu, Malem, and Utwe were taking notice and rethinking their stance. They asked us questions and contemplated our answers.

We were present at the October 1, 1959, meeting of the all-island Christian Endeavor committee when, after more deliberation, it was decided to begin young people's C. E. organizations in the remaining three villages. I attended the election of officers for the new Utwe group on Friday, November 6, and conducted their installation on Sunday, November 15. The officers of the Malem and Lelu groups, too, were officially installed on that day.

Finally, after two generations of young people asking for such a group for themselves, the adults had acquiesced. As had happened in Tafunsak, the groups in Malem, Utwe, and Lelu proved very quickly the wisdom of giving young people the opportunity to demonstrate their capabilities. They could be trusted after all to handle roles of leadership, to make mature decisions and to grow in faith together. In each village, non-church teenagers and young adults flocked to become part of the new youth-oriented organization.

EXTRAORDINARY COMMITMENT

Before going to Lelu for Christmas, our Wot staff had discussed a problem we always faced when the entire student body left the campus. Who would stay behind to feed the pigs and chickens? Who would serve as security guard while everyone else was gone? I asked the staff for volunteers. No one spoke up or raised a hand.

Later that day, our plantation foreman, Milton Timothy, pulled me aside to tell me quietly that he would like to stay when the rest of us left for Lelu; he had volunteered for this kind of assignment before. He had three children in the Christmas play, so I thought it was someone else's turn. I asked why it should be him and not another staff member.

Hesitantly, he told me, "When I made my commitment to try to live as Christ would have me live, I determined that I would always be willing to do the things that others did not want to do. This is my agreement with God. I want to stay."

Milton, the only member of the staff who was with us at Wot the entire time we were there, taught me many lessons. One of the first took place in the school's storeroom where the bags of rice, flour, and other supplies were kept. The students and staff were all busy elsewhere one afternoon, when I took it upon myself to clean this storeroom, where rats and cockroaches had made a mess of things. I was sweeping everything that littered the floor out the door, when Milton happened by.

"Oh, we can't throw out the rice!" he told me, looking at my pile of sweepings. "It is too precious." So he and I spent the next 15 minutes on our knees in the dirt picking up individual kernels of rice and placing them in a pan where they would be washed for cooking. He had gone through a war when it was practically impossible to feed his children. Obviously, I had never been in such an abysmal situation.

Before the war Milton had been Director of Education under the Japanese government. He spoke Japanese and had traveled to Japan. However, he had no English, so when the Americans arrived after the war, he was back to farming. But he never complained. His industry did not waver. He was constantly cheerful and supportive. He attended every staff meeting and worship service, his expression always open and alert. He and Pursis had 16 children; three of the younger ones—Paul, Filmore, and Ruth—were Lisa's and Lauren's constant play-companions, and two of them, Carlton and Myrle, were born at Wot while we were there. [Fifteen years later, someone had the brilliant idea of asking Milton to teach Japanese to Kosrae's high school students—a challenge he accepted.]

FUN NIGHT

All of us, staff and students alike, thoroughly enjoyed our fun nights. After a busy week filled with serious study and hard work, being able to gather on Friday night to play games, share funny stories or skits—to be silly together—completed our bonding as a big happy family. There was a marvelous variety of clowns on campus. Manapu Abraham, Siosi Aliksa, Paul Tilfas, and Natchuo Andrew were extraordinarily adept at improvisation and always in great demand. Skits were often repeated with hilarious variations. One favorite involved three, four, or more students standing in a line and interpreting some nonsense phrase for each other from Kosraean into English, then into Japanese or Samoan or Pohnpeian, or in whatever language they could come up with a word or a phrase. How we laughed!

SCHOOL BOARD FOR WOT

Though Pastor Alik Isaac continued to be our primary advisor and link to the island's churches, in 1960 we welcomed a newly appointed four-member School Board, courtesy of the all-island Church committee. These men represented the village churches: Zakias George of Tafunsak, Sru Likiaksa of Lelu, Kephas Charley of Malem, and Harold Edmond of Utwe.

These four men were a significant help to us. Together they served as our liaison with the all-island Church committee, and individually with their own village congregations. And they were hands-on participants in the life of the school, often appearing together or alone to help in whatever ways they could. They were a much-appreciated quartet of stalwart, involved churchmen.

NEW CHURCH DEDICATED IN UTWE

The time came to dedicate the new church in Utwe and we were invited to participate. In a regular weekly meeting of our staff, it was decided that Harrison, Erafe (who had returned from California in December), Caleb, and Srue—and those students with Utwe ties—would accompany Alice and me. The occasion was the subject of a newsletter distributed by the Missions Council in Boston:

On the early morning tide, Wednesday, February 3, Alice, Lisa, Lauren and I left the mission dock at Mwot, accompanied by 20 of our students and four staff members. For approximately two hours our canoes wound their way through the silent, narrow waterway of a dense tropical swamp. Shortly before noon we left the dark canal and crossed the glassy, sunlit harbor to Utwe, the smallest and most remote of the four Kusaien villages. Here we were to experience another new and exciting "first" for us: the dedication of an island church building.

Literally, the whole island population had gathered for the festivities, and now—the day before—was busy with final preparations. Large numbers of men were completing the long, thatch-roofed sheds which would house the various village delegations at the next day's feast. Women, in groups of 15 or 20, were making their way to or from the lagoon with their pandanas-fiber fish nets and "bustle baskets." From each newly built "oom" (Kusaien kitchen) pounding could be heard as stone mallets molded baked taro into the gummy, sweet Kusaien delicacy, fafa. Sitting along the trails, teenagers were busily braiding coconut frond trays, as well as flower leis and headbands, jabbering excitedly together as they worked.

In the center of the village, many happy hands swiftly put finishing touches to the church building itself. And, really, what a lovely church it is! All on its own, the Utwe congregation has erected a beautiful cement block building, with gleaming galvanized roofing and glass windows, the only building in Utwe thus complimented. For a people whose wealth is minimal, this was quite a feat. Begun in 1954, the men were now splashing on the last of the white coral paint to the outside walls, while inside, the women vigorously polished the handmade benches and carved chancel furniture. No one in Utwe even thought of sleep that night. By torchlight, great baskets of food were brought and lined up in the "village square" beside the church. From our upstairs guestroom window in the Sunday School building, Alice and I had an excellent view as, in the immediate foreground, pig after squealing pig was killed and roasted—over 200 of them!

By midmorning the next day the actual dedication service was begun. From the stirring processional hymn (the words of which Alice had written for the occasion) to the closing benediction, the deep sense of thanksgiving in the hearts of all was apparent. Benches in the back half of the sanctuary and woven mats on the floor of the front half were jammed tightly with worshipers, while at the doors and windows the faces of those too late to get inside reflected the excited reverence that characterized the day.

Certainly February 4, 1960, will be a day to live long in our memories. We praise God not only for the victory the completion of such a fine house of worship is, but for allowing us to be present on the day of the dedication.[1]

BREAKING GROUND FOR NEW SCHOOL BUILDING

On the 25th of that month, we broke ground for a school building at Wot. The large New England-style building which had been erected in 1909 by visiting carpenter George E. Bowker and his crew of Kosraean churchmen had been dismantled by the Japanese military in 1942 and carried off to be used as part of their Malem headquarters. The concrete steps, foundation, and pillars were still in place—silent but continual reminders of what had been. (Our students had filled the space inside the large, rectangular foundation with soil and used the area for growing sugarcane.) We were still using the chapel, the typhoon house and—weather permitting—the front lawn, for classes.

In the plans I drew, the new building would follow the downward curve of the Yonrak hill. Through the efforts of the school board, Kosrae's Christians pledged over $1,000 toward this project—a staggering amount at that time for these people.

The groundbreaking was an impressive occasion. Yekula's Royal Gifford (the public secondary school's new American teacher), Judge Linus George, Superintendent of Schools Florian Nena, Chief Magistrate Paul Sigrah, Pastor Frank Skilling, and Pastor Alik Isaac were there, along with many others. Before the symbolic shovels-full were dug up and turned, the students sang, I spoke, Erafe explained what the building would look like, and Harrison gave the prayer of dedication. It was a beautiful day. We were surrounded not only by the mountains, the ocean, and the sky, but by a "great cloud of witnesses" [Hebrews 12:1]—the many Kosraean, Marshallese, Gilbertese, Pohnpeian, and American saints who had studied, taught, and gone forth from this same hallowed spot. Their presence and influence permeated the entire campus.

The work began. Almost every week a different church group arrived to do its part—under the watchful eye of chief carpenter Erafe, who made the assignments and laid out the design. When no helpers were present, Erafe worked on his own, his enthusiasm never waning. While the excavation of the site took place, male students—during their work periods—began making concrete blocks at the wharf and carrying them up the hill. This transporting was usually accomplished by hanging four blocks—two in front and two in back—on a hefty bamboo pole balanced on a shoulder. Bags of cement and woven coconut baskets filled with sand and gravel were also carried up the steep, winding trail to the building site, as trenches for the footings were dug and forms for the pillars were constructed.

EASTER BAPTISMS

Several of our students were already members of the Church when they arrived at Wot and, as the months went by, the meaning of taking such a step frequently came up in Christian life classes and Sunday evening discussion groups. In Congregational tradition, they had all been baptized as infants. However, in place of confirmation, the Kosraean Church required a profession of faith and adult baptism when individuals chose for themselves the Christian life. After making their commitments for Christ before their peers, six students were baptized and became members of the Church during our Easter service on April 14: Grey Tolenoa, Printon Peter, Itchiko Luther, Simako Milton, Lucy Musrasrik, and Takae Joseph.

SEMESTER MOVES FORWARD

The regular school routine was often pleasantly interrupted. Fifty members of the Young People's Christian Endeavor Society of Utwe came to Wot March 14 to give us two full days of work in the gardens. On March 24 representatives of the Tafunsak Church arrived to present the school with a sleek new 40' canoe they had christened *Lisa M. Buck.*

There was some dissension on Kosrae during the first half of 1960 as the individual Young People's C. E. groups stumbled forward through the organizing process. I was frequently called to different villages to help explain things to the elders or to give guidance to the youth. Sometimes the young people complained that adult sponsors were refusing to allow them the freedom to make their own plans. Adults disapproved of certain innovations the young people suggested. With God's grace, we jumped the hurdles and ploughed through the problems. Fortunately, in the long run, the adults exhibited unusual patience, and the young people persevered and won the right to continue their own groups.

OUR FIRST GRADUATION

On June 2, 1960, our first class graduated. It was another stirring occasion as parents, grandparents, uncles and aunts, brothers and sisters, plus many others gathered from around the island, eager to be present at the ceremonies. Twenty-four of the students had finished the course. Alice had helped the girls sew lovely long white dresses, which they decorated with small red bows. The boys wore black pants, white dress shirts, every necktie that I owned—and shoes they had begged and borrowed from all over the island.

Of the 30 in that class at the first of the year, five had either been dismissed or had dropped out. Because he was younger than the others, we had transferred Marston Nena back a class. The 24 who graduated included 15 boys and nine girls. Shiro Milton Timothy was valedictorian and Holdon Jack Musrasrik, salutatorian. Magrina Wakuk, Walton Palik, and Yukiwo Tara tied for third highest grade-point average among the graduates.

In addition to the speeches of the valedictorian and salutatorian, Magrina, Noel, Connie, and Bardon shared memories of each of their four years at Wot— beginning in 1957. Pastor Frank Skilling brought greetings from the Church of Kosrae, and Florian Nena shared greetings from Kosrae's Board of Education. I delivered the commencement address and distributed diplomas to the graduates, many of whom were tearful.

Our guest of honor that day was Miss Margaret Hill, one of the Trust Territory administrators of education, who commented that, in her eight years in Micronesia, this was the first occasion on which she had seen Micronesians tearful in such a gathering. "Obviously, they really loved this school and what they have gotten here."[2]

Five of the graduates—Connie, Magrina, Holdon, Sisado, and Tulenna— were invited to return the next semester as special students for additional training and to work as tutors. Some of the others went right on to enroll at the Pacific Islands Central School (PICS) at Pohnpei. The graduates included future pastor Walton Kilafwa Palik. We were plenty proud of them all!

INDIGENOUS LEADERS CONFERENCE OF 1960

Pastor Alik Isaac and KCTS teacher Alik Palsis were unable to be present at the commencement festivities because the church committee had chosen them and Deacon Ernest Sigrah to represent Kosrae at the first Micronesian Indigenous Leaders Conference which took place in the Marshall Islands. Hosted by the United Church of Christ at Uliga, Majuro, June 3 to 6, the gathering gave delegates from the Marshalls, Kosrae, Pohnpei, Chuuk, and Palau the opportunity to meet one another, to share in worship, and to discuss matters of common interest and concern.

Transportation problems, coupled with complications inherent in a group gathered from five distinct language areas, were surmounted with grace, a lot of patience and excellent hospitality. Delegates were convinced that they should make the Indigenous Leaders Conference a biennial event in spite of the difficulties. They were well aware that the missionaries among them in Micronesia gathered every two years—why not the leaders of the island churches? They were also anxious about the possibilities of higher education for their young people and felt that together they could make more progress toward envisioned goals than they could as individual churches. A Committee on Higher Education became the primary product of their assembly that year.

TIME OUT FOR MISSION MEETING

From the earliest years of the Snows, the Gulicks, the Sturgeses, and their Hawaiian colleagues, it had been the practice of the missionaries to gather every two years for a meeting of the Micronesia Mission. As many of the missionaries as possible who were in the field at meeting time would make the effort to gather at one of the mission locations to report on their work, share ideas, and plan for the future. In addition, mission meeting was always an important time of fellowship, worship, and prayer. To bring the missionaries together for these meetings had been one of the purposes of the *Morning Stars* during the years that those mission vessels were in service.

After the *Morning Star V* was retired in 1905 and Wot's Marshall and Gilbert schools transferred from Kosrae back to those islands, the meetings of the missionaries often took place among those who worked within a given area, rather than everyone traveling to one place. During and between the two World Wars, there were no gatherings of the Micronesia Mission. There is no record of the Baldwin sisters ever having attended such a meeting during the 25 years of their active involvement at Wot—though they certainly had times of discussion and planning with Jessie Hoppin, and later with the Lockwoods. By 1947 these meetings were once more taking place every two years with Dr. Harold Hanlin presiding. He had been appointed by the American Board as Superintendent of the Micronesia Mission.

Alice, with the two little girls, left Kosrae May 12 to travel to Chuuk for this meeting. I remained at Wot to oversee graduation, then left for Pohnpei June 18 to join them. Due to erratic ship schedules from Pohnpei, I was too late for the meeting at Chuuk, but I did get to assist secretary Marge Terpstra put the minutes of the meeting into final form in Dr. Hanlin's Pohnpei workroom and get them ready for distribution. Marge and her husband Chet taught at the Pastors & Teachers Training School at Ohwa.

BACK HOME

We entered a whirlwind of activity upon our return to Wot. On July 26, 67 church leaders convened for a two-week retreat and planning conference. The first week in August, I went to each of the villages to interview prospective students. Church groups continued working on the foundation of the new school building. On August 4 the first concrete pillar was raised—and by August 11, 65 of them were in place!

Alice and I took a three-day leave over our fifth wedding anniversary, August 10, with Lisa and Lauren along, to get away to a small copra house that faced the sea on one of Utwe's reef islands, called Inkul Srisrik. We enjoyed our two days there, but we were not alone. As we tried to enjoy their habitat, thousands of mosquitoes enjoyed us. Finally, on the third day, we got into a canoe that Makato Edmond, owner of the little island, had left with me. We paddled down the channel, across the harbor, and took refuge in Utwe's Sunday School building.

I was proud that Alice and I had paddled the four of us all the way to Utwe—but instead of commending me as we pulled ashore at the village, my friends scolded me for allowing Lisa to fall asleep behind me in the stern of the canoe. "Your children should always be in front of you, where you can see them," they admonished us.

Joshua Phillip had returned from the Pastors & Teachers Training School, and we were pleased to have him become part of our Wot faculty. Alik Palsis took the year off, but Harrison was still teaching with us. Erafe was overseeing the progress of the new building. There were two grade levels at Wot during the 1960-1961 school year, with a total of 73 students.

We also welcomed new staff members that fall, all of them from Malem: Kun Aaron and his wife, Mabel, came to cook for the student body. Tulpe Robert was the new housemother. A staff position was added as we needed a mechanic to care for our newly acquired outboard motor, and to supervise our fleet of canoes and Wot's handsome new whaleboat. After only a few days with us it was apparent that Roland Stephen was the ideal person for that job. His wife, Lillian, was a valued help in supervising the girls' afternoon work program. Deckla had returned to her family in Lelu, so Kun and Mabel's just-graduated daughter, Sanahe, joined our family. As Deckla had been, Sanahe was a cheerful, attentive companion for Lisa and Lauren while Alice and I were teaching or otherwise occupied.

TIME TO CELEBRATE

The entire Wot family rejoiced with Harrison when he married Yamada Simeon Skilling October 27—and on November 15, Alice and I were in Tafunsak to celebrate the 6th anniversary of their young people's Christian Endeavor Society. These were significant events in the life of the Church and people from all over the island flocked to enjoy the ceremonies, songs, and feasting.

We also celebrated the baptism of nine of our students on October 23: Akiwo Likiaksa, Miosi Tulenna, Kasuo Isisaki, Natchuo Mongkeya, Kenye Alik Kefwas, Paul Tilfas, Lucy Likiaksa, Sepe T. Nena, and Masayuki Skilling.

TIME TO MOURN

Pastor Frank Skilling died December 2, 1960. He was 70 years old and had been a pastor three years. I took part in his memorial service in the Lelu church and was with those who, in a torrential downpour, accompanied his body to its final resting place in a very muddy grave at Sansrik.

WEEK OF PRAYER BAPTISMS

At the conclusion of our Week of Prayer services on January 8, 1961, 19 more of our students were baptized and became members of the Kosraean Church: Alma Melander, Neila Robert, Andrew Isaac, Sam T. Mike, Atilina Tamiko Clarence, Sepe K. Mongkeya, Hiroko Lambert, Sepe Moody, Julian J. Metwarik, Sra J. Palsisa, Kemwel Tilfas, Tatao M. Tulensru, Kenye Lucius, Tokiko Nelson, Kenye P. Asher, Tulpe Edmond, Lerina Musrasrik, Yosimi Roland, and Midio Tulen.

U.N. DIGNITARIES VISIT

We helped host a delegation of United Nations dignitaries on February 13. Periodically, these groups—composed of diplomats from three or four countries and their aides—appeared on Kosrae as part of their tour to observe and critique the efforts of the United States government's Department of the Interior to govern the islands of the Trust Territory.

WOT STUDENT GROUPS

Before traveling to Kosrae, Alice and I had visited various Congregational churches in different parts of the United States to explain our mission assignment and to garner interest for the work of the American Board. Four of these churches stayed in close contact with us during our years at Wot. The First Congregational Church of Swampscott, the First Congregational Church of North Weymouth, and the Rollstone Congregational Church of Fitchburg were all in Massachusetts. The fourth was the First Congregational Church of Indianapolis, Indiana. We built a fine rapport with each congregation and became good friends with the pastors and chairpersons of their mission committees. They sent school supplies, gifts for the students, other items that they thought might be useful, and things we specifically requested. We knew we could count on them, not only for assistance in the small and bigger things, but for prayer, which we needed and for which we were always grateful.

As our student body grew, we divided the young people into four groups named for the four churches—Indianapolis, North Weymouth, Rollstone, and Swampscott—for friendly competition in singing, work projects and to prepare fun night skits. As the months went by we found many uses for the groups. Some of our students corresponded with young people from these congregations, and each group developed an allegiance to his or her particular American church.

AN UPDATING

Throughout January, February, March, and April, large groups from Kosrae's four congregations continued to travel to Wot to work on the new school building emerging along the southwest edge of the Yonrak green. Some weeks the going seemed slow, other weeks we were amazed by how much progress was made.

In a Newsletter dated May 12, 1961, I wrote:

The mission hilltop is alive with activity these days. Besides the 93 members of our student body and staff who call this home, large groups of volunteer Kusaiean Christians are working hard to complete our new school building.

It is fascinating to watch them work. For reinforcing, they have rescued 500 iron rods from the old, bombed-out Japanese airstrip at Ponape. After these rods are transported on the deck of a field-trip ship, they have to be straightened and pounded by hand to knock off the rust, then painted. There are no cement mixers or electric saws, but what has never been used isn't missed. The giant timbers brought from our verdant Kusaie forests to be made into the beams and pillars are all hewn by hand. It's a wonder these carpenters don't lose their toes in the process of shaping the wood, for they stand right on the line they follow with their axes! The cement is mixed by shovel on large tins brought from the abandoned Air Force installation in Lelu. The wet cement is then passed by the buckets-full over their heads by shouting, laughing men and boys from the mixing area to where it is needed in the building. When two or more carpenters are hammering nails, they always pound together in rhythm. I shake my head in wonder at how they do that! It is completely unconscious on their part—automatic!

The women do a big share of the work. A long line of them winds up the mountain from the beach, each woman with a woven basket of sand or gravel on her hip. It is a good 10-minute walk up from the wharf area—and a steep climb at that—but they too are jubilant in their work. This joy these Christians radiate while working here at the mission is always a source of strength for us. They, as we, are eager to see this beautiful new building completed and in use.

The structure, 146 feet long and 28 feet wide, sits high on the bluff of our mountainside. It is being built on two levels, following the slope of the ground. The upper level houses three classrooms, which will be partitioned in such a way that they can be opened into one large assembly or recreational area. The lower level includes a library (so far without books for the shelves), an office, and a storeroom. A covered veranda runs the length of one side and windows run the length of the other—and what a view! An American class of youngsters might have a hard time concentrating on lessons with that exquisite scene of tropical foliage and blue, blue ocean beside them. These young people are content to keep their eyes glued to their textbooks. These windows are not glassed in, but rather—in keeping with the climate—are fitted with movable wooden louvers that let in the sea breezes but keep out the rain.

The villagers have divided the work into four parts—each village responsible for one complete section of the building. The bulk of the work has been completed. The people of Tafunsak have even finished painting their section. Since it has literally become "a race to the finish" among them, the Utwe folk are a bit embarrassed that it is only their fourth of the veranda which remains without roof. However, now that Easter is over, and if the ship scheduled for May 15th brings the needed supplies, the homestretch is sure to be covered swiftly. We've tentatively scheduled the dedication for October.[3]

FIGHT CULMINATES IN AN INSPIRING EASTER

Yekula students came to play baseball with us March 9 and 10. There was some rather blatant cheating on both sides and some irritating arrogance on the part of some team members when these instances were pointed out. Neither group was very happy with the results of the games, and there was a definite undercurrent of ill-will when the Yekula students climbed into their canoes to return to their own campus.

Then, on March 26, our students were in Tafunsak to present an Easter program of drama and song in the church there. Later that night, some of the

Yekula boys and some of the Wot boys got into a fight. The next day Yekula's Principal Shrew Jonas and I, with eight student leaders—four from each school—met together on the Yekula campus to see how we could make peace. We found a way that pleased both student groups and amazed the people of Kosrae, all of whom, of course, had heard about the fight.

We took the Wot student body to Pisin several days before Easter, and each day the Yekula students joined us there to learn our new Easter songs. On April 2, Easter Sunday morning, with Alice directing, the student bodies of Kosrae's two secondary schools stood at the front of the Lelu church and presented a joyous Easter program—together! It was one of the highlights of my years on Kosrae.

DEATH OF JACK YOUNGSTROM

With all of Kosrae, we were shocked and saddened by the sudden, tragic death of Jack Youngstrom on April 21. At the insistence of his uncle, Arthur Herman, Jack had left his home in Oakland, California, as a very young man to move to Kosrae and become his uncle's assistant in the older man's trading and planting company. For three years during World War II, Jack suffered great privation while incarcerated by the Japanese military. After ill-health drove Mr. Herman back to California in 1950, Jack worked hard to make his uncle's plantation productive and the trading company profitable, while enjoying his growing family. Jack was survived by his wife, Erwine, and his children: Mabel, Vernon, George, and Laura.

ALICE BEGINS BIBLE REVISION

In May, Alice began a project to translate a new version of the Kosraean Bible. As all languages, Kosraean is fluid. There were words that had been used by Benjamin Snow and Elizabeth Baldwin in their translations that Kosraeans no longer used, and some with meanings changed or lost. There were passages in the earlier Bible that followed too closely an English word order that was unnatural for Kosraean speakers. Ironically, as the years went by, readers were turning more and more to their English Bibles in an attempt to decipher Kosraean Bible verses.

Pastor Alik Isaac, who was frequently at Wot, worked with Alice as her primary consultant. They began and completed the three short letters of John and felt good about the results. By the time summer was over, they had completed Jude and the two letters of Peter.

In general, however, the leadership of the church looked with suspicion on a new translation of the Kosraean Bible. They felt that God's Word was being tampered with instead of clarified. It was a mark of his wisdom and commitment that Pastor Alik himself was enthusiastic about the project.

Alice also met during the summer with Kosrae's Department of Education personnel as they continued to grapple with a uniform spelling for the language.

ELDEN'S SUMMER JOBS

In mid-May, I accompanied our advanced students to Yekula where they took the PICS entry examination. On May 20 I participated in Yekula's graduation. We had no graduation at Wot that year, and by June 15 our students had left the campus for vacation. I attended sessions of the all-island church committee and several new-month meetings of the church membership, and visited the four communities to choose the new class of students for the fall semester at Wot.

In August, some of the students who were working through the summer helped refurbish the chapel. We re-varnished the walls and altar furniture, mended and dyed the chancel curtains, and painted the veranda pillars and the low wall separating the veranda from the chapel's interior. We also received a beautiful new Yamaha pump organ at the mission, purchased for us by an American family on Pohnpei.

On September 8, with Royal Gifford and Paul McNutt, I participated in the dedication of Utwe's new elementary school. On the 12th I led an orientation-retreat for the mission school staff. We began receiving students on the 14th, and, from the 26th through the 28th, hosted Dr. Elwell Pretrick of Pohnpei as he administered tests for tuberculosis to the student body and staff. When classes began there were 93 students in three grade levels.

Two more of our students were baptized on October 1: Nena T. Nena and Siosi Aliksa.

ESAU TILFAS AND ALIKSRU TOLENOA ORDAINED

On November 1, 1961, two respected deacons were selected to be Kosrae's 11th and 12th pastors. Esau Tilfas of Lelu and Aliksru Tolenoa of Tafunsak were ordained in a ceremony in the Lelu church at which Pastor Alik Isaac and I officiated. Pastor Esau was 67 and Pastor Aliksru was 61. More than 1,000 people were present for the ordination service and feast that followed.

WOT SCHOOL BUILDING DEDICATED

We had been using portions of the new building since the beginning of the fall semester. On November 8 we finally received the eight tables and 48 chairs ordered for the library. Other delays simply had to be accepted, given the isolated location of Kosrae, coupled with the further isolation of the mission school from Kosrae's port.

The Missions Council helped me spread the news of the dedication:

Before the passage of time brings a dimness to memory, we write you of the Dedication of our new Kusaie Christian Training School building. Yes—the dedication services and festivities finally took place yesterday, Thanksgiving Day, 1961.

By a unanimous decision of our staff, we dismissed classes for the week in order to prepare for the Big Day. The over-100 pairs of hands in our Mwot community each had a job to do. There was last-minute painting to be done; floors to be scrubbed; grass to be cut; ferns and flowers to be gathered and decorations made; firewood to be chopped; sugarcane to be cut and bundled; pigs to be rounded up, killed, and roasted; bread to be baked; fish to be caught; and song after new song to be practiced—all of the work done in a spirit of eagerness and thanksgiving for the day we had all looked forward to for so long.

The actual festivities began at 3 a.m. on November 23rd. The students and staff gathered on our mission mountaintop lawn and divided into the four KCTS campus groups: Rollstone, Indianapolis, North Weymouth, and Swampscott. Singing and marching until dawn, the groups wound up and down the Mwot trails serenading the several hundred visitors who had arrived for the dedication and bedded themselves down on their mats beneath the coconut trees and in the thatch guest houses at the wharf area.

At 9:15 a.m. the first bell pealed loud and long out across the lagoon, and the villagers began the climb up the hill to the site of the new school building. At 9:40 the second bell rang, and Alice began a 20-minute organ concert as people continued to arrive. The walls had been removed from between the three classrooms in order to accommodate the large gathering, but that room was soon jammed, and so were the lawn and garden areas on both sides. At exactly 10 a.m. the bell rang a third time, and from the chapel further up the hill marched the entire student body of 93 young people in procession, singing, in English, the stirring hymn: "All the Toil and Sorrow Done." The service lasted for two and a half hours, but each portion was short and varied enough so that the people were ready to sit for another hour or two! It was a thrilling service, and certainly a high point in our experience for both Alice and me. We praise God for abundant blessings!

Heavy, dark clouds hung over the mission hill the whole morning, but miraculously did not spill a drop until evening. They just served to keep the crowds cool as all gathered on Vesper Point [the lower end of the Yonrak ridge] to share in the dedication feast. The village churches joined the mission in gathering and preparing food: basket after basket of roasted pigs; boiled taro; rice and fish; oom'ed breadfruit; freshly baked bread, donuts, and biscuits; oranges; tangerines; pineapples; and sug-

arcane—and our Kusaien dessert, fafa.

Perhaps you would be interested to know that the single story, 146-foot by 28-foot building was erected for approximately $5,000. Of this, $2,000 was a gift from the American Board for the erasing of war damages; $2,000 was presented to the school in the form of materials and labor by the Kusaien Christians; and $1,000 was given by friends in the United States.

The weariness that we felt last evening was a kind of exhilarating weariness (if there is such a thing), as the great satisfaction of a tremendous job completed finally began to sink into our consciousness. We express to each of you our heartfelt thanks for your interest and prayers concerning this project.[4]

We were especially pleased to host Royal Gifford and Emi Mukaida at the dedication. At the time, they were the only other Americans living on Kosrae. Over the proceeding year, Mr. Gifford and I had developed a warm friendship, often consulting with each other about common concerns. Our ties with Miss Mukaida were strong as well. She was training teachers for the government school system, but was also a Congregational Church member and a stanch supporter of the Micronesia Mission through the Hawaii Conference of the United Church of Christ.

STAFF MEETINGS

Though they were sometimes lengthy—and occasionally heated—I remember our Wot staff meetings with a great deal of nostalgia. Two words come easily to mind as I contemplate these times of planning and pondering ideas together: Growth and gratitude.

We gathered in the mission house living room each Monday evening, in a circle on the floor mats, to discuss that week's schedule, the food situation, discipline issues, special programs, on-going problems, and new ones. The teachers, cooks, housemother, plantation foreman, and mechanic were all there to voice their opinions and share their concerns.

As in any such assembly, some talked more than others—but they all did talk, and we gained from one another's insights. Harrison had much to say and much to criticize. He was especially quick to pounce on innovations suggested by Erafe—and Erafe, who by nature was quieter and more sympathetic, would back off. Alik Palsis, with his one-line zingers, provided the comic relief that was sometimes needed. Joshua's thoughtful comments reflected his consistent willingness to cooperate and forgive, while Milton's support and calm reassurance could always be counted on. As the women began to realize that their opinions mattered, they began to express themselves, too—unusual in this culture. They shared openly and with an underlying wisdom that helped to keep us centered.

This seemed to surprise and please them, as well as their male colleagues.

These sessions gave us a solidarity of purpose and molded us into a concerned group of brothers and sisters, which was echoed in the relaxed and harmonious camaraderie of the student body.

HALLELUJAH!

The songs of choice among Kosraeans are those related to the Southern Gospel style. Kosraeans love the close, four-part harmony, and the moving alto, tenor, and bass parts which are sung in counterpoint to the melody of the sopranos. They have captured this style beautifully and made it thoroughly their own. Their singing is never dull or depressing.

From time to time, however, an American missionary or public school teacher has attempted to introduce a different style of music—and Christmas 1961 was one of those times. Alice took on the arduous project of teaching the students The Hallelujah Chorus from Handel's *Messiah*. Both she and the students gave it their ALL! Alice wrote out the four parts of the score using the Solfege System—"do-re-mi"—then spent hours in part-rehearsals with the sopranos one period and the tenors the next, then the altos, and finally an hour for the boys singing bass. Over and over they sang the same notes and remarkably, it all began to sound right. The students were not too sure what they thought of it at first, but when the parts were finally put together, they got very excited. No one on Kosrae had ever heard The Hallelujah Chorus—but they would hear it now! There would be other songs in our program but Handel's rousing anthem would be the climax.

In the meantime, I was working with the same students to prepare a dramatic presentation of six different Biblical Christmas scenes. Like students everywhere, they enjoyed dressing up in costumes—and they did a good job of memorizing, some lines in English and some lines in Kosraean, and convincingly acting the parts.

I also worked with the student body on the special processional we would use to enter the Lelu church for the Christmas service. Our chapel was not big enough to rehearse there, but the Yonrak slope was perfect. As the students marched down the green expanse of the lawn, they could easily see me as I led from the veranda of our new school building. It was December 19, and time was getting close.

"Let's do it again," I shouted—and everyone returned to the top of the hill to march down one more time while keeping their eyes on me as I marched parallel to them on the raised veranda—backward, in order to be facing them. Suddenly I disappeared from their view! I had marched in reverse right off the end of the veranda, falling seven feet down into a hibiscus bush. The singing stopped and there was deadly silence. When I peeked around the edge of the veranda with a sheepish grin, all 93 students erupted into a roar of laughter that I was sure could be heard in Utwe. They slapped each other—they rolled around on the grass—and the rehearsal was over!

We went to Lelu, and we processed into the church in fine order, faces forward—and Alice's 93-voice choir wowed all of Kosrae with a triumphant, a cappella rendition of The Hallelujah Chorus. Though clapping is generally frowned upon in church, more than 1,000 worshipers broke into hearty, spontaneous applause after the last resounding "HALLELUJAH!"[5] ✠

Notes - Chapter 16

1. Elden M. Buck, Newsletter, Missions Council, Congregational Christian Churches, Boston, Feb. 11, 1960
2. E. M. Buck, family correspondence, Kosrae, June 5, 1960
3. E. M. Buck, Newletter, Missions Council, May 12, 1961
4. Ibid, Nov. 24, 1961
5. The chronology and events recorded in this chapter are verified in the daily entries of the author's personal journals kept during the 1959-1962 period of his residency on Kosrae.

NUNAK YOHK KE CHAPTER 17
1961-1971

Committee lun Church Kosrae tuh sraklalak Lucius Charley in an principalla ke lutlut Wot in aolul Elden Buck meyen el ac sou lal ac som in mongla acn selos ke June. Lucius el mutaweak oru ma kunal in January oru el us sou lal ac som nu Wot.

Akilenyuk puseni mwet Kosrae su ke pacl se inge oasr ke mwet 2,500. Ke sripa se inge arulana iktokla lohm alu Lelu in karingin Christmas toeni. In sie meeting lun Committee lun Church Kosrae su orek Lelu ke March 30, 1962, elos tuh sramsramkin lac Christmas lalos nu ke yac sac ac toeni oana orek meet fahfahsru, ku kais sie church ac tari oru akfulat lalos ke church lalos sifacna. Tukun sramsram na yohk lalos, elos wotela mu in tufa fasrelik su ac pa inge pacl se oemeet Christmas Kosrae in tia toeni.

Un tulik akluo in srola ke kolyuk lal Pastu Elden ac sou lal tuh orek ke May 18, 1962, su tuh oasr tulik 27 pa srola inge. Kasuo Isisaki pa valedictorian ac Lerina Musrasrik pa tuh salutatorian. Elden ac Alice, us tulik luo natultal, Lisa ac Lauren, in folok mongla ke June 30. Ye kolyuk lal Lucius su principal ke lutlut se inge, ac wi kasru lun mwet luti ac mwet kasru wial, ac wi pa kutu sin tulik ma sasu srolla ke lutlut se inge, tuh oru in oasr tulik 99 tuh weang lutlut Wot ke September.

Ke sro lun u se ma tuh srolla ke May 1963, principal ke lutlut se Yekula ah, Mr. Royal Gifford, pa tuh oru sramsram in akkeye nu selos. Alwina Kephas pa tuh valedictorian ac Emiko Jim pa tuh salutatorian. Ke u se ma tu srolla ke 1964 ah, Arthur George pa tu valedictorian ac Clara Tulensru pa tuh salutatorian. Tukun lutlut ac tari ke 1964 ah, na Principal Lucius el folokla nu Malem, na Kingston Kintaro Phillip el tuh principalla. Yac 1965 pah tuh tui lutlut se Wot inge tukun ikak ke yac 86.

Tulik ma tuh wi lutlut se Wot inge tuh sokla in som wi lutlut in acn Micronesia—kutu som wela Pastors & Teachers Training School ac oayapa PICS fin acn Pohnpei, ac kutu nu Liebenzell Mission High School fin acn Palau: Bethania ikak nu sin tulik mutan fin an Bablethaup, ac Emmaus ikak nu sin tulik mukul fin an Koror. Kutu selos som wela lutlut Yekula na pwanang ke 1966 elos pa wi srolla oemeet ke lutlut se Yekula inge.

Anna Dederer pa missionary safla se supweyukla nu Kosrae sin American

Board. El isusla fin acn Germany ac el tuh supweyukme nu fin acn Mortlocks sin Liebenzell Mission ke 1934, na toko el som nu Chuuk ke 1939. Ke mweun akluo lun faclu, mwet mweun lun acn Japan tuh kalpousilya fin acn Chuuk. Ke wola pacl ah, el tafwella in oru orekma lal in kulansupu American Board fin acn Chuuk na pa inge pacl se el tuh akmusrala nu ke pastu. Ke 1954 el som nu fin acn Marshall ac orekma we ne ke supeyukla el nu Kosrae ke 1964. El tuh muta fin acn Pisin, ac yok na kasru lal nu sin mutan, mwet fusr, a mwet kol lun church.

Oasr mwet Kosrae tuh mukuila nu fin acn Ebeye in acn Marshall ke pulan pacl se inge, in orekma ke acn se lun U. S. Army fin acn Kwajalein. Ke sripen puseni mwet Kosrae fin acn we, oru Elden ac Alice Buck tuh kasrelos in mutaweak pac oru alu lalos ke kas Kosrae. Ke pal se inge fahfahsru nu ke yac meet ke 1970, Elden ac Alice—wi kasru lun kutu sin mwet Kosrae fin acn Ebeye—kasru in orala Kas in Kol lun Etawi, ac supwala in kasru mwet Kosrae ke yac nukewa.

Ke June 1966 tuh oasr toeni se lun mwet ke tuka in acn Micronesia inge ke ip lun alu, tuh orek fin acn Kosrae. Tuh oasr mwet tuku aol acn Marshall, Pohnpei, Chuuk, ac Palau nu ke meeting se inge. Pa inge pacl se oemeet Church Kosrae in karingin tukeni yok lun mwet kol ke alu fin acn Micronesia. Pastu Alik Isaac, Deacon Zakias George, ac Alik Palsis pa tuh aol Church Kosrae, ac Joseph Z. George el tuh aol ip lun mwet fusr.

Oayapa ke 1966, American Board—su pangpang misenge United Church Board for World Ministries—tuh oakiya Mizaph High School, Christian high school se fin acn Moen, Chuuk. Oasr tulik ma akilenyuk fin acn Kosrae tuh solla in som nu ke lutlut se inge. Inmasrlon tulik ma tuh som emeet pa Winston Likiaksa, Nena Shru Nena, ac Fred N. Skilling. Ke December 1966, Miss Dederer el tuh supalla Kun Caleb ac Joseph George in som nu ke lutlut se fin acn Rabaul, New Guinea su pangpang Malmaluan Youth Leadership Training Center.

Ke May 1, 1967, Isaiah Benjamin ac Harrison George tuh akmusralla elos nu ke pastu, oru elos pastu aksingoul tolu ac aksingoul akosr fin acn Kosrae. Pastu Isaiah el yac 75 ac Pastu Harrison el yac 35. Touyak lalos oru in oasr pastu lime-kosr fin acn Kosrae ke pacl se inge, oru pastu in tila forfor nu ke church saya, a elos mutana ke church lalos. Elos pah: Pastu Aliksru ke Church Tafunsak, Pastu Alik Isaac ac Pastu Esau ke Church Lelu, Pastu Harrison ke Church Malem, ac Pastor Isaiah ke Church Utwe.

Pus nunak sasu ma Pastu Harrison el srukak nu ke meeting lun mwet sropo Kosrae. Mwe naweyuk se oemeet el srukak ah pa ke Pre Lun Leum. El akilen mu fahkya uh arulana pisrpisr oru oana in wangin kalmeya. Mwet sropo wiyal kewa insese in oasr naweya. Sie pac mwe nunak ma Pastu Harrison el srukak ac akkeyeyuk sel Miss Dederer ah, pa wal lun "Lay Minister." Committee lun

Church Kosrae tuh insese mu in oasri wal lun lay minister in weang pastu ac deacon. Ke sripa se inge kais sie church ac tufah srukak mwet nu ke lay minister. Kunokon lalos pa in pwanak mwet nu ke alu uh, orani mwe sang ke pacl in alu, ac in kasru in kol pacl in alu.

Ke December 1969, Miss Dederer ac Dr. Hanlin tuh supalla Takeo Likiaksa ac Walton Palik in wi lutlut se pangpang Malua Theological College fin acn Western Samoa. Eltal wi lutlut se inge ke yac akosr. Ke 1970 Erafe Tosie el akmusrala nu ke pastu ac el pah pastu aksingoul limekosr fin acn Kosrae. Pacl se pacna inge pa Miss Dederer el aksafyela ma kunal fin acn Kosrae ac el folok nu California. El misa we ke October 21, 1976, ke el yac 74 matwa.

CHAPTER SEVENTEEN

CONNECTING BEYOND KOSRAE
1961-1971

PRINCIPAL LUCIUS CHARLEY

Our furlough was scheduled to begin at the completion of the school year, so as 1961 drew to a close, the KCTS school board—in consultation with the all-island church committee—was searching for a qualified person to become principal of the Wot school. The school board was unanimous in its selection of Lucius Charley, a respected public school teacher in Malem.

The new principal-in-waiting joined the staff at Wot in January 1962. His wife, Lily, and their younger children accompanied him, and were soon an integral part of campus life. Lucius and I worked side by side, anticipating the time when he would take the reins of the school as I departed.

OTHER TEACHERS, LEADERS, AND OFFICERS

A newly appointed school board was also in place. The church committee asked Sru Likiaksa to continue representing Lelu and Kephas Charley, Malem. Palikkun Nena now represented Utwe and Teroa Tolenoa, Tafunsak.

Through the efforts of Dr. Hanlin, there was a new teacher on the faculty. Dolbe Olter arrived in January from her home on Pohnpei. She was the sister of Baily Olter, who later became President of the Federated States of Micronesia. Sawan Sru and his wife, Kenye, were our new cooks. Harrison had the school year off, and Alik Palsis was back with us.

Our student officers were doing an outstanding job leading their classmates. Kasuo Isisaki was student body president. Kemwel Tilfas, Isao Mongkeya, Natchuo Mongkeya, Sam Tulensa, Atilina Lonno, Takae Olter, Yosimi Stephen, Kath Kilafwa Sikein, John Nena Mike, Lerina Musrasrik and Richard Tolenoa assisted as the student council. I was their advisor. Sephin Shrew was president of the Wot Christian Endeavor Society, assisted by Vice President Paul Tilfas, Secretary Siosi Aliksa, Treasurer Marston Nena, and committee members Sepe Nena, Hiroko Lawrence, and Sepe Sabel. Alice served as advisor.

TOGETHER OR SEPARATELY?

The swift growth of Kosrae's population brought with it an inevitable dilemma. Kosraean Christians continued to say that, though they had four meeting places, there was only one Church. On average Sundays, people were together in their own villages. Special days on the Church calendar—communion Sundays and baptisms, new-month services, Christmas, and Easter—were observed or celebrated with everyone together in Lelu. No one challenged this way of doing things—it had been this way for a hundred years. But it meant long walks or lengthy canoe trips for most of the membership, usually involving more than one day.

Now, on the most popular of these days, there could be more than 2,000 people attending. Church guest houses and other places to stay in Lelu were overcrowded, and more and more of the large island's people were questioning the need to go to Lelu. The church at Langosak could no longer accommodate all Kosraeans.

It had been discussed before, but at the all-island church committee meeting on March 30, 1962, an argument erupted. Could not the four churches celebrate Christmas in their own villages this year? Some members pled for the status quo—primarily the people of Lelu. It just wouldn't be Christmas, they felt, if everyone wasn't together in the main church. Others—mostly leaders from Tafunsak, Malem, and Utwe—countered that it certainly would be Christmas, and that more people would actually be able to enjoy it if the celebration took place simultaneously in four locations instead of being jammed into one.

Traditionally, each of the churches prepared a program of serpentine marches and new songs to present to the other three on Christmas. But these groups had become too large and unwieldy for a limited performing area. Each congregation could easily divide into two or more groups, in addition to Sunday School classes and Christian Endeavor societies. After a profoundly emotional struggle, the committee voted that Christmas would be celebrated by the congregations individually in their respective churches. But it was clear that the vote applied to 1962 only—the following Christmas, everyone was to gather in Lelu.

EASTER WEEK AT WOT

I was in my element during the weeks leading up to Easter. I had found three plays depicting events in the life of Jesus—the healing of blind Bartimaeus [Mark 10:46-52], the wedding in Cana of Galilee [John 2:1-11], and the raising of Jairus' daughter [Luke 8:40-42, 49-56]. The graduating class was divided into three casts who memorized their lines in English. A stage was erected at one end of the three-in-one room of our new building. The four campus clubs and the student body as a whole learned new and appropriate songs.

We issued an invitation to the villagers to come share the week with us, and by Monday, April 16—the first day of Holy Week—a large number of visitors were on campus for the first night's service and drama. Each day the number of visitors increased. On Tuesday evening Lucius Charley was formally installed as the new principal of KCTS, and the second drama performed. On Wednesday evening the students presented the third play, and we closed the program with a service of cleansing in preparation for observing the Lord's Supper the next evening.

The Church on Kosrae does not traditionally observe Maundy Thursday, but we at Wot did on this particular evening—a service done by candlelight. In a community that regularly used kerosene lanterns for nighttime illumination, the use of candles was not unusual. To use candles on the communion table was unique, however. The service was concluded as everyone held a candle and passed the flame—originating from a candle on the communion table—from one to the other, symbolizing our commitment to carry the light of Christ out into the world.

Seven students were baptized during this service: Alwina Kephas, Richard Tolenoa, Clara Tulensru, Tosiko Paliksru, Mitchiko Skilling, Yosiaru Nena, and Natchuo Andrew.

As the sun set on April 20, Alice and seven of the second-year students led the gathered community in a quietly compelling Good Friday service. Easter Sunday was a splendid day of celebration, culminating the week of five well-prepared and significant worship experiences.

OUR SECOND GRADUATION

Twenty-seven students received their diplomas from KCTS on Friday, May 18, 14 young men and 13 young women. These were the students who were with us longest at Wot, having begun their training in September 1959. At 10 a.m. they marched two by two from the chapel, passing under arches of red hibiscus and fern held aloft by pairs of second-year girls. Alice accompanied their march on the organ.

The families of the graduating students were well represented, in addition to leaders of the Kosrae Church and government. Pastor Aliksru Tolenoa gave the invocation; Pastor Esau Tilfas brought greetings on behalf of the Church; Principal Lucius Charley and I presented the diplomas; and Pastor Alik Isaac prayed the prayer of dedication and blessing for the new graduates. Kasuo Isisaki was valedictorian and Lerina Musrasrik, salutatorian. Following a feast of celebration, students and members of the staff gathered in a circle on the sloping green of Yonrak to sing together one last time and bid one another a tearful farewell.

PREPARING FOR DEPARTURE

After filling a large crate with personal belongings that would remain in the mission house during our furlough and then follow us to our next assignment, we packed our suitcases and moved to Pisin on May 31. We had expected to be there two weeks, but when the ship arrived, all space aboard was being utilized by a team of Air Force officers investigating the possibility of building a satellite-tracking station on Kosrae. The ship returned two weeks later to accommodate us, as well as Kosraean teachers and students on their way to summer school on Pohnpei.

In the meantime, we enjoyed our days at Pisin. I wandered with my camera, recording Erafe Tosie and Alik Frank Skilling as they shaped an eight-foot rough-hewn cross from a limb of one of Pisin's giant ituh [scientific name: *calophyllum inophyllum*] trees, to send to the First Congregational Church in San Antonio—a church that had been especially generous with the school at Wot. The cross was hung behind the altar on the chancel wall of the new sanctuary as a visual link between the Church on Kosrae and that congregation in Texas. [The pastor of the San Antonio church, Richard Engstrom, with his wife Nan, later taught at the Marshalls Theological College in Majuro.]

I planted two Norfolk pines in front of the Pisin house (by 2002, they had grown into towering sentinels) and assisted carpenters constructing a small, concrete storehouse beside the lagoon on Pisin. The building was to be used to store bags of rice, flour, and cement off-loaded from ships, keeping them secure and dry until they could be transported to Wot. I participated in the Yekula graduation on June 11 and on June 20 through 22, helped Principal Lucius register 46 new students for the fall term at Wot.

Alice met with the group that continued to search for an agreeable spelling for the Kosraean language. Aaron Sigrah, Florian Nena, Miles Benjamin, Salik Cornelius, Tosie Palikkun, and Pastor Alik Isaac were all part of that effort.

Throughout the month, there were farewell ceremonies in each of the villages. Alice, Lisa, Lauren and I had learned a favorite Kosraean gospel song, "Nga Konaok Inek Wo" (I Have Found the Good Way), to share with the various congregations, though it was sometimes difficult to sing through the emotion of our goodbyes. Church groups and individuals hosted feasts, and we were inundated with beautiful pieces of Kosraean handcraft. As they gave, many said, "Please share these with our friends in America, as you tell them about us." [The Kosraeans were not yet selling handcraft.] We were overwhelmed when the all-island church committee presented us with a bon voyage cash gift of $100—a gift from the heart of a gracious and generous people.

At 3:30 p.m. on June 30, Alice, Lisa, Lauren and I stood on the top deck of the M/V *Kaselehlia* as it slowly carried us away from the Lelu dock. We watched as the attractive young faces of our students, the worn and kindly faces of the leaders of the Church, and the pleasantly familiar faces of many other Christian brothers and sisters were no longer individually distinguishable.

The ship left the channel and turned northwest away from the island, we could distinguish the shiny white specks of the Wot buildings nestled in the jagged green of the mountains at the southwest corner of the island. On September 17, classes there would begin again with an anticipated group of 103 students in three class levels under the leadership of Lucius Charley. A fine contingent of teachers and staff members would be there to assist him, including some of our own former students.[1]

PRESSING ONWARD

The momentum generated during the our years at Wot continued into the new school year. Lucius was a capable leader who managed both the student body and staff with a firm and sympathetic hand. Joshua Phillip and Erafe Tosie were the leading faculty members, and recent graduates Siosi Aliksa, Walton Palik, Tulenna Palsis, and Yukiwo Tara proved to be valuable new members of the staff. Roland Stephen was back as chief mechanic; Aliksa Mongkeya was the new work foreman; Kenye Jacob Taulung was housemother; and Palsisa Talley and his wife, Sina, the cooks. Atchuo Kun Luey was storekeeper.

There was disappointment among the faculty and staff and sadness in the student body when only six of the 16 girls in the third-year class returned that September. Some parents still felt it better to find husbands for older girls instead of sending them to school. In spite of this, there were 97 in the student body. They elected Richard Tolenoa as their student council president. Officers assisting him were Arthur George, Masayuki Skilling, Mitchigo Simeon, Alwina Kephas, Nena Wilmer, Mary Kun Welly, Paliksru Albert, and Natchuo Andrew, with Principal Lucius staff advisor. President of Wot's Christian Endeavor Society for 1962-1963 was Tatasy Andrew. The C. E. executive committee included Conrad Albert, Joseph George, Yosiaru Nena, Elmina Milton, Ackley Kinere, and Tokiko Nelson. Siosi Aliksa served as their sponsor.

FREAK WAVES STRIKE WALUNG COAST

On October 13 and 14, a bizarre tide—or perhaps a type of tidal wave—did considerable damage to the dock area at Wot as well as to neighboring Walung settlements. One of the students, Joseph Zakias, wrote to us while we were studying at Northwest Christian College in Eugene, Oregon:

The waves were gigantic. It was scarey, but there was also some fun. We third-year boys were sleeping in Milton's house at the beach when a wave rushed in, thoroughly soaking us. As we tried to go back to sleep, an even larger wave rolled in and carried Andrew and Misima out into the taro patch. Andrew's sheet was swept off and later we found it over by the 55-gallon drums. Lots of things floated away on this tide. The walls of the house where the Malem people usually stay were carried out to sea. The water soaked everything in Roland's house—his chest and all its contents, his sheets and pillows. Lots of things were destroyed at Insief, too—including the houses of Salpasr and Horace and two of the houses in Leap. Hashime's house is gone.

There was also tragedy. The waves loosened the roots of a coconut tree in Tafunsak, causing it to fall, killing the two small daughters of Likunat and Likiaksru Lazarus of Utwe. Everyone is very sad about this terrible thing.[2]

NEWS OF FORMER STUDENTS

A number of recent Wot graduates were attending school at Pohnpei. Walton had completed his year in Pre-PICS and a semester at the Pastors & Teachers Training School before returning to help at Wot. Shiro Timothy was enrolled in PICS, followed there a short time later by Lerina Musrasrik, Simako Timothy, Connie Isaac, Kasuo Isisaki, and Yosino Weilbacher. Still later, Osamu Talley, Akiwo Likiaksa, Kemwel Tilfas, and Nena Wilmer were there. Upon graduating from PICS, Shiro became the recipient of an American Board scholarship, traveling to Dumagete in the Philippine Islands where, for three years, he attended Silliman University.

Other graduates had returned to their villages and were almost immediately pressed into service by their home churches. In January 1963 another former student, Yosimi Stephen, wrote to us: "The Malem church is really keeping us busy! We have responsibilities in the Young People's Christian Endeavor Society and most of us have been asked to teach Sunday School. This willingness of the older people to use us makes us very happy."[3]

From Utwe, Magrina Wakuk wrote: "I'm so proud of Takae and Agusta. Takae has married Kun Rendon and Agusta has married Atsiro Melander, so they are now part of Utwe instead of Malem. They are becoming more and more valuable to the people of this village and are kept very busy. Agusta is working with the Worship Committee of the Young People's C. E., and Takae is part of the Song Committee. Both are teaching Sunday School."[4]

In February, Erafe Tosie left the Wot faculty, and the church committee replaced him with Kingston Phillip. At this same time, Srue—the widow of Pastor Frank Skilling—accepted the invitation of Missionary Robert Simon at the Pastors & Teachers Training School on Pohnpei to become dean of women on that campus. She wrote: "My family wants me to stay on Kosrae and grieve some more, staying close to them, but I feel my life is God's and I can be more useful serving Him, even if it means going to a different island."[5] She was 68 years old.

Yekula's Royal Gifford was commencement speaker when the 1963 class graduated in May. Top scholastic honors went to Alwina Kephas, class valedictorian, and Emiko Jim, salutatorian. Though a few young people joined the student body that fall, others did not return. Plans for the school were indefinite, and no effort was made to select a new class to join the second- and third-year classes remaining on campus.

BETHANIA AND EMMAUS HIGH SCHOOLS

The Liebenzell Mission operated two high schools in Palau—Bethania, on the island of Bablethaup, was for girls, and Emmaus on Koror was for boys. In the early years of these schools, students were mostly Palauan, Yapese, and Chuukese, from the primary areas served by the Liebenzell Mission. The schools grew and so did their reputations. Both institutions were known for scholastic excellence and spiritual depth—a combination noted by Christian parents and church leaders in Pohnpei, Kosrae, and the Marshalls, who were soon seeking to enroll their own young people.

The first Kosraean to became a student at Bethania was Lucy Sam Musrasrik. Lucy had gone to Pohnpei several months after her 1962 graduation from KCTS, where she worked in Harold and Mary Ruth Hanlin's Kolonia home. In 1963, with Mrs. Hanlin's help, Lucy enrolled at Bethania, graduating in 1967. Initially it had been lonely for her, but two years after she reached Palau, 10 other Kosraean girls joined her on the campus: Adelyn Benjamin, Clara Tosie, Julia Nena, Kenye Palik, Mabel Youngstrom, Niome Likiak, Pastora Kephas, Sepe Killion, Sepe Robert, and Srue Noda. Most of these girls graduated in 1969. Srue Noda, who had enrolled as a 7th grader, graduated in 1971. Later, Brocula Killion enrolled, graduating in 1971. Principal Juanita Simpson maintained a concerned contact with the girls after they left the Bethania campus, visiting them several times at Kosrae and keeping in touch by letter.

Two Kosraean boys attended high school at Emmaus: Takeo Alik and Vernon Youngstrom.

A MOTHER ON POHNPEI

Former KCTS students attending The Pacific Islands Central School in Kolonia, Pohnpei, were finding a genial home-away-from-home at the Protestant Mission House. Mary Ruth Hanlin led several Bible study sessions and services for Kosraean students each week in the living room and on the lanai of the Hanlin home. Those who had attended school at Wot, as well as former Yekula students, were faithful in their attendance at these gatherings. The young people knew that there would be a friendly ear, something to eat, a quiet corner in which to study, and new songs to learn. Mary Ruth Hanlin maintained her low-key but much appreciated ministry, until her departure in 1973 to care for her father-in-law in Oklahoma City.

KOSRAE'S LAST AMERICAN BOARD MISSIONARY

In 1964, a vivacious and dedicated woman became the last missionary assigned to Kosrae.

After completing four years of seminary and a two-year nursing course, Anna Dederer had gone to Micronesia in 1934 with the Liebenzell Mission. She was assigned as a nurse and teacher in the Mortlock Islands. In 1939 she was reassigned to teach in the Liebenzell girls' school at Chuuk. Soon after her arrival, she survived when the boat in which she was traveling across the lagoon capsized in a storm. Tragically, a number of her students were trapped in the cabin and drowned.

Miss Dederer was at Chuuk when World War II began. Though she was a German national, she was incarcerated in 1942 by the Japanese military near her school on the island of Udot at the center of Chuuk's vast lagoon—suspected of being an American spy. She was forced to live in a wire pen backed by a small cave in which she slept. The place of her confinement was located between an area used to store drums of gasoline and a stockpile of ammunition. Anna never knew when an American bomb might be dropped to destroy the munitions and fuel, thus ending her life. She was given very little food—occasional scraps left by Japanese soldiers—and was not allowed to communicate with the local people.

On a day soon after she was imprisoned, a group of Chuukese walked past her makeshift jail, singing. The hymn tune was familiar to Anna, but the words—sung in the Chuukese language which the Japanese did not understand—went something like this: "Under the woodpile beside the big tree next to the fence, there is food for you. We will bring you more every day." So her friends kept her alive.[6]

After her liberation by American forces in 1945, Anna was determined to continue her work at Chuuk. As the U.S. Naval Administration was not allowing German missionaries to enter or remain in Micronesia without initiating the process of becoming American citizens, Anna took out citizenship papers. Then she went a step further, transferring from the Liebenzell Mission to the American Board. She continued to teach girls at Chuuk—but now at Kutchua on the island of Dublon [Tonoas], where the Baldwin sisters had first been assigned 60 years earlier.

When the Hanlin family reached Chuuk in December 1947 on their way to Kosrae, 14-year-old Alice was so captivated by Anna's enthusiasm and Christian commitment that she decided then and there to one day be a missionary "just like Aunt Anna." Alice began wearing her hair like Anna wore hers—pulled back in a bun at the nape of the neck—and looked forward to wearing the kind of "sensible missionary shoes" that Anna wore.

In 1948, Anna Dederer left Micronesia for the first time since arriving in 1934. She visited her family in Germany, then settled in New York City to fulfill the one-year residency required by the Immigration and Naturalization Service. Her sense of humor and unwavering devotion—combined with the harrowing personal experiences she recounted—made Anna a very popular missionary speaker. While headquartered in New York, she studied at Andover-Newton Theological School and, before returning to Chuuk the following year, was ordained a Congregational Christian minister in Honolulu's Church of the Crossroads.

After serving for 20 years at Chuuk, the now Rev. Anna Dederer was assigned in 1954 to be principal of the Marshall Christian High School at Rongrong in Majuro Atoll. During the last two of her nine years in the Marshall Islands, she assisted the church and school in Uliga, Majuro, the District Center, before the Micronesia Mission transferred her to Kosrae.

ANNA MAKES HER HOME ON PISIN

Wanting to see what sort of living arrangement she would have in her new location, Anna Dederer found a ride from Kwajalein to Kosrae aboard a U.S. Navy Search & Rescue training flight. Though she had only a few hours in Lelu, she was able to talk with Pastor Alik, Pastor Esau, Pastor Aliksru, and other church dignitaries. In a decision made jointly by the Micronesia Mission and the Church on Kosrae, Miss Dederer was not to be involved with the school at Wot, but would work directly with Kosrae's churches. Escorting her to Pisin where she would live, the leaders showed her the small concrete and screen mission house erected in 1959.

Like missionaries before her, Anna was delighted with Pisin, but felt the house inadequate for her needs. Could the Kosraean Christians add a second-floor bedroom to the little building and enlarge the kitchen? They readily assented. Grateful and pleased to have met her future colleagues, Anna continued aboard the seaplane to Pohnpei, where she stayed with Harold and Mary Ruth Hanlin while rounding up supplies and waiting for the Pisin renovation to be completed. Both she and her new friends at Kosrae were relieved and happy when the M/V *Kaselehlia* carried her back to her new place of service late in the year. The remodeled house was ready.

Only nine of the 46 missionaries who had lived on Kosrae before her had made their home on Pisin: Benjamin and Lydia Snow, Daniel and Doreka Opunui, George and Nancy Pierson, and J. W. and Kaholo Kanoa had lived there during the middle of the previous century. The missionaries operated a school for Pohnpeian girls at Pisin from 1889 to 1891. Jesse Hoppin had lived part-time at Pisin and part-time at Jaluit in the 1920s and 1930s. Most of the Wot missionaries had made Pisin their home away from home while they lived on Kosrae, but Anna Dederer was only the tenth to put down her roots on the little island in Lelu Harbor that Good King George had so generously presented to those first four missionaries in 1852.

As she settled into her new home, Miss Dederer began learning the Kosraean language. In addition to her fluency in German and English, she could already converse and preach in three Micronesian languages. Now, at 62, she tackled her fourth. The church committee assigned Robert Aliksa and his wife, Sarah, to stay with Anna at Pisin as language teachers, companions, and assistants.

MOTOR SCOOTER FLIPS

Miss Dederer had purchased a small motor scooter on Pohnpei, thinking that it would be a sensible means of transportation for her on Kosrae. There was, after all, a road that crossed the causeway from Lelu and continued to Tafunsak, and the machine could be carried by canoe to the far side of the harbor, where she could ride it from Sansrik to Malem and on to Utwe.

This decision to buy and then master a motor scooter was typical. Her bold determination when dealing with life's obstacles was a trait that colleagues had admired for years. Kosraeans watched amazed as she learned the tricks of operating her new conveyance. The tricks of the road were another matter.

Most of the roads built by the Japanese military during World War II had been bombed or had otherwise deteriorated. Without the appropriate equipment, restoring them was an extremely slow process. In 1964, Kosrae's roadways were not much more than footpaths along the edge of the island—sometimes sandy, in places rocky, frequently muddy. The three or four rickety trucks on the island, when actually operating, made slow progress along these tracks, crossing the many streams and rivers on precariously placed perforated steel runners supplied by the U.S. military. Often the profuse foliage along the way bent into the road to trace moist etchings on both sides of a moving vehicle. Mainly, these roads were for walking—no one had ever tried to negotiate them on a motor scooter!

One morning not long after Miss Dederer began using her scooter, she left Pisin to ride to Tafunsak for a meeting with church women. She carried her usual bag of books, papers, and extra clothing—and was grateful that the sun was shining. As she passed Sroanef, she came to a sandy stretch that was not packed as solidly as it appeared. By the time she realized this, it was too late. The motor scooter flipped in the sand and dragged her forward until she managed to extricate herself from the roaring, twisting machine.

The flesh was deeply scraped from one of her legs by the surface of the road, and the other leg badly burned by the engine. Her injuries required skin grafting. Her motor scooter was sold.

ROSE MACKWELUNG GOES TO ASIA

After establishing elementary schools in all four Kosraean municipalities in the years immediately after World War II and becoming Kosrae's first superintendent of schools, Rose Mackwelung—Missionary Jesse Hoppin's adopted daughter—turned her attention to training adults. She worked particularly hard to advance the educational, social and economic life of the women of Kosrae and Pohnpei. She organized women's clubs and served as advisor to the district administrator. In 1964, in honor of her achievement and superior public service, Rose Mackwelung was granted a United Nations Fellowship in Community Development, traveling to observe women's work sponsored by the U.N. in the Philippines, India, and Sri Lanka. She was the first Micronesian woman to receive such a fellowship.[7]

CENSUS OF 1964

The 1964 census recorded 3,245 persons living on Kosrae.

KOSRAEANS ON EBEYE

Kwajalein Island, at the southern tip of the Kwajalein Atoll in the Marshall Islands, was the site of the U.S. military's missile-testing program. Three miles up the reef was the island of Ebeye [EE-bye] which had the distinction of being the most densely populated island per-square-mile in all of Micronesia. Some 7,000 people were crowded onto Ebeye, a dot of land less than one-tenth of a square mile in area. Some of them were not there by choice. The U.S. Army had relocated them from islands in the northern part of the Kwajalein atoll and from Ellip—islands within the missile impact area. They were crowded in among the land-owning families on Ebeye. Other people came by the boatloads to Ebeye from all parts of eastern Micronesia to take advantage of jobs on the missile base. Though the pay was poor by American standards, the money received by the Army's locally hired employees—working primarily as maids and yard-men in the large, mostly civilian American community—provided more cash than the islands' inhabitants had ever handled.

Kosraeans, too, moved to Ebeye, where they bunched into tiny, makeshift lodgings. Those who were lucky joined the workforce that traveled to Kwajalein each morning by ferry. The Army's rules were strict. As it was a military base, only Kwajalein residents were allowed to shop at Surfway (the commissary), or Macy's (the post exchange). Those hired from the Micronesian community left the manicured ambience of Kwajalein each evening and returned to Ebeye. But as the new priority was making money, the dismal conditions there were tolerated.

Kosraeans on Ebeye regularly attended Sunday morning worship services with their Marshallese neighbors in the large United Church of Christ, located at the center of the island. Attendance of 1,000 on any given Sunday was not unusual. The strong desire to have a service in their own language, however, led to the creation of an Ebeye Kosraean Christian Endeavor society. Officers were elected and Sunday afternoon Kosraean services were begun, following the accepted pattern of worship used on their home island. Alice and I were assisting the group, as we had been reassigned by the Micronesia Mission following our furlough, and were now living and working on Ebeye.

Temporarily on Ebeye, Paul and Srue Sigrah, Joshua and Dora Abraham, Lupalik and Sepe Palsis, and Luther and Kenye Cornelius were all instrumental in helping the little group during its first months of existence. Leaders from among the more permanent Kosraean residents of Ebeye during the ensuing years included Aliksa and Lillian Tulensa, Alwin and Agusta Alik, Aspul and Mildred Benjamin, Gordon Benjamin, Franklin and Elizabeth James, Moses and Rhoda Cornelius, Sawan and Kenye Shrew, and Siosi and Diana Aliksa.

It was a source of some pride for the group that the daily Christian Endeavor topics and Scripture texts so important in the lives of all Kosraeans were originating on Ebeye, as various members of the Ebeye Kosraean community assisted Alice and me in the process of preparing these. The topics were chosen, translated, and assembled into printed booklets, then sent each year for use at Kosrae.

MEANWHILE, AT WOT

Arthur George graduated as valedictorian of the KCTS class of 1964, and Clara Tulensru was salutatorian. Family problems took Principal Lucius Charley back to Malem at the end of the school year, and Kingston Kintaro Phillip was appointed by the church committee to take his place. The 27 members of the class of 1965 elected Alexander Sigrah as student body president. The 16 boys worked hard in the gardens and the 13 girls did their part in maintaining the grounds around the school building, mission house, and chapel on Yonrak. There were fewer classes offered but the students persisted, graduating the following May with the distinction of being the last class to graduate in the 86-year history of the Wot mission school.

MIZPAH HIGH SCHOOL

The United Church Board for World Ministries, the entity into which the old American Board had been assimilated, opened Mizpah High School of Micronesia in 1966 on the island of Moen [Weno] at Chuuk. Under the direction of Paul Marshall, Mizpah's first principal, a campus was created with attractive, practical buildings positioned on the slope of a hill behind Logan Memorial Church. A group of highly trained teachers was sent to the school by the United Church Board. These men and women worked hard to make the school a superior place of learning for young people from throughout Micronesia for the decade of its existance.

Winston Likiaksa, Nena Shru Nena, and Fred N. Skilling were the first Kosraean students to be accepted for study there. They were later joined by Threadway Asher, Gerson Mongkeya, Kanston Palsis, Widmer Sigrah, Bob Skilling, and Madison Tosie.

PEACE CORPS ARRIVES

It was in 1966 that the Peace Corps reached Kosrae. President John Kennedy's dream-become-reality of sending American young people to assist in the development of emerging nations found a special niche in Micronesia. Population numbers on Micronesia's islands were small enough for Peace Corps volunteers to have considerable influence. A few of these young people—products of the ferment and clashes within American colleges and universities during the 1960s, and at times impatient with local custom, caused confusion. Many others, their youthful idealism tempered with open minds, a sensitivity to differing methods of perception, and a disposition to learn, were very effective.

Kosrae benefitted from most of the Peace Corps volunteers who were assigned there. These young Americans lived in local homes, were given Kosraean names, and were eagerly and willingly drawn into family circles. A few individuals among them criticized the Kosraean Church as too controlling and political, while a few others suggested that the Church was not spiritual enough, but many Peace Corps volunteers regularly attended Sunday services in their respective villages, sang in choirs, and participated in other church-related activities.

Doug Dunlap was among the first Peace Corps volunteers to be sent to Kosrae in 1966. He and his wife, Margaret, quickly became active in community life. "While teaching English at the Malem School, we became involved in a number of public health and community development projects. But most of all, we enjoyed being citizens of Malem, meeting neighbors, sharing friendship and hospitality, going to the Malem church, helping out on the famous village public work days, helping with community meals, and so on. It was a great experience."[8]

A few years after returning to the United States, Doug was reunited with Swinton Jack, a colleague and close friend from Malem, at a conference in New Mexico—a pleasant reunion neither man had expected. [Doug Dunlap later earned a Masters of Divinity degree from Harvard University and is an active United Church of Christ pastor in Wilton, Maine.]

A number of Peace Corps volunteers married Kosraeans, some of them settling permanently on Kosrae with their spouses, while others returned with their mates to the United States.

INDIGENOUS LEADERS CONFERENCE OF 1966

For the first time, Kosraeans welcomed a gathering of church leaders from beyond their shores when the Indigenous Leaders Conference met on Kosrae June 20-28. Pastor Alik Isaac, Deacon Zakias George, and Alik Palsis were Kosrae's official delegates—with Joseph George, youth delegate—but many others also attended the worship services, Bible studies, and business sessions of the conference. Members of all four congregations worked hard to feed and house the off-island visitors, most of whom had never been to Kosrae. Everyone delighted in the fellowship, food, singing, and studies.

Miss Dederer led a session on "The Place of Women in the Work of the Church." After much lively discussion, and some dissension, a motion was passed by the delegates that "There is no limit to the work of women in the

Church."[9] The delegates also deliberated the meaning of Christian marriage, especially relating to the responsibilities of parents whose adult children live openly with partners to whom they are not married, though this was a practice not yet seen on Kosrae.

"Church Members in Non-Christian Activities" was another topic debated by conference attendees. There was agreement that the use of "magic perfume, the worship of false spirits, the use of 'local medicines,' bingo, gambling, selling liquor and dynamiting for fish" were not acceptable activities for "those who hold a church office." Initially there was not clear agreement concerning "whether Christians should have a business, or whether they should hold offices in the government, either elected or as employees." The conference concluded that "Christians who hold government jobs, or are elected to government office, are serving the people and returning much of their goods for the work of the Church, and that being able to do government work is a talent given by God." The delegates passed a motion that it is "good for Christians to continue working in the government."[10]

MORE KOSRAEAN YOUTH TREK TO COLLEGE

During the summer of 1966, Miss Dederer was instrumental in introducing two young people who were ready for college—Penina Mackwelung and Alex Phillip—to the Protestant Chapel Scholarship Committee on the U.S. Army's Kwajalein missile base. This group provided financial assistance to both young people, not only while they worked toward their degrees at the University of Guam, but later as they took graduate courses—Penina at the University of Hawai'i and Alex at California State College in Hayward.

In December 1966, in consultation with the island's church leaders and Dr. Hanlin, Anna sent two young men, Kun Caleb and Joseph George, for a six-month course at the Malmaluan Youth Leadership Training Center in Rabaul, New Guinea—a facility of the Methodist Church in Australia. Travel, tuition, and living expenses for the two of them were underwritten by the Protestant Chapel Scholarship Committee at Kwajalein.

EMERGENCE OF HARRISON GEORGE

Harrison George was a man gifted with many ideas, and he possessed the additional gift of being able to expedite them. Given the reluctance of the collective Kosraean church leadership to allow change—or even to listen to recommendations for change—the giant strides made under the not-so-gentle prodding of this exceptional man were remarkable.

Born and raised in Malem, Harrison George attended Japanese elementary school in Lelu before the start of World War II. During the war he was required, with other boys his age, to catch crabs and gather coconuts for the Japanese military. Following the war he was a member of the second class to study at Wot. He was very bright and assertive, and during his last two years at the school while in his late teens, he continually clashed with Lucy Lanktree. She, in turn, deploring what she considered to be his judgmental attitude, would reprimand him harshly, occasionally reducing him to tears. On several occasions she threatened to terminate his studies at Wot.[11] Harrison was often intimidating, but that characteristic was counterbalanced by an ability to make people laugh. He could berate someone and in the next breath relate a story in such a way that the person was laughing in spite of the browbeating just endured.

Harrison was among the first Kosraeans to attend the Pastors & Teachers Training School on Pohnpei. By 1956 he had enrolled in Hawai'i's Maunaolu Bible College on Maui. He returned to Kosrae in the fall of 1959 to teach at Wot and to marry Yamada Simeon Skilling. After two years at Wot, Harrison returned to Malem and became an active, vocal part of the community and church. He developed into a sort of saddle burr—irritating many, while prompting them to action. He impressed people with his forthrightness, and, in spite of themselves, they were drawn to his suggestions because they recognized many of them as excellent. Malem's citizens elected him chief in 1962. From 1963 to 1966, he represented Malem in the Pohnpei District Legislature. In 1965 he began teaching in the Malem Elementary School, a paying job which provided his livelihood for the next 20 years.

ISAIAH BENJAMIN AND HARRISON GEORGE ORDAINED

On May 1, 1967, Isaiah Benjamin and Harrison George were ordained as the 13th and 14th pastors of the Church on Kosrae. Pastor Isaiah was 75 years old; Harrison was three weeks short of his 36th birthday. The ordination of the youthful Harrison proved the trend to ordain only older men was temporary. With the elevation of these two, the number of pastors was the largest it had ever been. There were now five men actively serving as ordained ministers of Kosrae's Church. Though there was no formal organization that bound them, everyone took for granted that, by reason of seniority, 60-year-old Alik Isaac was the lead pastor.

With this increase in the number of pastors, for the first time it become possible for each of the village congregations to have one or two pastors permanently assigned to it. This was a radically new pattern for the Church on Kosrae, and one that Pastor Harrison pushed vigorously. As the other four pastors were older, the idea was attractive to them. It would break a tradition that had been part of the Church from the beginning—that the pastors would travel among the four churches, equally pastors of all church members—but it would mean much less travel for them individually. The expansion of Kosrae's population was another factor.

By the fall of 1967, the pastors were all remaining in their own villages unless it was time for communion or a Sunday of particular significance, such as Easter. Pastor Aliksru in Tafunsak, Pastor Alik and Pastor Esau in Lelu, and Pastor Isaiah in Utwe conducted services as they had always been conducted. In Malem, however, Pastor Harrison took the reins of the church with considerable panache and began at once to translate the ideas of his active imagination into reality—though he was wise enough to begin with suggestions that were of a rather benign nature.

DECELERATING THE LORD'S PRAYER

One of Pastor Harrison's initial proposals concerned the Lord's Prayer. This teaching-prayer of Jesus was commonly used in Sunday morning worship services and always used to conclude the Christian Endeavor meetings each Sunday afternoon. The new pastor explained that the prayer had become so familiar and was repeated so quickly, worshipers were unaware of its meaning for them. "Slow down! Think what you are praying!" The people did. Within a few months—not only in the Malem church, but in all parts of Kosrae—the Lord's Prayer was recited deliberately, and noticeably much slower. And so it remains. (Young people, perhaps, were unaware of how this new ruling coincided with the ancient Kosraean preference for slow, quiet speech.)

WOT STUDENTS CONTINUE AT YEKULA

Six members of the Class of '67 at Yekula—the first students to graduate from that recently designated Kosrae High School—were young men who had attended the Kosrae Christian Training School at Wot. Principal Royal Gifford and Vice Principal Shrew Jonas welcomed these former mission school students. so eager to continue studying, into the government school. One of them, Yukiwo Tara, was Yekula's student body president that year. The others were Tatasy Andrew, Atchuo Luey, Walton Palik, Kemwel Tilfas, and Richard Tolenoa.

The class of 1968 included nine more young people who had previously studied at Wot: Paliksru Albert, Natchuo Andrew, Myra Lonno, Hemul Nena, Tulenna Palsis, Alexander Sigrah, Trime Tolenoa, Clara Tulensru, and Magrina Wakuk.

In the fall of 1968 the Kwajalein Protestant Chapel Scholarship Committee undertook the support of two more Kosraean students: Richard Tolenoa was sent to Malua Theological College in Western Samoa and Timothy Timothy to Maunaolu College on Maui.

LAY MINISTERS

Pastor Harrison, with the encouragement of Anna Dederer, began discussing a concept that was not new to Kosrae's leaders, but had never been brought forward as part of the agenda in the all-island church committee as something possible for their organization. For years laymen had regularly been used to lead services when a pastor could not be present. It had always been more common for worshipers to be in a service led by a deacon or another layman than it was to be in a service presided over by a pastor. Until 1967, there had never been enough pastors to go around.

As early as 1856, 10 years before he consecrated the first deacon and 12 years before the first pastor was ordained, Benjamin Snow began sending Kutuka and Notwe to lead Sunday services at Sansrik, while he conducted services in Lelu. He commissioned the couple as "lay ministers" even before they were officially baptized members of the Church!

Kosraeans were aware that Pohnpeian and Chuukese churches recognized a title given to those who served the Church as lay ministers. At Pohnpei, in fact, that title was positioned just below that of pastor and above deacon. The Kosraean leadership was reluctant to create a church title that would rank above deacon but—after a number of sessions with the missionary, and much discussion among themselves—it was decided in 1969 that the church would henceforth acknowledge "lay minister" as an authorized title or rank in the Church.

The English words "pastor" and "deacon" had been transliterated into the Kosraean language by Mr. Snow. So now, the English words "lay minister" were used to designate those who had been called to this new position. Just as men were ordained into the office of pastor or consecrated as deacons, lay ministers were now consecrated before the gathered church. At first, this service of recognition—always dignified—took place as part of an island-wide new-month service, but as the numbers of lay ministers increased, these services frequently took place in the worship setting of individual village churches.

More and more, the ranking of Kosrae's church leaders came to mirror the traditional chiefly system of years gone by—with one significant difference. In the old system, only those from chiefly families could attain rank. The church now afforded an avenue of mobility for those who would have had no opportunity for improving their status under the former system.[12]

Miss Dederer's suggestion, which was originally followed, was that there be no more than two or three lay ministers per congregation, but the number was gradually, then greatly, increased. Laymen had always been used as ushers and to collect offerings, but now only those laymen specifically named to the position of lay minister were used in these service-related roles. Individually, lay ministers also took turns leading worship, preaching, and presiding at services for shut-ins and those in the hospital, or jail.

Kosrae's first official lay ministers were: Dwight Sru Likiaksa and Lucian Robert in Lelu; Luther Cornelius and Swinton Jack Musrasrik in Malem; Daniel Seymor and Tulenna Palsis in Tafunsak; and Joel Kun Tilfas and Natchuo Andrew in Utwe.

WANING DAYS OF AN ERA

After the class of 1965 departed, the Wot campus was maintained for three years by a skeleton crew selected by the all-island church committee. Conferences were held during the summer months that—as in years gone by—were very popular with the participants. A woman who attended a 1968 conference for the youth of Malem and Utwe remembers: "We had a GREAT time studying the Bible, singing, sharing, working, and playing. For me, those two weeks at Wot were life-altering! It is impossible to overstate the value of that time together—and in that place! I had never been to Wot. All of us were aware that we were on 'hallowed ground'."[13]

Members of the church committee, while continuing to hope that the mission board would once again send personnel to staff a school at Wot, were beginning to grasp the reality that this would probably not happen. To the extent that she was able, Miss Dederer kept the committee apprised of the turmoil in the United States generated by assassinations and an unpopular war in Vietnam. She asked that they join her in praying for their American sisters and brothers in the United Church of Christ who found financial support for mission projects diminishing. At the same time they struggled to clarify a new interpretation of Mission—one that would remove them from the paternalism and arrogance that so often defined it in the past. But the agonized soul-searching going on within the mission board—in a radically different cultural setting thousands of miles away—was impossible for the islanders to empathize with or even to comprehend, given their own priorities and understanding of God's purposes. Looming in everyone's mind was the realization that, without missionary participation in a school at Wot, the property would revert to the original landowning families. The wording of the deed gave the Church no recourse. A sense of impotence and abandonment crept over them.

Everyone was grateful for the reassuring presence and tireless participation in their lives of Anna Dederer, but they knew that the time of her retirement was drawing near, and she would not be replaced.

TWO YOUNG MEN DEPART FOR SEMINARY

But new life was infusing the Church on Kosrae. One indication of this came at the end of that year when two of Kosrae's promising young men, Takeo Likiaksa and Walton Palik, were sent away by the Church specifically to study for the Christian ministry. A number of KCTS graduates—among them Erafe Tosie, Harrison George, Joshua Phillip, Katsisiro Tulensru, Bardon Musrasrik, and Yukiwo Tara—had studied at the Pastors & Teachers Training School at Ohwa, Pohnpei, but none had been sent beyond Micronesia for that purpose since Mr. Snow sent Paitok to Honolulu in 1862. Richard Tolenoa's departure for seminary the year before had been a personal goal unauthorized by the Church. Personal initiative was still a trait looked upon with suspicion.

There was another first involved. Though Walton was a graduate of KCTS and had spent some time at the Pohnpei school, Takeo was a product of Kosrae's newly emerging government school system—in particular, the high school at Yekula. That a person could pursue a church-related profession without having initiated the process in a mission school was an important statement. Anna Dederer was partially responsible for this step forward, as it was quite a jump for the Kosraean mind-set at the time. People took for granted that pastors got their start in mission schools. Miss Dederer, with the collaboration of Harold Hanlin, helped secure United Church Board scholarships for both young men and expedited their enrollment at Malua Theological College in Western Samoa—a school operated by the Western Samoa Congregational Churches.

On December 27, 1969, Takeo, age 25, and Walton, age 31, left Kosrae to begin their journey to Western Samoa. Accompanying Walton was his wife of two years, Tokiko, and their small daughter, Florence. The little group would be in Samoa for the next four years.

ERAFE TOSIE ORDAINED

Erafe Tosie decided in his early teens that he wanted to be a pastor, and was only 17 years old in 1949 when he left his home in Lelu to study at Wot. A handsome, lighthearted, friendly youth, he was popular with the other students and particularly with his missionary teachers. Mrs. Hanlin quickly took him under her wing as her own special project, and remained his lifetime mentor and friend. Until his death in 1952, Pastor Palik Kefwas had been a close companion and confidant; otherwise, Erafe had a turbulent relationship with the all-island church committee as his youth progressed. But, in spite of several votes of disapproval, he was able to spend four years during the mid-1950s at the Pastors & Teachers Training School on Pohnpei.

Erafe returned to Kosrae in 1958, teaching at Wot until 1963—with six months away during 1959 to attend several church-related work-camps in Southern California. He married Aklina Nena and became an elementary school teacher. He was teaching in Utwe when he was chosen for ordination in December 1970 at 38 years of age.

Pastor Harrison, just six months older than Erafe, was a friend and contemporary, though their friendship was occasionally strained. They attended KCTS and PTTS together. When it became apparent that Pastor Isaiah, now 78, was in much need of ministerial assistance in Utwe, Pastor Harrison pushed hard for Erafe's ordination. Pastor Isaiah, leaders of the Utwe congregation, and the all-island church committee agreed, and Erafe was ordained as Kosrae's 15th indigenous pastor. He continued teaching, but as Pastor Erafe, he had reached his life's goal.

One reason for Erafe's ordination was his position as a teacher in Utwe. By 1970, the other five pastors were even more convinced than they had been three years earlier, that it was much more effective and convenient for pastors to be assigned to specific congregations. Members of the four congregations were also finding it beneficial to have their pastors accessible.

ANNA DEDERER DEPARTS

Closing an illustrious career in Micronesia which spanned 36 years—the final six on Kosrae—Miss Dederer departed to become a resident of Plymouth Village, a community for retired church workers in Redlands, California. She died there six years later, on October 21, 1976, age 74.

INDIGENOUS LEADERS CONFERENCE OF 1970

The Kosrae Congregational Church sent a delegation of seven persons to the Indigenous Leaders Conference that met on Ebeye in the Marshall Islands, June 21-July 3, 1970. The delegates, led by Pastor Alik Isaac and his wife, Hannah, also included Kun Nena Sigrah, Sepe Kun Sigrah, Nena Charley, Sepe Lupalik Palsis, and Srue Frank Skilling.

Daily Bible study at the two-week conference was led by the Rev. James "Kimo" Merseberg of the United Church of Christ in Hawai'i. Two officials of the Woman's Board of Missions in Hawai'i were present as observers: Annie Kanahele and Albertine Loomis. Later in the month, the two women were briefly guests of the Church on Kosrae.

There were many questions and much agitated discussion at the conference, generated by the announcement that the United Church Board for World Ministries, which replaced the American Board of Commissioners for Foreign Missions in 1961, would no longer send missionaries to serve in Micronesia. For the time being, missionary teachers would remain at Mizpah High School at Chuuk, but Mizpah, too, was to be discontinued. Dr. Hanlin, Superintendent of the Micronesia Mission, explained to the delegates that the UCBWM planned to continue its involvement in Micronesia through its scholarship program.[14]

The Kosraean delegation, as well as delegations representing Pohnpei, Chuuk, Palau, Saipan, and all parts of the Marshall Islands, enjoyed the enthusiastic hospitality of their Ebeye hosts. They also delighted in a festive reception given in their honor by the Women's Protestant Chapel Fellowship at the officers' club on the U.S. Army's Kwajalein Missile Range.

KWAJALEIN PROTESTANT CHAPEL SCHOLARSHIP PROGRAM

By 1971 eight Kosraean young people had received, or were receiving, financial support in their college studies from the Kwajalein Protestant Chapel congregation. Kun Caleb and Joseph George had completed their course in Rabaul. In addition to Penina Mackwelung and Alex Phillip, who were still at the University of Guam; Richard Tolenoa in Western Samoa; and Timothy Timothy on Maui, two additional students were now underwritten by the chapel's scholarship program: Luey Luey was sent to Maui's Maunaolu College in 1970, and Winston Likiaksa had just enrolled in the University of Hartford in Connecticut. These scholarships were generous, covering tuition and the cost of books, travel, and dormitory and meal expenses, plus a stipend for incidentals.

Spanning a period of 20 years—1963-1983—there were 56 Micronesian recipients of Kwajalein Protestant Chapel scholarships,[15] representing many thousands of donated, dedicated dollars! ☥

Notes - Chapter 17

1. The chronology and events recorded in this chapter through May 1962 are verified in the daily entries of the author's personal journals kept during the 1959-1962 period of his residence on Kosrae.
2. Joseph Z. George, personal letter, Oct. 17, 1962, Kosrae (translated from Kosraean)
3. Yosimi R. Stephen, personal letter, Jan. 21, 1963, Kosrae (translated from Kosraean)
4. Magrina Wakuk, personal letter, Jan. 22, 1963, Kosrae (translated from Kosraean)
5. Mary Alice Hanlin Buck, personal correspondence to Mrs. Cruise, April 17, 1964, quote translated from Kosraean
6. *A.D. Magazine*, Sept. 1977, p. 51
7. Karen Reed Green, editor, "Glimpses Into Pacific Lives: Some Outstanding Women," Centers for National Origin & Sex Equity - Pacific, Honolulu, 1987. p. 51
8. Doug Dunlap, personal e-mail, Jan. 9, 2004
9. Minutes, "Indigenous Leaders Conference," Godaro Lorrin, secretary, Kosrae 1966, p. 2
10. Minutes, "ILC," Kosrae 1966, p. 4
11. Mary Alice Hanlin [Buck], personal diary, Kosrae, Jan. 1955, p. 124
12. James L. Lewis, "Kusaiean Acculturation 1824-1948," reprinted for Division of Land Management - Resources and Development, TTPI, Aug. 1967, p. 85
13. Eswina Jonas Smith, personal conversation, Sept. 20, 2003
14. "Minutes of the Missionary Meeting of the UCBWM and LM," Elfriede Schmidt, secretary, Chuuk, June 8-13, 1970, p. 9
15. Walter I. Wells, "Kwajalein Protestant Chapel Scholarship Committee, 20th Anniversary Booklet," unpublished, Kwajalein 1984

NUNAK YOHK KE CHAPTER 18
1971-1981

Pastu Harrison el tafwela in suk inkanek ma ac akwoyela mukuikui lun church. Yok finsrak lal tuh usyen mokuikui lun church in arulana wo ac fwel. Ke 1971, el ac mwet sropo wial (pastu Alik Isaac, Aliksru, Esau, ac Isaiah), tuh insesela in ekulla ine se ma orekmakinyuk nu ke Committee lun Church Kosrae nu ke "Kosrae Congregational Church Council"—ku KCCC. Members nu ke committee se inge oasr ke mwet singoul luo: Mwet sropo se, deacon se, ac lay minister se ke kais sie church akosr fin acn Kosrae. Elos akilen mu oiya se inge ac karingin tuh church nukewa in oana sie pusralos nu ke committee se inge. Pastu Harrison el tuh solla chairman lun committee se inge.

Ke 1972, Pastu Harrison el tuh nawela Pastu Calwin Edwin, su sie mwet sropo fin acn Pohnpei, el an karingin mukuikui ke alu lun mwet Kosrae ma muta fin acn Pohnpei. Yok aetui lal Pastu Calwin ac Pastor Harrison ke sripen elos tukeni lutlut Wot. El arulana elang ke kas Kosrae meyen el payuk nu sin mutan Kosrae se su inel pah Melina. Mwet kol ke church fin acn Pohnpei tuh arulana insese nu ke mukuila se inge, oru Pastu Calwin el mutaweak in oru ma kunal nu sin mwet Kosrae ma muta ac orekma fin acn Pohnpei. Elos tukeni oru ma kunalos arulana wo.

Pastu Esau Tilfas el misa ke August 3, 1972. Matwal ke pal se inge pa el yac 78. Pastu Esau el isusla fin acn Utwe ac tuku nu fin acn Lelu ke el fusr in wi orekma yorol Arthur Herman, mwet America se tuku orek business fin acn Finsrael. Pastu Esau ac sou lal tuh akwuki fin acn Otnaur se ma Lazarus su tamulel lal Esau sang el ac muta we. Ke Etawi Kosrae tu fasrelik nu in mura inge ke 1921, Pastu Esau pa tuh president se emeet ke Etawi Lelu. El tu akmusrala nu ke pastu ke 1961.

Mutan America ma kulansupu Protestant congregation fin acn Kwajalein tuh oraloselik nu ke u—fal nu ke tuka in acn Micronesia inge. U inge tu kupasryang in wi mutan ma tuku ekin missionary ac wi pa mutan kulansap lun church in tuka inge in welulos orekma. U se fin acn Kwajalein ma tu kapasryang nu Kosrae ah pangpang Etawi Circle. Kupasr se inge tuh orala in arulana fototo ac in yok akasrui inmasrlon mutan fin acn Kwajalein ac mwet kol ke Church fin acn Kosrae. Kutu kasru ma mutan Kwajalein inge oru nu sin Church Kosrae pa elos supu mwe luti nu ke Sunday School, book in kasru nu sin pastu, ac oayapa me sang ac me lung nu sin tulik ke pal in Christmas. Tuh arulana yok pac akilenyen kasru wowo ma mwet ekasr Kosrae inge—Erafe Tosie, Shrew Jonas, Aaron Sigrah, ac Joshua Phillip—tuh oru in lolngok nu yurin mwet ma wi Etawi Circle.

Ke 1973, tuh akilenyuk pac u sasu luo ma weang Church fin acn Kosrae: Alu lun Tulik Srisrik ac Choir ke Church ekasr inge. Meet liki pal se inge, tulik srisrik uh wi na mwet matu ke alu meet lalos ke Sunday. Sie lemlem sasu ma Pastu Harrison el srukak in naweyuk pa tulik sriksrik in tila wi mwet matu alu ke sripen matwelos. Mwet kol wiyal in pal sa akilen mu wo nunak se inge pwanang elos akkeyela. Pa oru fasru nu misenge tulik srisrik uh srisrila in tia wi mwet matu alu. Alu lalos uh karinginyuk sin lay minister. Ke pal se pana inge tuh akwuki Choir nu ke Church inge kewa elos in kasru on ke alu meet ke Sunday. Pus mwet tu akilen mu oiya na wowo se pac inge.

Ke kolyuk pac lal Pastu Harrison ke KCCC ke pacl se inge, elos tuh insesela in akpusyela pusen deacon ke kais sie church inge nu ke itkosr. Elos oayapa insesela in srukak kais itkosr deaconess nu ke kais sie church. Elos tu orekmakin yok mwe rit se in Orekma 6:1-6 ma srumun ke Mwet Sap elos tuh srukak deacon itkosr in kasrelos orekma in pa kololos nu ke sulala se lalos inge.

Ke December 1973, Takeo Likiaksa ac Walton Palik aksafyela lutlut lalos ke Malua Theological College fin acn Western Samos. Elos foloko sun acn Kosrae ke January 1974 tukin elos sisla yac akosr in wi lutlut se inge.

Ke 1975 Kasuo Isisaki ac Joshua Phillip tuh us mukul fusr 34, su elos nufon tuh wi lutlut meet Wot, in som sisla len luo fin acn Wot. Elos srike in sisla pulan pal se inge in aengani ac sramsramkin Kas in Bible in sifil akkeye lulalfongi lalos. Sayen ma inge elos tu sifil esamak pal lalos fin acn Wot ke elos lutlut ah. Ma inge kewa mokleak nunkalos in akilen koko lun God nu selos.

Good King George el tu sang acn Pisin nu sin missionaries ma tuku emeet nu Kosrae ke August 1852 ah. Ke May 21, 1973, tu ayaolla en mission board nu ke Church Kosrae in pa la acn Pisin. Oayapa in 1852 Benjamin Snow ac Daniel Opunui tuh molela acn Yenyen elos in orek ima srisrik lalos we. Ke May 19, 1975, tu ayaolla en mission board nu ke Church Kosrae in pa la acn we.

Pastu Harrison el oayapa tuh sramteak u se ma pangpang Women's Christian Association ke October 11, 1975. Tia mwet kol ke church nukewa insese nu ke mukuila se inge, tuh mutan Kosrae in pacl sa kewa arulana engan kac uh. Akiko Nena pa tuh solla president se oemeet lalos. Elos tu akfasrye tukeni lalos pacl se ke quarter se in lutlut ke Bible, on, ac pwapa nu ke ma elos enenu in oru. Elos srike in aknasnasye lukinum lun kais sie church, kasru katinmas ku mutan matu ma enenu kasru, ac kasru alu lun tulik ke Sunday School. Meeting lalos inge elos oru forfor ke church fin acn Kosrae inge kewa.

Pusen pastu ke Church fin acn Kosrae inge sifwil puseni. Ke December

3, 1977, Benjamin Benjamin el tuh akmusrala in kulansupu Church Utwe. Ke December 6, 1979, Aaron Sigrah el akmusrala in kulansupu Church Lelu, ac Kun Nena Sigrah el akmusrala in kulansupu Church Tafunsak. Ke pal se inge oasr mwet sropo oalkosr pa kulansupu Church Kosrae.

Ke pal se na ma Pastu Snow el us tuku Peng Wo se inge nu Kosrae ah, baptais lun tulik fusr el sie kunokon ma akfasryeyuk sin Church Kosrae oana ke orek fin acn America. Finne akilenyuk mu wangin fakya ke Wuleang Sasu tuh akilenyuk mu baptaisella sie tulik fusr el yok sripe ke orekma lun Church. In pal se inge Church Kosrae ekulla pac sie oiya ma orek fafasru meet me. Elos otella mu tulik uh in tila baptais meyen baptais ma na nu sin mwet sulala in auliyak in pangpang sie mwet lulalfongi. Tulik uh ac srakna filfilla papa ac nina in use nu yurin church in alu elosla. Tuh alu se inge ac tufa pangpang kisa ku sang kulo.

- CHAPTER EIGHTEEN -

INNOVATIONS AND RENEWAL
1971-1981

THE DRAMA OF WORSHIP

Pastor Harrison George sometimes consulted his ministerial colleagues about his ideas, but often he did not. He had a remarkable ability to judge the best time to move ahead on his own. Some of these unilateral decisions were made because he was well aware that his fellow pastors would not agree with him. Others were made in light of his growing sense of ownership of the Malem congregation.

Harrison was the first Kosraean pastor to contemplate the aesthetics or beauty of a worship service and its setting. He had a theatrical flair and had come to the conclusion that church services on Kosrae were in need of rejuvenation at least, if not redesigning. Was it not possible that the appearance of the worship area might either detract from, or enhance, a sense of God's presence and the possibility for inspiration? For the time being, the contents of worship would remain as they had been since instituted by Benjamin Snow, but Harrison was convinced that the trappings of worship needed some style.

Reflecting mid-19th-century Congregationalism, Kosrae's houses of worship were clean but without decoration. Each of the permanent church buildings erected after World War II had an altar raised on a platform or otherwise located in an elevated chancel alcove at the front of the worship area. Altars were sometimes draped, but otherwise there was no symbol or adornment, either on the altars or on the walls behind them. The pulpit, to one side, was used only during the Sunday morning service. A wood railing stretched across the front of the elevated area with an opening through which no one but the pastor or worship leader ever passed. A table or desk, usually covered with an embroidered white cloth, stood at the center on the floor level in front of the railing. Sunday School and Christian Endeavor were led from this table, as well as Meeting each Sunday afternoon and services on Wednesday and Friday.

Missionaries had used crosses and flowers on the altar of the Wot chapel, and Harrison had seen various styles of altar treatment as a student in Hawai'i. Bouquets of artificial flowers began appearing on the Malem altar and along the railing in front of the pulpit. Slowly the possibilities for decoration spread to other churches, though fresh flowers—of which Kosrae has an abundance—were seldom used. Artificial flowers lasted—fresh flowers do not.

Pastors traditionally wore long pants, and—by the late 1800s—suit jackets over white shirts, when leading Sunday morning worship. Shirts were always buttoned to the top. Gradually neckties were added during the years following World War II, but otherwise there was little variation. When coats, pants and shirts were unavailable, Kosrae's seamstresses were amazingly adept at producing the required garments. By 1971 in Malem, the deacon, as well as the pastor, was in suit and tie.

REVIVING THE MOTHER HUBBARD

After the war, when the shortage of clothing was over, Kosraean women began once more to wear white on communion Sundays. Dresses were simple. Puffed sleeves were short, and skirts were cut on the bias, to converve material. As time went by, it was increasingly common to see women in white on any Sunday, though colorful dresses were also worn.

Then Pastor Harrison proposed that his wife and the Malem deaconess use a specific pattern for their Sunday dresses—a "Mother Hubbard" design found commonly in Hawai'i, where the old missionary-introduced style later evolved into the fashionable and popular muumuu. On Kosrae, this same dress pattern had been used by earlier generations of church women. Gathered at the yoke with a large square collar hanging at the back, the material fell to the ankles with no waistline, incorporating as much as six yards of material. The fullness of these dresses and their long, two-tiered puffed sleeves made them quite striking.

At Pastor Harrison's urging, these old-fashioned garments soon became the dress-of-choice for Sunday in the other villages as well—worn not only by pastors' wives and deaconesses, but by many of the women. Among those who remembered the pattern was Katrina Mares Tosie, the mother of Pastor Erafe. She became the primary seamstress when this fashion revival began.

As months went by the dresses were derided by a few as "Malem dresses," and their popularity dipped among Tafunsak, Lelu, and Utwe women. But, conscientiously, pastors' wives and deaconesses in Malem continued wearing the dresses for Sunday morning worship, and the fashion took hold. Today the dresses are used by women leaders in all the villages, particularly for festive occasions of the Church.

NEW NAME FOR THE ALL-ISLAND CHURCH COMMITTEE

Pastor Harrison was increasingly concerned with reorganizing the all-island church committee. It was still controlled by the pastors and, indeed, existed only when they were present. In 1971 Harrison was finally able to wangle assent from the other pastors, arriving at a totally new arrangement. None of the four was enthusiastic about the plan. Pastor Isaiah and Pastor Esau, both in their late 70s, were no longer attending meetings, and Pastor Aliksru, 62, was in distant Tafunsak, but—persuaded by Pastor Harrison—they voted in favor. Only Pastor Alik had to be reckoned with. He was senior pastor and not enamored with some of Pastor Harrison's innovations. But Harrison knew how to finagle and flatter, and probably without understanding the younger pastor's full intent, Pastor Alik finally agreed.

As a result, Pastor Harrison became chairman of the new Kosrae Congregational Church Council, a group composed of one pastor, one deacon, and one lay minister from each of the four churches. For a few years, this leadership team, known as KCCC, operated smoothly, with members giving their approval to Pastor Harrison's agenda. Some of the changes authorized by the KCCC demonstrated their worthiness and became appreciated and successful aspects of Kosraean church life. They were logical steps waiting to be recognized and taken. Others, not so plausible, were tried but soon faded away.

LELU MEN'S COMMUNITY CHORUS AND BAND

A musical phenomenon was generating considerable excitement among the young men of Lelu in 1971—in fact, the entire village was enthralled.

The popular Lelu Men's Chorus had ordered musical instruments, augmenting their choir with a band. Not since the Lelu Marching Band had performed in the 1930s with instruments procured for them by Japanese merchants had such an attempt been made. The government participated with grant-in-aid money to help with equipment, and Fritz Weilbacher—a member of the band 40 years earlier—offered advice. Otherwise, the group was on its own.

The singular success of these young men in ordering trumpets, cornets, trombones, alto saxophones, and drums was bested only by their awe-inspiring determination to master musical instruments that most of them had never seen nor heard before. Each individual chose an instrument, read the instructions, and, with a great deal of tenacity, taught himself to play.

Officers for the group were: Edison Robert, president; Kasuo Isisaki, vice president; Dwight Likiaksa, secretary; and Masaki Thomson, treasurer. They met for rehearsals twice a week, alternating between Pisin and Edison Robert's home and, for more than a decade, performed all over Kosrae, delighting everyone who heard them.

KOSRAEANS ON POHNPEI

After Kosrae became part of the Ponape District of the U.S. Trust Territory of the Pacific Islands following World War II, a Kosraean community emerged in Kolonia, Pohnpei's primary town and district center. During the 1960s, a small Kosraean Christian Endeavor group had formed and, through the kindness of Pohnpei's church leaders, met regularly each Sunday afternoon in Pohnpei's "mother church" on Kolonia's waterfront.

By 1970, the group was meeting in its own community building in Duwenehue, the area of Kolonia designated for Kosraeans who worked for the district government. During a 1972 visit to Pohnpei, Pastor Harrison issued an invitation to one of his KCTS classmates, Calwin Gallio Edwin, a native Pohnpeian, to serve Kolonia's growing Kosraean community as pastor. After consulting with the leaders of the Pohnpei Church who had ordained him, Pastor Calwin accepted the call. With his Kosraean wife, Melina, beside him, Pastor Calwin—who had learned to speak Kosraean as a student at Wot—was the ideal leader for Pohnpei's Kosraean congregation, just as Pastor Harrison had anticipated.

DEATH OF PASTOR ESAU

Pastor Tilfas, age 74, died in his Otnaur home at mid-day on August 3, 1972, with his wife and other family members beside him. His body was carried to the Langosak church, where Pastor Alik Isaac conducted the memorial service, then returned for burial at Otnaur. He was the father of a large family of children, grandchildren, and great grandchildren that today numbers more than 500.

Born in Utwe, the grandson of Sepe Nuarpat, one of Kosrae's first Christians, Esau Tilfas moved to Lelu as a young man to work as a cook for Arthur Herman at the American trader's Finsrael headquarters. He had been recommended by his mother-in-law, Srasra Kir, a sister of Mr. Herman's second wife, Srue Kir. Esau and his wife, Kenye, built their home in Lelu at Otnaur, on a small parcel of land they purchased from Esau's older brother, Lazarus. Without much land, Esau had to work hard to feed his family, which grew to include 11 children. His humble, helpful demeanor won him a place in the hearts of those in the Lelu community, who were generous in assisting the family.

A faithful Christian, Esau was elected the first president of Lelu's Christian Endeavor society when C. E. was first divided into village groups in 1921. People were pleased when, on November 1, 1961, at age 67, he was ordained a pastor.

ETAWI CIRCLE

Seeking to build friendships and develop avenues of service with indigenous churches in Micronesia, members of the Women's Protestant Chapel Fellowship on Kwajalein divided themselves into five groups—called circles—averaging 20 members per group. First organized in the mid-1960s, the circles were named for missionary women in the islands with whom they had become identified. These American women, representing many denominations and church backgrounds, met monthly and actively involved themselves in the plans and needs of their missionary namesakes.

In spite of the sporadic shipping and mail service that still plagued Kosrae, the Anna Dederer Circle did an impressive job of keeping in touch with the island's last missionary while she remained at her post. By 1972, Miss Dederer had been gone for almost two years, and most of the other missionary women represented by Kwajalein circles were no longer in Micronesia. Not wanting to lose the cordial relationships they had developed with their Christian neighbors, the Women's Protestant Chapel Fellowship changed the names of their circles to reflect the island churches with which they had connections. The Anna Dederer Circle became the Etawi Circle. Etawi [e as in "ever"-TAH-wee], the Kosraean word meaning "to imitate," is used as the name for Kosrae's Christian Endeavor organization.

There were those on both Kosrae and Kwajalein who wondered if the warm association of the two island groups could be maintained without Anna Dederer as go-between. But the relationship thrived, largely because of the faithful correspondence between the American women and Kosrae's Church leaders. Letters from Erafe Tosie, Shrew Jonas, Aaron Sigrah, and Joshua Phillip delighted Etawi Circle members when they were received—often hand-carried by Kosraeans traveling to Ebeye.

The circle maintained its practice of sending Christmas treats for Kosrae's Sunday School children, books and classroom aids for teachers, and resources for pastors. Members of the circle also continued underwriting expenses for production of the annual Kas In Kol—the booklets containing daily topics and Scripture texts used by all Church and Christian Endeavor members on Kosrae. Translated by Alice Buck, with Kosraeans on Ebeye assisting her, the Kas In Kol were printed in Eugene, Oregon, and shipped to Kosrae. This help continued to be provided throughout most of the 1970s and was gratefully received by Christian Endeavor leaders on Kosrae.

The opening paragraph in a letter from Shrew Jonas to members of the Etawi Circle, dated January 29, 1973, is typical: "I thank God for the opportunity to greet you, and tell you of our great joy and happiness in receiving our Etawi topics. They reached us in time to distribute for the new year. We sincerely thank all of you who had a part in preparing and sending these books to us. Everyone here is excited about receiving them, and some are saying that it is like the days long ago when the Baldwin sisters provided our daily topics for us. I repeat, to each of you who has been involved in this project, thank you very much!"[1]

When these letters reached Kwajalein—always by ship—they were accompanied by baskets of oranges, tangerines, and limes; stalks of sugarcane; and boxes of delicate handcraft. Sometimes they were divided among the families of Etawi Circle members, who struggled to know just how to react to the overwhelming generosity of the Kosraean people. At other times they were used as prizes in the raffles that generated funds for circle projects.

CONGREGATION IN WALUNG

By 1973, records and correspondence mention Kosrae as having five congregations, with the fifth being a church in Walung, which was considered a branch of the Tafunsak church. Residents of the Walung coast had never had a building of their own in which to worship. Since they all had family and friends in Tafunsak, many traveled the four miles by boat to be in that village for Sunday. During the years of the mission schools, their custom was to worship at Wot. By 1974 their first meeting house had been erected.

JUNIOR CHURCH

One responsibility assigned to the lay ministers was to take turns leading a service for children while the Sunday morning worship service for adults was in progress. This was another of Pastor Harrison's ideas that once again highlighted his uncanny sense of knowing when the time was ripe for a certain innovation.

As long as church services had been conducted on Kosrae, children had been present. No one ever questioned this practice. In fact, children were usually the first to appear on a Sunday morning. They would fill the area in front of the pulpit, the boys on one side and the girls on the other, mirroring the arrangement of the adults behind them. They sat quietly on the ground and—as the years went by—on the floor and, still later, on sitting mats that were spread on the floor. They were remarkably well-behaved, sometimes falling asleep during the lengthy services.

Harrison described to his fellow pastors the practice of churches he had visited in Hawaiʻi, where special child-oriented services were conducted in another part of the church, while their parents and grandparents attended the main church service. By 1973, all four of Kosrae's congregations were providing such services for their children—toddlers through 7th and 8th graders—in a Sunday School or Christian Endeavor building next door to the church. In Lelu these groups consisted of several hundred children, while in Tafunsak, Malem, and Utwe, 70 or 80 were always present on any given Sunday. Their exuberant singing, easily heard by the adults, was never considered a distraction—only a source of pride, and an assurance that the needs of their children were being met.

CHURCH CHOIRS ORGANIZED

Another of Pastor Harrison's suggestions whose time had arrived was the organizing of church choirs.

Everyone on Kosrae sings. A natural ability to harmonize is practically universal among Pacific Islanders. It is a talent so incredible, in fact, that it has been the subject of studies by foreign musicologists. So—when members of a congregation can blend their voices in such a richness of sound, singing together with beauty and gusto—why the need for a choir?

But the Kosraeans loved the idea. The Malem congregation organized a choir in 1973, and soon after, the others enthusiastically organized their own—all for the specific purpose of providing special music during Sunday morning church services. The choirs gathered for rehearsals during the week, eagerly seeking new songs to learn and present. A friendly rivalry developed among the congregations that kept these groups of singers on their toes and thriving. Several choirs boasted as many as 60 members.

SEVEN DEACONS AND SEVEN DEACONESSES
PER CONGREGATION

Pointing his colleagues to the story in Acts 6:1-6 that describes the selection of the first deacons by the early Church, Pastor Harrison proposed that seven deacons instead of just one be consecrated by each congregation. The practical matter of the expanding number of Kosraeans made it a sensible proposal. Communion services had become very lengthy, as only the deacons and deaconesses were permitted to serve the gathered membership in Lelu. These few servers had to maintain their hold on the trays [communion trays are never touched by the congregants] as they pushed through the aisles and picked their way among worshipers crowded together on the floor.

Deaconesses were not mentioned in the Acts account, but given Kosrae's tradition of keeping the sexes separated in church, it was taken for granted that the Biblical number seven would apply to women as well.

Questions were raised among the laity, reflecting what many persons thought to be a startling proposal. As deacons were considered men of virtue, could the villages find that many individuals worthy of such responsibility? With the prodding of Pastor Harrison, and the realization that the rest of the pastors were of one mind on the issue, the church committee proceeded to select for each congregation six men and six women to join the single deacon and deaconess already in place. In general, people were pleased with this innovation, and though personal initiative was not a quality encouraged in the island culture, many privately expressed their admiration for Pastor Harrison and his talent for moving often intransigent leaders to get things done.

The number of persons seated in places of honor along the walls at the left and right front of Kosrae's churches dramatically increased. Because they ranked below pastors and deacons, and were often involved in their duties during services of worship, lay ministers were not accorded this honor.

TAKEO AND WALTON RETURN

In December, Takeo Likiaksa and Walton Palik graduated from Malua Theological College. Having lived on the Western Samoa campus for four years, they were anxious to get home. In January 1974—accompanied by Walton's wife, Tokiko, and their daughter, Florence—they reached Kosrae, warmly welcomed by their families and church friends.

Almost immediately Takeo left Kosrae again, this time for the University of Guam, where he enrolled in the spring semester as a junior. Harold Hanlin had arranged a mission board scholarship for him, augmented—through Dr. Hanlin's efforts—by the General Baptist Church on Guam. This congregation became Takeo's home-away-from-home, taking care of many of his needs and encouraging him in his studies. He graduated in December 1976, married Kioko Gifford Nena in 1977, and in 1978 was consecrated as a lay minister.

ICHY... NI... SANG... YONG KUMI

During Japanese times, each of Kosrae's four villages were divided into groups one, two, three, and four to expedite work projects. Before and during World War II, assignments for these groups were almost always dreaded because of the stern—and sometimes cruel—conduct of the work supervisors. During the post-war period, the groups were reorganized by the Kosraeans themselves and, surprisingly, they chose to keep the Japanese designations.

Originally considered community groups, all families within a village were assigned to one of the four. Church membership was not a consideration. As years passed, the composition of these groups did not change, but the lines between Ichy Kumi, Ni Kumi, Sang Kumi, Yong Kumi, and the Church became hazy. By 1974 in Lelu, the four groups were considered to be part of the total church program. In Malem and Utwe, however, the groups remained under the umbrella of the government office. Tafunsak disbanded their kumi and replaced them with neighborhood groups, called ota, which served the same purpose. Other villages began using neighborhood groups as well—but in addition to their kumi.

Whether kumi, ota, or both, the groups in all the villages were, and are, very active. An enormous amount of work is tackled—much of it pertaining to the improvement and beautification of public areas. Each group elects officers, and when these officers announce an assignment, the groups respond. Considerable competition is generated among the groups on any given work site—triggering excitement and energy in the Kosraean psyche. Since ancient times, Kosraeans have often assigned one or more persons to move along the sidelines when heavy work is undertaken to act as a combination cheerleader and clown, whipping the workers into almost a frenzy of activity. At times, a few will remain after a day's work to confirm that the project has been properly completed, but the work of these groups is consistently accomplished with pride.

These groups are in evidence during holidays and times of celebration when they work to prepare meals, erect temporary pavilions, or fulfill other assignments, and—because it is Kosrae—there is always festive singing. In fact, one of the primary areas of friendly competition between Ichy Kumi, Ni Kumi, Sang Kumi, and Yong Kumi is in their function as choirs!

NEW BRIDGES AND ROADS AND BUILDINGS AND LEADERS

The 1970s were exceptionally busy years for Kosrae. The new, concrete Dias Bridge spanning the mangrove channel that separated Finpukul and Mutunenea at the west end of Lelu Harbor opened the road connecting Tafunsak, and Lelu Island via its causeway, to the south side of the harbor and Malem and Utwe villages beyond. This road, in turn, opened up the vast public lands at Tofol, now designated as Kosrae's capital. Government buildings, a new high school, a hospital, a post office, and other public and private enterprises began to mushroom there above the harbor's mangrove fringe. The Church, too, was constructing. The new youth building at the Utwe Church was dedicated December 21, 1974.

During the 1960s, the Lelu congregation had erected a young people's Christian Endeavor building—the first congregation to do so—just a few feet south of the Langosak church, using poured concrete. Carpenters, just beginning to experiment with this method, were not pleased with the results. The building was hot, it was much too close to the main building, and the roof leaked. In the early 1970s, with the use of considerable muscle, that building was demolished and the area landscaped. A new youth building was construct-ed at a more reasonable distance to the south and placed perpendicular to the church. It was airier, more practical, and attractive. Young People's Christian Endeavor President William Tosie spearheaded this project, with a loyal group of helpers.

Next, a commodious two-story guest house, called "Sharon Inn," was built still further to the south. It proved its worth from the day it was dedicated in September 1975. Lelu began a tradition of assigning a church couple, or family, to live at Sharon Inn for one week—or considerably longer, if the family was available to remain there—to keep the premises neat and to act as hosts. It is a continuing tradition that is very effective.

There was an inflow of fresh leadership. Deacons consecrated at the December 1974 new-month meeting included: Kun Sigrah, Tafunsak; Milton Timothy and Kilafwa Palokoa, Malem; and Palikkun Nena and Benjamin Isaiah, Utwe. New deaconesses were Sepe Kun Sigrah, Tafunsak; Pursis Milton and Sra Tulen, Malem; and Florence Palikkun and Matline Kinshiro, Utwe.

Those chosen to join the Church Committee were Hamilton Jackson and Richard Tolenoa, Tafunsak; Walton Palik, Lelu; Basil Charley, Luther Cornelius, Austin Jonas, Likiak Phillip, Kun Lonno, and Palikkun Kephas, Malem; and Atino Poll, Mores Wakuk, Kinshiro Nena, and Joseph Wilmer, Utwe.

NOSTALGIA FOR WOT

Nine years after the last class graduated from KCTS, the future of the Wot campus was still in question. Letters from Kosrae frequently asked for prayer for those assigned to plan the school's future. Members of the church council felt themselves incapable of operating a school without help from the mission board—help they reluctantly began to realize would not be forthcoming.

A men's alumni group gathered to plan a work camp at Wot for the summer of 1975. Among the conveners were Kasuo Isisaki, a member of Kosrae's delega-tion to the Pohnpei District Legislature, and Joshua Phillip, Kosrae's librarian. They wrote a detailed report of what transpired:

Early in 1975, a number of former Wot students—either on government busi-ness or at leisure on their own—visited the old campus and found themselves enjoy-ing again the lush vegetation and peaceful atmosphere of that hallowed place. They began talking among themselves about the possibility of organizing a work camp there. In July, after some of them had returned from assignments beyond Kosrae,

Kasuo Isisaki called a meeting of the 1962 KCTS graduates to discuss such a gathering. At the same time, Joshua Phillip, without having heard Kasuo's idea, announced a meeting of all former Wot students for the same purpose. Kasuo and Joshua, each pleased to learn of the other's initiative, were convinced that it was not just coincidence. They felt that God was clearly in this plan. Together, they supervised the project to completion.

On July 28, a gathering took place of the 1962 male graduates, at which time four advisors were chosen: Joshua Phillip, Walton Palik, Alik Palsis and Donald Jonah. They selected Thursday and Friday, August 28 and 29 for the dates of their camp, and Food, Transportation, and Program committees were appointed. Each former student was asked to donate $5, if possible. The amount of $118.75 was collected, with $27.75 going for transportation and $65 for food, leaving a balance of $26. Everyone was asked to bring sleeping mats, plates and utensils, machetes, mosquito coils, Bibles and hymnals, pencils or pens, toilet tissue, and anything else they felt they might need.

Several other meetings were held as preparations progressed. A letter dated August 8 addressed to Kosrae's Church leaders, was finally answered on August 26 by Rev. Alik Isaac and Rev. Harrison George, giving the group official permission to proceed. On August 28, participants began traveling to Wot. Alokoa Talley, Siosi Aliksa and Kasuo Isisaki helped transport those from Malem and Lelu to Tafunsak. Noel Tulensru, Iwao Mongkeya, Natchuo Mongkeya, Hashime Vicente, and Johnson Taulung provided transportation from Tafunsak to Wot. Marston Nena, Tatasy Andrew, Likiak Tulenkun, and Nena Thomas provided transportation from Utwe to Wot. By 8 o'clock that evening, everyone had arrived.

Siosi Aliksa and his Food Committee were ready with the evening meal. Hashime Vicente and his Walung family provided an abundance of fish, and each camper brought bread and biscuits to share. Conrad Albert and Aruo Kun had stopped on the way to fish at Yela. Aruo speared a huge komokut [hump-head parrot fish]—perhaps 80 to 100 lbs—which he brought to the table. After the meal, Joshua Phillip led the evening worship. It had been a long day, but most found it impossible to sleep. They gathered in groups, reminiscing—what they looked like then, the mischief they got into, their work schedules and studies—agreeing that their years at Wot had been an extraordinary time for them. Many feelings were expressed—some happy and some sad—but all the attendees were grateful to be back at Wot.

Walton Palik led the morning worship on the 29th. As the worship proceeded, it became apparent that the boys had become men. After worship, everyone walked down to investigate their dilapidated dormitories. For most of them, it was 12 or 13 years since they had last bunked together there. Then everyone scattered: some went fishing, others to climb for breadfruit and coconuts, still others went to wield their machetes in the overgrown gardens. After the noon meal, the group cleaned around the school building. There was so much wild growth that they were unable to clear it all.

As they were working, the sad news of the death of Walton Palik's father reached them. Walton, accompanied by Ueta Palik and Kasuo Isisaki, departed immediately for Lelu. The group sent a 50-pound bag of rice and 19 cans of mackerel with them.

After the work period, everyone went to the river to bathe and get ready for supper. Marston and two others had caught a large kusrul [Napoleon wrasse] which was boiled, along with some pigeons that Higgin shot. These, with baked breadfruit, made a very tasty and full meal. After supper, it was time for fun-night, directed by Isao Mongkeya. Everyone laughed hard, especially at the antics of Grey Nena and Atchuo Luey.

At the conclusion of evening worship, led by Joshua Phillip, time was given for various ones to express their feelings about the camp. All agreed that they wanted to have another camp—very soon. It was pointed out, however, that since many of them were elementary school teachers, summer was the only time available. In addition to leaders Kasuo, Joshua, and Walton, there were 33 campers, each of whom filled out a questionnaire. Unanimously, they promised to live as Christian men before their children. Of the 33, 18 were members of the Church, 21 had government jobs, three were on the Church committee, and six were presidents or vice presidents of their Christian Endeavor groups. Thirty-one were married, and most of them had children. Only Yosino Abner and Atchuo Luey were unmarried—though Yosino announced that he had plans to marry very soon.

The evening was concluded with an election of officers: president, Kasuo Isisaki; vice president, Siosi Aliksa; secretary, Richard Tolenoa; and treasurer, Sephin Shrew. Everyone departed Wot on Saturday morning, August 30, those who lived in Malem were the last to reach home. Everyone in their home villages noticed the change in the camp's participants and the enthusiasm with which they returned to their families and responsibilities.[2]

DISPOSITION OF MISSION LAND

In 1972, with Dr. Hanlin serving as liaison, the mission board initiated the process of transferring property formerly held by the American Board to Kosraean ownership. The Determination of Ownership for Pisin was signed December 15th of that year. The Certificate of Title came through on May 21, 1973, granting legal ownership of that historic bit of land—given to Benjamin Snow in 1852 by Good King George—to the Church on Kosrae.

The Determination of Ownership for Yenyen, the small island Mr. Snow and Daniel Opunui had purchased in 1852 for use as their garden, was signed on May 1, 1973. The Certificate of Title was issued two years later, May 19, 1975, naming the Church legal owner of that significant but underused piece of land.

The wheels of justice turned much more slowly with reference to Wot. The reluctance of the Church to relinquish the land was the first hurdle. For most Kosraeans, it was simply inconceivable that there would be no more mission school there. It would take two decades of court cases and legal wrangling before a new Certificate of Title could finally be issued for that prime hillside property.

WOMEN'S CHRISTIAN ASSOCIATION

Pastor Erafe and Pastor Harrison attended the Aha Pae'aina, the annual assembly of the Hawai'i Conference of the United Church of Christ, June 13-18, 1975, at Kaumakapili Church in Honolulu. They were there as invited observers, and noted especially the active role in the conference of the Woman's Board of Missions. Church women seemed to be everywhere—not only hosting meals and singing in choirs, but leading workshops and worship services and participating as full delegates with the men in the discussions and decisions of the four-day meeting.

The two pastors—both public school teachers—returned to Kosrae in time to travel with other teachers to Pohnpei for the summer teachers' training session. One evening at Pohnpei, the pastors shared with their teacher-colleagues—Akiko Nena, Connie George, and Simako Holdon—how impressed they had been with the organization of the church women in Hawai'i. They described the considerable help and many worthwhile activities of the women at the Aha Pae'aina. Could the women of Kosrae be organized to assist and undergird their Church in a similar manner?

Back on their home island, the All-Kosrae Women's Choir—a popular group organized in 1971—met in Utwe on September 20th to elect new officers. Before they could begin, however, word arrived from Pastor Harrison asking them not to proceed. Instead, the women were instructed to gather at the Lelu church in three weeks to organize a Women's Christian Association for Kosrae. Pastor Harrison felt that the Women's Choir would make the ideal nucleus for the organization he envisioned.

On October 11, 1975, more than 200 women from all parts of Kosrae came together at Langosak to listen to Pastor Harrison explain his plan. Pastor Erafe stood with him that day, but some among the pastors and leaders of the church were opposed to the idea. The women wholeheartedly endorsed it. When called upon to select the women who would lead them, some felt that the pastors' wives and deaconesses should head the new organization. After much discussion it was decided that the new WCA would not be an arm of the Friday evening women's prayer meeting, which the pastors' wives and deaconesses already led. Instead, the women expressed their unanimous desire that the new group be a separate entity within the Church of Kosrae. The following young women were elected officers: Akiko Nena, president; Arue Cuffle, vice president; Kioko Cecilia Gifford, secretary; and Hattie Conrad, treasurer.

Participants were so excited by what was taking place, and had not noticed how much time was being consumed, that food had been forgotten! By the end of the lengthy proceedings, four or five women who had come from distant villages had fainted from hunger. Their Lelu friends hurried to feed them and make them comfortable.[3]

The WCA began meeting quarterly in one of the village churches for Bible study, singing, and planning. Their theme was "Christian Women Holding Hands around Kosrae." They beautified church yards, assisted women who were confined to their homes because of illness or age, paid special attention to the widows of their communities, and helped with Junior Church and Sunday School.

LESSON IN FORGIVENESS

In October 1976, I was in Saipan with some Americans from Kwajalein for whom I was leading a tour of Micronesia. I connected with the small, local Kosraean community—as I always did on my trips through Micronesia—and learned to my horror that a young man whose family I knew very well had been murdered in a fight aboard a ship in Saipan's harbor. Both young men, one Kosraean and the other Pohnpeian, worked together as sailors on a Trust Territory tanker. They had a history of getting drunk together during off hours. On this particular night, their drinking turned disastrous when they began arguing and then fighting. They both broke beer bottles, slashing at each other—the Pohnpeian youth delivering a fatal blow.

The young sailors had family members on Saipan. A sister of the murdered boy's deceased mother telephoned me at my hotel to ask that I join her and her family in a meeting she had called at her home with the family of the Pohnpeian perpetrator. I agreed—having no idea what to expect. When I arrived, a group of very somber, angry-looking young Kosraean men were seated in chairs around the living room. Whispering her greeting, the aunt motioned me to take a seat beside her.

Within minutes there was a light knock on the door, and 10 or 12 Pohnpeian men and women were ushered into the room. There were no greetings—they just sank to the floor in the middle of the room, the women crying softly. Then, from the group, a disheveled, devastated young man crawled toward the knees of the aunt, sobbing his apology to her. Sternly, she reached out and grabbed his head tightly in both hands. In an emotion-filled but surprisingly firm voice, she said: "Because of you, my son is GONE! From now on, YOU are my son!" ["Nephew" and "son" are the same word in Kosraean.] After several minutes, during which there was only the sound of weeping, she asked me to pray. God's presence in that prayer was but a shadow of the holy presence that radiated from the earnest compassion of that woman.

KUSAIE BECOMES KOSRAE

The celebrations that occurred during the first seven days of January 1977, when Kosrae became a district on its own, separated from Pohnpei, were unparalleled in the island's history. Two ships were tied side-by-side at Lelu's dock, with a third tied to buoys behind them. A fourth ship was anchored across the harbor toward Sansrik, with a smaller military vessel anchored nearby. The passengers who had arrived on these ships—some of them Kosraeans returning from other parts of Micronesia and the world—were wide-eyed, exuberant participants in the events of that week with the island's entire population.

High Commissioner Peter T. Coleman of the U.S. Trust Territory of the Pacific was an honored guest, along with officials from the U.S. Department of the Interior and State Department. There were military officers from Hawai'i, Kwajalein, and Guam—a U.S. Navy band being part of the Guam contingent. Visitors included officials from other areas of Micronesia, former missionaries, an entire shipload of people from Nauru, a large group representing the Kwajalein Protestant Chapel congregation, as well as friends of individual Kosraeans.

Kosrae sparkled, with the grounds of each of the four elementary schools— the centers of celebration—highly decorated with palm fronds, flowers and shells. Each location included a stage on which visiting choirs and local church and community groups performed songs, dances, and cultural demonstrations. There were concerts by the Lelu Men's Community Chorus and Band. There were speeches by visiting dignitaries, with Joab Sigrah and Jacob Nena working practically without a break as interpreters. There were parades, games, and canoe races—for which traditional long, sleek racing dugouts with outriggers had been especially constructed. There were picnics, barbeques, and feasts— food was everywhere. Worship in the village churches began each day, with invocations by various Kosraean pastors opening each event.

It had been an irritant to Kosraeans for 91 years to be classified as part of the Pohnpei District. For the first time since the Spanish arrived in 1886 and arbitrarily made Kosrae an administrative subdistrict of Pohnpei, Kosrae was on its own. The time was right. A new political reality was emerging from among the islands of the U.S. Trust Territory. The Northern Marianas had voted to become a commonwealth of the United States, while Palau and the Marshall Islands had chosen to be independent nations. As a separate district, Kosrae was preparing to join other islands in the Caroline group as part of an entity to be known as the Federated States of Micronesia.

Another irritant was salved that first week of January 1977. Since the day in the 1820s when they first stepped foot on Kosrae, foreigners had difficulty pronouncing the name of the island. Strong's Island was the name used by most non-Kosraeans, including missionaries, for the first 60 years of foreign contact. But even when they tried to correct this insult, most outsiders simply could not pronounce "Kosrae" [ko-SHRY, as in "eye"] with its unique "retroflexed 'r.'" So "Kusaie" [koo-SIGH] became the name the world used. For the Kosraeans, ever patient and courteous, it was unthinkable to correct these visitors, but they raised their eyebrows when it became known that the word pronounced "kusaie" in the Japanese language, meant "stink"! And when some early visitors tried to make a connection between Kosrae and Japan based on the mispronunciation of the island's name, Kosraeans shook their heads.

So, on January 1, 1977, it became "KOSRAE" for everyone—Kosraean or otherwise—to use. There need be no apologies for a beautiful, sentimental, comfortable, indigenous name just because some foreigners made no effort to pronounce it correctly. Now, when the pilot of a Continental Micronesia flight comes on the intercom to welcome his passengers to "CAUSE-ray," Kosraeans aboard shrug their shoulders and smile.

AIR SERVICE BEGINS FOR KOSRAE

But it was still a decade before Continental Micronesia jets would begin flying to Kosrae. Field-trip ships continued to make their sporadic visits with cargo and passengers, but in January 1977, Kosrae was the only major island in Micronesia that was not yet benefitting from air service. On June 25, 1973, a small amphibious med-evac plane out of Guam had crashed on take-off in Lelu Harbor, killing the patient, Kenye Abraham, her husband, Osamu Abraham, and a member of the crew. This disaster—witnessed by many, including the five young children of the Kosraean victims—had served as a tragic reminder of Kosrae's isolation from the rest of the world.

On May 1, 1977, a small aircraft owned and operated by Pacific Missionary Aviation came to the rescue. PMA began flying between Pohnpei and Kosrae once a week, giving Kosraeans speedy access to Pohnpei and making it possible for passengers to connect with the Continental Air Micronesia flights flying through Pohnpei six days a week—three days to Honolulu and the alternate days to Guam.

The Rev. Edmund Kalau, originally from Germany and formerly associated with the Liebenzell Mission, was the founder and president of Pacific Missionary Aviation. PMA, as it was known, was developed as a mission flight service, linking the more remote islands of Micronesia with district centers. An early brochure explains: "The planes provide emergency medical evacuations, air-sea search and rescue operations, medicine and food drops, church support, evangelistic outreach and inter-island passenger and cargo transport."[4] The commercial use of their planes generated funds for PMA ministries. Ed Kalau's son-in-law, Peter Reichert, was the first pilot to land a plane on Kosrae.

The first airstrip to accommodate these flights was built at Mokul, along the base of the mountains that rise above Tafunsak. But the airstrip had a flaw that caused an accident described by Harvey Segal in his *Kosrae, the Sleeping Lady Awakens*:

There was no windsock, rather four 55-gallon drums were filled with coconut husks and set afire at plane time so Peter could tell which way the wind was blowing. Often each plume of smoke was heading in a different direction because the strip was so close to the mountains that the winds were extremely variable. Matt Mix and Martin Christian of Pohnpei and Sam McPherson of Saipan were passengers with Peter on June 20, 1977, when the landing Dornier 28 plane got caught in a crosswind. The wind flipped the plane over, which threw everyone into a taro patch, scraped, scratched, and bruised, but not seriously hurt.[5]

The Tafunsak strip was abandoned. Work on an alternate landing site was already in progress. Dredged from the tideland south of Lelu Island, the new strip, running north and south, connected at a right angle to the middle of the Lelu causeway. Though this runway was also plagued with unpredictable wind currents, at 2,000 feet it was 1,000 feet longer than the Tafunsak strip. It was used weekly for the next six years.

Not only was the air service provided by PMA greatly appreciated and thoroughly used, but Pastor Kalau was a good friend of the Church on Kosrae. He, or one of his associates, conducted a number of conferences and workshops for pastors, deacons, and Church committee members on Kosrae, and often provided transportation free of charge for Kosraean participants to conferences held on Pohnpei. The PMA Good News Press print shop and bookstore, built on the site of the former Hanlin mission house in Kolonia, Pohnpei, provided Bible study and other church-related materials.

AHA PAEʻAINA MEETS ON KAUAI

The Kosrae Congregational Church was again invited to send observers to a meeting of the Hawaiʻi Conference of the United Church of Christ, in session June 13-19, 1977, in Lihue, Kauaʻi. Leaders of the Church chose Pastor Harrison George, Deacon Kun Nena Sigrah, and WCA president Akiko Nena to represent them. A deep impression was made by the fact that there were men and women also attending as observers representing the Roman Catholic Church and various Protestant denominations unfamiliar to Kosraeans. The Kosraeans had never participated in an ecumenical gathering and they reported feeling not only inspired and gratified, but overwhelmed and bewildered as well. They all agreed, however, that the experience was worthwhile.

BENJAMIN ISAIAH BENJAMIN ORDAINED

Pastor Benjamin Benjamin was ordained as Kosrae's 16th pastor on December 3, 1977. Pastor Benjamin's father, Pastor Isaiah, was 85 years old and confined to his home, so Erafe Tosie had been left as Utwe's only working pastor. Pastor Harrison, presiding officer of the KCCC, was anxious that each of the four villages have two active pastors. Benjamin, a 48-year-old Utwe native and former chief, who had taught in the Utwe Elementary School for many years, was the ideal candidate.

NEW ERA DAWNS

When those responsible for the functioning of the U.S. Trust Territory of the Pacific belatedly realized the value of having a government liaison on Kosrae, this official was always an American, called the District Administrator's Representative, or DistAd Rep. So the exciting new level of Kosrae's independence, initiated in January 1977, was solidly affirmed in November 1978 when Kosraeans went to the polls and, for the first time, elected a governor and lieutenant governor from among themselves. In a dignified ceremony on January 1, 1979—accompanied by understandable pride and great rejoicing—Jacob Nena was sworn in as governor of Kosrae, and Kun Nena Sigrah, as lt. governor. Governor Nena was a lay minister in the Lelu congregation, and secretary of the KCCC, the all-island Church council. First Lady Lerina, actively involved in all aspects of Church life, was a 1962 graduate of KCTS at Wot. Lt. Governor Sigrah was a deacon in the Tafunsak church, where Second Lady Sepe was a deaconess.

So with the inauguration, another shift was taking place—or, more accurately—it was a reversion to accepted practice prior to World War II. The siphoning of young adults from active involvement in the Church because of associations with non-church-oriented American advisors, stopped. Certainly there were Kosraeans in government who remained outside the Church, but as they matured, more and more of those who bore the responsibilities of public office were active participants in the life of their village congregations.

Late in 1979, Kosrae joined with Pohnpei, Chuuk, and Yap to form the Federated States of Micronesia when the FSM constitution was ratified.

AARON SIGRAH AND KUN NENA SIGRAH ORDAINED

On December 6, 1979, the Church on Kosrae ordained two new pastors. Aaron Sigrah, a respected deacon in the Lelu church and long-time principal of the Lelu Elementary School, became Kosrae's 17th ordained pastor. In the same service, Kosrae's lt. governor, Kun Nena Sigrah, became the 18th pastor of the Church on Kosrae.

MALEM CHURCH BUILDING ENLARGED

Members of the Malem congregation were struggling to contain their numbers within the walls of their existing church. From plans drawn by Pastor Harrison, carpenters extended both ends of the building. A new altar area was added to the front of the sanctuary. An enlarged entry area that incorporated the existing, and now reinforced, tower greatly enhanced both the interior and exterior appearance of the building and increased its size. The renovated building was dedicated in late 1980.

INFANT VS. ADULT BAPTISM

About this time Pastor Harrison initiated the most radical of his recommended changes for the Church on Kosrae. Since Benjamin Snow first organized it, individuals became members by stating publicly their acceptance of Jesus Christ as Lord of their lives, promising to live according to his purpose as revealed in New Testament Scriptures. Later, Mr. Snow introduced infant baptism, a central tenet of the Congregational Church in America, of which he was a part. Thus both adult and infant baptism became integral parts of Kosrae's Church.

How Pastor Harrison arrived at his conviction that only adults should be baptized is not clear. In his reading, in discussions with visiting clergymen, in observation of church practices in Hawai'i—or by an entirely different process—Pastor Harrison came to the conclusion that it was scripturally accurate to reserve baptism for those mature enough to understand what they were doing. For children, he suggested a service much like baptism, but without the water, at which time parents could express their thanks to God for their child and promise before God to raise the child in such a way that when the time was right, he or she would personally make the decision for Christian baptism.

As this change was contemplated, considerable discussion and argument took place in the Church council and beyond. To some it was unthinkable, not only that such a basic shift might take place, but that it was even being considered. Others turned to their Bibles, seriously reflecting on what they understood to be the policy and practice of the Early Church. Still others wrote letters to friends and former teachers beyond Kosrae seeking direction and advice.

There are no records available describing the details of the making of this momentous decision—but the decision was made, and Pastor Harrison's recommendation became the new practice of the Kosraean Church.

"MY ISLAND VISION, PAST AND FUTURE"

Flying from Kosrae on April 8, 1981 after a nostalgic, personal visit, Alice Buck sat in the co-pilot seat of the PMA plane and drank in the island's beauty as they circled—it was her first view of Kosrae from the air. Her mind brimming with memories and appreciation, she was inspired to express her thoughts in poetic form:

O Kosrae, you beautiful gem!
    Your emerald green mountains—
    your ferns, trees, and flowers
    nestled in fleecy clouds and azure blue ocean;
    recipient of rains, sunshine, cool breezes—
    all so quiet...yet energy potent!
    Waves splash on your encircling reef—
    a crocheted ruffle to your slip
    showing flirtatiously.
Ancient community of earnest smiles—
    language of vowels
    spoken in warm, soft voices;
    callouses on feet and hands,
    hard-working, devoted people.
    Yes, with squabbling and gossip,
        sickness,
            singing,

searching,
stretching.
Calmly acquiring new ideas, new ways.
Gracious...Serene...Persistent...
Looking to God in humble prayer
with sincere praise
asking for guidance.
Eternity experienced daily!
Divine dimensions in mortal grasp:
Nature—God—Spirit—Life—
MAGNITUDE in miniature
These are in me—HOORAY!
These have molded my life:
My parents' genes and example...
America's cultural mix and educational gifts...
Marshallese wit and expressiveness...
I am a special blend of all these traits.
Share—with abandon,
Receive—with grace and caution,
Delegate—with trust and joy,
Be persistent in seeing the good,
Apply whatever works,
Be equipped, prepared
mentally and physically;
natural—fully human/divine.
WOW![6] ☦

Notes - Chapter 18

1. Shrew Jonas, personal correspondence, Malem, Jan. 29, 1973
2. Kasuo Isisaki and Joshua Phillip, "Mwot Student Summer Camp 1975," unpublished report, translated from Kosraean
3. Akiko Nena, personal conversation, Kosrae, Oct. 4, 2004
4. Pacific Missionary Aviation brochure, P.O. Box 3290, Agana, Guam 96910
5. Harvey Gordon Segal, *Kosrae, the Sleeping Lady Awakens*, Kosrae State Tourist Division, 1995, p. 255
6. Mary Alice Buck, unpublished poem, "My Island Vision, Past and Future," April 1981

NUNAK YOHK KE CHAPTER 19
1981-1992

Pastu Isaiah Benjamin el misa ke August 20, 1981, ac Pastu Joshua Phillip el akmusrala ke December 5. In pacl se inge oasr mwet sropo oalkosr pa kulansupu Church Kosrae—kais luo mwet sropo ke mura kewa—ac pusialos tukeni orekma arulana wo. Tusruktu yok lainyal Pastu Harrison sin kutu sin mwet sropo inge, yokna ke us lal ke Kosrae Congregational Church Council. Mwet sropo ma tia wi KCCC inge pulakin mu tiana akilenyuk elos. Ke sripen Pastu Harrison el tiana srike in oasr aetuilla lalos oru Pastu Kun Sigrah ac Pastu Aaron mokleak in akwuki pac sie council lun pastu sayen pacna KCCC. Ke sripa se inge oru Church Kosrae tuh oan ye kolyuk lun u luo ke lusen pacl se.

Ke December 1982, Takeo Likiaksa ac Alik Palsis akmusrala nu ke mwet sropo—ac ke December 1983, Natchuo Andrew el akmusrala. Ke pacl se inge mutaweak in fwella inmasrlon mwet sropo

Ke August 1984, Alice Buck el tuh us mutan ekasr ma kol mutan ke Church Hawai'i in oru sie tukeni ma elos pangon SHINE nu sin mutan ke Church fin acn Kosrae. Mwet kol ke WCA pa tuh kasru pwapa nu ke forfor se inge. Tuh oasr mutan angaul tuh welulang Alice ac mutan ekasr ma sun acn Kosrae inge fwasreni tukeni muta ke Sharon Inn ke lusen len limekosr ma orek tukeni se inge. Oasr pac mutan 120 sayelos tuh fasr welulos alu, on, ac lutlut kais sie len. Lutlut ma orek inge ma ke oiyen sou Christian, karinginyen mano, sramsram nu sin mwet fusr, orekma lun deaconess, ac ma pac saya. Mutan Kosrae inge tuh arulana pwar ke ma orek inge. Oru elos tuh siyuk in oasr pac sie tukeni ah lalos tok. Alice el tuh akfasrye SHINE workshop se akluo su ma tuh orek pac fin acn Kosrae ke August 1986. El tuh sifil us mutan kol Hawai'i me ac oayapa South Pacific me in tuh akfasrye tukeni se inge.

Ke October 1984, tukeni se ma pangpang "Three-Way Conference" tuh orek fin acn Kosrae. Mwet ma wi tukeni se inge tuku ke alu fin acn Chuuk, Pohnpei, ac Marshall me. Oasr pac selos tuku ke United Church Board for World Ministries (su meet pangpang American Board), ac oayapa kutu ke Hawai'i Conference-United Church of Christ. U tolu inge—sin Micronesia, sin Hawai'i, ac sin United States mainland—tuh aol mwet ma tuh us Wosasu nu fin tuka inge, oayapa mwet ma tuh eis Wosasu fin tuka inge kewa. Tuh oasr mwet 87 orani nukewa delegates ac mwet ma tuku in tuh intoein tukeni se inge. Pastu

Kun Nena Sigrah pah tuh kol tukeni se inge ah. Church akosr fin acn Kosrae pah tuh karingin mwe mongo, acn in muta, ac program in akparyelos. Mwet nukewa ma tuh wi tukeni se inge ah arulana kaksakin mukuikui lun church ekasr ah, ac oayapa pwar lun mwet Kosrae in oru ma kunalos.

Pus mwet kol ke alu Kosrae tuh mutaweak fasri program se ma pangpang "Beyond the Reef" su ma orek fin acn Aurora, Oregon, ke June, July, ac August ke yac ekasr ke 1980. Program se inge ma akfasryeyuk sel Pastu David Bush, ac u se lal inge pah tuh moli forfor lun mwet som nu ke program se inge, muta lalos fin acn Hawai'i ke elos tui we, molin lutlut ac muta lalos fin acn Oregon. Pastu Bush el oayapa ikasla program se lal inge nu sin mwet kol alu fin acn Pohnpei ac Chuuk. Pus liki mwet 30 pah som nu ke program se inge Kosraela, ac pus selos kalkalwen in wi program se inge. Kutu mwet ma som wi inge pulakin mu luti ke Bible ma orek nu selos ah arulana wo ac elos srui la elos ku in wi. Oasr pac selos tiana sisya nunkalos ke program se inge meyen elos akilen mu sie pana luti lal Pastu Bush, yokna ke oiyen alu ma el oru inge. Oasr pac mwet kol ke alu Kosrae tiana insese nu ke kupasr se Church Kosrae orala nu sel Pastu Bush inge.

Ke July 1986, tukeni se oemeet lun Micronesia Council ke United Church of Christ tuh orek Majuro fin acn Marshall. Deacon Jacob Nena pa tuh aol Church Kosrae oemeet nu ke un mwet kol ke MCUCC. Ke November 1986, un mwet kol se inge tuh muta Kosrae in nawu tukeni yok se lun MCUCC ke yac tok ah.

Ke June 1987, Lucius Charley ac Salik Cornelius akmusralla ke Church Malem in mwet sropo ke Church Kosrae. Ke alu se inge, mutan kialos—Lilly Lucius ac Anako Salik—welulos aluiyukla nu ke nipastu. Oiya se inge ma pac akfwasryeyuk sel Pastu Harrison ac pa inge pacl se oemeet mutan kien mwet sropo in welulos akilenyuk in wi tapuk kunokon lun mukul tumalos.

Pastu Harrison el misa ke October 6, 1987, tukun pacl na loeloes el munasla ke mas lal. El yac 56 ke el misa ah. Pastu Aliksru Tolenoa el misa ke August 20, 1988—na oru Lupalik Palsis el akmusrala ke December 5 in aolul.

Ke 1989, mutan kien mwet sropo inge tuh orala u se lalos tukun elos tuh eis ku ke ma elos lutlut ka ke tukeni ma pangpang SHINE, ac oayapa ke elos liye tuh yokelik akilenyalos in akmusralla elos wi mukul tumalos. Elos ac srike in suk inkanek ma elos ac ku in sang kasru mukul tumalos ac oayapa mea elos ac ku in sang kasru WCA su ke pacl se inge oasr ke church kewa fin acn Kosrae.

Pastu Joshua Phillip el misa ke el yac 55 ke November 7, 1990. Walton Palik el akmusralla nu ke mwet sropo ke December ke pana yac sac. Pastu Aaron Sigrah el misa ke May 16, 1991. Ke December ke yac sac Kun Caleb el akmusralla in mwet sropo ke Church se fin acn Walung. In pacl se inge Church Walung, su kupasr na nu ke Church Tafunsak, mutaweak in yokelik ac kui.

In pacl se inge oasr mwet sropo 12 pa kulansupu Church Kosrae: Pastu Erafe, Pastu Takeo, ac Pastu Walton ke Church Lelu (Pastu Alik Isaac el srakna moul, tuh tila kulansap); Pastu Kun Sigrah ac Pastu Alik Palsis ke Church Tafunsak, ac Pastu Kun Caleb ke Church Walung (Pastu Lupalik el luman munasla pac ke pacl se inge); Pastu Lucius Charley ac Pastu Salik Cornelius ke Church Malem; ac Pastu Benjamin ac Pastu Natchuo ke Church Utwe.

– CHAPTER NINETEEN –

MAINTAINING TRADITION AND INTEGRATING THE NEW
1981-1992

DEATH OF PASTOR ISAIAH

After a decade of inactivity due to the infirmities of advancing age, Pastor Isaiah Benjamin died at 88 on August 20, 1981. The oldest son of Benjamin, who was the oldest son of the venerable Pastor Likiaksa, Pastor Isaiah had been a notable link to the earliest days of Kosrae's Church. His family buried him among his forebears at Melok, Utwe. His son, Pastor Benjamin Benjamin—ordained in 1977—carried on in his father's and great-grandfather's footsteps.

ORDINATION OF JOSHUA PHILLIP

On December 5, 1981—during the final new-month meeting of the year in Lelu—Joshua Likiak Phillip was ordained as Kosrae's 19th pastor. He was 46 years old when he joined Harrison George as the second pastor of the Malem church. The congregation was growing, with an increasing number of activities and programs, and was more than ready for him. Conscientious to a fault, Joshua had a concerned and humble demeanor that salved the hurts of many within his village church, as well as those in the wider island Church. He expended considerable effort acting as liaison and peacemaker between his talented but volatile colleague and the other Kosraean pastors, who were often bewildered, and frequently angered, by Pastor Harrison's unilateral decisions.

Pastor Joshua was a graduate of the Kosrae Christian Training School at Wot and the Pastors & Teachers Training School at Ohwa, Pohnpei. He had studied library science at the University of Guam and the East-West Center in Honolulu. In his secular career, he was Kosrae's first public librarian, a position he held for many years.

One of the few young men among his peers who had not taken time out from involvement in the Church, Joshua was an active Christian from his early youth. He taught at Wot from 1960 to 1963 and was superintendent of the island's Sunday Schools from 1966 to 1970 and secretary for the Kosrae Congregational Church Council from 1968 to 1971. In 1971 he was consecrated as one of Malem's deacons. His wife, Deaconess Katherine, was a daughter of Pastor Alik Isaac.

CONFLICT WITHIN THE PASTORS' GROUP

The year 1982 was not a particularly pleasant year in the life of the Church on Kosrae. A situation brought on by poor communication and personality differences among the pastors was thwarting progress among Kosrae's congregations, which were exhibiting signs of growth and eagerness for positive leadership. Individuals among the pastors, recognizing ripe potential in their churches, agonized over the state of affairs. Their frustration, however, seemed only to hobble them further.

Eight men now served Kosrae's four congregations, a number that could hardly have been imagined a decade earlier. The dream of Pastor Harrison that each church have a team of pastors had been attained: Pastors Alik Isaac and Aaron Sigrah were in Lelu; pastors Aliksru Tolenoa and Kun Nena Sigrah served in Tafunsak; pastors Harrison George and Joshua Phillip were in Malem; and pastors Erafe Tosie and Ben Benjamin were serving in Utwe. For the most part, each village team worked congenially, though little effort was made to communicate. It is difficult in Kosraean culture for individuals to speak openly or intimately with others, even within families. There are exceptions, of course, but they are rare.

As 1982 dawned, Harrison George was increasingly at odds with his seven colleagues, primarily over the organization of the KCCC. When it began 11 years earlier, each church was represented in the administrative body by three men: A pastor, a deacon, and a lay minister. The number of pastors was half of what it was 1982, and there were only one or two deacons per congregation. But with more pastors and a greatly increased number of deacons, many Church leaders were feeling excluded from the decision-making process. Overtures by various pastors and deacons, both outside and within the KCCC, were rejected or ignored by Pastor Harrison, who continued as chairman of the 12-member council.

Opposition to Pastor Harrison was led by pastors Aaron Sigrah and Kun Nena Sigrah. For Pastor Aaron it was a matter of traditional respect. He considered himself a father to Harrison and looked askance at what, to him, was an attitude of defiance that could not be tolerated. There was also the underlying matter of a Malem upstart ignoring the wishes of his Lelu superiors. For Pastor Kun Nena Sigrah the problem was one of logic and fairness. The changes and growth of the previous decade had given birth to a new reality. If each pastor was one among equals, then the organization that bound them should be updated. Pastor Kun's experience as a member of the Pohnpei District Legislature and as Kosrae's lt. governor gave him a wider vision and considerable clout.

Consistently rebuffed by Pastor Harrison, Pastor Aaron and Pastor Kun decided to organize a decision-making body that would reflect the majority point of view among the pastors. Thus the Kosrae Pastors' Council came into being, with each of the island's pastors a member. Pastor Harrison was invited to participate, but declined. So began a period of confusion unlike anything the Church on Kosrae had experienced. Two executive bodies were claiming authority over the island churches. Many people were sad and embarrassed and ardently prayed for a resolution that would bring healing to the Church.

It was relatively easy for the churches in Lelu, Tafunsak, and Utwe, where the proceedings of the KCCC were mostly ignored, but for Pastor Joshua, who had decided to take an active part in the new council, it was especially difficult. His decision, of course, drove a wedge between him and Pastor Harrison, who refused to allow Pastor Joshua to share announcements and reports from the Pastors' Council with the Malem congregation.

ORDINATION OF TAKEO LIKIAKSA AND ALIK PALSIS

There was optimism at year's end when two new men took their places on the roster of those who served as pastors. On December 4, 1982, Takeo Likiaksa, age 38, and Alik Palsis, 53, were ordained in Lelu before the gathered church as the 20th and 21th pastors of the Church on Kosrae.

Pastor Takeo was the first of Kosrae's pastors to have completed theological training beyond Micronesia, having graduated from Malua Theological College in Western Samoa and the University of Guam. In spite of his youth, Pastor Takeo was quickly recognized as a serious, wise, and insightful leader within the Pastors' Council and the Lelu congregation. Pastor Alik Isaac, now 75, was semi-retired in his Tenwak home. He and Pastor Aaron were grateful for their industrious new colleague. Pastor Takeo felt that he had arrived at his true calling.

Pastor Alik Palsis, also known as Alik Rupe, was from Tafunsak. Due to a misunderstanding among the leaders of the Tafunsak church in 1979, Alik had moved to Walung, where he was instrumental in energizing that small, isolated outpost of the Tafunsak congregation. Now he returned to his home village to work with Pastor Kun Nena Sigrah and to relieve some of the burden borne by Pastor Aliksru Tolenoa, who was in his 73rd year. The new Pastor Alik was a graduate of the Pastors & Teachers Training School and had been a teacher at KCTS, Wot. His secular career included elementary and high-school teaching, and service on the Land Commission, as a court judge, and as Kosrae's chief magistrate. His extemporaneous quips and comical way with words made him something of a public-speaking phenomenon on Kosrae, where humor in church is not encouraged.

A BETTER YEAR

If 1982 was characterized by discouragement and confusion, 1983 was one of rapid change and exhilaration. In the church, pastors Takeo and Alik Palsis entered positively into the activities of their respective congregations and the fledgling Pastors' Council. The Kosrae government inaugurated a new governor, Yosiwo George, a lay minister in the Malem church; and lt. governor, Moses Mackwelung, son of missionary Jessie Hoppin's adopted daughter, Rose.

DEACONESS ADELYN

Consecrated as a Lelu deaconess in January 1983 at age 32, Adelyn Noda was the youngest woman ever to be so honored.

Adelyn, a daughter of Pastor Ben Benjamin, spent part of her childhood in the Marshall Islands and at Pohnpei because of her father's work assignments. After completing her elementary education in Utwe, she attended Bethania High School in Palau. In 1972 she graduated from the Community College of Micronesia. During her college years on Pohnpei, she assisted Dr. Harold Hanlin in his Bible translation office.

Back on Kosrae, Adelyn taught high school English, eventually becoming head teacher in the English department in 1974. She went on to become a high-school counselor, and a member of the Kosrae Scholarship Board. In the Church, she served as vice chair of the Children's Sunday School Committee. A competent church musician, Adelyn delighted in composing songs for both children and adults.

Adelyn developed into a highly respected community and church leader. Kosraean parents began referring to her as a great role-model for their daughters. She was described by Ethel Simon-McWilliams, program director of the Pacific Center for National Origin & Sex Equity, as "a beautiful woman in all aspects of her life."[1] In her own words, Adelyn's goal was to "lead children to develop spiritually. Spiritual growth is very important at this time of rapid change in Kosrae."[2]

NATCHUO ANDREW ORDAINED

At the December 3 new-month service of the Kosraean Church, 38-year-old Natchuo Andrew, a lay minister in the Utwe congregation, was ordained as Kosrae's 22nd pastor. Deep-thinking and unassuming, Natchuo had been reluctant to accept the new position, but the Utwe church was without pastoral leadership. The Department of Education had transferred Pastor Erafe to Lelu, where he was also needed to assist pastors Takeo Likiaksa and Aaron Sigrah. Pastor Alik Isaac was inactive. Pastor Benjamin—who had lost a wife and then remarried—was living in Pohnpei for a season. Pastor Joshua's prayerful counseling finally assured Natchuo that his response should be affirmative.

Pastor Natchuo was a graduate of KCTS at Wot, Kosrae High School at Yekula, and the College of Micronesia at Pohnpei. He had worked as an elementary school teacher in Utwe and Lelu, and later—for 13 years—served as director of Community Development for Kosrae state.

In a letter to me on Kwajalein, Pastor Joshua wrote, "Last Saturday all Kosraean church members gathered in Lelu to ordain Natchuo Andrew as a pastor. I am especially pleased, as he was a student of mine at Wot in whom I saw great potential. Also, I am grateful and relieved to report that after the service, for the first time in many years, Pastor Aaron and Pastor Harrison sat and talked with each other. I thank God that I was able to see this happen."[3]

INCREASING LEVELS OF ACTIVITY

The rapid change and exhilaration continued into 1984. In conferences, seminars, and other gatherings, Kosraean Christians were having more and more contact with Christians beyond their island. As they traveled and observed, Kosraeans were becoming increasingly aware of the strength of their own Church and the extent of their involvement when compared with others. Realizing this pleased them, boosting their self-image and morale.

In June, Salik Cornelius wrote to me:

I want to describe some of the activities currently going on here at Kosrae. We are very busy. The new church building in Tafunsak is nearing completion. Not only are those in the Tafunsak church working hard on this project, but the Lelu, Malem, and Utwe churches are also heavily involved. The former Young People's Christian Endeavor building in Malem has been torn down to make room for a new two-story building. The Utwe choir is preparing to leave this Friday for their visit to Majuro. The Lelu choir is getting ready for their trip to Nauru the first week in August. The Malok Sokehs choir from Pohnpei is coming here the second week of August, hosted by the Malem church. Ten of us plan to go to Oregon the third week of July: three pastors, two deacons, two lay ministers, two members of the Women's Fellowship, and me. We are happy for the free tickets and the chance to see new places.[4]

SHINE! WORKSHOP

Alice Buck, with Hawai'i UCC colleagues Margery Terpstra, Kiku Kawata, and Kay Connor, had traveled to Majuro, Kosrae, Pohnpei, and Chuuk in July and August 1983, to discuss with leaders of the Women's Christian Fellowships in each area plans for conducting a series of workshops in Micronesia the following year. The Woman's Board of Missions in Hawai'i was looking forward to sponsoring the workshops. The plans had developed out of Alice's longing to give the women of Micronesia the opportunity to enjoy and be enriched by a woman-oriented event—something that had never taken place in those island churches.

In her background paper prepared to solicit funding and interest, Alice had written:

The people who live on the hundreds of tiny islands in the central Pacific known as Micronesia are coming to grips with the need to fashion a life for themselves that incorporates cherished traditional values as well as the new technologies and ideologies from the larger world beyond their reefs.

There is a growing awareness and a deepening concern among the island women about the current realities of materialism, alcoholism, and elitism, which contrast so strikingly with the inner serenity, dignity, and physical stamina that have characterized their people. Most Micronesian societies are matrilineal in the transference of land rights and tribal leadership. The women might be taking a greater role on community councils, in the church, and with the emerging independent governments, if education and motivation could be provided to develop their potential. Then the society as a whole will realize a healthier balance.[5]

At the same time, Alice had written to leaders of women's church groups in Micronesia:

Aloha and warm greetings from your sisters in Hawai'i. As Christian women living in the Pacific, we have many things in common: our history of strong ties through missionaries and mission schools, our commitment to experiencing and sharing God's love as revealed in the Bible, the Spirit which unites us across cultural and language differences, and our desire to know each other better and to learn from each other.

Because of these ties of faith and love, we are moved to make plans for renewed fellowship and service in the present. The executive board of the women's fellowships in Hawai'i has an idea they want to share with you. We hope you will be interested in this idea and will want to work with us to plan workshops, or retreats, or rallies, times that will give us opportunity to worship, study, sing, and play together.

Women in Hawai'i appreciate times of learning, prayer, relaxation, and play—away from home. Sometimes we gather for two or three days at a school or another place where there is a dormitory and a kitchen. We plan a program that will meet the needs we have and give us time and inspiration to grow and to think more clearly about possible solutions to problems we face—or ways we believe God wants us to change. We invite teachers and leaders who can guide us in worship and study. We would like to plan a program similar to this in 1984 for your women. To plan such a program, we feel it is very important for us to hear your ideas as well as tell you our ideas. So please let us know if you think your women will be interested, and if you are willing to work with us on the details.[6]

Leaders of the Women's Christian Association on Kosrae had cordially welcomed Alice and her planning committee in July 1983, and together they planned for Kosrae's SHINE! Workshop. Akiko Nena, as president of the WCA, chaired the local committee that included Matsuko Talley, Arue Cuffle, Irene George, Elmina Shrew, Srue Wilfred, Srue Joash, Kioko Likiaksa, Tulpe Tilfas, Lucy Aliksa, and Hattie Conrad. The Kosrae and Hawai'i planning teams, working as one, chose "Building a Christian Family" (Musai Sie Sou Christian) as the workshop theme. With their sisters at Pohnpei, Chuuk, and in the Marshalls, members of the committee also heartily approved of the English acronym that Alice and her Hawai'i partners had chosen as the umbrella title for the workshops: SHINE = Sincerity, Health, INtelligence, and Enthusiasm.

The Kosrae workshop took place August 6-10, 1984, and was an overwhelming success. Dr. Jean Renshaw, professor of Women's Studies at the University of Hawai'i, who had participated as a resource person, attributed this success to the "thoroughness of the preparation, the complete involvement of the local women in preparation and planning, and the integration of their concerns."[7]

Alice described the Kosrae workshop in her report to the Woman's Board of Missions:

Approximately 40 women packed small suitcases and spent the entire week, day and night, at Sharon Inn, a two-story guest house located beside the large Lelu church. For most, it was their first time "away from home"! Kosrae is only 42 square miles in size, and four of the five villages are now connected by road, so commuting each day was an option most husbands encouraged. Nevertheless, in spite of local custom, some men did see the benefits of their wives experiencing a time of complete refreshment and renewal—a back-to-school atmosphere of early morning exercise, clean-up, and morning group devotions before breakfast—and it was the wives of these men who were the 40 full-time participants. After breakfast each day the 120 others arrived to take part in that day's activities, on through the evening meal—then returned to their families for the night.

As the theme was developed, each woman became more aware of ways she could encourage her family by her own personal example, using positive care rather than negative criticism. The young women were especially eager to take part and showed great ability to organize and express themselves before the group. The older women were pleased with this, and shared responsibility gracefully.[8]

In addition to worship, each morning included two classes: Christian Family Relationships, and Women as Peacemakers in the Community. After lunch and rest, interest groups discussed topics including health issues, the role of deaconess, and community action. In the late afternoon there was recreation and singing and, after dinner, skits, entertainment, and evening worship. An all-day picnic August 10 at Kiel, a small reef island at the mouth of Okat Harbor, concluded the workshop.

Outside resource persons, in addition to Alice, included women leaders of church and community from Hawai'i and Fiji, and Lauren Buck, our 27-year-old daughter, whose enthusiastic song leading and youth-oriented idea sessions were very popular. Local resource persons included Julieta Fausto, Kieko Sigrah, Matlina Gaius, Solome Martin, Arue Cuffel, Antelise George, and Keti William.

Evaluation comments by participants included: "Please let this happen again!" "The government offers summer workshops, and now the Church has done the same. We're thrilled to see the Church involved in providing a relevant and uplifting experience such as this." "We had felt abandoned—orphaned—since the missionaries departed. Now we feel united, loved, and heard!" "The men need this, too!"[9]

Indeed, the men seemed to be a bit jealous of the serious study, the fun, and the fellowship that the women were obviously having in and around Sharon Inn. Even before the event took place, some men among Kosrae's church leaders were skeptical about one particular aspect of the announced workshop schedule. In June, the secretary of the Church council wrote to me, "We are anticipating the arrival of Alice and the women from Hawai'i. However, there is a question that was brought before the KCCC in May which I have been directed to ask you: Is it appropriate for our women to go from their homes and sleep in a place away from their husbands and children for an entire week?"[10]

THREE EQUAL PARTNERS

The historic mission boards that had nurtured the early Congregational Church in Micronesia were searching for new ways of relating to the island churches. At the same time, leaders of the Church in Micronesia were often puzzled about their status with the U.S. churches who had originally sent missionaries among them. Much of the wondering and confusion was the result of enormous changes that had taken place in the American Congregational Church in recent years.

In 1957, when the Congregational Christian Churches in the United States united with the Evangelical and Reformed Church (both of them united Churches), the United Church of Christ came into being. The mission boards of these uniting denominations, including the American Board of

Commissioners for Foreign Missions, were joined as the United Church Board for World Ministries. The Hawaiʻi Conference of the UCC evolved from the Hawaiian Evangelical Association, which had coordinated the first 50 years of the Micronesian Mission in partnership with the American Board. Though the HEA ceased to be officially responsible for missions and missionaries in 1901, it had maintained its historic ties by being friend and advocate to the emerging churches of the Marshalls and Eastern Caroline Islands, and continued to be the funnel through which materials and personnel entered Micronesia.

Gradually, Church leaders in Micronesia, in Hawaiʻi, and in the mainland U.S.A. came to the realization that there was, indeed, a way to maintain their historic ties while affirming their equality as partners in the Church of Jesus Christ. A new arena for communication, discussion and cooperation came into being. It was called the "Three-Way Conference."

THREE-WAY CONFERENCE

The Church on Kosrae hosted the Three-Way Conference October 7-11, 1984. Among the pastors and other church leaders on Kosrae—as well as among their colleagues from sister Micronesian churches and the United States—there was a sense of relief that this meeting was being held at Kosrae. Pastor Harrison had unilaterally pulled the Kosrae Congregational Church out of particiation in these conferences following an earlier meeting at Pohnpei. He, along with others, had been surprised when several resource persons from the Pacific Conference of Churches were seen smoking during breaks between sessions. Pastor Harrison found this unacceptable. Time and common sense mellowed his stance, and now members of the Kosrae Church were welcoming delegates, observers, and resource leaders to the first Three-Way Conference to meet in their midst.

Gathered were representatives of three entities: the Church in Micronesia, the United Church Board for World Ministries, and the Hawaiʻi Conference of the United Church of Christ. This was the fifth of the Three-Way Conferences, begun in 1971 to encourage continuing relationships and to coordinate the work of the Church in Micronesia.

Under the designation "Church in Micronesia" were representatives from the churches of the four areas of eastern Micronesia [excluding Kiribati] that had developed through the efforts of the American Board of Commissioners for Foreign Missions out of Boston and the Hawaiian Evangelical Association. These were the United Church of Christ in the Marshall Islands, the Kosrae Congregational Church, the Pohnpei United Church of Christ, and several groups representing the churches of Chuuk.

There were 87 delegates and official observers at this Three-Way Conference, and pastors Harrison George, Erafe Tosie, and Ben Benjamin were the delegates of Kosrae's Church. Official observers were Pastor Aliksru Tolenoa, Pastor Joshua Phillip, Pastor Takeo Likiaksa, Akira Timothy, Kun Luey, Simeon Sigrah, Ashley Jackson, Yukiwo Tara, Donald Jonah, Milton Timothy, Kun Abraham, and Judah Sigrah. Many guests arrived from Majuro aboard a chartered flight of the Airline of the Marshall Islands. Non-Kosraeans were housed at Lelu's Sharon Inn, and the Sandy Beach Hotel in Tafunsak.

Pastor Kun Nena Sigrah was the presiding officer of the conference. In a report published in *The Friend*, Dr. Teruo Kawata, Hawai'i Conference Minister, commented:

I was impressed with the quality of the leadership. The Chairman of the Conference, the Rev. Kun Sigrah, speaks six languages and translates from any one to the other instantly on his feet. He is a pastor of the Tafunsak Church and Land Commissioner for the State of Kosrae.

We were entertained royally by the four churches of Kosrae. They took turns preparing our meals. Each night we went to a different church for dinner, entertainment and the evening session. The Kosraeans are lavish in their hospitality and music is in their souls. Their churches are vigorous. In the smallest of the churches, in the evening program, there were about 200 children under ten years of age in attendance.[11]

Each of the delegations submitted agenda items for conference deliberation. Four concerns were brought before the conference by the Kosraean delegates: a desire to have a common Bible study calendar or topical resource for Micronesian churches to use for Sunday services and in Christian Endeavor groups; a need for information on dealing with sects; a question of the appropriateness of the Church accepting marriages performed by non-church officials; and a request for continuation of the immensely popular SHINE! Workshops for women.

Dr. Kawata's comments in *The Friend* continued:

The new nations of the Republic of the Marshall Islands and the Federated States of Micronesia are emerging. There is excitement and vision abroad as they seek to give form to their nations and take their places alongside the nations of the world. The Church, which is a major part of the life of the islands, is in a position to help shape the future and to help the people live creatively into this new future. The Church leaders are deeply aware of this opportunity and challenge. The Rev. Jude Samson, president of the United Church of Christ in the Marshall Islands, opened the conference with a homily on the prayer of our Lord "That they may all be one" (John 17:21). And from each of the other island groups came affirmations of that hope.

One of the major actions of the Conference was a vote to move towards the formation of a Council of these churches.[12]

And so the Micronesia Council of the United Church was conceived at Kosrae.

DEATH OF SRUE FRANK SKILLING

The Church on Kosrae lost one of its saints when death came to Srue Frank Skilling November 26, 1984, in Lelu, six weeks beyond her 89th birthday. The daughter of John Mackwelung and Sra Niarlang, Srue was raised by her adopted father, Deacon Alik Kefwas, Kosrae's foremost Bible teacher during the first 50 years of the 20th century. Srue attended the mission school at Wot, where she later worked for many years as a teacher. With her husband Frank, the oldest son of Pastor Fred Skilling, she spent several years as a missionary on Enewetak. Frank Skilling was ordained Kosrae's 10th pastor in 1957, but died just three years later. Instead of retiring, Srue continued her committed service to the church. When asked to be housemother at Ohwa Christian Training School and PTTS on Pohnpei, she accepted. During her last years she devoted her time to the children of Lelu, teaching them songs and telling them Bible stories during their after-school hours.

"BEYOND THE REEF"

The Rev. David Bush first appeared in Micronesia as a missionary-pastor in Nauru where he spent a number of years during the 1970s. Christians there, nurtured by the Church of England, objected to his rigid stance against smoking and drinking, and he was asked to leave. He traveled to Kosrae and was invited to stay at Pisin.

Pastor Bush was intrigued by Kosrae's singular mission-oriented history. He began developing a script for a movie depicting the life and work of Elizabeth and Jane Baldwin—a film that never materialized. Also, he was impressed with the level of devotion among Kosrae's Christians and recognized a conservatism that he felt was missing among Nauru's church members. He invited a pastor, a deacon, and a lay minister to a conference he was conducting in Fiji. Pastor Harrison George, Kephas Charley, and Salik Cornelius went from Malem, their transportation and expenses in Fiji paid by Pastor Bush. Donald Jonah, Thurston Siba, and Singkitchy George also attended, paying their own travel expenses. The Kosraeans enjoyed and appreciated the Fiji conference.

It was in Fiji that David Bush began discussing his plan to create, somewhere in the western United States, a place where Micronesian pastors and other church leaders could gather to study. Independently wealthy, he acquired several acres of farmland near Aurora, Oregon, on which he developed a conference center he called "Beyond the Reef." The buildings and program were reminiscent of an old-fashioned camp meeting.

The summers of three-month study periods began in 1982. All financial needs were taken care of by Pastor Bush: Plane tickets, Hawai'i housing and food while in transit, transportation in Oregon, food and housing at the conference center. There was no tuition. Pastor Bush and a colleague, Dr. Cetchell, were the primary teachers, with others lecturing on occasion. Courses included different Bible studies, and there was worship each morning and evening. This worship was in Pentecostal style, with which the Kosraean participants were uncomfortable. They tolerated it, however, feeling that the theology of their teachers, if not the worship practices, matched their own. They were also convinced when Pastor Bush told them that he had no intention of leading them out of the Congregational church; he said he wanted only to help strengthen the existing church, and them as leaders. His closest Kosraean friends insist that David Bush claimed no denominational affiliation. By 1985 a number of Kosraeans had taken advantage of the free airfare, accepting the opportunity to increase their knowledge of the Bible that study periods in Oregon gave them.[13]

Beyond the Reef offered two expense-free courses for Kosraean, Chuukese, Pohnpeian, Nauruan, and Solomon Island church leaders: A summer conference experience, and a three-summer course offering a certificate upon completion.

Kosraeans who participated in a summer conference at Beyond the Reef were: Palokoa and Mary Lou Charley, Justa Kilafwasru, Atchiro and Agusta Melander, Adelyn Noda, Alik and Joselyn Philip, Hiteo and Lillian Shrew, Palikkun and Sepe Shrew, Arue Cuffel, and Akira and Primrose Timothy.

Participating in the second option, and completing the three-year course to receive their certificates, were: Kun Caleb, Lucius Charley, Salik Cornelius, Nena Kilafwasru, and Joshua Phillip.

Those who participated in the second option, but for various reasons were unable to complete the three-year course, were: Austin Albert, Ben Benjamin, Harold Edmund, Harrison George, Singkitchy George, Nena Likiaklik, Justus Mongkeya, Alik Palsis, Aaron Sigrah, Judah Sigrah, Kun Nena Sigrah, Tulensa Sigrah, Ethan Skilling, Richard Tolenoa, and Erafe Tosie.[14]

During the mid-1980s, Pastor Bush went to Kosrae twice to lead workshops, though he was not welcomed by everyone. Among Kosrae's church leaders, there were those who disapproved of the Bush-Kosraean connection. They talked of problems of ethics and theology, questions concerning the legitimacy of Beyond the Reef, and of Mr. Bush himself, that were never answered to their satisfaction. On September 21, 1984, the Rev. Richard Engstrom, representing the United Church Board in Micronesia, sent a letter to David Bush in which he asked specific questions about Mr. Bush's background and intentions. The letter was never answered. [The Malem congregation sent David Bush an invitation to participate in the Sesquicentennial celebration in August 2002. He responded in the affirmative, but did not attend.]

PROBLEMS RESURFACE AMONG THE PASTORS

The easing of tension within the pastors' group in 1983 proved temporary. By 1986 disagreements among them had again escalated, this time to a level of hostility that caused open concern among other leaders of the Church. These were not arguments of theology, but problems of a very human nature, created by personality differences, the cultural reluctance to communicate, and more than a little hardheadedness. Pastors on the periphery found it practically impossible to intervene, while all the pastors made an effort to present a united front to the community and to Church visitors who arrived on island from time to time. But the disharmony was difficult to hide.

The dispute was, again, primarily between Pastor Harrison on one side and Pastor Kun Nena Sigrah and Pastor Aaron as leaders of the opposing side. They disagreed vehemently on the matter of seniority and on how the decision-making process should be implemented among the pastors. As before, Pastor Joshua was caught in the middle—between his colleagues in the other villages with whom he agreed, and his colleague in Malem with whom he had to work. It was his clear concept of right and wrong, his strong determination to "hold the fort," his deep spiritual commitment, and almost constant prayer, that made it possible for him to continue participating in both camps.[15]

As the months went by, those involved with the KCCC from villages other than Malem stopped participating and gradually the 1971-instituted Kosrae Congregational Church Council ceased to exist. Sadly, this turn of events was exacerbated by Pastor Harrison's deteriorating health due to diabetes. Very slowly, the Pastors' Council—smarting from the turmoil of the previous several years, but enlivened by their renewed determination to be truly one—became the unchallenged voice of authority for the Church on Kosrae.

SHINE! II

Following discussion of requests from Micronesian Church leaders and conscientious evaluation of SHINE! I, the Micronesia Committee of the Hawai'i Conference-UCC recommended that a second series of SHINE! workshops for the Church women of Micronesia be authorized for the summer of 1986. The first series had evoked such an enthusiastic response among the women and Church leaders of the Marshall Islands, Kosrae, Pohnpei, and Chuuk that there was a feeling among church leaders in Hawaiʻi that neglecting to follow through would show a lack of sensitivity to another great opportunity for mutual enrichment, outreach, and growth. Educational opportunities for adults in Micronesia were still meager, if they existed at all. SHINE! I had revealed that the women of Micronesia's Protestant churches were almost desperate to find ways of being more effective in nurturing their families. Women were more eager than ever for opportunities to learn and celebrate together.

At the close of the 1984 workshops, the women had expressed a desire to pursue the following subjects: Bible study, teaching techniques for Sunday School, parenting and family harmony, health and nutrition, youth activities, new songs for both adults and children, and leadership training. The Micronesia Committee asked that two other topics be included: Ways to relate to and encourage the young people of Micronesia who face problems that were unknown to their parents and the need for women to take a more active role on local church councils, as well as to be represented in the Micronesia Council of Churches.[16]

The Micronesia Committee asked Alice to coordinate all phases and plans for this second series of workshops, which she agreed to do. Several agencies that had provided funding for the earlier workshops were committed to other projects, so raising funds proved difficult. But Alice was in her element, and her joy and wholehearted enthusiasm proved contagious. The four individual workshops were designed in meetings with local planning groups on a trip to the islands in 1985. The necessary funds were raised, resource persons from both outside and within Micronesia were signed on, and by the summer of 1986 all was ready.

In mid-August, the women of Kosrae excitedly received the SHINE! II team. Almost all of those who had participated two years earlier were ready and waiting with others they had recruited. The women were thrilled to see Lauren Buck back again with her mother. The oldest among them were especially pleased to see Alice's sister, Ruth Ann Hanlin, now a chiropractic doctor and professional musician; she had been at Wot with her parents as a child. Leaders representing the Pacific Conference of Churches and the Pacific Theological College in Suva, Fiji, were also part of the team. Five days of prayer and inspiration, ideas and insight, laughter and singing, empowerment and blessing, reinvigorated the faith and renewed the hope of Kosrae's women.

MICRONESIA COUNCIL OF THE UCC

In July 1986, the inaugural meeting of the Micronesia Council of the United Church of Christ took place in Uliga United Church of Christ at Majuro in the

Marshall Islands. Member churches elected as the MCUCC's first board of directors the Rev. Jude Samson and the Rev. Pijja Matauto of the Marshall Islands; the Rev. Rufus David of Pohnpei; the Rev. Wie Fiti of Chuuk; and Deacon Jacob Nena of Kosrae.

In November these men gathered at Kosrae to plan the next General Assembly of the MCUCC for the summer of 1987. The Hawai'i Conference-UCC sent me to be laiason with the group. In my report, I wrote:

The meeting, which took place November 13-14, was characterized by warm camaraderie and a rather laid-back, but nonetheless enthusiastic, atmosphere. The business sessions were not rushed. Jacob Nena had prepared an agenda and a carefully planned schedule for the days on Kosrae. I was impressed again by Jude Samson's gift of leadership. Business proceeded in a friendly, no nonsense manner. Each member of the committee participated equally, with obvious pride in the responsibility placed upon each by the election at Majuro. Contributing to the up beat mood was their sense of excitement at being part of an organization of great promise for the future, which also affirmed continuity with a beloved history...

During the final session, committee members had a long and serious discussion of the pressures various infiltrating sects place upon them and their churches—a pressure not really felt by Hawai'i and mainland churches. As in the past, they expressed the desire to have training in what these sects stand for and how to resist the inroads they are making in small island communities. What encouraged me about this particular conversation was their maturity in admitting the need for lessons, not only on the sects, but also on handling rejection, anger, and other feelings and attitudes that often precipitate the movement of people from an established church to a sect.[17]

On Saturday the 15th, the visitors were pleased to participate in Kosrae's celebration of the 27th birthday of their young people's Christian Endeavor.

MEANWHILE, IN GOVERNMENT

Kosrae continued its march toward maturity in 1987 when Yosiwo George and Moses Mackwelung were elected to their second four-year terms as governor and lt. governor. And Kosraeans were rightfully proud when Hirosi Ismael—medical doctor turned politician—became the first Kosraean elected by his peers in the Congress of the Federated States of Micronesia to the position of vice president of the FSM.

...AND IN THE WCA

Kosrae's all-island Women's Christian Association had been active and growing since it was founded in 1975. Now, 12 years later, it was decided that each of the churches would be responsible for its own, separate, WCA. The core of the village groups was made up of women who had been active in the statewide organization: Alwina Aruo, Kenye Florian, Lerina Jacob, Matlina Gaius, Mina Austin, Mikal Joab, Rosa Alokoa, Srue Sisuwo, Tilda Thomas, and Yosimi Idosi in Lelu; Anako Salik, Arue Cuffle, Irene Rolle, Sepe Kilafwasru, and Yamada Harrison in Malem; Kamoa Alik, Sepe Kun Sigrah, Sepe Lupalik, Sra Alokoa, Srue Joash, and Srue Wilfred in Tafunsak; and Connie Natchuo, Kenye Benjamin, Lucy Aliksa, Matlina Alik, Mitchigo Hirosi, and Tulpe Sru in Utwe.

NIPASTU

Members of the Pastors' Council nodded their assent to one more innovation from the idea-filled mind of Pastor Harrison. From now on, when a new pastor was chosen, his wife would be included in the ordination ceremonies, consecrated alongside her husband to the position of "nipastu" [ni, as in "need"-PAS, as in "pass"-tu, as in "tumble"—the title is a derivative of the words for "mother-pastor"]. A pastor's wife had always held a place of honor among the people, but now she would be officially at the top, ranking above deaconess in the female hierarchy of the Church.

ORDINATION OF LUCIUS CHARLEY AND SALIK CORNELIUS

In 1987, aware that he was seriously ill and could no longer perform his pastoral duties, Pastor Harrison chose Lucius Charley and Salik Cornelius to be Kosrae's 23rd and 24th pastors. Lay leaders of the Malem congregation, members of the Pastors' Council, and Pastor Joshua agreed. Though acknowledged as pastors of the Church on Kosrae, the two men—both deacons who had worked for many years in the public school system—were ordained with the understanding that their primary area of responsibility would be the Malem congregation.

Lily Lucius and Anako Salik became the first two Kosraean women consecrated as nipastu when they stood, and then knelt, with their husbands before the altar in the presence of a congregation that packed the Malem church. This solemn ceremony on June 1, 1987, was the first time in the history of the Church on Kosrae that an ordination service was not held in Lelu.

DEATH OF PASTOR HARRISON

Just four months later, on October 6, Pastor Harrison died in the Pohnpei hospital from complications of diabetes. He was 56 years old. His body was returned to Kosrae by plane that afternoon and driven to the Malem church, where most of Kosrae went to pay their respects. The memorial service was held there October 7 at 11 a.m. with pastors Lucius Charley, Salik Cornelius, and Joshua Phillip presiding. Pastors Alik Palsis and Erafe Tosie officiated at the grave. Other pastors present were Aaron Sigrah, Kun Nena Sigrah, and Ben Benjamin.

Pastor Joshua—long over-shadowed by his outspoken colleague—and new pastors Lucius and Salik were on their own.

DEATH OF PASTOR ALIKSRU

Another death within the pastors' group took place August 10, 1988, when Pastor Aliksru Tolenoa died in his Tafunsak home at the age of 73. He had served with great dedication but little fanfare for 27 years, with his faithful and equally devout wife, Sepe, always beside him. There were only three pastors for the entire Church on Kosrae when Aliksru began his official ministry. He, Pastor Alik Isaac, and Pastor Esau took turns traveling to each of the villages and to Wot, mostly by foot or by canoe, to officiate at Sunday services. Pastor Aliksru—with his wide, infectious smile and humble, warm personality—was a favorite of many.

ORDINATION OF LUPALIK PALSIS

At the suggestion of Tafunsak church leaders, the Pastor's Council chose Deacon Lupalik Palsis to fill the position vacated by the death of Pastor Aliksru. He was ordained December 5, 1988. At 73 years of age, he was a peer and life-long colleague of the man he replaced. Pastor Lupalik, the 25th Kosraean to be ordained, also had a "Sepe" by his side. Sepe Lupalik Palsis, a woman of great spiritual insight, had been a deaconess in the Tafunsak church for almost 40 years.

KOSRAE BECOMES PART OF MICRONESIA'S AIRWAY SYSTEM

A dedicatory service to mark the beginning of the Kosrae airport project had been held at the Tafunsak site near Okat December 9, 1983. Work was already in progress. Even before the runway was completed, PMA flights from Pohnpei had begun using it, abandoning the small landing strip that jutted from the middle of the Lelu causeway. Air Marshalls' large propeller plane and Air Nauru's sleek passenger jet also began using the airstrip, though on no regular schedule.

In 1988 Air Micronesia's Continental jets began service to Kosrae, bringing more change—both fantastic and regrettable—than could have been imagined a year earlier. Flights arrived from Guam, Chuuk, and Pohnpei on Mondays, Wednesdays, and Fridays, continuing east. On Tuesdays, Thursdays, and Saturdays the plane came in from Honolulu, Majuro, and Kwajalein, then continued west. From the first, the Kosrae State Legislature made it clear that planes would not be serviced on Sundays, except in emergencies. Planes used the now-completed, paved, and illuminated 5,750 foot airstrip, which had been approved by the Federal Aviation Administration. It was built on tideland between the reef and the fringing mangroves at the northern edge of Okat Harbor. A handsome new terminal was dedicated that same year, and expansive dock facilities at the southwest end of the airfield were nearing completion.

The western approach to the airport brought flights directly over the old Morning Star Harbor at Yela, giving passengers who knew where to look an exquisite view of the historic Wot mission property—though now largely returned to the jungle. And from Wot, the Okat airfield was clearly visible, causing one to wonder what the students and missionaries of yore would think if they could see it now.

CENSUS OF 1988

The number of people on the island in 1988, as counted by the Kosrae Census Bureau, totaled 7,009. The population had more than doubled in 24 years—just one generation!

PASTORS' WIVES ORGANIZE

Empowered by the SHINE! Workshops and emboldened by the decision of the pastors' council to consecrate wives at the time of their husbands' ordinations, Kosrae's nipastu group made the decision "to DO instead of just BE,"[18] as one pastor's wife explained.

Since earliest times, Kosraean wives had accompanied their husbands when the men left the confines of the home village. Even when their husbands went to work in the banana or taro patch, wives ordinarily went along to help and provide companionship—and, perhaps, to be where their husbands could keep an eye on them. As Kosrae entered the post-World War II era, this custom changed for some. Husbands who worked in offices did not take their wives along, and certainly there were wives who attended church without their husbands—but still, it was expected that a pastor's wife, as always, would be with her husband when he was away from home.

When a pastor conducted a service in church or in a parishioner's home, his wife was there participating with him. When the pastors gathered for their quarterly council meeting, their wives were there, too. The women, however, were not present in these council meetings. Following an opening devotional in which they were included, they adjourned to one of the host church's out-buildings to wait for their husbands' meeting to conclude. Actually, these Pastors' Council meetings provided a good opportunity for the wives to be together as a group. Most of them looked forward to sharing family news, discussing church news from their common perspective as pastors' wives, and perhaps gossiping a bit.

Then it dawned on them that they could better use these hours they spent waiting for their pastor-husbands, by organizing themselves to pursue common objectives and to work on fund-raising ideas. In 1989 they formed their own group, elected officers, and began exploring ways to be productive. Interestingly, their first project was collecting money to buy refreshments for their husbands during the Pastors' Council meetings. They also used their group to coordinate the activities of the Women's Christian Associations in each village, for which they were responsible.

From among themselves, they elected officers: Anako Salik, president; Sepe Kun Sigrah, vice president; Mitchigo Hirosi, secretary; Mitchigo Asher, treasurer; and Kioko Takeo, bookkeeper.

HONOLULU KOSRAEANS

After the Compact of Free Association with the United States had been negotiated, Micronesians began slowly to immigrate to the United States—primarily Hawai'i—where they were now allowed to live and work without restriction. As the number of Kosraeans in Honolulu increased, they sought a place to gather for worship. At 4 p.m. on Sunday, January 3, 1982, they held their first service at the Korean Christian Church-UCC on Liliha Street where I was serving as senior pastor. Assisting me in sponsoring the group was Dr. Arthur Sigrah, who was in a graduate program at the University of Hawai'i, and his wife, Kimie. This couple was a great help in getting the group started and maintained. Attendance at services averaged 15 to 20 per Sunday; there were 47 on the rolls.

One of their first major activities was to host the visit to Hawai'i of 40 members of Lelu's Morning Star Choir—William Tosie, President—July 28-August 11, 1983. The group sang at Central Union Church, Korean Christian Church, Kawaiaha'o Church, First Samoan United Church of Christ, and at UCC Conference headquarters for the Woman's Board of Missions.

Officers for 1984 were Ben Jessie, president; Neimi Preston, vice president; Flora Stanton, secretary; Mina Kan, treasurer; Aimina Freddy, Worship Committee chair; and Eleanor Nakamine, song leader.

Members of the Korean Christian Church were hospitable and very generous with this group. They charged nothing for the use of their building, and when the Kosraean group in Honolulu sponsored a reprinting of the Kosraean hymnal, the Korean congregation provided an $8,000 interest-free loan until the books were printed, bought, and distributed.

The group met regularly at the Korean Christian Church until it ran out of steam after about four years, when faithful leaders returned to Kosrae. With my help, several attempts were made to restart it, and we finally saw it happen. On January 1, 1989, Honolulu's Kosraeans again began gathering each Sunday afternoon, this time in the Church of the Crossroads. Isamu Abraham, working toward his Ph.D. at the University of Hawai'i, was the backbone of this resurrected group. He served as president, set up the room, and cleaned up afterward. Floyd and Julia Alokoa were a big help, as were—again—Neimi, Eleanor, and Mina. From 40 to 50 people attended each Sunday.

After I moved to Hilo to become pastor of the First United Protestant Church-UCC in 1990, and members of the group found themselves having to pay a significant amount per week to continue using the Crossroads facility, they moved to Central Union Church where my daughter, the Rev. Lauren Buck Medeiros, was associate pastor. She welcomed and assisted them, and from then on, the group grew by leaps and bounds, often with several hundred people attending on any given Sunday.

[At the time of the Sesquicentennial the group was meeting in Kaumakapili Church, guided by Elwel Taulung, president. The group was soon to move into new facilities provided for them and the Honolulu Marshallese congregation by the Hawai'i Conference Foundation-UCC in the Kukui Building in downtown Honolulu. Christian Endeavor groups were also flourishing for Kosraeans in Kona under the leadership of Siosi Aliksa, and on Maui under the leadership Alik Nena.]

MODERN SCOURGE

During the early years of the Church on Kosrae, sickness and death were everyday occurrences. Illnesses introduced by foreigners took the lives of children, young adults, and the elderly with such frequency that Benjamin Snow was certain the Kosraean race would disappear. During the 1860s and 1870s, there were months when the Church buried more members than were being baptized.

Because there had been so much sickness during those years, by the time the whaling period ended, traditional care-givers had learned the benefits of some forms of hygiene. There was a renewal of the energetic work practices of old, and the people's diet of breadfruit, taro, fish, and fruit was a good one. By 1900, the health of the islanders was much improved and continued to improve well into the middle of the century. None of the students at Yekula and Wot during the 1960s were overweight. Young women, as well as young men, were accustomed to physical labor that kept their bodies toned and slender. Men and women stayed active into old age.

But from across the sea once again, came a distressing malady that began to take its toll. Without much thought, and often with considerable eagerness, large parts of the American diet and life-style were adopted by Kosraeans. Ship containers full of canned foods, cola, and refined sugar were off-loaded at Okat and trucked to the island's numerous little mom-and-pop stores. Next came—of all things—turkey tails, in great abundance! These grease-laden appendages, rejected by American consumers, were savored by almost everyone at Kosrae. Most islanders still planted their farm lands and gathered food from their gardens, but vehicles, outboard motors, weed-whackers, and power saws replaced muscles. Schools no longer had afternoon work programs, and more and more adults sat for much of the day behind their desks in offices. Rampant diabetes was the result of these new tastes and ways—amputation, kidney failure, and death were the consequences. By the 1980s, the Church on Kosrae was again burying too many of its young and middle-aged adults. In 1987, after treatment on Kosrae, in Hawai'i, and at Pohnpei, Harrison George, while still in mid-life, had been the first pastor to succumb to diabetes.

DEATH OF PASTOR JOSHUA

On November 7, 1990—three years after the death of Pastor Harrison—55-year-old Pastor Joshua Phillip lost his own battle with diabetes. With his death, the Malem congregation and the Church on Kosrae lost an ardent and compassionate leader. His body was tenderly transported from his home to the Malem church. There the women in his family sat around his body as a series of church groups entered to pay their respects and sing, while the men prepared the coffin and dug the grave.

ORDINATION OF WALTON PALIK

On December 1, 1990, 52-year-old Deacon Walton Palik was ordained in the Lelu church as Kosrae's 26th pastor. A tireless worker, Pastor Walton brought not only industry, but a humble, dedicated spirit to his role. He also brought with him his song-leading and -writing abilities and his resounding bass voice. Often Pastor Walton—when not presiding at a service—chose to sit with his choir rather than in the front area reserved for pastors and deacons. It became a custom adopted by other pastors who, like all Kosraeans, thoroughly enjoy singing.

DEATH OF PASTOR AARON

Pastor Aaron Sigrah, at age 73, died unexpectedly in his home at Pennem May 16, 1991. Diabetes was partially responsible. His body was taken to the Lelu church, where his family, friends, and parishioners gathered to pay their respects. Two of his seven sons were not on Kosrae. Tadasy, his oldest, was on Saipan, and Leon, the youngest, was stationed in the United States as a member of the U.S. Armed Forces. Though they missed the burial, both of them returned home as quickly as possible to be close to their mother, Ruth, and other family members, and to share in the traditions that were observed during the first several weeks following burial.

Leon Sigrah was not the only Kosraean in military service at this time. During the Gulf War almost 50 young men of the island were serving in the U.S. Army, Navy, or Marine Corps throughout the United States, Europe, and the Middle East.[19]

ORDINATION OF KUN CALEB

For a number of years, Deacon Kun Caleb, a staunch member of the leadership team in the Tafunsak church, had been assigned to assist the small but faithful group of Tafunsak parishioners who—because of the location of their homes and gardens—made up the Walung congregation. They worshiped in a small building at Insief, just west of the former mission school property at Wot.

The Walung coast, as it had come to be known, was accessible only by water from other parts of the island. Walung villagers commuted to and from Tafunsak by boat—some in traditional outrigger canoes, but most using outboard motor boats. Trips were dependent on the tides, though in emergencies it was possible to reach Walung by going beyond the reef through the Okat channel to the small and frequently treacherous Wot channel, then walking across the tidal area to the beach.

On December 17, 1991, the hopes of the isolated congregation were realized when Kun Caleb, age 49, was ordained as Kosrae's 27th pastor and specifically assigned to Walung. Officially, the congregation remained part of the Tafunsak church, and Pastor Kun was considered a member of the Tafunsak ministerial team, but in practice they were on their own—an active congregation and an energetic pastor making new things happen in their detached but vital community.

TWELVE PASTORS SERVING KOSRAE'S CHURCHES

With the ordination of Kun Caleb, 1992 arrived with the number of living Kosraean pastors at 12. Pastors Erafe, Takeo, and Walton served together in the Lelu church. Pastor Alik Isaac, now 84, was retired. Pastors Kun Sigrah and Alik Palsis were at the head of the Tafunsak church with Pastor Kun Caleb in Walung. Pastor Lupalik, at 76, was semi-retired. In Malem, Pastors Lucius and Salik worked together, while in Utwe it was Pastors Benjamin and Natchuo.

WOT PROPERTY RETURNED TO LANDOWNERS

In April 1992, Wot—the historic site of the primary mission school for eastern Micronesia and the place fondly referred to by elderly Christians in both the Gilbert and Marshall islands as "our Jerusalem"—was returned to the original landowning families. It had been 113 years since King Sru IV had taken the land by his powers of eminent domain and given it to Dr. Edmund Pease, who received it on behalf of the American Board as the location for the Micronesia Mission's Christian education center.

After a series of court cases in which Paul Sigrah and Alan Mackwelung also stated their claims to Wot, the court issued a Determination of Ownership on April 18, 1991, and the Certificate of Title on April 23, 1992, giving the property between the Wot River to the north and the Insief community to the south to the heads of three Walung families: Alik (Alikwan) Kefwas, Misima Palik Kefwas, and Stanley Taulung. The property on the north side of the river, called Len Wot, remained in litigation.

For more than four generations, the Church on Kosrae had been overshadowed by the mission school at Wot. The closing of the school and relinquishing of the property were wrenching procedures. There was little arguing—just sadness and disbelief. As time passed, however, the seismic jolt caused by the loss of Wot was dissipated by a growing awareness of all that was developing in the life of the Church. The leaders were capable, and people were responding with approval, a fresh fervor, and a new sense of confidence in themselves. ☧

Notes - Chapter 19

1. Karen Reed Green, editor, "Glimpses into Pacific Lives: Some Outstanding Women," Ethel Simon-McWilliams, program director, Centers for National Origin & Sex Equity - Pacific, Portland, CR, Feb. 1987, p. 52
2. Ibid, p. 53
3. Joshua Phillip, personal correspondence, Dec. 6, 1983, (translated from Kosraean)
4. Salik Cornelius, personal correspondence, June 28, 1984, (translated from Kosraean)
5. Mary Alice Buck, "Report of the SHINE! Workshops in Micronesia, July 10-Aug. 10, 1984," The Woman's Board of Missions of the Pacific Islands, Honolulu, p. 1
6. Ibid, Appendix A, p. 1
7. Jean R. Renshaw, in "Report of the SHINE! Workshops in Micronesia, July 10-Aug. 10, 1984," The Woman's Board of Missions of the Pacific Islands, Honolulu, Appendix G, p. 1
8. M. A. Buck, "Report of the SHINE! Workshops in Micronesia, July 10-August 10, 1984," p. 12
9. Ibid, p. 4
10. Salik Cornelius, personal correspondence, June 28, 1984, (translated from Kosraean)
11. Teruo Kawata, The Friend, Oct. 1984, pp. 2-3
12. Ibid, pp. 3-5
13. Salik Cornelius, personal conversation, Kosrae, Jan. 28, 2003
14. Nena T. Kilafwasru, personal conversation, Kosrae Village Resort, March 5, 2003
15. Joshua Phillip, personal correspondence, Feb. 13, 1986 (translated from Kosraean)
16. M. A. Buck, "Report of the SHINE! Workshops in Micronesia, July 10-Aug. 10, 1984," pp. 17-20
17. Elden Buck, report to the Hawai'i Conference UCC, Nov. 18, 1986
18. Anako Salik, personal conversation, Kosrae, Aug. 1, 2001
19. Harvey Segal, Kosrae, the Sleeping Lady Awakens, Kosrae State Tourist Division, 1995, p. 267

NUNAK YOHK KE CHAPTER 20
1992-2002

Tokin pacl na yohk, mwet sropo Kosrae sramsramkin in nawu koanon Bible Kosrae uh. Elos tuh insesela ke August 27, 1992 mu in tufa oasr naweyen koanon book se inge. Elos akilen la pus mwet fos ku tia na eis kalmen kas inge ke leng ma orek kac inge. Kutu leng inge ma orekla ke yac 140 somla sel Benjamin Snow. Kutu pac leng inge ma tuh orekla sel Mr. Channon yac 90 somla. Elizabeth Baldwin pa tuh orekma safla ke lungasyen Bible se inge ke 1926. Akilenyuk moniyuk lun mwet inge kewa ke lungasyen Bible se inge, tuh pulakinyuk pac lac srakpanu eneneyuk in sifil akwoyeyuk leng inge. Oayape ekla ke kutu kalmen kas inge oru eneneyuk pac in aksasuyeyuk kas in book se inge. Ke sripe inge kewa, mwet sropo Kosrae pulakin mu God El akinsewowoye sulala se lalos inge, meyen finsrak kac uh pa aksasu se inge ma orek in kalem nu sin fil misenge ac nu ke pac fil tok uh.

Nena T. Kilafwasru el tuh akmusrala nu ke mwet sropo ke December 5, 1992. Ke November 24, 1993, Pastor Lupalikk Palsis el misa.

Pus pac ma ekla ke mwet sropo Kosrae ke yac 1994 ac 1995. Asher Palik el akmusrala in sie mwet sropo ke December 6, 1994; ac Pastu Alik Isaac el misa ke July 5, 1995. Pastu Erafe Tosie el tuh masak ac ulla manol ke 1995, oru el tia ku in sifil oru ma kunal. Tokin yac 4 el misa ke August 19, 1999.

Leng ke Bible akfasryeyuk su tuh kolyuk sel Alice Buck ac wi pa kasru lal Dr. Stephen Hre Kio ekin Bible Society consultant. Elos inge pa tuh wi sramteak orekma se inge ah: Pastu Kun Nena Sigrah, Pastu Ben Benjamin, Pastu Salik Cornelius, Pastu Nena Kilafwasru, Judah Sigrah, ac Singkichy George. Buk inge pah elos tuh aksafyela oemeeta—Joshua, Mwet Nununku, ac Ruth—ac buk inge tu orekla ac kitakatelik. Tokin lay minister Judah el misa, Pastu Lucius Charley el tuh aolul nu ke orekma se inge. Apkuran in mwet sropo Kosrae kewa tuh wi committee se ma liye leng ma orek sin mwet leng inge in aksuwosye. Mwet sropo inge tuh pulakin mu ipin pa na lutlut ke Bible pah orekma se elos kuno-kono in oru inge. Elos oayapa pulakin mu tukeni lalos ke orekma se inge oru yokelik aetuila lalos nu sin sie sin sie.

Kais sie mwet pac ke Church Kosrae tuh oru pac kasru na yok lalos nu ke orekma se inge. Dr. Hre Kio el fak la el tufana liye kain akasrui lun mwet ke kain in mukuikui se inge fin acn Kosrae. Ke pacl nukewa Alice Buck el ac tuku nu Kosrae in oru ma kunal, wi kasru lun mwet sropo fin acn Kosrae, mwet ke alu kewa fin acn Kosrae kasrelos in kitelos mwe mongo ac oiya pac saya in akkeye orekma lalos.

Ke yac 1997, Church Lelu tuh srokakunla orekma se in aksralapyelik lohm in alu selos nu ke fit 20 nu ke siska luo ke lohm se inge. Ke akfulat lalos ke safla orekma se inge, tuh oasr sie mwet America su inel pa Thurston Clarke su tuh fak in sie buk ma el simis—el forfor nu ke acn puspis fin fwalu—el akilen acn Kosrae mu inmasrlon acn luo ma kulang oemeet fin falu nufon. El akkalemye pac lac oasr sie mwet fin acn Kosrae fak nu sel mu sripa se oru mwet Kosrae uh in kulang ouinge uh pa meyen elos lulalfongi ke God.

Lyndon Abraham ac Hirosi Ismael elos akmusrala nu ke mwet sropo ke December 5, 1997. Ke January 1, 1999, Arthur George el akmusrala nu ke mwet sropo; ac ke December 3 ke yac sac pana, Arnold Edwin el akmusrala nu ke mwet sropo. Pastu Lyndon el weang in kulansupu Church Lelu, Pastu Hirosi el weang in kulansupu Church Utwe, Pastu Arthur ke Church Malem, ac Pastu Arnold ke Church lun mwet Kosrae fin acn Pohnpei.

Church Malem tu oru musa na yok se ke iwen alu lalos, ac aksafyela ke lusen yac se, su elos tu aluela ke December 23, 1999. Lohm se inge pah yohk ac wo ata oemeet ke lohm alu fin acn Kosrae, ac orekma ke lohm se inge orek ke engan lun mwet in kasru. Lay minister Singkitchy George pah tuh kol planning committee nu ke musa se inge, ac kasreyuk sel lay minister Morgan Jonas.

Mwet pac ke Church Tafunsak kafofo pac in akwoye iwa lalos. Lohm in alu ke Church Walung tu aluiyukla ke August 21, 1998—ac iwen karingin mwet mutata nu ke Church Tafunsak tuh aluiyukla ke August 21, 2000.

Ke yac 1999 nu ke 2000, mwet ke church Lelu tuh nakla inalok se nu Pisin in akyokyelik acn lun church Lelu.

Ekyek ke mwet sropo sifilpa na pulakinyuk ke pacl se inge. Ke March 25, 2000, Pastu Lucius Charley el misa. Ke December 1, 2000, Tolenna Langu el aluiyukla nu ke mwet sropo. Ke December 13, Pastu Arthur George el tuh misa fin acn Guam. Tadasy Sigrah el tu aluiyukla nu ke mwet sropo ke May 1, 2002.

Orekma ke leng Bible tu aksafyeyukla ke August 9, 2002 ac itukyang nu in poun Bible Society fin acn Australia in aksafyela nu ke buk.

Ke August 21, tukin wik luo ke safla orekma se inge, Church Kosrae tuh akfulatye yac aksiofok lumngaul ke tuku lun Wosasu nu Kosrae. Ke sripen orek akfulat se inge in tuh falyang pac nu ke tuku lun mwet nu ke Micronesia Council ke United Church of Christ, oru pukanten mwet tuku nu Kosrae nu ke sripa luo inge. Akfulat orek sin kais sie church fin acn Kosrae ke on, drama, ac mwe mongo. Pus pac mwet sramsram srumun ke tuku lun Wosasu ac kaksakin God ke kolyuk ac akinsewowo Lal oru Church fin acn Kosrae kapkapak ac yokelik.

CHAPTER TWENTY

TRANSLATING, BUILDING, AND CELEBRATING
1992-2002

NEW TRANSLATION OF THE KOSRAEAN BIBLE

On August 27, 1992, the Pastors' Council made the decision to authorize a new translation of the Bible into the Kosraean language. Over the years, many Kosraeans had expressed dissatisfaction with their Bible. The most recently translated sections dated from Elizabeth Baldwin's work, completed in 1926. The four Gospels had been translated by Benjamin Snow in the 1860s and 1870s. Not only had the island's language undergone changes, as all languages do, but many of the terms and much of the wording of the original version were so stilted or so outdated that they were practically incomprehensible. For those who used English, it was much more satisfying to refer to a recent version of the Bible in English. Few thought that a new translation of the Bible into Kosraean was possible.

Two projects had served as catalysts to bring the matter of a new translation before the Pastors' Council. One was the Scrip-Pix project. Beginning in 1988, Alice Buck had worked with Dr. Howard Hatton of the United Bible Societies and several church leaders to produce colorful and easy to read Bible comics for the children and young people of Kosrae. Singkitchy George, Nena T. Kilafwasru, Akiwo Likiaksa, and Pastor Takeo Likiaksa had been translating words to appear in the "bubbles" within the comics. Alice had worked with Kosraeans in Honolulu, and later with several Kosraean students at the University of Hawai'i/Hilo Campus, to do the same. Nine Bible comics in the Kosraean language were completed and distributed: the Old Testament stories of Abraham, Joseph, Moses, David, Elijah, and Jeremiah and the New Testament stories of Jesus, Peter, and Paul. Adults as well as young people and children enjoyed the comics. It was exciting to read familiar stories in up-to-date language. The pastors took note.

A second project played into the picture. Pastor Salik Cornelius was teaching several well-attended Bible classes in Malem. As he delved into the Scriptures, he was surprised at the difficulty he was having as he tried to explain certain passages and Biblical concepts from the Kosraean Bible. At the same time, his right ankle and foot became painfully swollen—a problem doctors had difficulty diagnosing. He found himself sitting at home, unable to walk. To redeem the time, he began translating Genesis from the Today's English Version into Kosraean. He wrote to us, "I have to laugh at my situation. Perhaps through this strange illness, God is giving me the time to concentrate on translating."[1]

Invigorated by his work, Pastor Salik began talking about it with his fellow pastors—especially about the challenge he faced in searching for appropriate Kosraean words to use as he progressed.

In July 1990, Alice escorted Mrs. Consorcia Sanchez, the new executive secretary of the Micronesia Bible Society, on an introductory visit to Kosrae. In their meeting with the pastors, the subject of a new translation was broached and a strong interest was expressed by the Kosraeans. When Dr. Hatton was informed of this interest, he invited the Kosraeans to send two representatives to a translators workshop scheduled for the following year on Guam. From September 30 to October 6, 1991, Pastor Kun Nena Sigrah and Pastor Salik Cornelius, accompanied by Alice, participated in this workshop. Dr. Eugene Nida, preeminent Bible translation scholar, was their teacher.

Responding to a growing eagerness among Kosrae's Church leaders for a new translation of their Bible and wanting to help them proceed, the United Bible Societies appointed Dr. Stephen Hre Kio—a Biblical scholar born in Burma—to be the project's Bible Society consultant and asked Alice to oversee the work as project coordinator. On August 27, 1992, Dr. Hre Kio and Alice were on Kosrae to discuss details of the project with the pastors. That same day, in a meeting conducted by Pastor Alik Palsis, vice president of the Pastors' Council, the pastors of the Kosrae Congregational Church voted to commit themselves to the project.

Lay Minister Judah Sigrah and Pastor Kun Nena Sigrah were assigned as translators. The Old Testament books of Joshua, Judges, and Ruth were chosen to be translated first, as they are straight narrative. Stories are more easily translated than the Bible books of poetry (the Psalms, Song of Songs) or those packed with symbolism (Daniel, Revelation). The two men wrote out their suggested translations by hand in spiral notebooks. These were given to Singkitchy George, who entered the contents into a computer and then printed 12 copies of each. After the five pastors on the review committee had gone over the work, Alice went to Kosrae from our home in Hilo to read through the books with them. Completed, the books of Joshua, Judges, and Ruth were printed in booklet form by the Bible Society and distributed for members of the church to read and then share their impressions with committee members. The Kosrae Bible translation project was off to an encouraging start.

ORDINATION OF NENA T. KILAFWASRU

At the new-month meeting of the gathered Church in Lelu on December 5, 1992, a Malem elementary school teacher turned Department of Education liaison specialist, Nena Tulen Kilafwasru, was ordained Kosrae's 28th pastor. A youthful age 50 and another product of Wot, Pastor Nena brought refreshing exuberance to the pastor team in Malem. As the Tafunsak pastors did, the Malem pastors divided the community into sections, each presided over by one of the three. Families in a given section always knew which pastor would officiate at any funeral, wedding, celebration, or dedication service that took place among them.

DEATH OF PASTOR LUPALIK

On November 24, 1993—five years after his ordination—Pastor Lupalik Palsis died in Tafunsak at age 78. His passing left pastors Kun Nena Sigrah and Alik Palsis with an increased workload, but in emergencies, they could call on Walung Pastor Kun Caleb to assist.

ORDINATION OF ASHER PALIK

Since before the death of Pastor Lupalik, the need for another pastor in Tafunsak had been increasing. Asher Palik Asher, a great-grandson of Pastor Konlulu, was chosen. He was ordained in the Lelu church on December 6, 1994, age 59, as Kosrae's 29th pastor. Involved in health services during his adult life, Pastor Asher had been a hospital administrator on both Pohnpei and Kosrae, and later was appointed director of health services for Kosrae. He had been in the state legislature representing Tafunsak, and had served as its speaker.

Pastor Asher spent part of his childhood at Wot when his parents were assigned to work there with the Hanlin family. He had been a close friend of the Hanlin's son, John. Later, Pastor Asher had been a student at Wot. He studied at the Trust Territory Nursing School in Palau, took courses at the East-West Center in Honolulu, and studied management at the University of Hawai'i. His wife, Mitchigo, is a daughter of Pastor Palik Kefwas.

PASTOR ALIK ISAAC'S DEATH AND
PASTOR ERAFE'S STROKE

Death came quietly to Pastor Alik Isaac in his Tenwak home on July 5, 1995. He was 88 years old. His wife Hannah—born February 15, 1907, a daughter of

Pastor Fred Skilling—died March 19, 2002, at 95. They are buried side by side in the yard of the home they shared throughout the years of their marriage.

A devastating stroke incapacitated Pastor Erafe Tosie in 1995. He retired to his home at Yal, Lelu, to be cared for by his wife, Aklina, and their children. He died four years later, on August 29, 1999, at age 67. Pastor Erafe had been afflicted with epilepsy from his youth. It was a malady he had tried courageously to surmount, but he had found difficult to control in the isolated environment of Kosrae.

BIBLE TRANSLATION PROJECT PRESSES FORWARD

When a question arose among Tafunsak pastors over the extent of Pastor Kun Nena Sigrah's full-time involvement with the translation project, Pastor Ben Benjamin replaced Pastor Kun as one of the two Bible translators. Then, on March 16, 1995, lay minister and Bible translator Judah Sigrah died after a short illness. He had been doing an outstanding job. His work was clear, and he had a good sense of translation principles. It was common among Kosraean translators to follow too closely an English word order, in the mistaken assumption that it was "the correct way." This was a temptation that Judah carefully avoided. In keeping with Bible Society guidelines, he kept his vocabulary and wording within the range used by persons from 20 to 35 years of age—intelligible to those who did not attend church as well as to those who did. He worked hard to keep the text flowing in natural, everyday Kosraean.[2] Also, he was punctual in his correspondence with Alice and in passing on his work to Singkitchy George to be entered into the computer. He was sorely missed. Judah was replaced by Pastor Lucius Charley.

In 1996, when Pastor Ben asked for some time off, Pastor Kun Nena Sigrah—the problem in Tafunsak resolved—began working with Pastor Lucius. That same year, Pastor Kun attended a two-week translators' workshop in Honiara, Solomon Islands, along with Pastor Salik Cornelius. When they returned, Pastor Salik joined the ranks of translators. Pastor Nena Kilafwasru chaired the review committee that met to go over each translator's basic draft. After comments of the review committee were added, this became the committee draft. It was then sent to Alice, who maintained the manuscript at this draft level in her Hilo computer. Alice was now spending from two to five months each year at Kosrae, where the editorial committee met with her in the Lelu Church library—used as the Bible translation office—to produce the final draft. Dr. Hre Kio, in charge of more than 20 other translation projects in Asia and the Pacific, tried to meet with this committee for a week or two each year. When he was not present, Alice kept a detailed list of the committee's questions, which she referred to Dr. Hre Kio.

All of Kosrae's pastors were part of the editorial committee, with three or four scheduled to work with Alice on any given day when she was on Kosrae. With meticulous care, they read through the manuscript, fine-tuning it verse by verse, phrase by phrase. On the table around which they worked were copies of the old Kosraean Bible, the Today's English Version, the New Revised Standard Version, other English translations and versions, and the recent translations of the Marshallese and Pohnpeian Bibles, plus the all-important Bible Society Texts for Translators. The committee consulted each of these. As they worked, Alice entered the final, agreed-upon wording into her computer, stopping at the end of each paragraph to re-read aloud, without interruption, the text they had just completed. Committee members met each new challenge head-on and were pleased with the result of their efforts.

There were several significant side benefits for the editorial committee—and thus for the Church on Kosrae. For detailed, thought-provoking Bible study, there is no more enlightening method than the process of translating biblical texts. The pastors reveled in the education they were receiving. Over and over again, excited comments were made by committee members as they encountered new understanding and insights. Another benefit for the editorial committee was a new sense of camaraderie among themselves—the pastors were truly getting to know each other. They listened carefully to one another's ideas and concerns. Occasionally there was arguing, but they were aware that the resolution of any debate would be for their greater good and that of their parishioners. Often there was laughter as they struggled to bring startling new concepts into the Kosraean language.

CHURCH UNDERGIRDS TRANSLATION EFFORT

Each time members of the editorial committee met with Alice in Lelu, the five congregations were mobilized to take care of their mid-day meals. Usually, pastors and their wives from one of the villages took the first day, then families of deacons, deaconesses, lay ministers, and Christian Endeavor officers took their turns. Another village then swung into action. It was a system that worked beautifully. As many as 120 meals could be served during a specific series of meetings. Dr. Hre Kio commented several times that he had never seen such outstanding cooperation by a total church membership for a translation project in any of the areas he visited.

Sitting and standing around the edge of the room, the smiling host family would step forward to shake hands, place bands of flowers or rolled hand towels on the heads of Alice and committee members, then proceed to uncover the food. Occasionally a host chose to escort the committee to one of the four restaurants in the Lelu-Tofol area, where members of the family would be waiting with extra dishes brought in to augment the establishment's menu.

While members of the committee ate, the hosts sang. (Culturally, eating with your dinner guests shows a lack of respect and is considered impolite— though a shift to the American way is taking place.) Then came the speeches, first from the primary host, or head of the family. One or two other members of the family, including women, would take their turns. Thank you speeches from one, two, or more of the committee members came next. All such speeches followed a prescribed outline, beginning with an acknowledgment of God's presence and an expression of gratitude to God for the privilege of being together. What then followed could be surprisingly original. Sometimes certain memories were evoked; there might even be tears. At other times humorous stories were related, often about someone present.

In addition to the meals, the Church of Kosrae regularly donated money to help pay the expenses of the translation project beyond those budgeted by the Bible Society. These local funds were generously reinforced by gifts from the Kwajalein Chapel's Protestant congregation, Honolulu's Central Union Church, Hilo's First United Protestant Church, the Claremont United Church of Christ in California, and other agencies and individuals. From Kwajalein also came several computers (with experts to advise in their installation and use), air conditioners, and furniture.

PASTOR NENA REPRESENTS THE MCUCC IN TAHITI

Pastor Nena Kilafwasru was sent by the Micronesia Conference of the United Church of Christ to represent the churches of the Marshalls, Pohnpei, Chuuk, and Kosrae at the meeting of the Pacific Conference of Churches in Tahiti, March 3-13, 1997—the first Kosraean to be thus honored. Pastor Nena was serving as secretary of the MCUCC board of directors at the time he was chosen to be a part of this auspicious gathering of church leaders from around the Pacific.

LELU CHURCH SPREADS ITS WINGS

Members of the Lelu church celebrated the completion of an extensive renovation project on December 16, 1997. For months the men had toiled, building "wings" down both sides of their sanctuary, widening it by 20 feet on each side. Windows were relocated to the new outside walls, while large arches were opened in the original walls, joining the new with the old. Cleverly designed and implemented by Deacon Thurston Siba with the help of many, the worship area was not only enlarged, but enhanced.

ONE OF THE TWO FRIENDLIEST ISLANDS IN THE WORLD!

Traveling author Thurston Clarke, who was on Kosrae at the time of the dedication of the enlarged Lelu church, was trying to find and name the world's truly special islands. In his book, *Searching for Crusoe*, he recounts his visits to many islands in locations all over the world—off the coasts of the United States and the British Isles; in the Caribbean, the Mediterranean, and Indonesia; and throughout the Pacific. He selects 18 that, for him, represent a variety of themes—then he writes about each. Intriguingly, out of all the islands in the world, the two he selects as having the friendliest people are in Micronesia—both recipients of the 19th-century missionary efforts of the American Board of Commissioners for Foreign Missions and the Hawaiian Evangelical Association: Abemama in Kiribati [Gilbert Islands] and Kosrae.

ORDINATION OF LYNDON ABRAHAM AND HIROSI ISMAEL

Kosrae's 30th and 31th pastors were ordained in Lelu on December 5, 1997. Pastor Lyndon Percy Abraham, age 49, was assigned to Lelu, and Pastor Hirosi Harold Ismael, age 61, to Utwe.

Pastor Lyndon, a graduate of the University of Guam, had worked for a number of years as the Pohnpei District revenue officer. During his time on Pohnpei, he and his wife, Mesalina, were a faithful part of the leadership of Pohnpei's Kosraean congregation. He came back to Kosrae to accept the position of state finance officer. Later, he worked as the Kosrae branch manager for the Bank of FSM, and also had a term as Kosrae's lt. governor. At the time of his ordination, Pastor Lyndon was the postmaster and a deacon in the Lelu church.

Pastor Hirosi Ismael, a doctor, had studied in medical schools in Palau, Fiji, and New Zealand, and had practiced medicine in the hospitals of Chuuk, Pohnpei, and Kosrae. He retired from the medical profession to go into politics, representing the Pohnpei District and later Kosrae in the Congress of Micronesia. When the Federated States of Micronesia separated from the Marianas, Palau, and the Marshall Islands, Dr. Hirosi was appointed a delegate to the FSM Constitutional Convention. He was elected to the FSM Senate from Kosrae and appointed by his peers in congress to be vice president of the FSM national government. At the time of his ordination, Dr. Hirosi was a special assistant to the governor of Kosrae and a deacon in the Utwe church.

GUAM CHURCH ORGANIZED

Kosraeans living on Guam organized their church on February 25, 1998, under the direction of Deacon Wilton Mackwelung and his wife, Deaconess Daisy Mackwelung. There were approximately 40 members of the church, but many others attended services with them. The Guam Kosraean Christian Endeavor group was begun on October 3, 1988, with less than 20 members. Ten years later, more than 100 were attending, with double that number showing up on special Sundays. They celebrate April 26 (1992) as the birthday of their young people's group and April 27 (1996) as the birthday of the Women's Christian Association.

This Kosraean Church provides an extremely important service as it surrounds the young people who travel from Kosrae each year to study at the University of Guam. For almost all of these youth—some of whom drop out of school but remain to work—it is their first experience away from home, and the culture shock can be considerable. To have the Church there is often a lifesaver.

KOSRAEANS IN SEATTLE

The same year that Kosraeans on Guam organized their church, other Kosraeans were organizing 5,670 miles away in Seattle, Washington. Members of the Seattle Christian Endeavor Society mark their official beginning as June 12, 1998. Led by Clara Alanso Alokoa, Kosraeans who had settled in the area near the Seattle-Tacoma International Airport (SeaTac), had been holding services in homes of group members during the preceding year.

As numbers increased, Clara and Robin Benjamin located a community center they could rent—a building they are still using as their place of worship. The group averages 35 people each Sunday; on special days more than 50 show up. Robin W. Benjamin is president; Frank W. Benjamin, vice president; Jacob Tolman and Charleen Jacob Tolman, co-secretaries; and Sra M. Timothy is treasurer. Clara Alanso and lay minister Richard Tolenoa—both former Wot students—act as sponsors for the group.

DEDICATION OF WALUNG CHURCH

With Pastor Kun Caleb officiating, the Walung congregation dedicated their new church on August 21, 1998—Gospel Day. They had been working hard since their 1996 ground-breaking to find ways to generate money needed for materials, and then to transport those materials by boat the three miles down the lagoon from the Okat dock to their Insief building site. The building was lovingly and eagerly erected by the men of the church, with considerable help from relatives and friends in Tafunsak and the three other villages, many of whom returned on the day of dedication to join the festivities.

ORDINATIONS OF ARTHUR GEORGE AND ARNOLD EDWIN

A Wot mission school student who had graduated as valedictorian of his class, Arthur George worked almost two decades as a mechanic in the machine shops of Kwajalein Missile Range. Upon his return, he became active in his home church in Malem, rising to the position of deacon. On January 1, 1999, he was ordained at age 51, the 32nd pastor of the Kosraean church.

For the first time, the Church on Kosrae ordained a pastor specifically for a congregation on another island. In the Lelu church on December 3, 1999, Arnold Edwin became Kosrae's 33rd ordained leader—to be assigned to the Kosraean church on Pohnpei. Pastor Arnold, age 41, was the son of the long-time Pohnpeian pastor of the Kolonia Kosraean church, Calwin Edwin, and his Kosraean wife, Melina. After a particularly rough period in his youth, Pastor Arnold came under the influence of Pastor Edmund Kalau at Pacific Missionary Aviation. Under the missionary's prayerful guidance, and over a period of months, Arnold committed his life to Christ and made a complete turn-about in his conduct. [The Kosraean word for "conversion"—forla—literally means "to turn around."] He worked for several years as a printer for PMA. Pastor Arnold's wife, Selida, is a sister of Pastor Takeo's wife, Kioko.

The Kosraeans on Pohnpei dedicated their new church building on August 20, 1994. Planning ahead, they constructed the building so that someday in the future they can erect a sanctuary above it, using the current church as their Young People's Christian Endeavor room and fellowship area.

MALEM CHURCH CONSTRUCTION AND DEDICATION

The year 1999 was extremely busy for members of the Malem church and community as they constructed their new church building. After four years of intense fund raising, ground-breaking ceremonies were held on February 27, 1999. The congregation bought land from two neighboring families in order to have room for the building they needed, to be erected on the site of the church they had used since 1956. The purchase of this land involved the relocation of two graves. The congregation held a "goodbye service" in the old building—already encircled by the new building's foundation—on the last Sunday of March 1999. On the first Sunday of April, they began meeting in the young people's Christian Endeavor building, which could not hold the entire congregation. The overflow spilled out into tents placed there for that purpose. The old church was demolished, with the exception of the bell tower, which was renovated and included in the new building. With workers swarming over the site every day of the week but Sunday, the 60- by 130-foot building took only nine months to build.

With its handsome, wide windows; comfortably padded seating; and ceramic tile covering the entire 58- by 88-foot floor space, the sanctuary is unique on Kosrae. Money for materials ($313,856) was donated by members of the congregation; Kosrae's other churches; and individuals from all parts of Kosrae, as well as from Pohnpei, Guam, Hawai'i, and beyond. Most of the labor was done by volunteers.

A carefully prepared, professionally printed, 125-page report was distributed at the completion of the project. It contained a narrative of planning and accomplishment; lists of donors, receipts, and expenditures; copies of letters to and from contractors; floor and elevation designs; and other relevant information. Lay Minister Singkitchy George chaired the overall planning committee; Lay Minister Morgan Jonas served with him as vice chairman.[3]

There were no outstanding bills when the building was officially dedicated on December 23, 1999, with most of Kosrae in attendance. Two days later, believe it or not, the Malem congregation hosted the all-island Christmas celebration in their new church!

MR. SNOW AND THE BUILDING OF CHURCHES

The completion of yet another fine church building on Kosrae, constructed in its entirety by the people, is a reminder of a practice instituted by Benjamin Snow that has often been neglected in other mission areas around the world. The construction of church buildings by the indigenous people from the very inception of the Church among them was heartily encouraged by Kosrae's first missionary. The Kosraeans built their buildings themselves, using materials available to them. As a result, the mission boards never did pay for the erection of church buildings on Kosrae, beyond an occasional gift. Today the Kosraeans take a great deal of well-earned pride in their churches, the handsomest and best-cared-for buildings on the island.

A PARKING LOT AND OTHER PROJECTS
OF THE LELU CHURCH

Sentimental people were outnumbered by the practical-minded during the year 2000, when the tideland between the Langosak church on the western tip of Lelu Island and the historic, mission-related islet of Pisin was filled to create a parking lot for the automobiles of the Lelu church membership. Long neglected, Pisin lost its status as a separate island when Lelu's encircling road was moved from the front of the church to the outer edge of the new parking area. Now, Pisin is "just across the road"! There was grumbling among some of the leaders in other villages who felt that changes that affected Pisin—improvements or otherwise—were matters for the island-wide Church to decide. But the fill became fact and, indeed, serves an important function on Sundays and most evenings of the week. Plumeria trees and coconut palms have been planted, pleasantly delineating the outer edge of the new roadway, which is now paved.

During the same year, the men of the congregation worked Saturdays and most evenings to lay ceramic tile over a large part of the concrete floor fronting the altar. It is an area kept clear of benches because choirs, often boasting as many as 80 to 100 singers, stand there to perform. Tile was also placed down the long, wide aisle to the front door.

At this same time, Alice wrote of another project:

Last Saturday morning I was updating the Kosraean spelling file in the Lelu church library, which we use as our Bible translation office. About 75 men from of the Lelu congregation were laying the cement floor for a new toilet and shower facility. At noon they invited me to share lunch with them.

While I was savoring the soup, the senior pastor was thanking the workers. This was followed by pep talks from leaders of the three groups involved. Then the group that had prepared the meal came forward—about 25 members of the Lelu Young People's Christian Endeavor Society. All smiles in their grimy T-shirts, they sang two rousing songs. Everyone clapped and cheered in appreciation—the entire mood one of happy accomplishment!

I was so impressed that a hot Saturday morning spent mixing and pouring cement for a restroom-shower, was nevertheless an occasion for speeches of thanksgiving and special singing! What an enthusiastic, committed group of people.[4]

TAFUNSAK'S "WAITING HOUSE"

On Gospel Day, August 21, 2000, Tafunsak completed a three-year project under the supervision of Lay Minister Natchuo Mongkeya, the chief carpenter. Called the "Waiting House," it is a long, two-story building that looms above the newly paved road on the lagoon side of their church property. There are large Sunday School rooms upstairs and down, and above an open central court is a spacious room that accommodates church council meetings and choir rehearsals. One purpose of the building is to provide lodging for groups of church guests, a function it fulfills frequently.

Tafunsak's primary church building had been dedicated on Gospel Day 1991, after a decade of effort. Following ground-breaking in 1981, work crept along at a very slow pace, caused—many in Tafunsak readily admit—by haggling among the workers. Each man, it seemed, had a different idea of how to proceed. But it is a fine building, featuring an attractive altar railing and matching furniture of polished indigenous woods; Christmas lights blink through plexiglass from inside the pulpit.

The post-World War II church in Tafunsak, used since 1957, was renovated and rededicated on November 14, 1998, as the Young People's Christian Endeavor building.

TWO DEATHS AND THE ORDINATION OF TOLENNA LANGU

Changes continued to occur in pastoral leadership. On March 25, 2000, Pastor Lucius Charley died in his Malem home, age 81. He had suffered from dementia for several years.

Sixty-year-old Tolenna Langu, long-time Malem elementary school teacher and principal, was ordained as Kosrae's 34th pastor on December 1, 2000. A graduate of Kosrae High School at Yekula, George Washington High School on Guam, and the Community College of Micronesia at Pohnpei, Pastor Tolenna was a deacon when he was chosen pastor.

On December 13, 2000, Pastor Arthur George, age 53, died on Guam following a lengthy illness. Pastor Arthur's death, less than two years after his ordination, was reminiscent of the death of Lupalikkun George Lupalik, Kosrae's first pastor, who died in 1871, just a year and a half after he was ordained. Pastor Arthur's body was returned to Kosrae for burial at Funenea, Malem.

ORDINATION OF TADASY SIGRAH

On May 1, 2002, a retiring member of the Kosrae State Legislature, Tadasy Sigrah, was ordained as the 35th pastor in the 150-year history of the Church on Kosrae. Pastor Tadasy, age 60, is the eldest son of Pastor Aaron Sigrah.

NEW TRANSLATION COMPLETED

With the checking of the last two chapters of Proverbs (30:1—31:31), the editorial committee finished the new translation of the Kosraean Bible. It was 3 p.m. Friday afternoon, August 9, 2002. To mark the occasion, David and Julie Johannes hosted a dinner the next evening at their Island Café for all pastors and their wives, presidents of adult and young people's Christian Endeavor groups and their wives, and Alice and me. The food was plentiful and delicious, and there were many speeches of thanksgiving and joy. Only 10 years had passed since the project was begun—a rare accomplishment for a Bible translation committee, according to Dr. Hre Kio.

Most speeches on the night of August 10th mentioned Alice's consistently reliable work. Pastor Walton expressed himself with great emotion:

The Bible Society chose Mrs. Buck to be the coordinator for the translation project, which is going to benefit all of Kosrae. I have wondered how they found her—the one person who really knows Kosraean—to come and help us with this. God prepared her years ago—brought her to Kosrae when she was young, and she learned our language. Then she went away and worked elsewhere for many years. Now she has returned for this expressed purpose. To me, it is amazing!

Over 100 years ago our present Bible was translated. Many of the words are old and their meanings lost. But the words were appropriate for those days—it was the way our ancestors talked. I consider us extremely fortunate that Mrs. Buck uses Kosraean so well. She is a Kosraean expert! But that isn't all—she has studied and has helped us translate words of deep meaning and substance into our language. She has maintained a careful watch, making sure that we were true to the original languages of the Bible, while remaining true to our own. None of us could have done what she has done. With all my heart, I thank God for Mrs. Buck.[5]

COMPROMISE SPELLING

Though the entire translation was complete, the new Bible remained at least two years from publication. The glossary and cross-references, already begun, had to be finished. But the primary obstacle to publication was the Editorial Committee's decision to change the way the text was spelled, requiring a line-by-line, page-by-page re-spelling of the entire text from Genesis through Revelation.

Though Alice concurred with the decision, it nevertheless meant an additional year and a half of work for her. She tried to explain the situation to Lyn Saunders, her supervisor in the United Bible Societies office in Australia:

Some years ago, the Pacific Asia Language Institute at the University of Hawai'i was given the task of analyzing each of the Micronesian languages and making recommendations for more accurate orthographies. Diacritical marks used in spelling the Kosraean language [an orthography devised by Benjamin Snow] *were eliminated, and additional consonants added to differentiate between various vowel and consonant sounds, resulting in the lengthening of most words. Until recently, there has been strong opposition to this "new spelling." However, it has been taught in the elementary schools of this island for at least 15 years.*

During the 10 years of this project, our editorial committee has been reluctant to make a total shift to the new spelling. We felt that since the majority of adults use the old spelling—including those in government and the Legislature—it made sense to follow that spelling, with adjustments where needed to clarify "minimal-pair," monosyllabic words. I began organizing a Word List containing every word used in our translation, including every prefixed and suffixed form that appears—now 135 double-columned pages. Two years ago, as we again looked over this word list, the pastors recommended that any adjustments we proposed should correspond with the letter sequence of the new spelling. I printed Philippians in this alternate (or compromise) spelling and distributed it to church leaders in each village. The result was that they seemed so thrilled with the new clarity of the verses that they apparently did not notice the change in spelling!

Let me give you some examples: "tu" was formerly used for both "but" [pronounced "tuh"] and "stand" [pronounced "too"]. In our Word List they are now "tuh" and "tu" respectively. The word for "however" has traditionally been spelled "tusruktu"—but the new spelling uses "tuhsruhktuh." Those extra h's are not necessary, as there is no corresponding word where the u's have the "oo" sound. No Kosraean would mispronounce "tusruktu," or wonder what it meant. More absurd are longer words. "Clean" has been "nasnas," and "make-yourselves-clean" uses both a prefix and three suffixes: "aknasnasyekomwosla." The new spelling, dropping one letter, lengthens that to "ahknwacsnwacsyekowoslac"—though the additional letters are not needed for comprehension. The editorial committee has agreed that these long words will remain unchanged, as the new spelling is not needed for comprehension, and the lengthened words increase the volume of text.

It is unfortunate that these decisions could not be made at the beginning, but the intervening years have obviously softened the hard-core supporters of the old spelling, and only time can accomplish that. On the positive side, I sense a new appreciation for their own sound system, which the suggested changes reflect—much better than the system the first missionaries devised. That is GOOD. Initially, it will be awkward for anyone over 35 to read, and that is unfortunate, as it is such a wonderfully fresh translation. But our Statement of Principles clearly requires that the vocabulary be kept as nearly as possible within the range understood and used by persons from 20 to 35. Perhaps the younger generation may more readily claim the new translation as "theirs" when they realize the enormous switch that has been made, and that is good, too.

So—my work is cut out for me![6]

SOME REFLECTIONS OF GRATITUDE

Prior to the celebration of the sesquicentennial a number of individuals within the Kosrae Congregational Church shared feelings and opinions about their Church with me. Here is a sampling:

"The traditional way of doing things in our Church gives meaning to my life—to me."

"I am so grateful for our quiet, peaceful, worshipful Sundays."

"My church gives me many opportunities to serve God."

"I like the repetition in the activities of our Church. They help me feel secure. I am satisfied and at home."

"My church continually reminds me of the meaning of life, and how best to live mine."

"I am very proud of the active involvement of former Wot students in the life of our church."

"To me, God's presence is very real in the worship services and activities of my church."

"I love to sing!"

SOME CHALLENGES

There are criticisms to be heard. The fact that the Kosrae Congregational Church still has no charter, as required by the national government, bothers some individuals. Others are unaware that there is no charter, and many have no concept of what a charter is.

Some of the residents on the far side of Lelu Harbor, opposite Lelu village, complain about the drive to Langosak for services. (It is just over four miles from Sansrik to the Lelu church.) They ask why they can't have a meeting place of their own, closer to their homes—and be in relationship to the Lelu church much the same way the Walung congregation is related to the Tafunsak church. Sansrik was, after all, the location of the second congregation on Kosrae, when Mr. Snow began sending Kutuka and Notwe to conduct services there in 1856.

Many of the Church young people would like to use electric keyboards in their meetings, as they see and and hear visiting Marshallese church youth doing. A majority of church leaders continue to oppose this. Some are uncomfortable with the noise produced by the keyboards, while others point to a weakening of firm vocal sound when surrounded by the relentless electronic voice of the new machines.

There remain challenges of a much more critical nature. Spouse abuse still takes place on Kosrae, sometimes excused as the traditional way of "disciplining" a wife. Though physical abuse it is not as common as it was 40 years ago, it happens. Culturally, it is considered an extremely private matter, and is therefore practically impossible for the Church—or police—to address. Education

for both men and women is still needed—and surprisingly, some of this is coming by way of those who have experienced life in American society. Women,
especially, are beginning to understand that being beaten is not synonymous
with being married.

A problem leaders of the Church on Kosrae do grapple with is divorce. But
discussions lead to frustration as, officially, the Church does not recognize the
possibility. More and more young adults who are married on Kosrae face this
problem when one of them leaves the island and becomes involved with a third
party in another place. What does the spouse who is left behind do? Three
decades ago church leadership held parents responsible for the action of an
adult child who cohabited with someone who was not his or her spouse. Parents
would be disciplined by losing church rank until the matter was resolved in
accordance with rules. Now cohabitation is common, especially among young
people living away from Kosrae, and both parents and Church are hard-pressed
to know what to do.

Suicide, though not unknown in historic times, has reached a frightening
level among the island's young men. Many of Kosrae's citizens are discussing
this problem openly and with great concern. The subject is talked about in high
school, and a governor-appointed commission is wrestling with the issue. There
is also a new urgency among the young people's church groups and choirs to
reach out to all village youth, as it is pointed out that none of those who have
died in this violent manner were members of the Christian Endeavor.

Ministerial education, largely left to the missionaries through the earlier
years, received a positive nod from the Pastors' Council when, in the fall of
2002, four young men were sent to study at the fledgling theological school
at Ohwa, Pohnpei, chosen by their village pastors. George Rosen George was
sent from Lelu, Palsisa Olter from Malem, Sason Palsisa from Utwe, and Arnold
Caleb—the son of Pastor Kun Caleb—from Tafunsak-Walung.

CELEBRATING 150 YEARS OF CHURCH GROWTH

Overflowing with guests from the Marshall Islands, Pohnpei, Chuuk,
Hawai'i, and the mainland United States, the Kosrae Congregational Church
celebrated the 150th anniversary of the arrival of the Gospel August 18 through
22, 2002. The biennial meeting of the Micronesia Council of the United Church
of Christ met in conjunction with the celebration, with Pastor Kun Nena Sigrah,
general secretary of the MCUCC, presiding.

Non-Micronesian dignitaries attending the Sesquicentennial included the
Rev. Dr. Xaoling Zhu, Area Executive for East Asia and Pacific of the Common
Global Ministries Board; the Rev. Karl and Jan Whiteman, Wider Church

Ministries' liaison to Micronesia; the Rev. Lauren Buck Medeiros, the Rev. Fe' Nebres, and Deacon Shiro Timothy, Hawai'i Conference delegates; Milton Yee, Pacific Islander and Asian American Ministries (PAAM) representative; and Aulani Ho'omanawanui and Madeline Igawa representing Honolulu's Kawaiaha'o Church.

After the opening session in Lelu on Sunday morning, for which I was asked by Kosrae's pastors to give the keynote address, the festivities encircled the island with each congregation hosting the MCUCC meeting and Sesquicentennial activities on consecutive days: Utwe, Monday; Malem, Tuesday; Lelu, Wednesday; and Tafunsak-Walung, Thursday. Gospel Day, August 21, is a legal government holiday on Kosrae.

Lauren Buck Medeiros reported in *The Friend*:

We began each morning with a highly formalized roll call, speeches of welcome and greeting, introductions of various dignitaries of church and state, out-of-town guests, and songs—always songs! Sooner or later, there would be a prayer, and we would be invited to eat our breakfast. Breakfast was always a huge feast laid out on 15 feet or more of tables covered with food of all colors and textures and delicacies, fanned by smiling young Kosraean women.

The Micronesia Council of the United Church of Christ, meeting simultaneously with the celebration, took a definite second place to all of the excitement, but we met nevertheless! The four officers led the meetings with the formality and dignity of their years of ministerial leadership, and the delegations from Chuuk, Pohnpei, Kosrae, and the Marshall Islands each sat in their designated places around the tables. I was glad that they had honored the call for a woman delegate from each member island, and all but one had a youth delegate, as well. I say the meetings took second place, because we never seemed to get the business of the MCUCC fully addressed before it was time to adjourn for another feast and an afternoon filled with group after group presenting songs, performing clever skits, telling stories—variations of an old, old story, told in new ways.

The old story was about the arrival of the missionary ship, Caroline. The "new" was the way that story was dramatized by a variety of replicas of the Caroline. One day the Caroline was a hollow, boat-shaped lumber structure surrounding the "passengers" who had to lift and carry it as they "sailed" across the room. The next day, the Caroline was a real double-hulled yacht (donated to the Kosrae Church) sailing majestically into Lelu Harbor, carrying the costumed actors ready to play the parts of Benjamin and Lydia Snow, Daniel and Doreka Opunui, Berita and Deborah Kaaikaula, and the rest of the missionaries and ship's crew. Yet another day, the Caroline was a truck adorned with sheets on the sides to form sails, which drove into the stage area before anyone was ready, to the accompaniment of much laughter and shouts of joy!

How can one ever adequately describe the emotion welling up in the throats of Hawai'i delegates when, day after day, gratitude was expressed to our islands to the North for the great gift of the Good News—news that is lived fully in these islands, an inspiration to us and awakening the realization that the student has become the teacher! The moving story of Opukaha'ia, told to those of us who should know it, the story of Hawai'i and a great king addressing a letter to the chiefs and rulers of the islands beyond, the story of the commitment which enlivened those Hawaiian and American Christians 150 years ago, the litany of island names receiving the love of God in Christ Jesus, and powerful stories of the Kosraean leaders—chiefs and commoners—who were the real missionaries to their people and beyond.

There is no way to adequately describe it, other than to break forth into song: "Praise God from whom all blessings flow!" Oh, to capture a sliver of that joy, an ounce of that enthusiasm, to embrace with humility and pride that rich heritage which is all of ours—neighbors in the Pacific, siblings in the family of FAITH![7]

STILL THE ISLAND OF ANGELS

There are times when it seems the primary activity for Kosraeans is choir practice. Everyone sings, and everyone is a member of two or more choirs: A family choir, a neighborhood choir, or one of a multitude of church-related choirs. There are choir rehearsals at least once a week, and during the weeks before Christmas, Easter, and other significant holidays, there are nightly rehearsals. Three, four, or more choirs are often practicing simultaneously in the various buildings that belong to the churches, easily heard by one another. And it is not just an adult thing. Teenagers flock to choir rehearsals, where they meet and enjoy their peers. Each choir has officers, song writers, directors, those who choose the uniform to be worn when it comes time to perform, a food committee, a money committee and—as all choirs sing a cappella—the person designated to pitch the key.

Kosraeans sing of biblical history and New Testament precepts. They sing of forgiveness and Christ's invitation to discipleship. They sing of the responsibilities and joys of Christian living. They sing of God's unwavering goodness, of God's eternal presence. They sing of the wonder of God's love for them, their reciprocating love for God, and the love they have for one another as sisters and brothers. They sing in church, at home, at the hospital, and in jail. They sing their welcomes and farewells at the dock and the airport. They sing at school functions and government ceremonies, for visiting dignitaries, and at sports events. They sing at feasts and funerals. They go to other villages to sing; they travel by ship and plane to sing on other islands and in other countries. They sing without a book or paper in front of them, with hundreds of songs just waiting to be pulled from their mental files—songs that resonate with the depth and sincerity of their faith.

My minister at the Claremont, California, United Church of Christ, asked and answered a question in a recent sermon that swept me into a deep sense of thanksgiving for the Church on Kosrae. "How can we test the authenticity of faith?" The question was one I have found myself asking as I contemplate the Kosraean Church with its foibles, blind spots, and an isolation-reinforced theology that tends to be unbending. Dr. Henderson's answer to his own question touched my soul: "If it sings, it is authentic! If it sings, it is of God!"[8] By this definition, the Church on Kosrae is gloriously alive.

Yes, there is room for growth. As with all Christians, Kosraeans struggle with life's uncertainties and live through the tragic and the mundane. Yet this Church has emerged over the past 150 years propelled by men and women of profound spiritual dedication, who melded the best of what it means to be Kosraean with the heart of what it means to be Christian. They ARE an island of angels—human angels, with a marvelous, matchless, magnetic, SINGING witness to share with the world. As their voices soar, the authenticity of their faith is confirmed! ♀

Notes - Chapter 20

1. Salik Cornelius to Alice Buck, personal correspondence, June 6, 1990, translated from Kosraean
2. From "Statement of the Principals for the Translation of the Bible into Kosraean" translation committee, 1992
3. Singkitchy George, "Report Ke Loom Alu Malem 1999," Kosrae Printing
4. Alice Buck, unpublished paper, "Human Interest Stories at Kosrae," Oct. 1999
5. Walton Palik, speech, Sang Kumi supper, Lelu, May 29, 2002 (translated from Kosraean)
6. Alice Buck to Lyn Saunders, "Report from Kosrae," June 2, 2002
7. Lauren Buck Medeiros, The Friend, Sept. 2002, p. 2
8. Homer D. "Butch" Henderson, sermon, Claremont United Church of Christ, April 18, 2004

– APPENDIX –

THE KINGS of KOSRAE—1800-1957

1. Tokosra Sa I—circa 1800
   Awane Sa I*
   "Awane Sa The Great"—He was king
   at the turn of the century. It is said that
   a devastating typhoon took place during his
   reign that resulted in extreme hunger. There
   were many deaths from starvation, disease
   and killings.

2. Tokosra Likiak
   Awane Likiak
   The second son of High Chief Sipa, who
   was a son of Awane Sa I.
   Kasra: Mikiak Srusra

3. Tokosra Na
   Awane Na (or Noa)
   Nena, the third son of High Chief Sipa.

4. Tokosra Salik I
   Awane Salik I
   The fourth son of High Chief Sipa. He was
   the elderly, apparently senile king who
   ruled during the visits of the *Coquille* and
   Senyavin in 1824 and 1827.

5. Tokosra Sru I
   Awane Sru I
   The fifth son of High Chief Sipa.

6. Tokosra Sru II—1835-1837
   Awane Sru II
   The oldest son of Sru I. He was a cruel
   king and was deposed by Lupalik I.
   Kasra: Wa

7. Tokosra Lupalik I—1837-September 9, 1854
   Awane Lupalik I
   Known as "Good King George," he was the
   son of Sra Liat, daughter of Sru I and a sis-
   ter of Sru II. His father's name wasKilafwa.
   Kasra: Notwe Sruh

8. Tokosra Sru III—November 13, 1854-
   September 1856
   Awane Sru III
   Sefot—the Kanku, eldest son of Lupalik I.
   Kasra: Srue Nueliki

9. Tokosra Oa—1856-1858
   Awane Oa
   Alokoa—the Sesa. known as a foe of
   Lupalik I. He was a grandson of Awane Sru I.
   Kasra: Kenye Inrakunut

10. Tokosra Lupalik II—1858-1863
    Awane Lupalik II
    Grandson of Nena, Awane Na. He died
    suddenly while defying the church.
    Kasra: 1) Srue Nuwo, 2) Srue Nuweliki,
    3) Sepe Awe, 4) Notwe Sruh, 5) Sra Nuanwan

11. Tokosra Salik II—1863-1874
    Awane Salik II
    The Sipa—considered to be "royal" primarily
    through his wife who was a great-great-
    daughter of Awane Sru I. He was deposed
    by the people.
    Kasra: Sra Nuarar

12. Tokosra Sru IV—1874-1880
    Awane Sru IV
    Tulensa—a younger brother of Lupalik II.
    He was the Sigrah chosen by the church to
    be king, later deposed due to a misunder-
    standing concerning the Wot mission land.
    Kasra: Tulpe Srue "Fititi"

13. Tokosra Sru V—1880-1888
    Awane Sru V
    The Kanku, son of a brother of Lupalik I's
    mother. He abolished sunak.
    Kasra: Srue Intunmen

14. Tokosra Lupalik III—1888-1889
    Awane Lupalik III
    The son of Salik II. He lived for only six
    months after becoming king.
    Kasra: Sepe Insopus

15. Tokosra Sa II—1890-1910
    Awane Sa II
    Tulensa, nicknamed "Charley"—his grand-
    mother and Lupalik I's mother were sisters.
    His father and Awane Oa were brothers He
    had been living in Honolulu since 1863,and
    was brought back to Kosrae to become king.
    Kasra: Srue Nueliki

16. Tokosra Paliknoa—1910-1947
    Awane Paliknoa
    "King John Sigrah," the son of Tulensa
    Sigrah, Awane Sru IV. He was ordained a
    pastor of the Church on Kosrae April 1,
    1947, after which time he was technically
    no longer king. He died on April 19, 1957.
    Kasra: Hattie Harry Skillings

*The old Kosraean title for paramount chief, ruler,
or king was awa. The suffix ne denoted great respect.
Today awane is used to designate those who held the title
tokosra or king during life, but are now deceased.*

KOSRAE'S PASTORS—1869-2004

1. **Lupalikkun "George" Lupalik**
   Birth date: 1842
   Birth place: Posral, Lelu
   Father: Awane Lupalik I, "Good King George"
   Mother: Notwe Sru
   Wife: Kat "Kittie" Otnaur
   Children: none
   Schooling: Benjamin Snow, Lelu & Ebon
   Ordination: 1869, age 27
   Previous church position: First Kosraean Deacon
   Date of death: 1871, age 29
   Location of grave: unknown

2. **Likiaksa**
   Birth date: circa 1842
   Birth place: Utwe
   Father: Frenita
   Mother: unknown
   First wife: Tulpe Pisin
   Children: seven
   Second wife: Kenye
   Schooling: Benjamin Snow, Lelu
   Ordination: Oct. 1871, age 29
   Previous church position: Deacon
   Date of death: June 22, 1905, age 63
   Location of grave: unknown

3. **Konlulu**
   Birth date: unknown
   Birth place: Finnem, Lelu
   Father: Aliksru
   Mother: Nikalulu
   Wife: Kenye Wa Inkoeya
   Children: six
   Schooling: Benjamin Snow, Lelu & Ebon
   Ordination: May 20, 1894
   Previous church position: Deacon
   Date of death: 1903, age unknown
   Location of grave: Finnem, Lelu

4. **Likiaksa Yal**
   Birth date: unknown
   Birth place: Yal, Lelu
   Father: Kilafwa Furi
   Mother: unknown
   Wife: Tulpe Srue, "Handkerchief"
   Children: two stepsons
   Schooling: Wot Mission School
   Ordination: Nov. 18, 1903
   Previous church position: Deacon
   Date of death: Nov. 25, 1925, age unknown
   Location of grave: unknown

5. **Fred Skilling**
   Birth date: July 4, 1874
   Birth place: Utwe
   Father: Harry Skillings
   Father's birth place: Portland, Maine
   Mother: Sitoma "Jenny" Kanapu

   Mother's birth place: Nauru
   First wife: Sepe Intara Sampa
   Children: 11
   Second wife: Sepe Siminlik Sigrah
   Schooling: Wot Mission School
   Ordination: 1921, age 47
   Previous church position: President, Etawi All
   Date of death: Sept. 15, 1945, age 71
   Location of grave: Finpal, Lelu

6. **John Mackwelung Kasrlung**
   Birth date: unknown
   Birth place: Tafunsak
   Father: John Kasrlung
   Mother: Kenye Nikamro
   First wife: Sra Niarlang
   Children: three
   Second wife: Sepe Insopus
   Children: five
   Third wife: Tulpe Insrafofo
   Schooling: Wot Mission School
   Secular occupation: teacher; shark hunter
   Ordination: 1931, by the Church in the Marshalls
       1937, by the Church on Kosrae
   Previous church position: Deacon
   Date of death: April 19, 1957, age unknown
   Location of grave: Inpuspus, Tafunsak

7. **John Sigrah, Awane Paliknoa**
   Birth date: June 3, 1875
   Birth place: Lelu
   Father: Tulensa Sigrah, Awane Sru IV
   Mother: Tulpe Srue, "Fititi"
   Wife: Hattie Harry Skillings
   Children: 12
   Schooling: Wot Mission School
   Secular occupation: Chief Magistrate, king
   Ordination: April 1, 1947, age 72
   Previous church position: Deacon
   Date of death: April 19, 1957, age 81
   Location of grave: Kalung, Lelu

8. **Palik Kefwas**
   Birth date: Aug. 28, 1917
   Birth place: Yurlap, Lelu
   Adoptive father: Alik Kefwas
   Adoptive mother: Kenye Liokas
   Birth father: John Mackwelung Kasrlung
   Birth mother: Sepe Insopus
   Wife: Sarah Kilafwa Salik
   Children: nine
   Schooling: Wot Mission School
   Ordination: April 1, 1947, age 30
   Previous church position: Lay leader; Bible teacher
   Date of death: Dec. 19, 1952, age 35
   Location of grave: Insief, Walung

9. **Alik Isaac**
   Birth date: April 12, 1907
   Birth place: Lelu
   Father: Isaac Andrew Alik Kinsensoa

Mother: Srue Nuerma Kilafwa Wakuk
Wife: Hannah Fred Skilling
Children: seven
Schooling: Wot Mission School
Secular occupation: carpenter
Ordination: July 12, 1954, age 47
Previous church position: President, Etawi All
Date of death: July 5, 1995, age 88
Location of grave: Tenwak, Lelu

10. **Frank Skilling**
Birth date: Jan. 18, 1890
Birth place: Sansrik, Lelu
Father: Fred Skilling
Mother: Sepe Intara Sampa Paliknoa
Wife: Srue John Mackwelung
Children: six (two adopted in)
Schooling: Wot Mission School
Secular occupation: farmer; fisherman; teacher
Ordination: Dec. 2, 1957, age 67
Previous church position: Deacon
Date of death: Dec. 2, 1960, age 70
Location of grave: Sansrik, Lelu

11. **Esau Tilfas**
Birth date: March 9, 1894
Birth place: Utwe
Father: Tilfas Rebuk
Mother: Notwe Inwalpuk
Wife: Kenye Kir Nem
Children: 11
Schooling: Lelu Elementary School, Tara
Secular occupation: cook; farmer
Ordination: Nov. 1, 1961, age 67
Previous church position: Deacon
Date of death: Aug. 3, 1972, age 78
Location of grave: Otnaur, Lelu

12. **Aliksru Tolenoa**
Birth date: March 21, 1909
Birth place: Yeita, Tafunsak
Father: Tolenoa Palikkun
Mother: Tirime Akir
Wife: Sepe Nikisan Mongkeya
Children: nine
Schooling: Japanese Elementary School
Secular occupation: Chief, Tafunsak; Associate
    Trust Territory Judge
Ordination: Nov. 1, 1961, age 52
Previous church position: Lay minister
Date of death: Aug. 10, 1988, age 79
Location of grave: Finfoko, Tafunsak

13. **Isaiah Benjamin**
Birth date: Oct. 24, 1892
Birth place: Melok, Utwe
Father: Benjamin Likiaksa
Mother: Srue Dinah Palokoa
Wife: Notwe John Mackwelung
Children: 10

Schooling: Wot Mission School
Secular occupation: Chief, Utwe (under Japanese)
Ordination: May 1, 1967, age 75
Previous church position: Bible translator with
    Kefwas; missionary, Puluwat
Date of death: Aug. 20, 1981, age 88
Location of grave: Melok, Utwe

14. **Harrison George**
Birth date: May 22, 1931
Birth place: Malem
Father: Nena George Nena Sufafo
Mother: Kenye Niarkas Tulenkun Finkol
Wife: Yamada Simeon Skilling
Children: 10
Schooling: Kosrae Christian Training School,
    Wot; Pastors & Teachers Training School,
    Pohnpei; Maunaolu Bible College, Maui;
    Theological Center, Aurora, Oregon
Secular occupation: Malem Elementary School
    teacher; Chief, Malem; Clerk of Court
Ordination: May 1, 1967, age 36
Previous church position: Lay minister
Date of death: Oct. 6, 1987, age 56
Location of grave: Funenea, Malem

15. **Erafe Tosie**
Birth date: Nov. 25, 1931
Birth place: Tenwak, Lelu
Father: Mares Tosie
Mother: Katrina William Mongeya
Wife: Aklina Tolenoa Nena
Children: eight (three adopted in)
Schooling: Kosrae Christian Training School,
    Wot; Pastors & Teachers Training School,
    Pohnpei; Theological Center, Aurora, Oregon
Secular occupation: Utwe Elementary School
    teacher; Lelu Elementary School teacher
Ordination: Dec. 1970, age 39
Previous church position: Sunday School
    Superintendent, Utwe
Date of death: Aug. 29, 1999, age 67
Location of grave: Yal, Lelu

16. **Benjamin I. Benjamin**
Birth date: Dec. 24, 1929
Birth place: Melok, Utwe
Father: Isaiah Benjamin Likiaksa
Mother: Notwe John Mackwelung
First wife: Srue Tolenoa Nena
Children: 13 (one adopted out, two adopted in)
Second wife: Kenye Palikkun Nena
Children: seven
Schooling: PITTS, Chuuk; PICS, Pohnpei;
    MTEC CCM, Pohnpei
Secular occupation: Utwe Elementary School
    teacher; Chief, Utwe
Ordination: Dec. 3, 1977, age 48
Previous church position: Deacon

17. **Aaron Sigrah**
    Birth date: Feb. 13, 1918
    Birth place: Pennem, Lelu
    Father: Kun Miswan
    Mother: Sepe Siminlik Sigrah, Awane Sru IV
    Wife: Ruth Kilafwakun Basi Siba
    Children: 11
    Schooling: Wot Mission School; PICS, Chuuk
    Secular occupation: Principal, Lelu
        Elementary School
    Ordination: Dec. 6, 1979, age 61
    Previous church position: Deacon
    Date of death: May 16, 1991, age 73
    Location of grave: Sruosr, Lelu

18. **Kun Nena Sigrah**
    Birth date: Dec. 10, 1929
    Birth place: Bennem, Lelu
    Father: Nena Sigrah
    Mother: Sepe Jackson "Kapinta"
    Wife: Sepe Alan John Mackwelung
    Children: six (one adopted out)
    Schooling: PICS, Chuuk; University of Guam;
        East-West Center, University of Hawai'i
    Secular occupation: Tafunsak Elementary
        School teacher; Principal, Tafunsak
        Elementary School; Intermediate school
        teacher, Pohnpei; Vice Principal, Kosrae
        High School, Yekula; Vice Principal, Kosrae
        High School, Tofol; Pohnpei District
        Legislature, Kosrae Representative;
        Lt. Governor, Kosrae; Land
        Commissioner, Kosrae State Government
    Ordination: Dec. 6, 1979, age 50
    Previous church position: Deacon, (17 years,
        Secretary, Etawi All)
    Date of death: Oct. 29, 2002, age 72
    Location of grave: Keokat, Tafunsak

19. **Joshua Phillip**
    Birth date: July 3, 1935
    Birth place: Malem
    Father: Likiak Phillip Kir
    Mother: Sra Aaron Kungis
    Wife: Katherine Alik Isaac
    Children: seven
    Schooling: Kosrae Christian Training School,
        Wot; Pastors & Teachers Training School,
        Pohnpei; Theological Center, Aurora, Oregon
    Secular occupation: Kosrae Librarian
    Ordination: Dec. 5, 1981, age 46
    Previous church position: Deacon
    Date of death: Nov. 7, 1990, age 55
    Location of grave: Pilyuul, Malem

20. **Takeo Likiaksa**
    Birth date: June 23, 1944
    Birth place: Putuk, Lelu
    Father: Sru Likiaksa
    Mother: Sra Abraham Konlulu
    Wife: Kioko Cecilia Gifford Nena

Children: five (one adopted in)
    Schooling: Kosrae High School, Yekula; Malua
        Theological College, Western Samoa;
        University of Guam
    Secular occupation: Chief Librarian, Tofol;
        Principal, Lelu Elementary School
    Ordination: Dec. 4, 1982, age 38
    Previous church position: Lay minister

21. **Alik Palsis**
    Birth date: March 4, 1929
    Birth place: Wiya, Tafunsak
    Father: Tulen Rupe Palsis
    Mother: Srue Jackson "Kapinta"
    Wife: Kamoa Nena Tinteru
    Children: 11 (four adopted in)
    Schooling: Pastors & Teachers Training School,
        Pohnpei; PITTS, Chuuk; Theological Center,
        Aurora, Oregon
    Secular occupation: Tafunsak Elementary
        School teacher, Walung Elementary School
        teacher; Yekela High School teacher; Kosrae
        Land Commission; Judge, Kosrae; Chief
        Magistrate, Kosrae; Legislator, Tafunsak;
        Land Commission, Kosrae State Government
    Ordination: Dec. 4, 1982, age 53
    Previous church position: Deacon

22. **Natchuo Andrew**
    Birth date: April 22, 1945
    Birth place: Saulang, Utwe
    Father: Palikkun Andrew Alik Kinsensoa
    Mother: Tulpe Edmond Tulenkun
    Wife: Connie Joram Kinere
    Children: 11 (one adopted out, two adopted in)
    Schooling: Kosrae Christian Training School,
        Wot; Kosrae High School, Yekula; PICS,
        Pohnpei; College of Micronesia, Pohnpei
    Secular occupation: Utwe Elementary School
        teacher; Lelu Elementary School teacher;
        Director, Community Development
    Ordination: Dec. 3, 1983, age 38
    Previous church position: Lay minister

23. **Lucius Charley**
    Birth date: Sept. 20, 1918
    Birth place: Pilyuul, Malem
    Adoptive father: Nena Charley
    Adoptive mother: Sarah Lupalik Musrasrik
    Birth father: Palokoa Charley
    Birth mother: Kenye Fanny Kunsra
    Wife: Lily Moses Palokoa
    Children: nine
    Schooling: Wot Mission School; Marshall
        Theological College, Majuro; Theological
        Center, Aurora, Oregon
    Secular occupation: Malem Elementary
        School teacher; Clerk of Courts;
        Legislature, Malem
    Ordination: June 1, 1987, age 69
    Previous church position: Deacon

Date of death: March 25, 2000, age 81
Location of grave: Songto, Malem

24. **Salik Cornelius**
Birth date: April 18, 1930
Birth place: Malem
Father: Cornelius Palokoa Losakun
Mother: Kenye Charley
Wife: Anako Robert George
Children: four (three adopted in)
Schooling: PTTS, Chuuk; MTEC, Pohnpei;
CCM, Pohnpei; Theological Center,
Aurora, Oregon
Secular occupation: Utwe Elementary School
teacher; Malem Elementary School teacher;
Lelu Elementary School teacher; Tafunsak
Elementary School teacher; Principal, Utwe
Elementary School; Principal, Malem
Elementary School; Elementary School
Supervisor, Kosrae
Ordination: June 1, 1987, age 57
Previous church position: Deacon

25. **Lupalik Palsis**
Birth date: Aug. 29, 1915
Birth place: Wiya, Tafunsak
Father: Palsis Nena Rupe
Mother: Kenye Insuut
Wife: Sepe Tolenoa
Children: 11
Schooling: Palik Kefwas, teacher
Secular occupation: farmer
Ordination: Dec. 5, 1988, age 73
Previous church position: Deacon
Date of death: Nov. 24, 1993, age 78
Location of grave: Yeiua, Tafunsak

26. **Walton Palik**
Birth date: Aug. 23, 1938
Birth place: Pot, Lelu
Father: Kilafwa Palik George
Mother: Sra "Ule" Kun Miswan Sigrah
Wife: Tokiko Nelson Lakimis
Children: seven
Schooling: Kosrae Christian Training School,
Wot; Kosrae High School, Yekula; PTTS,
Pohnpei; Malua Theological College,
Western Samoa
Secular occupation: Chairman, Lelu Land
Commission
Ordination: Dec. 1, 1990, age 52
Previous church position: Deacon
Date of death: Feb. 16, 2005, age 66
Location of grave: Katemkosra, Lelu

27. **Kun Caleb**
Birth date: Jan. 30, 1942
Birth place: Lelu
Father: Seymour Kilingkun Albert
Adoptive grandfather: Caleb Jackson
Mother: Leah Abraham Konlulu

Wife: Rosa Alik Jonathan
Children: 11 (three adopted in)
Schooling: PICS, Pohnpei; Malmaluan, Rabaul,
New Guinea; Theological Center, Aurora,
Oregon
Secular occupation: elementary school teacher;
Kosrae High School teacher; Kosrae Mental
Health Coordinator
Ordination: Dec. 7, 1991, age 49
Previous church position: Deacon

28. **Nena T. Kilafwasru**
Birth date: Jan. 21, 1942
Birth place: Meoa, Malem
Father: Tulen Kilafwasru Job
Mother: Sra Tolenoa Pani
Wife: Justa Emos Elesha
Children: 10 (one adopted in)
Schooling: Kosrae Christian Training School,
Wot; PICS, Pohnpei; Theological Center,
Aurora, Oregon
Secular occupation: Malem Elementary
School teacher; Department of Education
Liaison Specialist; Kosrae Land Management
Ordination: Dec. 5, 1992, age 50
Previous church position: Lay minister

29. **Asher P. Asher**
Birth date: Dec. 14, 1935
Birth place: Yal, Lelu
Father: Palik Asher Konlulu
Mother: Sepe Fransilia Simuta
Wife: Mitchigo Palik Kefwas
Children: nine (two adopted in)
Schooling: Kosrae Christian Training School,
Wot; Ohwa Christian Training School,
Pohnpei; Trust Territory Nursing School,
Palau; East-West Center, University of
Hawai'i; University of Hawai'i, in Management
Secular occupation: Supervisor of Nursing,
Pohnpei Hospital; Hospital Administrator,
Pohnpei; Hospital Administrator, Kosrae;
Legislator, Tafunsak; Speaker, Kosrae
Legislature; Director of Health Services,
Kosrae
Ordination: Dec. 6, 1994, age 59
Previous church position: Lay minister

30. **Lyndon Abraham**
Birth date: Jan. 3, 1948
Birth place: Finpea, Lelu
Father: Percy Abraham Salik
Mother: Clara Nena Aliksa
Wife: Mesalina Tulensru Kun
Children: five
Schooling: Kosrae High School, Yekula;
University of Guam
Secular occupation: Pohnpei District Revenue
Officer; Kosrae State Finance Officer;
Kosrae Branch Manager, Bank of FSM;
Lt. Governor, Kosrae State;

Postmaster, Kosrae
Ordination: Dec. 5, 1997, age 49
Previous church position: Deacon

31. **Hirosi Harold Ismael**
Birth date: Nov. 30, 1936
Birth place: Pot, Lelu
Father: Ismael Tara Tepukue
Mother: Kenye Liokas Aaron
Wife: Mitchigo Simeon Skilling
Children: six (three adopted in)
Schooling: Ohwa Christian Training School,
    Pohnpei; Trust Territory Nursing School,
    Palau; Fiji School of Medicine; Colonia War
    Memorial Hospital, Fiji; Rotorua Hospital,
    New Zealand; Hamilton Hospital, New
    Zealand
Secular occupation: medical doctor at Chuuk,
    Pohnpei, Kosrae; Congress of Micronesia,
    Pohnpei District; Congress of Micronesia,
    Kosrae; Delegate, Constitutional Convention;
    Senator, Congress of the FSM; Vice President,
    FSM National Government; Special
    Assistant to the Governor, Kosrae; Super-
    intendent, Department of Health, Kosrae
Ordination: Dec. 5, 1997, age 61
Previous church position: Deacon

32. **Arthur George**
Birth date: Feb. 15, 1947
Birth place: Funene, Malem
Father: Roland Stephen George
Mother: Lillian Palokoa Charley
Wife: Estina Tulen Kephas
Children: five
Schooling: Kosrae Christian Training School,
    Wot
Secular occupation: mechanic; computer repair
Ordination: Jan. 1, 1999, age 51
Previous church position: Deacon
Date of death: Dec. 13, 2000, age 53
Location of grave: Funenea, Malem

33. **Arnold Edwin**
Birth date: Dec. 17, 1958
Birth place: Kolonia, Pohnpei
Father: Calwin Gallio Edwin
Mother: Melina Freddy Likiaksa
Wife: Selida Gifford Nena
Children: three (one adopted in)
Schooling: Pohnpei High School
Secular occupation: Micronesia Sales Co.,
    warehouse distributor
Ordination: Dec. 3, 1999, age 41
Previous church position: Deacon

34. **Tolenna Langu**
Birth date: July 10, 1940
Birth place: Pipi, Malem
Father: Jose Langu
Mother: Sra Tulenkun

Wife: Tamiko Clarence Lonno
Children: nine (one adopted out)
Schooling: Kosrae High School, Yekula; George
    Washington High School, Guam; CCM,
    Pohnpei
Secular occupation: Malem Elementary School
    teacher; Principal, Malem Elementary School
Ordination: Dec. 1, 2000, age 60
Previous church position: Deacon

35. **Tadasy Sigrah**
Birth date: Sept. 7, 1942
Birth place: Inkoanong, Lelu
Father: Aaron Sigrah
Mother: Ruth Kilafwakun Basi Siba
Wife: Kunie Norman Fred Skilling
Children: nine
Schooling: Kosrae High School, Yekula;
    CCM, Pohnpei
Secular occupation: general agriculture, Kosrae
    Government; Kosrae High School teacher,
    Yekula; Kosrae High School teacher, Tofol;
    Kosrae Legislature, Lelu
Ordination: May 1, 2002, age 60
Previous church position: Deacon

36. **Palokoa K. Charley**
Birth date: June 3, 1946
Birth place: Yewak, Malem
Father: Kilafwa Palokoa Charley
Mother: Margret Barney Tulenna
wife: Mary Lou Paliksru Sigrah
Children: six
Schooling: Kosrae Christian Training School,
    Wot; College of Guam
Secular occupation: Kosrae Branch Manager,
    FSM Social Security Office; businessman;
    store proprietor
Ordination: Dec. 7, 2002, age 56
Previous church position: Deacon

37. **Tulen Kinere**
Birth date: Oct. 25, 1942
Birth place: Lelu
Father: Stephen Kinere
Mother: Susie Kefwas
Wife: Tulpe Edmond Ned
Children: six
Schooling: George Washington High School,
    Guam; CCM, Pohnpei
Secular occupation: Walung Elementary School
    teacher; Lelu Elementary School teacher;
    Tafunsak Elementary School teacher;
    Principal, Tafunsak Elementary School;
    Department of Education
Ordination: Dec. 7, 2002, age 60
Previous church position: Deacon

38. **Edmond Salik**
Birth date: May 23, 1965
Birth place: Lelu

Father: Horace Salik
Mother: Sepe Joseph Skilling
Wife: Luilina Aliksru
Children: six
Schooling: Kosrae High School, Tofol;
    CCM, Pohnpei
Secular occupation: Captain, Kosrae Police
    Department
Ordination: Aug. 21, 2003, age 38
Previous church position: Deacon

39. **Willer W. Benjamin**
Birth date: Oct. 12, 1948
Birth place: Utwe
Father: Wilmer Isaiah Benjamin
Mother: Sra Nena Waguk
Wife: Sepe Joken Olter
Children: nine (one adopted out)
Schooling: Kosrae High School, Yekula;
    University of Guam
Secular occupation: Student Services
    Coordinator, College of Micronesia
Ordination: Dec. 1, 2003, age 55
Previous church position: Deacon

40. **Murtanel Tolenna**
Birth date: Dec. 3, 1953
Birth place: Malem
Father: Linter Tolenna
Mother: Srue Edmond Salik
Wife: Elsiner Lipan Kephas
Children: six (one adopted out)
Schooling: Kosrae High School, Yekula;
    MOC (Palau Community College)
Secular occupation: Livestock Administrator,
    Dept. of Agriculture; Acting Director,
    Dept. of Agriculture
Ordination: Aug. 21, 2004, age 50
Previous church position: Deacon

41. **Shiro M. Timothy**
Birth date: June 25, 1938
Birth place: Intea, Malem
Father: Milton Timothy
Mother: Pursis Cornelius Palokoa
Wife: Kensy Semeon Aaron
Children: seven (one adopted in)
Schooling: Kosrae Christian Training School,
    Wot; PICS, Pohnpei; Silliman University,
    Philippine Islands; University of Guam
Secular occupation: Elementary teacher Tafunsak,
    Utwe, Malem; Principal, Malem Elementary
    School; Malem Municipal Council
Ordination: Dec. 4, 2004, age 66
Previous church position: Deacon

42. **Siosi Aliksa**
Birth date: Dec. 3, 1941
Birth place: Katem, Lelu
Father: Aliksa Kanku
Mother: Flora John Paliknoa Sigrah

Wife: Diana Musrasrik Tinteru
Children: four (three adopted in)
Schooling: Kosrae Christian Training School, Wot
Secular occupation: Teacher, Kosrae Christian
    Training School; Hospital Corpsman,
    Kwajalein Missile Range; Kosrae Police
    Department; Hotel maintenance, Kailua-
    Kona, Hawai'i
Ordination: Dec. 4, 2004, age 62
Previous church position: Deacon

KOSRAE'S RESIDENT MISSIONARIES— 1852-1970

sponsored by
The American Board of Commissioners
*   for Foreign Missions/Congregational*
The United Church Board For World Ministries
The Hawaiian Evangelical Association
The Nan'yo Dendo Dan, Japan

Alphabetical listing of missionaries:

Abell, Annie Elizabeth—1894-1901 [#27]
Baldwin, Elizabeth—1911-1939 [#33]
Baldwin, Jane DuBois—1911-1941 [#34]
Buck, Elden Myrle—1959-1962 [#46]
Buck, Mary Alice Hanlin—1953-1955, 1959-1962
    [#45]
Cathcart, Lillian "Lillie" S.—1881-1887 [#13]
Channon, Irving Monroe—1890-1905 [#23]
Channon, Mary "May" Long Goldsbury—1890-
    1905 [#24]
Crosby, Ella Theodora Bliss—1886-1891, 1894-
    1896 [#17]
Dederer, Anna—1964-1970 [#47]
Forbes, Rachel Crawford—1889-1894 [#21]
Foss, Ida Creesey—1889-1892, 1894-1896 [#22]
Hanlin, Harold Francis—1948-1950 [#42]
Hanlin, Mary Ruth Martin—1948-1950, 1954-1955
    [#43]
Hemmingway, Lydia Esther Morehouse—1886-1887
    [#18]
Hoppin, Jessie Rebecca—1890-1912, 1913-1939
    [#25]
Kane, Emma—1897-1899 [#30]
Kanoa, J. W.—1855-1857, 1866-1867 [#7]
Kanoa, Kaholo—1855-1857, 1866-1867 [#8]
Lanktree, Lucy B.—1952-1954 [#44]
Little, Alice Cowles—1888-1893 [#20]
Lockwood, Eleanor "Nora" Illian—1928-1932 [#36]
Lockwood, George Carl—1928-1932 [#35]
McCall, Clarence F.—1936-1940 [#37]
McCall, Cora Campbell—1936-1940 [#38]
Olin, Jenny—1897-1911 [#31]
Opunui, Daniel—1852-1853 [#3]
Opunui, Doreka Kahoolua—1852-1860 [#4]
Palmer, Annette "Nettie"—1884-1886, 1889-1898
    [#16]
Pease, Edmund Morris—1878-1894, 1895-1897 [#9]

Pease, Harriet Almira Sturtevant—1878-1894 [#10]
Pierson, George—1855-1857 [#5]
Pierson, Nancy Shaw—1855-1857 [#6]
Rife, Clinton Francis—1894-1907 [#28]
Rife, Isadore Rote—1894-1906 [#29]
Smith, Sarah "Sadie" Louise Garland—1886-1891,
    1895-1896 [#19]
Snow, Benjamin Galen—1852-1862 (1862-1877)
    [#1]
Snow, Lydia Vose Buck—1852-1862 (1862-1877),
    1881-1882 [#2]
Suzuki, Ren—1940-1942 [#41]
Walkup, Alfred Christopher—1882-1889 [#14]
Walkup, Margaret Lavinia Barr—1882-1888 [#15]
Wells, Marion Parker Woodward—1909-1911 [#32]
Whitney, Joel Fisk—1879-1881 [#11]
Whitney, Louisa Maretta Bailey—1879-1881 [#12]
Wilson, Eleanor—1936-1941 [#39]
Wilson, Louise Eliza—1893-1909 [#26]
Yamada, Miss—1937-1939, 1941-1943 [#40]

Chronological listing of missionaries:

1. **Benjamin Galen Snow**—1852-1862,
    located at Pisin; 1862-1877 annually from Ebon.
    Born October 4, 1817, Brewer, Maine; son of
    Benjamin & Nancy Burrell Snow; Bowdoin
    College, Bangor Theological Seminary; married
    Lydia Vose Buck, September 1, 1851; ordained
    September 25, 1851, Brewer, Maine; sailed for
    Micronesia in November, 1851; arrived Kosrae
    August 21, 1852, age 34; transferred to Ebon,
    Marshall Islands, August 25, 1862; departed
    Micronesia October 31, 1877; died May 1, 1880,
    Robbinston, Maine, age 62; two children:
    Caroline, born Kosrae December 22, 1856;
    Fredrick Galen, born Kosrae March 9, 1858

2. **Lydia Vose Buck Snow**—1852-1862, Pisin;
    1881-1882, Marshallese school, Wot.
    Born October 26, 1820, Robbinston, Maine;
    daughter of Ebenezer & Mehitable Vose Buck;
    married Benjamin Galen Snow, September 1, 1851;
    sailed for Micronesia in November 1851; arrived
    Kosrae August 21, 1852, age 31; transferred to
    Ebon, Marshall Islands, August 25, 1862;
    departed Micronesia with her husband October
    31, 1877; returned to Kosrae September 24, 1881;
    departed Kosrae November 1, 1882; died in
    Maine, 1887, age 67; two children (see above)

3. **Daniel Opunui**—1852-1853, Pisin;
    native Hawaiian; Lahainaluna Seminary; married
    Doreka Kahoolua; arrived Kosrae August 21,
    1852; died Kosrae August 4, 1853, buried at
    Yenyen; one son: Galen, born Kosrae, 1853

4. **Doreka Kahoolua Opunui**—1852-1860, Pisin;
    native Hawaiian; married Daniel Opunui;
    arrived Kosrae August 21, 1852; departed
    Kosrae 1860; one son (see above)

5. **George Pierson**—1855-1857, Pisin;
    married Nancy Shaw; arrived Kosrae October
    6, 1855; departed; Kosrae November 3, 1857;
    died 1895; one daughter: Salome, born Kosrae
    August 31, 1856

6. **Nancy Shaw Pierson**—1855-1857, Pisin;
    married George Pierson; arrived Kosrae
    October 6, 1855; departed Kosrae November 3,
    1857; died 1892; one daughter (see above)

7. **J. W. Kanoa**—1855-1857, 1866-1867, Pisin;
    native Hawaiian; born 1823 Puna, Hawai'i;
    married Kaholo; arrived Kosrae October 6,
    1855, age 32; departed Kosrae November 3,
    1857; returned to Kosrae 1866, age 43; departed
    Kosrae 1867; married Mary [Gilbertese] after
    Kaholo's death; died June 30, 1896 Butaritari,
    Kiribati, age 73; eleven children, six lived to
    adulthood: Seoti; Emma, born Kosrae January
    8, 1857; Samuel; Rose; Harriet; Terekoma

8. **Kaholo Kanoa**—1855-1857, 1866-1867, Pisin;
    native Hawaiian; married J. W. Kanoa; arrived
    Kosrae October 6, 1855; departed Kosrae
    November 3, 1857; returned to Kosrae 1866;
    departed Kosrae 1867; died May 1875 in
    Butaritari, Kiribati; eleven children (see above)

9. **Edmund Morris Pease**—1878-1894,
    1895-1897, located at Marshallese school, Wot;
    Born December 6, 1828, Granby, Massachusetts;
    son of Asa & Abigail Smith Pease; Amherst
    College; Union Seminary NYC; Columbia
    University; College of Physicians & Surgeons
    NYC; U.S. Army doctor for four years; physician
    in New York City & Springfield, Massachusetts;
    married Harriet Almira Sturtevant, April 25,
    1877, Bordentown, New Jersey; arrived Kosrae
    October 12, 1878, age 50; departed Kosrae
    March, 1894 (returned for one year, 1895-1897);
    continued work on Marshallese Bible transla-
    tion in Claremont, California; died November
    28, 1906, Claremont, California, age 77; two
    sons: Edmund "Ned" Morris, born Ebon;
    Francis "Frank" Sturtevant, born Kosrae
    December 18, 1879 [Francis married Anna
    Forbes, born Kosrae March 4, 1890]

10. **Harriet Almira Sturtevant Pease**—1878-1894,
    Marshallese school, Wot; born Westport, New
    York, October 21, 1846; married Edmund Morris
    Pease, April 25, 1877, Bordentown, New Jersey;
    arrived Kosrae October 12, 1878, age 32; depart-
    ed Kosrae 1894; died January 9, 1933, Claremont,
    California, age 86; two sons (see above)

11. **Joel Fisk Whitney**—1879-1881, Marshallese
    school, Wot; born March 30, 1843, Wadhams
    Mills, New York; son of John Russell & Elmina
    Fisk Whitney; Middlebury College, Andover

Theological Seminary, ordained May 3, 1871, Wadhams Mills, New York; married Louisa Maretta Bailey, May 3. 1871, Wadhams Mills, New York; arrived Kosrae 1879, age 36; departed Kosrae 1881; pastorates in New England and New York, 1882-1905; died January 16, 1919, Royalton, Vermont, age 75; three children: eldest, John

12. **Louisa Maretta Bailey Whitney**—1879-1881, Marshallese school, Wot; married Joel Fisk Whitney May 3, 1871, Wadhams Mills, New York; arrived Kosrae 1879; departed Kosrae 1881; three children (see above)

13. **Lillian "Lillie" S. Cathcart**—1881-1887, Marshallese school, Wot; arrived Kosrae September 24, 1881; departed Kosrae September 1887

14. **Alfred Christopher Walkup**—1882-1889, Gilbertese school, Wot; born May 18, 1849, Nunda, Illinois; Beloit College, Chicago Theological Seminary; married Margaret Lavinia Barr, April 21, 1880; ordained June 4, 1880, Arronia, Kansas; arrived Kosrae August 13, 1882, age 33; departed Kosrae April 1889 died May 4, 1909, buried Ebon, Marshall Islands, age 59; three children (John M., born Gilbert Islands, 1881; Eleanor E. [Madison], born Kosrae 1883; Alfred William, born Kosrae, 1886

15. **Margaret Lavinia Barr Walkup**—1882-1888, Gilbertese school, Wot; born 1855; married Alfred Christopher Walkup, April 21, 1880; arrived Kosrae August 13, 1882, age 27; died August 16, 1888 Kosrae, buried at Wot, age 33; three children (see above)

16. **Annette "Nettie" Palmer**—1884-1886, 1889-1898, Pohnpeian & Girls' schools, Wot; born Hopkinton, New York, 1856; Manchester, New Hampshire High School; teacher Cedar Rapids, Iowa; arrived Kosrae 1884, age 28; departed Kosrae 1886; returned to Kosrae 1889; departed Kosrae 1893; died 1906 Pohnpei, buried Ohwa, age 50

17. **Ella Theodora Crosby [Bliss]**—1886-1891, 1894-1896, Marshallese school, Wot; born June 7, 1864, Georgetown, Massachusetts; Boston Common Schools; arrived Kosrae September 1, 1886, age 22; departed Kosrae April, 1891; returned to Kosrae August 15, 1894, age 30; departed Kosrae March 1896; married the Rev. Dr. Edwin Munsell Bliss, November 8, 1900, Brockton, Massachusetts; one daughter

18. **Lydia Esther Hemmingway [Morehouse]**—1886-1887, Girls' School, Wot; born July 22,

1838, Hartford, New York; Homer Academy, Lima Seminary; arrived Kosrae September 1, 1886, age 48; departed Kosrae March 1887; married D. L. Morehouse, 1888, LeRoy, Illinois

19. **Sarah "Sadie" Louise Smith [Garland]**—1886-1891, 1895-1896 Girls' School, Wot; born February 38, 1865, Boston, Massachusetts; Girls' High School, Boston; arrived Kosrae September 1, 1886, age 21; departed Kosrae April 19, 1891; returned to Kosrae 1895; departed Kosrae 1896; married Captain George F. Garland, September 3, 1891, Newton Centre, Massachusetts; died May 12, 1947, Lorrain, Ohio, age 82; three daughters: Dorothea Lakeman, June 8, 1894; Ruth, born Kosrae April 11, 1895; Elizabeth

20. **Alice Cowles Little**—1888-1893, Girls' School, Wot; born May 9, 1865, Janesville, Wisconsin; Oberlin College; arrived Kosrae July 1888, age 23; departed Kosrae February 8, 1893; died December 23, 1958, Oberlin, Ohio, age 93

21. **Rachel Crawford Forbes**—1889-1894, Girls' School, Wot; born May 9, 1867, Montreal, Canada; daughter of William & Isabel Ray Crawford; married John James Forbes, May 24, 1889 (John J. Forbes born December 10, 1859, Dumblade, Aberdeenshire, Scotland; died October 29, 1889 Kosrae, age 29 years, buried at Wot); arrived Kosrae 1889, age 22; departed Kosrae 1894; died October 31, 1952, Pomona, California, age 85; one daughter: Anna, born March 4, 1890, Kosrae [Anna married Francis Pease, born Kosrae Dec. 18, 1879. They lived in Claremont, California.]

22. **Ida Creesey Foss**—1889-1892, 1894-1896, Pohnpeian & Girls' schools, Pisin & Wot; born August 31, 1845, Marblehead, Massachusetts; Marblehead Academy; arrived Kosrae 1889, age 44; departed Kosrae for Mokil 1892; returned to Kosrae 1894; departed Kosrae 1896; died May 25, 1917, Melrose, Massachusetts, age 71

23. **Irving Monroe Channon**—1890-1905, Gilbertese school, Wot; born July 18, 1862, Durant, Iowa; son of James L. & Emma Adelaide Perkins Channon; Oberlin College, Oberlin School of Theology; married Mary Long Goldsbury, July 6, 1887, Minneapolis, Minnesota; ordained February 20, 1888, Rockport, Ohio; arrived Kosrae August 18, 1890, age 28; departed Kosrae August, 1905; 1907-1913 Ocean Island (Banaba); 1919-1932 founder/dean, Silliman Presbyterian College, Philippine Islands; died November 1, 1942, Oberlin, Ohio, age 80; nine children: Paul LeGrand, born U.S. April 29, 1888; Lillian Ruth [Hamilton], born U.S. May, 18, 1889; William Perkins, born

Kosrae December 14, 1890; Mary Goldsbury [Eglin], born Kosrae December 24, 1892; Hiram Bingham, born Kosrae July 15, 1894; Stephen Long, born Kosrae May 1, 1896; Eva Estella [Mau], born U.S. June 8, 1897; Grace Sweetzer [Morrison], born Kosrae December 10, 1899; Irving Monroe, Jr., born Kosrae January 25, 1902

24. **Mary "May" Long Goldsbury Channon**— 1890-1905, Gilbertese school, Wot; born March 26, 1865, Davenport, Iowa; daughter of James & Mary Rosaline Long Goldsbury; Oberlin College; married Irving Monroe Channon, July 6, 1887, Minneapolis, Minnesota; arrived Kosrae August 18, 1890, age 25; departed Kosrae August, 1905; died November 18, 1957, Oberlin, Ohio, age 92; nine children (see above)

25. **Jessie Rebecca Hoppin**—1890-1912, Girls' School, Wot; 1913-1939, half-time Jaluit/Pisin; born January 13, 1865, South Haven, Michigan; Oberlin College; 1887-1890 taught at Kawaiaha'o Seminary for Girls, Honolulu, Hawai'i; arrived Kosrae August 18, 1890, age 25; departed Kosrae 1912; returned to Kosrae/Jaluit 1913; departed Kosrae 1932; returned to Kosrae/Marshall Islands October 5th, 1933 as a retired missionary; returned to U.S. from Kosrae via Japan 1939; died January 14, 1949, Ashland, Wisconsin, age 84; one adopted [Gilbertese] daughter: Rose Kaumaip [Tulensa Mackwelung]

26. **Louise Eliza Wilson**—1893-1909, Girls' School, Wot; born October 25, 1868, Sonoma, California; arrived Kosrae July 3, 1893, age 24; departed Kosrae 1909; died March 13, 1935, Berkeley, California, age 66

27. **Annie Elizabeth Abell**—1894-1901, Girls' School, Wot; born September 6, 1863, Buffalo, New York; Oberlin College; 1892-1894, Kuchua Girls' School, Dublon, Chuuk; arrived Kosrae August 15, 1894, age 31; departed Kosrae 1901

28. **Clinton Francis Rife**—1894-1907, Marshallese school, Wot; born October 4, 1866, Fairfield County, Ohio; Rush Medical College, Chicago; married Isadore Rote, September 19, 1893, Warren, Illinois; ordained April 8, 1894, Barrington, Illinois; arrived Kosrae August 15, 1894, age 28; departed Kosrae May 1907 to Jaluit; died November 22, 1943, Naperville, Illinois, age 77; three children: John Alvin, born Kosrae May 13, 1896; Frances Luella, born Kosrae, January 13, 1899; Margaret "Maggie," born Kosrae

29. **Isadore Rote Rife**—1894-1906, Marshallese school, Wot; born October 1868, Green County, Wisconsin; Chicago Bible Training School; married Clinton Francis Rife, September 19,

1893, Warren, Illinois; arrived Kosrae August, 15, 1894, age 26; departed Kosrae March 1906; died May 8, 1961, Naperville, Illinois, age 92; three children (see above)

30. **Emma Kane**—1897-1899, Girls' School, Wot; native Hawaiian; Kamehameha Girls' School; arrived Kosrae August, 1897; departed Kosrae 1899

31. **Jenny Olin**—1897-1911, Girls' School, Wot; born May 1867, Sweden; Princeton, Mt. Holyoke College; arrived Kosrae August 1897, age 30; departed Kosrae July 1911; died September 2, 1911, Sydney, Australia, age 44

32. **Marion Parker Wells [Woodward]**— 1909-1911, Girls' School, Wot; born March 26, 1883, Holliston, Massachusetts; Northfield Seminary; arrived Kosrae December 16, 1909, age 26; departed Kosrae 1911; married the Rev. Frank J. Woodward, March 25, 1912 on Ocean [Banaba] Island; died March 7, 1948, West Newton, Massachusetts, age 64; four sons: the oldest two, Gordon & Leonard

33. **Elizabeth Baldwin**—1911-1939, Kosrae Christian Training School, Wot; born April 11, 1859, Newark, New Jersey; daughter of Samuel & Mary Baldwin; New York Missionary Institute; 1898-1910 Kuchua Girls' School, Dublon, Chuuk; arrived Kosrae September 6, 1911, age 52; retired on Kosrae April 16, 1936; died October 31, 1939 Kosrae, buried at Pukusrik, age 80

34. **Jane DuBois Baldwin**—1911-1941, Kosrae Christian Training School, Wot; born June 9, 1863, Newark, New Jersey; daughter of Samuel & Mary Baldwin; New York Missionary Institute; 1898-1910 Kuchua Girls' School, Dublon, Chuuk; arrived Kosrae September 6, 1911, age 48; retired on Kosrae April 16, 1936; departed Kosrae February 17, 1941; died July 5, 1949, Orange, New Jersey, age 86

35. **George Carl Lockwood**—1928-1932, Kosrae Christian Training School, Wot; born September 18, 1895, Fennville, Michigan; North Central, Oberlin School of Theology; ordained May 18, 1927, Jackson, Michigan; married Eleanor Illian; arrived Kosrae 1928, age 33; departed Kosrae 1932; Oberlin BD, 1934; died February 5, 1992, Lihue, Hawai'i, buried Hawaiian Memorial Park, Kaneohe, age 96; two daughters: Althea Orramell [McCleery], November 18, 1925; Winifred Alice [Marsh], September 2, 1928

36. **Eleanor "Nora" Illian Lockwood**—1928-1932, Kosrae Christian Training School, Wot; born May 8, 1898, Wisconsin; arrived Kosrae 1928, age 30; departed Kosrae 1932; died 1967, buried

Hawaiian Memorial Park, Kaneohe, age 69 two daughters (see above)

37. **Clarence F. McCall**—1936-1940, Kosrae Christian Training School, Wot; born August 11, 1881, Reform, Missouri; Westminister College, Oberlin Graduate School of Theology; married Cora Campbell 1908; 1908-1930 Christian Church/Disciples of Christ in Japan; 1930-1936 American Board of Commissioners for Foreign Missions in Japan; arrived Kosrae May 1936, age 54; departed Kosrae 1940; 1940-1949 pastorates in Ashland, Oregon & Spearfish, South Dakota; retired to Pilgrim Place, Claremont, California, May 1950; died July 27, 1962, Claremont, California, age 80; four children born in Japan: Merritt Campbell; Clarence F., Jr.; Robert Marshall; Frances McCall [Hudson]

38. **Cora Campbell McCall**—1936-1940, Kosrae Christian Training School, Wot; born November 17, 1878, Joliet, Illinois; Pomona College, University of California; married Clarence F. McCall 1908; 1908-1930 Christian Church/Disciples of Christ in Japan; 1930-1936, ABCFM in Japan; arrived Kosrae May, 1936, age 57; departed Kosrae 1940; retired to Pilgrim Place, Claremont, California, May 1950; died August 3, 1966, Claremont, age 87; two children (see above)

39. **Eleanor Wilson**—1936-1941, Kosrae Christian Training School, Wot; born November 3, 1891, Norwalk, Connecticut; Cambridge Latin School, Simmons College, Biblical Seminary in New York; 1925-1932 teacher/ principal Kobe Theological Seminary for Women, Japan; 1933-1935 Acting Associate Secretary ABCFM Boston; arrived Kosrae May 1936, age 45; departed Kosrae February 17, 1941; 1946-1961, Marshall Islands (1950-1951 Skipper, *Morning Star VI*); departed Micronesia 1961; 1961-1964 pastor Ko'olau Huiia Protestant Church, Anahola, Kaua'i; retired to Pilgrim Place, Claremont, California, November 1965; died February 24, 1972, Claremont, buried in Massachusetts, age 80

40. **Miss Yamada**—1937-1939, 1941-1943, Kosrae Christian Training School, Wot; arrived Kosrae 1937; departed Kosrae 1939; returned to Kosrae 1941; departed Kosrae 1943

41. **Ren Suzuki**—1940-1942, Kosrae Christian Training School, Wot; arrived Kosrae 1940; departed Kosrae 1942

42. **Harold Francis Hanlin**—1948-1950, Kosrae Christian Training School, Wot; born February 3, 1906, Mulhall, Oklahoma; son of John Gill & Mary LaJune Owens Hanlin; Johnson Bible College, School of Religion-Butler University, Phillips University; married Mary Ruth Martin, September 5, 1931, Oklahoma City, Oklahoma; Southern Baptist Theological College, PhD; Greek & Hebrew professor Johnson Bible College, Butler University; 1945-1947 chaplain U.S. Navy, Kwajalein, Guam; arrived Kosrae February 4, 1948, age 42; Skipper, *Morning Star VI* 1949-1950 ; departed Kosrae May 21, 1950; 1947-1980 ABCFM, UCBWM, UBS Micronesia; retired to Pilgrim Place, Claremont, California, 1980; died April 3, 1999, Pomona, California, age 93; three children: Mary Alice [Buck], December 24, 1932; John Martin, April 6, 1935; Ruth Ann, May 13, 1939

43. **Mary Ruth Martin Hanlin**—1948-1950, 1954-1955, Kosrae Christian Training School, Wot; born December 28, 1909, Witchita, Kansas; daughter of Joseph Lemmon & Eliza Abigail Fellow Martin; Oklahoma City University, Phillips University; married Harold F. Hanlin, September 5, 1931, Oklahoma City, Oklahoma; arrived Kosrae April 11, 1948, age 38; departed Kosrae March 10, 1950; returned to Kosrae August 19, 1954; departed Kosrae May 24, 1955; retired to Pilgrim Place, Claremont, California, 1980; died February 25, 2002, Claremont, California, age 92; three children (see above)

44. **Lucy B. Lanktree**—1952-1954, Kosrae Christian Training School, Wot; ABCFM in China; arrived Kosrae July 1952; departed Kosrae August 22, 1954; retired Walker Missionary Home, Auburndale, Massachusetts

45. **Mary Alice Hanlin Buck**—(1948-1950), 1953-1955, 1959-1962, KCTS, Wot; born December 24, 1932, Knoxville, Tennessee; daughter of Harold Francis & Mary Ruth Martin Hanlin, with them on Kosrae as a teenager April 11, 1948 to May 21, 1950; Oklahoma City University, Phillips University, Northwest Christian College; arrived Kosrae September 29, 1953, age 20; departed Kosrae May 24, 1955; married Elden M. Buck August 10, 1955, Fullerton, California; returned to Kosrae January 14,1959, age 26; departed Kosrae June 30, 1962; 1963-1968 Ebeye, Kwajalein, Marshall Islands; 1970-2003 United Bible Societies, Marshall Islands, Hawai'i; 1992-2002 on Kosrae five or six months of each year as Project Coordinator of the Kosraean Bible Translation Committee; retired to Pilgrim Place, Claremont, California, March 1999; died June 28, 2004, Claremont, California, age 71; three children: Lisa Lynette Buck [Haley], September 4, 1956; Lauren Yvonne Buck [Medeiros], February 8, 1958; Kyle Tolom, June 30, 1966 (adopted Kwajalein, January 27, 1968)

46. **Elden Myrle Buck**—1959-1962, Kosrae
Christian Training School, Wot; born April 12,
1931, Bell, California; son of Carlton C. &
Frieda Helen Claassen Buck; Phillips University,
Phillips Graduate Seminary, Institute of Church
Growth; married Mary Alice Hanlin August 10,
1955, Fullerton, California; arrived Kosrae
January 14, 1959, age 27; departed Kosrae June
30, 1962; 1963-1968 Ebeye, Kwajalein, Marshall
Islands; 1968-1981 Protestant Chaplain,
Kwajalein Missile Range; 1981-1997 UCC pas-
torates in Honolulu and Hilo, Hawai'i; retired
to Pilgrim Place, Claremont, California, March
1999; three children (see above)

47. **Anna Dederer**—1964-1970, Pisin; born July
21, 1902, Heinbronn, Germany; Liebenzell
Mission Seminary; Liebenzell Nurses' School;
1934 to Micronesia with the Liebenzell
Missionary Society, age 32; 1934-1939
Mortlock Islands; 1939-1948, 1950-1954
Chuuk; interned by the Japanese during WWII
Chuuk; Andover-Newton Theological School
transferred from Liebenzell Mission to the
American Board 1949; 1954-1961 Rongrong,
Majuro, Marshall Islands; 1961-1963 Uliga,
Majuro; arrived Kosrae May 1964, age 61;
departed Kosrae 1970; retired to Plymouth
Village, Redlands, California, 1970; died
October 21, 1976, Redlands, California, age 74

MORNING STARS—1857-1956

Morning Star I, 1856-1865
    Launched November 12, 1856, Mystic,
       Connecticut; two-masted square-rigged
       brigantine, 156 tons
    Cost: $18,351
    Capt. Samuel G. Moore, 1856-1858
    Capt. John W. Brown, 1858-1860
    Capt. Charles Wetherby Gelett, 1860-1865
    Sold in Honolulu, December 12, 1865

Morning Star II, 1866-1869
    Launched September 22, 1866, Boston,
       Massachusetts; two-masted square-rigged
       brigantine, 181 tons
    Cost: $23,406
    Capt. Hiram Bingham, Jr., 1866-1868
    Capt. Tengstrom, 1868-1869
    Wrecked Kosrae (off Lelu Harbor channel),
       October 18, 1869, no lives lost

Morning Star III, 1871-1884
    Launched February 27, 1871, Boston,
       Massachusetts; two-masted square-rigged
       brigantine, 181 tons
    Cost: $28,462
    Capt. Nathaniel Matthews, 1871-1872
    Capt. William B. Hallett, 1872-1874
    Capt. Charles W. Gelett, 1874-1875
    Capt. Andrew D. Colcord, 1875-1878
    Capt. Isaiah Bray, 1878-1883
    Capt. George F. Garland, 1883-1884
    Wrecked Kosrae (at Yela Harbor entrance),
       February 22, 1884, no lives lost

Morning Star IV, 1884-1900
    Launched August 6, 1884, Boston, Massachusetts;
       three-masted packet, 430 tons, 130-foot
       keel, auxiliary steam 150 horse-power; bow
       figurehead of a white-clad woman holding
       an open Bible
    Cost: $42,600
    Capt. Isaiah Bray, 1884-1886
    Capt. H. N. Turner, 1886-1887
    Capt. George F. Garland, 1887-1900
    Sold in San Francisco, May 1900

Morning Star V, 1904-1905
    Launched June 11, 1904, Boston, Massachusetts;
       (four-year-old *Sunbeam* out of Stonington,
       Connecticut); two-masted steamer (10 or
       11 knots an hour), 403 tons; 140 feet over
       all, 30-foot beam, nine-and-a-half foot draft
    Cost: $37,000 ($30,000 purchase price, $7,000
       repair/refitting)
    Capt. George F. Garland, 1904-1905
    Retired as impractical October 24, 1905
       (no coal available in Micronesia)
    Sold in San Francisco January 19, 1909

Morning Star VI, 1947-1952
    Launched July 17, 1947, Boston, Massachusetts;
       (previously the yacht *Norseman*, Boston);
       sixty-three-foot two-masted schooner, 29
       tons, three-cylinder diesel motor
    Capt. Price Lewis, 1947-1949
    Capt. Harold F. Hanlin, 1949-1950
    Capt. Eleanor Wilson, 1950-1951
    Capt. Creston Ketchum, 1951-1952
    Sank at sea in October 1952, 80 miles west of
       Majuro, no lives lost

KOSRAE'S CHURCH LEADERS at the time of the SESQUICENTENNIAL, August 21, 2002

ORDAINED PASTORS of the KOSRAE CONGREGATIONAL CHURCH

LELU:
1. Rev. Takeo Sru Likiaksa—Chairman, Church Council
2. Rev. Walton Kilafwa Palik
3. Rev. Lyndon Percy Abraham
4. Rev. Tadasy Aaron Sigrah

TAFUNSAK:
1. Rev. Kun Nena Sigrah—General Secretary, Micronesia Council of the UCC
2. Rev. Alik Rupe Palsis
3. Rev. Asher Palik Asher—Vice Chairman, Church Council

MALEM:
1. Rev. Salik Cornelius
2. Rev. Nena Tulen Kilafwasru
3. Rev. Tolenna Jose Langu—Secretary, Church Council

UTWE:
1. Rev. Benjamin Isaiah Benjamin
2. Rev. Natchuo Palikkun Andrew—Treasurer, Church Council
3. Rev. Hirosi Harold Ismael

WALUNG:
1. Rev. Kun Seymour Caleb

POHNPEI:
1. Rev. Arnold Calwin Edwin

PASTORS' WIVES—NIPASTU

LELU:
1. Nipastu Kioko Takeo Likiaksa, Bookkeeper, Nipastu
2. Nipastu (the late) Tokiko Walton Palik
3. Nipastu Mesalina Lyndon Abraham
4. Nipastu Kunie Tadasy Sigrah
5. Nipastu Ruth (the late) Aaron Sigrah
6. Nipastu Aklina (the late) Erafe Tosie

TAFUNSAK:
1. Nipastu Sepe Kun Sigrah, Vice President, Nipastu
2. Nipastu Kamoa Alik Palsis
3. Nipastu Mitchigo Asher Treasurer, Nipastu
4. Nipastu Sepe (the late) Lupalik Palsis

MALEM:
1. Nipastu Anako Salik Cornelius, President, Nipastu
2. Nipastu Jusda Nena Kilafwasru
3. Nipastu Tamiko Tolenna Langu
4. Nipastu Yamada (the late) Harrison George
5. Nipastu Estina (the late) Arthur George

UTWE:
1. Nipastu Kenye Benjamin Benjamin
2. Nipastu Connie Natchuo Andrew
3. Nipastu Mitchigo Hirosi Ismael, Secretary, Nipastu

WALUNG:
1. Nipastu Rosa Kun Caleb

POHNPEI:
1. Nipastu Selida Arnold Edwin
2. Nipastu Melina (the late) Calwin Edwin

DEACONS

LELU:
1. Thurston Basi Siba
2. Daniel Tosie Thomson
3. Paul Esau Tilfas
4. Jacob Nena Aliksa
5. Henry Noda Yamado Noda
6. Akiwo Sru Likiaksa
7. Idosi Jesse Kanku

TAFUNSAK:
1. Tulenna Rupe Palsis
2. Simeon Teye Sigrah
3. Roger Frank Skilling
4. Joseph Zakias George
5. Josaiah Hosea Saimon
6. Soloman Aliksa Mongkeya
7. Hanson Kun Sigrah

MALEM:
1. Hiteo Sapel Shrew
2. Palikkun Moody Shrew
3. Singkichy Palikkun George
4. Yosiwo Palikkun George
5. Bardon Samuel Musrasrik
6. Marumo Moses Lonno
7. Morgan Shrew Jonas
8. Austin Jonas (inactive)
9. Linter Tulenna Kilafwasru (inactive)
10. Roben Soloman Talley (inactive)

UTWE:
1. Wilmer Isaiah Benjamin
2. Kinshiro Palikkun Nena
3. Likiak Isaiah Benjamin
4. Godwin Joel
5. Tatasy Palikkun Andrew
6. Willer Wilmer Benjamin
7. Madison Tulenna Nena

WALUNG:
1. Alikwan Kefwas
2. Ezikiel David Nena
3. Edmond Horace Salik
4. Murtanel Linder Tulenna

POHNPEI:
1. Eden Harris Skilling

GUAM:
1. Wilton Saboar Mackwelung
2. Timothy Tulen Sopo Semuta

HONOLULU:
1. Shiro Milton Timothy

DEACONESSES

LELU:
1. Adelyn Henry Noda Yamado
2. Rosie Gifford Nena
3. Rosalia Reynold Tilfas
4. Alice Brian William
5. Kenye Itchigo Norio Skilling
6. Alwina Aruo Welly
7. Hattie Conrad Albert
8. Rebecca Kun Abraham (inactive)

TAFUNSAK:
1. Mersina Hamilton Jackson
2. Carsina Simeon Teye
3. Kenye Daniel Asu
4. Linda Obed Nena
5. Kiniko Tulenna Palsis
6. Kenye Roger Skilling
7. Yosiko Joseph George
8. Kenye Nena Tolenoa (inactive)
9. Notwe Zakias George (inactive)

MALEM:
1. Antilise Yosiwo George
2. Louisa Bardon Musrasrik
3. Srue Singkichy George
4. Sepe Kilafwasru Kilafwasru
5. Evelyn Mario Lonno
6. Lillian Hiteo Shrew
7. Sepe Palikkun Shrew
8. Betsy Swinton Musrasrik (inactive)
9. Clarese Roben Soloman (inactive)
10. Kenye Lambert Lawrence (inactive)
11. Kenye Lipan Kephas (inactive)

UTWE:
1. Agusta Atchiro Melander
2. Takae Kun Rendon
3. Hattie Godwin Joel
4. Martha Otniel Edmond
5. Sepe Wiler Benjamin
6. Tersina Keller Nena
7. Yosie Linus George
8. Florence Palikkun Nena (inactive)
9. Tulpe Sru Nena (inactive)
10. Sepe Likiak Benjamin (inactive)
11. Madlyne Kinshiro Nena (inactive)
12. Regina Elsworth Livae (inactive)

WALUNG:
1. Louise Sru Luke
2. Lulina Edmond Salik
3. Setsuko Ezikiel Nena
4. Elsiner Murtanel Tulenna
5. Sra Visente Taulung (inactive)

POHNPEI:
1. Julia Eden Skilling

GUAM:
1. Daisy Wilton Mackwelung
2. Elizabeth Timothy Semuta

LAY MINISTERS

LELU:
1. Aaron Royal Alokoa
2. Albert Thomas Welly
3. Alexander Herbert Sigrah
4. Alik Sam Isaac
5. Arthy Gifford Nena
6. Benjamin Joshua Abraham
7. Benskin Jesse Wakap
8. Berney Lucian Robert
9. Bolton Percy Abraham
10. Chang Bryan Alik William
11. Clanry Sru Likiaksa
12. Fred Simeon Skilling
13. Fores Kun Abraham
14. George Abner Esau
15. Gilton Abner Esau
16. Henry Edwin Robert
17. Hillman Aaron Sigrah
18. Huston Ekinaitus Elly
19. Inston Royal Alokoa
20. Jerson Tulensru Freddy
21. Joab Paul Sigrah
22. John Edwin Robert
23. John Brian Alik Willaim
24. Jonis Benjamin Joshua Abraham
25. Justus Siba Aktako
26. Kemwel Esau Tilfas
27. Kiosi Nena Florian
28. Masaki Tosie Thomson
29. Moses Yamado Noda
30. Nena Gifford Nena
31. Paliksru George Kanku
32. Ranson Reynold Tilfas
33. Reed Gifford Nena
34. Reedson Percy Abraham
35. Rensley Aaron Sigrah
36. Robert Sapino Sigrah
37. Salik Tosie Thomson
38. Salpasr Esau Tilfas
39. Sisumu Kilafwakur George
40. Switson Edison Robert
41. Tatchuo Herbert Sigrah
42. Weston Nelson Lakimis
43. William Kilafwa Palik
44. William Orlando Mares Tosie

TAFUNSAK:
1. Alik Sam Albert
2. Alik Harris Skilling
3. Alik Kilafwa Palsis
4. Alokoa Palokoa Joe
5. Ashley Hamilton Jackson
6. Edison Singeo Nena
7. Esah Rupe Palsis
8. Fred Roger Skilling
9. Gerson Alik Jackson
10. Harrison Nena Sigrah
11. Jack Kun Jack
12. John Tulensru Tolenoa
13. Jonah Obed Nena
14. Julian Jonah Metwarik
15. Julius Erwin Sigrah
16. Justus Kun Mongkeya
17. Kingsley Erwin Sigrah
18. Kun Palokoa Joe
19. Kun Kilafwa Mongkeya
20. Kun Stephen Kinere
21. Landson Kun Alik
22. Lupalik Nithan
23. Miles Aliksru Tolenoa
24. Miller Lupalik Palsis
25. Morris Oran George
26. Natchuo Alokoa Mongkeya
27. Nena Miosi Tolenoa
28. Obed Nena
29. Offanai Alik
30. Palikkun Lupalik Palsis
31. Richard Aliksru Tolenoa
32. Robert Hamilton Jackson
33. Seymour Tulensru Seymour
34. Skiller Kiyus Jackson
35. Stanley Kun Taulung
36. Tulensa Nena Sigrah
37. Webster Oran George
38. Wilfred Nimaiah Tulensru

MALEM:
1. Akira Milton Timothy
2. Alex Palokoa Phillip
3. Alokoa Lambert Talley
4. Arthur Austin Jonas
5. Benson Tulensa Langu
6. Carlton Milton Timothy
7. Gustin Kephas Charley
8. Jefferson Milton Timothy
9. Kalwin Lipan Kephas
10. Kilafwa Likiak Kilafwasru
11. Kilafwasru Tulen Kilafwasru
12. Kresma Kun Luey
13. Kun Joken Olter
14. McDonald Stephenson Ittu
15. Mario Theodore Lonnc
16. Midley Sapel Shrew
17. Milson Linder Tulenna
18. Minoru Kephas Charley
19. Mitchuo Milton Timothy
20. Nena Likiaklik Kilafwasru

21. Nena Shrew Tulenna
22. Paul Simeon Aaron
23. Remos Nena Livae
24. Robert Austin Jonas
25. Roldon Palokoa Timothy
26. Ruben Kilafwa Charley
27. Salik Albert Talley
28. Sanky Inos Sigrah
29. Sasaki Linus George
30. Simeon Joshua Phillip
31. Soloman Roben Talley
32. Takaki Likiaksa Phillip
33. Takasi Sapel Shrew
34. Tara Joses Charley
35. Tokowe Stephen George
36. Yasuwo Shrew Jonas

UTWE:
1. Albert Kun Tilfas
2. Atchiro John Melander
3. Clanry Kun Tilfas
4. Emius Thomas Nena
5. Ezra Sru Nena
6. Fred Otniel Edmond
7. Heuston Onosr Wakuk
8. Himul Walter Tulenkun
9. Hostino Elsworth Livae
10. Jefferson Benjamin Benjamin
11. Joel Kun Tilfas
12. John Martin Andrew
13. Keller Rebuk Nena
14. Kersin Ansin Tilfas
15. Kun Rendon Isaac
16. Likiak Lulu Tulenkun
17. Ludwig Lorena Tilfas
18. Marciano Kilafwa Waguk
19. Maxson Palikkun Nena
20. Mekanzie Nena Waguk
21. Milson Kinshiro Nena
22. Moses Rendel Alik
23. Nena Sru Nena
24. Nena Wilmer Benjamin
25. Orlando Tulenna Joseph
26. Patterson Benjamin Benjamin
27. Renster Palikkun Andrew
28. Rodney Makato Edmond
29. Sloving Kun Tilfas
30. Truman Morris Waguk
31. Tokiwo Nena
32. Vanston Tulensru Waguk
33. Vinton Likiak Benjamin
34. Winton Tulenna Clarence

WALUNG:
1. Elkena Alokoa Palsis
2. Harry Hamilton Jackson
3. Hashime Visente Taulung
4. Johnson Jacob Taulung
5. Kunio Sru Jerry
6. Leonard Clinton Benjamin
7. Misael David Nena

8. Nimos Horace Salik
9. Sailus Alik Kefwas
10. Samuel Zakias George
11. Swinfred Horace Salik
12. Timothy Hamilton Jackson

POHNPEI:
1. Reed Gifford Nena
2. Jefferson Benjamin Benjamin
3. Palikkun Alokoa George
4. Salik Aliksa Mongkeya

HONOLULU:
1. Elwel Alokoa Taulung
2. Himul Walter Tulenkun
3. Max Tupua
4. Robert Shrew Jonas

KONA:
1. Siosi Aliksa

KOSRAE CHRISTIAN ENDEAVOR OFFICERS

ALL-ISLAND ADULT CHRISTIAN ENDEAVOR SOCIETY:
1. Masaki Tosie Thomson, President
2. Tulensa Nena Sigrah, Vice President
3. John Bryan William, Secretary
4. Boldon Percy Abraham, Treasurer
5. Hanson Kun Sigrah, Secretary Treasurer
6. Switson Edison Robert, Worship Committee Chair (Alu)
7. Minoru Kephas Charley, Outreach Committee Chair (Fasr)
8. Natchuo Alokoa Mongkeya, Stewardship Committee Chair (Kasru)
9. Vanston Tulensru Wakuk, Children's Committee Chair
10. Kalwin Lipan Kephas, Special Projects Chair

LELU ADULT CHRISTIAN ENDEAVOR SOCIETY:
1. Weston Nelson Lakimis, President
2. Arthy Gifford Nena, Vice President
3. Berney Lucian Robert, Secretary

TAFUNSAK ADULT CHRISTIAN ENDEAVOR SOCIETY:
1. Robert Hamilton Jackson, President
2. Webster Oran George, Vice President
3. Edison Singeo Nena, Secretary

MALEM ADULT CHRISTIAN ENDEAVOR SOCIETY:
1. Morgan Shrew Jonas, President
2. Jefferson Milton Timothy, Vice President
3. Ruben Kilafwa Charley, Secretary

UTWE ADULT CHRISTIAN ENDEAVOR SOCIETY:
1. Maxon Palikkun Nena, President
2. Marciano Kilafwa Wakuk, Vice President

3. Milson Kinshiro Nena, Secretary

WALUNG ADULT CHRISTIAN ENDEAVOR SOCIETY:
1. Sailus Alikwan Kefwas, President
2. Nimos Horace Salik, Vice President
3. Timothy Hamilton Jackson, Secretary

POHNPEI CHRISTIAN ENDEAVOR SOCIETY:
1. Jefferson Benjamin Benjamin, President
2. Salik Aliksa Mongkeya, Vice President
3. Tilson Tulen Kephas. Secretary

GUAM CHRISTIAN ENDEAVOR SOCIETY:
1. Ezra Sru Nena, President
2. Likiaksa Himul Timothy, Vice President
3. Norman Harris Skilling, Secretary

SAIPAN CHRISTIAN ENDEAVOR SOCIETY:
1. Isamu Josaiah Abraham, President
2. Masayuki Alik Skilling, Vice President
3. Arson Likiaksru Joe, Secretary

EBEYE CHRISTIAN ENDEAVOR SOCIETY:
1. Samuel Tulen Tulensa, President
2. Elijah Franklin James, Vice President
3. Joseph Tulen Tulensa, Secretary

HONOLULU CHRISTIAN ENDEAVOR SOCIETY:
1. Elwel Alokoa Taulung, President
2. Dawson Nena Thomas, Vice President
3. Sepe Winson Elly, Secretary

KONA CHRISTIAN ENDEAVOR SOCIETY:
1. Siosi Aliksa, President
2. Bennett Ismael Alokoa, Vice President
3. Tulensru Selistin Likiaksa, Secretary

MAUI CHRISTIAN ENDEAVOR SOCIETY:
1. Alik Joseph Nena, President
2. Matthew Nena, Vice President
3. Srue Moleince Kephas, Secretary

SEATTLE CHRISTIAN ENDEAVOR SOCIETY:
1. Simeon Marcus Nedlic, President
2. Frank Wilmer Benjamin, Vice President
3. Jacob Tolman Luey, Secretary

LELU YOUNG PEOPLE'S CHRISTIAN ENDEAVOR SOCIETY:
1. Casey Jerson Freddy, President
2. Simpson Killion Abraham, Vice President
3. Clain Bryan William, Secretary
4. Ben Jesse, Sponsor

TAFUNSAK YOUNG PEOPLE'S CHRISTIAN ENDEAVOR SOCIETY:
1. Fred Roger Skilling, President
2. Skiller Kiyus Jackson, Vice President
3. Alik Harris Skilling, Secretary
4. Ashley Hamilton Jackson, Sponsor

MALEM YOUNG PEOPLE'S CHRISTIAN
ENDEAVOR SOCIETY:
1. Simeon Joshua Phillip, President
2. Skipper Sapel Ittu, Vice President
3. Arthur Alokoa Talley, Secretary
4. Kun Joken Olter, Sponsor

UTWE YOUNG PEOPLE'S CHRISTIAN ENDEAVOR
SOCIETY:
1. Maver Kun Jonathan, President
2. Grant Hirosi Ismael, Vice President
3. Patrick Wilmer Benjamin, Secretary
4. Madison Matthew Nena, Sponsor

WALUNG YOUNG PEOPLE'S CHRISTIAN
ENDEAVOR SOCIETY:
1. Joe Alwin Alik, President
2. Kenson Ezikiel Nena, Vice President
3. Caleb Kun Caleb, Secretary
4. Swinfred Horace Salik, Sponsor

**KOSRAE STATE GOVERNMENT
OFFICIALS**—with church offices noted

EXECUTIVE BRANCH
1. The Honorable Rensley Aaron Sigrah, Governor
    —Lay Minister, Lelu
2. The Honorable Gerson Alik Jackson, Lt. Governor
    —Lay Minister, Tafunsak
3. Singkitchy Palikkun George, Director, Dept. of
    Commerce & Industry—Deacon, Malem
4. Nena Shru Nena, Director, Dept. of Agriculture,
    Land & Marine Resources—Lay Minister, Utwe
5. Henry Edwin Robert, Director, Dept. of Education
    —Lay Minister, Lelu
6. Bruce Howell, Director, Dept. of Public Works
7. Nena Miosi Tolenoa, Director, Office of
    Community Affairs—Lay Minister, Tafunsak
8. Roland Bickett, Attorney General
9. Boldon Percy Abraham, Director, Dept. of
    Administration & Finance—Lay Minister, Lelu
10. Dr. Hirosi Ismael, Director, Dept. of Health
    Services—Pastor, Utwe
11. Aaron Fred Sigrah, Special Assistant to the
    Governor
12. Fred Simeon Skilling, Chief, Information &
    Protocol—Lay Minister, Lelu

LEGISLATIVE BRANCH
1. The Honorable Hiteo Sapel Shrew, Speaker,
    Seventh Kosrae State Legislature—Deacon,
    Malem
2. The Honorable Patterson Benjamin Benjamin, Vice
    Speaker—Lay Minister, Utwe
3. The Honorable Lyndon Hamilton Jackson, Floor
    Leader
4. The Honorable Albert Thomas Welly, Senator,
    Lelu—Lay Minister, Lelu
5. The Honorable Reedson Percy Abraham, Senator,
    Lelu—Lay Minister, Lelu

6. The Honorable Stephen Nelson Sigrah, Senator,
    Lelu
7. The Honorable Tadasy Aaron Sigrah, Senator, Lelu
    —Pastor, Lelu
8. The Honorable Thurston Basi Siba, Senator, Lelu
    —Deacon, Lelu
9. The Honorable Carson Kun Sigrah, Senator,
    Tafunsak
10. The Honorable James Rupe Palsis, Senator,
    Tafunsak
11. The Honorable Josaiah Hosea Saimon, Senator,
    Tafunsak
12. The Honorable Palikkun Moody Shrew, Senator,
    Malem
13. The Honorable Simeon Joshua Phillip, Senator,
    Malem—Lay Minister, Malem
14. The Honorable John Martin Andrew, Senator,
    Utwe—Lay Minister, Utwe

JUDICIARY BRANCH:
1. The Honorable Yosiwo Palikkun George, Chief
    Justice—Deacon, Malem
2. The Honorable Aliksa Bradley Aliksa, Associate
    Justice

MUNICIPAL GOVERNMENTS
1. The Honorable Vinson Moses Henry, Mayor, Lelu
2. The Honorable Julian Jonah Metwarik, Mayor,
    Tafunsak—Lay Minister, Tafunsak
3. The Honorable Maita Tulen Kilafwasru, Mayor,
    Malem
4. The Honorable Truman Morris Wakuk, Mayor,
    Utwe—Lay Minister, Utwe

DEPARTMENT/OFFICE AGENCIES
1. Landson Kun Alik, Executive Director, Kosrae
    Community Action Program—Lay Minister,
    Tafunsak
2. Simpson Killion Abraham, Administrator,
    Development Review Commission
3. Likiak Palikkun Wesley, Chief, Office of Planning
    & Statistics
4. Filmore Milton Timothy, Station Manager, Kosrae
    Broadcasting Authority
5. Robert Hamilton Jackson, Chairman, Kosrae
    Sports Council—Lay Minister, Tafunsak
6. Johnston Shrew Jonas, Associate Justice, Kosrae
    State Land Court
7. Jefferson Milton Timothy, Chief of Police—Lay
    Minister, Malem
8. Grant Hirosi Ismael, Administrator, Kosrae
    Visitors Bureau
9. Berlin Aaron Sigrah, Administrator, Kosrae
    Historical & Preservation
10. Robert Stanley Taulung, Administrator, Division
    of Marine Resources
11. Salpasr Esau Tilfas, Administrator, Division of
    Personnel & Employment Services—
    Lay Minister, Lelu

BIBLIOGRAPHY

Alexander, James M., *The Islands of the Pacific: From the Old to the New*, American Tract Society, New York 1895

American Board of Commissioners for Foreign Missions, "Micronesia," Yearbooks, Boston 1865, 1868

American Board of Commissioners for Foreign Missions, "Our Christian World Mission" position paper, Boston 1952

Ashby, Gene, editor, *Some Things of Value, Micronesian Customs as Seen by Micronesians*, by the Students and Former Students of the Community College of Micronesia, Education Department, Trust Territory of the Pacific Islands, Saipan 1975

Athens, J. Stephen, *Landscape Archaeology: Prehistoric Settlement, Subsistence, and Environment of Kosrae, Eastern Caroline Islands, Micronesia*, International Archaeological Research Institute, Inc., Honolulu 1995

Baker, Albert S., "The Third *Morning Star*," *The Friend*, Honolulu, Sept. 1942

Baldwin, Jane, unpublished correspondence, American Board of Commissioners for Foreign Missions archives, Houghton Library, Harvard University, undated

Baldwin, Jane, unpublished correspondence to Mary Channon, Feb. 7, 1940

Baldwin, Jane, unpublished correspondence to Carol Tompkins, April 29, 1941

Beardsley, Charles, *Guam Past and Present*, Charles E. Tuttle Company, Tokyo 1964

Bingham, Hiram, Jr., *Story of the* Morning Stars, *the Children's Missionary Vessels, with Sequels & a Supplementary Note*, The American Board, Congregational House, Boston 1907

Bishop, S. E., *The Friend*, Honolulu, Dec. 1889

Bliss, E. Theodora Crosby, *Micronesia: Fifty Years in the Island World*, American Board of Commissioners for Foreign Missions, Boston 1906

Buck, Elden M., "Kusaie Christian Training School," unpublished paper, Phillips University Graduate Seminary, Enid, Oklahoma 1957

Buck, Elden M., Newsletters, The Missions Council, Boston, Feb. 8, 1959, July 14, 1959, Feb. 11, 1960, Feb. 12, 1961, Nov. 24, 1961

Buck, Elden M., personal diaries, Kosrae 1958-1963

Buck, Mary Alice Hanlin, in "Children of Missionaries, Adjusting to Two Cultures," unpublished manuscript, Pilgrim Place, Feb. 2001

Buck, Mary Alice Hanlin, Children's Letters #55 & #83, Missionary Education Committee, Missions Council Research Department, Congregational Christian Churches, Boston 1959

Buck, Alice, coordinator, "Report of the SHINE! Workshops in Micronesia—July 10-Aug. 10, 1984, The Woman's Board of Missions of the Pacific, Honolulu 1984

Castle, George P., personal correspondence to Enoch F. Bell, American Board of Commissioners for Foreign Missions, Nov. 20, 1920

Channon, Irving M., personal correspondence to J. S. Emmerson, April 1, 1891

Channon, Irving M., personal correspondence, March 4, 1892, Jan. 16, 1892, Jan. 10, 1894

Channon, Irving M., report to the Hawaiian Evangelical Association, 1900

Channon, Mary L. G., "Memories of Kusaie, 1890-1905," unpublished, undated

Channon, Mary L. G., "My Trip to Ruk," July-Aug., 1892

Channon, Mary L. G., "Our Trip to Utwe," Kosrae, May 29, 1894

Channon, Mary L. G., personal correspondence, unpublished, undated, courtesy Mavea Hipps

Christian, F. W., *The Caroline Islands, Travel in the Sea of the Little Islands,* Frank Cass and Company Limited, London 1957 (first edition 1899)

Clark, E. W., unpublished correspondence to R. Anderson, ABCFM archives, Houghton Library, Harvard University, Nov. 4, 1852

Clarke, Thurston, *Searching for Crusoe, "A Journey among the Last Real Islands,"* Ballantine Books, Random House, Inc , New York 2001

Clyde, Paul H., *Japan's Pacific Mandate*, MacMillan, New York 1935

Colcord, Joanna C., unpublished "Journal of Mrs. Andrew D. Colcord, Aboard the Missionary Brig *Morning Star* on a Voyage to Micronesia, 1875," New York 1875

Cordy, Ross, *The Lelu Stone Ruins* (Kosrae, Micronesia) Asian and Pacific Archaeology Series, Number 10, Social Science Research Institute, University of Hawai'i at Mānoa 1993

Cordy, Ross & John, Teddy, "Interpretive Guidebook, Leluh Ruins," English Version, Leluh Ruins Landowners Corporation, Kosrae Historic Preservation Office 1984

Cormack, Maribelle, *The Lady Was a Skipper*, American Book, Stratford Press, New York 1956

Crawford, David and Leona, *Missionary Adventures in the South Pacific*, Charles E. Tuttle Company, Rutland, Vermont & Tokyo, Japan 1967

Crosby, E. Theodora [Bliss], "A Day in Kusaie, Micronesia," Committee on Junior Work, leaflet #3, Congregational House, Boston 1891

De la Porte, Philipp, personal correspondence to the Hawaiian Evangelical Association, May 30, July 26, Sept. 28, 1899

Ellis, Albert F., *Ocean Island and Nauru, Their Story,* Angus and Robertson Limited, Sydney 1935

Fairfield, Wynn C., "Christians from Boston," American Board of Commissioners for Foreign Missions, Boston 1944

Fischer, John L., *The Eastern Carolines,* Pacific Science Board, National Academy of Sciences—National Research Council, Human Relations Area Files, New Haven 1957

Foreman, Charles W., *The Island Churches of the South Pacific,* "Emergence in the Twentieth Century," Orbis Books, Maryknoll, New York 1982

Frear, Mary Dillingham, "Old Boards for New," in "Sixtieth Annual Report of the Woman's Board of Missions for the Pacific Islands," *Honolulu Star-Bulletin,* June 2, 1931

Garland, Sarah Smith, in *The Friend,* Honolulu, August 1905

George, Singkitchy P., "Report ke Loom Alu Malem 1999" Kosrae, Nov. 14, 1999

Green, Karen Reed, editor, "Glimpses Into Pacific Lives: Some Outstanding Women," Centers for National Origin & Sex Equity—Pacific, Northwest Regional Educational Laboratory, Portland, Oregon, Feb. 1987

Gulick, Luther, unpublished correspondence, American Board of Commissioners for Foreign Missions archives, Houghton Library, Harvard University, Aug. 26, 1852

Hall, Clarence W., "She Is Skipper of the *Morning Star,*" *Reader's Digest,* The Reader's Digest Association, Inc., Pleasantville, New York, Nov. 1957

Hanlin, Harold F., "Autobiography—Harold Francis Hanlin," unpublished manuscript, Claremont, California, Feb. 1986

Hanlin, Harold F., "Christmas In May," unpublished manuscript, Kosrae, May 23, 1948

Hanlin, Harold F., "Kusaie Christian Training School," *The Friend,* Honolulu, Dec. 1948

Hanlin, Harold F., "Micronesia—A Personal Viewpoint," unpublished paper, Claremont, California, undated

Hanlin, Harold F., Missions Council letters, Boston, Jan. 15, 1953, March 17, 1953

Hanlin, Harold F., "My Autobiography—Harold Francis Hanlin," unpublished manuscript, Claremont, California, June 1986

Hanlin, Harold F., circulated newsletter, Missions Council, Boston, March 11, 1950

Hanlin, Harold F., "Prayer Service in Kusaie," *The Friend,* Honolulu, Sept. 1948

Hanlin, Harold F., "The Passing of Kephas," *The Friend,* Honolulu, Dec. 1948

Hanlin, Mary Alice [Buck], "Alice in Wonderland," *Youth Magazine,* New York 1953

Hanlin, Mary Alice [Buck], "From Truk to Kusaie on the *Morning Star VI*—A Few Memories," *The Friend,* Honolulu, Aug. 1948

Hanlin, Mary Alice [Buck], Missions Council letter, Boston, Dec. 7, 1953

Hanlin, Mary Alice [Buck], personal diary, Kosrae 1953-1955

Hanlin, Mary Alice [Buck], personal newsletter, Nov. 17, 1954

Hanlin, Mary Ruth, unpublished "Five Year Diary," Jan. 1, 1948 through Dec. 31, 1952

Hanlin, Mary Ruth, unpublished report, "Kusaie Christian Training School," May 10, 1950

Hanlon, David, *Upon a Stone Altar, A History of the Island of Pohnpei to 1890,* University of Hawai'i Press, Honolulu, 1988

Hezel, Francis X., S. J., *Foreign Ships in Micronesia, A Compendium of Ship Contacts with the Caroline and Marshall Islands, 1521-1885,* Trust Territory Historic Preservation Office and U.S. Heritage Conservation and Recreation Service, Saipan 1979

Hezel, Francis X., S. J., *The New Shape of Old Island Cultures, A Half Century of Social Change in Micronesia,* University of Hawai'i Press, Honolulu 2001

Hezel, Francis X., S. J. and Berg, M. L., editors, *Winds of Change, A Book of Readings on Micronesian History,* Omnibus Program for Social Studies Cultural Heritage, U. S. Trust Territory 1980

Hoppin, Jesse R., personal letter to Wynn C. Fairfield, Kosrae, June 16, 1937

Hoppin, Jesse R., personal correspondence to the Hawaiian Evangelical Association, Feb. 1898, Jan. 22, 1900

Indigenous Leaders Conference minutes, Godaro Lorrin, secretary, Kosrae, July 1966

Jewett, Frances Gulick & Luther Halsey Gulick, "Missionary in Hawaii, Micronesia, Japan and China," Congregational Sunday School Publishing Society, Boston & Chicago 1895

Kahn, E. J., Jr., *A Reporter in Micronesia,* W. W. Norton & Company, Inc., New York 1966

Kerner, Myron, personal correspondence, United States Weather Bureau, Honolulu, March 1963

Ketchum, Creston Donald, *His Path Is in the Waters,* Prentice-Hall, Inc., New York 1955

Kiste, Robert C., and Marshall, Mac, editors, *American Anthropology in Micronesia: An Assessment,* University of Hawai'i Press, Honolulu 1999

Kosrae State Government, "Kosrae State Census Report, 1994 FSM Census of Population and Housing," Tofol, Kosrae, Oct. 1996

Levesque, Rodrigue, *Ships through Micronesia 1521-1991,* R.R.3, Gatineau, Quebec, Canada J8P 7G7, p. 71

Lewis, J. L., "Kusaien Acculturation," Coordinated investigation of Micronesian anthropology, Pacific Science Board, National Research Council, Washington 1948

Life and Light for Women, periodical published by the Woman's Boards of Missions, Boston

Lindemuth, Irvin Raymond, "Micronesia Missions: Proving Grounds of Christianity," unpublished thesis, Bangor Theological Seminary, Bangor, Maine, 1957

Lubbock, Basil, *Bully Hayes, South Sea Pirate*, Martin Hopkinson LTD, 23 Soho Square, London 1931

Loomis, Albertine, *To All People, A History of the Hawaii Conference of the United Church of Christ*, Honolulu 1970 (Kingsport Press, Inc., Kingsport, Tennessee)

Marvin, Mary A., editor, "A History of Missionary Work in Micronesia, 1852-1910," Vol. I, Vol. II, compilation of published materials from *Life and Light for Women*, and *The Missionary Herald* 1873-1910, Lancaster, Massachusetts

Micronesian Area Research Center, "Kusaie in the Nineteenth Century," University of Guam, undated

"Minutes of the Missionary Meeting of the UCBWM and LM," Elfriede Schmidt, secretary, Chuuk, June 8-13, 1970

Missionary Album, Portraits and Biographical Sketches of the American Protestant Missionaries to the Hawaiian Islands, Sesquicentennial Edition, Hawaiian Mission Children's Society, Honolulu 1969 (Edwards Enterprises, Inc., Honolulu)

The Missionary Herald, 1853 through 1910, published by the American Board of Commissioners for Foreign Missions, Boston

Missions Council, "The *Morning Stars*: God's Little White Ships, American Board of Commissioners for Foreign Missions, Boston undated

Moore, Robert W., "Our New Military Wards in the Pacific," *National Geographic Magazine*, Washington, D. C., Sept. 1945

Morris, Nancy J., "Hawaiian Missionaries Abroad, 1852-1909," Honolulu, Dec. 1987

Nawaa, Simeon K., "The Hawaiian Mission to Micronesia and Marquesas," Hawaiian Evangelical Association, Honolulu 1952

Olds, George, "A Letter from Kosrae," unpublished account, Nov. 1945

Oliver, Douglas L., *The Pacific Islands*, Harvard University Press, Cambridge 1951

Osborn, Fairfield, editor, *The Pacific World*, "Its vast distances, its lands and the life upon them, and its peoples*," W. W. Norton & Company, Inc., New York 1944

Pease, Edmund Morris, American Board of Commissioners for Foreign Missions Yearbooks Boston 1881, 1882, 1886

Pease, Edmund Morris, *The Friend*, Honolulu, May 1889

Pease, Edmund Morris, "Some Days on the *Morning Star*, 1893," Sunday School pamphlet "For Young People," Congregational House, Boston 1893

Peattie, Mark R., *Nan'yo, The Rise and Fall of the Japanese in Micronesia, 1885-1945*, University of Hawai'i Press, Honolulu 1988

Pierson, Delavan L., *The Pacific Islanders, From Savages to Saints*, Funk & Wagnalls Co., New York 1906

The PONAPE-PER, Kolonia, Pohnpei, Sept. 9, 1960

Price, Willard, *America's Paradise Lost*, The John Day Company, New York 1966

Price, Willard, *Japan's Islands of Mystery*, The John Day Co., New York 1944

Price, Willard, "Mysterious Micronesia: Japan's Mandated Islands," *National Geographic Magazine*, April, 1936

Price, Willard, *Pacific Adventure*, A John Day book, Reynal & Hitchcock, New York 1936

Rife, Clinton, *ABCFM Yearbook*, Boston 1906

Rivers, W. H. R., editor, *Essays on the Depopulation of Melanesia*, University Press, Cambridge 1922

Roberts, Myra Farrington, "The Micronesian Mission," unpublished personal reflections, 1896

Schaefer, Paul D., "Confess Therefore Your Sins —A Christian Rite of Passage and Kusaien Identity," Department of Anthropology, University of Minnesota 1973

Schaefer, Paul D., "From 'King' to Pastor: The Acquisition of Christianity on Kusaie," Department of Anthropology, University of Minnesota 1973

Segal, Harvey Gordon, *Kosrae: The Sleeping Lady Awakens*, Community College of Micronesia, Kosrae Tourist Division, Department of Conservation and Development, Kosrae 1989

Selvage, Irving L., personal correspondence to Elden Buck, Sept. 18, 2001

Sigrah, John P., unpublished "Record of Kusaie Girls' School up to the date of placing this bottle in the foundation," Kosrae, Nov. 30, 1909, courtesy Hashime Vicente

Snow, Benjamin G., "Annual Report, 1860," American Board of Commissioners for Foreign Missions, Boston 1860, 1868

Snow, Benjamin G., unpublished correspondence, American Board of Commissioners for Foreign Missions archives, Houghton Library, Harvard University, Dec. 1852, Oct. 1856, July 1858, June 1863

Snow, Lydia Vose Buck, unpublished correspondence to Dr. Pease, Robbinston, Maine, April 24, 1879, Hawai'i Mission Children's Society Library,

Honolulu

Snow, Mary Hitchcock [Mrs. Fredrick Galen], editor, "Incidents in the life of Mrs. Benjamin G. Snow," compiled from old letters for the Woman's Board Jubilee, Honolulu, June 1931

Strong, William E., *The Story of the American Board, "An Account of the First Hundred Years of the American Board of Commissioners for Foreign Missions,"* The Pilgrim Press, Boston 1910

Sturges, Albert, unpublished correspondence, American Board of Commissioners for Foreign Missions archives, Houghton Library, Harvard University, Sept. 1858

Trust Territory of the Pacific Islands, "Annual Report #13," Department of State publication #7183, Washington, D. C., May 1961

United Bible Societies, *The Book of a Thousand Tongues*, United Bible Societies, London 1972

Van Dusen, Henry P., *They Found the Church There*, Charles Scribner's Sons, New York 1945

Vincent, James M., editor, *Micronesia's Yesterday, Illustrations for an understanding of Micronesia's history*, Education Department, Trust Territory of the Pacific Islands, Saipan 1973

Walkup, Margaret Lavinia Barr, unpublished correspondence, American Board of Commissioners for Foreign Missions archives, Houghton Library, Harvard University, Jan. 12, 1884

Whitney, Louisa M., "Letter from Mwot, Kusaie," unpublished correspondence, March 26, 1880

Wiens, Herold J., Pacific Island Bastions of the United States, D. Van Nostrand Company, Inc., Princeton 1962

Williams, John, *A Narrative of Missionary Enterprises in the South Sea Islands*, J. Snow, 26 Paternoster Row and J. R. Liefchild, Piccadilly, London 1837

Wilson, Eleanor, "From Kusaie," unpublished manu script, Aug. 1948

Wilson, Eleanor, "Too Old? A Saga of the South Pacific," unpublished pamphlet, undated

Wilson, Scott, "Land, Activity and Social Organization of Lelu, Kusaie," Ph.D. dissertation, University of Pennsylvania 1968

Yanaihara, Tadao, *Pacific Islands under Japanese Mandate*, Oxford University Press, London 1940

– INDEX –

– ABOUT THE AUTHOR –

Elden Buck is a United Church of Christ clergyman with BA and BD degrees from Phillips University and Phillips Graduate Seminary. With his wife, Alice Hanlin Buck, he served the Church on Kosrae and in the Marshall Islands from 1958 to 1981. He was pastor of the Korean Christian Church/ United Church of Christ in Honolulu from 1981 to 1989 and of the First United Protestant Church/UCC in Hilo, Hawai'i from 1990 to 1998. Following his retirement in 1998, he spent many months on Kosrae researching and writing, while Alice Buck continued her work as coordinator of a new translation of the Kosraean Bible. Mrs. Buck died in 2004. Rev. Buck is the father of three adult children and has six grandchildren, two step-grandchildren, and a step-great-granddaughter. He lives in Claremont, California.